THE BALTIC STATES

A REFERENCE BOOK

D1124886

ESTONIAN ENCYCLOPAEDIA PUBLISHERS ■ LATVIAN ENCYCLOPAEDIA PUBLISHERS
■ LITHUANIAN ENCYCLOPAEDIA PUBLISHERS ■
TALLINN ■ RIGA ■ VILNIUS
1991

CONTRIBUTORS

The Republic of Estonia

Principal Authors: Küllo Arjakas, Hilja Jõgi, Jüri Kallasmaa, Tiia Karing, Kalev Keskküla, Jaan Kiivit, Lembit Koik, Arvo Kuddo, Viktor Masing, Teet Rajasalu, Maie Remmel, Sulev Teinemaa, Eerik Truuväli, Rein Zupping
Translators: Mare Kaljukaru, Peeter Mehisto, Tiia Raudma, Eve Tarm
Assistant Editors: Maarja Aasmäe, Ela Eelhein, Enn Hallikma, Janika Lõnsu, Aili Rosenberg, Helgi Tüksammel
Editors: Marje Jõeste, Ülo Kaevats

The Republic of Latvia

Principal Authors: Arnolds Klotiņš, Ābrams Kļockins, Jānis Lejnieks, Edgars Meļķisis, Indulis Ronis, Knuts Skujenieks, Ojārs Spārītis, Dzintra Stelpa, Bruno Strauks, Leons Taivāns, Viktors Tērauds, Eriks Tivums, Ivars Vīks
Translators: Ilze Freiberga, Maija Gulēna, Līga Korsts-Streipa, Lidija Ozola, Zane Ozola, Andris Vilsons
Assistant Editors: Ilze Freiberga, Zane Ozola, Elga Rusmane, Maija Sniega
Editors: Andrejs Urdziņš, Andris Vilks

The Republic of Lithuania

Principal Authors: Birutė Abraitienė, Giedrė Bufienė, Natalija Buivydaitė, Emilija Dagytė, Kęstutis Demskis, Petras Gaučas, Birutė Grabienė, Izidorius Ignatavičius, Arvydas Karaška, Jonas Klimas, Aldona Krutinienė, Bronislovas Kurkulis, Apolonija Kuzmickienė, Jonė Liandzbergienė, Gražina Marčiukaitytė, Danutė Rimšienė, Virginija Rupšienė, Evaldas Sinkevičius, Vytautas Spečiūnas, Stasys Stačiokas, Aldona Suščenkienė, Milda Šeškuvienė, Romas Šimkūnas, Jūratė Tamulaitienė, Nijolė Vadapalaitė, Irena Varnalytė, Antanas Vengris, Birutė Žalalienė
Translators: Vladas Dobilas, Auksė Kuokštienė, Šarūnas Papinigis, Antanas Paragys, Violeta Tamašauskienė
Assistant Editor: Raimonda Murmokaitė
Editors: Kęstutis Demskis, Mykolas Mikalajūnas

Design: Jüri Dubov, Heiki Looman, Inta Zaļaiskalne
Maps: Lauma Asare, Gaidīte Birziņa, Viktors Bukatičs, Mirdza Reča, Mudīte Reine, Rita Saurova, Izolde Slava

ISBN 5 — 89900 — 017 — 1
ISBN 5 — 89960 — 026 — 8
ISBN 5 — 89950 — 015 — 8

CONTENTS

ABBREVIATIONS

Acad. . . . . . . Academy, Academician
AD . . . . anno Domini
add. . . . . address
admin. . . . . . administration, administrative
agric. . . . . . . agriculture, agricultural
agron. . . . . . . agronomist, agronomy
approx. . . . . approximately
arch. . . . architect, architecture, architectural
Arm. . . . . Armenian
Assoc. . . . . Association
asst . . . . assistant

b. . . . . born
BC . . . . before Christ
Bd . . . . Board
biol. . . . . biology, biological, biologist
Blvd . . . . Boulevard
Bulg. . . . . Bulgarian
B/W . . . . black/white

c. . . . . country
capt. . . . . captain
CBd . . . . Council Board
Cent. . . . . Central
cent. . . . . century
Ch. . . . . Church
Chair. . . . . Chairman
champ. . . . . champion, championship
chem. . . . . chemical, chemistry, chemist
circ. . . . . circulation
cm . . . . centimetre
CM . . . . . . Council of Ministers
co . . . . company
corp. . . . . corporation
coll. . . . . collection
Commn . . . . Commission
comp. . . . . competition
constr. . . . . construction
contrib. . contributor, contribution, contributing
corr. . . . . corresponding
CP . . . . Communist Party
CPSU . . Communist Party of the Soviet Union
CSc. . . . . . Candidate of Sciences
Cttee . . . . Committee
cu . . . . cubic

Dem. . . . . Democratic
Dep. . . . . Deputy
dept . . . . department
dir . . . . director
DLP . . . . . Democratic Labour Party

Doc. . . . . Docent
Dr . . . . Doctor
DSc. . . . . . Doctor of Sciences

E . . . . East, Eastern
econ. . . . economic, economy, economist
ECP . . . . Estonian Communist Party
ed. . . editor, edited, editorial, educated
educ. . . . . . education, educational
EELC . Estonian Evangelican Lutheran Church
e.g. . . . . exempli gratia (for example)
E-in-C . . . . Editor-in-Chief
empl. . . . . employee
eng. . . . . engineer, engineering
Engl. . . . . English
ent. . . . . enterprise
EPF . . . . Estonian Popular Front
esp. . . . . especial, especially
Est. . . . . Estonian
est. . . . . established
equipm. . . . . . . equipment
et al. . et alibi (and elsewhere), et alii (and others)
etc. . . . . . et cetera (and so on)
excl. . . . . excluding
Exec. . . . . Executive
exh. . . exhibit, exhibition, exhibits

f. . . . . founded
Finn. . . . . Finnish
Fr. . . . . French
Fri . . . . Friday

g . . . . gram
gen. . . . . general
geogr. . . . geography, geographer
geol. . . . . geology, geologist
Ger. . . . . German
GNP . . . Gross National Product
govt . . . . government

h . . . . home
ha . . . . hectare
hist. . . . history, historical, historian
Hon. . . . . Honorary, honourable
hosp. . . . . hospital
Hung. . . . . . . Hungarian

i.e. . . . id est (that is, in other words)
ill. . . . illustration, illustrator, illustrated
incl. . . . . . including, inclusive
ind. . . . . . industry, industrial

indep.	independent, independence
inst.	institute
int.	international
inv.	invention, invent
invest.	investigation
It.	Italian
Jap.	Japanese
jr.	junior
kg	kilogram
km	kilometre
kW	kilowatt
kWh	kilowatt hours
l	litre
l.hr.	lunch hour
lab.	laboratory
Latv.	Latvian
LCP	Lithuanian Communist Party
LDLP	Latvian Democratic Labour Party
lg.(s)	language(s)
lic.	licence
lit.	literature, literary
Lith.	Lithuanian
LPF	Latvian Popular Front
Ltd	Limited
m	metre
Man.	Manager
math.	mathematics, mathematical, mathematician
max.	maximum
mech.	mechanics, mechanical, mechanic
med.	medical, medicine
mem.(s)	member(s)
mfrs	manufacturers
min.	minimum, minute
Min.	Minister, Ministry
mm	millimetre
Mon	Monday
Mt.	mountain
N	North, Northern
nat.	national
No, Nr.	number
Norw.	Norwegian
off.	office
orch.	orchestra
org.	organization
p.	page, pair
p.a.	per annum (per year)
Parl.	Parliament(ary)
part.	participated, participant
pat.	patent
perf.	perform, performed, performance
per.	person
PhD	Doctor of Philosophy
phil.	philosophy, philosopher
philol.	philology, philologist
phys.	physics, physical, physicist
POB	Post Office Box
Pol.	Polish
pol.	political, politic, politics
Pres.	President
prod.	production
Prof.	Professor
publ.	publication, published
publr(s)	publisher(s)
re-est.	re-established
ref.	re-founded
reg.	registered
reorg.	reorganize, reorganized
Rep.	Republic
Rom.	Romanian
RSFSR	Russian Soviet Federal Socialist Republic
Russ.	Russian
S	South, Southern
s	second
Sat	Saturday
SC	Supreme Council
sch.	school
sci.	science
SDP	Social Democratic Party
SDWP	Social Democratic Workers' Party
Sec.	Secretary
Sem.	Seminary
soc.	society
Span.	Spanish
spec.	specialist, specialized
sq	square
SSR	Soviet Socialist Republic
St.; SS.	Saint
SU	Soviet Union
Sun	Sunday
Sw.	Swedish
t	ton
tech.	technical
technol.	technologist, technological, technology
tel.	telephone
temp.	temperature
ThD	Doctor of Theology
ThM	Master of Theology
theol.	theology, theological
Thur	Thursday
transl.	translation, translated
TU	trade union
Tue	Tuesday
Turk.	Turkish
TV	television
u.	unit
Ukr.	Ukrainian
Univ.	University
UNO	United Nations Organization
UK	United Kingdom
US	United States
USA	United States of America
USSR	Union of Soviet Socialist Republics
vol.(s)	volume(s)
W	West, Western
Wed	Wednesday
wt	weight
WW	World War
YCL	Young Communist League
yr	year

THE BALTIC BRIDGE

The Baltic states exist. Why say it, if you believe it? No one says Sweden exists: it goes without saying. For the Baltic states, it has to be said, because their reemergence from the totalitarian grip of Soviet colonialism has been very recent. They were submerged to the point where their continued existence was not manifest. Our perception of the world always suffers some time lag, and the reestablishment of Lithuania, Latvia and Estonia has not yet sunk in — the more so, since the Soviet occupation forces still interfere. It will be a long time before the Baltic states will feel free and prosperous. But they exist.

So they exist. Who cares? You do, if you are still with me. It may be a casual scanning for business investment or new travel horizons or curiosity about what appears to be a resurrection, or annoyance with it, for whatever reason. Or the feeling that this is a place where you could pitch in and make a visible difference, precisely because the place is rather small and run down by the Soviet occupation. But it is a mess the Baltic people can sort out, when finally allowed to do so.

What sets the Baltic states apart? In what way are they unique? It begins with language. In a part of Europe which is largely Germanic or Slavic, the Baltic people are neither. Latvian and Lithuanian form the Baltic group of languages, a part of the large Indo-European family to which Slavic and Germanic also belong. Estonian is part of a completely different language family, the Finno-Ugric. An Estonian can make something out of Finnish, and a Latvian of Lithuanian, like a Frenchman can of Spanish. Russian is closer to English than to Estonian in its grammar and basic vocabulary. And Latvian, Lithuanian and Estonian all use the Latin script, like English — not the Russian Cyrillic.

Language isolation must have delayed Christianization of the eastern shores of the Baltic Sea. By 1200, it was the only European area west of the Volga where the ancient gods and spirits still were worshipped. Crusades against the eastern Baltic were engineered. In a magnificent anachronism, Lithuania struck back and created a huge pagan-ruled state in the midst of Christian Europe. Tourists can still admire the castles of the Lithuanian rulers, as they can the medieval town in Tallinn, Estonia, one of the best preserved in all of Europe.

The centuries that followed were unkind to the Baltic peoples. By 1800, the Russian Empire had conquered them, and the local power was in the hands of a German or Polish-speaking nobility. Only peasants spoke Lithuanian, Latvian or Estonian, and those peasants were serfs; this form of slavery never affected Finland and was all but gone in France while reaching its peak in the Baltic. By this time, the Lithuanians were staunch Catholics, while Latvians and Estonians were mainly Lutherans. During the late 1800s, a spectacular success story unfolded: within a few decades, those peasants became nations, with national cultures and a growing socio-economic basis for existence.

So what? The world has plenty of nations and cultures. But the world also has peasant populations, ranging from South America to Asia, often speaking a local language, in need of development. Their attempts to modernize, and the outside efforts to help them, have all too often led to very meager results. The success of the Baltic peasants is therefore of worldwide importance. They did something right, and the ingredients of their success story are worth studying so as to help a large chunk of humanity.

An important ingredient was that the Baltic peasants did not give up their language and all that goes with it: ancestral culture and self-identification. At first glance, they made economic development more difficult for themselves, by taking on the extra burden of simultaneously developing new literary languages rather than making use of German, Russian or Polish. How, then, did they develop so rapidly? Modernization can be a traumatic experience, because one's sense of identity is in danger. By hanging on to their languages, the Baltic peoples maintained a cultural compass. No parts of the population were left behind, because song festivals and folklore collection campaigns gave even the humblest sense of participation. The collection of Latvian folk songs gathered and published in seven thick volumes by Krišjānis Barons is unique in the world culture indeed. Faced with the apparent dilemma between economic modernization and maintaining their roots, the Baltic nations succeeded in having their cake and eating it too — like the Japanese.

In 1917, the Russian Empire first underwent a democratic revolution and then a communist counter-revolution which replaced democracy by one-party dictatorship and private enterprise by neo-feudal collectivism. The Baltic nations broke loose and formed independent states where their formerly suppressed languages and cultures could develop freely. Their wars of independence lasted from 1918 to 1920, against Soviet Russian invaders and at times also against German mercenary armies. The three self-made nations were gradually recognized by the great powers (by the United States only by 1922). The allegation that they were created at Versailles is a lie.

This period of independence lasted twenty years and was a success, compared to what preceded and followed. It was not all sweetness and light — how could it be, given people who only recently emerged from serfdom and tsarist rule, and who soon faced the Great Depression and the worldwide onslaught of fascism and communism. But they were catching up with their Scandinavian neighbours. By 1930, Latvia's per capita gross domestic product matched that of Norway. In 1939, however, a secret deal between Hitler and Stalin spelled the end of Baltic independence.

Annexation came in August. With little forewarning, the larger country invaded and annexed its neighbour. The small country had been as accommodating as it could, but now it was nonetheless accused of intolerable arrogance and provocation. The force ratio would have been overwhelming even if the victim had had time to mobilize, and any thought of armed resistance was futile. Within weeks, occupation was turned into annexation. The aggressor asserted that the annexed people warmly welcomed the act, and it ruthlessly crushed any manifestations to the contrary.

It certainly was August, but of which year? The story fits the Iraqi annexation of Kuwait in 1990 as well as the Soviet annexation of Lithuania, Latvia or Estonia in 1940. The fifty years of Soviet colonial rule that followed put the Baltic states back in every respect, compared to their neighbours in Finland and Sweden. War and Stalin's deportations removed one-third of the pre-occupation population. In their place, large numbers of colonists were pumped in. When mass terror subsided, the totalitarian mind control continued and discrimination against the Balts kept increasing.

Russian settlers fresh off the train received newly-built apartments, by-passing local people who sometimes had been on the waiting list for decades. In Latvia and Estonia, this discrimination in housing amounted to slow genocide, since cramped living reduced birth rates below reproduction level. To attract settlers, job openings in the Baltic states were at times advertised in Russia but not locally. Job discrimination almost eliminated the Balts from fields such as railroads, aviation and the merchant marine. These coastal nations with a maritime tradition celebrated by Hemingway were deprived of the use of the sea.

In the service sector language discrimination reached the point were colonial physicians, unable to understand the complaints of sick children, all too often chided the parents for not raising their children in the Russian language. Imagine, if you can, immigrant physicians in England asking their English patients to speak the immigrant language! In stores and post offices, customers asking for service in Estonian at times were told: 'Speak a human language!' The atmosphere of discrimination became such that, for some of the settlers, the occupied country's language was subhuman.

Such was the situation in the mid-1980s. In the late 1980s the Baltic states reemerged. As of late 1990, they had reasonably freely elected parliaments (supreme councils) and governments responsible to these parliaments. Their economies were still severely hampered by Soviet-imposed restrictions, and the occupation troops were still there, but privatization had begun. The Soviet government still had not recognized that their occupation of the Baltic states was as illegal as that of Kuwait by Iraq. However, these impediments were on their way out, because the independence of Latvia, Lithuania and Estonia was in the long-term interest of everyone — Russia, Western Europe, and the Balts.

For Russia, it is better to have 'four Finlands' rather than one Finland and three restive provinces. Geography makes Russia inevitably the main trade partner for the Baltic states. Freed from Soviet interference, the Baltic economies will expand, so that Russia will get more out of the Baltic states, even though it gets a thinner slice of that larger pie. Their location also imposes a 'Finlandized' foreign policy on the Baltic states. Mutual security needs may lead to an exchange of military bases. Cultural and educational autonomy for the local Russians is assured, given the Baltic exemplary track record in 1920—40 and the need to maintain good trade relations with Russia.

As for Western Europe, the dream of a common European home hinges on Baltic independence, because a home has rooms and not prison cells for some family members. The reappearance of the Baltic states on the map of Europe settles the last outstanding issue of WW II. Europe has always been more than its Atlantic seacost. Europe includes Liszt, Tchaikovsky, and Sibelius — and now Arvo Pärt of Estonia. It encompasses Bolyai's geometry, Mendeleyev's periodical table, and astronomy of Copernicus — and the first measurement of the distance of a fixed star, carried out at the Baltic university of Tartu. The symbolist art of Mikolajus Ciurlionis of Lithuania is Europe, the Europe that extends from the Atlantic to the Urals. But Europe has repeatedly been split into East and West — in 395, in 1054, and in 1945. The Baltic nations straddle the intra-European fault line, and they are familiar with both East and West as a battleground, cordon sanitaire — and a bridge. Indeed they will become more and more of a bridge as their liberation continues. Future history books may well write: This is where the two halves of Europe began to grow together — at the Baltic bridge in the new downtown of Europe.

Rein Taagepera, USA

Statistical Survey (area; population)

	Area ('000 sq km)	Population ('000)	Density (per sq km)	Year	Capital	Population ('000)	Year
USSR	22,402.2	286,717	12.4	1989	Moscow	8,967	1989
China	9,597.0	1,112,000[2]	115.0	1989	Peking	10,000[1]	1988
USA	9,363.2	246,900	26.4	1989	Washington	638	1986
						3,500[1]	1985
Sweden	449.9	8,526	18.9	1989	Stockholm	667	1987
						1,250[1]	1989
Japan	372.2	123,000	330.6	1990	Tokyo	11,719	1989
Norway	386.6	4,170	10.8	1989	Oslo	453.7	1988
Germany	356.8	79,700	248.0	1989	Berlin	3,200	1989
Finland	337.0	>4,970	14.7	1989	Helsinki	493.5	1989
						784.1[1]	1989
Poland	312.7	37,900	121.2	1989	Warsaw	1,652	1990
Austria	83.8	~7,600	90.6	1988	Vienna	1,500	1988
Lithuania	**65.2**	**3,675**	**56.6**	**1989**	**Vilnius**	**592.5**	**1990**
Latvia	**64.6**	**2,667**	**41.5**	**1989**	**Riga**	**916.5**	**1990**
Estonia	**45.2**	**1,565**	**34.9**	**1989**	**Tallinn**	**484**	**1990**
Denmark	44.5	5,130	115.3	1989	Copenhagen	1,300[1]	1989
Switzerland	41.3	6,600	159.8	1988	Bern	140	1988
						>300[1]	1988
Netherlands	41.5	14,760	355.7	1988	Amsterdam	955[1]	1988
Belgium	30.5	9,865	323.4	1989	Brussels	978[1]	1988
Luxemburg	2.6	370	143.9	1988	Luxemburg	80	1988

[1] With suburbs.
[2] With Taiwan ~1,132,000.

Distance in a Straight Line Between the Baltic Capitals and World Capitals (km)

	Riga	Tallinn	Vilnius
Amsterdam	1,320	1,440	1,350
Athens	2,090	2,360	1,860
Belgrade	1,360	1,170	1,650
Berlin	840	1,040	825
Bern	1,560	1,770	1,520
Brussels	1,430	1,590	1,470
Bucharest	1,380	1,650	1,140
Budapest	1,080	1,360	910
Buenos Aires	13,000	13,300	12,850
Cairo	3,090	3,330	2,810
Cape Town	10,400	10,700	10,100
Copenhagen	720	830	820
Damascus	2,900	3,200	2,650
Delhi	5,400	5,550	5,180
Dublin	1,940	2,000	2,050
Helsinki	360	85	610
Leningrad	500	330	660
London	1,660	1,770	1,710
Los Angeles	12,350	12,450	12,350
Madrid	2,680	2,890	2,670
Melbourne	14,900	15,100	14,700
Mexico City	12,030	12,200	12,000
Montreal	7,800	7,900	7,860
Moscow	830	860	780
New York	8,125	8,200	8,100
Oslo	840	790	1,040
Paris	1,670	1,840	1,680
Peking	7,550	7,600	7,475
Prague	970	1,220	900
Reykjavik	2,590	2,480	2,810
Rome	1,840	2,100	1,710
Seoul	8,550	8,550	8,450
Singapore	9,450	9,600	9,200

Distance in a Straight Line Between the Baltic Capitals and World Capitals (km)

	Riga	Tallinn	Vilnius
Sofia	1,560	1,850	1,520
Stockholm	440	375	680
Tashkent	3,925	4,050	3,780
Tirane	1,740	2,030	1,550
Tokyo	9,650	9,700	9,550
Vienna	1,070	1,340	950
Warsaw	560	820	390
Washington	8,650	8,760	8,650

Distance Along the Highway Between the Baltic Cities and Major European Cities (km)

	Riga	Tallinn	Vilnius
Amsterdam	1,859	2,166	1,686
Athens	3,144	3,451	2,909
Belgrade	1,847	2,154	1,674
Berlin	1,226	1,533	1,053
Bern	2,381	2,688	2,208
Bonn	1,950	2,257	1,777
Bordeaux	3,039	3,346	2,866
Bratislava	1,343	1,650	1,170
Brussels	2,130	2,437	1,957
Bucharest	1,960	2,267	1,787
Budapest	1,496	1,803	1,323
Geneva	2,619	2,926	2,446
Hamburg	1,648	1,955	1,475
Helsinki	1,093	786	1,393
Istanbul	2,842	3,149	2,669
Kaunas	194	501	95
Köln	1,922	2,229	1,749
Krakow	972	1,279	799
Leipzig	1,408	1,715	1,235
Leningrad	570	359	704
Liepāja	203	510	428
Madrid	3,726	4,033	3,553
Milan	2,388	2,695	2,215
Moscow	1,011	1,085	1,023
Munich	1,803	2,110	1,630
Münster	1,678	1,985	1,505
Odense	1,911	2,218	1,738
Paris	2,415	2,722	2,242
Plovdiv	2,434	2,741	2,261
Prague	1,403	1,710	1,230
Riga	—	307	300
Rome	3,034	3,341	2,861
Sofia	2,261	2,568	2,088
Strasbourg	1,944	2,251	1,771
Tallinn	307	—	605
Tartu	305	187	603
Toulouse	3,097	3,404	2,924
Vienna	1,408	1,715	1,235
Vilnius	300	605	—
Warsaw	654	961	481
Zagreb	1,865	2,172	1,692

REPUBLIC OF
ESTONIA

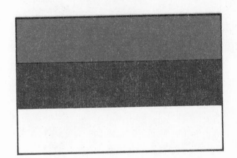

MU ISAMAA, MU ÕNN JA RÕÕM

(MY NATIVE LAND, MY PRIDE AND JOY)

Friedrich PACIUS/Johan Voldemar JANNSEN

Mu isamaa, mu õnn ja rõõm, kui kaunis oled sa!
Ei leia mina iial tääl see suure, laia ilma pääl,
mis mull' nii armas oleks ka, kui sa, mu isamaa!

Sa oled mind ju sünnitand ja üles kasvatand!
Sind tänan mina alati ja jään sull' truiks surmani!
Mull' kõige armsam oled sa, mu kallis isamaa!

Su üle Jumal valvaku, mu kallis isamaa!
Ta olgu sinu kaitseja ja võtku rohkest õnnista,
mis iial ette võtad sa, mu kallis isamaa!

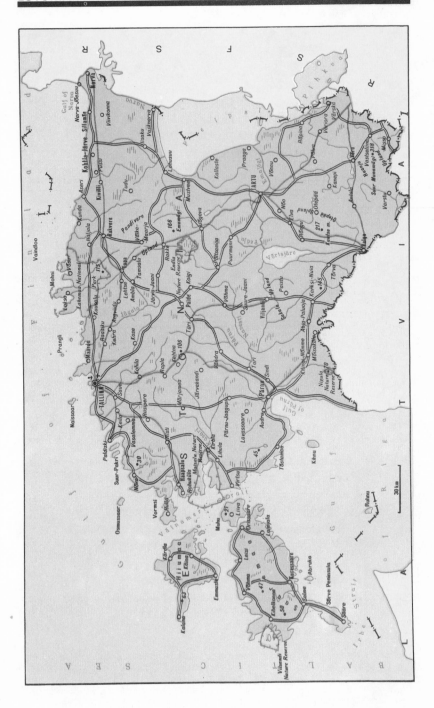

THE REPUBLIC OF ESTONIA, *Eesti Vabariik* in Estonian, lies on the eastern shores of the Baltic Sea. The name *Eesti* is apparently derived from the word *Aisti*, the name given by the ancient Germans to the peoples living north-east of Visla. The first to mention the Aisti was Tacitus, the Roman historian of the first century *(Aestii)*. The ancient Scandinavians called the land south of the Finnish Gulf *Eistland*, and the people *eistr*. The Latin name *Estonia* is used in many contemporary languages. The first known registration of Estonia on a map was by the Arab scholar al-Idrisi in 1154. The oldest surviving map was by the Antwerp astronomer Johann Portantius in 1573. Estonians, who belong to the Baltic-Finnic group of the Finno-Ugric peoples, as do the Finns and Hungarians, arrived on the territory of Estonia in the 3rd millennium BC.

Many wars have been fought in Estonia because of its strategic location. During the time of independence, before WW II, the territory of the Republic of Estonia covered 47,549 sq km — it is now 45,215 sq km. Therefore, Estonia is somewhat larger than Denmark, the Netherlands and Switzerland. Estonia is located between 57.30 and 59.49 latitude, and 21.46 and 28.13 longitude.The distance from east to west is 350 km and north to south 240 km. Estonia has many islands, large and small (over 1,500 in total) — the largest are Saaremaa (2,673 sq km), Hiiumaa (989 sq km), Muhu (200 sq km) and Vormsi (92.9 sq km). The sea islands total 4,133 sq km, the lakes 2,015 sq km (the largest are the Estonian parts of the Peipsi and Pihkva lake, and the Võrtsjärv). The length of the coast is 3,794 km, the land border is 633 km, of which 339 km is the southern border with Latvia and 294 km the eastern border with Russia (along the Narva River, and the Peipsi, Lämmijärv and Pihkva lakes).

According to the 1989 census, Estonia has a population of 1,565,662, of these 1,126,900 (71.6%) live in urban centres. The population density is 35 people per sq km. The ethnic composition: Estonians 963,269 (61.5%), Russians 474,815 (30.3%), Ukrainians 48,273 (3.1%), Byelorussians 27,711 (1.8%). Estonian is the state language. The main religious denominations are Lutheran, Orthodox and Baptist.

Administratively, Estonia is divided into 15 counties (*maakond*) and 6 towns (the other 27 towns are subordinate to the counties).The capital is Tallinn (1990 population: 484,400). The largest towns are Tallinn, Tartu (115,400), Narva (82,300), Kohtla-Järve (76,800), Pärnu (54,200), Sillamäe (20,700), Rakvere (20,100). The counties are divided into communes (*vald*).

The national holidays are January 1, February 24 (Independence Day), Good Friday, May 1, June 23 (Victory Day — the anniversary of the victory at the Battle of Võnnu in 1919, during the War of Independence), June 24, December 25 and 26.

The currency is the Soviet rouble.

LANGUAGE

Estonian is the language of the Estonian people and the official language of the Republic of Estonia. The Latin alphabet is used in written Estonian. Standard Estonian is based on the North Estonian dialect. Estonian belongs to the Baltic-Finnic group of the Finno-Ugric languages. Estonian is closely related to Finnish and distantly related to Hungarian.

Most of the vowel and consonant sounds of Estonian can be pronounced as either short, long or extra long. Changing the duration of a sound in a word can alter the grammatical function of the word, or change its meaning completely. Nouns are declined (there are 14 cases), and verbs conjugated generally by adding endings to root-words. The root changes in many words during declension and conjugation, with a vowel or consonant either being replaced by another, or disappearing completely. There are many post-positions and few prepositions in Estonian. 1/3 of the words in the vocabulary of standard Estonian is derived from root-words (by adding suffixes). A large number of words are formed by compounding roots. Most of the foreign words have been borrowed from German or Old-German. A number of international words entered Estonian as later borrowings, including about 700 from English. There are no articles or grammatical genders in Estonian.

The oldest known examples of written Estonian are the names, words and phrases registered in the 13th cent. chronicles. The earliest surviving Estonian text dates from the beginning of the 16th cent. Ferdinand Johann Wiedemann published a grammar in 1875 and a comprehensive Estonian — German dictionary in 1869. Many of the suggestions for language reform made by Johannes Aavik in the 1920s and 1930s were implemented in the written language. For example, the sentence structure was in some ways de-Germanized, and many newly created words came into use. In 1919 Estonian became the language of instruction at Tartu University. From 1920 to 1930, the scientific and academic vocabulary of Estonian was standardized under the direction of Johannes Voldemar Veski (over 100,000 terms). After WW II, a map of dialects, a grammatical textbook and many large dictionaries were published abroad by Estonians in exile, who had fled the Soviet occupation. In Estonia, Estonian language research is carried out at Tartu University, and at the Institute of Language and Literature, where the compilation of grammatical textbooks and dictionaries, and the standardization of Estonian are concentrated.

NATURE

GEOLOGICALLY, Estonia is situated on the level north-western part of the East-European platform on which there are only slight variations in elevation. The average elevation is only about 50 m. The elevation in south-eastern and eastern Estonia is higher than in western Estonia. The highest point (Suur Munamägi) is 318 m above sea level.
The extensive Ordovician limestone plateau in northern Estonia forms a steep bank — called the Baltic (North-Estonian) Glint (up to 56 m in height) — on the shores of the Gulf of Finland. A smaller Silurian limestone glint forms part of the northern coastline of the Estonian islands, Saaremaa and Muhu.
The most important mineral resources are embedded in the Ordovician bedrock of northern Estonia: oil shale or *kukersite* (reserves estimated at 6,000 million metric t) and phosphorite (700 million metric t). Limestone is used in the production of cement, lime, building stone, etc. The Cambrian blue clay, with outcrops on the north coast, is used in the manufacture of bricks, drainage pipes and cement.
During the glacial period, the territory of Estonia was covered on several occasions by a continental glacier. During the ice's retreat, bedrock was covered by moraine and sediments of glacial rivers and lakes. The quaternary deposits covering the limestone layers are initially thin, but become thicker towards the south (up to 200 m) — forming hilly morain terrain on the sandstone in southern Estonia. Peat is one of the more prevalent quaternary deposits. There are about 12,000 fens and bogs in a total area of 9,000 sq km, and the peat reserves total approximately 4,000 million metric t.
The coastline of the BALTIC SEA in Estonia is characterized by numerous bays, straits and islets. As a result of the gradual uplift of the earth's crust (3 mm a year in north-western Estonia) there are new islands constantly appearing, and the area of the older islands is increasing. The coastal sea in western Estonia is shallow and full of shoals. The Gulf of Riga, which is linked to the Baltic Sea by the Irbe Strait, is also shallow (max. depth 10 m).
Changes in sea water levels are not caused by tides but mostly by the wind. The height of waves may be up to 6 m during storms, normally the height is less than one metre.
The salinity of Baltic surface water is only 5 – 7 per thousand, and in the areas where rivers enter the sea, it is considerably less. The temperature of the surface water in summer is 16 – 19 °C on the average, and can reach a maximum of 26 °C. The Gulf of Finland and the Gulf of Riga freeze over only in exceptionally cold winters. The straits between islands and the mainland freeze over in mid-January, and the ice cover lasts on average for 3 months. The thickness of the ice near the coast can reach 80 cm by mid-March.
Coastal sea water is polluted at many locations. Swimming in summer is currently not recommended at the coastal resorts of Pärnu and Haapsalu.
The CLIMATE is determined by Estonia's location in the north-western part of the Eurasian continent in the vicinity of the North Atlantic. The closeness of the Baltic Sea has a strong influence on local climatic differences, especially in the coastal regions. The mean annual air temperature in the most western point (Vilsandi Island) is 6.0 °C, and in the most eastern points it is 4.2 to 4.5 °C. The maximum air temperature, measured at the same stations, is more even. The mean annual precipitation is, however, different — 500 mm on the coast to almost 700 mm in the uplands. Precipitation is the heaviest at the end of summer, and the lowest in spring.
The permanent snow cover becomes established in the south-eastern uplands at the beginning of December, at the earliest, and by the end of March, the snow can be half a metre in depth. In January there is snow throughout the land, and it usually melts at the end of March. In mild winters, there is often no lasting snow cover.
In Estonia, south-western and western winds prevail. Whirlwinds and heavy storms are rare. The last strong 'storm of the century' raged in western Estonia in the autumn of 1967.
In general, the climate in Estonia is similar to that in central Sweden (Stockholm) and southern Finland (Helsinki). In North America, the only area with an analogous climate is the north-east corner of the US.
Estonia is rich in INLAND WATER BODIES. There are over 1,400 natural and man-made lakes. The largest lake (Peipsi, 3,555 sq km, shared with the RSFSR) and the largest artificial water body Narva Reservoir (190 sq km, also shared with Russia) are located on the border with the RSFSR. The

maximum depth of both is 15 m. The deepest lake is Rõuge Suurjärv (38 m). The second largest lake, Võrtsjärv (270 sq km; 6 m deep) is well-stocked with fish. Smaller lakes in agricultural areas are affected by organic waste and the process of eutrophication is occurring.

In Estonia there are 420 rivers of over 10 km in length. Only three rivers have an average runoff at the river mouth of more than 50 cu m per s: Narva (399), Emajõgi (72) and Pärnu (64). The northern Estonian rivers which flow into the Gulf of Finland form picturesque waterfalls on the Glint. Some of the southern Estonian rivers (Ahja, Piusa, Võhandu) have scenic valleys with high outcrops of red Devonian sandstone and are partially restricted to the public.

With regard to zonal distribution of VEGETATION Estonia belongs to the northern part of the mixed forest zone. In prehistoric times the territory was covered with forests (with the exception of coastal marshes and treeless bogs which covered approximately 1/5 of the whole area). Coniferous trees — pines and spruces, as well as ash, maple, etc. — were predominant.

Now the forests cover approximately 40% of Estonia. This figure has almost doubled because the land belonging to private farms (abandoned because of forced collectivization) has been afforested, and grasslands have been overgrown with alder and birch. Wooded meadows in western Estonia which were formerly used for to provide hay, are now overgrown with mixed forests. Forest resources play an important role in the Estonian economy. The abundance of woodlands and shrubs has provided suitable habitats for game, and even for those animals which are already extinct, or very rare, in other European countries (e.g., wolf, lynx, bear, wild boar, elk, otter). During every hunting season, approximately 5,000 elk, 2,000 — 6,000 roe (deer), and 3,000 — 4,000 wild boar are shot.

The FLORA and FAUNA of Estonia have developed during the 10,000 years of post-glacial history. Native flowering plants number about 1500 species — due to the calcareous soils and the relatively mild climate, western Estonia is especially rich in flora.

59 plant and 198 animal species have been placed under state protection. There is currently 1 national park (Lahemaa, 649 sq km), 1 biosphere reserve, 1 water reserve, 5 state nature reserves (630 sq km in total) and 56 other nature reserves. The main problems today in preserving nature are the ever-increasing levels of air and water pollution.

POPULATION

The earliest signs of habitation in Estonia are from the 8th millennium BC. Approximately in the middle of the 3rd millennium BC, there was extensive migration by Finno-Ugric tribes from the east. These people mixed with the local population, and by the beginning of the 13th cent., a distinct ethnic group had developed in Estonia.

The first evaluations on the size of the population can be made on the basis of the Danish Assessment Book (*Liber Census Daniae*) and Henrik's Livonian Chronicle (*Heinrici Chronicon Livoniae*). According to the information in these books, the size of the Estonian population is assessed at 100,000 to 200,000 people. The following centuries — with many wars, epidemics, the Great Famine (1695 — 97), etc. — greatly affected the population developments. The effects are felt to this day : whereas in 1550 there were approximately the same numbers of Estonians and Finns, then today there are almost five times as many Finns as Estonians.

In the Middle Ages, the population was affected by immigration: Swedes, Germans and Latvians in the 14th and 15th cent.; and Russians and Finns from the end of the 16th cent. The historian Heldur Palli has estimated the population as follows:

in 1200	150,000 — 200,000	in 1698	330,000
1550	250,000 — 280,000	1712	150,000
1620 — 1640	70,000 — 100,000	1782	490,000
1695	400,000		

The population in the towns increased. In 1360, 860 people lived in Tallinn. In 1764, there were 6,521. In the 1st half of the 16th cent. there were 15,000 to 20,000 town dwellers — i.e., 6 — 8% of the Estonian population.

The first population count was conducted in Estonia in 1782. Therefore, from this time on, it is possible to be more precise in assessing population developments. In the period 1782 — 1858, the birth rate changed from 42 per thousand in 1796 to 29 in 1845. Due to many social-economic factors, the mortality rate varied even more. For example, the mortality rate in 1789 was 48.8 per thousand, but in 1797 it dropped to 21.9. In the above-mentioned period, the natural increase in population, during 10 of these years, was actually negative. The birth and mortality rates began to drop relatively quickly from 1880 onwards. In the years 1910 — 14, the birth rate was 25.0 per thousand, in 1920 — 24, 19.6, and from 1934 onwards, the rate was below 16 per thousand. In the 1930s, Estonia had one of the lowest birth rates in Europe. The mortality rate also dropped: 20 — 22 per thousand in the 1880s, 14 — 15 in the 1930s.

In the mid-19th cent. there was mass migration from Estonia — initially to Russia, but towards the end of the century, to other countries (primarily to the US). Migration to the West continued on a smaller scale between the two world wars: in the period 1920 — 39, the net migration was negative for eleven of the years. The ethnic composition in Estonia was relatively uniform. The 1934 census showed that Estonians formed 88.2% of the population. Of the national minorities, the Russians

formed the greatest proportion (especially in those districts bordering on the USSR) — 8.2% ; Germans formed 1.5% and the Swedes 0.7%.
The annexation of Estonia by the USSR in 1940 — and WW II — had a disastrous effect on the population. As a result of mass deportations (1940 — 41), the war and mobilization (1941 — 45), as well as mass emigration, the population of Estonia decreased from 1,136,000 in 1939 to 854,000 in 1945. Repressions continued in the 2nd half of the 1940s. Estonia lost a whole ethnic minority : in 1939 — 41 the local Germans left in response to Hitler's call. In 1943 — 44, as a result of a special agreement with Germany, the Swedes left *en masse*. 39,000 inhabitants (mainly Russians) were lost to Estonia when the border areas, where they lived, were added to Soviet territory. In 1945, Estonians formed approximately 94% of the population.
Since the Soviet occupation, and especially after the war, the population has been affected the most by the colonial assimilation policies of the USSR. Hundreds of thousands of people were brought into Estonia from central Russia, the Ukraine and Byelorussia. In the period 1945 — 50, the net migration was 240,000 people. In the whole of the period of Soviet occupation after the war, half a million more people have come to Estonia than have left. The percentage of Estonians in the population has dropped to 61.5%, according to the 1989 census. Russians form the largest minority (30.3%), followed by the Ukrainians (3.1%) and Byelorussians (1.8%). Heavy industry was introduced to Estonia by the central Soviet authorities — these factories are under all-Union control, their work-force consists mainly of the people brought into Estonia, and their output is largely meant for Soviet markets. The non-Estonian population is therefore dominant in the north-eastern Estonian industrial towns: e.g., Narva (96% non-Estonian). Estonians, however, form 87% of the rural population.
The total birth rate in Estonia in the period 1986 — 87 was 2,185; in 1989 it was even 2,312. This is quite high in comparison to other European countries. In recent years, however, the birth rate has suddenly decreased: whereas in 1987 and 1988 there were 25,100 births, in 1990 there were less than 23,000. The mortality rate has not changed significantly in the last 30 years. The average life expectancy in 1986 — 87 was 71.0 (66.4 for men and 75.1 for women). People in Estonia marry at a relatively young age: e.g., 28% of women born 1960 — 64 married before the age of 20, and 41% of men born 1955 — 59 married before the age of 23. The rates of divorce and illegitimacy are relatively high. There is a very high rate of abortions (in the 1980s, there were 120 to 140 abortions for every 100 births).
At the beginning of the 1990s, Estonia had a population of 1,576,000. The birth and migration rates have started to drop in recent years. A Republic of Estonia Immigration Law was passed in 1990, which establishes immigration quotas, and other measures to regulate the movement of people into Estonia. This law, in conjunction with changes in the socio-political situation, brought about a negative civilian net migration in 1990 — for the first time during the last 50 years.
Although there have recently been government moves to increase support for large families, there have not been corresponding significant changes in the demographic processes. The aging of the population is continuing, and the birth rate of the population is low.

POLITICAL SYSTEM

The November 16, 1988 Declaration on the Sovereignty of the Estonian SSR, together with amendments to the constitution, established that the Estonian SSR is the highest power on its territory, and that this is manifested in its structures of power, government and the courts. In order to regulate the future relations with the USSR, the idea of a Union Treaty was proposed. The central powers attempted to resolve the constitutional crisis by declaring the above-mentioned laws to be null and void.
The May 18, 1989 Law on the Bases for the Economic Independence of the Estonian SSR and the Resolution on the Transition to Economic Independence of the Estonian SSR were the legal bases for the realization of the principles of the sovereignty declaration in the economic area. Although the corresponding all-Union law was proposed on December 27, 1989, the subsequent laws and actions by the Soviet central administration made it impossible for the Republic to establish economic independence because of its continuing status as an imperial province.
The November 12, 1989 resolution by the Supreme Soviet of the Estonian SSR described the foreign policy and military actions of the USSR in 1940 as acts of aggression against the Republic of Estonia, as a military occupation, and as the annexation of the Republic of Estonia. The July 22, 1940 Resolution on Estonia Joining the USSR was declared null and void from the moment of its being passed.
The basis of the annexation of the Baltic States, the Secret Supplementary Protocol of the August 23, 1939 treaty between the USSR and Germany, was declared, by the USSR Congress of People's Deputies on December 24, 1989, to be illegal and null and void from the moment of signing.
Resolutions by the General Assembly of all elected representatives in Estonia, which met on February 2, 1990, and by the Supreme Soviet on February 23, 1990, contain the proposal to begin formal negotiations between the USSR and Estonia in order to restore the independence of the Republic of

Estonia *de facto* — based on the 1920 Tartu Peace Treaty between the Republic of Estonia and the Russian Federation.

On March 30, 1990, the newly elected Supreme Council (SC) declared Soviet power in Estonia to be illegal from the moment of its establishment, and declared the restoration of the Republic of Estonia (*restitutio in integrum*), together with a period of transition, which will end with the formation of the constitutional organs of state power of the Republic of Estonia.

On May 8, 1990, the term Republic of Estonia was restored as the name of the state, the use of current state symbols was terminated, and the first six paragraphs of the 1937 Republic of Estonia Constitution were put into effect — including the paragraph which determines the national status of Estonia: 'Estonia is an independent and sovereign republic, wherein the supreme power of the state is held by the people'.

The May 16, 1990 Law on the Bases for Provisional Government in Estonia contains two principally important paragraphs dealing with the system of government: 1) the subordination of the Republic of Estonia's bodies of state power, government, courts, and public prosecutor to the corresponding bodies in the USSR was terminated, and they were uncoupled from the Soviet systems; 2) all current normative acts are valid on Estonian territory unless they are annulled by the Estonian SC or by the Estonian government, or they are in conflict with these principles or with subsequent normative acts of the Republic of Estonia.

The above-mentioned last three legal acts have been declared illegal by USSR presidential decree.

On August 7, 1990, the SC passed a Resolution on the Relations Between the Republic of Estonia and the USSR which annulled the Estonian SSR 1978 Constitution and stated that the basis for regulating relations with the USSR cannot be the USSR Constitution or any USSR laws. The same resolution determined the basic principles and preliminary documents for negotiations with the USSR — to be held with the aim of restoring national independence. Negotiations began on August 23, 1990, but were already replaced, on the third meeting, by consultations between groups of experts. Imperial-minded forces have made numerous attempts to form alternative power structures, and have raised the question of the areas inhabited mainly by non-Estonians becoming autonomous and breaking away from the Republic of Estonia. Some local bodies have not recognized the legality of all Republic of Estonia laws on their administrative territories.

The 105-member SUPREME COUNCIL of the Republic of Estonia is the highest continually active legal body of state authority. The SC is elected for five years by registered voters in a general, direct and secret election. The SC elects, via secret ballot, the Chairman of the SC, the Speaker and 2 Deputy Speakers. The members of the SC can form factions, and belong to permanent or temporary committees.

The activities of the SC have shown that parliamentary democracy — as well as the separation of powers and the moves toward private property, privatization and the market economy — have been taken as a basis for the formation of new political structures. The legal system being established in the Republic of Estonia is based solely on the wishes of the Estonian people and the generally recognized principles of international law.

The Chairman of the Republic of Estonia SC represents the SC in internal and international contacts, signs the laws and other acts of the Republic, recommends the candidate for the position of government head to the SC, and chairs the meetings of the SC Presidium. The Chairman of the SC is Arnold Rüütel.

The Republic of Estonia SUPREME COUNCIL PRESIDIUM is responsible for the organizing of the work of the SC, and has other areas of authority determined by the law. The members are the Chairman of the SC, the Speaker, 2 Deputy Speakers and the chairmen of the permanent committees.

The Republic of Estonia GOVERNMENT is the state body with executive powers. The head of the government (prime minister) is nominated by the SC. The Prime Minister presents ministerial candidates to the SC for approval. The government consists of the Prime Minister and 21 ministers. There are 19 ministries. Two members of the government are ministers without portfolio.

In order to handle functions within the state authority, but which are outside the power of the various ministries, appropriate departments have been formed.

The head of the Republic of Estonia government (Prime Minister) is Edgar Savisaar.

The APPLICATION OF THE LAW belongs to the jurisdiction of the Supreme Court, and the town and county courts. Decisions in court cases are made by the judge and the assistant judges. All judges and Supreme Court assistant judges are elected by the SC. The town and county assistant judges are elected by the local inhabitants. There are preparations being made for law reforms, which will introduce changes in legislation and the court system.

The Public Prosecutor system consists of the State Prosecutors' Office and its subordinate town and county prosecutors' offices.

LOCAL GOVERNMENT allows local inhabitants independent decision-making on local issues, within the bounds of the Republic's laws. During the period of transition, the current Soviet system is being reorganized. According to the new system, the local government bodies include county, town, small town and commune councils; county, small town and commune elders and town mayors; county, town, small town and commune administrations; audit committees. Local government status is granted by the SC Presidium, according to the procedures determined by law. The transition to the new local government system is scheduled to be completed by the end of 1991.

HISTORY

ANCIENT TIMES (8th millennium BC – 13th cent. AD). After the last Ice Age, Estonia was inhabited by a people whose ethnic identity is unknown. There are signs of human activity from the middle of the 8th millennium BC. In the mid-3rd millennium BC, Comb Pottery people arrived from the east. They were the principal ancestors of the Estonians who have therefore lived on their land for 5,000 years. Estonians are one of the longest settled European peoples. By the beginning of the 13th cent., a nation had not yet developed, and the effect of Christianity was minor. There was a population of approximately 100,000.

RULED BY VARIOUS POWERS (13th cent. – 1918). EARLY FIGHT FOR INDEPENDENCE. At the end of the 12th cent., the German armed, religious expansion to the east increased. Warfare began at the beginning of the 13th cent., when the pagan society fought against the more advanced European society. German, Danish, Swedish, and Russian conquerors encountered armed resistance. By the year 1227, Estonia had been conquered, and this meant that Estonia's development became tied to that of Europe. The Estonian native inhabitants made numerous attempts to restore their independence – the largest, yet unsuccessful, attempt was the St. George Day Rebellion (1343 – 45).

MIDDLE AGES (1227 – 1558). After the conquest, small fuedal states were formed. Estonia was divided between Denmark (who sold its territory to the Teutonic Order in 1346), the Livonian Order (until 1237 the Order of the Knights of the Sword), and the bishops of Tartu and Saare-Lääne. Churches and stone fortresses were built, manor farms and nine towns were constructed (of these, 4 towns belonged to the Hanseatic League). The peasants were obliged to pay taxes, their legal status deteriorated, and by the beginning of the 15th cent., serfdom began to develop. Internal struggles continued between the Order, the bishops, the towns and the more powerful vassals; and Russia began to pose an external threat. The Reformation reached Estonia in 1523; the towns converted quickly to Lutheranism – whereas in the countryside, Catholicism remained for a longer period. The first known Estonian-language publication is from the year 1525.

THE LIVONIAN WAR AND THE PERIOD OF THE THREE KINGS (1558 – 1645). In 1558, Russian forces invaded Estonia and defeated the divided small states. In 1559, the Saare-Lääne Bishop sold his territory to Denmark. In 1561, northern Estonia yielded to Sweden and southern Estonia to Poland. By the year 1583, the Russian armies were forced out of Estonia. As a result of the Swedish – Polish wars, all of continental Estonia became Swedish territory in 1629. By the end of the wars, Estonia was devastated; the pre-war population of 250,000 – 280,000 had dropped to100,000. In 1645, the Island of Saaremaa also went under Swedish control.

THE SWEDISH ERA (1629 – 1710). In the interests of the Swedish rulers, the power of the aristocracy was somewhat curbed, and the taxation of the peasants was regulated. The freedom of movement of the peasants, which had increased during the wars, was again restricted. The peasants, however, began to understand that it was possible to be protected by the state. A basis was formed for Estonian-language schools; Tartu University opened its doors in 1632. The population grew to 350,000 – 400,000.

THE NORTHERN WAR AND THE RUSSIAN ERA (1700 – 1918). Estonia was effectively conquered by Russia in 1710. By surrendering, the Baltic-German aristocracy managed to preserve its privileges; due to the war, famine and plague, the population dropped to 140,000. In 1721, with the Nystad Peace Treaty, Estonia became part of Russia. In 1739, the first Estonian Bible was published. The power of the local aristocracy again strengthened over the land and the rural population. Serfdom spread, and state taxes increased. In the 1740s, classical serfdom was firmly in place.By the end of the 18th cent., serfdom's economic value was expended, and the government and some circles of the aristocracy, who were influenced by the ideas of enlightenment, attempted reforms which would limit serfdom. Village courts were established to regulate peasants activities, and this enabled some peasants to become prominent. Partial reforms, however, did not resolve the social and economic deadlock. The reforms of 1816 and 1819 freed the peasants from serfdom. Estonian schools were established across the country and the education level of the peasants rose quickly. The peasants were freed, but were unable to get land; rental agreements had the same, or even worse conditions. In the period 1820 – 40, the dissatisfaction of the peasants was expressed through activity in religious movements, in disturbances, emigration. The laws of 1849 and 1856 ensured a certain amount of land for the peasants, and rents began to be paid with money. The industrial revolution began slowly with the textile industry in 1830 – 40. The first railway was opened in 1870.

THE ERA OF AWAKENING (1860s – 1885). More peasants bought farms, Estonian-language journalism began (Johann Voldemar Jannsen), Estonian intelligentsia developed. At the beginning of the national movement, petitions were presented to the Russian central authorities; the era of awakening was effected through major national events: a collection for the establishment of an Estonian-language secondary school for peasants (Estonian Aleksander School), song festivals (from 1869), folklore collection. Agricultural and cultural societies and a national theatre were founded; research was begun into Estonian topics, such as philology, ethnology, history, etc. Estonians became aware that they constituted a nationality. A moderate group developed in the national movement

(Jakob Hurt), which emphasized the development of the spirit and culture. The more radical group (Carl Robert Jakobson) emphasized economic progress, the increase of the role of the peasants in society, and the removal of the privileges of the aristocracy. In 1884, the Estonian University Students Society's blue-, black- and white flag was consecrated. This later became the Estonian national flag.
ERA OF RUSSIFICATION (1885 – mid-1890s). Russian nationalism strengthened in order to tie the peripheral provinces to the centre. Although the Baltic-Germans' special status was restricted through reforms by the central powers, the intense Russification policies also suppressed the activities of the era of awakening. Russian became the language in government institutions and schools, local authorities became increasingly under the control of the Russian centre, the importance of the Russian officialdom increased. Organizations in the national movement were closed down; conversion to the Russian Orthodox Church was encouraged in a further attempt to Russify the indigenous population.
THE DEVELOPMENT OF A CIVIC SOCIETY (mid-1890s – 1917). In 1897, 986,000 people lived in Estonia – 90.6% were Estonians, with a 77.7% literacy rate (96.2% were able to read). Development began in the metal and machinery industries, as well as in ship-building. Estonia was one of the most industrialized areas in the Russian Empire, but the industries operated in the interests of Russia – with Russian raw materials and work-force, and the main markets being in Russia. In agriculture, there was a change of emphasis from grain growing to the dairy industry. Agricultural cooperatives flourished. The towns became more Estonian. A new generation of educated people, including politicians, quickly restored the awareness of national identity. Under the cover of Villem Reiman's teetotallers' movement, wider national cultural aims were proposed. Tartu became the centre of the national renaissance. Jaan Tõnisson, the editor of the Tartu newspaper *Postimees* (The Postman), fought against the effects of Russification, emphasized national virtues and the necessity of working together in an organized fashion, and actively took part in community activities. Konstantin Päts, the editor of the Tallinn newspaper *Teataja* (The Herald), emphasized economic demands. In 1905, the stormy events of the Russian revolution caused an increase in social activism and encouraged the development of democracy in society. Parties were formed, an all-Estonia representative body was elected – which split during the congress into the moderates (who were content with those concessions already made) and the radicals (who wanted to continue the revolution). During the counter-attack by the central powers, the battle moved to the rural areas, and 120 manors were burnt down. In the course of the suppressions, approximately 300 people were executed by the authorities. Despite the defeat, the development of a civic society continued: there was a differentiation into classes and social groups; the number of societies, cooperatives increased; more Estonians became involved in local government. Estonian-language education developed. At the beginning of WW I, the central powers restricted the influence of the Baltic-Germans. The war produced a cadre of Estonian soldiers and officers. As the war dragged on, there arose demands for autonomy (Jüri Vilms, 1916). After the collapse of tsarist power in 1917, the struggle between national forces and the Bolsheviks continued. On March 30, the Russian Provisional Government approved autonomy for Estonia, and the Land Council was elected as the people's representative. New parties were formed. Estonian servicemen formed national army units. The power of the Bolsheviks increased together with the growing chaos, and consequently they seized power in a bloodless coup in October. In Estonia, Bolshevik power was represented by the Estonian Soviet Executive Committee (Jaan Anvelt). The Soviets were unable to consolidate their control, and on November 15, the Land Council declared itself to be the supreme power in Estonia. In doing so, it declared for the first time the right of the Estonian people to self-determination. The Land Council was disbanded by the Soviets, but continued its activities underground.
THE BIRTH OF INDEPENDENCE (1918 – 20). The conviction to secede from Russia deepened in various spheres of the community. In February 1918, the peace talks between Soviet Russia and Germany broke down. The Russian forces and the Bolsheviks fled back to Russia in face of the advancing German army. Representatives of the larger parties in the Land Council formed the Estonian Salvation Committee, and on February 24, 1918, the Republic of Estonia was declared in Tallinn – and it became the first of the small national republics in Europe to be formed by oppressed peoples. A provisional government was nominated (Chair. K.Päts), and neutrality was declared in the Russian – German war. The Germans refused to recognize the new state and occupied Estonia. Supreme power was assumed by the German military government; the power of the aristocracy was restored and the manors were returned to the aristocracy. The economy was subjugated to the interests of Germany.
THE ESTONIAN WAR OF INDEPENDENCE. After the collapse of Germany in November 1918, the Estonian Provisional Government assumed power. Soviet Russia attacked Estonia – and in an attempt to conceal the aggression the Estonian Working People's Commune was set up. By the beginning of 1919, 1/3 of Estonia was under Soviet control. The Estonians counter-attacked and freed the land in three weeks. The Estonian defense force was led by Johan Laidoner. Assistance was provided by a British fleet, and volunteers from Finland and Scandinavia (4,000 men). The breakthrough came when Estonia mobilized all its resources. In the spring of 1919, there were 86,000 men in the Estonian army. In April 1919, the freely elected Constituent Assembly convened and passed a declaration of independence, a land reform bill and a constitution. In June and July of 1919, successful battles were conducted against the Baltic-German Landeswehr army in northern Latvia.

Military activity against Soviet Russia continued in autumn, and on February 2, 1920, the Tartu Peace Treaty was concluded, wherein Soviet Russia recognized the Republic of Estonia. The national self-determination of the Estonian people occurred whilst the War of Independence was being fought. **INDEPENDENCE** (1920 – 39). ECONOMY. The basis for the development of the economy was the radical land reform bill, which redistributed the land and inventory of the manors back to the people on the land. This brought about a lessening of social tensions and encouraged the stabilization of society. Specialization in butter and bacon production increased, and this constituted the major part of exports — the main markets being Great Britain and Germany. During the 1930s, grain production increased — most of the usable land was cultivable because of extensive soil betterment programmes. In the period 1923 – 24, more attention was paid to the domestic market. The industrial use of oil shale was initiated, the rail network was completed, the manufacture of foodstuffs, timber, paper and cellulose increased. In 1928, the official currency became the *kroon*, which was backed by gold reserves. The world-wide depression culminated in Estonia in 1932, and production dropped by 1/3 — particularly in areas geared for export. The speedy recovery which began in 1934 was assisted by government participation in the economy. With the assistance of German capital investment, the oil shale and phosphorite industries expanded. Construction increased, and modern plants produced many of the manufactured goods which needed to be imported in the 1920s.
INTERNAL POLITICS. The Constitution ensured a parliamentary system. Power lay with the 100-member *Riigikogu*, which was elected every 3 years by general and secret vote. The parliament was dominant over the government, and not having a head of state was peculiar to the system. The people were able to express their will during elections, in plebiscites and through citizens' initiative. During the 1920s, the right-wing parties strengthened at the expense of the centrist parties. The illegal ECP attempted a coup on December 1, 1924, with the assistance of the Comintern. After the coup's failure, the influence of the party decreased. The Depression destabilized the political system. The veterans (from the War of Independence) movement came to the fore (some influences from Italian fascism), and their draft constitution, which proposed strong presidential rule, was selected by a plebiscite. On March 12, 1934, Prime Minister K.Päts and armed forces chief J.Laidoner carried out a bloodless coup and disbanded the veterans' organization. During the subsequent 'period of silence', the parliament and parties were disbanded, and political rights were restricted. Legislative power was in the hands of the head of state, and the *Isamaaliit* (Patriotic League) was created as a widely-based organization to support the government. The National Assembly developed in 1937, and implemented in 1938 a new Constitution. A two-chamber parliament was created, which was, to a certain extent, dependent upon the president. In April 1938, K.Päts was elected president. The period of the Estonian authoritarian regime had been one of the most moderate amongst the numerous authoritarian regimes in Europe at the time. Once the situation had stabilized, both the Communists and the vaps (as members of the veterans' organization were called) were given amnesty.
CULTURE. National independence meant that, for the first time, national culture could properly develop. Estonian, as the national language, quickly developed into a language of research and scholarship; the amount of printed matter exceeded all which had previously been published. A network of cultural establishments was created; development was encouraged by following the principles of grass-roots activity and freely accessible contacts with foreign countries. Tartu University played an important role in scholarship and higher education. Notable achievements were made in medicine (Ludvig Puusepp), botany (Teodor Lippmaa), astronomy (Ernst Öpik). The best-known writers were A. H. Tammsaare and Friedebert Tuglas; amongst the artists: Eduard Wiiralt. Good results were achieved in sports: Kristjan Palusalu in wrestling, Paul Keres in chess, success great in rifle-shooting. The progressive 1925 law on cultural autonomy guaranteed the minorities (Jews, Swedes, Germans) the preservation of their cultures.
The culture and way of life in Estonia was similar to the generally accepted European standard.
FOREIGN POLICY. In January 1921, the Entente major powers granted recognition to Estonia. In September 1921, Estonia was accepted into the League of Nations. Initially the aim of Estonian foreign policy was the creation of the Baltic League (from Finland to Poland), but due to differing interests, this did not succeed. In 1923, the Estonian-Latvian League was formed, and in 1934, the cooperation treaty between Estonia, Latvia and Lithuania was signed. The unstable relationship with the USSR improved in the late 1920s – 1932, a mutual non-aggression pact was signed (extended in 1934). Relations with Poland were consistently good. At the end of the 1920s, approaches were made to Sweden — the Scandinavian countries, however, were not interested in a Baltic-Scandinavian League. The long-time Estonian orientation towards Great Britain changed in 1935 when, after the maritime treaty concluded between Great Britain and Germany, the Baltic Sea was included in the German sphere of influence. Estonia, isolated from the west, was caught between totalitarian USSR and totalitarian Germany. In December 1938, Estonia declared itself neutral.
SOVIET OCCUPATION (1940 –). According to the Hitler-Stalin Pact's secret protocol (signed on August 23, 1939), Estonia became part of the SU sphere of influence. The USSR, threatening force, obliged Estonia to sign an agreement on September 28, which resulted in 25,000 Red Army soldiers being brought into Estonia (the Estonian army was 15,000 men). The pact did not allow interference in the signatories' economy or system of government. In October 1939, the Baltic-Germans began to return to Germany. On June 16, 1940, the USSR presented a note to the Estonian government which included

an ultimatum that a new government be appointed and that more Red Army troops be allowed into Estonia. The government retired, and on June 17, the Red Army occupied Estonia. Andrei Zhdanov, one of Stalin's closest colleagues, conducted the events — organizing a demonstration of power on June 21 in Tallinn, and forcing K.Päts to appoint the new government which was formed in the Soviet Embassy. Johannes Vares-Barbarus became the Prime Minister. The new parliament was elected on July 14 — 15 — voting laws were broken, opposition candidates had their candidatures annulled, and an atmosphere of fear prevailed. This new parliament proclaimed the formation of the Estonian SSR on July 21, and nationalized industry, banks and the land — with no compensation being offered. On August 6, 1940, the Estonian SSR was incorporated into the USSR. As part of a totalitarian state, Estonia was no longer able to undergo normal development. Society was controlled, uncertainty increased, most of the community organizations were disbanded. The economy was centralized under Moscow's control. In the period July 1940 — June 1941, approximately 1,000 people were arrested and disappeared. During the mass deportations which began on June 14, 1941, over 10,000 people were sent to Siberia, without any legal procedures being utilized. People fled to the forests to escape the terror.

GERMAN OCCUPATION. German forces crossed the Estonian border on July 5, 1941. 35,000 people joined the retreating Soviet forces, as well as 33,000 Estonians who had been forcibly conscripted into the Soviet army. The Germans reached Tallinn on August 28. The Germans did not fulfil Estonians' hopes that the Republic of Estonia would be restored. Estonia became part of Ostland. The occupation was led by Commissar General Karl Sigismund Litzmann, who also commanded the Estonian Local Government. The economy was subjugated to the interests of the Reich, and nationalized property was not returned. Approximately 5,500 Estonians were executed in concentration camps. Because of the Red Terror which dominated in 1940 and 1941, there was voluntary enlistment into the German army. In 1942, the Estonian Rifle Corps was formed in the USSR; Estonians who fled to Finland fought in Karelia with the Finns, and from August 1944 in Estonia. In February 1944, the Red Army was again posing a threat to Estonia. 40,000 Estonians joined the army, and together with the German forces, they stopped the Red Army at the Narva River (north-eastern Estonia). Soviet bombing attacks on city residential areas followed. In August 1944, the Soviet army invaded southern Estonia. The German forces retreated, and the National Committee of the Republic of Estonia (formed in summer) attempted to restore independence with the assistance of western powers. A provisional government was appointed on September 18, with Otto Tief as Prime Minister. It was not possible, however, to defend the country — the Red Army reached Tallinn on September 22, and by the end of November, the whole country was under Soviet control. Fearing another Soviet occupation, approximately 70,000 people fled to mainly Germany and Sweden. During the war, the Swedish minority had been evacuated to Sweden.

AGAIN A SOVIET OCCUPATION — STALINISM (1944 — 55). Sovietization — which began in 1940 and which ignored the interests of Estonian society — continued. Forced industrialization, where oil shale production and electric power generation, as well as the machine industry, were rapidly expanded, meant the introduction of over 200,000 migrants from Russia. Specific policies, aimed at restricting the role of Estonians in society, as well as restricting Estonian culture, were implemented. The activity of farms was limited. In 1947 collectivization began. On March 25 — 26, 1949, at least 20,700 people were deported. In total, approximately 50,000 underwent repressions in the period 1944 — 53. Fear was responsible for the speedy collectivization of the villages in 1949. Until 1953, metsavennad (forest brethren) presented the Soviet authorities with armed resistance. At the end of the 1940s, there was a strong attack against national culture — cultural treasures were destroyed, and the aim was to sever cultural continuity. During the 8th Plenum of the ECP, Estonians from Russia — with Moscow's support — won the internal party battle, which resulted in the loss of any remaining autonomy and an all-out attack on Estonian national culture.

'THE THAW' (1956 — 68). In conjunction with a certain liberalization in the USSR, decentralization occurred in the economy. In 1957 the Estonian SSR National Economic Council was formed as a regional controlling body, and the economic indicators improved — developments also occurred in light industry. Investment in agriculture resulted in improvements, and the collective farm workers began to receive monetary payments, rather than just payments in kind. The constant campaigns and repeated re-organizations in Khrushchev's time had a negative effect. Very little liberalization occurred in the political sphere because the Russian-Estonians maintained their leading positions. There was an increased sense of security — those deportees who had survived were able to return to Estonia. The numbers of Estonians joining the ECP increased — in the hope that they would be able to democratize the party (society) from the inside (in 1966, 52% of the party members were Estonians). Continuity was restored in culture; it was possible to be freer in the interpretation of socialist-realist dogma; there was a noticeable amount of creative freedom. As society became more open, it was possible to follow new international trends.

THE INCREASE IN POLITICAL-ADMINISTRATIVE CONTROL (1969 — 85). The 1965 reform meant a return to centralized economic control. In the 1980s, Moscow controlled more than 90% of Estonian industry; possibilities for extensive development were exhausted, and Estonia had fallen further behind developed countries. The amalgamation of state farms in the 1970s resulted in the destruction of many historic settlements. The condition of the environment deteriorated because of large-scale production. As a whole, however, Estonia was still ahead on the Soviet productivity scale. The control of the ECP over society increased during the 1970s. Censorship increased, and creative freedom was restricted. At the end of the 1970s, the ECP, intending to increase the importance of Russian, began to restrict the use of Estonian. Dissatisfaction increased, and the dissident movement began. In 1980, 40 intellectuals — in an open letter — drew attention to the unresolved nationalities problem. In 1979, 1,465,800 people lived in Estonia, of whom 35.3% were non-Estonians. The Estonian leadership, obedient to Moscow, had not considered the interests of the Estonian people, and, in its ineptitude, had deepened the social-economic crisis.

THE RESTORATION OF A CIVIC SOCIETY (1986 — 90). By the mid-1980s, general stagnation prevailed. The glasnost encouraged by Moscow caused the central powers' intention to establish new phosphorite mines in northern Estonia to be made public. Mining in this area would have resulted in an ecological catastrophe (e.g., poisoning vital ground water supplies), as well as another influx of migrants. The dangers united the people, and massive protests occurred. On August 23, 1987 (anniversary of the Hitler-Stalin Pact), dissidents in Tallinn organized the first political demonstration. Plans for Estonian economic independence were fully supported. At the joint conference of the creative unions on April 1 — 2, 1988, a programme of action was presented: extending Estonian economic and political rights, halting the illegal flow of migrants, cultural independence. The Popular Front was founded on April 13, and united the masses. The national flag was restored. Criticism against the ECP leadership became more direct. During the summer of 1988, in a period of never-before-seen political activity, post-Stalinist society was thoroughly shaken, the historical memory of society was restored, compromised politicians were forced to resign. At a mass gathering organized by the EPF on September 11 — with 300,000 participants — radicals were already demanding political independence for Estonia. As a result of public pressure, the Supreme Soviet passed a sovereignty declaration on November 16, 1988, which acknowledged the supremacy of Estonian laws, and declared all resources in Estonia to be Estonian property. The new era of awakening caused Estonians to once again see themselves as a sovereign people, and the peaceful struggle to restore independent nationhood began. The Estonian problem began to receive international attention. In the years 1989 — 90, the civic society was restored: a free press developed, political parties were formed, society became more open, there were free elections. The ECP collapsed and relinquished its position of power. Historical truth was the basis for the Citizens Committees movement, which proposes the restoration of the Republic of Estonia on the basis of international law and Republic of Estonia citizenship. On August 23, 1989, the Popular Fronts from Estonia, Latvia and Lithuania organized a 600 km long human chain from Vilnius to Tallinn, demanding 'Freedom for the Baltic States'. On March 30, 1990, the new SC declared Soviet power in Estonia to be illegal, and declared a transition period for the restoration of the Republic of Estonia. The transition period will end with the formation of the constitutional bodies of power. On May 8, 1990, the flag and symbols of the Estonian SSR were abolished, and the official name of the country restoring its nationhood became the Republic of Estonia. There have been many changes in Estonia over the last three years, but Estonia has not yet managed to restore its nationhood. With 150,000 Soviet troops based on its territory, and no control over its borders, Estonia is still an occupied country.

NATIONAL ECONOMY

Estonia's gross domestic product (GDP) in 1989 amounted to 6,360 million roubles, or 4,017 roubles per capita. Nearly 80% of the GDP represented production, 20% was generated in the service sector.

By the mid-1960s, a Soviet-style structure had been developed for the Estonian economy, conforming to the central planning ideas then held in the USSR. This is clearly illustrated by the distribution of labour employed in various sectors of the economy (see Table 1). No significant changes occurred in the economic structure during the last 25 years. The service sector increased to some extent, while agriculture's share in employment declined. The number of people employed in industry grew until 1986 when it began to decrease.

In 1988, there were 291 independently operating industrial enterprises in Estonia, with some 230,000 employees producing 5,700 million roubles worth of manufactured goods. Additional manufactured goods were produced by collective farms, construction organizations and many cooperatives. Traditional Soviet classification of economic activity included among manufacturing industries such spheres as mining and electrical and thermal energy production (in the latter categories, however, only major power stations were included). A list of major industrial products are presented in Table 2. Estonia's list of industries (see Table 3) is headed by light industry and the food industry, which together account for 1/2 of the country's industrial output.

LIGHT INDUSTRY. Estonia's long-established textile mills (*Kreenholmi Manufaktuur* in Narva and *Balti Manufaktuur* in Tallinn, among others) maintain a leading position with considerable quantities of cotton material produced for export. Other important light industries are clothing and footwear. In the unbalanced Soviet market, Estonian light industrial products are in demand. Unfortunately, their mediocre quality makes them unsuitable for competition in foreign markets. Often they do not even satisfy the increasingly sophisticated needs of local consumers. Development in this sector is hampered by dependency on imported raw materials and technology.

EMPLOYMENT STRUCTURE

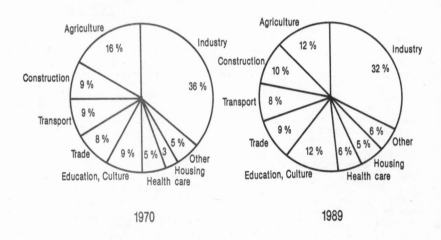

1970   1989

THE STRUCTURE OF INDUSTRIAL OUTPUT

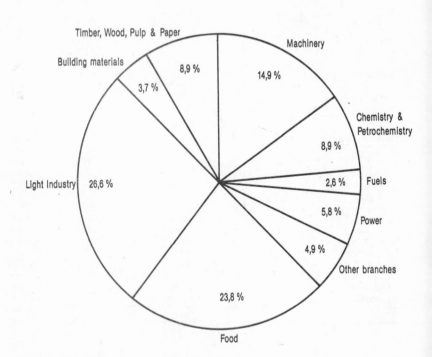

1988

Table 1
Distribution of Labour Force

	('000 persons)	
	1970	1989
Industry	246	270
Agriculture (excl. private farms)	109	92
Forestry	8	8
Transport and communications	65	73
Construction	65	73
Commerce, catering, distribution	58	75
Other production	9	15
Housing and municipal workers, vital services	24	38
Health care, sports, social services	34	48
Education, culture, arts, sciences	62	96
Banking, insurance	3	4
Government, administrative organs	16	19
Total	**698**	**814**

Table 2
Principal Industrial Products

	Unit of measurement	1980	1988
Electric energy (incl. power station consumption)	million kwh	18,898	17,627
Oil shale	million t	31,334	23,307
AC electric motors	u.	309,200	248,100
Excavators	u.	2,251	2,054
Air cooling equipment (for oil industry)	million roubles	34.0	45.8
Mineral fertilizers (recalculated for 100% active agent content)	'000 t	267.9	245.0
Sulphuric acid (as monohydrate)	'000 t	506.2	654.2
Varnishes, paints, solvents	t	3,744	3,831
Timber products	'000 cu m	2,530	2,700
Plywood	'000 sq m	30.3	32.9
Fibreboard	'000 sq m	3,813	16,777
Chip-board	'000 cu m	100.2	184.4
Cellulose	'000 t	86.5	94.2
Paper	'000 t	93.1	94.6
Skis	'000 p.	885	986
Cement	'000 t	1,213	1,200
Bricks	million u.	267.0	253.5
Roofing	'000 sq m	34,369	37,639
Window glass	'000 sq m	1,987	1,855
Textiles	million sq m	206.3	238.5
Footwear	million p.	5.8	6.8
Meat	'000 t	155.3	185.5
Butter	'000 t	30.4	32.5
Cheese	'000 t	12.1	17.4
Tinned food	million tins	317	355
Wine and spirits	million l	22.3	13.7
Cigarettes	million	4,456	4,735

Table 3
Categories of Industrial Output in 1988

	million roubles	%
Power	332	6
Fuels	145	3
Chemistry and petrochemistry	505	9
Machinery	844	15
Timber, wood products, pulp, paper	503	9
Building materials	210	4
Light industry	1,507	27
Food industry	1,349	24
Other	277	5

Local agriculture (meat and dairy industry), together with fishery products from the Baltic Sea as well as the Atlantic Ocean provide the basis for the Estonian FOOD INDUSTRY. A substantial part of the output is now being marketed in the SU, in spite of Estonia's own needs for meat, dairy products and quality fish products being left unsatisfied. Scarcity of raw materials limits the scope and speed at which these spheres can be developed. In future, therefore, attention must primarily focus on ways to better satisfy local demand. Chances of gaining entry into export markets (outside the USSR) will not only depend on product quality (one important aspect of which is the raising of sanitation standards at production sites), but also the extent to which agricultural production costs can be reduced. The fishing industry is nevertheless being regarded as the potential key to the world market. Another possible export sphere is the liquor industry. Though tobacco and confectionery production has proved remarkably efficient, the procurement of imported raw materials is causing difficulties.

The MECHANICAL ENGINEERING AND METALLURGICAL INDUSTRIES were until recently largely controlled by USSR ministries and government agencies. Leading sections in the mechanical engineering sector are instrument-making (measuring instruments, automation devices and control instruments for technological processes made by *RET*, *Tööstusaparaat*, etc.) and electrical engineering (*Volta* electric motors, electrical wires and cables made by *Eesti Kaabel*, lighting and other electrical fittings by *Estoplast*). Other products include excavators (*Talleks*), oil and gas processing equipment (Tallinn Engineering Plant), and food processing equipment (Pärnu Engineering Plant). Repairs of machinery and equipment have an important part in the activities of the mechanical engineering industry (facilities for marine and motor vehicle repairs). With the exception of repair works, the bulk of this sector's output has so far been earmarked for distribution to various parts of the SU. The foreign export share is insignificant, and growth is being held back by the inferior quality of current products and the orientation towards the Soviet market. For the industry to gain a foothold in the world market, its production would obviously have to be restructured and the need for metal as raw material substantially reduced.

Of importance to Estonia is the production of ELECTRICAL ENERGY from locally mined oil shale. Due to the extremely low prices which have been set for fuel and power products, their accorded share of the total value of industrial output has been small, given the fact that they require almost 1/3 of the industrial investment. This sector also causes great problems to natural resources and the environment. The annual output of oil shale extracted from 7 mines and 4 open-cut mines amounts to between 23 and 24 million metric t, of which close to 90% is burned into electric energy at the 2 thermal power stations Estonian Thermal Power Station and Baltic Thermal Power Station. The remainder is being processed into chemical products at 2 oil shale chemical plants. 1/2 of the generated electric power is supplied to neighbouring Latvia and the Russian Federation. If the atmospheric pollution caused by this industry is not significantly reduced (by 30% by the year 1992 and 50% by 1995, compared to 1980), the production of electric energy from oil shale will have to be reduced.

Estonia's resources of phosphorite provide local raw material for the CHEMICAL INDUSTRY. Phosphorite, used in the production of fertilizer, comes from the Maardu deposits, which are now being exhausted. Until now, the Maardu Chemical Plant has been the source of the most severe air, water and soil pollution in the Tallinn region. Production in this plant is moving into a reconstruction phase. The rich phosphorite reserves in Virumaa are waiting for an economically viable and ecologically acceptable technology to be developed. Nor has there yet been found a final solution to the problems involved in the enrichment of further processing of these deposits.

During the last few years the plastics industry has expanded its capabilities (the product line includes motorcycle and safety helmets, skiing and skating boots, toys, and washable wallpaper). A substantial part of the output goes to the Soviet market. However, packaging problems remain unsolved. The manufacture of varnishes and paints needs to be modernized, as does the range of detergents and other household chemicals. The future of the entire plastics and household chemical industry will depend on the availability of raw material.

The TIMBER, WOOD-PROCESSING, CELLULOSE AND PAPER INDUSTRIES utilize mainly domestic forest resources. Although the two Estonian cellulose plants at Tallinn and Kehra have caused considerable environmental problems, the future development of the cellulose and paper industries is regarded with optimism due to the existence of local raw material. An increase in the industry's potential is now on the agenda, with a view to entering the international market.

The furniture industry has undergone rapid development, helped by the establishment of a fibreboard plant at the village of Püssi. Today, fibreboard has almost entirely replaced natural timber in furniture-making. This has not been of benefit to the quality, however, due to the toxic glues used in the production of the board. Nevertheless, on the Soviet market, this type of mass-produced furniture continues to be in great demand, while domestic needs are left unattended. Looking ahead, it will be necessary to raise the quality of the furniture and to seek new markets abroad.

Technologically, the present state of the BUILDING MATERIALS INDUSTRY is extremely bad. The *Punane Kunda* cement plant needs to be replaced. So do many other run-down production facilities in the building materials sector (silica bricks, roofing tiles). The shortage and low quality of building materials are largely to blame for the slow development of Estonia's economy.

Estonian AGRICULTURE is specialized in cattle breeding. As a consequence of central planning, the targets for meat production were set to be extremely high. At present, this requires an annual import of more than 1 million t of grain feed. At the same time about 1/3 of the processed meat is taken out of the country. This type of agricultural structure is not suited to the nature of Estonia's cultivatable land. The total area of cultivatable land amounts to 1.36 million ha, of which 926,000 ha are arable land, 252,000 ha meadows and 181,000 ha pasture. Cereals and pulse crops are cultivated on approximately 400,000 ha, potato fields account for 55,000 – 60,000 ha, and 470,000 ha are for feed. The yield has fluctuated greatly during the last few years. The cereal crop has averaged 19 t per ha (after drying and cleaning), the potato yield 148 t per ha. During the last decades the number of cattle has risen (to 818,000 head in 1988); the proportional number of cows has, however, decreased. The ever-growing commitments to supply meat have been fulfilled primarily by increasing the number of pigs, which in recent years has risen to 1.1 million. Given development freedom, Estonian agriculture would be better off producing less meat and more milk. The dynamics of agricultural produce as well principal products are listed in Table 4.

Table 4
Principal Agricultural Products

	unit of measurement	1980	1988
Cereals	'000 t	196.2	204.4
Potatoes	'000 t	302.9	187.3
Vegetables	'000 t	80.5	75.1
Meat (slaughter weight)	'000 t	181.5	213.1
Milk and dairy products	'000 t	1031.6	1165.4
Eggs	million	406.2	436.9

Up to the mid-1980s Estonian agriculture underwent a process of production concentration into ever bigger collective farming enterprises, until a total of approximately 300 agro-industrial units was reached. The last five years has seen a reversal of this process. Agricultural production has been deconcentrated, beginning with the breaking up of the largest farms into smaller units and establishing family farms in outlying areas. In the most recent years the creation of private farms has dominated the picture, and at the end of 1990 Estonia had approximately 3,200 private farms. Agriculture has thus been the sector where the pace of the privatization process has been the fastest. Taking into account the limited availability of building materials and machinery, the addition of 1,000 new farms per year is considered a realistic prognosis for the near future.

Estonia's relatively dense road network facilitates TRANSPORTATION. The total length of the railway system is just over 1,000 km, all-weather paved roads 14,800 km. Motor vehicles dominate domestic freight-carrying with almost 100 million t of dispatched goods from a total of approximately 140 million t. Shipping leads in transportation turnover with close to 20,000 million t-km (from a total 30,000 million t-km carried annually). Sea transportation has increased in particular since the construction of Tallinn's New Harbour and the acquisition of more high-capacity vessels by the Estonian Merchant Shipping Agency. These ships carry grain from North America and also serve the West-African cargo routes. The railway is the second largest carrier with an annual turnover of 8,000 million t-km. Key problems in railway transportation are the scarcity of rolling stock and fluctuations in loads. In order to increase throughput, a second line of tracks is being laid along the Tallinn – Narva route.

The main form of transport for passengers are motor vehicles. Buses alone carry approximately 430 million passengers annually (from a total of 480 million travellers). Estonia has a notably high number of private cars – 135 per 1,000 inhabitants – which, though modest in comparison with other industrialized countries, still tops the Soviet list of republics.

Foreign travel – outside the SU – is an area where passenger transportation is crippled by problems. It is difficult to obtain train and airplane tickets. Boat connections between Tallinn and Helsinki, however, have become more frequent since joint shipping companies were established and additional ferries put into service. In 1990, a ferry service was opened between Tallinn and Stockholm. Tallinn has direct air links to Helsinki and Stockholm.

Business in the SERVICE SECTOR was formerly, with the exception of commercial enterprises, dependent on government financing.

Total turnover in retail trading was 3,100 million roubles in 1988, of which food catering accounted for slightly more than 300 million. There are 4,100 retail enterprises in Estonia and 2,500 establishments serving food; neither number suffices to cover existing needs, least of all in the towns. The problem is aggravated by the shortage of available goods which is the cause of queues. People are forced to go to several stores for their daily shopping and to wait for a long time for various goods to appear in the stores.

By the end of 1988, available HOUSING comprised of a total of 33.3 million sq m, or an average of 21.1 sq m living space per person. Government-owned, public and cooperative housing account for a major part (since private housing was nationalized at the start of the Soviet occupation in 1940) – 71% of all housing (82% in urban and 52% in rural areas). Rents have been relatively low, because housing costs have been largely financed by government subsidies. Low-cost, low-quality housing dominates the picture. Current plans propose to discontinue the present system of subsidies, and to sell off the bulk of government-owned and public housing units to their occupants.

EDUCATION has been free. In terms of quality, it has left something to be desired. General education is plagued by a shortage of school buildings, which forces many urban schools to operate in two shifts. Educational reform is now under way where the primary object is to modify the curriculum. In future, part of the educational system will probably require payment, which should help to enhance the value of the knowledge acquired.

HEALTH SERVICES have, up to now, also been free of charge. The main problem confronting the medical system is the shortage of technical equipment and drugs which makes it impossible to utilize the existing medical care potential. The introduction of a medical insurance programme is now being planned.

FINANCE. The current legal tender in Estonia is the Soviet rouble, which is issued by the Soviet State Bank, that also controls the money supply and the circulation. In reality, the monetary situation is catastrophic. The rouble, not being a convertible currency, has ceased to be the generally accepted means of exchange and is even being rejected by many Soviet state agencies and enterprises. Not merely inconvertible on the international market, the rouble is now inconvertible in domestic trade as well.

The banking system is in disarray. Several commercial banks have been established in Estonia, but since the Soviet State Bank still retains control over banking operations, the deliberate slowness with which foreign clearing accounts are settled in Moscow amounts at times to a virtual banking blockade.

The Estonian national budget is separated from the Soviet Union's budget, and will be subject to substantial structural as well as procedural changes. For 1991, however, the old structural pattern had to be retained, with a balance of 2,800 million roubles to be distributed.

Until 1990, one objective of the budget was the distribution of subsidies to the agricultural sector in compensation for the low state prices paid for its products. With the liberalization of price regulations and the gradual transition to free-market prices, these funds were at the end of 1990 being used to compensate low-income groups. Faced with the present difficulties and uncertainties, no prediction for the 1991 budget or revenues will carry any guarantee, and a new budget structure has therefore proved difficult to implement. The underlying principles have, however, already been formulated.

The 1989 aggregate profits of Estonian enterprises totalled 1,700 million roubles.

A consequence of the shortage of goods has been an increase in savings, which at the beginning of 1990 were estimated at 2,300 million roubles (or 1,464 roubles per person), despite last year's general awareness that interest rates (until recently averaging 2.5%) lagged behind inflation. This growth in holdings does not reflect any degree of prosperity, but the fact that people are not able to make use of their incomes. The first articles to disappear from stores were jewelry and any commodity that vaguely looked like an investment object. In early 1990, the fear of monetary reform and accelerating inflation turned into panic as people began to draw money from their bank accounts and hoard everyday consumer goods. The result was a total collapse of the consumer market.

The situation was further complicated by the liberalization of business and by the activities of cooperatives and small state enterprises. Although cooperatives were created on the assumption of their providing mainly consumer goods and services to the general public, they became very active suppliers of services to government enterprises. As a result, a large part of bank deposits held by state companies was converted into wages for cooperative staffs or into goods bought on the retail market. In the absence of normal business regulations the activities of the cooperatives and small enterprises therefore had a destabilizing influence on the consumer goods market.

There are no reliable long-term statistics for inflation. According to the estimates of the Estonian Statistics Department, 1989 saw an inflation rate of 3.1%. The official figures, however, do not include price rises in speculative trading. In the 2nd half of 1990, prices for several categories of food were raised. From IV quarter of 1989 to IV quarter of 1990, consumer prices increased more than by 60%.

FOREIGN TRADE RELATIONS. Until recently Estonia's foreign trade was characterized by net imports. In 1987, the value of imports was 3,600 million roubles, whereas exports were valued at 2,900 million roubles; these figures do not include service transactions. Fuel and raw materials account for nearly 40% of import expenditures. Machinery is, for the most part, also imported. Main export items are light industrial products, foodstuffs, machinery, chemical products, electric power, cellulose, paper and furniture.

In 1987, Estonian products were exported (to countries outside the USSR) to the sum of 218 million roubles while foreign goods at a cost of 660 million roubles (at domestic prices) were imported. Until recently, part of the imports were channelled through Soviet foreign trade organizations and paid for in Soviet roubles.

Although the trade deficit is somewhat smaller when calculated at world market prices, the shortage of hard currency is perceptible. The sale of services to foreign tourists does not, to any significant extent, reduce the imbalance.

In foreign trade relations Estonia's closest ties have to now been with Finland, followed by Germany and the Czecho-Slovakia.

CULTURE

ESTONIAN FOLK CULTURE. The oldest Estonian religious beliefs probably reach back to the Stone Age. These included the belief that the spirit of a witch could leave the body and gain wisdom from the place of the dead (shamanism); and the image of a tribal ancestor-animal (totemism). The cosmogonic myths about the creation of the world from the egg of a miraculous bird, and the creation of the Milky Way from a giant tree have been preserved in folklore, and are just as old. The cult of the dead had a central position in ancient times. The dead were believed to be under the control of evil forces, but also the controllers of this force. People turned towards the dead for assistance, and attempted to placate them with funeral rites and sacrifices. The home of the dead was imagined to be the funeral grove — in a forest of deciduous trees — where initially the body was placed (in later times, the dead were buried). Everything in nature was believed to have a spirit. These nature spirits were later treated as protective spirits, who were often referred to using the ancient German word *haldjas* (sprite). During the development of Estonian agriculture in the 1st millennium AD, spirits associated with the growth of crops and fertility attained pivotal importance. The most important holiday was Christmas, which was associated with fertility magic. The concept of Titanic heroes was borrowed from Scandinavia where it was widespread. After Christianity was introduced in the 13th cent., the belief in spirits blended with the cult of Catholic saints. The saints' name-days were celebrated using ancient pagan rites. The Lutheran Church was also unable to supplant the native beliefs; this occurred only in the 18th and 19th cent. when the Herrnhuter beliefs and later religious sects became more widespread.

The most original part of Estonian folklore, the runic folksong, originated in the 1st millennium BC as a result of the interaction between primitive Balto-Finnic singing (warbling, keening) and the songs of the Baltic tribes. Runic songs are based on the alternation of long and short syllables. The basic runic verse line is the trochaic tetrameter, with each line generally forming a conceptual whole. A song is constructed by the use of parallelism — the repetition, development and further definition of the concept of a line of verse in subsequent lines. The words are tied within the verse by alliteration and assonance. There are approximately 3,600 runic song types and 133,000 variations. The tunes have limited scope but are rich in variations. The oldest are songs with myth themes, spells and family ballads; with the coming of agriculture, work and ritual songs with a magic function developed. Most of the surviving songs are from the serfdom period, where the singers were mainly women, and the content female-oriented (there are no hero songs). Due to the conditions of serfdom, the songs were mainly elegy-style and satirical — rarely is there joy or love expressed. In the 19th cent., due to the influence of hymns, folksongs with rhyming lines became prevalent. These were more male-centered, and there is even some comedy. The tune was more complicated — often accompanied by a musical instrument (zither, violin, concertina). In folk stories the most common themes are legends — particularly place legends, and almost every larger rock, tree, body of water or hill has a legend associated with it. Heroic legends have blended with legends about hills. Estonian proverbs have been researched in detail, and 82,000 have been published.

Estonian folk culture has developed in contact with German and Slavic cultures. As a result of the German conquest in the 13th cent., Estonians remained peasants for centuries, and kept to their traditional culture. The towns on the other hand became German cultural provinces. Because the peasants were bound to the land, the differences between parishes (dialects and national dress) became more pronounced. Estonians lived in *rehi* dwellings, which consisted of three parts: in the centre of house (which had no chimney) there was a living-grain-drying room; at one end there was a threshing room, which was used in the winter as a barn; and in the other end there was a summer living room, without a fireplace (in the winter it was a storeroom). The buildings were built from logs, and had thatched roofs. Farms always had separate sauna buildings, which were also used to give birth and to treat illnesses. Farms were generally grouped as villages, but approximately 30% were isolated farms. Villagers used a common meadow and cooperated on major farming work. The most important event was a wedding — a performance with many definite traditions and players — which could last for up to a week. The effects of town culture were to be seen in handicrafts and clothing already in the 13th and 14th cent., but not in the farming practices. The town influences were immediately seen in the embroidery and lace used in the national costumes, as well as in the carved and burnt ornamental design on wooden beer mugs. A major change in folk culture occurred during the period of awakening (1860 — 80), when German cultural traditions were used as a cultural model.

EDUCATION. Latin-language cathedral and monastery schools were operating from the mid-13th cent., and Latin-language municipal schools from the 15th to 16th cent. Estonian peasant schools were founded after the decisions by the Livonian Diet in 1687, and the Estonian Diet in 1689, to establish a school in each parish. In 1688, there were 45 to 50 schools, where approximately 1,100 Estonian children studied (from a population estimated at 350,000 people). In 1641, the first Estonian primer was published. A major event in Estonian education occurred in 1630 when a secondary school was opened in Tartu; and in 1631 another one was opened in Tallinn. In 1632, on instruction from Swedish King Gustav II Adolph, the Tartu secondary school was changed into a university *Academia Gustaviana* (Tartu University). As a result of the Northern War, as well as famine and plague, at the beginning of the 18th cent., most of the schools were closed. Reading skills survived due to home and church confirmation instruction. In the 1780s, 45 – 50% of the population could read (at the same time in France, 47% of men and 27% of women could read). A stable school system began to take shape at the beginning of the19th cent. By the 2nd half of the 19th cent., a network of village and parish schools had been established. The language of instruction was Estonian. Secondary education developed: state secondary schools, secondary scientific schools, and private German schools were established. According to the 1897 census, 77.7% were literate, 96.2% could read. When the tsarist government began its Russification policies in the Baltic states in the 1880s, all schools were required to teach in Russian.

The independent Republic of Estonia introduced Estonian-language primary, secondary and higher education in 1919. An exemplerary 6-class primary school system was developed, with well-trained teachers and good quality textbooks. Primary education was free; education was compulsory from the age of 7 or 8 until 16. A network of vocational schools was established. Tartu University was developed into a national university, where, for the first time, Estonian topics – such as Estonian philology, ethnology and history – were researched and taught.

After the occupation of Estonia by the SU in 1940, the Soviet education system was established. The period 1940 – 87, was a period of uniformity in education. The Theology Faculty at Tartu University was closed. The Marxism-Leninism ideology was taught at schools; most of the textbooks were translated from Russian. Estonians and Russians were able to be educated in their native languages. The current education system covers pre-school (creches and kindergartens), general education, vocational education, secondary specialized education and higher education. The Estonian-language secondary school consists of 12 years of instruction (9 years in junior school + 3 years senior), Russian-language schools have 11 years. Handicapped children have special schools, and there are children's homes for orphans and uncared-for children. Special education is provided by music, art, sports, Sunday schools, etc. Skilled workers are trained by vocational secondary schools and technical schools; those with intermediate special education are trained at the medical, teachers and maritime colleges. In 1990, there were 561 schools in Estonia with 214,000 students, as well as 24,000 university students. Institutes of higher education are: Tartu University (1632), Tallinn Art University (1914), Tallinn Conservatoire (1919), Tallinn Technical University (1936), Tallinn Teacher Training Institute (1947), Estonian Evangelical Lutheran Church Theological Institute (1947), Estonian Agricultural Academy (Tartu, 1951).

Alternative education is becoming popular: e.g., the Old Town Primary School (1987) and the higher education, Estonian Institute of Humanities (1988).

SCIENCE. Estonia is located on the frontier between the church cultures of Roman Catholicism and Greek Orthodoxy. The geopolitical location of Estonia between East and West has substantially determined the development of scholarship in Estonia. The world view of Estonians, who were conquered in the 13th cent. by Catholic crusaders, was mythological – which was typical of pre-scientific cultures. Only in the fields of folk astronomy, medicine and phenology were there elements of objective knowledge. The European tradition of scholarship began with the founding of Tartu University in 1632. Prior to this, studies were undertaken in Western European universities, but this occurred only to a limited degree. In conjunction with the university, scholarship was cultivated in learned societies and publishing institutions. The history of Tartu University (and other bodies involved in learning) can be divided into 4 periods – determined by the political environment. The Swedish Period (1632 – 1710): normal scholarship with contemporary standards; no original work was done. The Baltic-German Period (1802 – 85): the contemporary learning standard was again reached quickly, and then the scientists rose to be amongst the leaders of the 19th cent. scientific revolution. The founders of the classical modern biology were Tartu University graduates Christian Pander and Karl Ernst von Baer; because of their, and Friedrich Bidder's, influence, the university remained in the forefront in the study of organisms – until the end of the period. Important achievements were also made in geography (Adam Johann von Krusenstern's group), in founding modern-day ecology and soil technology (Karl Ernst von Baer, Alexander von Middendorff, Carl Schmidt). The Russian (Russification) Period (1885 – 1918): the emphasis on natural science in the university was replaced by Slavic studies (Jan Baudouin de Courtenay). The Estonian Period (1918 –); learning developed in many areas; in periods with a favourable political situation, there has been more emphasis on national and regional scholarship – history, ethnology, Finno-Ugric linguistics. Estonian is a well-developed language for science. Tartu astronomers have remained in the forefront of their field – the main areas for research being stellar astronomy and cosmology (Wilhelm Struve, Johann Heinrich von Mädler, Ernst Öpik, Jaan Einasto). There have been successes in medical research (Ludvig Puusepp, Ain-Elmar Kaasik); as well as in chemistry (oil shale technology). The Nobel laureate Wilhelm Ostwald, one of the founders of physical chemistry, came from Tartu. Applied mathematics has generally been stronger than pure mathematics. The first cybernetics (computer science) institute in the SU was founded in Estonia (1961). There are many physics research centres. Science is well-developed in Estonia, and international contacts are increasing.

In 1990, there were 3 types of scientific research institutions in Estonia: the Estonian Academy of Sciences (1938), with 15 institutes; 7 institutes of higher education, with faculties and laboratories; and research departments of ministries and companies. Over 21,000 people worked in the higher education and research institutes – of these, 7,150 were researchers and academic staff (incl. 356

DSc. and 3,150 CSc.). There are difficulties in obtaining modern research equipment. The research system, which has developed in Estonia due to the requirements of the Soviet large-scale planned economy, has had very little association with the needs of the local Estonian community. When Estonia regains its independence, the scientific research system, and its functions, will need to undergo major changes.

LITERATURE. The first book with Estonian-language text (Lutheran catechism) was published in 1525. During the 16th to 18th cent., most of the literature was religious. In 1739, a successful Estonian translation of the Bible was published. Literature written by Estonians began in the period 1810 — 20 with the patriotic and philosophic poetry of Kristjan Jaak Peterson. In the mid-19th cent. Friedrich Robert Faehlmann published legends based on Greek and Finnish myths. The national epic *Kalevipoeg* (Son of Kalev, 1857 — 61) was written by Friedrich Reinhold Kreutzwald, based on themes from Estonian folklore. The epic consists of 19,023 runic verses and tells of the struggles and adventures of Kalevipoeg, the mythic Estonian ruler. The epic concludes with the invasion of foreign conquerors and the death of Kalevipoeg.

During the period of national awakening, the main theme in literature is the expression of love for the homeland, using a romantic style — the most prominent of the poets was Lydia Koidula. Juhan Liiv united the tragedy of his suppressed people with his own — in writing poems, which are effective in their simplicity. Eduard Vilde wrote the novel *Külmale maale* (To the Cold Land, 1896) as the first example of Estonian naturalism. Besides numerous novels, E.Vilde also wrote memorable plays. Another founder of Estonian play-writing is August Kitzberg (the tragedy *Libahunt* — Werewolf, 1912). Oskar Luts, with his colourful school tales (*Kevade* — Spring, 1912 — 13), has remained very popular.

The movement *Noor-Eesti* (Young Estonia), formed during the 1905 Revolution, was interested in literature from the aspect of aesthetics. Gustav Suits wrote philosophical lyrical poems using complicated forms; Friedebert Tuglas developed short stories with finely-worked composition. The movement *Siuru* (Wonderbird) had as its example the bohemian — one who follows creative urges and spiritual experiences. Marie Under wrote lyrical poetry and ballads, and her scale of emotions ranged from the raptures of love to deep tragedy. Henrik Visnapuu wrote of personal emotional experiences. The greatest Estonian novellist A. H. Tammsaare wrote the five-volume epic *Tõde ja Õigus* (Truth and Justice) in 1926 — 33, which gives an overview of both the philosophic development of the Estonian people, and the events, during the period 1870 — 1930. The other major novellists during the independence period were August Gailit, Albert Kivikas, August Jakobson, Mait Metsanurk, August Mälk. The prominent short-story writers were Karl August Hindrey, Peet Vallak and Karl Ast-Rumor.

In the 1930s, a new generation of poets, who declared the spiritual independence of writers, and emphasized the importance of art and form, made their debut: they appeared together in an anthology *Arbujad* in 1938. Betti Alver's lyrical poetry, which unites philosophical force with uncompromising ethics, attained great prominence during the years of occupation. Uku Masing's poetry with complex imagery reflects his religious experiences. Heiti Talvik, Kersti Merilaas and August Sang wrote lyrical poetry which was purely personal. The most prominent playwright during the 1920s and 1930s was Hugo Raudsepp. The most influential literary critics and scholars were G.Suits (professor of literature at Tartu University), F.Tuglas, Johannes Semper, August Annist and Ants Oras. By the end of the independence period, Estonian literature had attained a European standard.

In 1944, the majority of Estonia's leading writers (G.Suits, M.Under, H.Visnapuu, A.Gailit, A.Mälk, A.Kivikas) fled to the West in face of the Soviet invasion and occupation. The centre for literature in exile became Sweden. The central figure in exile literature became Bernard Kangro, a writer of elegies, lyrical poems, novels, scholar of literature and publisher. Karl Ristikivi achieved prominence with his historical-philosophical novels. Valev Uibopuu, Arvo Mägi, Arved Viirlaid, Helga Nõu and Raimond Kolk are prolific and versatile writers. Kalju Lepik uses varying styles and shades of emotion in his poetry. Ilmar Laaban has written surrealistic poetry; and Arno Vihalemm's poetry contains humorous absurdisms.

Literature in occupied Estonia was subjected to the strict control of the Stalinist regime, and it was possible to only publish works praising the system. Many writers were in prison; H.Talvik and H. Raudsepp died in Siberia. A new era in literature began during the liberalization of the Soviet regime in the 1960s. The most prominent representatives of the post-war generation were poet Debora Vaarandi and writer Juhan Smuul. Modernistic language imagery was introduced into Estonian poetry by Artur Alliksaar, who experimented with language opportunities; poet Paul-Eerik Rummo, who interpreted the spiritual revolution of the 1960s, and pantheistic poet and essayist Jaan Kaplinski. Hando Runnel writes political satires in the form of simple folk poems. Juhan Viiding (Jüri Üdi) uses the absurd and grotesque; Viivi Luik and Doris Kareva write about subtle emotional experiences. Jaan Kross is the best-known internationally — the central theme of his historical novels is the life and death struggle of Estonian men against the society of a large power. The current Estonian society has been reflected in the modernistic writings of Mati Unt, the existentialism of Arvo Valton, the humour and irony of Enn Vetemaa and the deep scepticism of Mats Traat. Lennart Meri has written about the history of the Baltic Sea peoples, using an essayistic style. One of the basic themes of literature during the last fifty years has been the historic injustice visited upon the

Estonian people, and the misanthropy of the Soviet regime — a theme which could only be expressed indirectly because of the Soviet censors.

Estonian literature has been translated mainly into the languages of the peoples in the SU and Eastern Europe. World literature has been translated into Estonian from approximately 50 languages.

ARCHITECTURE. Permanent settlement on Estonian territory dates from the end of the Bronze Age. Most of the population lived in villages consisting of log buildings; the most typical was a *rehi* dwelling, with a room which could be heated. With the coming of Christianity in the 13th cent., churches and monasteries were constructed. Building masters from Scandinavia and Germany directed architecture along Western European lines. GOTHIC prevailed from the 13th to the beginning of the 16th cent. Vaulting began to be used. Limestone was used in northern Estonia, and bricks in southern Estonia. The oldest stone churches (2nd half of the 13th cent., and 1st half of the 14th cent.) are very simple, with pleasing proportions. The Karja Church on the Island of Saaremaa is unique with its rich sculpture. Unique amongst northern European brick Gothic structures is the Jaani Church in Tartu (14th cent.) with its terracotta figures. The best preserved of the fortifications is the Kuressaare Episcopal Castle (14th cent.) in the Teutonic Order's architectural style. By the 14th cent., Tallinn had a complete city wall; in the 16th cent. the city wall was one of Northern Europe's largest and strongest. Of the towns dating from the Middle Ages, the Tallinn old town is the best preserved — with its churches, Town Hall (1404), guild buildings and numerous merchants' and craftsmen's residences, mainly from the 15th cent. From the RENAISSANCE period (2nd quarter of the 16th cent. until the 1630s), the best known is the Tallinn Blackheaded Fraternity Building (1597), executed by architect and sculptor Arent Passer from Holland. From the BAROQUE period(1630s to 1780s) in the town of Narva, only the restored Town Hall remains (1671, arch. Jürgen Teuffel). The Kadriorg Palace's (1720s, Niccolò Michetti) grand hall with its rich late-Baroque stucco decor is one of the most beautiful in Northern Europe. CLASSICISM (1780s to mid-19th cent.) is best represented in Tartu: Town Hall (1789, Johann Walter), dwellings, the university's monumental main building (1809, Johann Krause), and other buildings. Classicism was much used in the architecture of manor houses (Palmse, Saku). HISTORICISM and ECLECTICISM became prominent in the mid-19th cent. The brick Gothic style of northern Germany and Renaissance style was followed (Sangaste Castle, 1881, Otto Hippius). Baltic-German architects, educated at the Riga Polytechnic and St. Petersburg, were prominent. At the beginning of the 20TH CENT., the Estonian societies preferred the natio-nal-romantic designs of Finnish architects (the buildings were destroyed in WW II). The design of the current Estonian Drama Theatre building in Tallinn was influenced by *Art Nouveau* (1910, Aleksei Bubyr and Nikolai Vasilyev). At the start of the 20th cent., the first professional Estonian architects began activities; in the 1920s architects were educated in Tallinn. Initially, the style followed was late-*Art Nouveau* (Parliament Building in Tallinn on Toompea Hill, 1922, Eugen Habermann and Herbert Johanson); in the 1930s, functionalism became prevalent: the Tallinn Art House (1934, Edgar-Johan Kuusik, Anton Soans), Pärnu Beach Hotel (1937, Olev Siinmaa, A. Soans) and the elegant beach café with its mushroom-shaped balcony (1939, O. Siinmaa), school buildings in Tallinn, Rakvere, Pärnu. Local limestone was masterfully applied. In the 2nd half of 1930s, *Art Deco* became popular. Narva was completely destroyed during WW II; Tartu and Tallinn were full of ruins. Many renowned architects escaped Stalinist terror by fleeing to the West in 1944. After the war, the *Estonia* theatre and concert hall were restored (badly damaged by the Soviet bombing raid in 1944; project design by Alar Kotli). In the 1950s, the Soviet authorities aimed for cheap industrial housing construction. New identical suburbs were built. The Song Festival Amphitheatre, with its suspension engineering is, however, unique (1960, A. Kotli, Henno Sepmann).The principles of organic architecture were implemented by Valve Pormeister during the 1960s (Pirita Flower Pavilion, 1960). Modern trends (new-functionalism, etc.), are more in evidence in rural construction (admin. building in Rapla, 1977, Toomas Rein). The synthesis of utility and appropriateness in the environment is represented by the Pirita Sailing Centre (1980,Peep Jänes, Avo-Himm Looveer, H. Sepmann), Tallinn City Hall(1980) and National Library (1991, both by Raine Karp). During the 1980s, the rationalistic trend gave away to Postmodernism. Estonian architects have successfully participated in international competitions (e.g., Vilen Künnapu and Ain Padrik).

ART. The earliest finds of works of art are animalistic figures and metal ornaments. Especially interesting are the grave stones from the 13th cent. which are decorated with a combination of the ring (a pagan symbol) and the cross. Polychrome wooden altars and wood carvings have survived from the 14th and 15th cent. The oldest secular works of art are the benches in the Tallinn Town Hall (14th to 15th cent.). Most of the works of art created in the Middle Ages were done by foreign masters — most of the stone masons, however, were Estonians. Altars by Hermen Rode and Bernt Notke were brought to Tallinn from Lübeck; and from Brugge, the large wing altar created by the anonymous Master of the St. Lucia Legend. The first exponent of Renaissance art was the Tallinn artist Michel Sittow. The sculptor Arent Passer belonged to the Fontainebleau school. Wood carving flourished during the Baroque period — the most noteworthy masters were Elert Thiele (the Tallinn Town Hall frieze, 1667) and Christian Ackermann (altars and pulpits). Jewelry was fashioned using traditional Estonian silver designs. At the end of the 18th cent., the Christian Fick faience factory produced Rococo-style dinner services. The Tartu University drawing school, which was founded in 1803, was the first art school in Estonia, and the third official one in the Russian Empire; the most successful teacher was the graphic artist and painter Karl Senff. In Tartu, Georg Schlater founded in 1832 a lithographics workshop, and Ludwig Maydell in 1835 founded a woodcut workshop — the first in the Russian Empire. The brothers Gerhard and Karl von Kügelgen were renowned painters.

The first Estonian artists appeared in the 2nd half of the 19th cent. — Johann Köler and Amandus Adamson, who had studied at St. Petersburg, and sculptor August Weizenberg (educated in Munich). They are the founders of Estonian national art. During the 1890s, realism predominated. Local artistic life began at the start of the 20th cent. Ants Laikmaa founded his own studio school in 1903 in Tallinn. In 1906, the first general exhibition of Estonian art was held in Tartu. In 1914, the Tallinn Arts and Crafts School was founded. Interest towards modern art and national themes increased. Kristjan Raud was fully immersed in Symbolism and National Romanticism. The *Noor-Eesti* (Young Estonia) generation was interested in Nordic art. Nikolai Triik painted expressive portraits and landscapes. Konrad Mägi was a noteworthy colourist, who created neo-impressionist and expressionist paintings. Abstract expressionism is apparent in Ado Vabbe's works. The sculptor Jaan Koort was influenced by the simplicity of Egyptian sculpture. In 1919, the art school *Pallas* was founded in Tartu: the lecturers were K. Mägi, N. Triik, A. Vabbe and the sculptor Anton Starkopf. A large number of different movements appeared: e.g., the Estonian Artists' Group (Arnold Akberg, Eduard Ole, Märt Laarman, Jaan Vahtra) in 1923, which was based on Cubism and the principles of *Bauhaus*. German *Neue Sachlichkeit*, Expressionism, 1930s *Art Deco*, and the Parisian school of painting were all influential. Eduard Wiiralt, the most prominent Estonian graphic artist, was a graduate of the *Pallas* school, continued his studies in Dresden, and created particularly imaginative and grotesque works while he was living in Paris from 1925 to 1938. Adamson-Eric was very versatile; initially his paintings were in the *Neue Sachlichkeit* style, later in impressionist style, and he was an innovator in metal and leather handicrafts.

Artistic development ceased with WW II and the occupation of Estonia by the USSR. Many artists were killed — and many fled the country (Erik Haamer, Endel Kõks, Karin Luts, etc.). Many of those who remained were prevented from working in the artistic sphere. Official approval was accorded to those who had been evacuated to the SU during the war — e.g., Evald Okas, Aino Bach, Ferdinand Sannamees — and had been part of the Jaroslavl artistic ensemble. During the 1960s, art began to once again diversify, there were responses to international artistic trends, although these were restrained, softened and intertwined. Prominent colourists Aleksander Vardi and Elmar Kits created non-figurative art, Lepo Mikko attempted rational synthesis, Ilmar Malin had a surrealistic vision with the expression of the micro and macro worlds. Enn Põldroos' paintings are expressive and Olev Subbi's are harmonious. Surrealism is reflected in the works of painters Olev Maran, Jüri Palm, Tiit Pääsuke, and graphic artist Peeter Ulas; Malle Leis has an intense concept of reality, Toomas Vint has naivety. Vive Tolli and Kaljo Põllu have been inspired by ancient folklore. Jüri Arrak specializes in the grotesque. During the 1970s and 1980s, pop-art was echoed in the art of Ando Keskküla and Andres Tolts. Leonhard Lapin creates geometric art, and Avo Keerend creates abstracts. Tõnis Vint relies on the symbolism of signs, Raul Meel has a distinctive style with ready-made symbols. In sculpture, the grotesque, abstract, and pop-art are represented in the works of Ülo Õun, Edgar Viies, Jaak Soans. Siim-Tanel Annus has organized performances.

The designs of numerous craft artists are implemented mainly in the *Ars* workshops. The constructive clarity of the application of form is a feature of Estonian arts and crafts; as well as technical mastery and the utilization of the aesthetic features of the material. Traditional leather work is consistently popular (book-binding, albums, etc.) — Elo-Reet Järv's leather sculptures are very original.

Estonian artists have successfully participated in international graphics, ceramics and jewelry exhibitions. The high exhibition design standard of designers Mait Summatavet and Taevo Gans was apparent at the exhibitions in Spokane (1974) and Tokyo (1983).

MUSIC. The oldest form of Estonian folk music is probably the folk song in runic verse form — short tunes with a small range but rich in variations — which developed in the 1st millennium BC. In the 18th cent., this style was replaced by the rhymed folk song with a wider range. In the 1st half of the 19th cent., Estonians began to actively participate in choral music; and this era is also associated with the initial Estonian compositions of national music. The first Estonian choir was formed in Tallinn in 1823; the first brass band in 1848 in Torma. The first local song festival was organized in 1863. In 1869 the first Estonian Song Festival was held in Tartu — organized by the *Vanemuine* music society, which was formed in 1865. Estonia's first two original choral songs were performed there (by Aleksander Kunileid). In the last decades of the 19th cent., Estonian professional composers, Johannes Kappel, Miina Härma and Konstantin Türnpu (all graduates of the St. Petersburg Conservatoire), and Aleksander Läte (Dresden Conservatoire) composed mainly choral songs. A.Läte founded Estonia's first symphony orchestra in 1900 in Tartu. Rudolf Tobias wrote the first Estonian symphonic work (prelude 'Julius Caesar', 1896), piano concerto (1897) and oratorio (*Des Jona Sendung*, 1909). The first Estonian professional musicians were also educated at the St. Petersburg Conservatoire; the pianist brothers Artur and Theodor Lemba — and French horn player Jaan Tamm — all worked as professors. T.Lemba is the author of the first Estonian symphony (1908) and opera (*Lembitu tütar* — Lembitu's Daughter, 1908). The choral works by Mart Saar and Cyrillus Kreek raised the standards of choral music. In 1919, in the newly-independent Republic of Estonia, higher music schools were founded in Tartu and Tallinn. Two main creative schools developed: with Artur Kapp in Tallinn, and with Heino Eller in Tartu. In the classical clarity of form in A.Kapp's works, his symphonic works and the oratorio *Hiiob* (Job) stand out; the main work by his student Evald Aav is the opera *Vikerlased* (The Vikings). In the instrumental works of H.Eller, national intonations and 20th cent. modern forms are melded — his students, with their varying artistic expressions, have been instrumental in the development of Estonian music to this day.

In 1942, during WW II, those Estonian musicians who had been conscripted into the Red Army were formed into Estonian artistic ensembles, established in Jaroslavl in Russia — including the composers Eugen Kapp, Gustav Ernesaks and Hugo Lepnurm. Riho Päts, Tuudur Vettik and Alfred Karindi, who continued working in Estonia when the country was under German occupation, were persecuted by the Stalinist authorities after the war. Many fled to the West in 1944 to escape Soviet terror: Eduard Tubin, the noted symphonist and the author of the first Estonian ballet (*Kratt* — Goblin, 1943), went to Sweden; composers Roman Toi, Kaljo Raid and Udo Kasemets went to Canada. In the 2nd half of the 1950s, a new generation of composers appeared: Eino Tamberg aims for the synthesis of the arts; Jaan Rääts' works are urbanistic; Kuldar Sink tends towards orientalism; Veljo Tormis composes using traditional musical themes from the Estonians and from many of the small Finno-Ugric nationalities who are in danger of extinction; folksongs are also a basis for Ester Mägi; Arvo Pärt is the most famous (he lives in Berlin since 1980) — he began with a twelve-tone technique and has reached minimalism. Of the 1970s generation, Lepo Sumera's minimalistic and Raimo Kangro's works with their rich rhythms are of interest. Erkki-Sven Tüür is the best known of the younger composers. Conductor Neeme Järvi has contributed much to the introduction of Estonian music (he lives in the US since 1980). Eri Klas has been active as the lead conductor both in the *Estonia* theatre, as well as in the Stockholm Royal Opera and the Finnish National Opera. Estonian choirs have won numerous prizes at international competitions; of the conductors, the best-known are Gustav Ernesaks, Venno Laul and Tõnu Kaljuste. The high standard of organ music is reflected in the annual international organ music festival which has taken place in Tallinn since 1987. The *Hortus Musicus* old music ensemble is internationally known. Estonian musical scholarship was initiated by Elmar Arro (who later lectured at Vienna University); the first scholarly history of Estonian music was written in 1937 by Anton Kasemets. Noteworthy music scholars have been Juhan Aavik, Karl Leichter, Herbert Tampere, Leo Normet. Musical education is provided by 53 children's music schools, 2 music schools, a music secondary school and the Tallinn Conservatoire; concerts are organized by *Eesti Kontsert* (Estonian Concert).

SONG FESTIVALS. The tradition of Estonian song festivals began in 1869 in Tartu. Male choirs and brass bands participated in the first song festival; later festivals added mixed, female, children's, and boys' choirs. During the years of Soviet occupation, there were attempts to politicize the song festivals, and to suppress the national feelings which occurred during the festivals. The 1990 Song Festival was once again a real national event. There were 800 participants and an audience of 4,000 during the first song festival; nowadays there are 30,000 participants and more than 200,000 in the audience. The song festivals occur every 5 years. School children's song festivals have been held since 1961; and university students song festivals (called *Gaudeamus*) have been held, together with the Latvians and Lithuanians, since 1956.

THEATRE. The first known theatre performances in Estonia date from the 16th cent. In 1529, a school play was performed in Latin at the Tallinn Town Hall. Many western European travelling theatre troupes performed in Estonia during the 17th and 18th cent. In 1784, the local Baltic-Germans founded an amateur theatre in Tallinn. Estonian national theatre was born in the music societies; the first play to be performed was Lydia Koidula's *Saaremaa onupoeg* (The Cousin from Saaremaa) — in 1870 by the Tartu society *Vanemuine*. At the end of the 19th cent., August Wiera formed the *Vanemuine* theatre group, which gave regular performances. In 1906, the Tartu *Vanemuine* and the Tallinn *Estonia*, and in 1911 the Pärnu *Endla*, became professional theatres. The *Vanemuine* director Karl Menning was responsible for developing the theatre company into an ensemble with a consistently high professional standard. The *Estonia* company, however, was better known for its individual talented stars — e.g., Paul Pinna and Theodor Altermann, who were also directors. In 1907, *Estonia* began staging operettas; with operas in the following year, and ballets in 1922. In 1926, a permanent ballet troupe was formed by Rahel Olbrei. A ballet troupe was also formed by Ida Urbel at *Vanemuine* in 1935. In 1926, the *Draamateater* (Drama Theatre), Tallinn's second professional theatre was founded; and the expressionist *Hommikteater* (Morning Theatre) was active in the period 1921—24. Professional theatres were also founded in Viljandi and Narva. By 1940, Estonia had 11 professional and semi-professional theatres.

After Estonia was occupied by the SU in 1940, the theatre was subjected to ideological control. Estonian actors, who were evacuated during WW II to Russia — as well as those actors who were conscripted into the Red Army — were formed into an artistic ensembles. Many actors and directors fled to the West from the Stalinist terror in 1944. Estonian theatre was performed in the post-war displaced persons camps in Geislingen and Oldenburg (in Germany), and later in all the larger overseas Estonian centres. In post-war occupied Estonia, the transformation of the theatre according to Soviet ideology continued — mainly Russian plays were performed. *Estonia* was changed to a music theatre. Theatre life enlivened in the late 1950s — during the so-called thaw. Voldemar Panso brought new style to direction. In 1957, V.Panso founded a drama school at the Tallinn Conservatoire, and in 1965, he, together with his students, founded the Tallinn *Noorsooteater* (Youth Theatre). Avant-garde theatre reached Estonia at the end of the 1960s, with the work of the directors Evald Hermaküla and Jaan Tooming. The style of one of the currently prominent Estonian theatre directors, Mikk Mikiver, is more traditional; M.Mikiver's productions of plays which deal with the fate of the Estonian people have attracted much attention (e.g., *Pilvede värvid* — The Colours of the Clouds — by Jaan Kruusvall). Estonian ballet style has been determined by Ülo Vilimaa and Mai Murdmaa. The operatic standards have been improved due to the opportunity provided for many singers to train in Italy. The best-known names today are the actors Ita Ever, Jüri Järvet and Aarne Üksküla; the opera singers Anu Kaal, Mati Palm and Ivo Kuusk; and ballet dancers Kaie Kõrb and Tiit Härm. In 1990, there were 10 professional theatres in Estonia. Singers, musicians and actors are trained at the Tallinn Conservatoire; and ballet dancers at the Tallinn Choreography School.

CINEMA. 'Moving pictures' were shown for the first time in Estonia in 1896. The first movie theatre was opened in 1908. The first Estonian film-maker was the photographer Johannes Pääsuke, who made view-films and the first movie. During the independence period, documentaries and newsreels were produced regularly. The best cameramen were Konstantin Märska and Theodor Luts.

The first Estonian movie of the post-war Soviet occupation period was *Elu tsitadellis* (Life in the Citadel), which was made in cooperation with the Leningrad studio *Lenfilm* in 1947. Films with greater artistic merit were first produced in the 1960s. Kaljo Kiisk's themes have included social problems (*Hullumeelsus* — Lunacy, 1968), and an itinerant bohemian travelling around Estonia at the turn of the century (*Nipernaadi* — Happy-Go-Lucky, 1983). Grigori Kromanov's film *Viimne reliikvia* (The Last Relic, 1969) has been screened in 60 countries. Leida Laius' film *Naerata ometi* (Smile, Please, 1985, co-dir. Arvo Iho) and *Varastatud kohtumine* (A Stolen Meeting, 1988), have been well-received internationally. Peeter Simm has directed historically accurate films set in the 1940s and 1950s (*Ideaal maastik* — Ideal Country, 1980; *Inimene, keda polnud* — The Man Who Never Was, 1989). Arvo Iho analyzed two opposites from a Freudian viewpoint (*Vaatleja* — Observer, 1987). Jüri Sillart directed *Äratus* (Awakening, 1989) about the 1949 Stalinist mass deportations. Our well-known stage actors have also participated in films: Heino Mandri, Tõnu Kark, Maria Klenskaja, Elle Kull, Lembit Ulfsak, Suiev Luik.

Despite the restrictions imposed by political censorship, there have been noteworthy achievements in documentary film-making. Andres Sööt has created somewhat ironic documentaries with a social emphasis (*Jaanipäev* — Midsummer Day, 1978; *Reporter*, 1981; *Draakoni aasta* — Year of the Dragon, 1988). Mark Soosaar's films are experimental and innovative (*Kihnu naine* — Woman From Kihnu, 1974; *Kihnu mees* — Man From Kihnu, 1986; *Miss Saaremaa*, 1988). Peeter Tooming has a wonderful feel for the expressive possibilities of black and white film (*Hetked* — Moments, 1976; *Aastad* — Years, 1977). Rein Maran makes highly-rated nature films. Puppet film making was initiated in 1957 by Elbert Tuganov. Puppet films include works by directors Elbert Tuganov (*Verine John* — Bloody John, 1974), Heino Pars (*Nael* — Nail, 1972), Rao Heidmets (*Papa Carlo teater* — Papa Carlo's Theatre, 1988), Riho Unt and Hardi Volmer (*Sõda* — War, 1987). In 1971, Rein Raamat founded an animated film group. The most interesting animated films have been by Raamat (*Suur Tõll* — Tõll the Great, 1980; *Põrgu* — Hell, 1983) and Priit Pärn (*Kolmnurk* — Triangle, 1982; *Aeg maha* — Time Out, 1984; *Eine murul* — Picnic on the Grass, 1987). The puppet and animated films are considered to be Estonia's best output — they are more artistically mature and have received positive international recognition.

In the period 1955 — 89, the film studio *Tallinnfilm* has produced approximately 100 full-length and 20 short movies. The studio produces 15 documentaries and 5 to 6 animated films per year; *Eesti Telefilm* (Estonian TV Film) has produced 30 documentaries and music films.

PHOTOGRAPHY. The first daguerreotype camera was brought to Estonia in 1840. One of the first exponents of artistic photography was the 19th cent. Baltic-German artist Georg Friedrich Schlater from Tartu. Photography exhibitions have been organized in Estonia since the 1890s. Professional photography began at the start of the 20th cent. In the 1920s many amateur photography clubs were founded. The best known and most enterprising were the brothers Johannes and Peeter Parikas; Nikolai Nyländer's photographs received awards at over 80 international exhibitions. The first all-Estonia photography exhibition in the post-war Soviet occupation period was held in 1959. Current photographic developments have been most influenced by photography clubs and the members of the group Stodom (Kalju Suur and Peeter Tooming, AFIAP; Rein Maran). The 1980s were a period of variety and artistic maturity. Tõnu Noorits, Malev Toom, Ann Tenno, Tõnu Tormis, Peeter Langovits — amongst others — have received awards at international exhibitions. Consecutive photography exhibitions are displayed at the Kiek in de Kök cannon tower in medieval Tallinn; there is a permanent exhibition of Estonian photography at the Town Hall Prison. Since 1968, Estonia participates in the Baltic states artistic photography exhibition 'Land of Amber'; the exhibition 'Woman in Photography' has been held since 1983.

MUSEUMS. The initial material for the earliest Estonian museums was provided by the Baltic-German private collections. The first Estonian museum, the historical collection of items belonging to the Tallinn city apothecary Johannes Burchart, was opened in 1802. In 1803, the Museum of Classical Art and Antiquities at Tartu University was founded; in 1864, the Estonian Provincial Museum was opened in Tallinn (the current Estonian History Museum). The Estonian National Museum, which was founded in 1909, undertook regular searches for Estonian ethnographical and cultural-historical material and folklore. In 1919, the Estonian Art Museum was opened in Tallinn. There are many speciality museums in Estonia: Health Museum, Theatre and Music

Museum, Maritime Museum, Natural History Museum, etc. There are many local museums, and museums honouring cultural figures. Tallinn has an open-air museum at Rocca al Mare.

LIBRARIES. Books — in manuscript form — were brought to churches and monasteries in Estonia during the 13th cent. We know of the existence in 1251 of a cathedral school library in Pärnu. The first city library was founded in 1552 — the Tallinn Oleviste Library. Public libraries were opened during the 2nd half of the 18th cent. The Tartu University Library was opened in 1802, and it is the oldest Estonian research library. The Estonian National Museum's archive library was also a national library. During the Soviet occupation (beginning in 1940), the libraries were constantly 'cleaned' of banned literature, according to the lists produced by the official Soviet censors. Approximately 1/3 of the publications from the time of the independent Republic of Estonia were destroyed: 10 to 20 million books, and 5 to 6 million newspapers and journals. The largest libraries in Estonia today are the Estonian National Library (4.1 million items), Tartu University Library (4.9 million), Estonian Academy of Sciences Library (3.4 million). The most important public libraries are the Tallinn A.H. Tammsaare Library and the Tartu Oskar Luts Central Library. Very many Estonians have large personal libraries. The Estonian Librarians' Association is a member of IFLA.

ARCHIVES. The oldest surviving Estonian archive is a document collection from 1237 — belonging to papal legate Wilhelm of Modena. The first archives were part of churches and monasteries. A definite archival system was in place by the Swedish period (17th cent.). The Tallinn City Archives, founded in 1883, were the first to be scientifically organized. In 1921, the State Archives were founded in Tallinn (for central government departments), and the Central State Archives were founded in Tartu (for historical documents). WW II brought about the destruction — and the removal from Estonia — of much archival material. In 1944, the retreating Germans took with them many archives; these were returned to Tallinn in 1990. The Soviet occupation meant that archives came under the control of the Ministry of the Interior; archives were restricted, and documents were destroyed. Since the mid-1980s, the archives are once again open to researchers. There are currently 5 national central archives: Estonian Archives of History in Tartu, Estonian State Archives in Tallinn, Estonian Film Archives, Estonian Technical Archives and Tallinn City Archives.

THE PRESS. Journalism began in Estonia in the 17th cent. — in German. The first Estonian-language magazine *Lühhike öppetus* ... (Short Lesson ...) was published in 1766 — 67 in Põltsamaa; the first Estonian newspaper *Tarto maa rahwa Näddali-Leht* (Tartu Estonian Weekly) in 1806 in Tartu. The Estonian tradition to read newspapers and magazines regularly was formed due to the newspaper *Perno Postimees* (Perno Postman), founded by Johann Voldemar Jannsen in 1857. The newspaper *Sakala*, founded in 1878 by Carl Robert Jakobson, has an important place in Estonian journalism. By the end of the 19th cent., over 20 Estonian language newspapers were being published. In the 1st decade of the 20th cent. publishing and printing began to develop quickly in Estonia. Until 1917, the Estonian language media was controlled by the extremely strict censors of the Russian tsarist empire. In the Republic of Estonia, freedom of speech and the press were guaranteed by the Constitution; the publishing quality improved. In these favourable conditions, journalism developed quickly. Besides journalism in Estonian, there was also foreign-language journalism — in nine languages: German, Russian, Yiddish, Finnish, Swedish, English, French, Esperanto and Latvian. During the 1930s, the circulation of the larger newspapers was 15,000 — 45,000. There were many specialty — including academic — magazines. After Estonia was occupied by the USSR in 1940, almost all publications were closed — of all the magazines which were founded during the Republic of Estonia, only the literary journal *Looming* (Creation) has been continuously published. A Soviet system of journalism was installed and publications were again subject to censorship. During the so-called thaw — at the end of the 1950s and start of the 1960s — journalism had opportunities for development, and new publications appeared. The medium of television augmented printed media and broadcasting. Tartu University and the Tartu newspaper *Edasi* (Forward; now called *Postimees* — Postman) began sociological surveys. Journalism began to play an important role in the forming of public opinion. The 2nd half of the 1980s — when journalism once again had its independence restored — meant that journalism became the true intermediary of public opinion, as well as the consistent propagator of democratic thought. Journalism has become varied and interesting: with independent newspapers; economic and business newspapers; newspapers published by organizations, movements and political parties; by minority cultural societies, etc. Estonia has held one of the top positions in the SU for readership (in 1989, there were 152 magazines and 161 newspaper issues per 100 people in Estonia). The circulation of newspapers and magazines is relatively high — e.g., 175,000 for the mass circulation daily newspaper *Rahva Hääl* (Voice of the People); 180,000 for *Maaleht* (Country News). The Journalists' Union of Estonia is a member of IFJ.

RADIO AND TV. The first ESTONIAN RADIO broadcast was on April 11, 1924. Regular broadcasting began in 1926. Broadcasting has played an important role in the development of Estonian education and culture. After the occupation of Estonia in 1940 by the SU, radio also became part of the Soviet propaganda service. During the 2nd half of the 1960s, the style of programming on Estonian Radio began to again resemble that of other European broadcasters. Estonian Radio was the first in the SU to have advertising. Estonian Radio has 3 programmes (news, entertainment and cultural). There are transmissions in 8 languages. During 1990, there were 39 hours of transmission (24-hour period on 3 programmes), of which 17 hours was in stereo (stereo can be heard across Estonia).

ESTONIAN TV began transmission on July 19, 1955. *Eesti Telefilm* (Estonian TV Film) works as part of Estonian Television. Estonian Television has 1 programme which broadcasts in Estonian and Russian. There are 12 hours of broadcasting a day. Other channels carry transmissions from 2 Soviet Central Television channels, as well as from Leningrad Television. Finnish television programmes can be received in northern Estonia.

Estonian Radio and Estonian Television are members of OIRT; they have contacts with EBU and other broadcasting organizations.

RELIGION AND CHURCH

Christianity reached Estonia in the 11th cent. In the 2nd half of the 12th cent., the Roman Catholic Church began a mission which culminated in the 1220s with the conquering of the land and the conversion of the Estonians. The establishment of religious institutions was hindered for a long time by the disagreements between secular and church powers and the fact that Estonians objected to their conquered status. By the 15th cent., Estonia was completely integrated into the European spirit and culture. The 300 year-long Roman Catholic Church ecclesiastical institutions crumbled during the Reformation in the 1520s. Because of long-term warfare, reforms following on from the Reformation did not take effect until the period of Swedish rule. A state church was created, based on a strict Lutheran creed. A network of village schools was established, and Estonian religious literature was first published. In 1632, Tartu University was opened. The Bible was translated into Estonian (the New Testament was published in 1686, the whole Bible in 1739). Swedish Ecclesiastical Law was implemented, and it remained partially in force for almost 150 years.

During the Northern War in 1700 – 10, the land was devastated. The continuity of Estonian culture was guaranteed because of the traditions of the church. The privileges granted to the Baltic-German nobility by the Russian tsarist powers in 1743 also paralyzed church activities. The church lost its relative independence when the nobles were given the right to supervise the church, the schools and the hospitals. The difficult social condition of the peasantry created a receptive ground for the pietistic religious movements. The activities of the Herrnhuters (United Brethren) assisted in the growing awareness of the Estonian identity. From this followed the Estonians' own community activities (choirs, libraries, orchestras, societies), which prepared the ground for the national awakening and national independence. The 1832 ecclesiastical law reduced the Evangelical faith in Russia to the status of a tolerated religion. The relationship with the state Russian Orthodox religion soon developed into a serious problem for the official Lutheran Church. In the 1840s, there was extensive conversion to the 'tsar's religion', in the hope of improving the social condition which was due to the lack of legal rights. Those who were disappointed did not have the opportunity to return to the fold of the Lutheran Church. The proportion of Orthodox followers in the population rose to 20%. It was only the tolerance manifesto in 1905 which gave adults the right to choose their own faith. The ideology of the Estonian national awakening was Christian; in the forefront there was also the first generation of clergymen of Estonian descent. The patronage rights of the estate-owners, as well as the mainly German clergy caused an anti-clerical attitude amongst Estonian intellectuals, which was characteristic of the subsequent period. The tensions between the suppressed Estonians and the ruling Germans made themselves felt until 1939 when the Baltic German community left due to deteriorating political situation.

In 1919, the Lutheran Church was reorganized as a church of the Estonian people with an episcopal-synodical structure. It was now known as the Estonian Evangelical Lutheran Church. Control of the church passed into Estonian hands. In 1925 the church was separated from the state; but religious instruction remained in the schools and clergymen were trained at the Tartu University Theology Faculty. The Lutheran Church, to which over 80% of the population belonged, flourished due to the conditions of national independence. The achievements of the church in the short period of independence (1918 – 40) were remarkable.

When Estonia was occupied in 1940, the anti-Christian Soviet legislation was implemented. Work with children, youth, lay workers, publishing, etc. was banned; church property was nationalized; the Theology Faculty was closed. Only Sunday church services and presiding over funerals, etc. was allowed. In the 1940s, the church lost over 2/3 of its clergy, and the state interfered in the church's affairs. A certain religious revival manifested itself in 1956 – 59, but this was followed in the 1960s by the rapid alienation of the membership of congregations. In the 1970s, less than 10% of Estonians were prepared to publicly state that they were Christians. With the aid of repressions, Christianity and the church were isolated from society. The state's religious policy became tolerant in 1988. Repressive legislation was annulled in 1990. The Christian church is again ready to face the public; its influence in Estonian society is growing.

In Estonia the following congregations are active: Estonian Evangelical Lutheran Church, Orthodox, Evangelical Christian-Baptist, Methodist, Seventh Day Adventist, Old Believers, Pentecostalist, Roman Catholic, Word of Life and Seventh Day Baptist Congregations. There is a Jewish synagogue, as well as Islamic and Mormon congregations, and the Kuremäe Pühtitsa Orthodox Nunnery that are quite small in number.

SOCIAL WELFARE

HEALTH. The first hospices and asylums in Estonia were part of monasteries — first mentioned in 1237. The first apothecary shop was opened in 1422 in Tallinn. During the Middle Ages, the sick were treated by sauna-men, barbers and by the few trained doctors. The post of a town physician in Tallinn was created in the 15th cent. The first state hospitals in Estonia were founded in the 18th cent. The training of physicians began in Estonia in 1632 when Tartu University was founded. Qualified doctors were appointed as public health officers in the bigger towns at the end of the 19th cent. In 1905, medical districts were set up across Estonia.

During the period of the Republic of Estonia, medical care was provided by both state and private hospitals, and by private doctors. In 1940, Soviet authorities imposed a centralized medical system, and implemented free medical care. Because the health system received relatively little financial support, the rate of medical developments slowed. Developments in technical equipment have suffered the most. Emphasis was placed on increasing the number of doctors, and developing narrow fields of specialization. The basic unit of medical treatment has been the medical district, which gives primary care, mainly for internal diseases, to approximately 1,700 people in the towns and 3,000 people in rural areas. The medical district doctors in the towns work in polyclinics, and their main responsibilities are house calls and preliminary decisions on determining sick leave. In the event of sudden illness or accidents, first aid is provided by an emergency medical service. Specialized treatment is provided in the county and town hospitals. Highly specialized care is provided in the Tallinn and Tartu clinics.

Estonia has a relatively high number of doctors (39 doctors per 10,000 inhabitants) and relatively few auxiliary medical staff. The life expectancy of Estonians is lower than in the western world — 66 for men and 75 for women. Infant mortality is lower than in the USSR, but greater than in the western world — 14 — 16 deaths per 1,000 births. The main causes of death are cardiovascular diseases, cancer and accidents.

Currently there are moves to decentralize medical care, to increase the role of the family doctor and to develop a system of health insurance.

SPORT. Sport has been important part of life in Estonia. Taking part in sporting activities did not actually occur until the beginning of the 19th cent. — amongst Baltic Germans and at the University of Tartu. Sport became popular, both in the cities and in the country, towards the end of the 19th cent. Professional wrestlers, Georg Lurich, Georg Hackenschmidt and Aleksander Aberg were world class. Many sports were started at the turn of the century. A central sporting organization was formed in 1920 in newly-independent Estonia, and in 1923 the Estonian Olympic Committee was created. Estonian sports people took part in the Antwerp Olympics, and participated in European and world championships. Wrestling, weight-lifting and athletics were areas for Estonian success. The best result was by Kristjan Palusalu, who in the 1936 Olympics in Berlin became Olympic Champion in both freestyle and Greco-Roman wrestling, in the heavyweight division. The Estonian shooters team won the Argentine Cup twice in a row, and set many world records. The chess player Paul Keres, who came to prominence in 1936, remained amongst the best in the world for 40 years. Estonia had close sporting and competition ties with many countries — both near and far.

In 1940, the Estonian sporting bodies were forcibly incorporated into the USSR system. For decades Estonian international contacts were severed, sportsmen and women were forced to represent the SU. The more prominent were the wrestlers Johannes Kotkas (3 times European champion, and 1952 Olympic champion in the heavyweight division) and August Englas (World champion in 1953 and 1954 in the mid-heavyweight division), the weight-lifter Jaan Talts (3 times World- and 4 times European champion, Olympic champion in 1972 in the mid-heavyweight division). Other fields have also produced champions — cyclists Aavo Pikkuus and Erika Salumäe, volleyball player Viljar Loor, basketballer Tiit Sokk, chess player Jaan Ehlvest.

In 1989, Estonian sports were reorganized, the National Olympic Committee was restored. Estonian sportsmen's and women's international ties are being reinstated and extended, and competition is again taking place under the national colours of blue, black and white. The following table represents the gold medals won by Estonian amateur sportspeople in the period 1920 — 90 (4 medals from previous times are included):

	Gold	Silver	Bronze
Olympic Games	18	17	21
World championships	142	76	66
European championships	153	86	58
Total	313	179	145

TOURISM. Estonia has a long tradition of tourism. Summer holidaymakers have visited the western and northern beach resorts of Haapsalu, Pärnu, Kuressaare and Narva-Jõesuu for more than 150 years. In 1936 in Estonia, there were 7 travel bureaus and 372 tourist accommodation sites, with 372 to a six-month stay. Tourism was coordinated in the Republic of Estonia by the Central Tourist Office. This office published a magazine *Loodushoid ja Turism* (Nature Conservation and Tourism). In 1939, Estonia became an associate member of the *Alliance Internationale de Tourisme*. In the same year, the USSR established its military bases in Estonia, and foreign tourism was terminated.

After the occupation of Estonia by the USSR, all tourism and holiday organization was placed under the control of Moscow through the all-Union companies (*Intourist, Sputnik*) and the trade unions. Almost all foreign exchange was utilized by Moscow, so only a very small proportion was left to the tourism centres. Due to these policies tourism has not provided the desired economic end result. Regulations restricted the freedom of activity of the tourism enterprises and reduced interest in developing local tourism centres. Extensive picturesque coastal areas and islands became restricted military zones and are out of bounds both to locals and tourists.

Tallinn is one of the favourite tourist destinations. The ancient old town is a great attraction, and it received a gold medal in 1980 for the preservation of its unified architectural identity. Estonia has beautiful landscapes, Hanseatic architecture, long traditions of folk-music and folk-dance festivals, and experience in organizing sailing regattas and conferences. Many harbours were opened to foreign sailing enthusiasts during 1990.

Tourism has been coordinated since May 1990 by the newly-formed State Department of Tourism, whose responsibilities are the development of tourism and the implementation of government tourism policies. There are currently almost 300 joint ventures, companies and travel agencies dealing with tourism. There were over 200,000 foreign visitors to Estonia during 1990. There are particularly close contacts with Sweden and Finland. Regular ferry transport — as well as air transport — links Tallinn with Helsinki and Stockholm. During 1990, on the route Tallinn-Helsinki, *Georg Ots* carried 283,600 passengers, *Tallink* carried 182,500, and *Helta* ships 16,700. On the route Tallinn—Stockholm, *Nord Estonia* carried 91,400 passengers.

USEFUL INFORMATION FOR A VISITOR

ESTONIAN PLACES OF INTEREST

1 Ambla Church (13th cent.) **2** Angla Wind Mills **3** Endla Nature Reserve **4** Hüpassaare — composer Mart Saar's Museum **5** Juuru — Mahtra Rural Museum **6** Jõgeveste — Count Michael Andreas Barclay de Tolly's Museum (Commander in the Russian Army) **7** Jägala Waterfall (Estonia's highest) **8** Järva-Madise — writer A. H. Tammsaare's Museum **9** Kaali Lake — meteor crater **10** Kaarma Church (13th cent.) **11** Karja Church (13th cent.) — one of Northern Europe's best examples of sculpture in Gothic rural churches **12** Karksi Castle ruins (13th cent.) **13** Keila Waterfall **14** Koeru Church (13th cent.), tavern and coach stop (19th cent.) **15** Koguva village-museum **16** Kuremäe — Pühtitsa Orthodox Convent (1892) **17** Kurgja — Carl Robert Jakobson's Farm Museum **18** Kõpu Lighthouse (16th cent.) — oldest maritime object in the Baltic states **19** Käina — composer Rudolf Tobias' Museum **20** Lahemaa National Park **21** Matsalu Nature Reserve **22** Muhu Church (14th cent.) **23** Muuga Kabelikivi — one of the largest rocks in Northern Europe **24** Märjamaa Church (14th cent.) **25** Nigula Nature Reserve **26** Nõo Church — oldest surviving brick church in Southern Estonia (approx. 1300) **27** Otepää stronghold and the ruins of the bishop's castle, Pühajärv Lake **28** Padise Monastery ruins (14th cent.) **29** Paide Castle ruins (13th cent.) and Church (1786) **30** Palamuse — Parish School Museum **31** Palmse Manor House **32** Panga Scarp — Saaremaa's highest **33** Porkuni Bishop's Castle ruins (15th cent.) **34** Põltsamaa Castle ruins (14th—18th cent.) **35** Pöide Church (13th cent.) **36** Rakvere Castle ruins (13th cent.) **37** Rannamõisa Scarp **38** Ridala Church (13th cent.) **39** Ruhnu Church (17th cent.) — oldest surviving example of wooden architecture **40** Rõuge lakes and stronghold **41** Rägavere Manor **42** Sagadi Manor, Estonian Forestry Museum **43** Saka—Onti-ka—Toila limestone escarpment — highest part of the Northern Estonia Glint **44** Saku manor **45** Sangaste Manor (19th cent.) **46** Saue Manor **47** Suure-Jaani — Kapp Museum (composers) **48** Suuremõisa Manor (2nd half of the 18th cent.) **49** Suur Munamägi — highest mountain in Estonia and the Baltic states (318.1 m), observation tower, museum **50** Taebla — artist Ants Laikmaa's museum **51** Toolse Castle ruins (15th cent.) **52** Valjala Stronghold (12th—13th cent.) — one of the strongest fortresses of the ancient Saaremaa people — and church (13th cent.) **53** Vasknarva Castle ruins (15th cent.) **54** Vastseliina Bishop's Castle ruins (14th—15th cent.) **55** Viidumäe Nature Reserve **56** Viki — Mihkli Farm Museum **57** Vilsandi Nature Reserve **58** Vormsi Church (14th cent.) **59** Ülenurme — Estonian Agricultural Museum

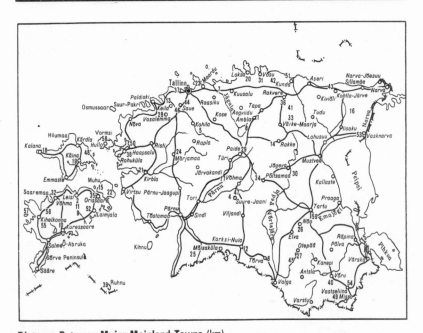

Distance Between Major Mainland Towns (km)

	Haap-salu	Narva	Paide	Pärnu	Rak-vere	**Tal-linn**	Tar-tu	Val-ga	Vil-jandi	Virt-su	Võru
Haapsalu	—	311	156	109	196	**99**	265	249	187	77	303
Narva	311	—	201	296	118	**212**	182	268	233	361	251
Paide	156	201	—	95	83	**92**	102	152	71	160	171
Pärnu	109	296	95	—	178	**128**	171	140	93	74	194
Rakvere	196	118	83	178	—	**97**	123	211	139	242	192
Tallinn	**99**	**212**	**92**	**128**	**97**	—	**187**	**238**	**158**	**137**	**255**
Tartu	265	182	102	171	123	**187**	—	86	77	243	69
Valga	249	268	152	140	211	**238**	86	—	80	214	75
Viljandi	187	233	71	93	139	**158**	77	80	—	167	125
Virtsu	77	361	160	74	242	**137**	243	214	167	—	268
Võru	303	251	171	194	192	**255**	69	75	125	268	—

To find the distance to **Kuressaare** (Saaremaa) from any of the above towns, read its distance to **Virtsu** and add 85 km (incl. 7 km by sea from Virtsu to Kuivastu); the distance to **Kärdla** (Hiiumaa) is similarly found by adding 57 km to the distance to **Haapsalu** (incl. 22 km by sea from Rohuküla to Heltermaa). The distance route across the 6 km Soela Strait, may be cut to 100 km.

TALLINN

TELEPHONE DIRECTORY

EMERGENCIES (same tel. nrs used throughout Estonia)

Fire	01	Gas leakage	04
Police	02	Directory assistance	
Ambulance	03	(for non-residential nrs)	09

GENERAL INFORMATION

Taxis	430 330, 603 044	Pharmacies	441 813
Trains	446 756	Telegraph	066
Home delivery of tickets	448 087	Long distance	
Buses (inter-city)	422 549, 448 087	in Estonia and SU	
Aeroflot	421 265	(if requiring operator assistance)	07
International flights	211 945	in Harju county	08
Passenger harbour	449 427	International long distance	007
Traffic police	445 450	Directory assistance	
Lost property office	433 127	(private subscribers)	065

CITY CODES (from Tallinn dial 8 and wait for dialtone)

Kaunas 0127   Leningrad 812   Moscow 095   Riga 0132   Vilnius 0122

Haapsalu	. . . 247	Paide	. . . 238	Tartu	. . . 234
Jõgeva	. . . 237	Põlva	. . . 230	Valga	. . . 242
Kuressaare	. . . 245	Pärnu	. . . 244	Viljandi	. . . 243
Kohtla-Järve	. . 233	Rakvere	. . . 232	Võru	. . . 241
Kärdla	. . . 246	Rapla	. . . 248		
Narva	. . . 235	Sillamäe	. . . 249		

International telephone code to Estonia 7 — 014, to Tallinn 7 — 0142

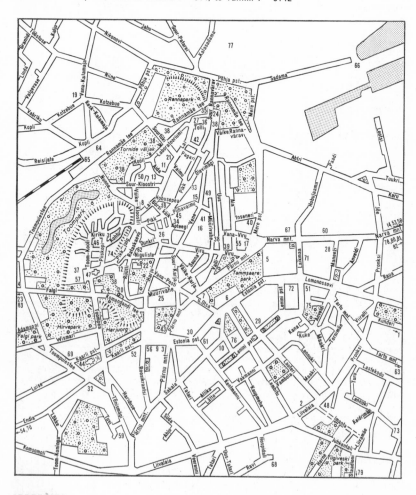

ADDRESSES

HOTELS

1 KUNGLA Kreutzwaldi 23, tel. 421 460; **2 OLÜMPIA** Kingissepa 33, tel. 602 438; **3 PALACE** Vabaduse väljak 3, tel. 444 761; **4 TALLINN** Toompuiestee 27, tel. 604 332; **5 VIRU** Viru väljak 4, tel. 652 081; **SPORT** Regati 1, tel. 238 598

RESTAURANTS

EESLITALL Dunkri 4, tel. 446 309; **GLORIA** Müürivahe 2, tel. 446 950; **GNOOM** Viru 2, tel. 442 488; **KARJA KELDER** (beer cellar) Väike-Karja 1, tel. 440 280; **KEVAD** Lomonossovi 2, tel. 425 549; **KOLM KANNU** (beer restaurant) Nunne 12, tel. 441 597; **KULLASSEPA KELDER** Kullassepa 9, tel.

442 240; **KUNGLA** Kreutzwaldi 23, tel. 422 506; **MAIASMOKK** Pikk 16, tel. 601 396; **MARGARETA** (pizza restaurant) Pärnu mnt. 14, tel. 666 704; **NORD** Rataskaevu 3, tel. 444 695; **NOMME** Jaama 2, tel. 510 083; **OLÜMPIA** Kingissepa 33, tel. 602 490; **PALACE** Vabaduse väljak 3, tel. 443461; **PIRITA** Merivälja tee 5, tel. 238 102; **RAE** Vabaduse väljak 7, tel. 666078; **RAEKOO** Dunkri 5, tel. 444 350; **RATASKAEVU** Dunkri 8, tel. 448 426; **REEDER** Vene 33, tel. 446 518; **SUB MONTE** Rüütli 28, tel. 666 871; **TALLINN** Toompuiestee 27, tel. 604 308; **VANA TOOMAS** Raekoja plats 8 (Town Hall Sq.), tel. 445 818; **VIRU** Viru väljak 4, tel. 650 776

CAFÈS

HARJU Suur-Karja 4; **KADRIORG** Narva mnt. 90; **MEREKOHVIK** Mere pst.20; **MOSKVA** Vabaduse väljak 10; **NARVA** Narva mnt. 10; **NEITSITORN** Komandandi 3; **PÄRL** Pikk 1; **TALLINN** (night club) Harju 6; **TELETORN** Kloostrimetsa tee 58; **CARINA** Pirita tee 26; **VIGRI** (children's) Narva mnt. 19

SNACKBARS AND BARS

ARABELLA (ice-cream) Dunkri 5; **GRILLBAAR** (fish) Pärnu mnt. 19; **KARIKABAAR** Kuninga 3; **KASTANIBAAR** Toompuiestee 7; **KAROLIINA** (wine-bar) Harjumägi 1; **KIKAS** (grill) Liivalaia 29; **KULLER** (beer) Kallaku 1; **MÜNDI BAAR** Mündi 3; **PIKK JALG** Pikk jalg 16; **REGATT** Merivälja tee 1; **SAIAKÄIK** Saiakang 5; **SININE BAAR** Pirita tee 28; **TALLINN** Harju 6; **TARTU** Tartu mnt. 6; **TOOMBAAR** Toom-Kooli17; **ULVI** Pühavaimu 7; **VIRMALINE** (ice-cream) Sauna 5

THEATRES AND CONCERT HALL

6 ESTONIA Estonia pst. 4, (opera and ballet) tel. 444 424, (concert hall) tel. 441 308; **7 ESTONIAN DRAMA THEATRE** Pärnu mnt. 5, tel. 443 378; **8 PUPPET THEATRE** Lai 1, tel. 601 633; **9 RUSSIAN DRAMA THEATRE** Vabaduse väljak 5, tel. 443 716; **10 VANALINNASTUUDIO** Sakala 3, tel.448 408, 442 525; **11 YOUTH THEATRE** Lai 23, tel. 609 624

MUSEUMS

12 ADAMSON-ERIC MUSEUM Lühike jalg 3, Wed — Sun 11 — 18, tel.445 838; **13 ARTS AND CRAFTS MUSEUM** Lai 17, Wed — Mon 11 — 18, tel. 445 989; **14 ESTONIAN ART MUSEUM** Weizenbergi 37, Wed — Mon 11 — 18, tel. 426 240; **15 CITY MUSEUM** Vene 17, Wed — Mon 10.30 — 17.30, tel. 445 856; **16 DOMINICAN MONASTERY** Vene 16, June 1 — Oct 1, Tue — Sun 11 — 17; **17 FIRE STATION MUSEUM** Vana-Viru 14, Tue — Sat 12 — 18, tel. 444 251; **18 HISTORY MUSEUM** (Great Guild House) Pikk 17, Thu — Tue 11 — 18, tel. 443 446; **19 KALAMAJA MUSEUM** Kotzebue 28, Wed — Mon 10.30 — 17.30, tel. 602 741; **20 KIEK IN DE KÖK** (cannon tower) Komandandi tee 2, Tue — Fri 10.30 — 17.30, Sat — Sun 11 — 16, tel. 446 686; **21 NATURAL HISTORY MUSEUM** Lai 29, Wed — Mon 10 — 17.30, tel. 444 223; **22 NIGULISTE CHURCH** (St. Nicholas) Niguliste 13, Thu — Sun 11 — 18, Wed 14 — 21, tel. 449 911; **23 OPEN-AIR MUSEUM at Rocca al Mare,** Vabaõhumuuseumi tee 12, May — Oct, Tue — Sun, tel. 555 024; **24 MARITIME MUSEUM** Pikk 70, Wed — Sun 10 — 18, tel. 601 803; **25 THEATRE AND MUSIC MUSEUM** Müürivahe 12, Wed — Sun 10 — 18, tel. 442 132; **26 TOWN HALL** Raekoja plats 1, Mon — Fri 11 — 18, tel. 440 819; **OLD TOWN PRISON** Raekoja 4, Thu — Tue 10.30 — 17.30; **HEALTH MUSEUM** Lai 28, Tue — Sat 10 — 16; **KUNSTIHOONE** (art gallery) Vabaduse väljak 8, Wed — Sun 12 — 19, Mon 12 — 18, tel. 445 054; **ART SALON** Vabaduse väljak 6, Mon 12 — 18, Wed — Sun 12 — 19; **LASTE KUNSTIMAJA** (children's art) Kuninga 6, Wed — Mon 12 — 18, tel. 446 873; **DRAAKONI GALERII** (art) Pikk 18, Tue — Fri 11 — 18, Sat 11 — 16; **VAALGALERII** (art) Väike-Karja 23, Wed — Fri 14 — 19, Sat — Sun 12 — 16; **PIRITA CONVENT** (ruins) Pirita, Tue — Sun 11 — 19; **PETER THE GREAT'S HOUSE** Mäekalda 2, Wed — Sun 11 — 18, tel. 425 480; **MAARJA-MÄE CASTLE** Pirita tee 56, Wed — Sun 11 — 17, tel. 237 071; **A.H.TAMMSAARE MUSEUM** Koidula 12, Wed — Mon 11 — 18, tel. 427 208; **FRIEDEBERT TUGLAS MUSEUM** Väikese Illimari 12, Mon — Fri 10 — 17, tel. 510 243; **EDUARD VILDE MUSEUM** Roheline aas 3, Wed — Mon 11 — 18, tel. 426 300; **KRISTJAN RAUD MUSEUM** K. Raua 8, Wed — Mon 11 — 18, tel. 511 881; **ESTONIAN EXHIBITIONS** Pirita tee 28, Tue — Sun 11 — 19, tel. 238 271

ARCHIVES

27 CITY ARCHIVES Tolli 4, tel. 601 744; **28 STATE ARCHIVES** Maneeži 4, tel. 441 118

LIBRARIES

29 ACADEMY OF SCIENCES LIBRARY Lenini pst. 10, tel. 440 649; **30 CITY LIBRARY** Estonia pst. 8, tel. 443 085; **31 NATIONAL LIBRARY** Kiriku plats 1, tel. 442 094; **32 NATIONAL LIBRARY** Tõnismägi 2

ARCHITECTURAL MONUMENTS

33 BLACKFRIARS HOUSE (Oleviste Guild) Pikk 26; **34 RAEAPTEEK** (Town Hall Apothecary) Raekoja plats 11; **35 SUUR RANNAVÄRAV** (gate in city wall) and **PAKS MARGAREETA** (Fat Margaret; tower); **36 'THREE SISTERS'** (buildings) Pikk 71; **37 TOOMPEA CASTLE** ; **38 CITY WALL TOWERS** ; **39 VIRU VÄRAV** (gate)

CHURCHES

40 ADVENTIST, METHODIST CONGREGATIONS Mere pst. 3; **41 CATHOLIC CHURCH** Vene 18; **42 OLEVISTE** (Baptist) Lai 50; **43 JAANI** (Lutheran) Vabaduse väljak; **44 KAARLI** (Lutheran) Toompea 10; **45 PÜHAVAIMU** (Holy Spirit; Lutheran) Pühavaimu 2; **46 TOOMKIRIK** (Lutheran Cathedral) Toom-Kooli 6; **47 ALEXANDER NEVSKY CATHEDRAL** (Orthodox) Lossi plats 10; **48 KAZAN** (Orthodox) Imanta 33; **49 NIKOLSKY** (Orthodox) Vene 18; **50 PREOBRAZHENSKY CATHEDRAL** (Orthodox) Suur-Kloostri 14; **JEWISH SYNAGOGUE** Lasteaia 9

INSTITUTIONS OF HIGHER EDUCATION

51 ART UNIVERSITY Tartu mnt. 1; **52 CONSERVATOIRE** Kaarli pst. 3; **53 TEACHER TRAINING INSTITUTE** Narva mnt. 25; **54 TECHNICAL UNIVERSITY** Ehitajate tee 5

ADMINISTRATIVE BUILDINGS

55 CITY COUNCIL Vana Viru 12; **56 CITY GOVERNMENT** Vabaduse väljak 7; **57 GOVERNMENT AND SUPREME COUNCIL** Lossi plats 1a; **58 PRESIDIUM OF THE SUPREME COUNCIL** Weizenbergi 39

BANKS AND CURRENCY EXCHANGE

59 UNION BALTIC BANK Tõnismägi 16; **60 BANK OF ESTONIA FOREIGN DEPARTMENT** Narva mnt. 7; **CURRENCY EXCHANGE:** harbour passenger terminal, Viru Hotel, Olümpia Hotel, Tallinn Hotel; **61 ESTONIAN SOCIAL BANK , USSR STATE BANK OF THE ESTONIAN REPUBLIC** Estonia pst. 13; **62 TARTU COMMERCIAL BANK** Dunkri 9; **BANK OF ESTONIA** Kentmanni 13

TRANSPORT

63 BUS TERMINAL Lastekodu 47, tel. 422 549; **64 BUS STATION** next to railway terminal; **65 RAILWAY TERMINAL** Toompuiestee 35, tel. 446 756; **66 HARBOUR** (passenger) Sadama 21, tel. 449 427; **GAS STATIONS** Kadaka 66b, tel. 532 134; Laki 22, tel. 614 359; Leningradi mnt. 58, tel. 212 160; Paldiski mnt. 96, tel. 559 191; Pärnu mnt. 141, tel. 529 200; Pärnu mnt. 552, tel. 519 067; Regati 1, tel.238 404; Rummu tee 2, tel. 238 002; **CAR SERVICE** Pärnu mnt. 232, tel. 529 225; Veerenni 54, tel. 556 579; Ülemiste tee 1, tel. 215 421

CAMPING SITES: CAMPING Kloostrimetsa tee 56a, tel. 238 686; **PEOLEO** Pärnu mnt. 555, Laagri, tel. 556 566; **RANNAMÕISA** Tabasalu, tel. 470 332

TOURIST FIRMS

ESTONIAN TOURS Foreign Tourist Company, Roosikrantsi 4b, tel. 448 718, fax 442 034; **ESTONIAN SPUTNIK TRAVEL BUREAU** Kentmanni 20, tel. 440 500, fax 440 290; **ESTRAVEL Ltd.** Roosikrantsi 12, tel. 771 460, fax 238 636; **INTOURIST** Viru väljak 4, tel. 650 873, fax 440 416; **MAINOR MEELIS Ltd** Kuhlbarsi 1, tel. 424 808, fax 421 829; **ESTONIAN TOURIST** Republican Company, Pikk 71, tel. 602 444, fax 440 533; **TALLINN INTOURBUREAU** Kreutzwaldi 23, tel. 425 594, fax 425 594; **TALLINN TRAVEL BUREAU** Toompuiestee 17a, tel. 446 509; **RAETURIST** Raekoja plats 18, tel.444 333, fax 441 100; **JALO MATKAD** Travel Agency, Raekoja plats 17, tel. 446 344, fax 446 344

OTHER

67 CENTRAL POST OFFICE Narva mnt. 1; **ADDRESS OFFICE** Narva mnt. 31; **68 CENTRAL HOSPITAL** Ravi 18; **69 DENTAL CLINIC** Toompuiestee 4; **70 EMERGENCY HOSPITAL** Sütiste tee 19; **71 SERVICE CENTRE** Laikmaa 5; **72 DEPARTMENT STORE** Lomonossovi 2; **73 CENTRAL MARKET** Turu põik 2; **74 ACADEMY OF SCIENCES** Kohtu 6; **75 TRADE UNION HOUSE** Tartu mnt. 4; **76 SAKALA CULTURAL CENTRE** Lenini pst. 12; **77 LINNAHALL** (concerts and sports) Mere pst. 20; **78 KADRIORG STADIUM** Roheline aas 24; **79 KALEV STADIUM** Staadioni 3; **80 SONG FESTIVAL AMPHITHEATRE** Pirita tee; **81 METSAKALMISTU** (cemetery) Kloostrimetsa tee 36; **82 BOTANIC GARDENS** Kloostrimetsa tee 44; **83 ZOO** Paldiski mnt. 145; **OLYMPIC SAILING CENTRE** Regati 1

TARTU

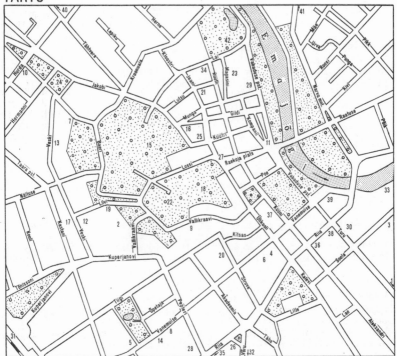

HOTELS

1 TARU Rebase 9, tel. 737 00; **2 PARK** Vallikraavi 23, tel. 336 63; **3 TARTU** Soola 3, tel. 320 91

RESTAURANTS. CAFÈS

TARVAS Riia 2, tel. 322 53; **KAUNAS** Narva mnt. 2, tel. 346 00; **KASEKE** Tähe 19, tel. 703 86; **VOLGA** Küütri 1, tel. 339 60; **PÜSSIROHUKELDER** Lossi 28, tel. 341 24; **HUMAL** (beer restaurant) Küütri 12, tel. 344 11; **RUKKILILL** Tuglase 2; **SÄDE** Küüni 2; **TEMPO** Küütri 6; **VIKERKAAR** Näituse 7

THEATRES AND CONCERT HALL

4 VANEMUINE Vanemuise 6, tel. 329 68; **5 VANEMUINE** (small hall) Vanemuise 45a; **6 CONCERT HALL** Vanemuise 6, tel. 755 64

MUSEUMS

7 CITY MUSEUM Oru 2, Wed — Sun 11 — 18, Mon 11 — 17, tel. 320 33; **8 FRIEDRICH REINHOLD KREUTZWALD LITERARY MUSEUM** Vanemuise 42, Mon — Fri 10 — 16, tel. 333 96; **9 ART MUSEUM** Vallikraavi 14, Tue — Sun 11 — 18, tel. 325 21; **10 ANTON STARKOPF MUSEUM** Vilde 2, Wed — Mon 11 — 18, tel. 620 64; **11 KIVISILLA GALERII** (art) Raekoja plats 18, Tue — Sun 11 — 18, tel. 330 63; **12 ESTONIAN NATIONAL MUSEUM** Veski 32, Wed — Sun 11 — 18, tel. 322 54; **13 KARL ERNST VON BAER'S HOUSE** Veski 4, Mon — Fri 13 — 17, tel. 335 14; **14 ZOOLOGY MUSEUM** Vanemuise 46, Tue — Sun 10 — 16, tel. 347 44; **15 TARTU UNIVERSITY HISTORY MUSEUM** (Cathedral) Toomemägi, Wed — Sun 11 — 17, tel. 326 35; **16 TARTU UNIVERSITY CLASSICAL ART AND ANTIQUITIES MUSEUM** Ülikooli 18, Tue — Fri 11 — 16.30, Sat 10 — 13.30, tel. 314 14; **17 STUDENT MUSEUM** Veski 61, Tue — Sat 11.30 — 16; tel. 330 03; **18 TARTU OBSERVATORY** Toomemägi, Wed — Mon 11 — 16, tel. 349 32; **ESTONIAN NATIONAL MUSEUM** Raadi; **OSKAR LUTS MUSEUM** Riia 38, Wed — Mon 11 — 17, tel. 337 05; **KARL RISTIKIVI MUSEUM** Hermanni 18; **SPORTS MUSEUM** Riia 27a, Wed — Sat 11 — 19, Sun 10 — 15.30, tel. 346 02; **AGRICULTURAL MUSEUM** Ülenurme, Tue — Sat 10 — 16, tel. 123 96

ARCHIVES: 19 ESTONIAN ARCHIVES OF HISTORY Liivi 4, tel. 324 82

LIBRARY: 20 TARTU UNIVERSITY LIBRARY Struve 1, tel. 324 67

ARCHITECTURAL MONUMENTS

21 JAANI CHURCH Rüütli; **22 OLD ANATOMICUM** Toomemägi

CHURCHES

23 USPENSKY CHURCH (Orthodox) Magasini 1; **24 CATHOLIC CHURCH** Veski 3; **PAULUS CHURCH** (Lutheran) Riia 27; **PEETRI CHURCH** (Lutheran) Narva mnt. 104; **JÜRI CHURCH** (Orthodox) Narva mnt. 103; **ADVENTIST, METHODIST CONGREGATIONS** (Alexander Nevsky Church) Sõbra 19a; **BAPTIST CONGREGATION** Võru 18; **BAPTIST CONGREGATION** Tähe 66

INSTITUTIONS OF HIGHER EDUCATION

25 TARTU UNIVERSITY Ülikooli 18; **26 ESTONIAN AGRICULTURAL ACADEMY** Riia 12

ADMINISTRATIVE BUILDINGS

27 CITY GOVERNMENT (Town Hall) tel. 331 28; **28 COUNTY GOVERNMENT** Riia 15, tel. 315 55

BANK: 29 TARTU COMMERCIAL BANK Munga 18, tel. 331 97

TRANSPORT

30 BUS STATION Turu 2, tel. 324 06; **31 RAILWAY STATION** Vaksali 6, tel. 399 50; **32 AIRPORT** Tõrvandi, tel. 324 45; **33 RIVER HARBOUR** Turu 2, tel. 332 34; **TAXIS** Riia 20, tel. 338 67; **GAS STATIONS** on the corner of Võru and Aardla, tel. 739 13; Külitse, tel. 973 44; Väike Ringtee, tel. 288 64; **CAR SERVICE** Sepa 21, tel. 748 16

OTHER

34 POST OFFICE Lai 29; **ADDRESS OFFICE** Gildi 12; **TRAVEL BUREAU** Lai 35, tel. 345 64; **35 TARTU CLINICAL HOSPITAL** (emergency) Puusepa 8; **36 SERVICE CENTRE** Riia 4; **37 GOODS HALL** Küüni 7; **38 DEPARTMENT STORE** Riia 2; **39 MARKET HALL** Vabaduse pst. 1; **TARTU UNIVERSITY STADIUM** Staadioni 21; **TAMME STADIUM** Kungla 1; **40 SONG FESTIVAL GROUNDS; 41 RAADI CEMETERY; 42 BOTANIC GARDENS** Lai 40, Wed — Fri 9 — 16, Sat — Sun 10 — 16, tel. 326 43

PÄRNU

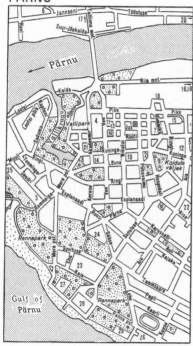

HOTELS: 1 PÄRNU Rüütli 44, tel. 421 45; **2 VÕIT** Kuninga 25, tel. 431 69; **3 KAJAKAS** Seedri 2, tel. 430 98

RESTAURANTS

HERMES Riia mnt. 74, tel. 426 81; **NEPTUN** Ranna pst. 3, tel. 434 85; **POSTIPOISS** Vee 12, tel. 402 04; **PÄRNU** Rüütli 44, tel. 422 30; **RANNAHOONE** Ranna pst. 3, tel. 402 22; **TALLINN** Akadeemia 5, tel. 404 68

CAFÈS AND BARS

ARA BAAR Riia mnt. 28; **ATLANTIKA** Tallinna mnt. 2; **EKSPRESSBAAR** Tallinna mnt. 14; **FLORETT** Nikolai 26; **HUMAL** (beer) Auli 1a; **HÕBE** Hõbe 2; **HÜDRA** Vingi 13; **KOHVIBAAR** Mere pst. 22; **KUNGLA** Rüütli 31; **PÄRNA** Riia mnt. 71; **PÜHAVAIMU** Pühavaimu 21; **ROOSI BAAR** Roosi 12; **ROOSIKELDER** Kuninga 18; **VAHTRA BAAR** Kerese 4; **VIDEOBAAR** Seedri 2; **VIDEOSALONG** Ranna pst. 3

THEATRE: 4 ENDLA Keskväljak 1, tel. 424 80

MUSEUMS

5 LOCAL MUSEUM Rüütli 53, Wed — Fri 11 — 18, Sat — Sun 11 — 17, tel. 434 64; **6 LY-**

DIA KOIDULA MUSEUM Jannseni 37, Wed — Sun 10 — 17, Sat 10 — 16, tel. 416 63; **7 PUNANE TORN** (Red Tower) Hommiku 11, Wed — Sun 12 — 17

ARCHITECTURAL MONUMENTS: 8 TALLINNA VÄRAV (Tallinn Gate); **9 LYDIA KOIDULA MONUMENT**

CHURCHES

10 ELISABETH (Lutheran) Nikolai 22; **11 KATARIINA** (Orthodox) Vee 16; **12 PREOBRAZHENSKY** (Orthodox) Aia 5; **BAPTIST CONGREGATION** Henno 3; **ADVENTIST CONGREGATION** Karja 3; **METHODIST CONGREGATION** Karja 3

ADMINISTRATIVE BUILDINGS: 13 CITY GOVERNMENT (Town Hall) Malmö 4, tel. 411 38; **14 COUNTY GOVERNMENT** Akadeemia 2, tel. 401 03

BANK: PÄRNU COMMERCIAL BANK Rüütli 51

TRANSPORT

15 BUS STATION Ringi 3, tel. 415 54; **16 RAILWAY STATION** Tammiste, tel. 407 33; **17 AIRPORT** tel. 407 52; **TAXIS** tel. 412 40; **18 GAS STATION** Hommiku, tel. 405 37; **19 GAS STATION** Riia mnt., tel. 219 06; **20 GAS STATION** Niidu, tel. 428 77; **CAR SERVICE** Tallinna mnt. 89a, tel. 433 58

OTHER

21 MAIN POST OFFICE Akadeemia 7; **ADDRESS OFFICE** Pikk 18; **POLYCLINIC** Suur-Sepa 16, tel. 420 02; **22 MARKET** Suur-Sepa 18; **TRAVEL BUREAU** Kuninga 32, tel. 427 50; **23 — 26 SANATORIUMS** ; **27 BEACH SALON** Mere pst. 22, tel. 419 43; **28 MUD BATHS; 29 BEACH PAVILION**

HAAPSALU

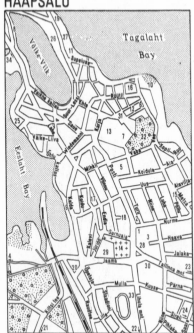

HOTELS: 1 HOTELL Posti 71, tel. 448 47; **2 PENSION 'PIPI'** Posti 37, tel. 451 74

RESTAURANTS: 3 MARITIMA Tallinna mnt. 1, tel. 444 45; **4 PARALEPA** tel. 440 54

5 CULTURAL CENTRE: Posti 33, tel. 440 82

MUSEUM: 6 LOCAL MUSEUM (old Town Hall) Kooli 2, Wed — Sun 11 — 18, tel. 445 65

ARCHITECTURAL MONUMENTS

7 HAAPSALU BISHOP'S CASTLE ; 8 CYRIL- LUS KREEK MONUMENT AND HOME; 9 ERNST ENNO MONUMENT ; 10 RUDOLF TOBIAS MONUMENT ; 11 PETER TCHAI- KOVSKY MEMORIAL BENCH

CHURCHES

12 JAANI CHURCH (Lutheran); **13 TOOM- KIRIK** (Lutheran Cathedral); **14 ALEXANDER NEVSKY CHURCH** (Orthodox); **15 BAPTIST CONGREGATION ; 16 ADVENTIST CONGRE- GATION ; 17 METHODIST CONGREGATION**

ADMINISTRATIVE BUILDINGS

18 CITY GOVERNMENT Posti 67a, tel. 454 03; **19 COUNTY GOVERNMENT** Sadama 28, tel. 568 84

TRANSPORT

20 BUS STATION Raudtee maja 1, tel. 449 46; **RAILWAY STATION** Raudtee maja 1, tel. 458 01; **21 ROHUKÜLA HARBOUR** tel. 911 38; **22; 23 GAS STATIONS** Lihula mnt. 11, tel. 551 02; Tallinna mnt. 73; **CAR SERVICE** Tallinna mnt. 73, tel. 562 65

OTHER

24 POST OFFICE Tamme 21a; **25 POLYCLINIC** Suur-Liiva 15, tel. 445 02; **26 SANATORIUM 'LAINE'** Sadama 18, tel. 456 39; **27 MUD BATHS** ; **28 SHOPPING CENTRE** Tallinna mnt. 1; **29 MARKET; 30 SERVICE CENTRE** Posti 79; **31 CASTLE COURTYARD; 32 COUNT'S GARDEN; 33 SPORTS HALL AND STADIUM** ; **34 BEACH** ; **ESTONIA TRAVEL Ltd** POB 67, tel. 451 91, fax 568 01; **ROOSTA CAMPING** Ehitajate tee 3, tel. 937 32, 972 30, fax 569 66

NARVA

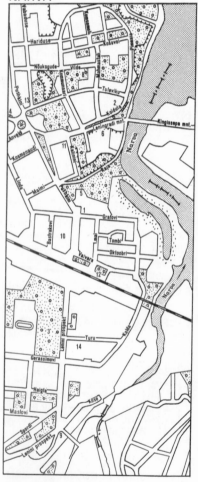

HOTELS: 1 NARVA Pushkini 6, tel. 227 00; **2 VANALINN** Koidula 6, tel. 224 86

RESTAURANTS. CAFÉS. BARS

BALTIKA Pushkini 10, tel. 315 31; **JOALA** Kreenholmi 6, tel. 335 63; **REGATT** Anveldi 26, tel. 401 55; **SOPRUS** Anveldi 5; **VIKERKAAR** Võidu prospekt 1; **NARVA** Pushkini 6; **OKSANA** Tallinna mnt. 19; **BISTROO** Pushkini 10; **KEVADE** Nõukogude 6; **RANDEL** Leningradi 2; **TEMPO** Tallinna 56

CULTURAL CENTRES

3 V. GERASIMOV Lenini prospekt 8, tel. 331 92; **4 ENERGEETIK** Võidu prospekt 2, tel. 245 41; **5 OKTOOBER** Pushkini 8, tel. 312 27

MUSEUMS

6 TOWN MUSEUM (in the Narva Castle) Leningradi mnt. 2, Sat—Tue 10—18, tel. 332 01; **7 MUSEUM OF THE KREENHOLMI MANUFAKTUUR** Lenini prospekt 18, Tue—Sun 10—18, tel. 241 18

ARCHITECTURAL MONUMENTS

8 TOWN HALL Raekoja väljak 1; **9 MONUMENT COMMEMORATING THE STRIKE AT THE KREENHOLM IN 1872**

CHURCHES

10 VOSKRESENSKY CATHEDRAL (Orthodox) Bastrakovi 4; **BAPTIST CONGREGATION** 1. Jõe 42; **METHODIST, ADVENTIST CONGREGATIONS** Fedjuninski 4

ADMINISTRATIVE BUILDING: 11 CITY GOVERNMENT Peetri väljak 5, tel. 224 04

TRANSPORT

12 BUS STATION Vaksali 2, tel. 315 95; **RAILWAY STATION** Vaksali 2, tel. 314 54; **AIRLINE BOOKINGS** tel. 468 57; **GAS STATIONS** Tallinna mnt. 70, Tallinna mnt. 81; **CAR SERVICE** Kirovi 1, tel. 490 49

OTHER

13 TELEGRAPH Tuleviku 3, tel. 222 85; **14 MARKET** Kalda 3; **POLYCLINIC** Komsomoli 3, tel. 224 43; **TOURIST FIRM 'NARVA'** Peetri väljak 5, tel. 220 12

VILJANDI

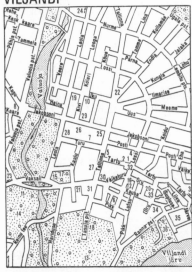

HOTEL: 1 VILJANDI Tartu 11, tel. 538 52

RESTAURANTS. CAFÈS. BARS

2 VILJANDI Tartu 11, tel. 547 95; **3 VIKER-KAAR** Roo 5, tel. 529 09; **4 VILJANDI** Lossi 31; **5 MULGI KELDER** Tartu 44; **6 KIRSIMÄE** Lossi 7; **7 KOIT** Turu 6; **8 SUVI; 9 DRAAKON** Tartu 34; **10 LEOLA**

THEATRE: 11 UGALA Vaksali 7, tel. 536 17

MUSEUM: 12 LOCAL MUSEUM Laidoneri plats 12, Thu—Mon 10—17, tel. 526 63

ARCHITECTURAL MONUMENTS

13 VILJANDI CASTLE RUINS ; 14 INDEPEN-DENCE WAR CEMETERY ; 15 CAPTAIN ANTON IRV'S MONUMENT ; 16 ARTIST JOHANN KÖLER'S MONUMENT

CHURCHES

17 PAULUS CHURCH (Lutheran) Kiriku 5; **18 JAANI CHURCH** (Orthodox) Mäe 8; **19 ADVENTIST, BAPTIST CONGREGATIONS** Uku 11a

ADMINISTRATIVE BUILDINGS

20 CITY GOVERNMENT Linnu 2, tel. 539 80; **21 COUNTY GOVERNMENT** Vabaduse plats 2, tel. 533 46

TRANSPORT

22 BUS STATION Ilmarise 1, tel. 539 80; **23 RAILWAY STATION** Metalli 1, tel. 538 25; **AIRLINE BOOKINGS** Tartu 14, tel. 539 85; **24 GAS STATION** Tallinna 99a, tel. 542 50; **CAR SERVICE** Tallinna 97, tel. 536 56

OTHER

25 POST OFFICE Tallinna 11; **26 EMERGENCY MEDICAL AID ; 27 DEPARTMENT STORE** Tallinna 3; **28 MARKET** Turu plats 1; **29 SERVICE CENTRE** Jakobsoni 11; **30 TRAVEL BUREAU** Tallinna 6, tel. 544 18; **31 VABADUSE PLATS ; 32 KESKVÄLJAK ; 33 LINNA VÄLJAK; 34 TREPIMÄGI ; 35 STADIUM ; 36 ROWING CENTRE**

KURESSAARE

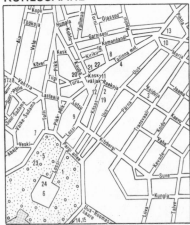

HOTEL: 1 LOSSI Lossi 27, tel. 544 43

RESTAURANT. CAFÈ

2 RESTORAN Raekoja 1, tel. 551 39; **3 VESKI** Pärna 19

CULTURAL CENTRES: 4 KULTUURIMAJA Tallinna 6, tel. 542 38; **5 KUURSAAL** Pargi 2, tel. 597 49

MUSEUMS

6 SAAREMAA MUSEUM (Kuressaare Episcopal Castle) Lossihoov 3, Wed—Sun 11—17.30, tel. 563 07; **7 KURESSAARE CITIZENS' MUSEUM , ART GALLERY** Pargi 5, Wed—Sun 11—17.30, tel. 596 71

CHURCHES

8 LAURENTSIUS CHURCH (Lutheran) Tallinna 13; **9 NIKOLAI CHURCH** (Orthodox) Lossi 8; **10 BAPTIST, METHODIST, ADVENTIST CONGREGATIONS** Karja 1

ADMINISTRATIVE BUILDINGS

11 CITY GOVERNMENT (Town Hall) Tallinna 2, tel. 542 66; **12 SAARE COUNTY GOVERNMENT** (Knights' Building) Lossi 1, tel. 542 44

TRANSPORT

13 BUS STATION Pihtla tee 25, tel. 573 80; **14 AIRPORT** Roomassaare 1, tel. 542 61; **TAXIS** tel. 549 39, 573 89, 555 77; **15 GAS STATION** Roomassaare, tel. 555 75; **CAR SERVICE** Kalevi 2, tel. 574 57

OTHER

16 POST OFFICE Torni 1; **17 HOSPITAL** Aia 25, tel. 592 01; **18 SANATORIUM** Kastani 20, tel. 594 04; **19 DEPARTMENT STORE** Raekoja 1; **20 SHOPPING CENTRE** Kauba 2; **21 WEIGH-HOUSE** Tallinna 3; **22 MARKET HALL** Tallinna 5; **23 TRAVEL AGENCY 'THULE'** Pargi 1, tel. 574 70; **SAAREMAA TRAVEL BUREAU** Pärna 2, tel. 579 70; **24 SONG FESTIVAL STAGE**

KÄRDLA

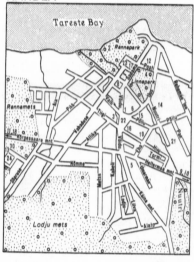

RESTAURANT. CAFÈ

1 RESTORAN Keskväljak 1, tel. 915 62; **2 RAN-NAPAARGU** Lubjaahju 5, tel. 912 87

3 CULTURAL CENTRE: Võidu 22, tel. 911 90

CHURCHES: 4 CHURCH (Lutheran); **5 BAP-TIST, ADVENTIST PRAYER HOUSE**

ADMINISTRATIVE BUILDINGS: 6 CITY GOV-ERNMENT Uus 1, tel. 913 73; **7 COUNTY GOVERNMENT** Nõukogude väljak 5, tel. 913 68

TRANSPORT

8 BUS STATION Võidu 1, tel. 911 37; **9 AIR-PORT** tel. 913 77; **10 HELTERMAA HARBOUR** tel. 942 12; **TAXIS** tel. 911 39; **11 GAS STA-TION** Kõrgessaare mnt. 47, tel. 913 59; **CAR SERVICE** Hellamaa, tel. 946 72

OTHER

12 POST OFFICE Posti 7; **13 TELEGRAPH** Nõukogude väljak 9; **14 HOSPITAL** Rahu 2, tel. 914 49; **15 DEPARTMENT STORE** Uus 2; **16 MARKET** ; **17 TOURIST FIRM 'DAGO'** Vabriku väljak 1, tel. 912 41; fax 991 42; **18 MALVASTE TOURIST CENTRE** tel. 915 25; **19 STADIUM** ; **20 SPORTS HALL** Nõukogude väljak 11, tel. 914 35; **21 KEK SPORTS HALL** ; **22 KESKVÄLJAK** ; **23 VABRIKUVÄLJAK; 24 NÕUKOGUDE VÄLJAK; WESTERN ESTONIA BIOSPHERE RESERVE** tel. 991 36

GOVERNMENT

REPUBLIC OF ESTONIA SUPREME COUNCIL: Lossi plats 1a, Tallinn 200100
Chairman — Arnold Rüütel
Secretariat . . . . tel. 426 200; telex 173647 VIKING; fax 436 389
Press Attaché — Raul Mälk . . . . tel. 424 882
Presidium of Estonian Supreme Council: Weizenbergi 39, Tallinn 200100

PERMANENT COMMITTEES

Administrative Reform Committee — Andrus Ristkok 606 486
Defence Committee — Rein Tamme 606 341
Economic Committee — Ants Veetõusme 606 315
Environment Committee — Andres Tarand 606 779
Ethics Committee — Villu Jürjo 606 748
Ethnic Relations Committee — Sergei Sovetnikov 606 797
Foreign Affairs Committee — Indrek Toome 444 089
Labour Committee — Lehte Sööt-Hainsalu 606 388
Legal Committee — Tõnu Anton 606 318
Media Committee — Rein Veidemann 449 565
Research, Education and Culture Committee — Jaak Jõerüüt 606 410
Rural Affairs Committee — Juhan Telgmaa 606 739

REPUBLIC OF ESTONIA GOVERNMENT: Lossi plats 1a, Tallinn 200100
Chairman — Edgar Savisaar
Secretariat . . . . tel. 606 735; fax 606 249, 440 372
State chancellery . . . . tel. 606 766
Press Secretary — Juhan Hindov 606 734

MINISTRIES

MINISTRY OF AGRICULTURE: Lai 39/41, Tallinn 200102
Minister — Harri Õunapuu . . . . tel. 441 166; telex 173216 TOMAT SU; fax 440 601
Department of Foreign Relations . . . . tel. 601 210; telex 173216 TOMAT SU; fax 602 160

MINISTRY OF COMMERCE: Kiriku 6, Tallinn 200103
Minister — Ants Laos . . . . . . tel. 443 941; telex 173623 ZEFIR; fax 448 091
Department of Foreign Relations . . . . tel. 445 921

MINISTRY OF CONSTRUCTION: Harju 11, Tallinn 200001
Minister — Gennadi Golubkov . . . . tel. 440 577

MINISTRY OF CULTURE: Suur-Karja 23, Tallinn 200001
Minister — Lepo Sumera . . . . . . tel. 445 077; telex 173260 HELI SU; fax 440 963
Department of Foreign Relations . . . . tel. 448 311

MINISTRY OF ECONOMICS: Komsomoli 1, Tallinn 200100
Minister — Jaak Leimann . . . . . tel. 683 444; telex 173106 PLAAN SU; fax 682 097

MINISTRY OF EDUCATION: Kingissepa 60, Tallinn 200103
Minister — Rein Loik . . . . tel. 437 760; fax 437 892
Department of Foreign Relations . . . . tel. 437 715

MINISTRY OF THE ENVIRONMENT: Toompuiestee 24, Tallinn 200110
Minister — Tõnis Kaasik . . . . . tel. 452 507; telex 173238 METS SU; fax 453 310
Department of Foreign Relations . . . . tel. 452 693

MINISTRY OF FINANCE: Kohtu 8, Tallinn 200100
Minister — Rein Miller . . . . tel. 452 801; fax 452 992
Department of Foreign Trade and Finance . . . . tel. 451 950

MINISTRY OF FOREIGN AFFAIRS: Lossi plats 1a, Tallinn 200001
Minister — Lennart Meri . . . . . . tel. 443 266; telex 173269 EVM SU; fax 441 713

MINISTRY OF HEALTH: Lossi plats 7, Tallinn 200100
Minister — Andres Ellamaa . . . . tel. 445 123; fax 440 869

MINISTRY OF INDUSTRY AND ENERGY: Lomonossovi 29, Tallinn 200104
Minister — Jaak Tamm . . . . . . tel. 423 550; telex 173278 AKTIV SU; fax 425 468
Department of Foreign Relations . . . . tel. 421 133

MINISTRY OF THE INTERIOR: Pikk 61, Tallinn 200101
Minister — Olev Laanjärv . . . . tel. 663 262, 663 459; fax 602 785
Department of Foreign Relations . . . . tel. 663 676

MINISTRY OF JUSTICE: Pärnu mnt. 7, Tallinn 200104
Minister — Jüri Raidla 445 120

MINISTRY OF LABOUR: Lomonossovi 29, Tallinn 200104
Minister — Arvo Kuddo 423 434
Foreign Relations Consultant 422 945

MINISTRY OF SOCIAL SECURITY: Estonia pst. 15, Tallinn 200001
Minister — Siiri Oviir 666 930

MINISTRY OF SUPPLY: Kiriku 2/4, Tallinn 200100
Minister — Aleksander Sikkal . . . . . tel. 421 597; telex 173145 FOND; fax 450 540

MINISTRY OF TRANSPORT AND COMMUNICATION: Viru 9, Tallinn 200100
Minister — Tiit Vähi . . . . tel. 443 842; fax 449 206
Department of Foreign Relations . . . . tel. 441 487; fax 449 206

REPUBLIC OF ESTONIA SUPREME COURT: Pärnu mnt. 7, Tallinn 200104
Chief Justice — Jaak Kirikal . . . . tel. 442 931

REPUBLIC OF ESTONIA PUBLIC PROSECUTOR'S OFFICE: Wismari 7, Tallinn 200100
Prosecutor General — Leo Urge 445 226

REPUBLIC OF ESTONIA STATE ARBITRATION: Pärnu mnt. 20, Tallinn 200105
Head Arbitrator — Anatoli Berezi 442 362

STATE SECURITY COMMITTEE (KGB): Pikk 57, Tallinn 200001
Chairman Major-General — Rein Sillar 443 400

MILITARY COMMISSARIAT FOR THE ESTONIAN SSR: Narva mnt. 8, Tallinn 200100
Commander Major-General — Rein Põder 444 406

STATE DEPARTMENTS

DEPARTMENT OF STATE PROPERTY: Komsomoli 1, Tallinn 200100
General Director — Ardo Kamratov 682 974

NATIONAL GRAIN BOARD: Toomkuninga 20, Tallinn 200100
General Director — Mati Allas . . . . tel. 453 376, 452 436; fax 452 616

NATIONAL MARITIME BOARD: Viru 9, Tallinn 200100
General Director — Nathan Tõnnisson . . . . tel. 442 725, 443 003, 444 669; fax 449 206

NATIONAL TOURIST BOARD: Suur-Karja 23, Tallinn 200101
General Director — Tiia Karing . . . . tel. 441 239; fax 440 963

CUSTOMS DEPARTMENT: Kohtu 8, Tallinn 200100
General Director — Tõnis Härm . . . . tel. 452 767

DEPARTMENT OF ARCHIVES: Maneeži 4, Tallinn 200102
General Director — Peep Pillakd . . . . tel. 424 928; fax 432 295

DEPARTMENT OF AVIATION: Viru 9, Tallinn 200100
General Director — Rein Järva . . . . tel. 441 785; fax 449 206

DEPARTMENT OF COMMERCIAL LICENSING: Komsomoli 1, Tallinn 200100
General Director — Mati Jürgens . . . . tel. 682 920

DEPARTMENT OF EMPLOYMENT: Lomonossovi 29, Tallinn 200104
General Director — Vello Rääk 422 945

DEPARTMENT OF FOREIGN ECONOMIC RELATIONS: Komsomoli 1, Tallinn 200100
General Director — Mehis Pilv . . . . tel. 683 559; fax 682 097

DEPARTMENT OF HOUSING AND MUNICIPAL SERVICES: Harju 11, Tallinn 200001
General Director — Toivo Lippmaa . . . . tel. 445 173

DEPARTMENT OF LANGUAGE: Roosikrantsi 6, Tallinn 200106
General Director — Mart Rannut 446 906, 441 800

DEPARTMENT OF STATISTICS: Endla 15, Tallinn 200106
General Director — Rein Veetõusme . . . tel. 453 889; telex 173302 FAIL SU; fax 453 923

DEPARTMENT OF TECHNICAL INSPECTION: Lossi plats 4, Tallinn 200103
General Director — Ölo Tambet . . . . tel. 606 715

FIRE AND RESCUE DEPARTMENT: Raua 2, Tallinn 200106
General Director — Ants Muna 663 986

FOREST DEPARTMENT: Toompuiestee 24, Tallinn 200001
General Director — Enn Tasso . . . . tel. 452 982; telex 173238 METS SU; fax 453 310

IMMIGRATION DEPARTMENT: Vana-Viru 12, Tallinn 200001
General Director — Andres Kollist . . . . tel. 444 473

LAND DEPARTMENT: Mustamäe tee 51, Tallinn 200006
tel. 528 401; telex 173216 TOMAT SU; fax 528 400

POLICE DEPARTMENT: Pikk 19, Tallinn 200001
General Director — Jüri Nurme . . . . tel. 663 815

PRICING DEPARTMENT: Toompea 1, Tallinn 200001
General Director — Peeter Tammistu 443 733

REGISTRY OF BIRTHS, DEATHS AND MARRIAGES: Lossi plats 1a, Tallinn 200001
General Director — Kersti Hiedel 606 701

ROAD ADMINISTRATION: Pärnu mnt. 24, Tallinn 200001
General Director — Jüri Riimaa . . . . tel. 445 829; fax 440 357

SPORTS DEPARTMENT: Regati pst. 1, Tallinn 200103
General Director — Mati Mark . . . tel. 238 059; telex 173236 SPORT SU; fax 238 355

TAXATION DEPARTMENT: Kohtu 8, Tallinn 200100
General Director — Villar Aron . . . . tel. 452 329

REPRESENTATIVES OF ESTONIA ABROAD

SOVIET UNION
PERMANENT MISSION OF THE ESTONIAN GOVERNMENT TO THE SOVIET UNION:
Sobinovski pereulok 5, Moscow 103009
Permanent Representative — Jüri Kahn . . . . tel. 290 50 13; fax 202 38 30

LITHUANIA
PERMANENT MISSION OF THE ESTONIAN GOVERNMENT TO LITHUANIA:
Turniškiu 20, Vilnius 232016
Permanent Representative — Mart Tarmak . . . . . . tel. 764 896; fax 769 848

RUSSIAN FEDERATION
PERMANENT MISSION OF THE ESTONIAN GOVERNMENT TO THE RUSSIAN FEDERATION:
Sobinovski pereulok 5, Moscow 103009
Permanent Representative — Jevgeni Golikov . . . . . . tel. 290 50 13; fax 202 38 30

DENMARK
BALTIC CULTURAL AND INFORMATION CENTRE:
H. C. Andersens Boulevard 38, 1553 Copenhagen V
Representative — Arvo-Jürgen Alas . . . . tel. 931 867; telex 40072 DK; fax 913 099
Baltic Chambers of Commerce. Representative — Anu Pärt

FINLAND
ESTONIAN CULTURAL OFFICE: Mariankatu 8B C13, 00170 Helsinki
Director — Kulle Raig . . . . tel. 179 719; fax 669 615
EMBASSY OF THE SOVIET UNION: Tehtaankatu, 1B, 00140 Helsinki
Representative of the Ministry of Foreign Affairs of Estonia —
Johannes Johanson . . . . tel. 661 448, 661 449

FRANCE
ESTONIAN INFORMATION BUREAU: 30, Rue de l'Aude, 75014 Paris
Representative — Malle Talvet . . . . tel. and fax 3314 327 01 68

SWEDEN
ESTONIAN INFORMATION BUREAU: Rädmansgatan 18, 11425 Stockholm
Representative — Aadu Must . . . . tel. 109 981, 109 986; fax 107 744
EMBASSY OF THE SOVIET UNION: Kungsgatan 48, Stockholm
3rd Secretary — Eimar Rahumaa . . . . tel. 130 440

UNITED STATES
CONSULATE GENERAL OF THE REPUBLIC OF ESTONIA (1918 – 40):
Rockefeller Plaza 9, New-York, N. Y.
Consul General — Ernst Jaakson . . . . . . tel. 212 – 247 14 50; fax 212 – 262 08 93

REPRESENTATIVES OF FOREIGN STATES IN ESTONIA

FINLAND
CONSULATE GENERAL OF THE REPUBLIC OF FINLAND IN LENINGRAD TALLINN BRANCH:
Kingissepa 12, Tallinn 200001
Consul — Eija Kauppi . . . . tel. 449 522, 446 869; fax 446 392

SWEDEN
CONSULATE GENERAL OF THE KINGDOM OF SWEDEN IN LENINGRAD TALLINN BRANCH:
Endla 4a,Tallinn 200001
Consul — Häkan Damm . . . . tel. 450 350; telex 173124 SVNSK SU; fax 450 676

LATVIA
PERMANENT MISSION OF THE REPUBLIC OF LATVIA TO ESTONIA:
Permanent Representative — Aldis Bērziņš . . . . tel. 237 665

LITHUANIA
PERMANENT MISSION OF THE REPUBLIC OF LITHUANIA TO ESTONIA:
Vabaduse väljak 10, Tallinn 200001
Permanent Representative — Sigitas Kudarauskas 448 917, 666 634

DENMARK
DANISH CULTURAL INSTITUTE: Vana-Viru 4, Tallinn 200101
Secretary — Silvi Teesalu . . . . . . tel. 446 836; telex 173134 ESTO SU; fax 601 247

FINLAND
FINNISH CULTURAL BUREAU: Vana-Viru 12, Tallinn 200010
Head — Riitta Koivisto-Arhinmäki . . . . tel. and fax 449 237

NORDIC COUNCIL OF MINISTERS
INFORMATION OFFICE: Tolli 3, Tallinn 200101 . . . . tel. 601 238

BUSINESS DIRECTORY

INDUSTRIES

Further information on Estonian businesses available from the Gen. Computation Centre of the State Dept of Statistics: Endla 15, Tallinn 200106; tel. 450 573, the Register of Businesses, consultant: Jüri Rebane, and from the Estonian Chamber of Commerce and Ind.

ESTONIAN CHAMBER OF COMMERCE AND INDUSTRY. F. 1925 as a Public Law Chamber of Commerce; Mem. of the Int. Chamber of Commerce 1927 – 40; observer of the Nordic Chamber of Commerce. Links with the Int. Chamber of Commerce, the Eurochamber of Commerce, the Baltic Chamber of Commerce and with all business communities of the world regions. Assoc. of Est., Latv. and Lith. Chamber of Commerce est. 1989; Est.-American Chamber of Commerce est. 1990. Pres. Peeter Tammoja. **Add.** Toom-Kooli 17, Tallinn 200106; tel. 444 929; telex 173254 KODA SU; fax 443 656.

ESTONIAN SMALL BUSINESS ASSOCIATION (EVEA). Est. 1988; organizes small-business owners in Estonia and abroad. Man. Dir Vello Vallaste. **Add.** Kuhlbarsi 1, Tallinn 200104; tel. 431 577; telex 173254 KODA SU; fax 771 675.

ENGINEERING

BALTIJETS Production Association. Est. 1947. Gamma therapy equipm., gamma defectoscopes, radiation meters, monitoring and control instruments for other non-electrical parametres, vacuum pumps, radioisotropic generators and other electronic devices. Export to 11 c. Man. Dir Valeri Chetvergov. **Add.** Linda 2, Narva 202000; tel. 318 45.

DESINTEGRAATOR Scientific Production Association. Est. 1974. Design and prod. of disintegrators and devices based on them. Foreign partners in Finland, Germany and Austria. Man. Dir Jüri Eelma. **Add.** Leningradi mnt. 71, Tallinn 200104; tel. 211 001; telex 173214 VASAR SU; fax 211 008.

DVIGATEL All-Union State Plant. Est. 1899. Gen. machinery. Foreign partners in Cuba, Czechoslovakia and Hungary. Man.Dir Vladimir Yarovoy. **Add.** Suur-Sõjamäe 10, Tallinn 200090; tel. 210 160; fax 210 965.

EESTI KAABEL. Est. 1924. Cables and wires from copper and aluminium for 30 different purposes, incl. elevator and power cables, wires for installations, lighting, communications and assembly lines. Man.Dir Valeri Malyshko.

Add. Jõe 4, Tallinn 200102; tel. 422 049; fax 422 049.

ESTEL Electrical Engineering Works Manufacturing Group. Est. 1870. Development and manufacture of semiconductor devices and converters based on them. Company-owned research inst. Man.Dir Vladimir Miroshnichenko. *Add.* Telliskivi 6, Tallinn 200110; tel.495 410; telex 179234 ESTEL SU; fax 495 489.

ESTRE Factory. Est. 1944. Repair of tractor engines and their assemblies; design, prod. and marketing of machinery; prod. of gas oxygen. Man.Dir Valter Teppan. *Add.* Vasara 50, Tartu 202400; tel. 735 42; fax 708 68.

ETKVL KIT. Est. 1936. Food, beverage and tobacco processing equipm., wheeled containers and wire products for retail businesses. Man.Dir Uno Tänav. *Add.* Kesk-Sõjamäe 3, Tallinn 200104; tel. 211 440; fax 215 468.

ILMARINE. Est. 1859. Equipm. for ind. boilers: cleaning devices for heated surfaces, oil and gas burners; safety and ignition devices, automatic control panels. Household goods: stoves, electric saws, lawn mowers. Semifinished and finished cast-iron and steel products. Partnership in Finland, Sweden,Germany, Bulgaria, P.R. of China. Man.Dir Toomas Talving. *Add.* Mustamäe tee 5, Tallinn 200108; tel. 495 000; fax 496 062.

PIONEER Tooling Works. Est. 1965. Press tools, dies and injectionmoulds; sales, installation and service of various foreign CNC electric discharge machines (EDM) on the Soviet market, incl. staff training. Man.Dir Vladimir Frishman. *Add.* Marja 7, Tallinn 200108; tel. 494 314; fax 494 763.

RET Tallinn Radioelectronics Manufacturing Corporation. Est.1935. Electronic control and instrumentation products. Man.Dir Aleksandr Plushchayev. *Add.* Narva mnt. 11, Tallinn 200102; tel.422 051; fax 448 969.

TALLEKS Association. Est. 1944. Excavators, cast-iron semifinished and finished goods. Trading partners in all E-European c., Iraq, Jemen, Egypt, Finland, Norway. Man.Dir Paul Treier. *Add.* Mustamäe tee 12, Tallinn 200100; tel. 449 048; telex 173201 VKFT; fax 498 285.

TALLINN ENGINEERING PLANT. Est. 1865. Cooling equipm. and components, ultrasonic devices, compact disintegrator mills,chem. ind. equipm., heating ovens, central-heating boilers and radiators, semifinished and finished steel castings. Man.Dir Aleksei Moroz. *Add.* Kopli 68, Tallinn 200110; tel. and fax 444 621.

TARTU EXPERIMENTAL AUTOMOBILE REPAIR PLANT. Est. 1949. Motor vehicle bodies, trailers and semitrailers, specialised transport vehicles and equipm.; repair and maintenance of motor vehicles; repair of engines, turbines, pumps, etc. Man.Dir Sulev Piibar. *Add.* Riia 24, Tartu 202400; tel. 320 30.

TARTU INSTRUMENT FACTORY Leaseholders' Organization. Est. 1958. Control equipm. for technol. and prod. processes. Chair. of the Bd Kaido Klaassen. *Add.* Kastani 42, Tartu 202400; tel.325 30; fax 343 39.

TERAS Ltd. Est. 1944. Metal constr., tools and accessories, knitting machines, hairdressers'

equipm. and home appliances. Trading partners in Finland and Hungary. Man.Dir Alvar Hirtentreu. *Add.* Rännamõisa tee 4, Tallinn 200109; tel. 559 133; fax 330 103.

TÖÖSTUSAPARAAT Industrial Engineering. Est. 1945. Electromagnetic flowmeters, calorimeters, gasmeters, noncontact transducers and limit switches for automated systems and process control. Man.Dir Anatoli Makarov. *Add.* Masina 1, Tallinn 200001; tel. 424 955; fax 426 570.

VASAR Production Association. Est. 1946. Doorlocks, padlocks and carlocks; safety belts for high-level constr. work, gardening tools (lawn mowers), various fastening components, aluminium utensils, wire, galvanic coatings. Export to Finland, Sweden, Germany, Denmark, Canada, Cuba; import from Finland, Germany, Switzerland. Man.Dir Ants Viigisalu. *Add.* Pärnu mnt. 139c, Tallinn 200013; tel. 555 143; telex 173166 VASAR; fax 557 596.

VOLTA Plant. Est. 1899. Gen. and special-purpose electric generators and motors, miniature electric motors, home appliances (electric wafflers and radiators). Man.Dir Boris Churikov. *Add.*Tööstuse 47, Tallinn 200110; tel. 446 002.

VÕIT Tartu Agricultural Machine Works. Est. 1885. Farming and forestry machines and spare parts, gardening tools. Man.Dir Kalju Kaljuste. *Add.* Kalmistu 21/23, Tartu 202400; tel. 328 08.

VÕRU GAS ANALYSERS PLANT. Est. 1959. Monitoring and control equipm. for non-electric parametres. Export to 15 c. Man.Dir Einar Kuuse. *Add.* Kreutzwaldi 59, Võru 202710; tel. 215 21.

BALTIC MARINE REPAIR PLANT. Est. 1947. Marine constr. and repair; dyed-metal castings, forgings, cast and moulded metal products. Man.Dir Fyodor Berman. *Add.* Kopli 103, Tallinn 200017; tel. 479 408; telex 173120 REM; fax 493 496.

LOKSA MARINE REPAIR PLANT. Est. 1905. Const. and repair of ships and floating structures. Man.Dir Aleksandr Kustov. *Add.* Tallinna 2, Loksa, Harjumaa 203020; tel. 752 41.

EXPERIMENTAL SPORTS-BOAT BUILDING YARD. Est. 1946. Racers and cruisers, launches, rowboats and motorboats, boat and yacht parts. Trading partners in Poland, Finland, Sweden, Norway and Hungary. Man.Dir Hans Nukki. *Add.* Maleva põik 3, Tallinn 200110; tel. 474 616; telex 173212 RUMB; fax 474 616.

VIHUR Experimental Sports Equipment Plant. Est. 1975. Electronic equipm., calculators, sports cars and racing motorcycles, incl. spare parts. Automobile maintenance and repair. Trading partners in Finland. Man.Dir Taivo Tandre. *Add.* Kreutzwaldi 4, Tallinn 200102; tel. 432 880; telex 173187 VIHUR SU.

MINING & ENERGETICS

EESTI FOSFORIIT Production Association. Est. 1920. Phosphorite mining, prod. of phosphorous and mixed fertilizers, road metal prod. Man.Dir Aleksandr Revkuts. *Add.* Fosforiidi 4, Maardu 200901; tel. 234 146.

EESTI PÕLEVKIVI Production Association. Est. 1945. Oil-shale mining and refining (7 underground and 4 open-pit mines). Annual output nearly 24 million metric t. 14,000 employees. Man.Dir Otto Sullakatko. *Add.* Lenini 10, Kohtla-Järve 202020;tel. 266 54.

ORU PEAT WORKS. Est. 1963. Peat and peat briquet prod. Man.Dir Anatoli Lepetkin. *Add.* Oru, Ida-Virumaa 202020; tel. 271 41.

SANGLA PEAT WORKS. Est. 1924. Farming peat and peat briquet prod., metal processing. Man.Dir Rein Lettens. *Add.* Puhja sjk., Tartumaa 202466; tel. 512 60.

TOOTSI PRODUCTION ASSOCIATION. Est. 1937. Peat, peat briquets; mica, peat, graphite and other mineral-based products; textile products. Man.Dir Arvo Luberg. *Add.* Tootsi, Pärnumaa 203470; tel. 662 21; fax 435 54.

BALTIC THERMAL POWER STATION. Est. 1959. Prod. and distribution of electric energy; supplier of steam and hot water to buildings. Capacity 1,624 MW. Man.Dir V. Terentev. *Add.* POB 18, Narva 202000; tel. 933 62.

ESTONIAN THERMAL POWER STATION. Est. 1969. Prod. of electric energy. Capacity 1,610 MW. Man.Dir Konstantin Senchugov. *Add.* POB 28, Narva 202000; tel. 282 22.

IRU THERMAL POWER STATION. Est. 1978. Prod. of electric power (capacity 460 MW) and thermal power for heating (1,085 Gcal/h). Man.Dir Janis-Aivar Balodis. *Add.* Leningradi mnt. 103, Tallinn 200103; tel. 612 256.

CHEMICAL INDUSTRIES

FLORA Production Association. Est. 1889. Paints and household chem., candles, perfumes and cosmetics, non-toxic pesticides (more than 200 plant protection agents). Foreign trade partners in Germany, Sweden, Finland, Austria, France, Switzerland, Italy, USA, Norway, Denmark, Ireland, Egypt, Czecho-Slovakia, Hungary and Poland. Man.Dir Elmar Kruusma. *Add.* Tulika 19, Tallinn 200109; tel. 472 448; telex 173256 SU FLORA; fax 491 021.

EKE-SADOLIN S.P. Soviet-Finnish joint venture. Est. 1987. Paints,varnishes, enamels and organic solvents; prod. and repair of special machinery and equipm.; import-export transactions. Man.Dir Aivar Ild. *Add.* Haigru 9a, Tallinn 200006; tel. 423 082; telex 173268 SADEK SU; fax 448 493.

KIVIOLI OIL-SHALE CHEMICAL PLANT. Est. 1922. Synthetic detergents, pesticides and agrochem. products, other oil-shale-derived chem. Man.Dir Eberhaard Vaas. *Add.* Turu 3, Kiviöli 202040; tel. 570 29.

KOHTLA-JÄRVE OIL-SHALE CHEMICALS PRODUCTION ASSOCIATION. Est. 1924. Oil-shale gas and oil, antiseptic impregnants, anti-erosion chem., electrode coke, rubber softeners, mastics, synthetic resins, carbamide, benzene and toluene. Man.Dir Nikolai Kutashov. *Add.* Narva mnt. 14, Kohtla-Järve 202020; tel. 445 45.

TALLINN CHEMICAL AND PHARMACEUTICAL PLANT. Est. 1914. Pharmaceuticals and cosmetics. Trading partners in Finland, Poland, Czecho-Slovakia, Hungary and Yugoslavia. Man.Dir Aare Loog. *Add.* Tondi 33, Tallinn 200109; tel. 557 366; telex 173293 TAFA SU; fax 557 366.

BUILDING MATERIALS

AHTME BUILDING MATERIALS PLANT. Est. 1961. Building components of concrete, lime and gypsum. Man.Dir Aleksandr Vorobyov. *Add.* Ahtme, Kohtla-Järve 202020; tel. 224 05.

ASERI CERAMICS WORKS. Est. 1922. Bricks, plates, roofing tiles and other ceramic constr. material; ceramic pipes, gutters, tubular fittings. Man.Dir Ivo Tomeri. *Add.* Tehase 1, Aseri, Ida-Virumaa 202043; tel. 513 82.

JÄRVAKANDI TEHASED Window Factory. Est. 1879. Window panes, glass balls, glass insulators, timber constr. components (window-frames, doors). Man.Dir Ando Lillioja. *Add.* Järvakandi, Rapla maakond 203504; tel. 773 77; telex 173242 GLASS SU.

NARVA BUILDING MATERIALS PLANT. Est. 1969. Building components of concrete, lime and gypsum (bricks, roofing tiles, plates, etc.) and various other products (sculptures, furniture, bas-relief works). Man.Dir V. Sukhov. *Add.* POB 3, Narva 202000; tel. 333 01.

PALIVERE BUILDING MATERIALS PLANT. Est. 1974. Firebricks, blocks, plates and other building materials; lime processing, electronic measuring tools and instruments, special cargo transportation. Man.Dir Hanno-Mati Saar. *Add.* Lähtru tee 15, Palivere, Läänemaa 203150; tel. 941 91.

PÜSSI FIBREBOARD PLANT. Est. 1975. Chipboards and fibreboards. Man.Dir Aleksander Uedom. *Add.* Maidla tee 7, Püssi, Ida-Virumaa 202041; tel. 224 05.

SILIKAAT. Est. 1910. Silica bricks, roofing and insulating materials, linoleum, pavement and mosaic tiles, sand and lime. Trading partners in Finland and Sweden. Man.Dir Leonhard Liiv. *Add.* Pärnu mnt. 238, Tallinn 200107; tel. 511 144; fax 558 850.

TEKT Tallinn Construction Ceramics Plant. Est. 1955. Bricks, floor and roofing tiles, various other ceramic constr. products; tableware and other household ceramics. Trading partners in Finland. Man.Dir Andres Suurküla. *Add.* Maleva 2, Tallinn 200017; tel. 473 608; fax 441 910.

PAPER & PRINTING

KEHRA PULP AND PAPER MILL. Est. 1936. Sulphate pulp, kraft paper, tissue-paper and crepe paper, other paper products. Dir Žanna Botvinkina. *Add.*Anija mnt. 10, Kehra, Harjumaa 202240; tel. 765 408.

KOHILA PAPER MILL. Est. 1893. Ill. paper, writing-paper, wallpaper, cardboard, corrugated paper, paper bags, other paper products. Foreign partners in Switzerland. Dir Igor Gnatyshin. *Add.* Tööstuse 17, Kohila, Rapla maakond 203420; tel. 335 64.

TALLINN PULP AND PAPER MILL. Est. 1839. Paper, pulp. Foreign partners in Finland. Man.Dir Ernst Vaher. *Add.* Masina 20, Tallinn 200104; tel. 424 477; fax 424 303.

PRINTERS

ÜHISELU. Est. 1633. Books, booklets. Man.Dir Gunnar Otsa. **Add.** Pikk 40/42, Tallinn 200001; tel. and fax 442 589.

VABA MAA. Est. 1920. Stationery, books. Man.Dir Ain Puusep. **Add.** Pikk 58, Tallinn 200001; tel. 442 428.

OKTOOBER. Est. 1922. Postcards, posters, labels, in colour. Man.Dir Vladimir Hazinski. **Add.** Kreutzwaldi 24, Tallinn 200105; tel. 423 119, 421 570; fax 422 483.

TARTU PRINTERS. Est. 1959. Books, newspapers, journals. Man.Dir Kalle Rannu. **Add.** Ülikooli 17/19, Tartu 202400; tel. 332 14.

PUBLISHERS AND PRINTERS OF THE CENTRAL COMMITTEE OF THE ECP. Est. 1962. Newspapers and journals, in colour. Man.Dir Valeri Chernyshev. **Add.** Pärnu mnt. 67a, Tallinn 200090; tel. 681 119.

TALLINN BOOK PRINTERS. Est. 1985. Books, booklets, posters, in colour. Man.Dir Jüri Simsel. **Add.** Laki 26, Tallinn 200108; tel. 598 058; fax 537 181.

FURNITURE, HOUSEWARE, PLASTICS

KOHTLA-JÄRVE FURNITURE FACTORY. Est. 1979. Kitchen furniture. Man.Dir Ülo Nappa. **Add.** Ehitajate tee 131a, Kohtla-Järve 202020; tel. 438 01.

NAROVA. Est. 1955. Upholstered and wooden furniture; racquets. Man.Dir Valeri Myachin. **Add.** Tiimani 1, Narva 202000; tel. 318 34; fax 403 37.

STANDARD Furniture Designers and Manufacturers. Est. 1946. Design and manufacture of furniture. Man.Dir Ronald Ilves. **Add.** Kopli 21, Tallinn 200110; tel. 441 266; telex 173218 BIRCH.

TALLINN PLYWOOD AND FURNITURE FACTORY. Est. 1877. Prod. of plywood, parquet, mirrors, living and bedroom furniture. Trading partners in Sweden, Finland, Germany. Man.Dir Nikolai Grigorev.**Add.** Pärnu mnt. 69, Tallinn 200106; tel. 681 542; fax 681 977.

TARMEKO Timber Products. Est. 1947. Lumber, cut timber, compressed wood, wooden containers, furniture, turnery blanks, wooden toys. Trading partners in Finland, Sweden and Germany. Man.Dir Olev Nigul. **Add.** Sõbra 56, Tartu 202400; tel. 745 80; fax 322 35.

TARMEL Ltd. Est. 1925. Furniture elements, table-tennis racquets, wooden articles, mattresses, wooden containers. Trading partners in Sweden and Finland. Man.Dir Ain Saarmann. **Add.** Pärnu mnt. 158, Tallinn 200107; tel. 555 888; telex 173893 TARM; fax 555 629.

WERMO, Võru Woodworking Association. Est. 1947. Furniture, wooden containers and cut timber, lumber prod. Trading partners in Sweden, Finland, USA, Germany. Man.Dir Lembitu Luts. **Add.** Räpina mnt. 12, Võru 202710; tel. 211 60; fax 313 72.

VIISNURK Ltd. Est. 1945. Living room furniture, skis, chipboard and fibreboard. Trading partners in Finland, Sweden, Germany. Man.Dir Richard Mutso. **Add.** Suure-Jõe 48, Pärnu 203600;

tel.400 83; telex 173116 VIRO SU; tel. and fax 439 64.

TALLINN PIANO FACTORY. Est. 1950. Pianos and other keyboard instruments, kannels (Est. zithers). Export to Canada, USA, Austria, Switzerland, Germany, Finland. Man.Dir Jaan Läheb. **Add.** Kungla 41, Tallinn 200004; tel. 449 337; telex 173278 AKTIV SU; fax 449 337.

TARBEKLAAS (Household glass). Est. 1934. Glass and glassware. Trading partners in Finland and Sweden. Dir Tõnu Roondi. **Add.** Marati 12; Tallinn 200110; tel. 473 222; fax 474 994.

ESTIKO. Est. 1918. Plastic toys, household goods, etc.; plastic film and tubing. Trading partners in Finland. Man.Dir Kalju Hellenurm. **Add.** Tehase 16, Tartu 202400; tel. 707 24; fax 738 64.

ESTOPLAST. Est. 1959. Lighting fixtures and switches. Trading partners in Germany, Czecho-Slovakia, Hungary and Finland. Man.Dir Üllas Täht. **Add.** Türi 10, Tallinn 200107; tel. 556 557; telex 173231 PLAST; fax 558 886.

NORMA Production Association. Est. 1891. Safety belts, toys, metal containers (pails, boxes, barrels), metal kitchenware, flash-bulbs. Man.Dir Udo Käär. **Add.** Laki 14, Tallinn 200108; tel. 445 757; fax 492 792.

SALVO. Est. 1948. Plastic vessels, kitchen utensils and bathroom items, safety helmets, warning triangles, slalom and hockey boots, toys, wooden and textile souvenirs. Man.Dir Aleksei Nõomaa. **Add.** Leningradi mnt. 81, Tallinn 200104; tel. 323 150; telex 173202 SALVO; fax 321 583.

TALLINN AUDIOCASSETTE FACTORY. Est. 1971. Gramophone records, audiocassette manufacture and copying, studio recordings, plastics products. Man.Dir Jüri Lang. **Add.** Lohu 12, Tallinn 200026; tel. 537 296; telex 173205 THAKT; fax 537 086.

RAKVERE Production Association. Est. 1945. Store furnishings, cooling and freezing equipm.; beer, grain coffee, jersey fabrics and garments, woollen fabrics. Man.Dir Teet Ottin. **Add.** Lauristini 3, Rakvere 202100; tel. 433 66; fax 433 66.

VIKERO Industries. Est. 1945. Custom furniture, yarn and wool, jersey fabrics and garments. Man.Dir Kalju Loo. **Add.** Tallinna mnt. 8, Pärnu 203600; tel. 405 84.

TEXTILES, CLOTHING, LEATHERWARE, FOOTWEAR

ARENG Textiles. Est. 1963. Wools and yarns, rugs and carpets, jersey fabrics and garments, leather and imitation leather bags and suitcases. Man.Dir Avo Kivimäe. **Add.** Pikk 14, Tartu 202400; tel. 331 63.

BALTI MANUFAKTUUR Textile Factory. Est. 1898. Cotton yarns, cotton lining material and fabrics, nonwovens. Export to Portugal, Turkey, Austria. Man.Dir Jaagu Kurg. **Add.** Kopli 35, Tallinn 200090; tel. 493 511; fax 444 126.

KEILA Factory. Est. 1918. Wools and yarns, woollen fabrics. Man.Dir Anatoli Belov. **Add.** Pärnu mnt. 132, Tallinn 200013; tel.557 150.

KREENHOLMI MANUFAKTUUR Cotton Association. Est. 1857. Cotton yarns and fabrics, flanelette blankets, silk fabrics, nonwoven materials and household textiles. Trading partners in Japan, Sweden, Germany, Finland, Switzerland and Hungary. Export to 20 c. Man.Dir Oleg Klushin. *Add.* Lenini 20, Narva 202000; tel. and fax 241 65.

MARAT Factory. Est. 1940. Knitwear. Trading partners in Germany, Finland, Sweden. Man.Dir Ants Kapral. *Add.* Tartu mnt. 63, Tallinn 200105; tel. 421 010; fax 432 924.

MISTRA Tallinn Nonwovens Engineering and Manufacture. Est. 1960. Tufted carpets, needlework carpeting, nonwovens; development of light-ind. technol., design of nonwoven- manufacturing machinery, constr. projects. Export to Finland, Denmark, Germany, Italy, Czecho-Slovakia. Man.Dir Argo Sillaots. *Add.* Laki 15, Tallinn 200108; tel. 537 009; telex 173122 MIKO; fax 597 536.

PUNANE KOIT Textile Factory. Est. 1919. Hosiery, synthetic silk. Man.Dir Jaan Mark. *Add.* Kotzebue 11, Tallinn 200110; tel. 443 227; fax 445 725.

PÄRNU LINEN PRODUCTS Ltd. Est. 1919. Spun linen, linen yarns and fabrics. Trading partners in Sweden. Man.Dir Boris Gelman. *Add.* Tööstuse 38, Pärnu 203600; tel. 416 81; fax 416 07.

SINDI TEXTILE FACTORY. Est. 1833. Woollen fabrics, nonwovens,textile finishing. Man.Dir Neeme Roosimägi. *Add.* Pärnu mnt. 40, Sindi 203490; tel. 512 63, 514 68; fax 514 08.

SULEV Factory. Est. 1936. Cotton terrycloth, synthetic fur,decorative curtains and drapes, clothing articles. Trading partners in Finland, Norway, Sweden. Man.Dir Väino Mets. *Add.* Nurme 1a, Haapsalu 203170; tel. 445 49; fax 457 56.

TEKSTIIL Factory. Est. 1963. Woollen and cotton fabrics, carpets and carpeting material, knitted and crocheted fabrics and garments. Man.Dir Henno Hommuk. *Add.* Vana-Viru 6, Tallinn 200001; tel. 445 325.

BALTIKA Clothing Company. Est. 1928. Men's, ladies' and children's outdoor wear (excl. furs). Trading partners in Finland, Sweden. Man.Dir Meelis Milder. *Add.* Veerenni 24, Tallinn 200106; tel. 683 231; fax 448 572.

TALLINN FASHION HOUSE. Est. 1957. Clothing and footwear design, fashion shows and exh., clothing manufacture, fashion magazine publ. Man.Dir Tiina Tibar. *Add.* Suur-Karja 13, Tallinn 200001; tel. 444 354; fax 446 334.

VILHELMINE KLEMENTI CLOTHING COMPANY. Est. 1970. Ladies' and men's wear. Import of textiles from Japan, Germany, Norway, Finland. Export of finished goods to Finland, Sweden. Man.Dir Rein Pikner. *Add.* Akadeemia tee 33, Tallinn 200108; tel. 531 150; fax 531 037.

WALKO Ltd. Est. 1963. Men's, ladies' and children's outdoor wear. Man.Dir Sander Karu. *Add.* Sepa 7, Valga 202500; tel. 403 51; fax 410 01.

ELKAR Factory. Est. 1945. Footwear, furriery, tannery. Man.Dir Eduard Veisman. *Add.* Kastani 48/50, Tartu 202400; tel. 703 38.

KOMMUNAAR Leather and Footwear Factory. Est. 1877. Natural and synthetic leather footwear, bags, suitcases; wholesale dept. Trading partners in India, Finland, Italy, Hungary. Man.Dir Laine Reisin. *Add.* Laki 12, Tallinn 200108; tel. 598 307; fax 539 858.

NARVA BOX-CALF FACTORY. Est. 1984. Tannery, leather and non-leather footwear (excl. rubber). Trading partners in Italy and Finland. Man.Dir Mikhail Kuzmich. *Add.* POB 17, Narva 202000; tel. 496 86.

PÕHJALA Rubber Manufacturing. Est. 1924. Rubber footwear, rubber consumer articles. Trading partners in Sweden, Finland. Man.Dir Talip Beknazarov. *Add.* Marati 5, Tallinn 200102; tel. 474 931.

LINDA. Est. 1963. Leather and imitation leather bags and suitcases, gloves, belts, etc.; fur garments (coats, hats, collars); tannery. Trading partners in Finland, Italy, Germany. Man.Dir Osmar-Paul Soidla. *Add.* Maakri 19/21, Tallinn 200105; tel.421 256; fax 423 305.

HANDICRAFT & JEWELRY

ARS Tallinn Combine. Est. 1944. Decorative fabrics and carpets,ceramics, painted porcelain, leathercraft, textiles (incl. traditional costumes); interior decorating of public rooms. All hand-made, using natural materials. Designer products in limited editions. Man.Dir Vello-Maide Koore. *Add.* Pärnu mnt. 154, Tallinn, 200107; tel. 555 043; fax 557 033.

ARS-JUVEEL Jewelry Workshop, Est. Artists' Union. Est. 1987. Precious metal and stone jewelry, non-ferrous metal souvenirs, emblems, medals, cups; designer metalcraft in limited editions. Trading partners in Finland, Sweden and Canada. Man.Dir Raivo Lillemets. *Add.* Hobusepea 2, Tallinn 200001; tel. and fax 601 912.

ARS-MONUMENTAAL Sculpture Workshop, Est. Artists' Union. Est. 1987. Bronze sculpture casting, stone sculpture modelling, glass inlay; exh. arrangements. Man.Dir Andres Arnover. *Add.* Raja 11a,Tallinn 200026; tel. 531 255.

JUVEEL Production Association. Est. 1923. Silver tableware and jewelry, German silver tableware. Trading partners in Finland, Sweden, Czecho-Slovakia. Man.Dir Rein Mikli. *Add.* Kadaka tee 36,Tallinn 200108; tel. 490 121; telex 173886 JEWEL SU; fax 597 345.

UKU Association of Folk Art Craftsmen. Est. 1966. Knitted and crocheted garments; handwoven runners; wooden, metal and leather folk art items. Export to Scandinavia and Central Europe; import from Finland and Germany. Man.Dir Juhan Kajandu. *Add.* Lomonossovi 29, Tallinn 200104; tel. 421 359.

FOODSTUFFS, TOBACCO & SPIRITS

TALLINN GRAIN PROCESSING PLANT. Est. 1829. Concentrated fodder,flour, cereals. Man. Dir Vladislav Levchenko. *Add.* Pärnu mnt. 390, Tallinn 200107; tel. 511 479.

TAMSALU GRAIN PROCESSING PLANT. Est. 1961. Concentrated fodder, flour; storage of agric. produce, grain storing service. Man.Dir Aadu Jaansoo. **Add.** Tööstuse 15, Tamsalu, Lääne-Virumaa 202300; tel. 305 83.

TARTU GRAIN PROCESSING PLANT. Est. 1940. Flour, concentrated fodder. Man.Dir Leonhard Puksa. **Add.** Väike Kaar 33, Tartu 202400; tel. 338 42.

VILJANDI GRAIN PROCESSING PLANT. Est. 1941. Concentrated fodder, flour; wholesale dept, storage facilities for agric. products. Man.Dir Vassili Kislenko. **Add.** Vilja 11a, Viljandi 202900; tel.535 95.

LEIBUR Bakery Products. Est. 1762. Bread and pastry; macaroni, noodles and other flour-based products. Man.Dir Kalju Urva. **Add.**Kadaka tee 76a, Tallinn 200108; tel. 531 359; telex 173484 BATON; fax 531 359.

STANDARD Bread Factory. Est. 1945. Bread, cakes and pastry; softdrinks. Man.Dir Rein Hallik. **Add.** Viljandi tee 13, Türi 202810, Järvamaa; tel. 786 90.

PAIDE DAIRY PLANT. Est. 1963. Milk products, cheese, butter. Man.Dir Jaan Käär. **Add.** Prääma tee 1, Paide 202820; tel. 417 88.

POLVA DAIRY PLANT. Est. 1965. Milk products and butter. Man.Dir Enn Sokk. **Add.** Jaama 20, Põlva 202600; tel. 957 61.

RAKVERE MEAT PROCESSING PLANT. Est. 1890. Meat products and sausages. Man.Dir Olev Rohumäe. **Add.** Näpi tööstusrajoon, Rakvere 202100; tel. 434 13.

TALLINN MEAT PROCESSING PLANT. Est. 1941. Meat and meat products; wholesale service. Man.Dir Lembit Kivisild. **Add.** Ülemiste tee 5, Tallinn 200104; tel. 213 058; fax 211 292.

TARTU MEAT PROCESSING PLANT. Est. 1928. Meat and sausages. Man.Dir Ilmar Ulp. **Add.** Teguri 43, Tartu 202400; tel. 706 42.

VALGA MEAT AND DAIRY PRODUCTS. Est. 1911. Meat products sausages, canned food, dairy products. Man.Dir Kustas-Reedik Närska. **Add.** Metsa 19, Valga 202500; tel. 436 90; fax 402 34.

VÕHMA MEAT PROCESSING PLANT. Est. 1928. Meat products and sausages. Trade partners in Sweden and Denmark. Man.Dir Arvi Kotsar. **Add.** Tallinna 40, Võhma alev, Viljandimaa 202870; tel. 232 43.

TARTU CANNED FOOD FACTORY. Est. 1946. Canned vegetables and meat; fruit preserves, fruit drinks, soft drinks, potato chips, food additives. Man.Dir Matti Holter. **Add.** Põllu 2, Tartu 202400; tel.321 16.

ESTKOMPEXIM. Soviet-Swiss joint venture. Est. 1988. Prod. and retailing of ice-cream, milk and meat products; foreign trade; agency services. Man.Dir Lembit-Olav Uusna. **Add.** Jaama 1a,Tallinn 200107; tel. 512 220; telex 173113 KOMEX SU; fax 528 872.

LEEK Tobacco Factory. Est. 1921. Tobacco products. Man.Dir Boris Lev Oks. **Add.** Kunderi 8, Tallinn 200104; tel. 422 421; telex 173170 LEEK SU; fax 423 060.

LIVIKO. Est. 1901. Alcoholic beverages, yeast, carbon dioxide, grain spirit and ind. spirit. Trade partners in Norway, Netherlands, Canada, USA, Italy and Finland. Man.Dir Udo Themas. **Add.** Masina 11, Tallinn 200104; tel. 422 467; telex 173216 TOMAT SU; fax 432 352.

BUILDING & CONSTRUCTION

BUILDING AND CONSTRUCTION ADMINISTRATION, EKE Co-Operative. Est. 1972. Constr. of buildings and building elements, civil constr., designing and eng. Man.Dir Villu Aabne. **Add.** Madara 27, Tallinn 200109; tel. 449 519; fax 442 941.

HARJU KEK Co-Operative. Est. 1964. Constr., constr. material, electrotech. and electronics ind. Trading partners in Finland, Sweden, Norway and Germany. Man.Dir Jüri Kalmet. **Add.** Paldiski mnt. 21, Keila, Harjumaa 203053; tel. 745 850; telex 173259 PULT SU; fax 771 652.

PAIDE KEK Ltd. Est. 1959. Gen. constr. works, road repairs; timber, concrete and reinforced concrete products; metal structures. Trading partners in Finland and Sweden. Exec. Man.Toomas Agasild. **Add.** Mäo, Järvamaa 202820; tel. 216 68.

TARTU KEK Co-Operative. Est. 1957. Gen. and special constr. works, designing and eng. Trading partners in Sweden. Chair. of the Bd Jaak Kalm. **Add.** Riia 132, Tartu 202400; tel. 735 94; fax 314 88.

VILJANDI KEK Co-Operative. Est. 1957. Gen. constr. works, constr. elements of concrete, lime, gypsum (bricks, roofing tiles, slabs, etc.), metal structures, etc. Foreign partners in Finland, Sweden, Austria, Germany. Man. Olavi Liivandi. **Add.** Männimäe tee 28, Viljandi 202900; tel. and fax 531 04.

TARTU MAJA Design & Construction. Est. 1987. Gen. constr. works, designing and eng. Foreign partners in Finland, Sweden, Germany, Hungary. Man. Olari Taal. **Add.** Betooni 9, Tartu 202400; tel. 289 57; telex 173138 TARM SU; fax 629 70.

MAAEHITUSTRUST Building Trust. Est. 1977. Gen. constr. works, rebuilding and extensions, repairs. Man. Mart Keek. **Add.** Lutsu 14, Tartu 202400; tel. 335 32; fax 325 19.

TALLINN BUILDING TRUST. Est. 1944. Constr. of residential, commercial, public buildings, etc.; ind. facilities; pipelaying. Trading partners in Finland. Man. Ants Raja. **Add.** Narva mnt. 40, Tallinn 200102; tel. 422 124.

TÖÖSTUSEHITUS Industrial Construction Trust. Est. 1976. Ind. and civil constr., pipes and electricity connections. Man.Dir Eduard Dobolin. **Add.** Jaama 1a, Tallinn 200107; tel. 512 660.

MATEK S.P. Soviet-Finnish joint venture. Est. 1988. Prefabricated houses and parts, building and insulating materials, polyurethane foam makroflex. Man.Dir Ivo Kaasik. **Add.** Haigru 8, Tallinn 200006; tel. 498 133; telex 173210 MATEK SU; fax 479 951.

EESTI MAAPARANDUSPROJEKT Land Reclamation Project. Est. 1966. Land and forest reclamation; projects relating to irrigation, farm roads, water works, fish ponds and peat mining; blueprints for land reclamation and water farming projects, incl. technol. and field studies.

Man.Dir Valdo Urbel. **Add.** Mustamäe tee 33, Tallinn 200006; tel. 528 406.

EESTI PROJEKT Project Institute. Est. 1944. Designs for residential and public buildings, urban planning and development. Man.Dir Hans Rohtmaa. **Add.** Lenini pst. 8, Tallinn 200105; tel.425 973; fax 432 244.

EESTI PÕLLUMAJANDUSPROJEKT Agricultural Project Institute. Est. 1951. Land and soil studies, land development projects, land reservation, topographic studies, preparation of documents. Man.Dir Aadu Sutt. **Add.** Mustamäe tee 51, Tallinn 200006; tel. 528 414; fax 528 400.

EESTI RESTAURAATOR Restoration Company. Est. 1950. Research, projection, preservation and restoration of arch. monuments; consultancy in arch. matters. Gen.Dir Arsi Kook. **Add.** Lai 29, Tallinn 200001; tel. 446 474; fax 446 678.

EESTI TÖÖSTUSPROJEKT Industrial Projects Institute. Est. 1944. Arch. and constr. designs for ind. and civil objects. Trading partners in Finland. Man.Dir Udo Lall. **Add.**Lenini pst. 5, Tallinn 200105; tel. 440 855; telex 173109 PROJEKT.

EKE PROJEKT Project Institute. Est. 1966. Designs for residential, public and agric. buildings, eng. projects. Trading partners in Finland, Sweden, USA, Canada, Germany, Norway. Man.Dir Enn Parbo. **Add.** Kingissepa 12, Tallinn 200106; tel. 683 720; telex 173352 AT; fax 683 750.

KOMMUNAALPROJEKT Municipal Project Institute. Est. 1941. Arch., constr. and restoration designs for ind. and civil constr. Man.Dir Endel Paalmann. **Add.** Lai 27, Tallinn 200001; tel. 446 294; telex 173312 ELLIPS; fax 440 348.

TRANSPORT

ETKVL AUTO Co-Operative. Est. 1921. Road haulage; metal containers (cases, pails, barrels); prod. of components and lifting equipm. for motor vehicles; maintenance and repairs; gen. constr. work. Trading partners in Finland. Man.Dir Raimu Aas. **Add.** Tähetorni 21, Tallinn 200107; tel. 513 628; fax 532 096.

MOOTOR Bus Company. Est. 1990. Passenger bus service. Man.Dir Hugo Osula. **Add.** Suur-Sõjamäe 4, Tallinn 200109; tel. 211 409; fax 215 520.

PÄRNU BUS AND TAXI FLEET. Est. 1960. Passenger transportation by bus and taxi; wholesale of used motor vehicles; maintenance and repair; driver training and consultancy. Man.Dir Ülo Tomson. **Add.** Mere 7, Pärnu 203600; tel. 223 86.

SAAREMAA AUTOMOBILE BASE. Est. 1944. Maintenance and repair, lorry transportation, special cargo vehicles, passenger transportation by bus and taxi. Man.Dir Karli Valt. **Add.** Pihtla tee 20, Kuressaare 203300; tel. 541 14.

TALLINN BUS COMPANY. Est. 1945. Passenger bus service. Man.Dir Mati Mägi. **Add.** Kadaka tee 62a, Tallinn 200026; tel. 532 063; fax 532 277.

TARTU BUS AND TAXI FLEET. Est. 1954. Passenger bus and taxi service, excursion service. Man.Dir Vello-Lembit Teemusk. **Add.**Ringtee 14, Tartu 202400; tel. 713 72.

TARTU AUTOVEOD Motor Transport Company. Est. 1944. Road haulage. Trading partners in Austria and Sweden. Man.Dir Heiti Aarsalu. **Add.** Aardla 23, Tartu 202400; tel. 727 20.

TURIST Bus Company. Est. 1979. Excursion service. Man.Dir Rein Vinni. **Add.** Kadaka tee 72c, Tallinn 200108; tel. 593 584.

ESTONIAN SHIPPING COMPANY. Est. 1940. Cargo and passenger transportation (incl. tourist and excursion service). Chief Exec. Toivo Ninnas. **Add.** Estonia pst. 3/5, Tallinn 200101; tel. 443 802; fax 424 958.

BALTLINK Ltd, Soviet-Finnish-Austrian joint venture. Est. 1988. Cargo haulage; tourist transportation, travel agencies; import-export. Man.Dir Jaan Orro. **Add.** Tartu mnt. 13, Tallinn 200105; tel. 421 003; telex 173211 LINK SU; fax 450 893.

EESTI-ESTLINE Ltd, Estonian-Swedish joint venture. Est. 1989. Passenger and cargo transportation between Tallinn and Stockholm. Man.Dir Harri Enula. **Add.** Sadama 29, Tallinn 200103; tel. 449 051; fax 425 352.

TALLINK Soviet-Finnish joint venture. Est. 1989. Shipping, ferry operations. Man.Dir Peeter Veegen. **Add.** POB 3495, Tallinn 200090; tel. 440 770; telex 173176 TALIK SU; fax 445 224.

AGRICULTURE & FISHERIES

At the beginning of the 1990s, the Soviet farming of Estonia was in poor condition and great rearrangements had begun. There is a gradual transition from coercively established collective farms — sovkhozes and kolkhozes — to various forms of small-scale production (co-operatives, joint-stock companies, farms, etc.). The future belongs basically to well-organized farms. Privatization has been put into motion that will continue in the process of the radical proprietary and agrarian reforms. The transition from large-scale production to new farms of enterprises is characterized by the following data:

Form of managing	The end of 1989	1 January 1991
Kolkhozes	200	214
Sovkhozes	126	108
State farms (former sovkhozes)	—	4
Inter-farm organizations	26	19
Co-operatives	—	15
Agro-firms	—	3
Farms	1050	3590

Information on the farming is available from the following organizations:

ESTONIAN AGRICULTURAL PRODUCERS' CENTRAL UNION. F. 1990. Chair. Andres Varik. **Add.** Lai 43, Tallinn 200100; tel. 602 045.

ESTONIAN AGRICULTURAL SERVICE ASSOCIATION. F. 1990. Man.Dir Kaljo Lauri. **Add.** Lai 39/41, Tallinn 200100; tel. 448 798.

ESTONIAN FARMERS' CENTRAL UNION.
F. 1989. Man.Dir Jaan Leetsar. *Add.* Saku, Harjumaa 203400; tel. 721 783; telex 173216 TOMAT SU; fax 451 669.

ESTONIAN FOOD INDUSTRY ASSOCIATION
'ASTO'. F. 1990. Chair. Aksel Treimann. *Add.* Lomonossovi 29, Tallinn 200104; tel. 422 246; fax 421 977.

ESTONIAN PROVINCIAL INDUSTRIES AS-SOCIATION.
F. 1989. Man.Dir Anu Hämalane. *Add.* Lomonossovi 29/426, Tallinn 200104; tel. 422 004; fax 442 325.

The Estonian fishermen are organized (January, 1991) into: 7 kolkhozes, 2 joint-stock companies and 1 co-operative. Information available from:

ESTONIAN FISHERY ASSOCIATION.
F. 1962. Chair. Heino Palu. *Add.* Kingissepa 14, Tallinn 200106; tel. 683 442; telex 173289 ERKS SU; fax 682 283.

FINANCIAL INSTITUTIONS

BANK OF ESTONIA. F. 1990. Pres. Rein Otsason. *Add.* Kentmanni 13, Tallinn 200100; tel. 445 331; telex 173146 EPANK SU; fax 443 395.

BANK OF TALLINN. F. 1990. Exec. Dir Jüri Trumm. *Add.* Vabaduse väljak 10; tel. 449 983.

COMMERCIAL BANK OF THE ESTONIAN SMALL BUSINESS ASSOCIATION (EVEA Bank). F. 1989. Chair. of the Bd Boris Spungin. *Add.* Narva mnt. 40, Tallinn 200106; tel. 422 122; telex 173184 EVEA SU; fax 421 435.

ESTONIAN COMMERCIAL BANK OF IN-DUSTRY. F. 1988. Chair. of the Bd Aleksandr Gellart. *Add.* Suur-Karja 7, Tallinn 200001; tel. 442 410; fax 440 495.

ESTONIAN PROVINCIAL BANK. F. 1990. Exec.Dir Harry-Elmar Volmer. *Add.* Estonia pst. 11, Tallinn 200105; tel. and fax 441 797.

ESTONIAN SAVINGS BANK. F. 1920. Chair. Ruslan Dontsov. *Add.* Kinga 1, Tallinn 200100; tel. 441 758.

ESTONIAN SOCIAL BANK. F. 1990. Chair. of the Bd Saima Strenze. *Add.* Estonia pst. 13, Tallinn 200100; tel. 446 900; fax 445 255.

ESTTEXPANK. F. 1989. Chair. Mart Sild. *Add.* Sakala 1, Tallinn 200100; tel. 666 657.

SOUTH-ESTONIAN DEVELOPMENT BANK. F. 1990. Man. Toomas Lehiste.*Add.* Kesk 42, Põlva 202600; tel. 962 39.

TARTU COMMERCIAL BANK. F. 1988. Chair. of the Bd Rein Kaarepere. *Add.* Munga 18, Tartu 202400; tel. 331 97; telex 173107 MONEY SU; fax 335 93; **Tallinn office:** Dunkri 9, Tallinn 200105; tel.446 977. Branch offices in Jõgeva, Põlva, Otepää and Narva-Jõesuu.

UNION BALTIC BANK Ltd. F. 1990. Chair. Valentin Porfiryev. *Add.* Tõnismägi 16, Tallinn 200001; tel. 682 233; fax 444 778.

THE USSR STATE BANK OF THE ESTONIAN REPUBLIC. F. 1940. Chair. Galina Litvinova. *Add.* Estonia pst. 13, Tallinn 200100; tel. 445 124.

WEST-ESTONIAN BANK. F. 1990. Dir Aare Sosaar. *Add.* Karja 27, Haapsalu 203170; tel. 440 91; fax 450 76. Branch offices in Orissaare, Lihula and Märjamaa.

SCIENTIFIC & RESEARCH CENTRES

ESTONIAN ACADEMY OF SCIENCES. F. 1938; 52 acad.; 4 divisions: Astronomy and Phys. (3 inst.), Informatics and Eng. Sci. (2 inst.), Biol., Geol. and Chem. (6 inst.), Humanities and Social Sci. (4 inst.). Pres. Arno Köörna. The Acad. publishes 9 scientific journals. Total staff at the Acad. inst.: 4,446, incl. 1,400 scientists. *Add.* Presidium of the Est. Acad. of Sci.: Kohtu 6, Tallinn 200106; tel. 443116; telex 173257 NAUKA; fax 442 149.

INSTITUTE OF ASTROPHYSICS AND AT-MOSPHERIC PHYSICS, Est. Acad. of Sci. F. 1946; 78 scientific staff (6 DSc., 42 CSc.). Fields of research: astrophys. (structure of galaxies, evolution, phys. of stars' atmospheres), atmospheric phys. (radiation distribution, surface energy), biophys. Scientific collaboration within the Int. Astronomical Union and the Int. Meteorological and Atmospheric Phys. Assoc. Dir Tõnu Viik. *Add.*Tõravere observatorium, Tartumaa 202444; tel. 101 74, 334 39; fax 102 05.

INSTITUTE OF PHYSICS, Est. Acad. of Sci. F. 1973; 135 scientific staff (14 DSc., 83 CSc.). Research in: solid state phys., laser spectroscopy and optics, theoretical phys., phys.-related instrument building (VUV spectrometry, lasers, cryotechnl.). Scientific collaboration with USA, Germany, Netherlands, Sweden, Canada and Switzerland. Dir Arvi Freiberg. *Add.* Riia 142, Tartu 202400; tel. 281 53, 281 06; telex 173200 LASER SU; fax 722 27.

INSTITUTE OF CHEMICAL PHYSICS AND BIOPHYSICS, Est. Acad. of Sci. F. 1980; 96 scientific staff (6 DSc., 34 CSc.). Research in:chem. phys. (radiospectroscopy of condensed media, automatization of scientific research, high-temp. superconductivity, environmental protection); phys.-chem. biol. and biotechnol. (fermentative catalysis, preparative biochem., microbiol. synthesis, molecular neurobiol.). Scientific collaboration with Finland, Sweden, Germany, Hungary, Poland, USA and USSR. Dir Endel Lippmaa. *Add.* Lenini pst. 10, Tallinn 200001; tel. 441 304; fax 440 640.

ESTONIAN BIOCENTRE, Est. Acad. of Sci. F. 1986; 22 scientific staff (one DSc., 3 CSc.). Research in: molecular biol., cell biol., genetics and biotechnol. Scientific collaboration with Finland, Sweden, UK, USA and Germany. Dir Richard Villems. *Add.* Tähetorn Toomel, Tartu 202400; tel. 336 35, 319 80; telex 173243 TAUN SU; fax 354 30.

SPECIAL CONSTRUCTION BUREAU, Est. Acad. of Sci. F. 1963; 117 scientific staff. Research in: creation of excimer lasers and laser distance-spectrometry as well as preparative liquid chromatography. Dir Karl Saar. *Add.* Akadeemia tee 19, Tallinn 200108; tel. 537 171; fax 527 204.

INSTITUTE OF CYBERNETICS, Est. Acad. of Sci. F. 1960; 76 scientific staff (7 DSc., 39 CSc.). Research in: information technol., software eng., automatic control, math., mech. Scientific cooperation at Euromech colloquia 241 (1988),

256 (1989), IFAC 11th World Congress (1990). Close collaboration with Finland (automatic control), Sweden (software), UK (information technol., mech.) et al. Dir Ülo Jaaksoo. **Add.** Akadeemia tee 21, Tallinn 200108; tel. 525 435; telex 173267 IFAC SU; fax 527 901.

COMPUTER R&D DIVISION 'EKTA', Inst. of Cybernetics. F. 1976; 100 scientific staff (3 DSc., 34 CSc.). Research in: cybernetics,automation, electronics and electronic eng. Scientific collaboration with Finland, Sweden and UK. Dir Kalju Leppik. **Add.** Akadeemia tee 21/1, Tallinn 200026; tel. 536 373; telex 173267 IFAC; fax 527 555.

INSTITUTE OF THERMAL PHYSICS AND ELECTROPHYSICS, Est. Acad. of Sci. F. 1937; 79 scientific staff (5 DSc., 38 CSc.). Research in: electrophys. (super conductive transformers, phys. of semiconductor structures); systems studies of energy technol.(fuel econ. and optimization of electric energy systems); thermal phys. (turbulent flow aeromech., burning of lowyield solid fuels). Scientific collaboration with Finland, Sweden, Denmark, Germany, Hungary, UK, Canada, Latvia, Lithuania and USSR. Dir Paul Tamkivi. **Add.** Paldiski mnt. 1, Tallinn 200031; tel. 452 544; fax 452 435.

INSTITUTE OF CHEMISTRY, Est. Acad. of Sci. F. 1947; 142 scientific staff (7 DSc., 72 CSc.). Fields of research: search for synthesis and effect of bioactive compounds, synthesis and technol. of organic compounds, chem. of oil shales, phys.-chem. invest., environmental chem. Scientific collaboration with France, Sweden, USA, Germany, Netherlands and Finland. Dir Jüri Kann. **Add.** Akadeemia tee 15, Tallinn 200108; tel. 536 450, 536 430; fax 536 371.

EXPERIMENTAL PLANT FOR ORGANIC SYNTHESIS AND BIOPREPARATIONS,Inst. of Chem. F. 1979. Chem. reagents and ultrapure substances; pharmaceutical components; perfumery products. Dir Kalev Beek. **Add.** Männiku tee 104, Tallinn 200107; tel. 517 885.

INSTITUTE OF GEOLOGY, Est. Acad. of Sci. F. 1947; 88 scientific staff (5 DSc., 49 CSc.). Research in: complex geol. studies of Estonia and neighbouring areas, rational use of mineral resources and environmental protection, regularities of organic evolution. Scientific collaboration with USSR, Lithuania, Latvia, Finland, Sweden, Norway, Germany, France, UK, USA and Canada. Dir Rein Vaikmäe. **Add.** Estonia pst. 7, Tallinn 200101; tel. 444 189.

INSTITUTE OF EXPERIMENTAL BIOLOGY, Est. Acad. of Sci. F. 1957; 63 scientific staff (7 DSc., 32 CSc.). Research in: genetical and physiological bases of productivity in agric. plants and animals, biol. and infectious characteristics of primitive animals. Scientific collaboration with Czecho-Slovakia, Hungary, Germany and Finland. Dir Aavo Aaviksaar. **Add.** Instituudi tee 11, Harku alevik, Harjumaa 203051; tel. 512 456.

INSTITUTE OF ZOOLOGY AND BOTANY, Est. Acad. of Sci. F. 1946; 84 scientific staff (9 DSc., 53 CSc.). Research in: dynamics and prognosis of evolutionary processes, rational use and protection of biol. resources, ecology of biol. systems and problems of anthropogenic dynamics. Scientific collaboration with Netherlands, Poland, Germany, Finland, UK, Czecho-Slovakia. Dir Andres Koppel. **Add.** Vanemuise 21, Tartu 202400; tel. 313 31; fax 334 72.

TALLINN BOTANICAL GARDENS, Est. Acad. of Sci. F. 1961; 27 scientific staff (one DSc., 16 CSc.). Research in: introduction of plants; environmental conditions and bio-indication; human interference with ecosystems in natural and artificial habitats. The nursery constitutes a separate dept. Scientific collaboration with USSR, Finland and USA. Dir Heiki Tamm. **Add.**Kloostrimetsa tee 44/52, Tallinn 200019; tel. 238 913; fax 238 468.

INSTITUTE OF ECOLOGY AND MARINE RESEARCH, Est. Acad. of Sci. F.1990; 45 scientific staff (3 DSc., 36 CSc.). Research in: terrestial and marine ecosystems, evaluation of marine environment and bioresources, econ. prognosis, substance turnover and energy flow of natural and technogenic processes. Scientific collaboration with Finland, Sweden, Germany and Poland. Dir Mati Punning. **Add.** Paldiski mnt. 1, Tallinn 200031; tel. 451 634; fax 453 748.

INSTITUTE OF ECONOMICS, Est. Acad. of Sci. F. 1947; 87 scientific staff (8 DSc., 51 CSc.). Research in: prognosticating development and location of productive forces, and working out long-term planning fundamentals; improvement of public and ind. econ. and management mechanisms; environmental econ. Scientific collaboration with Finland, Poland, Hungary, Yugoslavia, Czecho-Slovakia and USSR. Dir Olev Lugus. **Add.** Estonia pst. 7, Tallinn 200105; tel. 444 570; fax 442 835.

INSTITUTE OF HISTORY, Est. Acad. of Sci. F. 1947; 80 scientific staff (9 DSc., 48 CSc.). Research in: Est. hist. from prehistoric to the present time, incl. archeology, ethnology, hist. of culture, art and public educ.; hist. of the Baltic Sea c. Scientific collaboration with Finland, Sweden and Germany. Dir Rein Helme. **Add.** Rüütli 4, Tallinn 200101; tel. 446 594; fax 443 714.

INSTITUTE OF PHILOSOPHY, SOCIOLOGY AND LAW, Est. Acad. of Sci. F.1988; 43 scientific staff (6 DSc., 25 CSc.). Research in: phil. of sci.; youth, family and cultural sociology; nat. relations; mechanisms of transition from totalitarianism to democracy; legal regulation of new social relations. Scientific collaboration with Finland, USA and Denmark. Dir Priit Järve. **Add.** Estonia pst. 7, Tallinn 200101; tel. 605 139; fax 446 608.

INSTITUTE OF LANGUAGE AND LITERATURE, Est. Acad. of Sci. F. 1947; 101 scientific staff (7 DSc., 51 CSc.). Research in: lgs and folklore of Estonians and other Finno-Ugric peoples; Est. lit.; automatized preparation of dictionaries. Scientific collaboration with Finland and Hungary. Dir Tõnu Seilenthal. **Add.** Roosikrantsi 6, Tallinn 200106; tel. 442 076.

ESTONIAN INSTITUTE OF FORESTRY. F. 1969; 50 scientific staff (2 DSc., 29 CSc.). Research in: forest management and productivity improvement; management of protected-areas, protection of plants and animal species. Scientific collaboration with Finland, Sweden, Poland, Germany, Latvia, Lithuania and Russia. Dir Ivar Etverk. *Add.* Röömu tee 2, Tartu 202400; tel. 363 81.

ESTONIAN RESEARCH INSTITUTE OF AGRICULTURE AND LAND RECLAMATION. F. 1946; 153 scientific staff (9 DSc., 80 CSc.). Research in: agric. plant cultivation (agrochem., land development, land tillage, mechanization, soil analysis, plant protection, horticulture, variety cultivation, econ.). Scientific collaboration with Netherlands, Sweden, Germany and Finland. Dir Valdek Loko. *Add.* Saku sjk., Harjumaa 203400; tel. 721 408, 721 630.

INSTITUTE OF EXPERIMENTAL AND CLINICAL MEDICINE. F. 1947; 93 scientific staff (15 DSc., 53 CSc.). Research in: pollution by cancerogenes in bodies of water, cancer epidemiology, hygiene and occupational pathology in the oil-shale ind., toxicology, pulmonology, gastroenterology, Est. curative mud. Scientific collaboration with Finland, Germany and Sweden. Dir Toomas Veidebaum. *Add.* Hiiu 42, Tallinn 200107; tel. 514 300.

ARNOLD SEPPO LABORATORY AND CLINIC FOR METALLOSTEOSYNTHESIS RESEARCH. F. 1978; 20 scientific staff (one DSc., 5 CSc.). Research in: surgical treatment of bone fractures; conservative and operative treatment of osteomyelitis and orthopaedic diseases; treatment of burns. Scientific collaboration with USA, Finland, Sweden, Italy and Switzerland. Dir. Rein Raie. *Add.*Tõnismägi 5a, Tallinn 200001; tel. 682 798, 683 132.

INSTITUTE OF GENERAL AND MOLECULAR PATHOLOGY, Tartu Univ. F. 1979; 108 scientific staff (4 DSc., 31 CSc.). Research in: genetics, biotechnol., immunology, immunochem., cell biol., microbiol., endocrinology, pharmacology, cardiology, neurology, enterology. Scientific collaboration with Finland, Sweden and Germany. Dir Aavo-Valdur Mikelsaar. *Add.* Veski 34, Tartu 202400; tel 323 87, 353 47; fax 303 65.

ADOLF MÖLDER ANIMAL BREEDING AND VETERINARY SCIENCE RESEARCH INSTITUTE. F. 1947; 121 scientific staff (11 DSc., 68 CSc.). Research in: racial characteristics and performance of livestock and poultry; feeding, nutritive value of feeds, animal diseases and treatment; environmental protection; automatization of farm work; econ. Scientific collaboration with Canada, UK, Netherlands, Denmark, Norway, Sweden, Czecho-Slovakia and Finland. Dir Elmar Valdmann. *Add.* Kreutzwaldi 1, Tartu 202400; tel. 324 52; fax 348 97.

RESEARCH AND DESIGN INSTITUTE OF SILICATE CONCRETE. F. 1961; 151 scientific staff (2 DSc., 35 CSc.). Research in: technol. and equipm. for autoclaved foam concrete, silica bricks and high-dispersive filler materials, designs for factories. Scientific collaboration with USA, Germany, Switzerland, Finland, Poland and Hungary. Dir Vyacheslav Shlyk. *Add.* Männiku tee 123, Tallinn 200012; tel. 517 259; fax 529 662.

ESTONIAN INSTITUTE FOR INFORMATION. F. 1972; 35 scientific staff (2 DSc., 16 CSc.). Research in: information systems design, on-line database services, information policy, environment pollution (esp. atmospheric), protection of metals from corrosion. Scientific collaboration with Poland, Hungary, Germany, Czecho-Slovakia and Finland. Acting Dir Gustav Laigna. *Add.* Tõnismägi 8, Tallinn 200106; tel. 440 513; telex 173178 BINOM SU; fax 682 057.

ESTONIAN MANAGEMENT INSTITUTE. F. 1978. Research in: entrepreneurship in Estonia (incl. co-operatives and ltd liability companies), innovation policy, successful management. Scientific collaboration with Finland, Sweden, Norway, USA, Canada and Czecho-Slovakia. Acting Dir Jüri Truusa. *Add.* Sütiste tee 21, Tallinn 200108; tel. 521 619; fax 521 625.

ESTONIAN INSTITUTE. F. 1989; 13 staff; initiates and promotes bilateral scientific and cultural exchange with other c. Founder and Dir Lennart Meri; Sec. Gen. Henno Rajandi. *Add.* Sakala 3, tuba 15; tel. 443 555; fax 691 877.

INSTITUTIONS OF HIGHER EDUCATION

TARTU UNIVERSITY. F. 1632; 9 faculties: Hist., Med., Biol. and Geogr., Philol., Phys. and Chem., Physical Educ., Econ., Math., and Law; 1,230 academic staff (incl. 104 Prof., 290 Asst Prof.); 8,000 students (5,770 full-time, 2,230 correspondence); joint projects with 60 univ. and research inst. in Europe and N-America. Rector Jüri Kärner. *Add.* Ülikooli 18, Tartu 202400; tel. 348 66; telex 173243 TAUN SU; fax 354 40; public relations office tel. 354 21.

TALLINN TECHNICAL UNIVERSITY. F. 1936; 6 faculties: Energy, Automation, Mech., Chem., Constr., and Econ.; 816 faculty and scientific staff (39 Prof., 300 Asst Prof.); 9,049 students (5,314 full-time, 1,382 evening, 2,353 correspondence). Scientific collaboration with Finland, Hungary, Netherlands, UK, USA, Sweden, Bulgaria, Czecho-Slovakia, Poland and Germany. Rector Olav Aarna. *Add.* Ehitajate tee 5, Tallinn 200108; tel. 537 258; telex 173101 STJUD SU; fax 532 446.

ESTONIAN AGRICULTURAL ACADEMY. F. 1951; 9 faculties: Agron., Econ., Forestry, Agric. Eng., Agric. Mechanization, Zoo Eng., Veterinary Med., Humanities, and Extramural Studies; 361 faculty and scientific staff (23 Prof., 114 Asst Prof.); 4,130 students (2,819 full-time, 1,311 correspondence). Scientific collaboration with Sweden, Finland, Germany, Hungary, Poland, Ireland, USA, UK, Denmark, Netherlands, Japan, Czecho-Slovakia. Rector Olev Saveli. *Add.* Riia 12, Tartu 202400; tel. 318 00, 714 97; telex 173839 ADER SU; fax 315 73.

TALLINN TEACHER TRAINING INSTITUTE. F. 1947; 6 faculties: Lgs, Math. and Phys., Pedag., Cultural Educ., Sports, and Preparatory and Supplementary Training for Educ. Management; 424 faculty and scientific staff (9 Prof., 107 Asst Prof.); 3,589 students (2,324 full-time, 1,265 correspondence). Scientific collaboration with USA, Switzerland, Germany, UK and Finland. Rector Rein Virkus. *Add.* Narva mnt. 25, Tallinn 200001; tel. 425 868; fax 425 339.

TALLINN ART UNIVERSITY. F. 1914; 12 depts: painting, sculpture, graphic art, ceramics, glass work, metal work, leather work, textiles, costumes, arch., interior decoration and furniture design, ind. art; 130 faculty staff (22 Prof., 50 Asst Prof.); 534 students (467 full-time, 67 evening). Scientific collaboration with Finland, Sweden, Germany, USA, Norway, Poland, Hungary, Czecho-Slovakia, Belgium and Netherlands. Rector Jaak Kangilaski. *Add.* Tartu mnt. 1, Tallinn 200105; tel. 432 664, 432 655.

TALLINN CONSERVATOIRE. F. 1919; 10 depts: piano, organ, string instruments, wind instruments, vocal, composition, music sci., choir conducting, music teaching, drama; 120 faculty and scientific staff (21 Prof., 34 Asst Prof.); 450 students (370 full-time, 80 correspondence). Scientific collaboration with Germany, Finland, Lithuania, Latvia and Russia. Rector Venno Laul. *Add.* Vabaduse pst. 130, Tallinn 200009; tel. 514 598.

ESTONIAN EVANGELICAL LUTHERAN CHURCH THEOLOGICAL INSTITUTE. F. 1946; Faculty of Theol., incl. Sacred Music and Religious Pedag.; 6 Chairs; 6 Prof., 4 Asst Prof.; 78 students; 2 scholars in Helsinki, 1 in Birmingham, 1 in Chicago. Bible transl. research in collaboration with Finland. Curator Jaan Kiivit. *Add.* Kiriku 8, Tallinn 200106; tel. 451 682; fax 601 876.

ESTONIAN INSTITUTE OF HUMANITIES. F. 1988; 3 faculties: Philol., Phil. and Hist.; 10 Chairs; 71 academic staff; 108 students. The first privately owned, wholly indep. inst. of higher educ. in the Baltic states. Collaboration with USA, Italy, Finland and Japan. Chair. of the Bd Rein Raud. *Add.* POB 3320, Tallinn 200001; tel. 449 331; fax 443 713.

ESTONIAN BUSINESS SCHOOL (EBS). F. 1988 as a private school; the first 29 graduate students got their 'Graduate Diploma in Int. Business' in 1989; in 1990 the EBS started its 2-year Int. MBA programme, a year later — 4-year Bachelor of Business Admin. programme. Teaching lg. is English, in 1991 the first acad. programme in German was added into EBS's schedule. Founder and Pres. Madis Habakuk. *Add.* Lenini pst. 12, Tallinn 200001; tel. 666 696, 446 038; telex 173269 EVM SU; fax 446 038.

VOLUNTARY ORGANIZATIONS

ESTONIAN ENGINEERS' ASSOCIATION. F. 1988; 662 mems; Pres. Harald Velner. *Add.* Tönismägi 7, Tallinn 200106; tel. 449 411; telex 173267 IFAC SU; fax 527 901.

ESTONIAN SCIENTISTS' ASSOCIATION. F. 1989; 450 mems; Co-Chair. Peeter Saari, Ain Raitviir, Jaan Laas. *Add.* Lenini pst. 10, Tallinn 200101; tel. 448 640; fax 442 835.

ESTONIAN MEDICAL ASSOCIATION. F. 1988; 1,500 mems; Pres. Rando Truve. *Add.* Vana-Viru 12, Tallinn 200001; tel. 449 132.

ASSOCIATION OF NATIONAL MINORITIES OF ESTONIA. F. 1989. Pres. Hagi Shein. *Add.* Faehlmanni 12, Tallinn 200100; tel. 430 741; fax 434 155.

OPEN ESTONIA FOUNDATION. F. 1990. Arranges and sponsors foreign fellowships for college seniors, graduates and postgraduates. Supports major educ., cultural and econ. projects. Financed by George Soros (USA). Chair. of the Bd Raoul Üksvärav. *Add.* Olevimägi 12, Tallinn 200101; tel. 601 895; fax 601 998.

ESTONIAN CULTURAL FOUNDATION. F. 1987. Chair. Jaak Kangilaski. *Add.* Olevimägi 14, Tallinn 200100; tel. 449 512; fax 601 247.

ESTONIAN CHILDREN'S FUND. F. 1988. Chair. Rein Agur. *Add.* Sakala 3, Tallinn 200105; tel. 443 310.

ESTONIAN PENSIONERS' UNION. F. 1990. Chair. Harri Kärtner. *Add.* POB 2956, Tallinn 200032.

UNION OF ESTONIAN SOCIETIES OF THE DISABLED. F. 1989. Chair. Mihkel Aitsam. *Add.* Tatari 14, Tallinn 200001; tel. 442 804.

ESTONIAN COMMITTEE OF THE RED CROSS. F. 1919. Chair. Ursel Vagur. *Add.* Lai 17, Tallinn 200101; tel. 444 265.

ESTONIAN SOCIETY FOR NATURE CONSERVATION. F. 1966. Chair. Jaan Eilart. Affiliation: E-European Cttee of Int. Union for Conservation of Nature and Natural Resources. *Add.* Koidu 80, Tallinn 200007.

ESTONIAN HORTICULTURAL AND APICULTURAL UNION. F. 1975. Chair. Jüri Amur. *Add.* Mustamäe tee 60, Tallinn 200108; tel. 477 243.

ESTONIAN UNION OF CONSUMERS' CO-OPERATIVES. Chair. Andres Aruvald. *Add.* Narva mnt. 7, Tallinn 200102; tel. 438 201; fax 421 578.

POLITICAL ORGANIZATIONS

ESTONIAN COMMUNIST PARTY (CPSU). F. 1990; 15,000 mems (1990); 1st Sec. of the Cent. Cttee Lembit Annus. *Add.* Lenini pst. 9, Tallinn 200100; tel. 445 311.

ESTONIAN COMMUNIST PARTY. F. 1920, in 1940–90 it was a part of CPSU; 5,000 mems (1990); 1st Sec. of the Cent. Cttee Enn-Arno Sillari. *Add.* Lenini pst. 9; tel. 445 258.

ESTONIAN SOCIAL DEMOCRATIC PARTY. F. 1990; 320 mems (1990); mem. of Socialist International 1990; Chair. Marju Lauristin. *Add.* POB 3437, Tallinn 200090; tel. 421 150; fax 444 902, 449 565.

ESTONIAN RURAL CENTRE PARTY. F. 1990; 250 mems (1990); Chair. Ivar Raig. *Add.* Aiandi 2a, Saku, Harjumaa 203400; tel. 721 783, 442 835; Rahukohtu 1–15, Tallinn 200001; fax 442 835.

ESTONIAN LIBERAL DEMOCRATIC PARTY. F. 1990; 300 mems (1990); observer of Liberal International 1990; Chair. Paul-Eerik Rummo. *Add.* POB 2, Tallinn 200090; tel. 445 909, 606 401; telex 173298 EPARL SU; fax 440 963.

ESTONIAN CHRISTIAN DEMOCRATIC UNION. F. 1989; 300 mems (1990); Chair. Illar Hallaste. *Add.* Rahukohtu 1–33, Tallinn 200001; tel. 444 896, 606 463.

ESTONIAN NATIONAL INDEPENDENCE PARTY. F. 1988; 750 mems (1990); Chairperson Lagle Parek. *Add.* Endla 6 – 4, Tallinn 200001; tel.452 472; fax 452 864.

ESTONIAN ENTREPRENEUR PARTY. F. 1990; 250 mems (1990); Chair. Tiit Made. *Add.* Pikk 68, Tallinn 200001; tel. 609 620.

ESTONIAN CONSERVATIVE PARTY. F. 1990; 80 mems (1990); Chair. Enn Tarto. *Add.* POB 3, Tallinn 200090; tel. 452 318.

REPUBLICAN COALITION PARTY. F. 1990; 160 mems (1990); Chair. Leo Starkov. *Add.* Vana-Viru 12, Tallinn 200100; tel. 442 644; fax 449 032.

POPULAR FRONT OF ESTONIA. F. 1988; eleven mem. bd; leaders Edgar Savisaar, Ignar Fjuk, Mati Hint. *Add.* Uus 28, Tallinn 200101; tel. 449 236; fax 448 442.

INTER-MOVEMENT OF THE WORKING PEOPLE OF THE ESTONIAN SSR. F.1988; coordinating cttee, in fact led by Jevgeni Kogan, Juri Rudyak; tel. 212 029, 426 156.

ESTONIAN HERITAGE SOCIETY. F. 1987; 3,000 mems (1990); Pres. Trivimi Velliste. *Add.* POB 3141, Tallinn 200090; tel. 449 216.

UNION OF WORK COLLECTIVES. F. 1988; more than 1,000 collectives (400,000 workers), econ.-pol. org.; Chair. Ülo Nugis. *Add.* Vana-Viru 12, Tallinn 200100; tel. 442 644; fax 449 032.

UNITED COUNCIL OF WORK COLLECTIVES. F. 1988; group of 100 business 'organizations' subordinate to Soviet cent. authorities; Chair. of the Exec. Bd Sergei Petinov. *Add.* Killustiku 3, Tallinn 200014; tel. 212 029.

ESTONIAN GREEN MOVEMENT. F. 1988; Chair. Tõnu Oja. *Add.* POB 300, Tartu 202400; Struve 2, Tartu 202400; tel. 301 98; Dir Valdur Lahtvee, Tallinn tel. 492 087.

MEMENTO, Est. Union of Illegally Repressed People and Their Supporters. F. 1989; 4,000 mems (1990); Chair. Aadu Oll. *Add.* POB 3410, Tallinn 200090; tel. 496 923.

ESTONIAN WOMEN'S UNION. F. 1989; 10 mem. leadership Council, leaders Ene Grauberg, Klara Hallik, Lehte Sööt-Hainsalu. *Add.* POB 3002, Tallinn 200090; tel. 443 169.

ESTONIAN CITIZENS' COMMITTEES. F. 1989; a movement of legal citizens of the Republic of Estonia (1918 – 40) and their descendents (non-Soviet quasi-parliament); Chair. Tunne Kelam. *Add.* Narva mnt. 5a; Tallinn 200090; tel. 666 731.

ESTONIAN TRADE UNION HEAD OFFICE. Chair. Siim Kallas. *Add.* Tartu mnt. 4, Tallinn 200100; tel. 425 100.

RELIGIOUS ORGANIZATIONS

CONSISTORY OF THE EVANGELICAL LUTHERAN CHURCH OF ESTONIA. Archbishop Kuno Pajula. *Add.* Kiriku 8, Tallinn 200106; tel. 451 682; fax 601 876.

COUNCIL OF THE RUSSIAN ORTHODOX DIOCESE. Bishop Kornelius. *Add.*Pikk 64 – 4, Tallinn 200001; tel. 601 747.

PÜHTITSA CONVENT OF THE DORMITION OF THE MOTHER OF GOD (Russian Orthodox). Est. 1891. 160 novices and nuns (14 serve in Jerusalem). Mother Superior (Igumenja) Varvara. *Add.* Kuremäe,Ida-Virumaa 202035; tel. 921 24.

ASSOCIATION OF THE ESTONIAN EVANGELICAL CHRISTIAN BAPTIST COMMUNITIES. Chair. Ülo Meriloo. *Add.* Pargi 9, Tallinn 200016; tel. 513 005.

ESTONIAN UNION OF THE SEVENTH-DAY ADVENTISTS. Chair. Rein Kalmus. *Add.* Mere pst. 3, Tallinn 200001; tel. 447 879.

METHODIST CHURCH OF ESTONIA. Superintendent Olav Pärnamets. *Add.* Apteegi 3, Tallinn 200001; tel. 449 246.

CULTURAL INSTITUTIONS

MUSEUMS

ESTONIAN NATIONAL MUSEUM. Est. 1909; 25 staff. Research in Est. and other Finno-Ugric peoples' ethnology and cultural hist. as well as corresponding studies of ethnic minorities living in Estonia. Coll. of 898,434 items, incl. 104,781 objects. Publ., since 1959, a yearbook. Dir Aleksei Peterson. *Add.*Veski 32, Tartu 202400, tel. 342 79.

ESTONIAN MUSEUM OF ART. Est. 1919; 32 scientific staff. Est., W-European and Russ. paintings, graphic art, sculpture and applied art, totalling 54,208 works. Engaged in collecting, studying and exh. Est. folk art. Dir Marika Valk. *Add.* Weizenbergi 37, Tallinn 200103; tel. 426 246.

F. R. KREUTZWALD MUSEUM OF LITERATURE. Est. 1940; 24 scientific staff (4 CSc.); Est., Finno-Ugric and Baltic folklore, lit. and cultural studies in manuscript and print; audiocassettes and records, photographs, films and works of art; largest coll. of Est. folklore (1,118,800 p.); bibliographic archives holding the most complete coll. (846,765 items) of old Est. lit. and periodicals. Scientific collaboration with Finland (Finnish Lit. Soc., Tuglas Soc.) and Sweden (Baltic Inst., Baltic Archives). Dir Peeter Olesk. *Add.* Vanemuise 42, Tartu 202400; tel. 300 35.

LIBRARIES

ESTONIAN NATIONAL LIBRARY. Est. 1918; 374 staff; 4.1 million items; archives contain one copy of every Est. and Estonian-related publ. Complete sci. library, scientific dept of Est. book-publ. hist., centre of Est. state bibliography and publ. statistics. Scientific collaboration with Finland, Canada and USA. Dir Ivi Eenmaa. *Add.* Tõnismägi 2, Tallinn 200001; tel. 448 778.

LIBRARY OF THE ESTONIAN ACADEMY OF SCIENCES. Est. 1946; 168 staff; 3.4 million items. Estonia's largest coll. of foreign-lg. scientific publ., extensive section on Baltica (material publ. in or about the former Baltic Provinces of Estonia, Livonia and Courland). Scientific collaboration with Finland and Sweden. Dir Maive Dobkevich. *Add.* Lenini pst. 10, Tallinn 200105; tel. 440 649.

TARTU UNIVERSITY LIBRARY. Est. 1802; 320 staff; 4.9 million items; Estonia's oldest scientific library; holds publ. from the 15th cent. onward; rare books on the Baltic c.; manuscripts donated by individuals attached to the univ.; art works. Exchange of publ. with 400 partners. Dir Malle Ermel. *Add.* Struve 1, Tartu 202400; tel. 325 77, 353 79.

ARCHIVES

ESTONIAN ARCHIVES OF HISTORY. Est. 1921; 3,192 records with 1,872,639 items dating from 1240 to 1917 (personal and church records up to the present day); library of 182,927 vols. Oldest original document is a 1240 royal decree on church titles by King Erik IV of Denmark. Scientific collaboration with Swedish and Finnish archives. Dir Endel Kuusik. *Add.* Liivi 4, Tartu 202400; tel. 324 82.

ESTONIAN STATE ARCHIVES. Est. 1921; 4,209 records with 2,386,834 items dating from 1917. Dir Heino Valmsen. *Add.* Maneeži 4, Tallinn 200107; tel. 441 118.

TALLINN CITY ARCHIVES. Est. 1883; 997 records with 287,356 items; library of 15,200 vols. Holds the hist. archives of the City of Tallinn from the 13th cent. on, the oldest original being a document by the Papal Legate William of Modena dated 1237. Scientific collaboration with Sweden, Finland and Germany. Dir Jüri Kivimäe. *Add.* Tolli 4, Tallinn 200001; tel. 601 744.

CREATIVE SOCIETIES

ESTONIAN ARCHITECTS' UNION. Est. 1921; 336 mems; Chair. Ike Volkov. *Add.* Lai 29, Tallinn 200110; tel. 442 337; fax 441 179.

ESTONIAN ARTISTS' UNION. Est. 1944; 636 mems; Chair. Ando Keskküla. *Add.* Vabaduse väljak 6, Tallinn 200105; tel. 445 014.

ESTONIAN COMPOSERS' UNION. Est. 1944; 88 mems; Chair. Jaan Rääts. *Add.* Lauteri 7, Tallinn 200105; tel. 444 103.

ESTONIAN DESIGNERS' ASSOCIATION. Est. 1989; 138 mems; Chair. Hugo Mitt. *Add.* Paldiski mnt. 161 – 26, Tallinn 200035; tel. 590 453; telex 173271 RADIO SU 'Design'; fax 434 172.

ESTONIAN FILM-MAKERS' UNION. Est. 1962; 144 mems; Chair. Rein Maran. *Add.* Uus 3, Tallinn 200101; tel. 445 337, 666 011; telex 173 213 KINO SU; fax 601 423.

ESTONIAN THEATRE UNION. Est. 1945; 1,200 mems; Chair. Mikk Mikiver. *Add.* Uus 5, Tallinn 200001; tel. 441 519; fax 443 584.

ESTONIAN WRITERS' UNION. Est. 1922; 195 mems; Chair. Vladimir Beekman. *Add.* Harju 1, Tallinn 200001; tel. 444 583.

ESTONIAN JOURNALISTS' UNION. Est. 1919; 1,306 mems; Mem., IFJ. Chair. Märt Müür. *Add.* Narva mnt. 30, Tallinn 200010; tel. 443 889, 425 758; fax 433 585.

ESTONIAN MUSIC ASSOCIATION. Constituted 1987. Mems: Choir Assoc., Folk Dance and Folk Music Soc., Men's Choir Soc., Music Teachers' Union, Piano Teachers's Assoc., Violin Teachers'Assoc. Chair. Venno Laul. *Add.* Tõnismägi 10, Tallinn 200001; tel. 681 679; telex 173260 HELI SU; fax 449 147.

ESTONIAN GEOGRAPHICAL SOCIETY, Est. Acad. of Sci. F. 1955; 548 mems. Comprehensive research in Est. geogr.; publ. yearbook; Chair. Jaan-Mati Punning. *Add.* Lenini pst. 10, Tallinn 200105; tel. 605 739.

MOTHER TONGUE SOCIETY, Est. Acad. of Sci. F. 1920; 422 mems, 4 hon. mems. Collects dialect material through correspondents; publ. dialect compilations and a yearbook; Chair. Henn Saari. *Add.* Roosikrantsi 6, Tallinn 200106; tel. 449 331.

SOCIETY OF ESTONIAN REGIONAL STUDIES, Est. Acad. of Sci. Ref. 1990; 150 mems. Chair. Vello Lõugas. *Add.* Estonia pst. 7, Tallinn 200101; tel. 440 475.

PERIODICALS

AKADEEMIA. From 1937 to 1940, resumed publ. 1989; monthly; organ of the Est. Writers' Union; articles, commentary, essays on acad. topics by Est. and foreign authors; in Est.; circ. 6,000; E-in-C Ain Kaalep. *Add.* Küütri 1, Tartu 202400; tel. 311 17, 313 73.

EESTI LOODUS (Estonian Nature). F. 1933; monthly; publ. by the Est. Acad. of Sci. and the Min. of Environment; popular sci.; in Est.; circ. 31,000; E-in-C Ain Raitviir. *Add.* Veski 4, Tartu 202400; tel. 323 68.

KEEL JA KIRJANDUS (Language and Literature). F. 1958; monthly; publ. by the Est. Acad. of Sci. and the Est. Writers' Union; Est. lg. and lit. related topics; in Est.; circ. 2,400; E-in-C Aksel Tamm. *Add.* Roosikrantsi 6, Tallinn 200106; tel. 449 228.

KULTUUR JA ELU (Culture and Life). F. 1958; monthly; Est. hist. and cultural affairs, memoirs, biographies, travel; in Est.; circ. 16,000; E-in-C Sirje Endre. *Add.* Narva mnt. 5, Tallinn 200090; tel. 442 900; fax 449 558.

LINGUISTICA URALICA. F. 1965; quarterly; articles, in Engl., Ger., Russ., Fr., on Finno-Ugric and Samoyedic lgs; circ. 1,230; E-in-C Paul Kokla. *Add.* Roosikrantsi 6, Tallinn 200106; tel. 440 745.

LOOMING (Creation). F. 1923; monthly; the Est. Writers' Union's journal with original pieces and lit. analyses, articles on arts subjects, transl.; in Est.; circ. 12,600; E-in-C Andres Langemets. *Add.* Harju 1, Tallinn 200090; tel. 443 262.

OIL SHALE. F. 1984; int. quarterly; articles on geol., mining, chem. and processing methods, combustion, econ. and ash utilization of oil shale and bituminous sands; circ. 1,000; E-in-C Ilmar Öpik. *Add.* Akadeemia tee 15, Tallinn 200108; tel. 537 084; fax 536 371.

VIKERKAAR (Rainbow). F. 1986; monthly; works by young writers: poetry, short stories, essays, transl. and reviews; in Est. and Russ.; circ. 10,000 (Est. ed.) and 5,000 (Russ. ed.); E-in-C Toivo Tasa. *Add.* Toompuies tee 30, Tallinn 200031; tel. 445 826.

NEWSPAPERS

EESTI EKSPRESS (Estonian Express). F. 1989; weekly; in Est.; circ. 60,000; E-in-C Ivo Karlep. *Add.* Kentmanni 20, Tallinn 200001; tel. 666 864, 666 219.

EESTI ELU. ESTONIAN LIFE. F. 1989; semimonthly; pol. and cultural affairs; in Est. and Engl.; circ. 20,000; E-in-C Madis Jürgen. *Add.* Narva mnt. 5, Tallinn 200090; tel. 445 466; fax 449 558.

THE ESTONIAN INDEPENDENT. F. 1990; weekly; publ. by the Est. news agency *ETA* and the *Perioodika* publ. house; in Engl.; circ. approx. 8,000; E-in-C Tarmu Tammerk. *Add.* Pärnu mnt. 67a, Tallinn 200090; tel. 683 074; telex 173193 ETA; fax 691 537.

MAALEHT (Country News). F. 1987; weekly; in Est.; circ. 180,000; E-in-C Olev Anton. *Add.* Toompuiestee 16, Tallinn 200106; tel. 453 521.

MOLODEZH ESTONII (Youth of Estonia). F. 1950; 5 days a week; in Russ.; circ. 75,000; E-in-C Sergei Sergeyev. *Add.* Pärnu mnt. 67a, Tallinn 200090; tel. 681 431.

POSTIMEES (Postman). F. 1857; daily; Tartu's local newspaper; in Est.; circ. 120,000; E-in-C Mart Kadastik. *Add.* Gildi 1, Tartu 202400; tel. 333 53.

PÄEVALEHT (Daily). F. 1905; daily; in Est.; circ. 100,000; E-in-C Margus Mets. *Add.* Pärnu mnt. 67a, Tallinn 200090; tel. 681 235; fax 442 762.

RAHVA HÄÄL (The Voice of the People). F. 1940; daily; organ of Est. SC and govt; in Est.; circ. 175,000; E-in-C Toomas Leito. *Add.* Pärnu mnt. 67a, Tallinn 200090; tel. 681 202; fax 448 534.

SIRP (The Sickle). F. 1940; weekly; cultural affairs; in Est.; circ. 30,200; E-in-C Toomas Kall. *Add.* Toompuiestee 30, Tallinn 200031; tel. 601 703.

SOVETSKAYA ESTONIA (Soviet Estonia). F. 1940; daily; organ of the Est. SC, the govt and the Cent. Cttee of the ECP; in Russ.; circ. 40,000; E-in-C Voldemar Tombu. *Add.* Pärnu mnt. 67a, Tallinn 200090; tel. 681 171.

ÕHTULEHT (The Evening Gazette). F. 1944; daily; in Est. and Russ.; circ. 76,400 (Est. ed.) and 41,700 (Russ. ed.); E-in-C Endel Lepisto. *Add.* Pärnu mnt. 67a, Tallinn 200090; tel. 681 154; fax 441 924.

ÄRIPÄEV (Daily Business). F. 1989; weekly; business and finance; in Est.; circ. 20 – 25,000; E-in-C Hallar Lind. *Add.* Raua 1a, Tallinn 200010; tel. 431 201; fax 426 700.

PUBLISHERS

EESTI RAAMAT. F. 1940. Belles-lettres, juvenile and children's books. Dir Roman Siirak. *Add.* Pärnu mnt. 10, Tallinn 200090; tel. 443 937.

ESTONIAN ENCYCLOPAEDIA PUBLISHERS. F. 1991. Encyclopaedias and reference books. Chair. of the Bd Ülo Kaevats. *Add.* Pärnu mnt. 10, Tallinn 200090; tel. 449 469; fax 445 720.

KOOLIBRI. F. 1991. Textbooks. Dir Ants Lang. *Add.* Pärnu mnt. 10, Tallinn 200090; tel. 445 223.

KUNST. F. 1958. Art books. Dir Sirje Helme. *Add.* Lai 34, Tallinn 200001; tel. 602 035.

KUPAR, Est. Writers' Union Co-Operative. F. 1987. Est. contemporary prose. Chair. Enn Vetemaa. *Add.* Harju 1, Tallinn 200001; tel. 446 832.

OLION. F. 1989. Pol., econ., guide-books, postcards. Dir Heino Kään. *Add.* Pikk 2, Tallinn 200090; tel. 445 403.

VALGUS. F. 1965. Popular sci. and dictionaries. Dir Arvo Heining. *Add.* Pärnu mnt. 10, Tallinn 200090; tel. 443 702; fax 445 197.

PERIOODIKA. F. 1964. Newspapers, periodicals, guide-books, pol.; children's books in foreign lgs. E-in-C of the Book Publishing Dept Anatoli Mikhailov, tel. 602 194. Dir Uno Sillajõe. *Add.* Pärnu mnt. 8, Tallinn 200090; tel. 441 262.

NEWS AGENCY, RADIO & TV

ESTONIAN TELEGRAPH AGENCY (ETA). F. 1918. Distributes text and photographic information as well as advertisements to Est. newspapers, TV, radio and foreign news agencies. Co-operation agreement with Reuters 1922 – 40, re-est. 1991; collaborates with Latv. and Lith. news agencies – a jointly operated news service, *Baltija* was est. in 1990. Gen.Dir ETA, Aimar Jugaste. *Add.* Pärnu mnt. 67a, Tallinn 200001; tel. 681 301; telex 173193 ETA, SU; fax 682 201.

ESTONIAN NATIONAL RADIO. F. 1926. Broadcasts in Est. (3 programmes), Russ., Finn., Sw., Engl., Esperanto, Ukr. and Byeloruss. Mem., OIRT. Publishes *Raadioleht* programme guide. Gen.Dir Peeter Sookruus. *Add.* Lomonossovi 21, Tallinn 200100; tel. 434 115, 434 222; telex 173 271 RADIO SU; fax 434 457.

ESTONIAN NATIONAL TELEVISION. F. 1955. Programming in Est. and Russ. Mem., OIRT. Weekly TV guide *Televisioon* (in Est. and Russ.). Gen.Dir Mart Siimann. *Add.* Faehlmanni 12, Tallinn 200100; tel. 434 113; telex 173271 RADIO SU; fax 434 155.

SPORTS & TOURISM ORGANIZATIONS

KALEV Sports Association. Est. 1901. Chair. Tõnu Murashev. *Add.* Pärnu mnt. 41, Tallinn 200103; tel. and fax 442 987.

ESTONIAN CENTRAL SPORTS UNION. Est. 1922. Chair. of the Bd Tiit Nuudi, Sec. Gen. Toomas Tõnise. *Add.* Regati pst. 1, Tallinn 200103; tel. 237 959; telex 173236 SPORT SU; fax 238 355.

ESTONIAN OLYMPIC COMMITTEE. Est. 1923. Pres. Arnold Green. *Add.* Regati pst. 1, Tallinn 200103; tel. 237 277; fax 238 100.

DYNAMO Sports Association. Est. 1940. Chair. Ivar Hallop. *Add.* Pikk 37, Tallinn 200101; tel. 601 965.

JÕUD Rural Sports Association. Est. 1946. Chair. Ants Saar. *Add.* Toompuiestee 21, Tallinn 200106; tel. 451 615; fax 451 496.

ESTONIAN ASSOCIATION OF TRAVEL AGENTS. Pres. Daisi Järva. *Add.* Pikk 71, Tallinn 200101; tel. and fax 425 594.

ESTONIAN MARINE TOURISM ASSOCIATION. Chair. Mart Kutsar. *Add.* Regati pst. 1, Tallinn 200103; tel. 421 003; fax 450 893.

BALTIC-TOURS. Soviet-Finnish joint venture. Est. 1989. Hotel accomodation and tourist service; restaurants, bars, cafeterias; import-export transactions; tourist transportation and excursions. Dir Mait Metsamaa. *Add.* Vene 23b, Tallinn 200003; tel. 446 331; telex 173885 TOURS SU; fax 440 760.

FINEST HOTEL GROUP S.P. Soviet-Finnish joint venture. Est. 1988. Hotel and restaurant management and tourist service; car rentals; fast-food pizza chain. Man.Dir Toomas Sildmäe. *Add.* Pärnu mnt. 22, Tallinn 200001; tel. 451 510; telex 173252 FINES SU; fax 446 029.

FINEST TARTU HOTELS F.S.P. Soviet-Finnish joint venture. Est. 1989. Hotel management, tourism, catering service. Dir Mart Raik. *Add.* Rebase 9, Tartu 202400; tel. 755 66, 739 51; telex 173104 TARU SU; fax 740 95.

CONSULTING COMPANIES

MAINOR. Est. 1979. Activities: improvement of econ. system, management, solving the personnel and social problems, development of data processing and foreign relations, advertising,

rendering operative help to the concern. Has 30 daughter firms. Foreign partners in Finland, Sweden, Norway, USA, Germany, Austria, England, Taiwan, Bulgaria, Hungary, Czecho-Slovakia. Pres. Ülo Pärnits. *Add.* Kuhlbarsi 1, Tallinn 200104; tel. 425 294; 431 700; telex 173112 MELIS SU; fax 433 122.

EKE ARIKO Ltd. Est. 1977. Activities: public opinion researches, management consultation, entrepreneurship development, int. business projects, manager training in Estonia and abroad. Foreign partners in Finland, Germany, Hungary. Chair. of the Bd Jüri Läänesaar. *Add.* Tartu mnt. 16, Tallinn 200105; tel. 427 480, 682 173; fax 684 905.

KODAMU Ltd. Est. 1987. Activities: foreign econ. and legal advisory, partner search, purveyance of preliminary information, marketing studies; personnel training, org. of educ. abroad; transl. services; publ.; business tourism; wooden products. Foreign partners in Sweden, Finland, Germany, USA, Norway. Chair. of the Bd Lauri Hink. *Add.* Toompuiestee 18, Tallinn 200031; tel. 450 392, 444 388; telex 173177 KODAM SU; fax 449 900.

WHO'S WHO

▪ **AARNA, Olav,** eng. scientist; b. 1942; ed. Tallinn Tech. Univ.; DSc. (Tech.), Prof.; Tallinn Tech. Univ., 1966 — , Rector, 1991 — ; research on math. models and control of chem. ind. processes; evaluation of state of continuous technol. processes. *Add.* Ehitajate tee 5, Tallinn 200108; tel. 532 427.

▪ **AASMÄE, Hardo,** Mayor of Tallinn, 1990 — ; b. 1951; ed. Tartu Univ.; CSc. (Geogr.); Consultancy *Mainor,* 1977 — 90, Scientific Dir, 1989 — 90; Mem. of Bd, EPF; scientific articles on geogr. and regional sci. and essays. USSR People's Deputy, 1990 — . *Add.* Vabaduse väljak 7, Tallinn 200100; tel. 444 955.

▪ **AAVIKSAAR, Aavo,** biochemist; b. 1941; ed. Tartu Univ., Max Planck Inst. of Biochem., Bristol and Rockefeller Univ.; DSc. (Chem.), Prof.; Dept Head, Inst. of Cybernetics, 1973 — 80; Lab. Head, Inst. of Chem. and Biol. Phys., 1980 — 91; Dir, Inst. of Experimental Biol., 1991 — ; research into protein chem., the mechanisms of selectivity of biocatalysis, separation and purification of natural bioactive substances and elucidation of the mechanisms of their biol. activities. *Add.* Instituudi tee 11, Harku , Harjumaa 203051; tel. 512 456.

▪ **ABEN, Hillar,** eng. scientist; b. 1929; ed. Tallinn Tech. Univ.; DSc. (Tech.); Mem., Est. Acad. of Sci.; Mem., Finn. Acad. of Tech. Sci.; Dept Head, Inst. of Cybernetics, 1960 — , Dir, 1976 — 89; research in the fields of photoelastics and operations research. *Add.* Akadeemia tee 21, Tallinn 200026; tel. 525 933.

▪ **ADAMSON, Mari,** textile artist; b. 1908; ed. State Arts and Crafts Sch., Pallas; Prof.; Art Prod. Combine, Workshop Dir, 1944 — 50; Tallinn Art Univ., 1944 — 77, Dept Head, 1964 — 77;

created tapestries, fabrics, monotypes, inspired by folklore and ornaments. 1st prize at a doll show in Antwerp, 1934; diplome d'honneur at Parisian World Exh., 1937; purchase award at the Lódż Tapestry Triennial, 1975. *Add.* (h) Tehnika 15 — 8, Tallinn 200031; tel. 450 067.

▪ **ALAS, Arvo-Jürgen,** Representative of Baltic Cultural and Information Centre in Denmark, 1990 — ; b. 1943; ed. Leningrad Univ., philol.; mag. *Noorus,* 1971 — 81; Est. Writers' Union, 1981 — 84; transl. of Scandinavian lit. *Add.* H.C.Andersens Blvd 38, 1553 Copenhagen V; tel. 4533 931 867; telex 40072 DK; fax 4533 913 099.

▪ **ALEXIUS II** (Aleksei Ridiger), Patriarch of Moscow and All Russia, 1990 — ; b. 1929; ed. Leningrad Religious Acad.; Metropolitan of the Russ. Orthodox Ch. for Tallinn and Estonia, 1968 — 88; Metropolitan of Leningrad and Novgorod and Ruler of the Tallinn and Est. Bishopric, 1988 — 90; Mem. of the Holy Synod.

▪ **ALLAS, Mati,** Gen. Dir, Nat. Grain Bd, 1990 — ; b. 1947; ed. Est. Agric. Acad., eng. of mech.; Dep. Cereal Products Min. Est. SSR, 1985 — 90. *Add.* Toomkuninga 20, Tallinn 200100; tel. 453 376.

▪ **ALLIKMETS, Lembit,** pharmacologist; b. 1936; ed. Tartu Univ., postgraduate studies at Yale, New York and Wisconsin Univ. (USA); DSc. (Med.), Prof.; Tartu Univ., 1963 — , Dept Head, 1972 — , Dean of Faculty, 1975 — 84, 1989 — ; Memberships: Soc. of Biol. Psychiatry (USA), Int. Soc. on Research of Aggression, Int. Soc. on Research of Emotions; Chair., Est. Pharmacology Soc.; research on pharmacology of nemoleptics, adaptation of receptors to long-term treatment with psychotropics. *Add.* Ülikooli 18, Tartu 202400; tel. 325 78, 320 43.

- **ANDREJEV, Viktor,** Dep. Speaker, Est. SC, 1990 — ; b. 1948; ed. Tallinn Tech. Univ., mining eng.; CSc. (Tech.); Skochinski Inst. of Mines, 1975 — 90; CPSU; research on oil-shale mining. **Add.** Lossi plats 1a, Tallinn 200100; tel. 606 797.
- **ANDRESEN, Lembit,** education spec.; b. 1929; ed. Tallinn Teacher Training Inst.; DSc. (Pedag.), Prof.; Tallinn Teacher Training Inst., 1959 — , Dept Head, 1969 — 71; research into hist. of sch. in W-Europe and Baltic States. **Add.** Narva mnt. 25, Tallinn 200102; tel. 523 945.
- **ANNUS, Lembit,** 1st Sec., Cent. Cttee ECP (CPSU), 1990 — ; b. 1941; E-in-C, *Eesti Kommunist* journal, 1983 — 89; Mem., Politbureau CPSU Cent. Cttee, 1991 — . **Add.** Lenini pst. 9, Tallinn 200100; tel. 445 311.
- **ANTON, Tõnu,** Chair., Est. SC Legal Cttee, 1990 — ; b. 1953; ed. Tartu Univ., lawyer; Tartu City Govt, 1975 — 90; Tartu Univ., 1979 — . **Add.** Lossi plats 1a, Tallinn 200100; tel. 606 318.
- **ANTSON, Ants,** speed skater; b. 1938; ed. Tallinn Teacher Training Inst.; Dir, Sports Dept, Tallinn October District, 1977 — ; medals: Olympic gold 1500 m, 1964; world champ.: bronze 1500 m, 5000 m, 1964; European champ.: gold, all-round, 1964; USSR champ.: gold, all-round, 1967; world records: sprint 176,300 points and 3000 m 4:27.3; 1964. **Add.** Vabaduse väljak 10, Tallinn 200001; tel. 666 798.
- **ARENG, Kuno,** choir conductor; b. 1929; ed. Tallinn Conservatoire; Prof.; Tallinn Conservatoire, 1962 — ; conductor, Est. Nat. Male Choir, 1966 — 89; chief conductor, Tallinn Chamber Choir, 1978 — ; 1st prize: Arezzo Int. Choir Festival, 1971, and in Tallinn, 1972; 2nd prize: Cork Choir and Folkdance Festival, 1982; conductor at the Song Festivals. **Add.** Kaarli pst. 3, Tallinn 200001; tel. 445 814.
- **ARON, Villar,** Gen. Dir, State Taxation Dept, 1990 — ; b. 1935; ed. Tartu Univ., financier; Min. of Finance, Dept Head, 1965 — 79, Dep. Min., 1979 — 90. **Add.** Kohtu 8, Tallinn 200100; tel. 452 862.
- **ARRAK, Jüri,** painter, metal and graphic artist; b. 1936; ed. Tallinn Art Univ.; has painted grotesque compositions, portrait and figure paintings; drawings, printgraphic, ill. to books, exlibrises, jewelry with miniatures; artist of several films. **Add.** (h) Tammsaare tee 72 — 50, Tallinn 200034; tel. 526 235.
- **ARUVALD, Andres,** Chair., Est. Union of Consumers' Cooperatives, 1984 — ; b. 1939; ed. Tallinn Tech. Univ., eng.; Est. Union of Consumers' Cooperatives, 1976 — ; USSR People's Deputy, 1989 — . **Add.** Narva mnt. 7, Tallinn 200102; tel. 438 200.
- **BASKIN, Eino,** actor and producer; b. 1929; ed. Est. Theatre Inst.; Est. Drama Theatre, 1951 — 57, 1970 — 80; founder and Artistic Dir, theatre *Vanalinnastuudio*, 1980 — ; directed comedies and satires. **Add.** Sakala 12, Tallinn 200001; tel. 448 408.
- **BEEKMAN, Aimeé,** writer, Vladimir Beekman's wife; b. 1933; ed. Moscow Cinematography Inst.; has written many novels on the problems of the modern woman. **Add.** Writers' Union, Harju 1, Tallinn 200001; tel. 446 832.
- **BEEKMAN, Vladimir,** writer; b. 1929; ed. Tallinn Tech. Univ., chem. eng.; Chair., Est. Writers' Union, 1983 — ; has written poetry, novels, travel stories and books for children; has transl. from Sw. (the most part of Astrid Lindgren's books) and Russ. **Add.** Writers' Union, Harju 1, Tallinn 200001; tel. 446 832.
- **BERNSTEIN, Boris,** art critic; b. 1924; ed. Leningrad Univ.; CSc. (Arts), Prof.; Tallinn Art Univ., 1951 — ; research on Est. contemporary painting and graphic arts as well as methodology and theory problems of art. **Add.** (h) Mustamäe tee 161 — 5, Tallinn 200029; tel. 535 005.
- **BOGOVSKI, Pavel,** morphologist; b. 1919; ed. Alma-Ata Med. Inst.; DSc. (Med.), Prof.; Inst. of Experimental and Clinical Med., 1949 — , Dir, 1974 — 91; Int. Agency for Research on Cancer in Lyon, 1968 — 74; research on cancer causing effects of ind. substances and environmental factors, on modifying factors of cancer genesis, on progression of tumours. **Add.** Hiiu 42, Tallinn 200107; tel. 514 300.
- **BRONSTEIN, Mikhail,** economist; b. 1923; ed. Leningrad Univ., agrarian econ.; DSc. (Econ.), Prof.; Mem., Est. Acad. of Sci.; Tartu Univ., 1949 — , Dept Head 1961 — ; 380 scientific publ., incl. 12 monographs; EPF, *Vaba Eesti* Movement; Mem., Int. Assoc. of Agrarian Econ., 1979 — . USSR People's Deputy (Econ. Reform Cttee), 1989 — . **Add.** Ülikooli 18, Tartu 202400; tel. 337 26.
- **DOBKEVICH, Maiva,** Dir, Library of Est. Acad. of Sci., 1984 — ; b. 1942; ed. Tartu Univ.; Library of Est. Acad. of Sci., 1967 — . **Add.** Lenini pst. 10, Tallinn 200105; tel. 440 649.
- **EENMAA, Ivi,** Dir, Est. Nat. Library, 1984 — ; b. 1943; ed. Tartu Univ., Moscow Inst. for Culture; CSc. (Pedag.); Est. Nat. Library, 1973 — ; Mem., IFLA. **Add.** Tõnismägi 2, Tallinn 200001; tel. 448 778.
- **EESPERE, Rene,** composer; b. 1953; ed. Tallinn Conservatoire; Tallinn Conservatoire, 1979 — , Dept Head, 1987 — ; composed short ballets, oratoria, chamber music, choir music and children's songs. **Add.** Vabaduse pst. 130, Tallinn 200103; tel. 514 597.
- **EHLVEST, Jaan,** chess player; int. grand master; b. 1962; ed. Tartu Univ., psychologist; 4th at World Cup tournament,1990; European Junior champ., 1983; Mem. of USSR gold-winning team at the 1988 Chess Olympics. **Add.** Tallinna Malemaja, Vene 29, Tallinn 200001.
- **EIGI, Ado,** architect; b. 1938; ed. Tallinn Art Univ.; Kirov Fishing Cooperative design office, 1973 — 90, arch. firm *A.E.B.*, 1990 — ; designed prod., admin., commercial buildings and treatment centres; work contains new functional and post-modern elements; prize winner Sofia Interarch '87. **Add.** (h) Weizenbergi 20a — 5, Tallinn 200010; tel. 424 663.
- **EINASTO, Jaan,** astronomer; b. 1929; ed. Tartu Univ.; DSc. (Phys. & Math.), Prof.; Mem., Est. Acad. of Sci.; Inst. of Astrophys. and Atmospheric Phys., 1952 — , Dept Head,

1977 — ; Acad. Sec., Est. Acad. of Sci. Division of Phys. and Astronomy, 1987 — ; studies on composition of galactic systems, theoretical verification of the existence of the Galaxy's massive corona (1974). *Add.* Tõravere, Tartumaa 202444; tel. 310 97.

■ **ELLAMAA, Andres**, Min. of Health, 1990 — ; b. 1944; ed. Tartu Univ., neurosurgeon; CSc. (Med.), Tallinn State Hosp., 1968 — 74, 1974 — 80; Dept Dir, Tallinn Emergency Hosp., 1980 — 90; research on surgical treatment of spinal column lesions and diseases; Vice-Pres., Est. Med. Assoc., 1988 — 90; EPF. *Add.* Lossi plats 7; Tallinn 200100; tel. 445 123.

■ **ENDRE, Sirje**, E-in-C, *Kultuur ja Elu* mag., 1986 — ; b. 1945; ed. Tartu Univ., journalist; newspapers *Noorte Hääl* and *Kodumaa*; mag. *Kultuur ja Elu*, 1979 — ; founder of *Eesti Elu* 'Est. Life' newspaper; Dep. Chair. of the Exec., Council of Estonia. *Add.* Narva mnt. 5, Tallinn 200090; tel. 437 768.

■ **ENGELBRECHT, Jüri**, eng. scientist; b. 1939; ed. Tallinn Tech. Univ.; DSc. (Phys. & Math.), Prof.; Mem., Est. Acad. of Sci.; Inst. of Cybernetics, 1969 — ; Mem., European Mech. Council, Acoustics Inst. (UK); Foreign Mem., Accademia Peloritana (Italy); research in the fields of constant environmental mech. and the wave theory. *Add.* Akadeemia tee 21, Tallinn 200108; tel. 527 905.

■ **ERELT, Mati**, linguist; b. 1941; ed. Tartu Univ.; DSc. (Philol.); Inst. of Lg. and Lit., 1969 — , Dept Head, 1983 — ; research on the syntax and semantics of the Est. lg. *Add.* Roosikrantsi 6, Tallinn 200106; tel. 446 947.

■ **ERMEL, Malle**, Dir, Tartu Univ. Library, 1990 — ; b. 1949; ed. Tartu Univ.; Tartu Univ. Library, 1974 — . *Add.* Struve 1, Tartu 202400; tel. 325 77, 353 79.

■ **ERNESAKS, Gustav**, conductor and composer; b. 1908; ed. Tallinn Conservatoire, Prof.; Tallinn Conservatoire, 1944 — 72, Dept Head, 1946 — 48 and 1951 — 61; Est. Nat. Male Choir, 1944 — , founder and chief conductor; organiser and chief conductor of Song Festivals; 5 operas, 5 cantatas, approx. 300 songs for choirs, 6 books on current public affairs. *Add.* Choral Society, Tönismägi 10, Tallinn 200001; tel. 681 667.

■ **ETVERK, Ivar**, forest scientist; b. 1932; ed. Est. Agric. Acad.; DSc. (Agric.), Prof.; Est. Inst. of Forestry, 1969 — , Dir, 1990 — ; research on forest selection, forest policies and management of forest; has written humorous short stories. *Add.* Rõõmu tee 2, Tartu 202400; tel. 363 75.

■ **EVER, Ita**, actor; b. 1931; ed. Moscow A.Lunacharsky Theatre Inst.; Est. Drama Theatre, 1953 — ; roles: Kattrin, Masha, also roles in comedies and films; Grand Old Lady of the Est. theatre today. *Add.* Pärnu mnt. 5, Tallinn 200001; tel. 442 065.

■ **FJUK, Ignar**, architect and politician; b. 1953; ed. Tallinn Art Univ.; Dept Head, *Eesti Maaehitusprojekt* Inst.; Dir, Dept of Arch., Min. of Constr., 1988 — 90; Chair., Cultural Council of Creative Soc., 1987 — 89; Mem. of Bd, EPF,

1990 — ; co-author of Estonia's Declaration of Sovereignty (Nov. 16, 1988); designs for residential and community buildings; co-draftsman of the Tallinn city plan; has published articles on arch. USSR People's Deputy, 1989 — ; Est. SC Deputy, 1990 — . *Add.* Uus 28, Tallinn 200001; tel. 449 236.

■ **FREIBERG, Arvi**, physicist; b. 1948; ed. Tallinn Tech. Univ.; DSc. (Phys. & Math.); Inst. of Phys., 1971 — , Dir, 1989 — ; research on interactions of electrons and photons in crystals with additives and on extremely fast relaxation processes in condensed substance. *Add.* Riia 142, Tartu 202400; tel. 281 02, 310 73.

■ **FREY, Toomas**, ecologist and forester; b. 1937; ed. Est. Agric. Acad.; DSc. (Biol.), Prof.; Inst. of Zoology and Botany, 1968 — 83; Tartu Univ., 1983 — , Lab. Head, 1990 — ; Min. of Environment, 1990; Est. Scientists' Assoc.; quantitative methods of plant research, prod. biol., ecology; Est. Green Movement. *Add.* Tiigi 61, Tartu 202400; tel. 343 81.

■ **GANS, Taevo**, interior decorator and designer; b. 1941; ed. Tallinn Art Univ.; *EKE Projekt* Inst., 1969 — 74, *Ars* combine, 1974 — ; designed whole rooms, furniture, light fixtures, and exh. (incl. Soviet pavilion in Spokane, 1974, Est. exh. in Soviet pavilion in Tokyo, 1983, Est. exh. at Turkish Izmir Fair, 1977). *Add.* (h) Hiiu 11 — 2, Tallinn 200016; tel. 513 063.

■ **GOLIKOV, Jevgeni**, Permanent Representative to the Russian Federation, 1991 — ; b. 1946; ed. Tartu Univ., journalist, sociologist; CSc. (Phil.); Est. Agric. Acad., 1972 — 83; Consultant, Presidium of the Est. SSR Supreme Soviet, 1982 — 88; Consultant, Presidium of the Supreme Soviet of the USSR, 1988; Cent. Cttee of the ECP, 1989; Dep. Ed., the *Poliitika*, 1989 — 1991. *Add.* Sobinovski pereulok 5, Moscow 103009; tel. 290 50 13; fax 202 38 30.

■ **GOLUBKOV, Gennadi**, Min. of Constr., 1990 — ; b. 1937; ed. Mari Teacher Training Inst.; Aseri Ceramics Works, 1961 — 90, Dir, 1983 — 90; EPF; ECP; USSR People's Deputy, 1989 — . *Add.* Harju 11, Tallinn 200001; tel. 440 577.

■ **GRÄZIN, Igor**, lawyer; b. 1952; ed. Tartu Univ.; DSc. (Law), Prof.; Tartu Univ., 1978 — , Dept Head, 1986 — 89; Notre Dame Univ. Indiana, USA, 1990 — ; *Vaba Eesti* Movement; research into law and into phil. and epistemological aspects of legal sci. USSR People's Deputy, 1989 — . *Add.* Ülikooli 18, Tartu 202400; tel. 352 64.

■ **GREEN, Arnold**, Pres., Est. Olympic Cttee. 1989 — ; b. 1920; ed. CPSU Cent. Cttee Higher Party Sch.; Dep. Chair., CM Est. SSR, 1953 — 58, 1960 — 84; Foreign Min. of the Est. SSR, 1962 — 90. *Add.* Regati pst. 1, Tallinn 200103; tel. 237 277.

■ **HABAKUK, Madis**, economist; b. 1938; ed. Tallinn Tech. Univ.; DSc. (Econ.), Prof.; Tallinn Tech. Univ., 1966 — 78; Dept Head, Est. Management Inst., 1978 — 88; founder and Pres., Est. Business Sch., 1988 — ; UN expert, 1982 — ; research on management and planning. *Add.*

Lenini pst. 12, Tallinn 200001; tel. and fax 446 038.

■ **HALLASTE, Illar,** Chair., Est. Christian Dem. Union, 1988 — ; b. 1959; ed. EELC Theol. Inst.; Torma Maarja parish, 1983 — 88; Kadrina parish, 1988 — ; Council of Estonia; Est. Heritage Soc. Est. SC Deputy, 1990 — . *Add.* Rahukohtu 1, Tallinn 200100; tel. 606 463.

■ **HALLIK, Klara,** social scientist; b. 1933; ed. Tartu Teachers' Inst., Tallinn Teacher Training Inst., CPSU Cent. Cttee Social Sci. Acad.; CSc. (Hist.), Prof.; Tallinn Tech. Univ., 1965 — 88; Inst. of Phil., Sociology and Law, 1988 — ; research on ethnic relations and social theory; USSR People's Deputy, 1989 — ; EPF. *Add.* Estonia pst. 7, Tallinn 200101; tel. 605 130.

■ **HÄRM, Tõnis,** Gen. Dir, State Customs Dept, 1990 — ; b. 1936; ed. Tartu Univ.; CSc. (Law); Tallinn Tech. Univ., 1967 — 90; research on keynesianism, neokeynesianism and neoconservatism. *Add.* Kohtu 8, Tallinn 200100; tel. 452 767.

■ **HELME, Rein,** Dir, Inst. of Hist., 1990 — ; b. 1954; ed. Tartu Univ.; CSc. (Hist.); Dept Head, Est. State Archives, 1987 — 90; research on the 1812 Napoleonic invasion of Russia. *Add.* Rüütli 6, Tallinn 200101; tel. 446 594.

■ **HELP, Toomas,** linguist; b. 1960; ed. Tartu Univ.; Inst. of Lg. and Lit., 1984 — ; research of the grammatical structures of the Est. lg. *Add.* Roosikrantsi 6, Tallinnn 200106; tel. 446 947.

■ **HERMAKÜLA, Evald,** producer and actor; b. 1941; ed. Tartu Univ., geol.; theatre *Vanemuine*, 1971 — 83; Est. Drama Theatre, 1983 — , chief producer, 1988 — ; initially produced plays in avangardist style, later returned to more traditional styles. *Add.* Pärnu mnt. 5, Tallinn 200001; tel. 442 065.

■ **HIEDEL, Kersti,** Gen. Dir, State Registry of Births, Deaths and Marriages, 1985 — ; b. 1944; ed. Tartu Univ., lawyer. *Add.* Lossi plats 1a, Tallinn 200001; tel. 606 701.

■ **HINDOV, Juhan,** journalist; b. 1952; ed. Tartu Univ., econ. geogr.; *Eesti Maaehitusprojekt* Inst., 1976 — 80; Est. Radio int. news dept, 1980 — 89; Press Sec., Rep. of Estonia Govt, 1990 — . *Add.* Lossi plats 1a, Tallinn 200100; tel. 606 734.

■ **HINT, Mati,** linguist and politician; b. 1937; ed. Tartu Univ.; CSc. (Philol.), Asst Prof.; Inst. of Lg. and Lit., 1966 — 75; Tallinn Teacher Training Inst., 1974 — ; research on Est. lg., articles on lg. and nationalities policies; Dep. Chair., Est. SC Presidium Lg. Defense Commn; Mem. of the Bd, EPF, 1988 — ; freedom prize of the Paul Lauritzen Foundation (Denmark), 1990. *Add.* Narva mnt. 25, Tallinn 200102; tel. 423 116.

■ **HIZHNYAKOV, Vladimir,** physicist; b. 1938; ed. Tartu Univ.; DSc. (Phys. & Math.), Prof.; Mem., Est. Acad. of Sci.; Inst. of Phys., 1960 — ; research in solid state phys. and theoretical spectroscopy. *Add.* Riia 142, Tartu 202400; tel. 281 64.

■ **IHO, Arvo,** film dir and cameraman; b. 1949; ed. Moscow Cinematography Inst.; *Tallinnfilm*, 1970 — 71, 1975 — ; made films psycho-analyzing the relationship between mid-dle-aged woman and young men; 1st prize at Rouen festival, 1990. *Add.* Harju 9, Tallinn 200001; tel. 449 994.

■ **JAAKSON, Ernst,** Consul-Gen. of the Rep. of Estonia (1918 — 40) in New York, 1968 — ; b. 1905; ed. Columbia Univ., B.Sc., econ.; diplomatic corps of Estonia, 1929 — ; Sec. in the New York Consulate-Gen., 1932 — 39, Consul, 1939 — 65, chargé d'affaires (for the Consul-Gen.), 1965 — 68. *Add.* Rockefeller Plaza 9, New-York, N. Y.; tel. 212 247 1450; fax 212 262 0893.

■ **JAAKSOO, Ülo,** eng. scientist; b. 1939; ed. Tallinn Tech. Univ.; DSc. (Tech.), Prof.; Mem., Est. Acad. of Sci.; Inst. of Cybernetics, 1961 — , Dir, 1989 — ; Vice-Pres., Est. Acad. of Sci., 1990 — ; research on management theory and computer-aided design. *Add.* Akadeemia tee 21, Tallinn 200108; tel. 525 435.

■ **JAANSON, Jüri,** oarsman; b. 1965; *Dynamo* Sports Club, Pärnu; winner of the 1st World Cup, 1990, gold medal at the world champ., 1990, bronze single blade, 1989, silver at the Goodwill Games, 1990, and gold in the USSR 4-man double blade team, USSR champ., 1986, 1987, 1989. *Add.* Tööstuse 27, Pärnu 203600; tel. 437 97.

■ **JÄNES, Peep,** architect; b. 1936; ed. Tallinn Art Univ.; *Eesti Projekt* Inst., 1963 — 68 and 1975 — ; designed public buildings, dwellings, cottages, sports facilities, vacation areas; prize winner Sofia Interarch' 83 for Tallinn Olympic Sailing Centre, part. in UNESCO's London comp., 1961. *Add.* (h) Ranniku tee 29 — 6, Tallinn 200021, tel. 232 026.

■ **JÄRV, Elo-Reet,** leatherworks artist; b. 1939; Tallinn Art Univ.; has made relief surfaced boxes, book covers and unique sculptural compositions; diploma at the applied arts exh. in Erfurt, 1982; personal exh. in Finland, 1982 — 83. *Add.* (h) Veerenni 1 — 21, Tallinn 200007; tel. 684 772.

■ **JÄRV, Rein,** Gen. Dir, State Dept of Aviation, 1990 — ; b. 1937; ed. Moscow Aviation Inst. *Add.* Viru 9, Tallinn 200100; tel. 441 785.

■ **JÄRVE, Priit,** Dir, Inst. of Phil., Sociology and Law, 1989 — ; b. 1941; ed. Tartu Univ., philol.; CSc. (Phil.); Dept of Sci. and Higher Educ., ECP Cent. Cttee, 1972 — 80; Research Dir, Inst. of Hist., 1982 — 89; works on cognition theory, psychology of phil. problems and social phil. *Add.* Estonia pst. 7, Tallinn 200105; tel. 443 078.

■ **JÄRVET, Jüri,** actor; b. 1919; ed. Est. Theatre Inst.; Est. Drama Theatre, 1952 — 65 and 1970 — ; roles: Claudius, Polonius, Willie; success as movie actor ('Solaris', 'King Lear'). *Add.* Pärnu mnt. 5, Tallinn 200001; tel. 442 065.

■ **JÄRVI, Neeme,** conductor; b. 1937; ed. Leningrad Conservatoire; Tallinn Conservatoire Hon. Dr; chief conductor, Est. State Symphony Orch., 1963 — 79; chief conductor, *Estonia* theatre, 1963 — 75; emigrated 1980; chief conductor, Gothenburg Philharmonic Orch., 1981 — ; chief conductor, Scottish Nat. Symphony Orch., 1984 — 88; 1st prize at the VI Int. Conductors' Comp., Accademia Nazionale di Santa Cecilia,

1971; the Northern Cross from the Swedish Kingdom, 1990. **Add.** c/o Van Walsum Management, 40 St. Peter's Road, London, W6 9 BH, England; tel. 741 5 905 (Sweden).

▪ **JÖERÜÜT, Jaak,** writer; b. 1947; ed. Tallinn Tech. Univ., econ.; Sec. of the Bd, Est. Writers' Union, 1977 — 90; Chair., Est. SC Research, Ed. and Culture Cttee, 1990 — ; Liberal-Dem. Party; Council of Estonia; has written prose about psychological problems in contemporary urban soc. Est. SC Deputy, 1990 — . **Add.** Writers' Union, Harju 1, Tallinn 200001; tel. 446 832.

▪ **JUGASTE, Aimar,** Gen. Dir. Est. Telegraph Agency, 1990 — ; b. 1957; ed. Tartu Univ., journalist; newspaper *Edasi,* 1981 — 90. **Add.** Pärnu mnt. 67a, Tallinn 200001; tel. 442 657.

▪ **JÜRGEN, Madis,** E-in-C, *Eesti Elu* 'Est. Life' newspaper, 1989 — ; b. 1962; ed. Tartu Univ., journalist; *Kultuur ja Elu* mag., 1985 — 89. **Add.** Narva mnt. 5, Tallinn 200090; tel. 445 466; fax 449 558.

▪ **JÜRGENS, Mati,** Gen. Dir, State Dept of Commercial Licencing, 1990 — ; b. 1947; ed. Tallinn Tech. Univ., electrical eng.; Est. SSR Planning Cttee, 1978 — 88; Est. SSR Fuel and Energetics Cttee, 1988 — 90. **Add.** Komsomoli 1, Tallinn 200100; tel. 683 560.

▪ **JÜRJO, Villu,** clergyman, Chair., Est. SC Ethics Cttee, 1990 — ; b. 1950; ed. EELC Theol. Inst.; Urvaste parish, 1985 — ; Christian Dem. Union. **Add.** Lossi plats 1a, Tallinn 200100; tel. 606 748.

▪ **KAAL, Anu,** singer (soprano); b. 1940; ed. Tallinn Conservatoire, postgraduate studies at La Scala Opera Sch.; theatre *Estonia,* 1963 — ; Tallinn Conservatoire, 1984 — ; roles: Gilda, Violetta, Luisa, Zerlina, Adele. **Add.** Estonia pst. 4, Tallinn 200105; tel. 444 709.

▪ **KAALEP, Ain,** writer; b. 1926; ed. Tartu Univ., philol.; Transl. Office Head, Tartu Univ., 1976 — 83; E-in-C, journal *Akadeemia,* 1989 — ; has written elegiacs in classical poetic form; has transl. classical poetry from different lgs. **Add.** Küütri 1, Tartu 202400; tel. 313 73.

▪ **KAASIK, Ain-Elmar,** neurologist and neurosurgeon; b. 1934; ed. Tartu Univ., postgraduate studies at univ. clinics of Lund, Sweden, Pennsylvania, USA; DSc. (Med.), Prof.; Uppsala Univ. Hon. Dr; Tartu Univ., 1967 — , Dept Head; 220 publ. on pathogenesis and treatment of neurological diseases, with special emphasis on pathophysiology of cerebral vascular circulation and metabolism; Soc. of Scandinavian Neurosurgeons. **Add.** Puusepa 2, Tartu 202400; tel. 282 49.

▪ **KAASIK, Tõnis,** Min. of Environment, 1991 — ; b. 1949; ed. Tartu Univ.; CSc. (Geogr.); Est. Management Inst., 1986 — 88; Cttee of Nature Conservation, 1988 — 90; Gen. Dir, State Dept of Water Resources, 1990 — 91; research in ecology and environment protection. **Add.** Toompuiestee 24, Tallinn 200100; tel. 452 507.

▪ **KADASTIK, Mart,** journalist; b. 1955; ed. Tartu Univ.; newspaper *Postimees,* 1977 — , E-in-C, 1983 — . **Add.** Gildi 1, Tartu 202400; tel. 321 26.

▪ **KAEVATS, Ülo,** E-in-C, Est. Encyclopaedia, 1989 — ; b. 1947; ed. Tartu Univ., phys., phil.; CSc. (Phil.), Asst Prof.; Inst. of Hist., 1972 — 82; Est. Acad. of Sci. Phil. Dept, 1982 — 90; EPF, Chair. of the Programme Cttee, 1988 — 90; research in the methodology of sci., journalism. **Add.** Pärnu mnt. 10, Tallinn 200090; tel. 449 469; fax 445 720.

▪ **KAHK, Juhan,** historian; b. 1928; ed. Tartu Univ.; DSc. (Hist.), Prof.; Mem., Est. Acad. of Sci.; Foreign Mem., Finnish Acad. of Sci.; Inst. of Hist., 1954 — 74, Dir, 1968 — 74; Acad. Sec., Est. Acad. of Sci. Division of Humanities and Social Sci., 1974 — 87; Inst. of Phil., Sociology and Law, 1987 — ; research on econ. development of farms and estates in Estonia, and rural movements in the 18th and 19th cent. **Add.** Estonia pst. 7, Tallinn 200101; tel. 605 736.

▪ **KAHN, Jüri,** Permanent Representative of the Est. Govt to the USSR, 1990 — ; b. 1953; ed. Tartu Univ., math.; CSc. (Econ.); Inst. of Econ., 1977 — 89; research on building econ.; USSR People's Deputy and Mem. of the USSR Supreme Soviet,1989 — . **Add.** Sobinovski pereulok 5, Moscow 103009; tel. 290 50 13; fax 202 38 30.

▪ **KALJO, Dimitri,** geologist; b. 1928; ed. Tartu Univ.; DSc. (Geol.), Prof.; Mem., Est. Acad. of Sci.; Inst. of Geol., 1957 — ; Acad. Sec., Est. Acad. of Sci. Division of Biol., Geol. and Chem., 1990 — ; research on Ordovician and Silurian system in Estonia; Int. Geol. Union, Int. Paleontology Assoc. **Add.** Estonia pst. 7, Tallinn 200101; tel. 449 982.

▪ **KALJUSTE, Tõnu,** choir conductor; b. 1953; ed. Tallinn Conservatoire; founder and chief conductor, Est. Philharmonic Chamber Choir, 1981 — ; 1st prize at the int. choir festival Tallinn '75 and at the B.Bartók IX Int. Choir Comp., 1980. **Add.** Lühike jalg 9, Tallinn 200001; tel. 448 926.

▪ **KALL, Toomas,** writer; b. 1947; theatre *Vanalinnastuudio,* 1980 — 87, E-in-C, newspaper *Sirp,* 1990 — ; has publ. coll. of humorous stories and plays. **Add.** Toompuiestee 30, Tallinn 200031; tel. 441 416.

▪ **KALLAS, Siim,** Chair., Est. TU Head Office, 1989 — ; b. 1948; ed. Tartu Univ., financier; Min. of Finance, 1975 — 79; Chair., Cent. Office of Savings Banks, 1979 — 86; EPF; *Vaba Eesti* Movement; Est. Heritage Soc. USSR People's Deputy, 1989 — . **Add.** Tartu mnt. 4, Tallinn 200100; tel. 425 100.

▪ **KALLAS, Teet,** writer; b. 1943; written numerous novels on city life; Est. SC Deputy, 1990 — ; EPF. **Add.** (h) Raua 51 — 5, Tallinn 200010; tel. 431 016.

▪ **KAMRATOV, Ardo,** Gen. Dir, Dept of State Property, 1990 — ; b. 1954; ed. Tallinn Tech. Univ.; CSc. (Econ.); Tallinn Tech. Univ., Dept Head, 1986 — 90; research on decentralization of ind. and privatization of property. **Add.** Komsomoli 1, Tallinn 200100; tel. 682 974.

▪ **KANGILASKI, Jaak,** art critic; b. 1939; ed. Tartu Univ.; CSc. (Arts), Prof.; Tartu Univ., 1967 — 71; Tallinn Art Univ., 1971 — , Rector, 1989 — ; research on contemporary 20th cent.

art trends. **Add.** Tartu mnt. 1, Tallinn 200105; tel. 432 664, 432 655.

■ **KANGRO, Raimo,** composer; b. 1949; ed. Tallinn Conservatoire; Est. Composers' Union, 1977 — 85; operas, concertos, piano sonatas in impulsive and rhythmical style. **Add.** Composers' Union, Lauteri 7, Tallinn 200107; tel. 444 103.

■ **KANN, Jüri,** chemist; b. 1938; ed. Tallinn Tech. Univ.; DSc. (Biol.); Tallinn Tech. Univ., 1961 — 88, Dept Head, 1985 — 88; Dir, Inst. of Chem., 1988 — ; research in food chem. and technol.; Chair. of the Bd, Est. Chem. Soc. **Add.** Akadeemia tee 15, Tallinn 200108; tel. 536 450.

■ **KAPLINSKI, Jaan,** writer; b. 1941; ed. Tartu Univ., philol.; has written pantheistic phil. poetry (9 coll. in Est., 2 in Engl., 2 in Finn. and 1 in Russ.) and essays on culture, pol. and ecology. **Add.** (h) Nisu 33 — 9, Tartu 202400; tel. 287 55.

■ **KAREVA, Doris,** writer; b. 1958; ed. Tartu Univ., philol.; has written discrete emotional poetry. **Add.** (h) Kärberi 39 — 104, Tallinn 200038.

■ **KARING, Tiia,** Gen. Dir, Est. Tourist Bd, 1990 — ; b. 1945; ed. Tartu Univ., econ. geogr.; CSc. (Econ.); Inst. of Econ., 1969 — 90; research on organizing tourism and recreation ind. in Estonia. **Add.** Väike-Karja 23, Tallinn 200101; tel. 441 239.

■ **KARLEP, Ivo,** E-in-C, *Eesti Ekspress,* 1991 — ; b. 1954; ed. Tallinn Tech. Univ., econ., Tartu Univ., journalist; *Rahva Hääl* (daily), 1980 — 86. **Add.** Pärnu mnt. 22, Tallinn 200001; tel. 666 219.

■ **KÄRNER, Jüri,** biologist; b. 1940; ed. Tartu Univ., postgraduate studies at Helsinki Univ.; DSc. (Biol.), Prof.; Tartu Univ., 1962 — , Dept Head, 1981 — 86, Vice-Rector, 1986 — 88, Rector, 1988 — ; research on cytology and evolutionary biol. **Add.** Ülikooli 18, Tartu 202400; tel. 348 66; telex 173 243 TAUN SU; fax 354 40.

■ **KARP, Raine,** architect; b. 1939; ed. Tallinn Art Univ.; *Eesti Projekt* Inst., 1963 — 90; Intermed Assoc., 1990 — ; designed large scale public buildings (Tallinn Concert and Sports Hall, 1980; Est. Nat. Library, 1991), apartment buildings; gold medal, Sofia Interarch '83; part. in Paris Bastille Sq Opera comp., 1983. **Add.** (h) Viimsi tee 45, Tallinn 200021; tel. 231 435.

■ **KELAM, Tunne,** Chair., Council of Estonia, 1990 — ; b. 1936; ed. Tartu Univ., hist.; Est. Encyclopaedia, 1964 — 79; Ranna state farm, 1980 — 88; Est. Nat. Indep. Party. **Add.** Narva mnt. 5a; Tallinn 200001; tel. 666 731.

■ **KESKKÜLA, Ando,** painter; b. 1950; ed. Tallinn Art Univ.; Asst Prof.; chief artist, Est. Art Fund, 1976 — 86; Tallinn Art Univ., 1985 — ; Chair., Est. Artists' Union, 1989 — ; initially influenced by pop art, later by urban reality; group exh. in Belgium, Bulgaria, Germany, Denmark and France. **Add.** Vabaduse väljak 6, 200105; tel. 445 014.

■ **KIIK, Heino,** writer; b. 1925; ed. Est. Agric. Acad., agron.; has written novels depicting acute social problems in Estonia during the Soviet period; has worked as a publr. **Add.** (h) Sütiste tee 26 — 5, Tallinn 200034; tel. 522 038.

■ **KIISK, Kaljo,** film dir and actor; b. 1925; ed. Moscow A.Lunacharsky Theatre Inst.; Est. Drama Theatre, 1953 — 55; *Tallinnfilm,* 1955 — ; created films about turning points in this cent. in Estonia, filmed lit. classics, played tragically comic roles in film and on stage. **Add.** Harju 9, Tallinn 200001; tel. 449 994.

■ **KIIVIT, Jaan,** theologian and pastor; b. 1940; ed. EELC Theol. Inst., Asst Prof.; Tallinn Holy Spirit parish, 1965 — ; Theol. Inst., 1978 — , Curator, 1990 — ; research on practical theol., has ed. yearbooks of EELC as well as a series of theol. textbooks for high sch.; transl. from Ger. and Finn. **Add.** Kiriku 8, Tallinn 200016; tel. 440 479.

■ **KILVET, Krista,** Dep. Min. of State, 1990 — ; b. 1946; ed. Tartu Univ.; philol.; Est. Radio, 1967 — 90; Mem. of the leadership, Est. Women's Union. **Add.** Lossi plats 1a, Tallinn 200100; tel. 606 723.

■ **KIRIKAL, Jaak,** Chief Justice, Supreme Court of the ESSR and the Rep. of Estonia, 1988 — ; b. 1939; ed. Tartu Univ., lawyer; CPSU Cent. Cttee Higher Party Sch.; Chair., Kohtla-Järve People's Court, 1965 — 70; Dep. and 1st Dep. of Justice Min. of ESSR, 1976 — 88; Co-founder, Est. Acad. Law Soc. and Est. Lawyers' League. **Add.** Pärnu mnt. 7, Tallinn 200104; tel. 442 931.

■ **KIVI, Raul-Levroit,** architect; b. 1920; ed. Tallinn Tech. Univ.; chief arch., *Eesti Projekt* Inst. Tartu Dept, 1950 — 72; *Eesti Ehitusmälestised,* 1972 — 82; designed apartment buildings and plan for downtown and old town Tartu; publ. arch. articles; spoken at UIA, ICOMOS and ICOM conferences. **Add.** (h) Veski 4a — 2, Tartu 202400; tel. 323 68.

■ **KIVIMÄE, Jüri,** Dir, Tallinn City Archives, 1990 — ; b. 1947; ed. Tartu Univ.; CSc. (Hist.); Asst Prof.; Est. Encyclopaedia, 1970 — 75; Inst. of Hist., 1975 — 90; Tartu Univ., 1972 — ; works on the hist. of the Baltic Sea c. 1400 — 1600, on ancient Est. cultural and econ. hist.; Chair., Baltic-German Cultural Soc. **Add.** Tolli 4, Tallinn 200001; tel. 601 744.

■ **KLAS, Eri,** conductor; b. 1939; ed. Tallinn Conservatoire, Leningrad Conservatoire; theatre *Estonia,* 1965 — , chief conductor, 1975 — ; chief conductor, Stockholm Royal Opera, 1985 — 89; chief conductor, Finnish Nat. Opera, 1989 — ; Swedish Royal Nordic Star Medal, 1989; Promoter of Est. musicians' int. relations. **Add.** Estonia pst. 4, Tallinn 200105; tel. 448 585.

■ **KOGAN, Jevgeni,** Co-leader of the Inter-Movement of the Working People of the Est. SSR; b. 1954; ed. Tallinn Tech. Univ., ship repair tech.; Est. Shipping Co, 1972 — 82; Est. Fish Processing Ind., 1982 — . USSR People's Deputy, 1989 — . **Add.** Tallinn tel. 212 029.

■ **KOKLA, Paul,** linguist; b. 1929; ed. Tartu Univ.; CSc. (Philol.); Inst. of Lg. and Lit., 1960 — ; journal *Linguistica Uralica,* 1965 — ; E-in-C, 1990 — ; research on Mari and Baltic-Finnic lgs. **Add.** Roosikrantsi 6, Tallinn 200106; tel. 440 745.

■ **KOLLIST, Andres,** Gen. Dir, State Immigration Dept, 1990 — ; b. 1948; ed. Tartu Univ.; CSc. (Chem.); Inst. of Chem., 1975 — ; research on biopolymers and red seaweed; Mem., Int. Lectin Soc. **Add.** Vana-Viru 12, Tallinn 200001; tel. 444 473.

■ **KOMISSAROV, Kalju,** producer and actor; b. 1946; ed. Tallinn Conservatoire; Youth Theatre, chief producer, 1974 — 87; Tallinn Conservatoire, 1984 — , Dept Head, 1986 — ; theatre *Ugala*, 1987 — ; has concentrated on pol. themes, had roles in his own prod., produced films. **Add.** Jakobsoni 18, Viljandi 202900; tel. 520 74.

■ **KOOLMEISTER, Indrek,** lawyer; b. 1949; ed. Tartu Univ.; CSc. (Law), Asst Prof.; Est. Acad. of Sci., 1973 — 78 and 1981 — 85, Tartu Univ., 1985 — ; legal councillor, Tartu City Govt, 1990 — ; research in state and admin. law; *Vaba Eesti* Movement. **Add.** Raekoda, Tartu 202400; tel. 331 22.

■ **KOORNA, Arno,** economist; Pres., Est. Acad. of Sci., 1990 — ; b. 1926; ed. Tartu Univ.; DSc. (Econ.), Prof.; Mem., Est. Acad. of Sci.; Tartu Univ., 1953 — 65; Inst. of Econ., 1965 — , Dir, 1966 — 73; Presidium of Est. Acad. of Sci., 1973 — ; research into quality-related econ., state prod. efficiency, and sci. policy. **Add.** Kohtu 6, Tallinn 200100; tel.442 129.

■ **KOPPEL, Andres,** biologist and ecologist; b. 1950; ed. Tartu Univ.; CSc. (Biol.); Tartu Univ., Dept Head, 1983 — 88; Inst. of Zoology and Botany, 1975 — 83, Dir, 1989 — ; research on gen. ecological problems, plant ecology and ecophysiology; Est. Scientists' Assoc. **Add.** Vanemuise 21, Tartu 202400; tel. 328 28.

■ **KÕRB, Kaie,** ballet dancer; b. 1961; ed. Tallinn Choreography Sch.; theatre *Estonia*, 1980 — ; roles: Quiteria, Odette — Ottilie, Giselle; 3rd prize at Moscow Int. Ballet Contest, 1985. **Add.** Estonia pst. 4, Tallinn 200105; tel. 444 709.

■ **KORNELIUS** (civilian name Viacheslav Jakobs), Bishop of Tallinn Orthodox Ch., 1990 — ; b. 1924; ed. Leningrad Religious Seminar; elder priest at Haapsalu Maria Magdalena Ch., 1948 — 51; priest in Vologda, 1951 — 57; pol. prisoner, 1957 — 60; elder priest at Tallinn John the Baptizer Ch., 1960 — 90. **Add.** Pikk 64, Tallinn 200001; tel. 601 747.

■ **KOTKAS, Johannes,** wrestler; b. 1915; Dynamo Sports Club, Tallinn,1961 — ; medals: Olympic gold, Greco-Roman heavyweight, 1952; world champ.: silver, 1953; European champ., 1938, 1939, 1947; USSR champ.: Greco-Roman, gold, 1946, 1948, 1950 — 53, 1955, 1956; free-style, silver, 1947; hammer, silver, 1943. **Add.** Pikk 37, Tallinn 200101; tel. 601 950.

■ **KRISTOFFEL, Nikolai,** physicist; b. 1932; ed. Tartu Univ.; DSc. (Phys. & Math.), Prof.; Inst. of Phys., 1955 — , Dept and Lab. Head, 1976 — ; Tartu Univ., 1976 — ; studies on theory of crystals with impurity centre and ferroelectric phase transition. **Add.** Riia 142, Tartu 202400; tel. 281 64.

■ **KROSS, Jaan,** writer, Ellen Niit's husband; b. 1920; ed. Tartu Univ., lawyer; Hon. Dr, Helsinki and Tartu Univ.; Est. Writers' Union,

1976 — , Dep. Chair. of the Bd, 1981 — ; has written hist. novels and short stories depicting the lives of prominent hist. figures from Estonia; his novel, 'The Emperor's Lunatic', has been transl. into 6 lgs; Amnesty International's lit. award, 1990; pol. prisoner, 1946 — 54. **Add.** (h) Harju 1 — 6, Tallinn 200001; tel. 441 697.

■ **KRUMM, Lembit,** eng. scientist; b. 1928; ed. Tallinn Tech. Univ.; DSc. (Tech.), Prof.; Mem., Est. Acad. of Sci.; USSR Acad. of Sci. Siberian Dept Transportation Energy Inst., Lab. and Dept Head, 1962 — 81; Dept Head, Inst. of Thermal Phys. and Electrophys., 1981 — ; research on large electroenergetic systems. **Add.** Paldiski mnt. 1, Tallinn 200031; tel. 451 568.

■ **KRUUSVALL, Jaan,** writer; b. 1940; ed. Moscow M.Gorky Inst. of Lit.; journal *Looming*, 1981 — 87; has written short stories and miniatures with elaborated form as well as plays depicting the tragedy of the Est. farmers during and after WW II. **Add.** (h) Veimeri 34 — 117, Tallinn 200035.

■ **KUDDO, Arvo,** Min. of Labour, 1990 — ; b. 1954; ed. Moscow Univ., demographer; CSc. (Econ.); Inst. of Econ., 1981 — 90; research on Est. demographic processes and social policies. **Add.** Lomonossovi 29, Tallinn 200001; tel. 423 434.

■ **KULBACH, Valdek,** eng. scientist; b. 1927; ed. Tallinn Tech. Univ.; DSc. (Tech.), Prof.; Mem., Est. Acad. of Sci.; Tallinn Tech. Univ., 1955 — , Dept Head, 1975 — ; research on solid constr. **Add.** Ehitajate tee 5, Tallinn 200026; tel. 537 076.

■ **KÜNNAPU, Vilen,** architect; b. 1948; ed. Tallinn Art Univ.; *EKE Projekt* Inst., 1969 — ; designed private homes, treatment centres, public buildings; part. in La Villette park comp. in Paris, 1982, special award Rovaniemi Artic Centre, 1983; 2nd prize Los Angeles W-Coast Gateway comp., 1988 — 89; part. in shows Finland (9 arch. from Tallinn, 1985), Modern Redux in New York, 1986, Stockholm, 1988; publ. articles on arch. **Add.** (h) Raua 8 — 3, Tallinn 200010; tel. 424 706.

■ **KURREL, Ede,** metal artist; b. 1909; ed. State Arts and Crafts Sch.; Asst Prof.; Tallinn Art Univ., 1946 — 68; a founder of professional Est. jewelry art; first to cultivate filigree technique; silver medal in Paris, 1937, gold medal at Brussels World Exh., 1958. **Add.** Vabaduse väljak 6, Tallinn 200105; tel. 445 014.

■ **KUUSIK, Endel,** Dir, Est. Archives of Hist., 1985 — ; b. 1950; ed. Tartu Univ., hist.; Est. Archives of Hist., 1982 — . **Add.** Liivi 4, Tartu 202400; tel. 324 82.

■ **KUUSK, Ivo,** singer (tenor); b. 1937; ed. Tallinn Conservatoire; Asst Prof.; theatre *Vanemuine*, 1967 — 78; theatre *Estonia*, 1978 — ; Tallinn Conservatoire, 1979 — , Dept Head, 1982 — ; roles: Albert Herring, Alfredo, Faustus; has produced operas. **Add.** Estonia pst. 4, Tallinn 200105; tel. 444 709.

■ **LAANJÄRV, Olev,** Min. of the Interior, 1990 — ; b. 1942; ed. Acad. of the USSR Min. of the Interior, colonel; Min. of the Interior, 1965 — , Head of Dept on organized crime,

1989 — 90. **Add.** Pikk 61, Tallinn 200100; tel. 663 611.

■ **LAAR, Mart,** historian; b. 1960; ed. Tartu Univ.; Co-founder of Est. Heritage Soc., 1987, Mem. of its leadership; compiler of Soviet-period memoirs; Council of Estonia; Est. SC Deputy, 1990 —. **Add.** (h) Pärnu mnt. 195 — 6, Tallinn 200016; tel. 510 854.

■ **LAISK, Agu,** plant physiologist; b. 1938; ed. Tartu Univ., phys. DSc. (Biol.); Inst. of Astrophys. and Atmospheric Phys., 1961 —, Lab. Head, 1985 —; research on radiation regime of vegetation and on photosynthesis of plants. **Add.** Töravere, Tartumaa 202444; tel. 280 21.

■ **LAIUS, Leida,** film dir; b. 1923; ed. Est. Theatre Inst., Moscow Cinematography Inst.; Est. Drama Theatre, 1951 — 55; *Tallinnfilm,* 1960 —; analyzes female psychology; 1st prize at Los Angeles Int. Women's Film-makers Festival, 1989. **Add.** Harju 9, Tallinn 200001; tel. 593 367 (h).

■ **LANGEMETS, Andres,** lit. critic, E-in-C, *Looming* journal, 1988 —; b. 1948; ed. Tartu Univ., philol.; *Keel ja Kirjandus* journal, 1976 — 87; publ. critiques of current Est. fiction and 2 coll. of poetry. **Add.** Harju 9, Tallinn 200090; tel. 443 262.

■ **LAOS, Ants,** Min. of Trade and Commerce, 1989 —; b. 1943; ed. Tallinn Tech. Univ., chem.; Dir, Pärnu Brewery, 1975 — 78; Min. of Food Ind. Est. SSR, 1979 — 86; Dep. Chair., Agric. Ind. Cttee of Est. SSR, 1986 — 89. **Add.** Kiriku 6, Tallinn 200103; tel. 443 941.

■ **LAPIN, Leonhard,** graphic artist and arch.; b. 1947; ed. Tallinn Art Univ.; Restoration Bd, 1971 — 74; created mostly geometric, constructive art and designed private homes. Publ. articles on arch. theory and criticism. **Add.** (h) Graniidi 19 — 3, Tallinn 200004; tel. 601 645.

■ **LASSMANN, Peep,** piano player; b. 1948; ed. Tallinn Conservatoire; Asst Prof.; Tallinn Conservatoire, 1973 —, Dept Head, 1987 —; soloist and ensemble-player. **Add.** Vabaduse pst. 130, Tallinn 200103; tel. 513 779.

■ **LAUL, Venno,** choir conductor; b. 1938; ed. Tallinn Conservatoire; Prof.; Tallinn Conservatoire, 1972 —, Rector 1982 —; founder and chief conductor, Est. Boys' Choir, 1971 —, Chair., Est. Music Soc., 1987 —; gen. conductor of Song Festivals; Mem. of Man. Bd, *Europa Cantat;* Mem. of Man. Bd, Int. Federation of Choral Music; Assoc. of American Choir Conductors. **Add.** Vabaduse pst. 130, Tallinn 200103; tel. 514 510.

■ **LAURISTIN, Marju,** politician and sociologist; b. 1940; ed. Tartu Univ.; CSc. (Philol.), Asst Prof.; Tartu Univ., 1970 —, Dept Head, 1987 — 90; Dep. Speaker, Est. SC, 1990 —; one of founders of EPF and Mem. of its 1st and 3rd Man. Bd; Chair., Est. SDP, 1990 —; Council of Estonia, 1990; USSR People's Deputy and Mem. of USSR Supreme Soviet, 1989 —; research into mass-media and cultural sociology. **Add.** Lossi plats 1a, Tallinn 200100; tel. 606 356.

■ **LEIMANN, Jaak,** Min. of Econ., 1990 —; b. 1941; ed. Tallinn Tech. Univ.; DSc. (Econ.); Research Dir, Consulting Co *Mainor,* 1979 — 87;

Dir, Est. Man. Inst., 1987 — 90; research on management and the training of managers. **Add.** Komsomoli 1, Tallinn 200103; tel. 683 445.

■ **LEISSON, Enn,** journalist; b. 1942; ed. E-Siberian Cultural Inst.; leader of Est. building team at Baikal — Amur railway, 1975 — 86; Est. TV, 1987 — 90; Vice-Pres., Est. Assoc. of Nat. Minorities; EPF; Council of Estonia 1990. Est. SC Deputy, 1990 —. **Add.** Lossi plats 1a, Tallinn 200100; tel. 606 754.

■ **LEITO, Toomas;** journalist; b. 1946; ed. Tartu Univ.; Head of ECP Cent. Cttee Propaganda Dept, 1985 — 87; E-in-C, newspaper *Rahva Hääl,* 1987 —; ECP. **Add.** Pärnu mnt. 67a, Tallinn 200090; tel. 681 202.

■ **LEPNURM, Hugo,** organist and composer; b. 1914; ed. Tallinn Conservatoire; Prof.; Tallinn Conservatoire, 1936 —; Vice-Chair., Soc. of Organists at USSR Music Soc., 1987 —; cantatas, organ concerto, songs for choirs; articles and book on organ playing. **Add.** Vabaduse pst. 130, Tallinn 200103; tel. 514 514.

■ **LEPP, Andres,** model aircraft flier; b. 1943; ed. Tallinn Tech. Univ., mech.; Dir, Tech. Bureau, Est. Assoc. for the Blind, Tartu Factory, 1987 —; world champ. in the glider model class, 1989, European champ., 1990; as mem. of the USSR team at the world champ., gold medal, 1969, 1975, 1981, 1989, silver, 1977, 1981; 2 inv. in model aviation. **Add.** Ringtee 1, Tartu 202400; tel. 745 05.

■ **LEPPIK, Kalju,** Dir, Computer R & D Division *EKTA,* Inst. of Cybernetics, 1976 —; b. 1931; ed. Tallinn Tech. Univ., electrical eng.; Inst. of Cybernetics, 1957 — 76. **Add.** Akadeemia tee 21/1, Tallinn 200026; tel. 536 373.

■ **LEVANDI, Allar,** Nordic skiier; b. 1965; Olympic bronze, 1988, 2nd in the 1990 and 5th in the 1991 World Cup; team bronze for USSR at the 1987 world champ. **Add.** Regati pst. 1, Tallinn 200019; tel. 238 623.

■ **LIIDJA, Georg,** physicist; b. 1933; ed. Tartu Univ.; DSc. (Phys. & Math.), Mem., Est. Acad. of Sci.; Inst. of Phys., 1957 — 82, Dept Head, 1966 — 82; Inst. of Chem. and Biol. Phys., 1982 —, chief research worker, 1986 —; initiated research studies on low temps in Estonia. **Add.** Lenini pst. 10, Tallinn 200105; tel. 605 538.

■ **LILJE, Peeter,** conductor; b. 1950; ed. Tallinn Conservatoire, Leningrad Conservatoire; Est. State Symphony Orch., chief conductor, 1980 — 90; Oulu Symphony Orch., Finland, chief conductor, 1990 —. **Add.** (h) Narva mnt. 38 — 2, Tallinn; tel. 422 622.

■ **LILLE, Ülo,** chemist; b. 1931; ed. Tallinn Tech. Univ.; DSc. (Chem.), Prof.; Mem., Est. Acad. of Sci.; Inst. of Chem., Lab. Head, 1975 —; research into oil-shale oil and synthesis of prostaglandin. **Add.** Akadeemia tee 15, Tallinn 200026; tel. 529 244.

■ **LIND, Hallar,** E-in-C, *Äripäev* newspaper, 1989 —; b. 1950; ed. Tartu Univ., lawyer; Man. Ed., *Noorus* mag., 1977 — 86; newspaper *Rahva Hääl;* Est. Radio. **Add.** Raua 1a, Tallinn 200010; tel. 431 201.

■ **LIND, Vello,** agronomist; b. 1936; ed. Est. Agric. Acad.; CSc. (Agric.); Dir, Ranna collective farm, 1968 — 81; Dep. Chair., Agric. Ind. Cttee, 1983 — 89; Min. of Agric., 1981 — 83, 1990 — 1991; World Poultry Farmers' Assoc.; Research Dir, *Eesti Põllumajandusprojekt* Inst., 1991 — ; Est. Soc. for Nature Conservation. *Add.* Mustamäe tee 51, Tallinn 200006; tel. 604 921.

- **LIPPMAA, Endel,** physicist, chem. and politician; b. 1930; ed. Tallinn Tech. Univ.; DSc. (Phys. & Math.), Prof.; Mem., Est. Acad. of Sci., Hon. Dr, Jyväskyla Univ.; Inst. of Cybernetics, Dept Head, 1961 — 80; Acad. Sec., Est. Acad. of Sci. Division of Phys., Math. and Tech. Sci., 1977 — 82; Dir, Inst. of Chem. and Biol. Phys., 1980 — ; Foreign Min. without portfolio of Rep. of Estonia, 1990 — ; USSR People's Deputy, 1989 — ; research on nuclear magnet resonance and relaxation, high temp. super conductivity and biophys.; Mem., AMPERE, ISMAR, American Phys. Soc. and American Chem. Soc.; Mem. of the ed. bd of several scientific journals.; UK Royal Soc. medal in chem., 1989. *Add.* Lenini pst. 10, Tallinn 200001; tel. 441 304; fax 440 640.

- **LIPPMAA, Toivo,** Gen. Dir, State Dept of Housing and Municipal Services, 1990 — ; b. 1937; ed. Tallinn Tech. Univ., econ.; Min. of Public Housing; Est. Municipal Heating Utilities Prod. Assoc. *Add.* Harju 11, Tallinn 200001; tel. 445 173.

- **LOIK, Rein,** Min. of Education, 1989 — ; b. 1950; ed. Tartu Univ., econ.; Dep. Chair., Tallinn People's Deputies Council Planning Commn, 1980 — 85; Dept Head, Est. SSR Planning Cttee, 1985 — 88. *Add.* Kingissepa 60, Tallinn 200103; tel. 437 760.

- **LOKO, Valdek,** agronomist; b. 1938; ed. Est. Agric. Acad.; CSc. (Econ.); Est. Research Inst. of Agric. and Land Reclamation, 1966 — , Dir, 1990 — ; research on math. methods of ind. econ. and on using computer technol. in agric. *Add.* Saku sjk., Harjumaa 203400; tel. 721 630, 721 383.

- **LOONE, Eero,** philosopher; b. 1935; ed. Moscow Univ.; DSc. (Phil.), Prof.; Tartu Univ., 1966 — , Dept Head, 1986 — ; research on methodology of hist. *Add.* Ülikooli 16, Tartu 202400; tel. 353 65.

- **LOOR, Viljar,** volleyball player; b. 1953; ed. Tallinn Tech. Univ., econ.; Asst Dir, Agro Co., 1987 — ; team gold for USSR at the 1980 Olympics, world champ., 1978, 1982, European champ., 1975, 1977, 1979, 1981, 1983, World Cup winner 1977, 1981. *Add.* Vabaõhukooli tee 68, Tallinn 200020; tel. 238 072.

- **LOTMAN, Yuri,** scholar of lit. and structuralist; b. 1922; ed. Leningrad Univ., DSc. (Philol.), Prof.; Corr. Fellow of British and Norwegian Acad., Mem., Est. Acad. of Sci.; Tartu Univ., 1954 — , Dept Head, 1960 — 76; one of the founders of structural semiotics, research on 18th and 19th cent. Russ. lit., cultural typology and poetry in film; his studies have been transl. into many lgs; Vice-Pres., Int. Assoc. for Semiotic Studies, 1967 — ; Hon. Mem., Semiotic Soc. of America; Mem., Modern Lg. Assoc. of America. *Add.* Ülikooli 18, Tartu 202400; tel. 351 83.

- **LÕUGAS, Vello,** archeologist; b. 1937; ed. Tartu Univ.; CSc. (Hist.); Inst. of Hist., 1961 — ; Est. Heritage Soc.; Chair., Soc. of Est. Regional Studies. *Add.* Rüütli 28, Tallinn 200001; tel. 440 716.

- **LUGUS, Olev,** economist; b. 1935; ed. Tartu Univ.; CSc. (Econ.); *Viisnurk*, 1953 — 62; Inst. of Econ., 1962 — , Dept Head, 1971 — 85, Research Dir, 1985 — 89, Dir, 1989 — ; research on econ. of forest complex, improvement of econ. mechanism. *Add.* Estonia pst. 7, Tallinn 200101; tel. 444 570; fax 442 835.

- **LUIK, Viivi,** writer; b. 1946; has written emotional poetry, focusing on pressures emerging from the conflict of nature and technocratic soc., her novel 'The Seventh Spring of Peace' has been transl. into 3 lgs. *Add.* Writers' Union, Harju 1, Tallinn 200001; tel. 446 832.

- **LUSHCHIK, Cheslav,** physicist; b. 1928; ed. Leningrad Univ.; DSc. (Phys. & Math.), Prof.; Mem., Est. Acad. of Sci.; Inst. of Phys., 1954 — , Lab. Head, 1960 — ; research in phys. of luminescent ionic crystals. *Add.* Riia 142, Tartu 202400; tel. 289 46.

- **MADE, Tiit,** politician and econ.; b. 1940; ed. Tallinn Tech. Univ.; CSc. (Econ.), Asst Prof.; Tallinn Tech. Univ.; 1967 — 74 and 1977 — 79; USSR Embassy in Sweden, 1974 — 77; Est. Inst. of Information, 1979 — 85; Inst. for Teachers' Post-Graduate Training, 1986 — 90; int. affairs analyst, studies on int. econ.; Chair., Est. Entrepreneur Party, 1990 — . USSR People's Deputy (Cttee for External Affairs), 1989 — ; Est. SC Deputy, 1990 — . *Add.* Lossi plats 1a, Tallinn 200100; tel. 606 754.

- **MÄGI, Ester,** composer; b. 1922; ed. Tallinn Conservatoire; Asst Prof.; Tallinn Conservatoire, 1954 — 84; symphonic and chamber music, based on Est. folk tunes. *Add.* Composers' Union, Lauteri 7, Tallinn 200107; tel. 444 103.

- **MÄGI, Paul,** conductor; b. 1953; ed. Tallinn Conservatoire, Moscow Conservatoire; theatre *Estonia*, 1984 — 90; USSR Min. of Culture Symphony Orch., 1985 — 88; chief conductor, Latv. Nat. Symphony Orch., 1990 — ; jazz violinist. *Add.* (h) Sütiste tee 14 — 20, Tallinn 200034; tel. 529 787.

- **MÄLK, Raul,** Press Sec. of the SC of Estonia, 1990 — ; b. 1952; ed. Tartu Univ., econ.; Est. Radio, 1977 — 90. *Add.* Weizenbergi 39, Tallinn 200100; tel. 424 882; telex 173182 EVYNP; fax 436 389.

- **MARAN, Olav,** painter; b. 1933; ed. Tallinn Art Univ.; mag. *Pikker*, 1959 — 65; began with abstract compositions, later his still-lifes contain magical realism. *Add.* (h) Saturni 13 — 3, Tallinn 200001; tel. 453 097.

- **MARAN, Rein,** film dir and cameraman; b. 1931; ed. Moscow Cinematography Inst.; Est. Acad. of Sci., 1958 — 67; *Tallinnfilm* and *Eesti Telefilm*, 1970 — 89; Chair., Est. Film-makers' Union, 1990 — ; created documentary and scientifically accurate nature films; won int. film festival awards. *Add.* Uus 3, Tallinn 200001; tel. 445 337.

- **MARGNA, Udo,** biologist; b. 1934; ed. Tartu Univ.; DSc. (Biol.); Mem., Est. Acad. of Sci.;

Inst. of Experimental Biol., 1959 —, Research Dir, 1966 — 87, chief researcher, 1987 — ; Scientific Sec. Gen., Est. Acad. of Sci., 1990 — ; research into the metabolism of polyphenols. *Add.* Instituudi tee 11, Harku, Harjumaa 203400; tel. 512 490.

▪ **MARK, Heinrich,** Prime Min. (and Acting Pres.) of the Est. Govt in exile, 1990 — ; b. 1911; ed. Tartu Univ., lawyer; Chair., 1945 — 81, Hon. Chair., 1982 —, Est. Council in Sweden; Gen. Sec., Est. Nat. Council, 1951 — 79; Mem., Est. Govt in exile, 1953 — ; Dep. Prime Min., 1971 — 90. *Add.* (h) Gimmerstavägen 20 — 11 S — 125 71 Älvsjö, Sweden; tel. 08 477 924.

▪ **MARK, Mati,** Gen. Dir, State Sports Dept, 1990 — ; b. 1941; ed. Tallinn Teacher Training Inst., teacher of physical ed.; Chair., Est. Sports Cttee, 1984 — 90; Vice-Pres., European Shooting Union. *Add.*Regati pst. 1, Tallinn 200103; tel. 238 059.

▪ **MARTIN, Jüri,** biologist; b. 1940; ed. Tartu Univ.; DSc. (Biol.); Mem., Est. Acad. of Sci.; Tallinn Botanical Gardens, Scientific Sec., 1969 — 75, Research Dir, 1975 — 78, Dir, 1978 — 89, Lab. Head, 1978 — ; research on lichenology, biogeochem., and ecology; Chair., Est. Cttee of the UNESCO 'Man and Biosphere' programme. *Add.* Kloostrimetsa tee 44, Tallinn 200019; tel. 239 001.

▪ **MASSO, Valjo,** agric. scientist; b. 1933; ed. Est. Agric. Acad.; DSc. (Agric.), Prof.; Animal Breeding and Veterinary Sci. Research Inst., 1958 —, Dept Head, 1971 — ; research on admin. of large-scale farming. *Add.* Kreutzwaldi 1, Tartu 202400; tel. 613 08.

▪ **MEEL, Raul,** graphic artist and painter, Mari Saat's husband; b. 1941; ed. Tallinn Tech. Univ.; self-taught artist; combines intuition and constructivism; in graphics prefers serigraphy, in painting acrylics; works are usually part of a series; prize winner Krakow Graphic Arts Biennials, 1971, 1972, Frechen, 1974; exh. in Ljubljana, 1971, 1975, Venice, 1972, Italy, 1973, Hungary, 1977, USA, 1979, 1985; works in Museum of Modern Art in New York, Guggenheim and Georges Pompidou Centre. *Add.* (h) Akadeemia tee 60 — 66, Tallinn 200026; tel. 536 224.

▪ **MERESTE, Uno,** economist; b. 1928; ed. Tallinn Tech. Univ., Tartu Univ., geogr.; DSc. (Econ.), Prof.; Tartu Univ., 1954 — 64; Dept Head, Tallinn Tech. Univ., 1964 — ; publ. about 50 books on methodology of econ. analysis, statistical methods of research, demography and on theoretical and math. geogr. *Add.* Kopli 101, Tallinn 200037; tel. 476 561, 474 053.

▪ **MERI, Lennart,** Foreign Min., 1990 — ; writer; b. 1929; ed. Tartu Univ., hist.; Hon. Dr, Helsinki Univ.; Corr. Fellow of European Acad. of Sci. and Arts; studio *Tallinnfilm*, 1963 — 71, 1976 — 78; has written travel stories, lit. essays and made films depicting the hist. of Finno-Ugric people and nations living by the Baltic Sea; EPF; Council of Estonia. *Add.* Lossi plats 1a, Tallinn 200100; tel. 443 266.

▪ **METS, Margus,** E-in-C, newspaper *Päevaleht*, 1990 — ; b. 1961; ed. Tartu Univ., journal-

ist; newspaper *Rahva Hääl*, 1985 — 89. *Add.* Pärnu mnt. 67a, Tallinn 200090; tel. 681 233.

▪ **MIKELSAAR, Aavo-Valdur,** physician, geneticist; b. 1941; ed. Tartu Univ., Univ. of Vienna Inst. of Histology and Embryology; DSc. (Biol.); Tartu Univ., 1965 — ; Inst. of Gen. and Molecular Pathology, 1979 —, Dir, 1988 — ; research on human, med. and cytogenetics as well as biotechnol. *Add.* Veski 34, Tartu 202400; tel. 323 87, 353 47.

▪ **MIKIVER, Mikk,** producer and actor; b. 1937; ed. Tallinn Conservatoire; Youth Theatre, 1965 — 74; Est. Drama Theatre, 1974 —, chief producer, 1977 — 85; Chair., Est. Theatre Union, 1987 — ; has produced nat. plays, depicting turning points of the Est. hist.; USSR People's Deputy, 1989 — . *Add.* Pärnu mnt. 5, Tallinn 200001; tel. 442 065.

▪ **MIKK, Arne,** producer; b. 1934; ed. Tallinn Conservatoire; theatre *Estonia*, 1952 —, chief producer, 1977 — ; Chair. of the Bd, Estonia Soc., 1990 — ; Sec., USSR Theatre Union; traditional-style prod. *Add.* Estonia pst. 4, Tallinn 200105; tel. 448 585.

▪ **MILLER, Rein,** Min. of Finance, 1990 — ; b. 1938; ed. Tartu Univ., financier; Dept Head, Min. of Finance, 1966 — . *Add.* Kohtu 8, Tallinn 200001; tel. 452 801.

▪ **MITT, Hugo,** designer; b. 1957; ed. Tallinn Art Univ.; Tallinn Art Univ., 1982 — ; *MaDis* Firm, 1985 — ; Chair., Est. Designers' Union, 1990 — ; has designed ind. products and created graphic art works in a free style. *Add.* Tartu mnt. 1, Tallinn 200001; tel.432 639.

▪ **MUDIST, Peeter,** painter; b. 1942; ed. Tallinn Art Univ.; created impulsively naive figure compositions and portraits, granite sculpture; prize winner, Baltic Painting Triennial, 1981. *Add.* Vabaduse väljak 6, Tallinn 200105; tel. 445 014.

▪ **MURDMAA, Mai-Ester,** choreographer; b. 1938; ed. Moscow A.Lunacharsky Theatre Inst.; theatre *Estonia*, 1964 —, chief choreographer, 1974 — ; original and modern choreography; has also produced in New York, Helsinki et al. *Add.* Estonia pst. 4, Tallinn 200105; tel. 444 709.

▪ **MUST, Aadu,** Representative of Est. Information Bureau in Sweden, 1990 — ; b. 1951; ed. Tartu Univ., hist.; CSc. (Hist.), Asst Prof.; Tartu Univ., 1976 — ; research on medieval hist. and archivism. *Add.* Rådmansgatan 18, 11425 Stockholm; tel. 109 981, 109 986.

▪ **MUSTONEN, Andres,** musical dir and violonist; b. 1953; ed. Tallinn Conservatoire; old music ensemble *Hortus Musicus*, founder and conductor, 1972 — ; has performed at int. music festivals, lectured in Finland, Sweden and USA. *Add.* Lühike jalg 9, Tallinn 200001; tel. 440 719.

▪ **MUTT, Mihkel,** writer; b. 1953; ed. Tartu Univ., philol.; lit. review *Looming*, 1977 — 86; written ironical-grotesque prose about current life of the educated. *Add.* (h) Harju 1, Tallinn 200001; tel. 446 832.

▪ **MÜÜR, Märt,** journalist, Chair., Est. Journalists' Union, 1989 — ; b. 1942; agron., film dramatist and dir; ed., Est. TV, 1975 — 89; creator of popular series on Est. TV; creator of documentaries; deported to Siberia 1949 — 57. **Add.** Narva mnt. 30, Tallinn 200010; tel. 449 889, 425 758.

▪ **MÜÜRSEPP, Ilmar,** spec. in veterinary sci.; b. 1931; ed. Est. Agric. Acad.; DSc. (Veterinary); Animal Breeding and Veterinary Sci. Research Inst., 1961 — ; research into methods and implementation of embryo transplants. **Add.** Kreutzwaldi 24b, Tartu 202400; tel. 933 30.

▪ **NIIT, Ellen,** writer, Jaan Kross's wife; b. 1928; ed. Tartu Univ., philol.; has written prose and poetry for children that has been transl. into many different lgs as well as patriotic poetry for adults. **Add.** (h) Harju 1 — 6, Tallinn 200001; tel. 441 697.

▪ **NINNAS, Toivo,** Chief Exec., Est. Shipping Co, 1987 — ; b. 1940; ed. Far-East Higher Nautical Sch.; Gen. Dir, Finn.-Est. Corp. Ltd *Saimaa Lines*, 1980 — 86; USSR People's Deputy, 1989 — . **Add.** Estonia pst. 3/5, Tallinn 200103; tel. 443 802.

▪ **NIRK, Endel,** scholar of lit.; b. 1925; ed. Tartu Univ.; DSc. (Philol.); Inst. of Lg. and Lit., 1953 — 72; Tallinn Teacher Training Inst., 1976 — 81; research on the hist. of early Est. lit. and the development of the Est. novel. **Add.** (h) Seene 28, Tallinn 200016; tel. 511 309.

▪ **NORMET, Ingo,** producer, son of Leo Normet; b. 1946; ed. Moscow A.Lunacharsky Theatre Inst.; theatre *Endla*, 1969 — , chief producer, 1982 — ; uses improvisation in his prod. **Add.** Keskväljak 1, Pärnu 203600; tel. 566 93.

▪ **NORMET, Leo,** composer and music expert; b. 1922; ed. Tallinn Conservatoire; CSc. (Arts), Prof.; Tallinn Conservatoire, 1954 — ; 2 operas, operettas, solo songs; research on non-European music and 20th cent. European music. **Add.** Vabaduse pst. 130, Tallinn 200103; tel. 514 597.

▪ **NUGIS, Ülo,** Speaker, Est. SC, 1990 — ; b. 1944; ed. Byeloruss. Polytech. Inst., eng.; plant *Ehitusdetail*, Dir, 1974 — 80; Dir, Ski Factory, 1980 — 86; Gen. Dir, *Estoplast*, 1986 — 90; Chair., Union of Work Collectives, 1988 — ; Rep. Coalition Party. **Add.** Weizenbergi 39, Tallinn 200010; tel. 426 280.

▪ **NURME, Jüri,** Gen. Dir, State Police Dept, 1990 — ; b. 1952; ed. Tallinn Teacher Training Inst., physical ed. instructor; Ministry of the Interior, 1976 — 90. **Add.** Pikk 19, Tallinn 200001; tel. 663 815.

▪ **OIM, Haldur,** linguist; b. 1942; ed. Tartu Univ.; DSc. (Philol.), Prof.; Tartu Univ., 1969 — ; research on semantic structure and computational linguistics. **Add.** Ülikooli 18, Tartu 202400; tel. 351 24.

▪ **OLESK, Peeter,** Dir, F. R. Kreutzwald Lit. Museum, 1990 — ; b. 1953; ed. Tartu Univ. philol.; publishing house *Eesti Raamat*; Tartu Univ., 1985 — , Tartu City Council; research on Est. lit. and criticism, hist. of textology, scientific policies of Estonia; Corr. Mem., Finn. Lit. Soc. **Add.** Vanemuise 42, Tartu 202400; tel. 300 35.

▪ **OLL, Aadu,** Chair., *Memento* (Est. Union of Illegally Repressed People and their Supporters), 1989 — ; b. 1932; ed. Moscow Poly-

tech. Inst. for Corr. Students, Moscow Inst. for Standardization and Metrology, machine building eng.; Orotukan Machine Building Plant, Magadan district, 1956 — 70; Special Design Bureau of the USSR Machine Building Min., 1977 — 89; Tallinn Pelgulinn Hosp., 1989 — ; pol. prisoner, 1950 — 56. **Add.** Sõle 16, Tallinn 200006; tel. 496 923.

▪ **ÖPIK, Ilmar,** eng. scientist; b. 1917; ed. Tallinn Tech. Univ.; DSc. (Tech.), Prof.; Mem., Est. Acad. of Sci., 1968 — , Vice-Pres., 1977 — 1987; E-in-C, 'Oil Shale' journal, 1984 — ; research in oil-shale energetics and technol. **Add.** Akadeemia tee 15, Tallinn 200108; tel. 537 084.

▪ **OTS, Arvo,** eng. scientist; b. 1931; ed. Tallinn Tech. Univ.; DSc. (Tech.), Prof.; Mem., Est. Acad. of Sci.; Tallinn Tech. Univ., Dept Head, 1968 — ; research on oil shale as a fuel and on the solid fuel burning theory. **Add.** Ehitajate tee 5, Tallinn 200026; tel. 474 095.

▪ **OTSASON, Rein,** Pres., Bank of Estonia, 1989 — ; b. 1931; ed. Tallinn Tech. Univ.; DSc. (Econ.); Inst. of Econ., 1963 — 71, Dir, 1984 — 1988; Chair., Est. SSR State Planning Cttee, 1988 — 89; Dep. Chair., Est. SSR CM, 1989; *Vaba Eesti* Movement; Pres., Est.-Austrian Soc.; 120 scientific publ., mostly on microecon. USSR People's Deputy, 1989 — . **Add.** Lossi plats 1a, Tallinn, 200100; tel. 445 331.

▪ **OUNAPUU, Harri,** Min. of Agric., 1991 — ; b. 1947; ed. Est. Agric. Acad., agron.; Rapla Regional Agro-Ind. Union, 1981 — 89, Chair.; Rapla county elder, 1989 — 91. **Add.** Lai 39/41, Tallinn 200102; tel. 441 166.

▪ **OVIIR, Siiri,** Min. for Social Security, 1990 — ; b. 1947; ed. Tartu Univ., lawyer; High Court, 1975 — 90; Mem. of the Bd, Est. Women's Union. **Add.** Estonia pst. 15, Tallinn 200001; tel. 666 930.

▪ **PÄÄSUKE, Tiit,** painter; b. 1941; ed. Tallinn Art Univ.; Asst Prof.; Tallinn Art Univ., 1971 — ; work contains figurative and abstract expressiveness; personal exh. in Helsinki, 1983, 1989, Oulu, 1983, Trento, 1990; prize winner, Baltic Painting Triennial, 1978. **Add.** Vabaduse väljak 6, Tallinn 200105; tel. 682 850.

▪ **PADRIK, Ain,** architect; b. 1947; ed. Tallinn Art Univ.; *Eesti Projekt* Inst, 1966 — 68; *EKE Projekt*, 1968 — ; designed public buildings, private homes, cottages; part. in La Villette park comp. in Paris, 1982; special award Rovaniemi Artic Centre, 1983; 2nd prize Los Angeles W-Coast Gateway comp., 1988 — 89; part. in shows in Finland, Germany, USA. **Add.** (h) Hospidali 4 — 3, Tallinn 200007; tel. 447 316.

▪ **PÄI, Leo,** internist; b. 1920; ed. Tartu Univ.; DSc. (Med.), Prof.; Tartu Univ., 1957 — , Dept Head, 1957 — 90; research on rheumatic diseases; Mem., European League Against Rheumatism (EULAR) and USSR Acad. of Med.; Mem., the Commn on Rheumatic Problems. **Add.** Puusepa 6, Tartu 202400; tel. 283 01.

▪ **PAJULA, Kuno,** Archbishop of Est. Evangelical Lutheran Ch., 1987 — ; b. 1924; ed. EELC Theol. Inst., Göttingen Univ.; Tallinn Jaani parish, 1957 — 87. **Add.** Kiriku 8, Tallinn 200106; tel. 451 682.

- **PALM, Jüri,** painter and graphic artist; b. 1937; ed. Tallinn Art Univ.; created figurative panel paintings and graphic art for books and prints; influenced by surrealism and pop art; 1st prize, Baltic Painting Triennial, 1987; part. in exh. in Stockholm, Kiel and Philadelphia. **Add.** (h) Härma 15/Võru 16–144, Tallinn 200010; tel. 321 544.

- **PALM, Mati,** singer (bass-baritone); b. 1942; ed. Tallinn Conservatoire, postgraduate studies at La Scala Opera Sch.; theatre *Estonia,* 1967–; roles: Attila, the Dutchman, Boris Godunov; has perf. at the Savonlinna Opera Festival; 2nd prize at the Viñas Int. Comp. in Barcelona, 1972. **Add.** Estonia pst. 4, Tallinn 200105; tel. 444 709.

- **PALM, Viktor,** chemist; b. 1926; ed. Leningrad Univ.; DSc. (Chem.), Prof.; Mem., Est. Acad. of Sci.; Tartu Univ., 1952–, Dept Head, 1960–; research on organic compounds and reactions. USSR People's Deputy, 1989–. **Add.** Jakobi 2, Tartu 202400; tel. 312 52.

- **PAREK, Lagle,** Chairperson, Est. Nat. Indep. Party, 1989–; b. 1941; Est. Arch. Memorials Inst., 1972–83; deported for pol. reasons, 1949–54, pol. prisoner in Novosibirsk, Russia, 1983–87; Council of Estonia. **Add.** Endla 6–4, Tallinn 200001; tel. 452 472.

- **PARK, Andrus,** philosopher; b. 1949; ed. Tartu Univ.; DSc. (Phil.), Prof.; Mem., Est. Acad. of Sci; Tartu Univ., 1973–90; Est. Acad. of Sci, 1982–, Mem. of Presidium, 1987–, Acad. Sec., Humanitarian and Social Sci. Division, 1990–; Fellow, Woodrow Wilson Int. Centre for Scholars, Washington, D.C., 1990–91; research in phil. of hist., sci. policy, pol. sci.; Mem., Ed. Bd of the 'Nationalities Papers'. **Add.** Kohtu 6, Tallinn 200106; tel. 449 370.

- **PARMASTO, Erast,** expert in mycology; b. 1928; ed. Tartu Univ.; DSc. (Biol.), Prof.; Mem., Est. Acad. of Sci.; Inst. of Zoology and Botany, 1955–, Dept Head, 1973–, Dir, 1985–90; Acad. Sec., Est. Acad. of Sci. Geology and Chem. Division, 1973–81; Vice-Pres.,Int. Mycology Assoc., 1978–; research on the phylogenesis, systematics and ecology of higher basidiomycetes. **Add.** Vanemuise 21, Tartu 202400; tel. 732 72.

- **PÄRN, Priit,** film dir, artist, cartoonist; b. 1946; ed. Tartu Univ., biol.; Tallinn Botanical Gardens, 1970–76; *Tallinnfilm,* 1976–; created witty, satirical, paradoxical animated films redolent of cartoons; won many int. film festival awards. **Add.** Harju 9, Tallinn 200001; tel. 449 477.

- **PÄRNITS, Ülo,** Pres., Consultancy *Mainor,* 1979–; b. 1936; ed. Tallinn Tech. Univ., chem.; Tartu Univ., psychologist; CSc. (Econ.); Maardu Chem. Factory, 1963–70; Development and Consulting Centre, Dept Head, 1971–79; research on human resources in ind., Chair. of the Bd, Tarmel Ltd and Walko Ltd; Vice-Pres., Est.-Swedish Assoc. of Econ. **Add.** Kuhlbarsi 1, Tallinn 200104; tel. 425 294; fax 433 122.

- **PÄRT, Anu,** Representative of Est. Chamber of Commerce and Ind. in Denmark, 1991–; b. 1963; ed. Leningrad Univ., philol.; Est. Chamber of Commerce and Ind., 1987–. **Add.** Toom-Kooli 17, Tallinn 200106; tel. 444 661.

- **PÄRT, Arvo,** composer; b. 1935; ed. Tallinn Conservatoire, Hon. Dr; emigrated in 1980; has composed music with ethical foundation, initially in twelve-tone technique, later in aleatoric style, beginning from mid-1970s started to compose music in minimalism, the so-called tintinnabul-style; recordings of his works have won int. prizes. **Add.** Universal Edition AG, Karlsplatz 6, A–1015 Vienna; tel. 658 695.

- **PEEGEL, Juhan,** philologist and writer; b. 1919; ed. Tartu Univ.; DSc. (Philol.), Prof.; Mem., Est. Acad. of Sci.; Tartu Univ., 1953–, Dept Head, 1979–86; research on hist. of Est. journalism and the poetic lg. of folk songs; has written home inspired prose and a novel depicting Estonians in WW II. **Add.** Ülikooli 18, Tartu 202400; tel. 351 18.

- **PETERSON, Aleksei,** ethnographer; b. 1931; ed. Tartu Univ.; Dir, Est. Nat. Museum, 1958–; studies on Est. and other Finno-Ugric nations' hist. of constr. and agric. implements; Mem., Finn. Heritage Soc. **Add.** Veski 32, Tartu 202400; tel. 322 54.

- **PETERSON, Karl,** microbiologist and epistolarian; b. 1927; ed.Tartu Univ.; DSc. (Veterinary), Prof.; Est. Agric. Acad., 1951–; research on salmonella in fowl and cattle diseases. **Add.** Leningradi mnt. 84, Tartu 202400; tel. 338 88.

- **PIIRIMÄE, Helmut,** historian; b. 1930; ed. Tartu Univ.; DSc. (Hist.), Prof., Hon. Dr, Uppsala Univ.; Tartu Univ., 1956–; research on 17th cent. econ. hist. and Tartu Univ. hist. **Add.**Tartu Univ. Hist. Museum, Toomemägi, Tartu 202400; tel. 391 71.

- **PILLAK, Peep,** Gen. Dir, State Dept of Archives, 1991–; b. 1957; ed. Tartu Univ., hist.; Dept of Archives, 1983–; articles on hist. and archives. **Add.** Maneeži 4, Tallinn 200102; tel. 424 928; fax 432 295.

- **PILV, Mehis,** Gen. Dir, State Dept of Foreign Econ. Relations, 1990–; b. 1947; ed. Tallinn Tech. Univ., electrical eng.; CSc.(Tech.); Est. SSR CM, 1974–85; USSR Cultural and Scientific Centre in Helsinki, 1985–89. **Add.** Komsomoli 1, Tallinn 200001; tel. 683 559.

- **PÕDER, Rein,** Commander, Major-Gen., Military Commissariat for Est. SSR, 1987–; b. 1942; ed. Leningrad Higher Armed Forces War Sch., Frunze Acad.; platoon commander, 1976–78, divisional commander, 1981–84, head, Soviet army's war educ. dept, 1984–86, dep. corps commander, 1986–87; CPSU. **Add.** Narva mnt. 8, Tallinn 200100; tel. 445 367, 425 707.

- **PÕLDROOS, Enn,** painter; b. 1933; ed. Tallinn Art Univ.; Asst Prof.; Tallinn Teacher Training Inst., 1961–66; Est. Artists' Union, Exec. Sec., 1967–71, 1982–89, Chair., 1985–89; Tallinn Art Univ., 1973–86; figurative works, rich in contrasts; awarded at the Baltic Painting Triennial, 1969, 1st prize, 1975; Mem. of the Bd, EPF; Est. SC Deputy, 1990–. **Add.** (h) Ranniku tee 29–9, Tallinn 200021; tel. 232 009.

■ **PÕLLU, Kaljo,** graphic artist, b. 1934; ed. Tallinn Art Univ.; Prof.; Tartu Univ., art programme dir, 1962 — 75, Tallinn Art Univ., 1975 — ; created prints, exlibrises, book ill.; uses archaic mythical, folklore motifs; in 1978 began expeditions to Finno-Ugric and Samoyed areas, copied 4 — 5,000 yr old cave drawings in Karelia; personal exh. in Norway and Finland, 1984, Hungary, 1985, Sweden, 1985 — 88; part. in the XIV Ex-libris Congress Exh. in Denmark, Ljubljana X and Krakow VI Graphic Arts Biennials, Katowice Intergrafia '76. **Add.** Vabaduse väljak 6, Tallinn 200105; tel. 445 054.

■ **PORMEISTER, Valve,** architect; b. 1922; ed. Tallinn Art Univ.; *Eesti Maaehitusprojekt* Inst., 1952 — ; designed buildings which compliment their natural surroundings. **Add.** (h) Lootuse pst. 22, Tallinn 200012; tel. 511 523.

■ **PORT, Mart,** architect; b. 1922; ed. Tallinn Tech. Univ.; Prof.; chief arch., *Eesti Projekt* Inst., 1961 — 65, Tallinn Art Univ., 1965 — ; worked on city planning, designed city building complexes, apartment buildings, public buildings. **Add.** Lai 29, Tallinn 200110; tel. 442 337.

■ **PUNNING, Mati,** glaciologist; b. 1940; ed. Tartu Univ.; DSc. (Geogr.), Prof.; Inst. of Geol., 1970 — 87; Dep. Dir, Inst. of Thermal Phys. and Electrophys., 1987 — 90; Dir, Inst. of Ecology and Marine Research, 1990 — ; research, incl. 5 monographs on Quaternary era geocronology, paleogeography, climatology, glaciology and ecology of E-European plains, Spitzbergen and the Arctic Ocean islands; Pres., Est. Soc. for Geogr.; Int. Union of Geophys. **Add.** Paldiski mnt. 1, Tallinn 200031; tel. 453 416.

■ **PUUSTAK, Kaisa,** graphic artist; b. 1945; ed. Tallinn Art Univ.; Tallinn Art Univ., 1975 — 80; created classically exact still-lifes; 1st prize at Baltic Graphic Arts Triennial, 1983. **Add.** (h) Nõmme tee 48 — 10, Tallinn 200034; tel. 552 846.

■ **RÄÄK, Vello,** Gen. Dir, State Dept of Employment, 1990 — ; b. 1953; ed. Tallinn Tech. Univ.; CSc. (Econ.); Design and Technol. Inst. for Service Min., 1987 — 90. **Add.** Lomonossovi 29, Tallinn 200104; tel. 422 945.

■ **RAAM, Villem,** art and arch. hist.; b. 1910; ed. Tartu Univ.; Hon. Dr, Turku Univ.; Dir., Est. Museum of Art, 1940 — 41; Est. Arch. Memorials Inst., 1956 — 82; pol. prisoner, 1941 — 56; has studied and popularized medieval arch. of Estonia; Mem., Finn. Heritage Soc.; lectures and reports in Finland, Sweden, Hungary, Poland, Canada, USA, France, Denmark, Austria, Germany. **Add.** Vanemuise 75 — 5, Tallinn 200009; tel. 516 093.

■ **RAAMAT, Rein,** film dir and artist; b. 1931; ed. Tallinn Art Univ.; *Tallinnfilm*, 1957 — 89; *Stuudio B*, 1989 — ; animated films reflect a masterful use of figurative art; won numerous awards at int. film festivals. **Add.** Sakala 3, Tallinn 200001; tel. 691 529.

■ **RÄÄTS, Jaan,** composer; Chair., Est. Composers' Union, 1974 — ; b. 1932; ed. Tallinn Conservatoire; Prof.; Tallinn Conservatoire, 1968 — 70, 1974 — ; has composed instrumental music (8 symphonies, 6 string quartets, 9 piano sonatas). **Add.** Composers' Union, Lauteri 7, Tallinn 200107; tel. 444 103.

■ **RAIDLA, Jüri,** Min. of Justice, 1990 — ; b. 1957; ed. Tartu Univ., lawyer; CSc. (Law); Dep. Chair., Halinga collective farm, 1982 — 87; Pärnu District Cttee, 1987 — 89; Chair., Pärnu County Council, 1989 — 90. **Add.** Pärnu mnt. 7, Tallinn 200104; tel. 445 120.

■ **RAIE, Rein,** traumatologist and orthopaedist; b. 1941; ed. Tartu Univ.; DSc. (Med.), Prof.; Leningrad Turner Inst. for Children's Orthopaedics, 1972 — 86; Dir, Seppo Lab. and Clinic for Metallosteosynthesis Research, 1986 — ; research, incl. 2 monographs on spine pathology and arm surgery. **Add.** Tönismägi 5a, Tallinn 200001; tel. 682 798.

■ **RAIG, Ivar,** economist, Chair., Est. Rural Centre Party, 1990 — ; b. 1953; ed. Est. Agric. Acad.; CSc. (Econ.); Inst. of Econ., 1977 — ; EPF; Council of Estonia; Chair., Est. Rural Centre Party, 1990 — ; research on agric. and econ. policies. USSR People's Deputy, 1989 — ; Est. SC Deputy, 1990 — . **Add.** Estonia pst. 7, Tallinn 200101; tel. 605 173.

■ **RAITVIIR, Ain,** biologist; b. 1938; ed. Tartu Univ.; DSc. (Biol.); Inst. of Zoology and Botany, 1961 — 90; E-in-C, *Eesti Loodus* review, 1990 — ; Chair., Est. Scientists' Union; research on mycology and theoretical biol. **Add.** Veski 4, Tartu 202400; tel. 323 68.

■ **RANDALU, Kalle,** pianist; b. 1956; ed. Tallinn Conservatoire; Tallinn Conservatoire, 1984 — 88; Berlin Acad. of Arts, 1990 — ; 1st prize at Int. Comp. of Pianists in Munich, 1985; 4th prize at the Tchaikovsky Comp. in Moscow, 1982; 3rd prize at the Schumann Comp. in Zwickau, 1981.

■ **RANNAP, Jaan,** writer; b. 1931; ed. Tallinn Teacher Training Inst., math.; mag. *Põhjanael*, 1955 — ; has written prose for children, mostly humorous adventure stories. **Add.** (h) Ädala 5 — 12, Tallinn 200006; tel. 492 226.

■ **RANNUT, Mart,** Gen. Dir, State Dept of Lg., 1990 — ; b. 1959; ed. Leningrad Univ., philol.; Inst. of Lg. and Lit., 1982 — 90; works on lg. policy, phonology and phonetics. **Add.** Roosikrantsi 6, Tallinn 200106; tel. 446 906, 441 800.

■ **RÄTSEP, Huno,** linguist; b. 1927; ed. Tartu Univ.; DSc. (Philol.), Prof.; Mem., Est. Acad. of Sci.; Tartu Univ., 1954 — , Dept Head, 1975 — ; research on Est. syntax and etymology. **Add.** Ülikooli 18, Tartu 202400; tel. 321 24.

■ **RAUD, Eno,** writer; b. 1928; ed. Tartu Univ., philol.; has written children's books for different age groups, many of which have been transl. into other lgs. **Add.** (h) Harju 1 — 28, Tallinn 200001; tel. 449 263.

■ **RAUD, Irina,** Chief Arch. of Tallinn, 1990 — ; b. 1945; Tallinn Art Univ.; *Eesti Projekt* Inst., 1969 — 90, Tallinn's Dep. Mayor, 1990 — ; USSR People's Deputy, 1989 — ; primarily designed detailed plans for cities and neighbourhoods. **Add.** Vabaduse väljak 7, Tallinn 200100; tel. 443 165.

■ **RAUD, Rein,** writer; Chair. of the Bd, Est. Inst. of Humanities, 1989 — ; b. 1961; ed.

Leningrad Univ., philol.; produced lyric poetry; transl. from Jap., Chinese and other lgs. *Add.* POB 3320, Tallinn 200001.

▪ **RAUKAS, Anto,** geologist; b. 1935; ed. Tartu Univ.; DSc. (Geol.), Prof.; Mem., Est. Acad. of Sci.; Dept Head, Inst. of Geol., 1965 — ; Chair., *Teadus* (Science), 1991 — ; Soc. research on Est. and neighbouring area quaternary geol. *Add.* Estonia pst. 7, Tallinn 200101; tel. 605 182.

▪ **REBANE, Ilmar,** lawyer; b. 1912; ed. Tartu Univ.; DSc. (Law), Prof.; Tartu Univ., 1945 — 50, 1954 — ; research on gen. and theoretical problems of penal law; Chair., Est. Academic Soc. of Law, 1988 — . *Add.* Ülikooli 18, Tartu 202400; tel. 321 54.

▪ **REBANE, Karl,** physicist; b. 1926; ed. Leningrad Univ.; DSc. (Phys. & Math.), Prof.; Mem., Est. Acad. of Sci.; Mem., USSR Acad. of Sci.; Inst. of Phys., 1956 — , Dir, 1973 — 76, Dept Head, 1977 — ; Est. Acad. of Sci., Vice-Pres., 1968 — 73, Pres., 1973 — 90; research on the phys. of solid substance and the theory of spectrums. *Add.* Riia mnt. 142, Tartu 202400; tel. 310 73.

▪ **REIN, Toomas,** architect; b. 1940; ed. Tallinn Art Univ.; Asst Prof.; *Eesti Maaehitusprojekt* Inst., 1960 — 67; Tallinn Art Univ., 1970 — ; arch. firm *Toomas Rein & Toomas Kivi*, 1988 — ; designed public buildings, apartment buildings, resorts, private homes; silver medal, Sofia Interarch '87; part. at exh. in Finland (9 arch. from Tallinn, 1984), France, Bulgaria, Belgium, Poland, Italy. *Add.* Lai 29, Tallinn 200110; tel. 446 119.

▪ **REINTAM, Loit,** soil scientist; b. 1929; ed. Est. Agric. Acad.; DSc. (Biol.), Prof.; Mem., Est. Acad. of Sci.; Est. Agric. Acad.,1954 — , Dept Head, 1965 — ; research on Est., Far-E and E-Siberian soil. *Add.* Viljandi mnt., Eerika, Tartu 202400; tel. 284 28.

▪ **REMMEL, Mart,** linguist, b. 1944; ed. Tartu Univ.; CSc. (Philol.); Inst. of Lg. and Lit., 1969 — ; research on computer linguistics and acoustics. *Add.* Roosikrantsi 6, Tallinn 200106; tel. 449 282.

▪ **RIIMAA, Jüri,** Gen. Dir, State Road Admin., 1990 — ; b. 1942; ed. Tallinn Tech. Univ., highway eng.; Gen. Dir, Corp. Est. Highways, 1988 — 90. *Add.* Pärnu mnt. 24, Tallinn 200001; tel.445 829.

▪ **RISTKOK, Andrus,** Chair., Est. SC Admin. Reform Cttee, 1990 — ; b. 1949; ed. Tartu Univ., geogr.; CSc. (Econ.); Inst. of Econ., 1973 — 87; Head, Pirgu Development Centre, 1988 — . *Add.* Weizenbergi 39, Tallinn 200100; tel. 606 486.

▪ **ROSS, Juhan,** physicist; b. 1925; ed. Tartu Univ.; DSc. (Phys. & Math.), Prof.; Dept Head, Inst. of Astrophys. and Atmospheric Phys., 1958 — ; research on plant cover radiation regimes math. photosynthesis models. *Add.* Tõravere, Tartumaa 202444; tel. 102 78.

▪ **RUMESSEN, Vardo,** music expert and piano player; b. 1942; ed. Tallinn Conservatoire; Tallinn Conservatoire, 1975 — ; firm *Eesti Kontsert*, 1990 — ; research on Est. music, presentations at scientific conferences in Stockholm, Washington, etc.; Council of Estonia; Est. Nat.

Indep. Party. *Add.* Estonia pst. 4, Tallinn 200105; tel. 440 603.

▪ **RUMMO, Paul-Eerik,** writer; b. 1942; ed. Tartu Univ., philol.; consultant to the Govt of Rep. of Estonia, 1989 — ; Chair., Est. Liberal Dem. Party, 1990 — ; Council of Estonia; has written poetry uniting Est. classical poetic traditions with modern system of symbols. *Add.* Writers' Union, Harju 1, Tallinn 200001; tel. 446 832.

▪ **RUNNEL, Hando,** writer; b. 1938; has written poetry in simple verse based on folk songs containing moral and pol. satire as well as children's books; Council of Estonia. *Add.* (h) Uus 63 — 53, Tartu 202400; tel. 362 27.

▪ **RÜÜTEL, Arnold,** Chair., Rep. of Estonia SC, 1983 — ; b. 1928; ed. Est. Agric. Acad., DSc. (Agric.); Rector, Est. Agric. Acad., 1969 — 77; Est. SSR Supreme Soviet Presidium, 1969 — 79; 1st Dep. Chair., Est. SSR CM, 1979 — 83; USSR Supreme Soviet Deputy, 1984 — 89; Dep. Chair., USSR Supreme Soviet Presidium, 1983 — 89; Council of the Baltic States, 1990 — ; studies on technol. and econ. of dairy farming. USSR People's Deputy, 1989 — . *Add.* Weizenbergi 39, Tallinn 200100; tel. 426 389.

▪ **RÜÜTEL, Ingrid,** music and folklore expert, Arnold Rüütel's wife; b. 1935; ed. Tartu Univ.; CSc. (Philol.); Inst. of Lg. and Lit., Dept Head, 1987 — ; Foreign Mem., Finn. Kalevala Soc. and Soc. for Finn. Lit.; research on Est. folk music; one of the organisers of *Baltica* folklore festivals. *Add.* Roosikrantsi 6, Tallinn 200106; tel. 441 528.

▪ **SAAR, Karl,** Dir, Est. Acad. of Sci. Special Constr. Bureau, 1990 — ; b. 1945; ed. Tallinn Tech. Univ., power eng.; CSc. (Tech.); Tallinn Tech. Univ., 1969 — 81, Special Constr. Bureau, 1981 — . *Add.* Akadeemia tee 19, Tallinn 200108; tel. 538 150.

▪ **SAARI, Henn,** linguist; b. 1924; ed. Tartu Univ.; CSc. (Philol.); Inst. of Lg. and Lit., 1975 — ; Chair., Mother Tongue Soc., 1990 — ; worked on the regulation of lg. in theory and practice. *Add.* Roosikrantsi 6, Tallinn 200106; tel. 446 153.

▪ **SAARI, Peeter,** physicist; b. 1945; ed. Tartu Univ.; DSc. (Phys. & Math.); Mem., Est. Acad. of Sci.; Inst. of Phys., 1968 — , Lab. Head, 1976 — 81, Dir, 1981 — 88; Chair., Est. Sci. Foundation, 1990 — ; research on laser spectroscopy of crystals, holography and nonlinear optics; one of the discoverers of heat luminescence. *Add.* Riia 142, Tartu 202400; tel. 281 75.

▪ **SAARMA, Jüri,** psychiatrist; b. 1921; ed. Tartu Univ.; DSc. (Med.), Prof.; Tartu Univ., 1945 — ; research on clinical psychiatry, psychopathology and psychopharmacology; Corr. Mem., USSR Acad. of Med.; Mem., Int. Soc. of Higher Nervous Activity, Psychiatric Foundation of Finland, Psychiatric Soc. of Finland, Royal Soc. of Psychiatrists of Belgium, Soc. of Psychopharmacology of Turkey, Canadian Soc. of Psychiatrists. *Add.* Raja 31, Tartu 202400; tel. 288 67.

▪ **SAARMA, Mart,** molecular biol.; b. 1949; ed. Tartu Univ.; DSc. (Biol.), Prof.; Mem., Est.

Acad. of Sci.; Tartu Univ., 1971 — 77; Inst. of Phys., 1977 — 80; Lab. Head, Inst. of Chem. and Biol. Phys., 1980 — ; Dir, Helsinki Univ. Inst. of Biotechnol., 1990 — ; research on molecular mechanisms of nerve cell differentiation, structure of plant viruses and molecular mechanisms of plant virus resistance; Mem. of the ed. bd of several journals. *Add.* Akadeemia tee 23, Tallinn 200026; tel. 529 562; fax 529 579; Karvaamokuja 3, 00380 Helsinki, Finland; tel. 4346 041; fax 4346 046.

▪ **SAAT, Mari,** writer, Raul Meel's wife; b. 1947; ed. Tallinn Tech. Univ.; CSc. (Econ.); Inst. of Econ., 1970 — ; has written prose depicting the psychological and moral problems of modern urban dwellers. *Add.* (h) Akadeemia tee 60 — 66, Tallinn 200026; tel. 536 224.

▪ **SALUMÄE, Erika,** cyclist; b. 1962; ed. Smolensk Teacher Training Inst.; medals: Olympic gold, sprint, 1988; world champ.: gold, 1987, 1988; silver, 1984, 1986; many world records. *Add.* Rummu tee 3, Tallinn 200019.

▪ **SALUPERE, Vello,** internist; b. 1935; ed. Tartu Univ.; DSc. (Med.), Prof.; Tartu Univ., 1963 — , Dept Head, 1977 — ; research on gastroenterology. *Add.* Puusepa 6, Tartu 202400; tel. 284 97.

▪ **SALURI, Rein,** writer; b. 1939; ed. Tartu Univ., biol.; journal *Looming,* 1977 — 82; has written psychological and hist. short stories and plays. *Add.* (h) Harju 1 — 4, Tallinn 200001; tel. 446 179.

▪ **SAPAR, Arved-Ervin,** astrophysicist; b. 1933; ed. Tartu Univ.; DSc. (Phys. & Math.); Mem., Est. Acad. of Sci.; Dept Head, Inst. of Astrophys. and Atmospheric Phys., 1968 — ; research on cosmology, the atmosphere of stars theory and radiation transmission theory. *Add.* Tõravere, Tartumaa 202444; tel. 104 65.

▪ **SAVELI, Olev,** agric. scientist; b. 1938; ed. Est. Agric. Acad., livestock expert; DSc. (Agric.), Prof.; Dep. Chair., Agric. Ind. Cttee, 1986 — 88; Rector, Est. Agric. Acad., 1988 — ; Est. Rural Union; Pres., Academic Agric. Soc.; research in cattle breeding. *Add.* Riia 12, Tartu 202400; tel. 318 00.

▪ **SAVISAAR, Edgar,** Chair., Rep. of Estonia Govt, 1990 — ; b. 1950; ed. Tartu Univ., hist.; CSc. (Phil.), Asst Prof.; Chair., Est. SSR State Planning Cttee; Dep. Chair., Est. SSR CM, 1989 — 90; founder and leader of EPF; Mem., Baltic Council, 1989 — ; publ. works on global problems, policies for youth and public affairs. USSR People's Deputy, 1989 — ; Est. SC Deputy, 1990 — . *Add.* Lossi plats 1a, Tallinn 200100; tel. 445 051.

▪ **SEILENTHAL, Tõnu,** linguist; b. 1947; ed. Tartu Univ.; CSc. (Philol.), Asst Prof.; Tartu Univ., 1976 — ; lector of Est. at Helsinki Univ., 1978 — 81, Jyväskyla Univ., 1985 — 89; Dir, Inst. of Lg. and Lit., 1989 — ; research on the morphology of Finno-Ugric lgs, esp. Handi; has written books about Estonia and the Est. lg.; Mem. of several Hung. and Finn. research centres; Hon. Mem. of the Kalevala Soc.; Helsinki Univ. Order of Merit. *Add.* Roosikrantsi 6, Tallinn 200106; tel. 443 472.

▪ **SERGEYEV, Sergei,** E-in-C, newspaper *Molodezh Estonii,* 1989 — ; b.1953; ed. Moscow Polygraphy Inst.; newspaper *Molodezh Estonii,* 1979 — . *Add.* Pärnu mnt. 67a, Tallinn 200090; tel. 691 212.

▪ **SIIMANN, Mart,** Man. Dir, Est. TV, 1990 — ; b. 1946; ed. Tartu Univ.; philol. and psychology; Tartu Univ., 1975 — 82; Est. TV, 1982 — 87; Est. Radio, 1987 — 89; Mem., Intervision Bureau; Mem., OIRT Admin. Council. *Add.* Faehlmanni 12, Tallinn 200100; tel. 434 102.

▪ **SIKKAL, Aleksander,** Min. for Supply, 1990 — ; b. 1952; ed.Tallinn Tech. Univ., econ. *Add.* Kiriku 2/4, Tallinn 200100; tel. 421 597.

▪ **SILLA, Raiot,** hygienist; b. 1928; ed. Tartu Univ.; DSc. (Med.), Prof.; Research Dir, Inst. of Preventive Med., 1957 — ; research on the relationship between youth health, environment and living conditions; Chair., Est. Soc. of Hygienists. *Add.* Inst. of Preventive Med., Paldiski mnt. 52, korpus 6a, Tallinn 200109; tel. 493 184.

▪ **SILLAR, Rein,** Chair., State Security Cttee (KGB), 1990 — ; Major-Gen.; b. 1948; ed. Tartu Univ., lawyer; State Security Cttee, 1971 — ; ECP. *Add.* Pikk 57, Tallinn 200001; tel. 443 400.

▪ **SILLARI, Enn-Arno,** 1st Sec., Cent. Cttee of ECP, 1989 — ; b. 1944; ed. Kaunas Polytech. Inst., eng. of textile ind.; textile factory *Keila,* 1968 — 74; Exec., Cent. Cttee of ECP, 1974 — 81; Instructor CPSU Cent. Cttee, Moscow, 1981 — 1984; 1st Sec., Tartu City Cttee of ECP, 1984 — 86; 1st Sec., Tallinn City Cttee of ECP, 1986 — 89; Mem., Supreme Soviet of Est. SSR, 1985 — 90; Mem., CPSU Cent. Cttee, Mem., Politbureau CPSU Cent. Cttee, 1990 — . *Add.* Lenini pst. 9, Tallinn 200100; tel. 445 118; fax 448 554.

▪ **SILLASTU, Heinart,** pulmonologist; b. 1929; ed. Tartu Univ.; DSc. (Med.), Prof.; Tartu Univ., 1954 — ; councillor in the Council of the European Region of the Int. Union Against Tuberculosis and Lung Diseases, 1982 — ; research on tuberculosis and chronic bronchial obstruction; Hon. Mem., Finnish Assoc. of Lung Doctors, Hungarian Med. Assoc. for Tuberculosis and Lung Diseases, Med. Assoc. of Argentina; Foreign Mem., Finnish Anti-Tuberculosis Assoc. *Add.* Ülikooli 18, Tartu 202400; tel. 342 85 (h).

▪ **SIMM, Helle,** hydrobiologist, and chem.; b. 1920; ed. Tartu Univ.; DSc. (Biol.), Prof.; Mem., Est. Acad. of Sci.; Inst. of Zoology and Botany, 1950 — , Lab. Head, 1960 — 72; research on bio-chem. of med. plant and the formation of the chem. composition of Est. surface water. *Add.* Vanemuise 21, Tartu 202400; tel. 348 07.

▪ **SIMM, Peeter,** film dir; b. 1953; ed. Moscow Cinematography Inst.; *Tallinnfilm,* 1976 — ; created retrospective films on recent Est. past. *Add.* Harju 9, Tallinn 200001; tel. 449 994.

▪ **SINK, Kuldar,** composer; b. 1942; ed. Leningrad Conservatoire; oriental influence apparent in his works, 2 ballets, 2 chamber symphonies, chamber music; works played at int. music festivals. *Add.* Composers' Union, Lauteri 7, Tallinn 200107; tel. 444 103.

■ **SOANS, Jaak,** sculptor; b. 1943; ed. Tallinn Art Univ.; Tallinn Youth Centre, 1965 – 74; Tallinn Art Univ., 1968 – ; created monumental and yarn sculptures (using ready made objects in the latter); made the A.H.Tammsaare (1978) monument in Tallinn; part. in int. congress in sculpture in Toronto, 1978. *Add.* (h) Imanta 39 – 41, Tallinn 200001; tel. 432 195.

■ **SOKK, Tiit,** basketball player; b. 1964; *Kalev* Sports Club team, 1981 – ; team gold for USSR at the Olympics, 1988, silver at the world champ., 1986, bronze at the European champ., 1990. *Add.* Regati pst. 1, Tallinn 200019; tel. 237 026.

■ **SOOKRUUS, Peeter,** Gen. Dir, Est. Radio, 1990 – ; b. 1950; ed. Tartu Univ., hist.; Est. Radio, 1978 – 82, Head of journalism dept, ECP Cent. Cttee, 1984 – 89. *Add.* Lomonossovi 21, Tallinn 200100; tel. 427 128.

■ **SOOSAAR, Mark,** film dir and cameraman; b. 1946; ed. Moscow Cinematography Inst.; *Eesti Telefilm,* 1970 – 78; *Tallinnfilm,* 1979 – ; created unique dramatized documentary films in colour; 1974 Grand Prix Intervision VII for 'People and the Sea'; *Add.* Harju 9, Tallinn 200001, tel. 445 029.

■ **SÖÖT, Andres,** film dir and cameraman; b. 1934; ed. Moscow Cinematography Inst.; *Tallinnfilm,* 1954 – 57, 1963 – 72, 1980 – ; *Eesti Telefilm,* 1972 – 80; through masterful editing created excellent portraits and unique documentary films which lean toward being chronicles of their time. *Add.* Harju 9, Tallinn 200001; tel. 445 029.

■ **SÖÖT-HAINSALU, Lehte,** Chair., Est. SC Labour Cttee, 1990 – ; b. 1938; ed. Tartu Univ.; writer; Sec., Est. Writers' Union Tartu Dept; publ. essays and articles on social themes, coll. of poems, prose and children's books; Est. Women's Union. *Add.* Lossi plats 1a, Tallinn 200100; tel. 606 388.

■ **SOVETNIKOV, Sergei,** Chair., Est. SC Ethnic Relations Cttee, 1990 – ; b. 1931; ed. Tartu Univ.; Dir, Narva Polytech. College, 1964 – 90; CPSU. *Add.* Lossi plats 1a, Tallinn 200100; tel. 606 797.

■ **STOLOVICH, Leonid,** philosopher; b.1929; ed. Leningrad Univ.; DSc. (Phil.), Prof.; Tartu Univ., 1953 – ; publ. studies on the hist. and theory of esthetics and esthetics in educ. *Add.* Ülikooli 16, Tartu 202400; tel. 313 14.

■ **SULLING, Toomas-Andres,** cardiac surgeon; b. 1940; ed. Tartu Univ., Helsinki Univ.; DSc. (Med.), Prof.; Tartu Univ., 1969 – ; Dir, Est. Heart Centre; research on coronary surgery; Mem., Int. Soc. for Cardiovascular Surgery and European Assoc. for Cardio-Thoracic Surgery. *Add.* Sütiste tee 19, Tallinn 200106; tel. 525 702; fax 525 908.

■ **SUMERA, Lepo,** Min. of Culture, 1989 – ; composer; b. 1950; ed. Tallinn Conservatoire, Asst Prof.; Tallinn Conservatoire, 1978 – ; has composed ballets, symphonies and film scores; Est. Liberal Dem. Party. *Add.* Suur-Karja 23, Tallinn 200001; tel. 445 077; fax 440 963.

■ **SUMMATAVET, Mait,** designer; b. 1938; ed. Tallinn Art Univ.; Prof.; Art Fund, 1967 – 72; *Ars* combine, 1972 – 87; Vice-Rector, Tallinn Art Univ., 1987 – ; designed lights, interior design of *Ugala* theatre in Viljandi and Arts and Crafts Museum in Tallinn; designed exh., e.g., Siberia exh. in Tokyo, 1973, Soviet pavilion in Spokane, 1974; part. in furniture fair *Habitare '87* in Helsinki. *Add.* (h) Ranniku tee 29 – 4, Tallinn 200021; tel. 232 000.

■ **TAAGEPERA, Rein,** political scientist; b. 1933 in Tartu; ed. Toronto Univ.; PhD. (Phys.), M.A. (Int. Relations), Univ. of Delaware; E.I. DuPont Co, Wilmington, 1964 – 70; Univ. of California, Irvine, 1970 – , Prof. of Social and Pol. Sci., 1978 – ; spec. in worldwide analysis of electoral rules; co-author (1983, with Romuald Misiunas), 'The Baltic States: Years of Dependence 1940 – 1980'; Tuglas Prize for short stories (Est. Writers' Union, 1990). *Add.* 18191 Mayapple Way, Irvine, CA 92715, USA; tel. (714) 786 9291 (h); fax (714) 856 8441.

■ **TALTS, Jaan,** weightlifter; b. 1944; Dir, Elite Sports Sch., 1989 – ; medals: Olympic gold, heavyweight, 1972, silver, light heavyweight, 1968; world champ.: gold, heavyweight, 1969, 1970, 1972; silver, light heavyweight, 1968; European champ.: gold, light heavyweight, 1968; heavyweight, 1969, 1970, 1972; USSR champ.: gold, light heavyweight, 1967, 1968; heavyweight 1972; first heavyweight to exceed 500 kg, 1967; 40 world records. *Add.* (h) Ranniku tee 22, Tallinn 200021; tel. 232 191.

■ **TAMBERG, Eino,** composer; b. 1930; ed. Tallinn Conservatoire; Prof.; Tallinn Conservatoire, 1968 – , Dept Head, 1978 – 87, 1989 – ; has composed 3 operas, 3 ballets, 3 oratoriums, 2 symphonies, 2 violin concertos, romantic cycles. *Add.* Vabaduse pst. 130, Tallinn 200103; tel. 514 597.

■ **TAMBET, Ülo,** Gen. Dir, State Dept of Tech. Inspection, 1990 – ; b. 1932; ed. Tallinn Tech. Univ., mt. eng. *Add.* Lossi plats 4, Tallinn 200103; tel. 606 715.

■ **TAMKIVI, Paul,** eng. scientist; b. 1927; ed. Tallinn Tech. Univ.; DSc. (Tech.); Inst. of Thermal Phys. and Electrophys., 1955 – , Dir, 1989 – ; research on semi-conductor transformers, electrical frequency filters, tractable electrical gears and plasma technol. *Add.* Paldiski mnt. 1, Tallinn 200031; tel. 452 544.

■ **TAMM, Aksel,** lit. critic.; b. 1931; ed. Tartu Univ.; E-in-C, publishing house *Eesti Raamat,* 1966 – 82; E-in-C, journal *Keel ja Kirjandus,* 1983 – ; Int. Assoc. of Lit. Critics. *Add.* Roosikrantsi 6, Tallinn 200106; tel. 449 228.

■ **TAMM, Boris,** eng. scientist; b. 1930; ed. Tallinn Tech. Univ.; DSc. (Tech.), Prof.; Mem., Est. Acad. of Sci.; Tallinn Tech. Univ., 1954 – 57, Rector, 1976 – 90; Inst. of Cybernetics, 1960 – 76, Dir, 1969 – 76, Chief Scientist, 1991 – ; Acad. Sec., Division of Informatics and Eng. Sci., Est. Acad. of Sci., 1991 – ; research on automation, tech. cybernetics, software eng.; Mem., Bd of IFAC, Pres., 1987 – 90; Foreign Mem., Finnish Acad. of Tech. Sci.; Hon. Dr, Budapest and Helsinki Tech. Univ. *Add.* Akadeemia tee 21, Tallinn 200108; tel. 525 724; fax 527 901.

▪ **TAMM, Heiki,** biologist; b. 1941; ed. Tartu Univ.; CSc. (Biol.); Tallinn Botanical Gardens, 1971 – , Dir, 1991 – ; research on ecosystems modified by human interference; publ. and broadcasts on nature-related subjects. **Add.** Kloostrimetsa tee 52, Tallinn 200019; tel. 238 081.

▪ **TAMM, Jaak,** Min. of Ind. and Energy, 1990 – ; b. 1950; ed. Tartu Univ., social psychology; CSc. (Psychology); Consulting Co *Mainor,* 1981 – 86; Dir, *Kodamu* Constr. Co, 1987 – 90. **Add.** Lomonossovi 29, Tallinn 200104; tel. 423 550.

▪ **TAMM, Jüri,** athlete; b. 1957, ed. Kiev Sports Inst.; Kiev Sports Club *Burevestnik;* medals: Olympic bronze, hammer, 1980, 1988; Universal Games: silver, 1981; USSR Cup winner, 1979; world record (80,46 m), 1980.

▪ **TAMME, Rein,** Chair., Est. SC Defence Cttee, 1990 – ; b. 1940; ed. Tallinn Tech. Univ., constr. eng.; Est. Consumers' Cooperatives Union, 1964 – 89; EPF; Council of Estonia. **Add.** Lossi plats 1a, Tallinn 200100; tel. 606 341.

▪ **TAMMERK, Tarmu,** E-in-C, newspaper 'Estonian Independent', 1990 – ; b. 1961; ed. Tartu Univ., philol.; newspaper *Kodumaa,* 1985 – 90. **Add.** Pärnu mnt. 67a, Tallinn 200090; tel. 683 074.

▪ **TAMMISTU, Peeter,** Gen. Dir, State Pricing Dept, 1990 – ; b. 1953; ed. Tallinn Tech. Univ., econ.; Min. for Meat and Milk Prod., 1977 – 81, State Prices Cttee, 1981 – 89; Min. of Trade, 1989 – 90. **Add.** Toompea 1, Tallinn 200001; tel. 443 733.

▪ **TAMMOJA, Peeter,** Pres., Est. Chamber of Commerce and Ind., 1989 – ; b. 1953; ed. Tallinn Tech. Univ., Moscow Foreign Trade Acad. **Add.** Toom-Kooli 17, Tallinn 200001; tel. 444 929.

▪ **TARAND, Andres,** Chair., Est. SC Environment Cttee, 1990 – ; b. 1940; ed. Tartu Univ.; CSc. (Geogr.); Tallinn Botanical Gardens, 1965 – 68, 1970 – 90, Dir, 1989 – 90; publ. approx. 80 scientific and as many popular articles and essays; EPF; Green Movement; Council of Estonia. **Add.** Lossi plats 1a, Tallinn 200100; tel. 606 779.

▪ **TARMAK, Jüri,** athlete; b. 1946; ed. Leningrad Univ.; CSc. (Econ.), Asst Prof.; Leningrad Univ., 1975 – ; Dir, Broker Baltic Ltd, 1990 – ; medals: Olympic gold, high jumps, 1972; European indoor champ.: silver, 1971, bronze, 1972; USSR indoor champ.: gold, 1972. **Add.** (h) Lenini pst. 15 – 18, Tallinn 200001; tel. 447 745.

▪ **TARMAK, Mart,** Permanent Representative of the Est. Govt to Lithuania, 1990 – ; b. 1955; ed. Tartu Univ., chem., Vilnius Univ., philol.; Inst. of Chem. and Biol. Phys., 1978 – 81, newspaper *Sirp,* 1981 – 90; EPF Foreign Sec., 1988 – 90; Ed., newspaper *Vaba Maa,* 1989. **Add.** Turniškių 20, Vilnius 232016; tel. 764 896; fax 769 848.

▪ **TARTO, Enn,** Chair., Est. Conservative Party, 1990 – ; b. 1938; Tartu Branch of Est. Heritage Soc., Mem. of the Bd, *Memento,* Council of Estonia; pol. prisoner, 1956 – 60, 1962 – 67, 1983 – 88. **Add.** Ülikooli 15 – 2, Tartu 202400; tel. 322 63.

▪ **TARVEL, Enn,** historian; b. 1932; ed. Tartu Univ.; DSc. (Hist.); Dept Head, Inst. of Hist., 1960 – ; research on rural and gen. hist. **Add.** Rüütli 28, Tallinn 200001; tel. 443 620.

▪ **TASA, Toivo,** E-in-C, *Vikerkaar* journal, 1990 – ; b. 1951; ed. Tartu Univ., philol.; Dep. Ed., *Keel ja Kirjandus* journal, 1984 – 90; transl. of Ger. lit. **Add.** Toompuistee 30, Tallinn 200031; tel. 445 826.

▪ **TASSO, Enn,** Gen. Dir, State Forest Dept, 1990 – ; b. 1950; ed. Est. Agric. Acad., forestry eng.; Min. of Forestry and Nature Protection, 1985 – 90; Chair., Est. Forest Soc. **Add.** Toompuiestee 24, Tallinn 200001; tel. 452 982.

▪ **TEDER, Inge,** art critic; b. 1931; ed. Tartu Univ.; Dir, Est. Museum of Art, 1965 – 91; research on Est. decorative art; Mem., ICOM. **Add.** (h) Kentmanni 9 – 2, Tallinn 200001; tel. 661 702.

▪ **TEDRE, Ülo,** folklorist; b. 1928; ed. Tartu Univ.; CSc. (Philol.); Inst. of Lg. and Lit., 1954 – , Dept Head, 1962 – ; research on Est. runic songs. **Add.** Roosikrantsi 6, Tallinn 200106; tel. 444 650.

▪ **TEINBERG, Rein,** veterinary scientist; b. 1935; ed. Est. Agric. Acad.; DSc. (Agric.), Prof.; Est. Agric. Acad., 1964 – 79; Dept Head, Inst. of Experimental Biol., 1979 – ; E-in-C, Est. Agric. Encyclopaedia, 1990 – ; research on zoogenetics and selection, publ. 140 studies. **Add.** Lenini pst. 9, Tallinn 200100; tel. 444 703.

▪ **TELGMAA, Juhan,** Chair., Est. SC Rural Affairs Cttee, 1990 – ; b. 1946; ed. Est. Agric. Acad., mechanizer; Dir, Torma collective farm, 1976 – 90. **Add.** Lossi plats 1a, Tallinn 200100; tel. 606 739.

▪ **TIKS, Mihkel,** E-in-C, 'Theatre. Music. Cinema' mag., 1988 – ; b. 1953; ed. Tartu Univ., journalist; basketball player in *Kalev* club, 1973 – 83; has written novels and plays. **Add.** Narva mnt. 5., Tallinn 200090; tel. 440 472.

▪ **TITMA, Mikk,** sociologist; b. 1939; ed. Tartu Univ.; DSc. (Phil.), Prof.; Tartu Univ., 1963 – 75; Dept Head, Inst. of Hist., 1975 – 88; Ideology Sec., Cent. Cttee of ECP, 1988 – 90; Inst. of Phil., Sociology and Law, 1988 – ; research, incl. 30 monographs, on social policies and sociology; *Vaba Eesti* Movement. Est. SC Deputy, 1990 – . **Add.** Mündi 3, Tallinn 200001; tel. 448 428.

▪ **TOLLI, Vive,** graphic artist, b. 1928; ed. Tallinn Art Univ.; Tallinn Art Univ., 1988 – ; created prints using corrosion techniques, ill. books; silver medal, int. book art show in Moscow, 1975, Golden Apple award, Bratislavia BIB '77; medals, Florence Graphic Arts Biennial, 1972, Malbork, 1969, 1971, prize winner, Ljubljana Graphic Arts Biennial, 1965, Heidelberg, 1980; special award, Krakow, 1984. **Add.** (h) Bornhöhe 32, Tallinn 200019; tel. 239 961.

▪ **TOMINGAS, Rein,** architect; b. 1944; ed. Tallinn Art Univ.; *EKE Projekt* Inst., 1968 – ; designed agric. and public buildings, cultural and sport centres, private homes; created sculpture. **Add.** (h) Sõpruse pst. 186 – 43, Tallinn 200029; tel. 526 351.

▪ **TÕNNISSON, Nathan,** Gen. Dir, Nat. Maritime Bd, 1990 — ; b. 1948; ed. Odessa Inst. of Navigation Eng.; Est. Shipping Co, 1970 — 90. *Add,* Viru 9, Tallinn 200100; tel. 442 725.

▪ **TONURIST, Igor,** ethnographer and expert of folk music; b. 1947; ed. Moscow Univ.; Inst. of Hist., 1969 — ; chief conductor, folk music band *Leegajus,* 1970 — ; studies on popular musical instruments. *Add.* Rüütli 28, Tallinn 200001; tel. 445 997.

▪ **TOOME, Indrek,** Chair., Est. SC Foreign Affairs Cttee, 1990 — ; b. 1943; ed. Tallinn Tech. Univ., ind. electronic eng.; 1st Sec., Est. YCL Cent. Cttee, 1972 — 78; Est. SSR CM Dep. Chair., 1984 — 87, Chair., 1988 — 90; Ideology Sec., ECP Cent. Cttee, 1987 — 88; Chair., *Vaba Eesti* Movement; USSR People's Deputy, 1989 — . *Add.* Lossi plats 1a, Tallinn 200001; tel. 444 089.

▪ **TOOMING, Jaan,** producer and actor; b. 1946; ed. Tallinn Conservatoire; theatre *Vanemuine,* 1969 — 74 and 1975 — ; expressive and even shocking prod. *Add.* Vanemuise 7, Tartu 202400; tel. 338 85.

▪ **TOOMING, Peeter,** film dir, cameraman, photographer; b. 1939; ed. Tartu Univ., philol.; *Tallinnfilm,* 1961 — ; works include documentaries on photographical and ecological subjects, photograph albums and articles on the hist. of photography; co-founder of the *Stodom* photographers' group; personal exh. in Italy, Austria, Poland, England, etc.; int. awards; AFIAP. *Add.* Harju 9, Tallinn 200001; tel. 445 029.

▪ **TORMIS, Veljo,** composer; b. 1930; ed. Moscow Conservatoire, Dept Head of the Man. Bd, Est. Composers' Union, 1974 — ; has composed choral pieces based on Finno-Ugric nations' folk music, an opera, a cantata-ballet; his works have been presented at int. music festivals. *Add,* Lauteri 7, Tallinn 200107; tel. 444 103.

▪ **TOUGU, Enn,** eng. scientist; b. 1935; ed. Tallinn Tech. Univ.; DSc. (Tech.), Prof.; Mem., Est. Acad. of Sci.; Dept Head, Inst. of Cybernetics, 1976 — ; Acad. Sec., Est. Acad. of Sci., Division of Informatics and Eng. Sci., 1987 — 90; research on systems programming and artifical intelligence; Assoc. for Logic Programming, Assoc. for Computing Machines, IFIP WG5.2; mem. of various scientific journals' ed. bd. *Add.* Akadeemia tee 21, Tallinn 200108; tel. 525 728.

▪ **TRAAT, Mats,** writer; b. 1936; ed. Moscow M.Gorky Inst. of Lit.; has written novels, short stories and poetry, critically depicting recent and contemporary Est. soc. *Add.* (h) Oru 16, Tallinn 200010; tel. 426 541.

▪ **TRASS, Hans-Voldemar,** botanist; b. 1928; ed. Tartu Univ.; DSc. (Biol.), Prof.; Mem., Est. Acad. of Sci., Dept Head, Tartu Univ., 1956 — ; Chair., Est. Soc. for Nature Studies; research into lichenology and geobotany. *Add.* Lai 40, Tartu 202400; tel. 352 40.

▪ **TRUVE, Rando,** surgeon; b. 1936; ed. Tartu Univ.; DSc. (Med.); Dept Dir, Pelgulinna Hosp., Tallinn, 1971 — ; research on surgical treatment of stomach and gall-bladder diseases; founding mem. of the Est. Med. Assoc. and Pres., 1990 — . *Add.* Sõle 16, Tallinn 200108; tel. 496 784.

▪ **TULVISTE, Peeter,** psychologist; b. 1945; ed. Moscow Univ.; DSc. (Psychology), Prof.; Tartu Univ., 1969 — , Dept Head, 1988 — ; Clark Univ. (USA), 1990 — 91; research on the development of sensory perception; transl. of fiction. *Add.* Tiigi 78, Tartu 202400; tel. 300 63.

▪ **TÜÜR, Erkki-Sven,** composer; b. 1959; ed. Tallinn Conservatoire; 2 symphonies, instrumental music influenced by rock style, film music. *Add.* Composers' Union, Lauteri 7, Tallinn 200107; tel. 444 103.

▪ **UIBO, Andres,** organist; b. 1956; ed. Tallinn Conservatoire; Tallinn Niguliste Museum-Concert Hall, 1981 — ; chief producer, *Esto-Muusika* Firm, 1989 — ; one of Tallinn Int. Organ Festival organisers. *Add.* Niguliste 13, Tallinn 200001; tel. 449 911.

▪ **ÜKSKÜLA, Aarne,** actor; b. 1937; ed. Tallinn Conservatoire; theatre *Endla,* 1968 — 78; Tallinn Conservatoire, 1978 — 85; Est. Drama Theatre, 1985 — 89, theatre *Vanalinnastuudio,* 1989 — ; roles: George (Albee's 'Who is Afraid of Virginia Woolf?'), the man with the contrabass (Süskind's 'Contrabass'). *Add.* Sakala 12, Tallinn 200001; tel. 448 408.

▪ **ÜKSVÄRAV, Raoul,** economist; b. 1928; ed. Tallinn Tech. Univ.; DSc. (Econ.), Prof., Hon. Dr, Turku Trade Univ.; Tallinn Tech. Univ., 1958 — 89, Dept Head, 1969 — 89; Research Dir, Est. Management Inst., 1989 — ; research on ind. econ. and admin. management. *Add.* Sütiste tee 21, Tallinn 200108; tel. 521 616.

▪ **ULAS, Peeter,** graphic artist; b. 1934; ed. Tallinn Art Univ.; Asst Prof.; Tallinn Teacher Training Inst., 1963 — ; created graphic art through various techniques; uses corrosion technique to prepare large scale graphic prints; ill. books; 1st prize, Baltic Graphic Arts Triennial, 1968. *Add.* (h) Nõmme tee 48 — 32, Tallinn 200034; tel. 552 843.

▪ **UNDUSK, Jaan,** scholar of lit.; b. 1958; ed. Tartu Univ.; CSc. (Philol.); Inst. of Lg. and Lit., 1982 — ; has implemented modern theoretical research methods for studying Est. lit. *Add.* Roosikrantsi 6, Tallinn 200106; tel. 446 067.

▪ **UNT, Mati,** writer and producer; b. 1944; ed. Tartu Univ., philol.; theatre *Vanemuine,* 1966 — 71; Youth Theatre, 1974 — ; has written prose in modern form depicting the psychology of contemporary urban dwellers; his novel 'The Autumn Ball' has been transl. into 7 lgs; has dramatized and produced the world classics. *Add.* Lai 23, Tallinn 200001; tel. 609 624.

▪ **URGE, Leo,** Prosecutor Gen. of the ESSR and the Rep. of Estonia, 1987 — ; b. 1941; ed. Tartu Univ.; Pärnu City Prosecutor, 1971 — 85; Tallinn City Prosecutor, 1985 — 87. *Add.* Wismari 7, 200100 Tallinn; tel. 442 652.

▪ **UUDMÄE, Jaak,** athlete; b. 1954; ed. Est. Agric. Acad., econ.; Otepää City Govt, 1990 — ; medals: Olympic gold, triple jump, 1980; Universal Games: silver, 1979; European Cup: gold, 1981; European indoor champ.: silver, 1977, 1980, bronze, 1979. *Add.* Lipu väljak 9, Otepää 202513; tel. 555 81.

▪ **VAARANDI, Debora,** writer; b. 1916; has written poetry relating the topic of the home to gen. phil. problems. **Add.** (h) Kuristiku 10, Tallinn 200100; tel. 426 557.

▪ **VÄÄRTNÕU, Eli,** architect; b. 1939; ed. Tallinn Art Univ.; *EKE Projekt* Inst., 1967 −; designed apartment buildings, resorts, treatment centres; silver medal, Sofia Interarch '87. **Add.** Kingissepa 12, Tallinn 200206; tel. 683 812.

▪ **VAGA, Voldemar,** art historian; b. 1899; ed. Tartu Univ.; DSc. (Arts), Prof.; postgraduate studies at Sorbonne Univ. and École du Louvre; Tartu Univ., 1923 − 69, Dept Head, 1944 − 50; research on medieval Est. arch. and the 19th cent. Baltic-German fine arts; author of the first 'Gen. Hist. of Art' in Est. in 1938 and of 'Est. Art' in 1940. **Add.** Jakobsoni 3, Tartu 202400; tel. 718 97.

▪ **VÄHI, Tiit,** Min. of Transportation, 1989 − ; b. 1947; ed. Tallinn Tech. Univ., eng. of precision mech.; Valga Motor Depot, 1972 − 89, Dir, 1976 − 89. **Add.** Viru 9, Tallinn 200100; tel. 443 842.

▪ **VAHTRE, Sulev,** historian; b. 1926; ed. Tartu Univ.; DSc. (Hist.); Tartu Univ., 1955 −, Dept Head, 1989 − ; research on rural and urban hist. of Estonia. **Add.** Tartu Univ. Hist. Museum, Toomemägi, Tartu 202400; tel. 352 68.

▪ **VAIKMÄE, Rein,** naturalist; b. 1945; ed. Tallinn Tech. Univ.; CSc. (Geogr.); Tallinn Tech. Univ., 1969 − 73; Inst. of Geol., 1973 −, Dir, 1990 − ; research into implementation of isotropic methods in paleoclimatology, hydrogeol. and environmental studies. **Add.** Estonia pst. 7, Tallinn 200101; tel. 605 120.

▪ **VAINIKKO, Gennadi,** mathematician; b. 1938; ed. Tartu Univ.; DSc. (Phys. & Math.), Prof.; Mem., Est. Acad. of Sci.; Tartu Univ., 1963 − 65, 1967 −, Dept Head, 1971 − ; Vice-Pres., Est. Acad. of Sci., 1990 − ; research on gen. theory and practice of approximation methods. **Add.** Liivi 2, Tartu 202400; tel. 351 58.

▪ **VAINO, Karl,** CPSU functionary; b. 1923; ed. Tomsk Railway Transportation Eng. Electro-Mech. Inst., CPSU Cent. Cttee Higher Party Sch.; ECP Cent. Cttee, 1948 − 88; 1st Sec., ECP Cent. Cttee, 1978 − 88; Soviet communist colonial Russification policy leader; CPSU Cent. Cttee in Moscow, 1988 −.

▪ **VALDMANN, Elmar,** physiologist; b. 1928; ed. Est. Agric. Acad.; DSc. (Biol.), Prof.; Animal Breeding and Veterinary Sci. Research Inst., 1952 −, Dir, 1976 − ; Chief Exec., *Eesti Loomakasvatus* (Est. Animal Breeding) Sci. Prod. Assoc., 1988 − ; research on the physiology of farm animals; Mem., Lenin All-Union Agric. Acad. **Add.** Kreutzwaldi 1, Tartu 202400; tel. 324 52, 624 53.

▪ **VÄLJAS, Vaino,** politician and diplomat; b. 1931; ed. Tartu Univ.; CSc. (Hist.); ECP Cent. Cttee, 1961 −, Sec., 1971 − 80, 1st Sec., 1988 − 90, Chair., 1990 − ; USSR Ambassador to Venezuela, 1980 − 86, Nicaragua, 1986 − 88; Est. SC Deputy, 1990 − , USSR People's Deputy, 1989 − . **Add.** Lossi plats 1a, Tallinn 200001; tel. 444 089.

▪ **VALK, Heinrich,** artist and politician; b. 1936; ed. Tallinn Art Univ.; Art Fund,

1972 − 76; 1st Sec., Est. Artists' Union, 1976 − 79; Est. SC Deputy, 1990 − ; Mem., 1st Man. Bd of EPF, 1988 − 90; Liberal Dem. Party; publ. coll. of cartoons. **Add.** Lossi plats 1a, Tallinn 200001; tel. 606 754.

▪ **VALK, Uno,** sylviculturist; b. 1922; ed. Tartu Univ.; DSc. (Biol.), Prof.; Inst. of Zoology and Botany, 1948 − 69; Dept Head, Inst. of Forestry, 1969 − ; research into utilization of moors and bogs as well as into draining, fertilizing and development of forests. **Add.** Rõõmu tee 2, Tartu 202400; tel. 363 81.

▪ **VALMSEN, Heino,** Dir, Est. State Archives, 1985 − ; b. 1929; ed. Tartu Univ., lawyer. **Add.** Maneeži 4, Tallinn 200107; tel. 441 118.

▪ **VALTON, Arvo** (real name Vallikivi), writer; b. 1935; ed. Tallinn Tech. Univ., mining eng.; Moscow Cinematography Inst.; studio *Tallinnfilm*, 1975 − 88, Est. Writers' Union, 1988 − ; has written existentialist short stories, novels and aphorisms; deported 1949 − 54. **Add.** Harju 1, Tallinn 200001; tel. 446 832.

▪ **VARE, Raivo,** Min. of State, 1990 − ; b. 1958; ed. Tartu Univ., lawyer; Est. SC Presidium, 1980 − 90. **Add.** Lossi plats 1a, Tallinn 200100; tel. 444 898.

▪ **VARVARA** (Trofimova), Mother Superior, the Pühtitsa convent; b. 1930; joined the Pühtitsa convent in 1952, in 1955 went to Vilnius Mary Magdalene Nunnery, where she was ordained a nun in 1958; was appointed mother superior of the Pühtitsa Nunnery in 1968 by Patriarch Alexius. **Add.** Kuremäe, Ida-Virumaa 202035; tel. 921 24.

▪ **VEETOUSME, Ants,** Chair., Est. SC Econ. Cttee, 1990 − ; b. 1949; ed. Tartu Univ., econ.; Tartu Dept of the USSR State Bank, 1978 − 87; Chair. of the Bd, Tartu Commercebank (1st in USSR), 1989 − 90; Chair., Council of Bank of Estonia, 1991 − ; deported 1949 − 54. **Add.** Lossi plats 1a, Tallinn 200100; tel. 606 315.

▪ **VEETOUSME, Rein,** Gen. Dir, State Dept of Statistics, 1991 − ; b.1947; ed. Tallinn Tech. Univ., eng., econ. **Add.** Endla 15, Tallinn 200106; tel. 453 889.

▪ **VEIDEMANN, Rein,** Chair., Est. SC Media Cttee, 1990 − ; b. 1946; ed. Tartu Univ., scholar of lit.; CSc. (Philol.); E-in-C, *Vikerkaar* journal, 1986 − 90; research into theory and hist. of lit. criticism; Mem., 1st and 3rd Man. Bd of EPF, 1988 − 90, 1991 − ; Vice-Chair., SDP. **Add.** Lossi plats 1a, Tallinn 200100; tel. 606 356.

▪ **VEIDERMA, Mihkel,** chemist; b. 1929; ed. Tallinn Tech. Univ.; DSc. (Tech.), Prof.; Mem., Est. Acad. of Sci.; Tallinn Tech. Univ., 1960 −, Dept Head, 1971 − ; Vice-Pres., Est. Acad. of Sci., 1987 − ; research on the chem. and technol. of phosphates. **Add.** Kohtu 6, Tallinn 200100; tel. 445 810.

▪ **VELLISTE, Trivimi,** Pres., Est. Heritage Soc., 1987 − ; b. 1947; ed. Tartu Univ., philol.; newspaper *Sirp*, 1976 − 87; Vice-Chair., Council of Estonia. **Add.** POB 3141, Tallinn 200090; tel. 449 216.

▪ **VETEMAA, Enn,** writer; b. 1936; ed. Tallinn Tech. Univ., chem. eng.; Tallinn Conservatoire, composer; Chair., Est. Writers' Union Co-Operative *Kupar*; has written humorous and satirical novels and plays on topics of contemporary life. *Add.* (h) Harju 1 — 5, Tallinn 200001; tel. 444 466.

- **VIIDING, Juhan,** writer and actor; b. 1948; ed. Tallinn Conservatoire, Drama Dept; Est. Drama Theatre, 1972 — ; has written poetry depicting the paradoxes and grotesqueness of reality; roles: Hamlet, Peer Gynt. *Add.* Pärnu mnt. 5, Tallinn 200001; tel. 442 065.
- **VIIK, Tõnu,** astronomer; b. 1939; ed. Tartu Univ.; CSc. (Phys. & Math.); Inst. of Astrophys. and Atmospheric Phys., 1971 — , Dir, 1985 — ; research, incl. 4 monographs on radiation distribution in the atmospheres of stars and planets; Mem., Int. Union of Astronomers (IAV), European Soc. for Astronomy. *Add.* Tõravere Observatory, Tartumaa 202444; tel. 348 53, 102 65.
- **VIIRES, Ants,** ethnographer; b. 1918; ed. Tartu Univ.; DSc. (Hist.), Hon. Dr, Helsinki Univ.; Inst. of Hist., 1956 — ; research on the hist. of material culture of Est. and other Baltic nations. *Add.* Rüütli 28, Tallinn 200101; tel. 605 440.
- **VIITSO, Tiit-Rein,** linguist; b. 1928; ed. Tartu Univ.; DSc. (Philol.), Prof.; Inst. of Lg. and Lit., 1973 — ; Helsinki Univ.; 1989 — ; research on Baltic Finno-Ugric lgs and their phonology. *Add.* (h) Vikerkaare 23, Tartu 202400; tel. 622 47.
- **VILIMAA, Ülo,** ballet dancer and ballet master; b. 1941; ed. Tallinn Choreography Sch.; theatre *Vanemuine*, 1962 — , chief ballet master, 1974 — ; has produced Est. ballets, short ballets and musicals. *Add.* Vanemuise 7, Tartu 202400; tel. 338 85.
- **VILLAKO, Kaljo,** roentgenologist and gastroenterologist; b. 1919; ed. Tartu Univ.; DSc. (Med.), Prof.; Hon. Dr, Tampere Univ.; Tartu Univ., 1955 — , Dept Head, 1980 — 90; research on the spread of gastritis; Mem., European Gastroclub, 1971; Hon. Mem., Finnish Assoc. of Internists, 1981. *Add.* Puusepa 8, Tartu 202400; tel. 284 62.
- **VILLEMS, Richard,** biologist; b. 1944; ed. Tartu Univ.; DSc. (Biol.), Prof.; Mem., Est. Acad. of Sci.; Foreign Mem., Sweden's Royal Acad. of Sci.; Tartu Univ., 1968 — 76; Inst. of Phys., 1976 — 80; Inst. of Chem. and Biol. Phys., 1980 — 86; Dir, Est. Biocentre, 1986 — ; research on molecular biol. *Add.* Tähetorn Toomel, Tartu 202400; tel. 319 80; telex 173243 TAUN SU; fax 354 30.
- **VINT, Tõnis,** graphic artist; b. 1942; ed. Tallinn Art Univ.; his work contains art nouveau elegance ritualistic symbols and signs; deep interest in the Far East. *Add.* (h) Lomonossovi 14 — 20, Tallinn 200001; tel. 422 887.
- **VIRKUS, Rein,** education spec.; b. 1930; ed. Tallinn Teacher Training Inst.; CSc. (Pedag.), Prof.; Tallinn Teacher Training Inst., 1974 — , Rector, 1979 — ; research on comparative pedag. *Add.* Narva mnt. 25, Tallinn 200001; tel. 425 868.
- **VOLKOV, Igor,** Chair., Est. Arch. Union, 1990 — ;b. 1951; ed. Tallinn Art Univ.; chief arch., Halinga collective farm, 1984 — 87; designed rural buildings and private homes, publ. arch. articles and a coll. of poetry; Dir, country band *Kukerpillid.* *Add.* Lai 23, Tallinn 200110; tel. 601 977, 442 337.
- **VOLMER, Arvo,** conductor; b. 1952; ed. Tallinn Conservatoire, Leningrad Conservatoire; theatre *Estonia*; Est. State Symphony Orch., 1988 — ; conducted at the Finnish Nat. Opera and in Denmark; 4th prize at the IX Malko Int. Comp. for Young Conductors in Copenhagen, 1989. *Add.* Lomonossovi 21, Tallinn 200100; tel. 434 420.

REPUBLIC OF
LATVIA

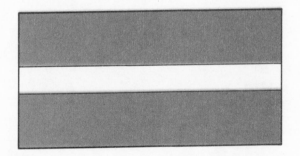

DIEVS, SVĒTĪ LATVIJU!
(GOD BLESS LATVIA)

Kārlis BAUMANIS

Dievs, svē - ti Lat - vi - ju, mūs dār - go tē - vi - ju, svē - ti jel Lat - vi - ju, ak

svē - ti jel to! to! Kur latvju mei - tas zied, kur latvju dē - li dzied,

laid mums tur lai - mē diet, mūs Lat - vi - jā! Lat - vi - jā!

Dievs, svētī Latviju,
Mūs' dārgo Tēviju,
Svētī jel Latviju,
Ak, svētī jel to!

Kur latvju meitas zied,
Kur latvju dēli dzied
Laid mums tur laimē diet —
Mūs' Latvijā!

Friedrich PACIUS / Johann Voldemar JANNSEN
Vincas KUDIRKAS
Kārlis BAUMANIS

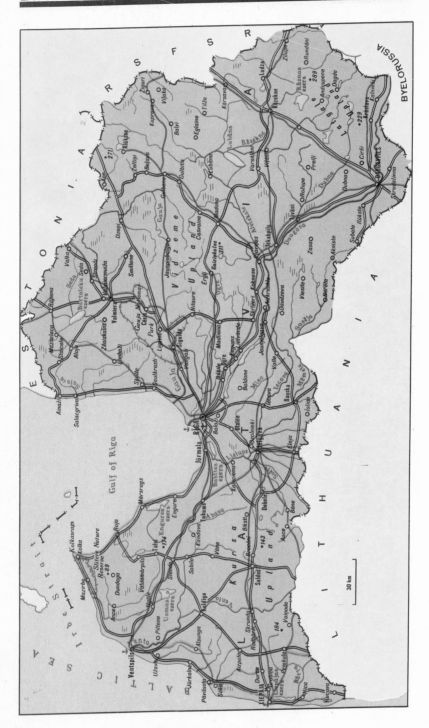

THE REPUBLIC OF LATVIA lies on the eastern coast of the Baltic Sea. Since ancient times, with its coastline exceeding 500 km and easily accessible ports, Latvia has been a significant link between the states surrounding the Baltic Sea and Russia. The Baltic Sea has always been of great importance in political, economic and cultural life of the country. The overall length of Latvia's boundaries exceeds 1,800 km. Latvia is bounded by Estonia (on the north), Lithuania (on the south), Russia and Byelorussia (on the east). It is rather 210 km across the widest part of Latvia and 410 km in a straight line from the east extreme to the westernmost point.

The territory of Latvia covers 64,600 sq km. Among the independent European states only Denmark, Switzerland, the Netherlands, Belgium, Albania and Estonia as well as 8 tiny countries are smaller in size. The population of Latvia totalled to 2,686,000 in 1990.

The capital of Latvia is Riga with the population of 916,500 in 1990, that constitutes 34% of the total population. The largest cities: Daugavpils (128,200), Liepāja (114,900), Jelgava (75,100), Jūrmala (66,400), Ventspils (50,400), Rēzekne (42,900).

The official state language: Latvian.

Religious affiliation: Lutheran, Russian Orthodox, Roman Catholic.

State holiday: November 18 — Proclamation Day of the Republic of Latvia.

Monetary unit: rouble.

LANGUAGE

The Latvian language belongs to the Baltic language group of the Indo-European language family. It is one of the two still living Baltic languages, the other one being Lithuanian. Latvian is the native language of about 1,690,000 people in the Republic of Latvia. Additionally, 260,000 in Latvia, 20,000 in the USSR and 95,000 people abroad speak Latvian either as the first or second language. The language has developed on the basis of the geographical closeness of its nationalities (Selonians, Semigallians, Couronians, Latgallians). Traditionally three main dialects have been distinguished — the Central dialect (the basis for the literary language), the High (or East) dialect and the dialect of the Livs.

The Latvian language is an inflective language with several analytical forms. It has 48 phonemes: 12 vowels, 10 diphthongs and 26 consonants. Germanic influences are observed in its syntax, in the vocabulary most loanwords come from the German, Russian, Livian and Estonian languages. The evolution of the written Latvian (its orthography) has undergone three periods: Old Latvian (16th cent. — middle of 19th cent.), New Latvian (middle of the 19th cent. to the 1880s), and the present-day literary language or Standard Latvian (in use since the 80s and 90s of the 19th cent.). The basis of the written language is the Latin alphabet; in 1908 the 2nd Commission of Orthography of the Riga Latvian Society (K.Mīlenbahs, J.Endzelīns) adopted the present-day orthography.

The contemporary Latvian language finds itself in a complicated situation. Its natural environment has been deteriorating, since almost 1/2 of the inhabitants of Latvia do not speak Latvian, there is a rapid increase in the pollution of the language with Russicisms, slang and barbarisms. In order to save the Latvian language, a law giving Latvian the status of the official state language was passed in 1989.

NATURE

Latvia lies on the western edge of the East European Plain. The ice-cover of the Quarternary Period, the last of which retreated from Latvia some 10,000 to 12,000 years ago, has been of great importance in the formation of its natural conditions. The outcrops of the Ice Age throughout Latvia's territory (with the exception of the Coastal Lowlands) have shaped the present-day principal relief formations. 57% of Latvia's territory is located up to 100 m above the sea level, 40.5% from 100 m to 200 m, hardly 2.5% ever reaches 200 m.

RELIEF, HYDROGRAPHICAL NETWORK, CLIMATE. The difference between the natural regions and their classification in Latvia are determined by the direct influence of the Baltic Sea and the change of natural conditions from the West to the East, where the influence of the Atlantic Ocean is lessened and the continentality of the climate increases. The country is divided into the Coastal Lowlands and three main inland regions — the Western Latvia, Middle Latvia and Eastern Latvia.

The Coastal Lowlands comprise the region of the Baltic seashore and the Gulf of Riga, from Lithuania to the border of Estonia. Its width is 2 to 50 km, the height varying from 5 to 60 m above the sea level. Of the inland regions, the Western Latvia has the least formational contrast, its highest point being Krievukalns (184 m above the sea level), which is located in the Western Kursa Upland. The Middle Latvia displays a rich variety of contrasts in the relief of its natural regions. The Zemgale Plain is in the southwestern part of the Middle Latvian Lowlands. Its northern part is slightly below the sea level, the southern part approximately 25 m above the sea level. The Vidzeme Upland is the highest part of Latvia (Gaiziņkalns — 312 m above the sea level), with a highly segmented and uneven relief formation. The largest part of its surface is higher than 180 m above the sea level. In the Eastern Latvia the Latgale Upland is the dominating, with a medium height of 170 — 180 m above the sea level. The second highest point in Latvia, Lielais Liepukalns (289 m above the sea level), is located in this area.

The hilly, uneven relief, the damp climate, as well as the geological development, have encouraged the formation of a ramified system of rivers. There are 12,000 rivers in Latvia, although only 17 rivers ʹ ʹ ʹonger than 100 km, and only the Daugava (357 km in the territory of Latvia) and the Gauja are longer than 200 km. The discharge of rivers during the spring reaches 45 — 55% of the annual discharge, during the winter it is 15 — 20%. The rivers containing the most water are the Daugava and its tributary Aiviekste, as well as the Lielupe, Gauja and Venta.

The lakes and reservoirs take up 1.7% of the territory of Latvia. There are more than 3,000 lakes and reservoirs larger than 1 ha, 14 lakes and the reservoirs of 3 hydroelectric power stations on the Daugava are larger than 10 sq km. Most of the lakes are shallow, with a medium depth of 1 — 5 m. Only 8 lakes have a medium depth of more than 10 m, the deepest being the Drīdzis (65 m). Lakes are concentrated mainly in the uplands (more than 40% in the Latgale Upland), as well as in the Coastal Lowlands.

Latvia's climate is determined by its geographical location in the northwest of the Eurasian continent, and by its closeness to the Atlantic Ocean. Latvia is crossed by an average of 120 — 140 cyclones annually, which cause frequent meteorological changes. Due to the influence of cyclones, the summer temperatures are slightly lower, but winter temperatures higher than the average at middle latitudes. The range of temperature in January varies from $-2.6\,°C$ in Liepāja to $-6.6\,°C$ in Daugavpils, in July correspondingly from $+16.8\,°C$ to $+17.6\,°C$. The average annual percipitation reaches 600 — 650 mm. Under the influence of frequent thaws, the depth of snow is not great — 15 — 20 cm; in the Vidzeme Upland it reaches an annual average of 50 cm.

SOIL, FLORA AND FAUNA. The most widely distributed bedrock of Latvia's soils is moraine loam (largest areas are found in the Zemgale Plain and the Lubāns Plain), as well as sandy bedrock (Coastal Lowlands). More than 1/2 of Latvia's soil consists of podsolic humus. It constitutes about 1/3 of the total area of the arable land. The most fertile soil is that of carbonate humus (7% of the arable land), the largest continuous areas of which are located in the vicinity of Dobele, Jelgava and Bauska. The total woodland area covers 41% of the territory of Latvia. 1/2 of it consists of pines, and to a lesser degree, of birches and firs. The greatest density of woodland occurs in the north of Kurzeme and in the northern parts of Vidzeme, as well as in the lower reaches of the Gauja and Daugava. Swamp and marsh-land occupies approximately 10% of Latvia's territory, mainly in the Coastal Lowlands and in the East Latvian Lowland.

There are about 14,000 animal species registered in Latvia. During the 20th cent. two species have been reaclimatized: in 1911 the wild boar was brought in from Poland, the Eurasian beaver — from Norway in 1927 and from the RSFSR in 1952. During the last 20 — 30 years the brown bear has reentered the territory of Latvia, as well as the ondatra. The routes of the migratory birds pass along the Baltic Sea and over Latvia.

NATURAL RESOURCES AND USEFUL MINERALS. Latvia is not rich in useful minerals. Peat, some 530,000,000 t of which there is an industrial stock, is the only combustible mineral of economic importance. The largest peat deposits are found in the Riga district (the Cena Heath — 32,000,000 t) and in the districts of Preiļi, Ludza, Valka and Aizkraukle. Most important in the economy of the Republic is the production of raw building materials. Dolomite is found mainly in the central and eastern parts of Latvia. Industrial stock of dolomite that can be utilized in construction is valued at 137,000,000 cu m, the largest being the Aiviekste deposits in the Aizkraukle district — 52,000,000 cu m and the Birze deposits in the Jēkabpils district — 29,000,000 cu m. Limestone is widely found in the southwestern part of Latvia. Industrial stock of limestone has been estimated at about 81,800,000 t, of which 81,000,000 t are to be found in the Kūma deposits of the Saldus district. Gypsum deposits are located in the Riga and Bauska districts and their industrial stock consists of 55,000,000 cu m. Clay deposits are found in many parts of the Republic, and their industrial stock is valued at 85,000,000 t. The biggest are the Kuprava deposits in the Balvi district — 19,000,000 t. There is a considerable amount of gravel and sand in the Republic, as well as mineralwater and medicinal mud.

ENVIRONMENTAL PROTECTION, ECOLOGICAL SITUATION. There are almost 700 territorial and other nature objects under state protection in Latvia (their total area being larger than 4,000 sq km), as well as almost 300 endangered species of flora and fauna. The largest areas are occupied by the Gauja National Park and by 5 reserves — Slītere, Grīņi, Moricsala, Krustkalni and Teiči. As of 1990, the Northern Vidzeme Regional Nature Protection Complex, which includes the largest part of Limbaži and Valmiera districts and the northwestern part of the Valka district, is being developed.

Here the necessary preconditions for the organization of a biospheric reserve will be created. Although an elevated level of environmental pollution is typical of a large part of the Republic, nevertheless, the average level of air pollution is considerably lower than that of many European countries (Germany, Sweden and the southern part of Finland, etc.). The total amount of pollution, that reaches the atmosphere, surpasses 600,000 t annually. The least favourable situation in Latvia has developed in Riga, Olaine, Liepāja and Daugavpils.

A much more serious problem is connected with water pollution. The lack of local waste conversion equipment and the present non-effective operation of what is available, as well as the use of chemical fertilizers, herbicides and pesticides in agriculture have created a situation in which, according to specialists, more than 185,000 t of various pollutants reach the rivers, lakes and water reservoirs. During the last years due to agricultural runoff there has been a sharp deterioration in the ecological situation of the smaller and medium sized rivers, and consequently an increase in the eutrophication of lakes. Approximately 87% of all lakes in Latvia are considerably eutrophic (the overgrowth surpasses 30% of the area of all lakes). Most pollutants from the rivers of Latvia end up in the Gulf of Riga, where a complicated ecological situation has developed. One of the main pollutants of the Gulf of Riga is Riga itself, which as late as 1991 functioned without a combined city waste conversion equipment system. As a result, the recreational use of the Gulf of Riga is considerably limited. In some areas of Latvia (Riga, Liepāja, Olaine, Inčukalns) pollution of the subsoil water has begun. Nor, from the ecological viewpoint, have the questions of energy production, the conversion and utilization of toxic waste, the storage of radioactive matter, and the ecological problems created by the Soviet army in the Republic of Latvia, been solved.

POPULATION

The national census, held in Latvia on January 12, 1989, registered a population of 2,680,000, the number of permanent inhabitants being 2,667,000. That is the largest number of inhabitants that has ever lived within the territory of Latvia.

Population ('000, within the present borders of Latvia)

1914	2,493	1950	1,943
1920 (June 14)	1,596	1959 (Jan. 15)	2,093
1935 (Feb. 12)	1,905	1979 (Jan. 17)	2,521
1940	1,886	1989 (Jan. 12)	2,680

As compared to other European nations (except for Estonia), the increase in the population during the post-WW II years has been dominated by an increase on account of immigration. Until 1989, due to migration Latvia had the highest growth of population in all of Europe. Throughout the years, the main flow of migration has been from the nearest regions of the Russian SFSR, the Byelorussian SSR and the Ukrainian SSR. The natural increase in population from the late 1950s to the 1980s was on a continual decrease.

Increase in Population (annual average)

	1959 – 69	1970 – 78	1979 – 88
Total increase ('000)	24.6	17.4	16.0
Natural increase ('000)	10.3	5.8	6.7
% of total increase	41.9	33.3	41.9
Increase due to migration ('000)	14.3	11.6	9.3
% of total increase	58.1	66.7	58.1

The number of people in the cities during the post-war period, mainly due to migration, were on a constant increase. In the country, because of poor socio-economic conditions, the population decreased. The most rapid decrease took place after WW II caused by the terror and deportations of the inhabitants of the Republic, which were organized by the Latvian CP and supported by the Latvian SSR government. Another reason was the development of a misguided system for the management of the rural areas during the 1970s, as well as the forced construction of industrial enterprises in the largest cities, especially in Riga.

Population Distribution Between Town and Country

	1935	1959	1979	1989
Total population ('000)	1,905	2,093	2,521	2,680
Urban ('000)	709	1,114	1,726	1,906
% of total population	37.2	53.2	68.5	71.1
Rural ('000)	1,196	979	795	774
% of total population	68.2	46.8	31.5	28.9

Since the beginning of WW I almost throughout the 20th cent. there has been a considerable disproportion in the male/female composition of the Latvian population.

Sex Ratio

	1935	1959	1979	1989[x]
Males ('000)	890	919	1,161	1,239
%	46.7	43.9	46.0	46.5
Females ('000)	1,015	1,174	1,360	1,428
%	53.3	56.1	54.0	53.5

[x] Permanent population.

In the Republic approximately 25,000 marriages take place annually, more than 10,000 end in divorce. 56.5% of the population of Latvia in 1989 were of an employable age, 22.8% were younger than of working age, 20.7% — older. The process of the ageing of population continues.

Age Distribution (%)

	1930	1959	1979[x]	1989[x]
Total population	100	100	100	100
0 — 19 years old	32.1	30.0	28.1	28.4
20 — 59 years old	55.0	55.0	55.1	54.2
60 years old and older	12.9	15.0	16.8	17.4

[x] Permanent population.

The average expected age for women in 1989 was 75.2 years, for men — 65.3 years of age. In no European country, in which the state has been named after its native population, with the exception of Latvia, Estonia (61.5% Estonians in 1989), Moldavia (64.5%) and the Ukraine (72.7%), do its native inhabitants represent fewer than 3/4 of the population. The nationalistic politics practiced in the USSR have led the Latvian nation to the border of extinction: the question is truly not that of any further evolution of the Latvian nation, as of its very survival. Even on the terms that in an independent Latvia any kind of immigration be discontinued (with the exception of those Latvians returning to their home-country), during the next 30 years the number of Latvians within the total population of the Republic will increase by only a few percent.

National Composition of Population

	1935		1959		1979		1989	
	('000)	%	('000)	%	('000)	%	('000)	%
Latvians	1,473	75.5	1,292	62.0	1,344	53.7	1,388	52.0
Russians	206	10.6	556	26.6	821	32.8	906	34.0
Byelorussians	27	1.4	62	2.9	112	4.5	120	4.5
Ukrainians	—	0.0	29	1.4	67	2.7	92	3.5
Poles	49	2.5	60	2.9	63	2.5	60	2.3
Lithuanians	23	1.2	32	1.5	38	1.5	35	1.3

The distribution of the population is quite uneven. The average density within the Republic is 41 persons per sq km. Almost 1/2 of the total population of the Republic lives in the agglomeration of Riga (Riga, Jelgava, Jūrmala and other neighbouring cities and villages within a distance of 40 — 70 km), that constitutes approximately 6% of Latvia's territory. In the Riga district which makes up the largest part of the agglomerative territory, the density is 50 persons per sq km, the lowest is in the Western Latvia, Ventspils district — 6 persons per sq km.

STATE STRUCTURE

State and administrative structures of the Republic of Latvia, their formation, basic principles and development have been determined by the Declaration on the Renewal of the Independence of the Republic of Latvia passed by the Supreme Council (SC) of the Latvian SSR on May 4, 1990. State structure of the Republic, still in the process of formation, is characterized by firm rejection of the Soviet totalitarian system and socialist dogmas in state policy violently imposed on Latvia; by re-creation of political plurality, multi-party system and democratic parliamentarian statehood, and setting up independent administrative bodies. Implementation of these basic principles can be guaranteed by the re-establishment of the *de facto* independence of the Republic of Latvia. In the Declaration the SC, expressing the will of the people, declared that the liquidation of the statehood and sovereignty of the Republic of Latvia proclaimed in 1918, its incorporation into the SU in 1940 and setting up of the Soviet regime in Latvia are illegal acts resulting from the USSR aggression and occupation contrary to the will of the Latvian people. The SC declared null and void from the moment of inception the decision by the People's Parliament (*Saeima*) from July 21, 1940, on the Republic of Latvia joining the Union of Soviet Socialist Republics and reinstated the official name of the Republic of Latvia, abbreviated as Latvia.

The Declaration being the basic document of the transition period with constitutional significance, states that Articles 1, 2, 3 and 6 of the 1922 Constitution (*Satversme*) have re-established authority, according to which Latvia is an independent, democratic republic (Article 1); the sovereign power of the Latvian state belongs to the people of Latvia (Article 2); the territory of the Latvian state consists of Vidzeme, Latgale, Kurzeme and Zemgale, within the boundaries stipulated by international treaties (Article 3). Article 6, which states that the *Saeima* is elected by universal, equal, direct and secret vote on the basis of proportional representation, will be applied when electing the new *Saeima*. During the transition period constitutional and legal acts of the Latvian SSR can also be implemented, insofar as they do not contradict the above-mentioned Declaration and Articles 1, 2, 3 and 6 of the Constitution (*Satversme*) of the Republic of Latvia.

In the course of the creation of new state structures and demolition of the totalitarian rule in the Republic of Latvia, internationally accepted principles of the division of legislative, executive and judicial powers are used.

During the transition period till the election of new *Saeima* supreme state power in Latvia is held by the SC of the Republic. It is authorized to accept for trial any case of social and state significance and to decide on this matter. 201 deputies were elected to the Parliament of Latvia in March 1990; 138 of these were the supporters of the LPF. Presidium of the SC, consisting of the Chairman, 2 Deputy Chairmen, Secretary and 15 members, leaders of standing commissions, has been set up for organizing the work of the SC and implementing variety of delegated authority.

With the legislative bodies being independent and well-established, the formation of the executive structures in the Republic is a complicated process including dismantling of the former totalitarian government bodies, disintegration from the executive institutions of the USSR, suspending their functions on the territory of Latvia, setting up new administrative and state structures, both local and national. The Council of Ministers is the highest executive body in the Republic of Latvia, accountable to the SC. It organizes and coordinates the activities of 19 republican ministries, various state committees and separate departments. In the transition period disintegration from the USSR structures in the sphere of court and legal supervision is taking place. In October 1990, the Prosecutor's Office of the Republic of Latvia, independent of that of the USSR, was set up and the Prosecutor General was appointed. Parallel USSR Prosecutor's offices still exist and are active in the Republic.

With the elimination of the leading role of the Communists in the multi-party system of the Republic took root and numerous public organizations and movements were formed. Leading positions are taken by the LPF, Latvian National Independence Movement, Latvian Party of the Greens, LSDWP, LDLP, as well as CPSU-oriented CP of Latvia which represents the interests of the USSR.

HISTORY

THE PERIOD UNTIL THE DEVELOPMENT OF THE LATVIAN STATE. The present-day Latvia's territory has been inhabited since 9,000 BC. About 3,000 BC there lived the ancestors of the Baltic Finns, but during the 1st half of the 2nd millennium BC the territory was entered by the first pre-Baltic tribes. The culture of the Baltic (Selonians, Semigallians, Couronians, Latgallians) and Finno-Ugric (Livian) tribes was formed; the first formations of government occurred. This independent evolution was interrupted by the feudal German aggression in the Baltics. The conquered territory was named Livonia, and regular economic and cultural ties with the more developed European regions were established. However, this national yoke was a significant hindrance to the historical development of the Baltic peoples. Riga became a large trading centre; though, since the middle of the 14th cent. the trade and property rights of the non-Germans of Riga were restricted. The social structure of the Baltic inhabitants was deformed, the native inhabitants were represented mainly by peasantry which, during the 15th and 16th cent. came under the yoke of serfdom. After the War of Livonia (1558 – 83), the newly formed Duchy of Pārdaugava and the Duchy of Kurzeme and Zemgale came under the rule of Rzeczpospolita and there arose the possibility to unite the lands populated by Latvians into a joint state. After the Polish – Swedish War (1600 – 29) and the Armistice of Altmark (1629) Sweden acquired Riga and, with the exception of Latgale, the better part of the Duchy of Pārdaugava. This historical segregation of Latgale hindered the consolidation of the Latvian people. The inclusion of Latvian territories into the Russian Empire began after the Great Northern War (1700 – 21). Since the end of the 18th cent., there began a period of change from feudalism to capitalist industrialism in Latvia. After the abolition of serfdom, industry began to develop at a rapid rate, the population increased. The process of consolidation of the Latvian nation took place during the 19th cent. In the middle of the 19th cent. there arose a national awakening, that was firmly tied to the wide-ranging efforts of the Neo-Latvians, such as Kr.Valdemārs, Kr. Barons, J.Alunāns, A.Kronvalds, R.Tomsons and K.Kalniņš to achieve for the Latvian nation the same rights other nations enjoy. These efforts also signalled the beginning of a fight for national self-determination. The unification and Russification policies begun by the Russian Empire endangered both the autonomy of the Balto-Germanic provinces, as well as the nationalistic movements of the Baltic peoples. The huge landed estates of the German barons caused a sharp lack of available farm-land in Latvia. A hallmark of the Latvian social structure was the relatively large percentage of the land-less and city workers (up to 60% of the population). The autocratic character of the Russian Empire channelled the frustrations of the population into illegal revolutionary activities. The first leftist political parties in Latvia were organized: the Latvian Social Democratic Union (1903), and in 1904, when the various Social Democratic parties joined into one, the Latvian SDP became the most influential. The Revolution of 1905 in Latvia was a fight for social and nationalistic liberation. The question of national statehood became quite universal among the people.

WW I (1914 — 18) was a difficult time for the Latvian people; Kurzeme was occupied by Germany, and was threatened with colonization. The threat of division brought about a new outburst of national self-confidence; Battalions (later regiments) of Latvian Riflemen were formed for the protection of the fatherland. The heroism and selflessness of the Latvian Riflemen was wasted by the tsar's generals mainly on poorly planned and bungled military operations. During the 1917 Russian Revolution, the slogan was advanced 'Free Latvia within free Russia'. The Latvian Social Democrats remained the most influential, but to a large degree supported the Bolsheviks. After the October armed overthrow, the Iskolat Republic was formed in the unoccupied part of Latvia. The Iskolat rule (Chair. F.Roziņš) was inimical to the work toward independence by the Latvian Provisional National Council and the Riga Democratic Bloc.

THE PERIOD OF INDEPENDENCE. After the November Revolution in Germany, a historically favourable situation developed for the realization of the rights of self-determination for the Latvian nation. Of large importance was the support of the Entente. Latvian political parties formed into the Latvian People's Council which, on November 18, 1918, for the first time proclaimed the national independence of Latvia. The Latvian Army, which had a decisive role in the struggle for freedom, was formed. The existence of the new Latvian state was threatened by the army of Soviet Russia, supported by the Latvian Bolsheviks, as well as by parts of the German army, with whom were the sympathies of the Baltic Germans. As the German occupation army retreated, the Red Army, formed to a great part by the Latvian Riflemen, entered Latvia. The resumption of Soviet power in Latvia was announced on December 17, 1918, by a manifesto of the Latvian Soviet government. There was some leftist sentiment in a part of Latvia's population. The Constitution of the Latvian Socialist Soviet Republic was based on that of the Russian Socialist Federated Soviet Republic; its army formed part of the Red Army. The Soviet government (Chair. P.Stučka) liquidated private land ownership, confiscated country estates with their entire inventories, nationalized industrial and trade companies, railways, banks and other credit associations. The nationalized land was divided among Soviet and rented farms; the farmers did not receive land into ownership. The government of the Latvian Socialist Soviet Republic subjected their actions to a Utopian ideology, which it tried to bring to life with tyrannical methods. That was the main reason for the fall of Soviet power. On May 22, 1919, Riga was occupied by R. von der Goltz's armed forces during the reign of the so-called Niedra's government. For several days, the terror of the German Landeswehr raged in the city. At a time, when Latvia once again was threatened to come under the yoke of Russia and German gentry, the Latvian nation united around the Latvian Provisional Government for the decisive battle against the armies of R. von der Goltz and P.Bermondt-Avalov. A victory over Bermondt, and a course toward an independent Latvia, assured the Provisional Government of the Republic of Latvia the support of the nation's majority. The war activities on the Latgale front were also successful. On January 13, 1920, the Latvian Soviet government announced its dissolution in Veļikije Luki. On August 11, 1920, a peace treaty was signed between Latvia and the Soviet Russia, in which Soviet Russia recognized Latvia's independence and relinquished any and all rights of the previous tsarist Russian government toward Latvia's territories. On September 22, 1921, Latvia was admitted to the membership in the League of Nations. The Latvian Constitution (*Satversme*) of 1922 stated that Latvia was a democratic, parliamentary republic.

The first Prime Minister of Latvia was K.Ulmanis, but the first President and Chairman of the Latvian People's Council and the Constitutional Assembly was J.Čakste. Although the war had devastated Latvia's agriculture un totally destroyed its industries (bulk of factories had been evacuated to Russia), after radical agrarian reform and other far-reaching reforms Latvia became a highly developed state with a flourishing national culture. Latvia had an active social and political life; there were many political, social and cultural organizations. During the years of the world economic crisis, the social and political conflicts were noticably intensified. On May 15, 1934, an overturn of the government took place; K.Ulmanis' authoritarian regime was formed, the parliament was dismissed, political parties and some organizations were closed. A tendency toward state control of the economic and social life was strengthened. Latvia's foreign policy was shaped for the protection of peace and safety of the state. During the 1930s, Latvia had been recognized as an independent state by all the independent states of that time. As early as 1928 there were 21 foreign embassies in Latvia (among them those of Belgium, France, Germany, Great Britain, Japan, the Netherlands, Sweden, the USA and the USSR), as well as 45 consulates-general, consulates and vice-consulates. In 1939, there were 16 Latvian embassies that represented Latvia in 25 countries, as well as 194 consulates in various countries. Much credit for the development of the Latvian state and toward its strengthening must be given to the Foreign Minister Z.A.Meierovics.

THE EVENTS OF 1939 — 40. At the end of the 1930s, the international situation of the Republic of Latvia became unstable; this was determined by the breakdown of the Versailles agreements, as well as the system of treaties between Germany and the USSR (the Treaty of Non-Aggression, August 23,

1939; the Treaty on Friendship and Existing Borders, September 28, 1939). Based on these treaties, Eastern Europe was divided between the USSR and Germany into spheres of influence. Yielding to the SU demand a treaty of mutual assistance was forcibly signed during the September and October of 1939, which gave to the SU the right to bring in its army troops and to build military bases; Latvia became a virtual Soviet dominion. In accordance with the treaty of September 28, 1939, the repatriation of the Baltic Germans began.

On June 16, 1940, the Soviet government presented to the government of the Republic of Latvia an ultimatum that demanded establishing pro-Soviet regime and admit more Soviet troops throughout Latvia. On June 17, an unprovoked aggression was carried out against Latvia, and Latvia was occupied by the Red Army troops. On June 20, the Latvian People's Government, which attempted to legitimize the annexation of Latvia into the USSR, was formed; on July 14–15, parliamentary elections were proclaimed. The Soviet-sponsored list of candidates put up by the Latvian Workers' Bloc was the only list registered and permitted into the polls. The electoral platform of the Latvian Workers' Bloc called for the formation of a close alliance between Latvia and the USSR, one that would assure the independence of Latvia and the immunity of the state. The newly elected People's Parliament (*Saeima*) on July 21, 1940, disregarding the Constitution of 1922, proclaimed the establishment of Soviet power in Latvia and carried a decision to join the USSR; the Latvian SSR was created. Such a decision did not correspond with the electoral platform or the authority of the deputies. On July 11, 1940, Latvia was incorporated into the Baltic War Region even though only on August 5, 1940, the Supreme Soviet had admitted the Latvian SSR into the USSR. Although the largest part of the people acted loyally toward the new government, extensive atrocities took place, reaching a culmination during the unlawful deportations on June 14, 1941, when almost 15,000 of Latvia's inhabitants were deported. A considerable number of the Latvian Army officers (the Latvian Army had been converted into the Red Army 24th Territorial Riflemen's Corps) were deported and a part of them were shot (in Litene and elsewhere). For this reason the year has been remembered by the Latvian nation as the 'Year of Horror'.

WORLD WAR II. Within a few days after the Nazi attack on the USSR the war zone entered Latvia's territory, however, general mobilization was not proclaimed in Latvia. National army units were disbanded, a large part of officers were unfoundedly repressed. Many Latvian citizens were later mobilized into the *SS* legion. During the German occupation, Latvia was incorporated as an administrative territorial unit in *Reichskomissariat Ostland.* Local collaborationists took an active part in the mass murders of people. Many crimes against humanity were committed both during the USSR and subsequent Nazi occupation.

As early as the beginning of the first occupation there were attempts to organize Latvian resistance movement. However, only in 1943 did the diplomatic representatives of the Republic of Latvia abroad manage to contact political activists in occupied Latvia and suggested the formation of an illegal political organization, the Central Council of Latvia. The aims of this organization were the restoration of the Republic of Latvia.

Since the SU was an ally in the fight against Nazi Germany, some Latvians became part of the Red Army. There were also resistance groups in Latvia, controlled by the Latvian CP.

THE PERIOD OF SOVIET OCCUPATION. THE DECLARATION OF INDEPENDENCE. After the liberation of Latvia (July, 1944 – May, 1945) the number of inhabitants had decreased by 1/3, the larger part of the intelligentsia living in emigration. The Stalinist regime was restored, wide-range repressions took place. A forced general collectivization was connected with a new wave of deportations on March 25, 1949 (more than 42,000 people were deported). The industrialization of the Republic was speeded up without any economic substantiation. The process of healing begun in Latvia during 'the spring of Khrushchev' was interrupted by the restoration of Neo-Stalinism. During the plenum of the Latvian CP Central Committee in 1959, the leaders of the Latvian CP and the Latvian SSR were accused of 'bourgeois nationalism' and dismissed from their leading positions in the Republic. The forced speed-up of the Republic's industries intensified, which promoted a huge mechanical increase in population, sharpening the social and national problems. By the end of the 1970s, Latvia had arrived at the point of a social, economic and ecological crisis. The movement of reconstruction during the 2nd half of the 1980s, which opened the way to democratization, permitted the voicing of the wishes of the people for self-determination, and thus created the necessary pre-conditions for a national reawakening, as well as for the renewal and resurrection of the Latvian state. On May 4, 1990, the name of the Republic of Latvia was renewed, and the Declaration on the Renewal of the Independence of the Republic of Latvia was adopted. Consultative meetings with the government of the USSR concerning possible times and places for meetings between the two states have begun, and an increased activity in Latvia's foreign policy has been observed.

In the public opinion poll held on March 3, 1991, 73.7% of voters expressed their support for the renewal of independence of the Republic of Latvia.

NATIONAL ECONOMY

The development of Latvia's national economy has been greatly influenced both by its geographical position and political, social and economic situation. Climate has a favourable impact on agriculture in general, dairy farming and pig-breeding, being the leading branches. Advantageous geographical location of Latvia on the eastern shores of the Baltic Sea and at the crossing of ancient trade routes from Russia to Western Europe has determined the development of a significant transport network. Limited natural resources on the one hand and considerably well-developed infrastructure on the other have facilitated the creation and speedy progress of processing industries.

In the early 20th cent., the territory of Latvia was one of the best industrially-developed provinces of the Russian Empire. During the WW I, more than 500 industrial enterprises alongside with the technological equipment were moved from Latvia to the Central Russia. In the period of Latvia's independence while the former economic ties with Russia were loose, industrial production was local-market-oriented and based mainly on highly skilled domestic labour force. Traditional industries were those of timber and paper (29% of the totally employed in 1939), light (22.9%) and food (17.6%). Agricultural produce accounted for 53.5% of Latvia's export values in 1939 (including dairy produce and meat exports), timber industries gave 35.5%; engineering enterprises (producing mainly bicycles and radio receivers) constituted only 1.4% of external trade.

Since the mid-1940s, Latvia has been an integral part of the vast but ineffective national economy of the SU. Due to the political and economic considerations of the USSR the national economy of Latvia was subjected to crude distortions. Completely neglecting the vital interests and needs of the Latvian nation, forcible industrialization was started which, in its turn, brought about influx of manpower and mass-scale oversaturation of Latvia with immigrants from different regions of the USSR. Between 1940 and mid-1980s, the number of industrially-employed workers increased 3.7 times. In the 2nd half of the 1980s these numbers tended downwards (by 43,400 in 1984 — 88) while today there is a constant increase of the employed in the social services like catering for the population (by 17% in 1960 and 24.2% in 1989). A notable decrease of the employed in the state sector of the national economy is observed lately, at the same time a rapid increase of working population engaged in cooperative sector can be characterized by the following — 28,700 persons in 1988 and 135,000 in 1990.

Gross National Product and National Income in 1989 (%)

	GNP	National Income
Industry	60.3	45.2
Agriculture	20.4	25.0
Construction	7.2	8.8
Transport and communications	5.5	7.3
Other branches	6.6	13.7
Total	100	100

Economically Active Population ('000 persons)

	1985	1988	1989
Workers and employees engaged in the national economy	1,231	1,213	1,171
Industry (production staff)	416	392	374
Agriculture	118	108	102
Construction	102	115	114
Transport	109	93	88
Communications	20	18	17
Trade and public catering, material and technical provision and realization, supplies	119	124	122
Health services, sports and social insurance	73	78	79
Education	92	102	102
Culture	15	16	17
Art	6	7	7
Science	33	32	31
Administration	28	21	17
Farmers (on collective farms)	138	141	146
Total	1,369	1,354	1,317

INDUSTRY of the Republic produces comparatively limited range of specified items. Local natural resources supply feedstock only for 2/5 of the overall industrial output. Approximately 1/4 of the overall output produced in the Republic is exported and the same amount of produce consumed in the Republic is imported. Considerable transportation costs make production ineffective and enterprises non-paying. 20% enterprises with over 1,000 workers each account for 2/3 of fixed assets, labour force and industrial output, the latter in 1989 was 59 times as much as in 1940. Most rapid rates of advance are characteristic of machine-building, metal working, chemical and petrochemical industries. Economic progress of these branches is related mainly to extensive methods of transformation. By 1990, the wearing-out level of fixed assets has reached the critical point and just

10 – 12% of all technological equipment can produce foreign market competitive goods. Low quality of industrial output is greatly determined by technological backwardness of industry. Success in further development of the national economy of Latvia lies in scientific approach to the production processes, revitalization of the production and high-technology output by all industries and enterprises in the years ahead. Latvia's biggest industrial centre is Riga, several important enterprises are operating also in Liepāja, Ventspils, Valmiera and Daugavpils.

Distribution of Labour Force in Industries ('000 persons)

	1985	1988	1989
Electric engineering	7.0	6.5	6.9
Machine building and metal working	160.6	153.3	147.2
Chemical and petrochemical	24.9	23.9	23.2
Timber, pulp and paper	37.6	36.9	33.8
Building materials	19.8	19.3	18.0
Light	81.9	74.3	70.0
Food	49.0	45.6	43.1
All industries	**415.7**	**392.1**	**373.7**

Industrial Output

	1985	1988	1989
Electricity generated (million kWh)	4,961	5,110	5,801
Steel ('000 t)	550	559	555
Rolled ferrous metals ('000 t)	823	848	795
Diesel engines and generators ('000 u.)	11.2	9.7	7.8
Electric bulbs (million u.)	66.3	43.4	38.4
Industrial robots (u.)	378	132	78
Automatic telephone exchanges ('000 no)	719	734	647
Telephones ('000 u.)	2,801	2,727	2,900
Refrigerating equipment ('000 sets)	100.2	110.2	94.6
Electric railway cars (u.)	499	561	505
Diesel engine train cars (u.)	72	72	60
Buses ('000 u.)	15.2	17.6	17.0
Mineral fertilizer spreaders ('000 u.)	27.7	25.4	21.5
Milking equipment ('000 u.)	29.5	32.2	25.1
Chaindrives (million m)	33.2	35.4	38.5
Mineral fertilizers ('000 t)	169	176	188
Synthetic fiber and thread ('000 t)	50.3	52.0	50.9
Synthetic resins and plastics ('000 t)	35.0	40.0	37.9
Varnishes and paints ('000 t)	54.2	52.6	53.2
Sawn timber ('000 cu m)	866	1,024	825
Plywood ('000 cu m)	107	113	95
Woodwaste plates ('000 cu m)	131	228	226
Cellulose ('000 t)	69.0	62.2	51.9
Paper ('000 t)	167	153	138
Cement ('000 t)	787	825	776
Bricks (million u.)	377	447	466
Radio receivers ('000 u.)	1,570	1,762	1,486
Cassette recorders ('000 u.)	36.1	80.8	94.9
Washing machines ('000 u.)	647	657	612
Motorbicycles ('000 u.)	194	196	182
Cotton fabric (million sq m)	61.3	59.2	55.6
Silk fabric (million sq m)	26.0	27.8	27.7
Linen (million sq m)	19.3	19.6	19.8
Knitwear (million u.)	44.5	42.8	43.0
Socks and stockings (million p.)	75.8	78.3	78.8
Footwear (million p.)	10.6	10.3	10.2
Matches ('000 boxes)	576	577	582
Linoleum (million sq m)	6.7	7.6	7.8
Meat ('000 t)	242.5	263.6	254.5
Sausages ('000 t)	54.4	61.0	61.0
Tinned meat (million tins)	10.7	11.3	12.0
Butter ('000 t)	44.6	47.1	46.7
Whole-milk products ('000 t)	540	577	576
fat cheese ('000 t)	23.0	24.7	24.8
tinned milk (million tins)	80.3	90.8	92.4

	1985	1988	1989
Sugar ('000 t)	249	243	248
Fish catch ('000 t)	538	559	547
Fish preserves (million tins)	239.5	226	233
Tinned fruit and vegetables ('000 tins)	81.9	122.7	166

AGRICULTURE. Cultivated lands occupy 2,570,000 ha (1989; 3,710,000 ha in 1940); 1,680,000 ha of these are fields, 264,200 ha meadows and 599,800 ha pastures. Post-war slowdown in development hit the agriculture of the Republic, due to which output increased just 1.5 times between 1939 and 1989. Cattle-breeding went up 1.9 times, but plant-growing only by 14% in the same period. Vast drainage network (1,541,000 ha in 1989) and soil fertilizing (8 times increase as compared with 1940) did not ensure a boost in productivity and rich harvests. The share of cattle-breeding in gross agricultural output today is 69%. Before WW II Latvia figured in the world as a prominent dairy producer. In the post-war period the number of head of cattle, pigs and poultry went up considerably; a key factor of this steep rise was extensive use of concentrated fodder brought in from other parts of the SU. In 1988, 35% of state-purchased meat, 36% of milk and 14% of potatoes were taken out of the Republic and delivered to the consumers in the USSR. Today 1/4 of meat and milk produced in the Republic comes from individual farmers and subsidiary farms.

Land Use ('000 ha)

	1985	1988	1989
Cereals	727	656	680.5
rye	101	101	129
barley	397	353	332
oats	92	66	75
Industrial crops	30	31	30
Potatoes	95	88	85
Vegetables	12	12	11
Fodder crops	789	864	819
Perennial fodder grasslands	176	181	181
Total	**1,653**	**1,651**	**1,625**

Principal Crops ('000 t)

	1985	1988	1989
Grain	1,294	1,142	1,597
Flax	4.0	4.6	5.9
Sugar beets	356	455	395
Potatoes	1,272	1,110	1,315
Vegetables	217	214	220
Fodder root-crops	1,056.8	1,348.7	1,425.2
Ensilage crops	298.2	353.8	216.2
Maize	1,394.7	1,600.7	1,533.7

Crop Production (100 kg per ha)

	1985	1988	1989
Cereal crops	22.1	21.5	23.5
Flax fibre	2.8	3.6	4.6
Sugar beets	263	333	294
Potatoes	135	127	155
Vegetables	165	159	185
Fodder root-crops	331	395	412
Ensilage crops	113	87	116
Maize	290	342	332
Perennial fodder grass hay	39.7	40.0	43.4

Livestock ('000 head, end of the year)

	1985	1988	1989
Cattle	1,485	1,460	1,472
Cows	563	543	544
Pigs	1,721	1,620	1,555
Sheep	177	160	159
Goats	5	5	5
Horses	33	33	32
Poultry	12,667	12,209	11,246

Livestock Products

	1985	1988	1989
Meat ('000 t)	324.0	344.4	331.3
beef and veal	126.5	136.1	129.1
pork	151.8	160.3	154.3
mutton and lamb meat	4.3	4.0	4.0
poultry	39.9	42.4	42.6
Milk ('000 t)	1,956.9	1,974.0	1,976.8
Eggs (million)	880.3	920.0	890.0
Wool (t)	437	382	370
Honey (t)	—	—	2,806

TRANSPORT. The Republic has a highly ramified transport network. There are 37 km of railroads and 288 km of hard-surfaced motor roads per 1,000 sq km (Estonia and Lithuania have 328 and 321 km respectively). Railway network serves the purpose of transporting freights within the SU and to the principal ports for export shipments. Grain, fuel and building materials rank among the most important freights. More than 4/5 of the total number of railway passengers use suburban trains for daily commuting and reaching recreation areas. Due to the sharp rise in oil exports through the ports of the Republic, the transportation of goods by sea has increased 14-fold in 1960 – 89. In 1989, the total volume of 38,000,000 t, including 32,000,000 t of oil products and 2,000,000 t of chemicals and fertilizers was transported through the ports of Latvia, mainly Ventspils. River navigation system operates solely for the needs of the national economy and for passenger transportation. 2/3 of all industrial freights are delivered by motor-vehicles. Alongside with a recent drop in the number of trucks (61% in 1989), the average freight capacity has increased (5,1t). Interurban passenger communication has been ensured by a well-developed bus transport. The total length of airlines connecting Riga with 85 cities in the USSR is 81,000 km. Since 1990, first international flights take passengers from Riga to Helsinki, Stockholm, Copenhagen, New York and back. The completion of the gas-main accounted for decrease in the supplies of coal and oil products for heating, thus relieving additional resources for various means of transport. The gas-main from Polock to Ventspils fully handles the whole Soviet oil shipments.

	1985	1988	1989
Traffic roads (km, end of the year)			
railways	2,384	2,384	2,397
electrified railways	248	267	271
motor roads	20,500	20,500	20,600
inland waterways	347	347	347
airlines	83,000	82,000	81,000
gas-mains	832	1,110	1,121
Freight transportation (million t)			
railway	22.4	20.3	20.5
sea	32.4	38.0	36.6
inland waterways	4.0	4.3	3.9
motor vehicles	85.5	90.2	85.4
total	**144.4**	**152.8**	**146.5**
Freight turnover (million t-km)			
railway	19,900	21,700	21,100
sea	66,600	67,600	65,200
inland waterways	200	300	300
motorways	2,300	2,400	2,400
total	**89,100**	**92,000**	**89,000**
Passenger conveyance (million)			
railway	134.0	140.8	135.0
inland waterways	0.9	1.0	0.8
buses	510.6	569.5	575.0
trolley-buses	207.8	218.4	217.9
trams	217.2	244.4	241.2
air	0.9	1.0	1.1
total	**1,091.1**	**1,195.5**	**1,189.1**
Passenger traffic (million passenger-km)			
railway	5,214	5,761	5,449
inland waterways	22	17	13
buses	5,266	5,821	5,877
air	2,853	3,237	3,283
total	**13,355**	**14,836**	**14,622**

Interrepublican exchange topped 9,100,000,000 roubles in 1988, the imported goods reaching 4,600,000,000 and exported goods — 4,500,000,000 roubles. Power industry, metallurgy and machine-building mainly account for the excess import share of this exchange. Latvia produces an ample amount of goods for the all-Union market, among which passenger carriages (31% in 1989), automatic telephone exchanges (22%), telephones (58%), refrigerating equipment (29%), milking equipment (43%), diesel engines and generators (16%), buses (19%), mopeds (57%), radio receivers (17%) and washing machines (9%) rank among the most important items. 3/5 of the goods taken out of the Republic are produced by Riga enterprises.

FOREIGN TRADE. Industrial goods worth 334,000,000 roubles or 2% of the GNP were exported from Latvia in 1989. The output of machine building industry worth 16,700,000 roubles or 1% of the gross product was sold abroad for hard currency (Lithuania sold 9.1%, but Estonia — 0.6%). Exports in 1989 included 514,000 radio receivers, 19,000 washing machines, 1,500 minibuses, 5,100 mopeds, 16 railway carriages, 1,900 manure spreaders, 19,000,000 boxes of tinned milk, 1,000 t of cheese, 5,000 t of fat, and fish produce worth 63,000,000 roubles. Imported goods account for 7% of the total consumption or 1,400,000,000 roubles. Consumer goods, raw materials for food industry (raw sugar, grain, coffee and cocoa beans), communication systems, technical equipment for textile industry, electronic computer technology, cars, wool, volatile oils constitute the bulk of import. 15 Latvian enterprises have established direct business contacts with firms abroad, the number of joint ventures rising to 30 by January 1,1990.

FINANCE AND CREDIT. The centralized state fund of money resources comprises the Budget of the Republic of Latvia and 584 budgets of local authorities, which are independent and form a system of budgets in Latvia.

The Budget is controlled by the Finance Ministry of the Republic of Latvia, the Finance Board, finance departments and finance inspection departments. The banks perform compiling and execution of the Budget.

Property and personal insurance is performed by the Latvian State Insurance Company *Latva*. Pensions and sickness benefits are paid from the state insurance budget, which is formed from social taxes.

The Bank of Latvia controls money circulation, crediting, supervises all the banks of the Republic. For the time being, coins and notes, that are in circulation in the Republic of Latvia, are made in the USSR. Exchange rates are determined by the USSR State Bank. Practical work is carried out by Industrial and Constructional Bank, Agro-Industrial Bank, Housing, Public Services and Social Development Bank, commercial and cooperative banks. They settle accounts, grant credits, issue money from the budgets, perform international financial operations.

One-year credits are granted to enterprises, organizations, cooperatives, peasants and craftsmen for the purchasing of circulating means and long-term credits for basic means and for construction and reconstruction work.

CULTURE

FOLKLORE. Folklore provides basis both for Latvian folk art and professional art. The Folklore department of the Latvian Academy of Sciences cherishes the rich heritage of about 1,400,945 folk songs, 30,285 melodies, 35,955 fairy tales, 574,234 riddles, 57,592 folk tales and 33,139 anecdotes. Folk song, sometimes shortly and euphonically called *Daina*, undoubtedly is the most peculiar, highly developed and well-investigated folklore genre. Folk song (*Daina*) is plainly distinguishable from other genres with its stylistically well-preserved form. More than 90% of them are created in trochaic metre. Being of ancient origin, its form and style display mythological world perception from the times of the so-called Indo-European community as well as established religious system of the Baltic peoples. Later Latvians started differentiating between city folklore and traditional folk song. Nowadays classical folk song is considered to be a lyric and philosophical poetry.

The first piece of folklore published in 1632 is folk song, but the first collection was issued in 1807 (by G.Bergmanis). Since the middle of the 19th cent. systematic collection and preserving of folklore has been taken over by the Latvians. A very important role befalls to F.Brīvzemnieks, later — to Kr.Barons, who has been entrusted with the heritage of folk songs by his pre-decessors. It resulted in the most complete collection of folk songs *Latvju dainas* (Latvian Folk Songs; 1894 — 1916). From the point of view of its scientific classification and artistic value there is no analogous literary monument in the world literature. In 1979, a new edition of Latvian folk songs, based on the collection of Kr.Barons, has been started (~1,200,000 units; 6 vols have already appeared).

In Latvian fairy tales the mythological trend is more internationalized. Thus local colouring, moral percepts, and ethnical peculiarities are of greater importance than originality of plot. The most complete publication is *Latviešu tautas pasakas* (Latvian Fairy Tales; 1891 — 94) compiled by A.Lerhis-Puškaitis in 5 parts and *Latviešu pasakas un teikas* (Latvian Fairy Tales and Folk Tales; 1920 — 37) compiled by P.Šmits in 15 volumes.

The most ancient layer of riddles and magic words has much in common with folk song both in form and inner structure. Folklore samples of less distant period of time are closer to colloquial speech and contemporary way of living.

The beginnings of professional approach to collecting and preserving of folklore heritage date back to the end of the 19th cent. The contribution of J.Lautenbahs-Jūsmiņš (comparative folklore studies, typology), P.Šmits (mythology), L.Bērziņš (poetic studies of folk song), P.Birkerts (people's philosophy), K.Straubergs (people's customs and magic) is remarkable.

The activities of folklore ensembles, groups of folklore friends as well as dance folklore groups (*Iļģi, Skandinieki, Dandari*) acquire increasing importance in cherishing and handing down the deep-rooted folklore traditions. Plenty of folk ensembles have appeared at enterprises and schools and the number of groups is growing constantly.

EDUCATION. The activities of the Catholic clergy in the territory of Latvia marked the beginnings of school system in the 13th cent. (1211 — the Riga Dome School). The first secular school was the Peter's School (1353). The first schools for Latvian children appeared during the 2nd half of the 16th cent. (the school attached to St.Jacob's Church). Lessons in the Russian language were introduced in 1789, at the same time the network of Latvian schools became larger. The *Academia Petrina* (in Jelgava), founded in 1775, turned into an important research centre. Russification imposed by the authorities began to intensify during the 1860s — in 1865 in Latgale it was forbidden to print any book in the Latin alphabet, but starting with 1887 all instruction at schools in Vidzeme and Kurzeme was in the Russian language (this was repealed at the beginning of the 20th cent.). At that time many Latvians obtained their education outside the Latvian territory — in Tērbata (Tartu), St.Petersburg, also in Moscow. During the 2nd half of the 19th and at the beginning of the 20th cent., special educational establishments (trade schools, naval colleges) were started. In 1862, the Riga Polytechnic was founded; a definite system of education was being developed.

After the proclamation of the Republic of Latvia (1918), extensive school building programme was carried out, free and compulsory pre-school education for children 7 years of age, and elementary school education for children from 8 – 14 years of age was established. For those wishing to obtain further education there were secondary and trade schools, technical schools and universities. The opportunities existed of studying abroad. The curriculum was based upon classical study programmes, besides there existed voluntary organizations for pupils and students — the Scouts and Guides Associations, fraternities and sororities, etc. After Latvia was incorporated into the USSR, the Latvian educational system was destroyed and subordinated to the authoritarian USSR system of education. The result — a low level of general education, poorly prepared specialists. In order to provide efficient education and bring it closer to that of Western Europe, radical changes in the existing curricula and institutions have been made since 1990. During the academic year of 1989/90, 45,600 students were enrolled in the various institutions of higher education (61.5% full-time students, 7.7% evening students, 30.8% correspondence students). There are 17 university students per 1,000 of the population of Latvia.

Institutions of Higher Education (October 1, 1990)

	Year	Faculty	Students	Lecturers
Riga Technical University	1862	10	13,000	1,000
University of Latvia	1919	13	12,586	816
Latvian Academy of Music	1919	3	895	166
Latvian Academy of Arts	1919	10	350	84
Latvian Academy of Agriculture	1939	9	6,167	467
Latvian Institute of Physical Culture	1946	1	1,250	122
Latvian Academy of Medicine	1950	4	2,530	399
Daugavpils Pedagogical Institute	1952	5	2,846	210
Liepāja Pedagogical Institute	1954	3	2,658	141
Riga Civil Aviation Engineering Institute	1960	4	4,100	460

SCIENCE. The beginnings of professional scientific research in Latvia have been pin-pointed in the 16th cent. Initially they consisted mainly of a take-over of the more widespread theories of Western European scientists, later, since the foundation of the *Academia Petrina* in Jelgava (1775), the development of original scientific ideas and their recognition began. Essential to the development of science during the 18th and 19th cent. was the collaboration with Tērbata (Tartu) University and St.Petersburg's Academy of Sciences — the largest scientific centres of that time in the northern Baltics. After the Riga Polytechnic was founded in 1862, science expanded successfully into new fields as engineering, biology and chemistry. During the period F.Bucholtz, K.Kupffer, P.Walden, W.Ostwald, H.Pflaum, K.A.Bischoff, F.Canders, and others worked in Latvia. Around the end of the 19th cent., there began an intensive study of Latvian folklore and linguistics (K.Mīlenbahs, J.Endzelīns, Kr.Barons, P.Šmits).

Since 1918, when the Republic of Latvia proclaimed its independence, and 1919, when the University of Latvia was established, a steady progress of scientific activities was achieved, a new generation of Latvian scientists started their work. Great success was attained in the field of Baltic philology, medicine, various branches of the technical sciences, chemistry, biology, and agriculture. After Latvia was incorporated into the USSR (1940), the organization, leadership and development of sciences in Latvia was subordinated to the corresponding institutions of the SU, whose interests, as a rule, did not coincide with those of Latvia. A wide network of various scientific research organizations was established, however, the subjection of them to different ministries and committees, duplication of effort, lack of co-ordination, etc., did not favour research work. The leaders are the scientific research institutes and centres of the Latvian higher educational establishments and the Academy of Sciences, which carry out research in the traditionally developed field of physics, chemistry, biology, medical as well as technical sciences, obtaining internationally acknowledged results, especially in microbiology, polymer mechanics, wood chemistry, semi-conductor physics and medicine. Orthopaedic surgeon V.Kalnbērzs, physicists E.Siliņš, E.Blūms, chemists J.Stradiņš, E.Grēns, E.Lukevics, microbiologist R.Kārkliņš are widely known not only in Latvia, they have acquired worldwide reputation. The long-term plans of Latvian scientists are tied to expected cooperation and to hoped-for partners among the more developed nations, both on the level of research and on that of bringing the results into production.

LITERATURE. Since the Lutherans tended to preach in local languages (later this principle was taken over by the Catholics as well), Latvian orthography and literature began to gain ground in Martin Luther's teachings throughout the Baltics. The first significant texts in Latvian come from the beginning of the 16th cent., the first book recorded, a Lutheran mass, was burnt in Lübeck in 1525. The first book that has survived — the Small Catholic Catechism — was published in Vilnius in 1585. One of the most distinguished figures of the literature and linguistics of the 17th cent. is K.Fürecker, who lifted the poetics of Latvian spiritual songs unto an excellent level; however, the most notable event of the 17th cent. was the translation of the Bible (1691) by E.Glück, done from the original languages, without the help of any in-between language (German or Latin). The work of E.Glück is still one of the corner-stones of Latvian poetics and literary style. The 18th cent. gave to Latvian literature the outstanding writer of religious works and enlightener G.F.Stenders who, with the help of his secular poetry and in a sentimental manner developed in the Latvian serf an individual sense of the world. It must be added, that the number of people in the provinces of Latvia and Estonia who could read exceeded that in Germany, England and France of that time. G.H.Merkel, the enlightener and defender of the Latvian people, who wrote only in German but nevertheless belongs to Latvian literature, should also be mentioned.

The first writers of Latvian descent appear at the end of the 18th cent. — Ķikuļa Jēkabs, a weaver, and J.N.Ramanis, a debased clergyman and teacher. These writers produced only hand-written manuscripts, and their activities are rooted in the unofficial literature of the Herrnhuters. The first Latvian poet, widely popularized during his time, was Neredzīgais Indriķis (Indriķis the Blind), with the publication of whose collection of poetry in 1806 began the dominance of the Latvians in their own literature. Until the middle of the 19th cent., Latvian literature was represented by such energetic and versatile self-educated writers as A.Līventāls, A.Leitāns, E.Dinsberģis. In 1856, J.Alunāns, a student at Tērbata (Tartu) University, published a book of verse *Dziesmiņas* (Songs), that proved the feasibility of the Latvian language and literature within the context of the Europe of that time, and which quite validly is called the turning-point of professional Latvian poetry. J.Alunāns, together with others who shared his views — representatives of the first generation of the intelligentsia, as Kr.Valdemārs and Kr.Barons, furthered the awakening of the Latvian people and gave an impetus to the next period in Latvian literature. From this combination of patriotism, historical remembrances and the progressive ideas of the time, came the eminent poets of this period of National Romanticism — Auseklis, who is known for his heroic ballads based on history and mythology, and A.Pumpurs, whose epic poem *Lāčplēsis* (Bearslayer, 1888) was raised by the Latvian people into the realm of a national epos. In 1879, there appeared the first significant Latvian novel — *Mērnieku laiki* (The Times of the Land-Surveyors) by brothers Kaudzītes, whose characters, interwoven with religious piety and social satire, have become part of Latvian folklore.

The beginnings of the Latvian national theatre can be traced to the 1870s (Ā.Alunāns); however, the development of modern and full-blooded Latvian literature did not begin until the turn of the century. A short, bright and ahead-of-the-times episode was the poetry of E.Veidenbaums, unpublished but widely known throughout his lifetime. The scepticism and acuteness of its typically critical outlook and analysis keeps it actual, especially among the youth. The name of R.Blaumanis is towering above a host of other prose-writers for his novelletes which, both for their literary technique and psychological depth, are equal to Chekhov's and Maupassant's short stories. Moreover, R.Blaumanis, a dramatist of talent, exercised a powerful influence on theatre life of the time — his folk comedy, *Skroderdienas Silmačos* (Tailor's Days in Silmači, 1902), the socio-psychological dramas *Indrāni* (The Indrāni, 1904) and *Ugunī* (In the Fire, 1905) are still of great literary value. J.Poruks, the first great Latvian poetic individualist, attempted to grasp and describe his time philosophically. Aspazija was also a change-of-the-century poetess, and the greatest woman-writer of the time, who blended poetry and drama in her creative genius both as a romantic rebel and a socially engaged critic. Her spouse, J.Rainis, greatly inspired by Aspazija, was a poet, playwright, journalist and philosopher, who became the synthesis of two centuries of Latvian literature. J.Rainis' authority in the Latvian nation can be compared to that of Goethe, Dante and Pushkin in their respective countries. The plays *Uguns un nakts* (Fire and Night, 1904), *Jāzeps un viņa brāļi* (Joseph and His Brothers, 1914), as well as the volumes of poetry *Gals un sākums* (The End and the Beginning, 1912) and *Piecas Dagdas skiču burtnīcas* (Dagda's Five Notebooks, 1925) are an original quintessence of the 20th cent. European literature. Among the contemporaries of J.Rainis one must mention F.Bārda, a symbolically pantheistic poet, K.Skalbe, a lyricist and master of the fairy tale, J.Akuraters, V.Plūdonis, authors of virtuoso ballads, all — deeply nationalist poets with an original nationalistic style.

Latvia proclaimed its independence on November 18, 1918, and there a new and prolific period in Latvian literature began. In the multi-coloured panorama of the poetry of the 1920s and 1930s especially outstanding is J.Sudrabkalns, with his original and lyrically expressionistic manner, and A.Čaks, who, in his turn, developed his imagist experience. A.Čaks' most important work, the ballad cycle *Mūžības skartie* (Those Marked by Eternity, 1938), is dedicated to the Latvian Riflemen of WW I. The talents of both outstanding poets were distorted by the Soviet cultural politics. An original adapter of French culture was E.Virza, who attempted to combine strict classical forms with the spirit of national domination. The English pre-Raphaelist influence can be felt in the poetry and short stories of E.Ādamsons. This period produced one more outstanding Latvian short-story writer — J.Ezeriņš.

The occupation of Latvia in 1940 and WW II destroyed the process of evolution in literature. Paradoxically, during the German occupation the literary, theatre and musical life, since the Nazi administration did not pay any undue attention to Latvian cultural activities, was revitalized. In its turn, Latvian literature had to pay dearly for this activity upon the return of Soviet power. At the end of WW II, many writers were forced to emigrate, others were deported. The 1940s and 1950s was the time of censorship and organized literature. The outstanding epic prose-writer of his time, A.Upīts, having published the historical novel *Zaļā zeme* (The Green Land, 1945), turned into the central figure of the destructive Soviet literary criticism. Similarly, the popular novelist and author of *Zvejnieka dēls* (The Fisherman's Son, 1933), V.Lācis, during the Soviet regime served in responsible government posts and adapted his previous writings to Soviet requirements, produced new works without any visible literary value. After Stalin's death and the coming to power of N.Khrushchev, a thaw began in Latvian literature which, although short-lived, was nevertheless able to produce some tenacious, vital shoots, primarily in poetry. A distinguished representative of the period was O.Vācietis, a temperamental, spontaneously free poet who tore down more than one psychological and stylistic hedge of literature. V.Belševica, through difficult inner struggles and reflections, rose through the years to a revelation of the tragedy of today's humanity, to a judging of the conscience. I.Ziedonis' prose and poems are remarkable for seismographically sensitive resonances of social tendencies. In the realm of the story during the 1960s and 1970s, lasting values are created by E.Vilks, M.Birze. A.Bels' acutely constructed novels-parables, Z.Skujiņš' panoramas of social genre and history display a reporter's precision, but R.Ezera's psychologically centered works are written with literary excellence. During the 1970s and 1980s, a new generation of literary mature poets (U.Bērziņš, L.Briedis, J.Rokpelnis), who actively and noticably widen the poetic tradition, enter the field of poetry. In prose fiction a large number of women-writers make their debut during the 1980s, among them A.Neiburga stands out with her psychological depth.

Latvian literature in the diasporus developed along a parallel line. During the 1940s, this part of Latvian literature, by absorbing the experience of Anglo-Saxon literature, evolved at a most intensive level. Some writers (V.Strēlerte, M.Zīverts, A.Eglītis) continued to cultivate the traditions established in Latvia, others, the younger ones (L.Tauns, G.Saliņš, O.Stumbrs), fashioned a totally new style of poetry. During later periods the difference between the two divisions of Latvian literature begins to lessen, a tendency is observable for both to meld into one joint literary consciousness.

ARCHITECTURE. The most ancient architectural monuments in Latvia come from the Neolithic period (Sārnate Settlement). Fortified settlements and towns date from the Iron Age. The peasants of the early feudal period lived in scattered homesteads, while craftsmen and tradesmen settled in villages close to the castles. The Latvian national architecture was typically wooden with many features common with other countries surrounding the Baltic Sea. The buildings were constructed of either vertically or horizontally laid logs, practically without ornament, the main distinction being an original formation of pillars, corners of buildings and ridge crosses. During the period of feudalism the professional architecture gradually merged with that of folk; the stylistic forms, changing from one culture into another, became more simplified. The first German settlers of the 12th cent. brought the technology of limestone trim and introduced brick building traditions.

The principles of Romanesque architecture, which came from the architectural centres of Scandinavian countries and Germany, were carried out in sacral buildings (the Church of Ikšķile, 1186; Church of St. George in Riga, 1208) and in the city fortifications. The architecture of Riga, which was a typical Western European trade and crafts centre of the Middle Ages and later a member of the Hanseatic League, began in 1201 and influenced the development of architectural and building techniques throughout the Baltic territories. The Cathedral of the Archbishop of Riga (Riga Dome) displaying coexistance of two styles — Romanesque and Gothic was begun in 1211. The Church of St. Jacob in Riga (1225), Church of St. Simon in Valmiera (1283) and Church of St. John in Cēsis (1284) also have the typical basilican form.

During the Gothic period of the 15th cent., wooden and *fachwerk* buildings began to be replaced with brick buildings, and gable-type houses ('Three Brothers'; Mazā Pils Street 17, 19, 21). An outstanding monument is the Church of St. Peter in Riga, from which all churches acquired their slender, pyramidal late-Gothic-style brick steeples.

In the period of the Renaissance two cultural centres developed in Latvia — one in Riga and the other in Jelgava, in the Court of the Duchy of Kurzeme. The best examples of the architecture of that time have not survived. Of original construction is the Ecke Convent building in Riga, Skārņu Street 22 (1592).

During the Baroque period the regional differences between Swedish-occupied Vidzeme and Riga, the independent Duchy of Kurzeme and Latgale increased. Swedish city builders modernized the fortifications of Riga by constructing the Citadel (1652). The citizens of Riga built luxurious dwelling-houses — Reuthern's House (Mārstaļu Street 2/4, 1685) and Dannenstern's House (Mārstaļu Street 21, 1696). The stone churches of Kurzeme were decorated with wood carvings of the Dutch school (Ēdole, 1648; Ugāle, 1694), Polish Baroque can be seen in the Catholic church at Skaistkalne (1692). The grandiose conception of F.B.Rastrelli puts its stamp on the palaces of Rundāle and Jelgava (1730 — 60).

Russian Classicism followed the incorporation of Latvia into the Russian Empire, making use of government-approved models of architecture became obligatory. However, K.Haberland, the first city architect born in Riga, developed a type of apartment building in the form of the Civic Classicism (Šķūņu Street 17, 19, 1788).

The growth of capitalism promoted rapid urbanization, especially in Riga which, during the 19th cent. became Russia's most important port of export. In 1856, the city architect J. Felsko and engineer O.Dīce drew up a project of reconstruction, city fortifications were torn down and the Ring of Boulevards and canals was developed that put Riga next to such European city as Vienna. Eclecticism became the dominating style of the period. At the beginning of the 20th cent., two sources of Latvian architecture — that of the traditional styles and folk architecture was joined by the third — that of the industrial revolution of the Western world.

The Jugendstil (*Art Nouveau*) came as a rejection of historical architecture, its rationalistic trend abandoned any kind of ornament (Factory VEF, Riga, P.Bērenss, 1913). Special notice must be given to National Romanticism. Latvian architects K.Pēkšēns, E.Laube and A.Vanags, under the influence of Finnish architecture of the time, created their own architecture of original form and content (secondary school, Tērbatas Street 15/17; dwelling houses, Brīvības Street 47, 58, 62).

The founding of the Latvian state is marked by the construction of the Brethren Cemetery and the Monument to Freedom. An attempt to create a modern and national architecture was furthered by P.Kundziņš' Open-Air Museum of Ethnography in Riga (1924). Rationalism held a strong position, as attested by Central Market (P.Dreijmanis, 1930), the multifunctional Association Building in Daugavpils (V.Vitands, 1936), as well as the schools built by A.Grīnbergs in Riga and T.Hermanovskis' apartment buildings and private residences. The demand for a nationally conservative architecture, which increased after President K.Ulmanis' *coup d'état* of 1934, was met by E.Laube (the reconstruction of the Riga Castle, 1938), A.Klinklāvs (the Ministry of Finance building, 1939), F.Skujiņš' in the demiclassic forms.

WW II and the occupation of Latvia accounted for the emigration of an absolute majority of Latvian architects. The crisis was intensified by the elimination for several years of the Faculty of Architecture at the Latvian University. Soviet retrospective architectural models were imported, and under that influence the first high-rise building of the Academy of Sciences (O.Tīlmanis, K.Plūksne, V.Apsītis, 1958) was erected in Riga. The decree of the Central Committee of the CPSU of 1954 exchanged the eclectic architectural forms for ascetic, even utilitarian ones. Apartment construction was dominated by large ready-made panel buildings, concentrated into residential areas of *Āgenskalna priedes, Ķengarags, Pļavnieki, Zolitūde*. The better traditions of rational architecture were renewed during the 1960s, with the development of shop interior design in the centre of Riga (Dz.Driba, M.Ģelzis), public buildings: concert hall *Dzintari* (M.Ģelzis, A.Vecsīlis, 1960), restaurant *Sēnīte* (L.Skuja, 1967), the Art Theatre (M.Staņa, I.Jākobsons, H.Kanders, 1975), hotel *Rīdzene* (Z.Kalinka, J.Ģertmanis, V.Kadirkovs, 1985). Multi-storeyed buildings in the International style were projected by A.Reinfelds and J. Vilciņš, more originality is shown by the grouping of TV buildings (A.Purviņš, B.Maike, V.Kadirkovs, 1987). Sculptural possibilities in architecture have been used by architects G.Asaris, I.Strautmanis, O.Ostenbergs, O.Zakamennijs at the Salaspils Memorial Ensemble. Local tendencies during the 1970s made a timid appearance in the Art Salon in Riga (A.Kalniņš) and in the Lielupe Café (L.Alksnis). They acquire a more brilliant form during the next decade, together with the entrance of Postmodernism into Latvia, first, in rural architecture — dwelling houses in Mārupe (A.Skujiņa, A.Marinska, 1984), the administrative building in Renda (L.E. Tīkmanis, 1987), Druva School (T.Timpars, 1989), then in Riga — the administrative building in Peldu Street (J.Skalbergs, A.Zavadskis, P.Birulis, 1988). Within the wide postmodernism scope of Latvian modern architecture high-tech tendencies (Motor Museum in Riga, V.Valgums, A.Briedis, 1988) exist side by side with the radically eclectic work of U.Šēnbergs. The Design Office *V-10* in Liepāja produces contextual work. As a result, we can safely forecast the rebirth of the tradition of a free-style Latvian architectural classicism.

ART. The same as at Altamira, Spain, the first artist in the Latvian territory was a hunter, and his conception of the Universe, the world, and himself in it is fixed in the archeological testimonies of the Mesolithic era. Between 7,000 and 3,000 BC elk, deer, waterfowl and snakes were reproduced as totem-like figurines in bone, antler or amber. The replica of the anatomical human figure dating from 3,000 to 2,000 BC was still far-removed from the mastery of Egyptian or Mesopotamian stonecutters, the sculptural figures cut in bone or amber were rough. Applied arts blossomed during the period of intensive metal workmanship (5th cent. AD), the jewelry makers towering above the masters of pottery, weaving and wood-carving. With a few modifications, the basic samples of ancient Latvian jewelry have survived to our times and are still popular today. Before German conquest, Baltic, among them Latvian, ornament remained at the stage of plant, animal or geometric stylization; the reproduction of the human figure was not typical.

The German spiritual and military expansion of the 12th cent. was a determining factor in Latvia joining the processes of Western European culture. The peculiar status of a territory the fruits of which we are still gathering today came into being, namely, we have kept the individuality of a borderland, a country still not totally assimilated. The portrait of a piper found scratched into the clay wash of the wall of a metal foundry at Tērvete has the character of chance, yet it must be considered as an example of the earliest regional art in which the samples of Western culture have guided the hand of an anonymous artist toward reproducing a Gothic ornament, articles of clothing, as well as making an attempt at characterization and typification so necessary to portrait painting. Under German, Swedish, Polish and Russian rule a continuous and natural development of the ethnic Baltic tribes has been able to continue and grow under conditions of the strictest social differentiation. In either subdued or open form the art of the natives coexists with the dominant styles of art. Amalgamation of folk art and that of the settlers has taken place as anonymous Baltic artists absorbed powerful influences from various art styles and simplified them. Baroque architecture, decorative woodcuts, the love for the applied arts, contrasts and the modelling of combined convex and concave forms are carried over to ceramics even in the 20th cent. by reproducing the inner feeling of this splendid sense for style. By transferring the art language of the top layers into untypical genres and modes of expression, a pagan-like colourful synchronization of folk styles has appeared. And the other way round. In a patriarchal, agricultural way of life, where rational functionalism and constructionism tested at practice, holds the leading role, ornament ranks as the second. The first pieces of art displaying Romanesque and Gothic style, produced in an atmosphere of hurried colonization, have the quality of simplicity brought by the expansion of the warriors, missionaries and tradespeople.

At the end of the 18th and during the 1st half of the 19th cent., a number of artists who brought with them the mastery and experience gained during their studies in St. Petersburg, Dresden, Berlin and Paris, resided in Latvia. Various influences and traditions episodically flashed up and disappeared. Several painters, as regards their artistic mastery, balanced between dilettantism and primitive art, but their achievements under Latvian (and European) art conditions should not be underestimated (J.K.Brotze's cultural landscapes in 10 vols).

During the period of general national awakening in the middle of the 19th cent., Latvian culture absorbed and intensively followed the most noteworthy influences of world art; however, this was still a period of more or less talented reproduction of various academic impressions (J.Roze, K.Hūns, J.Feders, R.Zariņš). Only at the end of the century did there appear in the so-called Baltic provinces a call for independence in the artistic reflection of national history. In 1896, filled with a romanticized heroization of the past (Ā.Alksnis, A.Baumanis), preferring characterization of realistic environment (J.Rozentāls, J.Valters), and following the postimpressionistic tendencies widespread in Europe and those of Jugendstil (V.Purvītis), several artists manifested themselves in the first important group show in Riga. The first Latvian professional sculptors (G.Šķilters, T.Zaļkalns, B.Dzenis) were strongly influenced by the School of O.Rodin.

During protest and military campaigns of the Revolution of 1905, WW I and the following fights for liberation a new process of cultural consolidation took place against the background of both an anti-German and anti-Russian frame of mind. It manifested itself in short excursions into Sybolism, Expressionism as well as timid searches for artistic enrichment in the aesthetic of decadents. In the current of the gently counterpoised, perfect tonal painting of Latvian art an obvious bright spot is the infatuation for Postimpressionism displayed by J.Kazāks and J.Grosvalds in their creation; besides, some individual fauvist, cubist and constructivist work, produced in the spirit of creative experimentation, must be mentioned. Without losing the traditions of an excellent academic schooling, Latvian art between the two world wars balanced itself between the lush colouring of the Belgians and Flemish and the ponderous expression of aestheticized farming existence (Ģ.Eliass, J.Tīdemanis, L.Liberts), as well as the new stylization of the new applied arts and ethnographical forms interpreted in the so-called *Art Deco* manner (S.Vidbergs, graphics; A.Beļcova, ceramics; N.Strunke, painting; R.Suta painting and ceramics; A.Cīrulis, painting, applied arts and stained glass). On the whole, the sentiment was definitely lyrical, with overtones of pantheism, which expressed itself in an intensified interest in landscapes, still lifes and marine paintings and which was essential to the Academy of Arts established in 1919.

After the October Revolution, those artists remaining in Russia took on the politicized canons of Soviet art and quickly lost the traditions of the national school (V.Andersons, K.Veidemanis). A few individuals (G.Klucis), having delved into the expressive artistic possibilities of Constructivism, creatively introduced the use of photo montage and collage into the genre of advertising and propaganda.

A high level of achievement was shown by Latvian sculptors during the years of independence. The monuments to popularly honoured celebrities and memorial ensembles to those who died during

WW I and the fights for liberation reach the level of perfection with the inherent depth of feeling for the national tragedy and humane emotions (Brethren Cemetery; K.Zāle, 1924 – 36) and the peaceful reflection of the national, humane pathos (Monument to Freedom; K.Zāle, 1931 – 35).

Bright witnesses to flourishing of culture during the period between world wars were the stage designers, who inculcated an adoring love for theatre which, as a legend, has survived to the end of the 20th cent. Internationally distinguished masters were L.Liberts at the National Opera with his exotically bright and orientally refined stage decorations and J.Muncis, a stage designer of the Art Theatre. The latter was in perfect command of any modern trends of scenography and produced exceptional stage sets for patriotic mass productions.

WW II dispersed many talented Latvian artists throughout the world. Those who had obtained their education and had developed their artistic outlook in Latvia, did not break their ties with the Latvian society in exile and predominantly tended to reorientate themselves in their art towards reproductional nature and the daring innovations of the 1930s. The younger generation, depending upon its upbringing and social environment, has integrated into its foreign surroundings and has adapted to the demands of the international art market. That accounts for the dualistic and complicated question of what part the work of the artists in exile might hold in the total over-view of Latvian culture.

Applied arts during the post-WW II period in Latvia exist on two separate levels. One, consisting of a large group of artists and amateurs, continues to cultivate all possible variations of the traditional forms and techniques of folk crafts. The other focuses the attention on the production of objects of modern design and stylistic decoration, and is represented mainly by artists with an academic education whose creativity often comes from international movements.

The excellent quality of graphic arts, based on the well-tended etchings of the old masters R.Zariņš and A.Apinis and the perfection of wood-cuts made by O.Ābelīte, J.Plēpis and P.Upītis, is of surprising stability. The dominance of realistic tradition has ensured Latvian graphic arts with a long-lasting stylistic and qualitative integrity. Artists of the 1970s (G.Krollis, L.Zikmane, N.Petraškevics) perfected the various etching techniques and worked toward deepening of their associative pictorial style. Likewise, having surmounted the threshold of this revelation of an illustrative content, Latvian poster art enters a contemporary stage of laconic expression (G.Kirke). If the art of the 1930s can be noted by the historic genre and its expansion on a wide, emotional scope tied to the growth of the national self-confidence of the time, then after WW II, in the environment of fear and apathy of the Republic incorporated into the USSR, official support was gained by works filled with pathos, historical tendentiousness and bias, and inspired by the ideology of the CP. Artists who were conformist amateurs were forced to imitate examples of the Soviet art of the 1920s and 1930s. This atmosphere of the trade-off and political speculation lasted until the end of the 1950s, when a new generation found original, legal and individual 'break-out' possibilities and began, within the poetical frame of the so-called harsh or biting style, to romanticize individual episodes of the nationalistic history (I.Zariņš, Ģ.Vilks) in painting as well as in monumental sculpture (A.Terpilovskis, A.Dumpe). However, similarly to the pre-war period, the biggest demand was for portraits and reproduction of nature in a lyrical manner, through which an oppressed social consciousness could utter some individual protest or show the feelings of a belittled and derogated love for one's country.

The social stagnation of the 1970s intensified the production of pseudo-philosophical and non-conflict officially ordered work (Dž.Skulme), that placed cultural tradition into a secondary, decorative role. Artists searched for ways out in individual speculation, realm of subjective form, and turned toward the development of their artistic mastery; however, that was a hermetically restricted, local and self-satisfied phenomenon. One can observe the beginnings of a thorough search made by separate individuals in the direction of the content and form of their art (photo realism – I.Lancmanis, B.Vasiļevskis, M.Polis, metaphoric, fantastic realism – M.Tabaka), the enrichment of which is bound to an unadvertised look into the processes of world art.

During the next to the last decade of this century, an explosive expansion of Latvian art took place, in the direction to the West, as well as in the fact that the shutters of our own windows were thrown open, so that we finally could enter the panoramic landscape of Western culture. The artists of the middle and older generations, without loss of their national identity and professionality, are still resisting the enticement of the production of marketable art for mass consumption, while the younger generation flits in bewilderment between the basic notions of the world's art lexicology, keeping of themselves little but the workmanship provided by a good academic education. In the meantime, the Western world discovers in wonder the region of East European cultures as their long-past childhood and the maximalism of their youth, one that contains much moving naiveté and the freshness of feeling possible in a society still untouched by postindustrialism.

MUSIC. Fragments that have been preserved from the steeple music, peculiar to Latvian medieval cities, date back to the Middle Ages, collections of church songs – to the 16th cent. Baroque instrumental music was dominating in the Court of the Duchy of Kurzeme, where during the 17th and 18th cent. there operated military and symphonic orchestras as well as opera and ballet performances, using J.Fischer's and F.A.Veichtner's compositions were staged. The majority of works by the notable representative of the Northern European school of piano concertos –

J.G.Müthel were composed in Riga, where he lived for 35 years (since 1753). A great treasure is more than 250 well-preserved historical organs, built mostly in the 17th — 19th cent.

Until the 19th cent., Latvian folk music was the only mode of musical expression for the native population, since professional music, begun with the introduction of Christianity by the feudal aggressors, belonged to the ruling minority of the other-language (mainly German) culture and practically did not touch the native population that were deprived of their rights. That is the reason for the extensive wealth in the manner of expression and genres of folk music as well as for the presence of exceedingly ancient elements found in Latvian folklore. Archeology dates the first musical instruments in Latvia from the Neolithic era. Since the Middle Ages the most typical Latvian folk instrument is the *kokle* that is kindred to the Finnish *kantele*. Deep-rooted traditions of folk music had developed before the crusaders' invasion of the Baltics during the 13th cent., namely — half recitative, improvised archaic burdona and ritual solo songs connected to the family, its annual celebrations and the work processes. This music, kept within the primitive and Middle Age range of tonality, has witnessed a renaissance in the present-day movement of folklore popularization. The most recent stratum of music developed during the 17th and 18th cent. under the influence of Western European professional music. It has had a most influential role in the reawakening of Latvian national music in the 19th cent. City folklore is considered alien to Latvian culture and has been neither recorded nor preserved.

The Latvian national school of composers belongs to the newer professional trend taking roots in the era of Romanticism. It has much in common with the tendencies dominating in the professional music of small European nations. Latvian folklore, National Romanticism as well as aptness to Classicism and programme music adopted from the period of studies at St. Petersburg's Conservatoire lies on the basis of Latvian professional music. Alongside with the first arrangements of folk song for four-part choirs by J.Cimze and K. Baumanis (the author of the national anthem *Dievs, svētī Latviju* — God Bless Latvia), songs by A.Jurjāns are not forgotten. The greatest credit for Latvian choral music and chamber music belongs to J.Vītols and E.Melngailis, likewise that for solo songs, operas, ballets and symphonic music — to A.Kalniņš and Jānis Mediņš. In the period between the two world wars Latvian professional music was enriched with impressionistic and postimpressionistic tendencies — mainly in the symphonic creations by Ā.Skulte and J.Ivanovs.

With the forcible annexation of Latvia to the USSR (1940) the creation of Latvian composers is brought under strict ideological control; much has been created though almost no pieces of parmanent artistic value appear. The crucial events of 1944 in Latvia account for the political emigration of about 1/3 of Latvian composers. Although in the post-war period musical compositions by Latvian composers display the main modernistic nuances dominating in the European music, Latvian professional music has preserved moderate post-avant-garde and neo-classical features. Nowadays it has acquired both — lucidly fine and ethically suggestive content. The most distinguished contemporary Latvian composers are: P.Dambis, I.Kalniņš, R.Kalsons, R.Pauls, P.Plakidis, P.Vasks, I.Zemzaris, as well as J.Kalniņš, T.Ķeniņš and G.Pone residing abroad.

Towards the close of the 17th cent., several musical societies were established, but since 1760 special season-tickets for symphonic concerts were introduced. The Riga German Theatre (1772 — 1924) possessed drama, ballet and opera companies. The performances staged there were characterized by a contemporary repertoire and such celebrities as R.Wagner (1837 — 39) and B.Walter (1898 — 1900) conducting the orchestra. Since the beginning of the 19th cent., world-famous musicians started performing in Riga.

The origin of choral activities in Latvia dates back to the 1st half of the 19th cent., but since 1873 Song Festivals held every five years have become national-scale. With thousands of participants (about 15,000) performing on an open-air stage the festival has reached the ordinal numeral of 20 in 1990, thus proving the popularity of choral music and turning it into the leading genre of Latvian music. The 2nd half of the 19th cent. witnessed the first concerts of instrumental music as well as performances of musical plays and operas (the first Latvian-language opera was staged in 1893). Since 1901, the symphonic seasons have become quite a tradition in Jūrmala musical life. In 1913, the Latvian Opera Company was formed in Riga. Moreover, in the 1920s and 1930s, the artistic level of the newly established company reached that of Warsaw and Helsinki opera companies. In the 1960s — 1980s, the repertoire has been enriched with the performances of contemporary operas; besides, undertaking extensive tours abroad, Riga Ballet Company enjoys high international esteem. Latvian Academy of Music, Latvian Composers' Union, Latvian Radio with its performing staff and musicians, Latvian Philharmonic, National Symphonic Orchestra, several chamber orchestras, professional choirs, Latvian Music Society have contributed greatly to the development and prosperity of Latvian music. Various international music festivals and competitions held in Riga have become traditional. A characteristic feature of the 1980s and 1990s is secession of Latvian music institutions from the corresponding ones operating in the USSR and establishing direct contacts with the institutions and musicians abroad.

THEATRE. The first theatre performance in Latvia is dated to 1205. In the following centuries mysteries, Shrovetide-plays as well as other drama forms widespread in Western Europe were performed to the audience. Since the 17th cent., guest-performances delivered by the High German, Italian and English professional troupes were quite popular, too. In the 2nd half of the 18th cent. a permanent German theatre company has been set up and consequently a new theatre building has been erected in 1863 (today the National Opera House). At the same time, drawing inspiration from folklore, the first Latvian theatre performances were given in the provinces. The presentation of F.Schiller's play *Laupītāji* (The Robbers) is considered to be the first theatre performance in the Latvian language. It was staged in the Dikļi estate (Vidzeme) by a Latvian serfpeasant J.Peitāns, who was also the translator of the play.

The beginnings of the professional theatre have been traced to the end of the 1870s, when on the initiative of the so-called Neo-Latvian movement, Latvian bourgeoisie started establishing creative societies, in charge of which theatre companies prospered later. Thus in 1870, the Riga Latvian Theatre has been set up. The company was run by the first Latvian professional actor and director — Ā.Alunāns — a writer of standing reputation. Soon, due to the successful stage productions by Ā.Alunāns and natural talent for performing, theatre gained a wide popularity throughout Latvia. Passion for theatre, even its adoration with Latvians has survived up to nowadays and has become a remarkable phenomenon in the history of theatrical art. The Riga Russian Theatre has been dating its history since 1883, but in 1902 the second Latvian professional theatre has been founded. At the turn of the century the Latvian professional theatre enjoyed a constellation of stage celebrities, the undying fame and divine presence of who has not faded yet. D.Akmentiņa, B.Rūmniece, J.Skaidrīte, A.Mierlauks, T.Banga, J.Duburs are great names for the Latvian stage.

Gradually professional theatre companies were set up in the provinces. Alongside with the plays by world-famous playwrights, those by Aspazija, R.Blaumanis were included in the theatre repertoires, but since 1911, productions of J.Rainis' plays have had a long run and a great success. WW I and the subsequent events account for a large-scale dispersion of Latvian theatre people abroad. The number of actors residing in Russia was particularly large; thus up to the notorious year of 1937, a professional Latvian theatre company was functioning there.

During the 20 years of Latvia's independence, the number of professional theatre companies is increasing rapidly. Thus the problem of providing actors with the due professional training ranks among the most acute ones. Various groups are organized and courses of lectures are delivered by B.Skujeniece and Zeltmatis. Nevertheless, two theatre companies, namely that of the National Theatre (set up in 1919; dir. A.Amtmanis-Briedītis) and the Art Theatre (1920; E.Smiļģis) stand out against the background of theatre life of that time. If the stagings at the Art Theatre were notable for their brilliant theatric scenes, perfect form and stage-setting, then the National Theatre displayed the idiosyncrasy and way of living of the Latvian people mostly; therefore dramatic tension and hopeful humanity goes hand in hand. Likewise, both the theatre companies differentiate between the playwrights. Plays by J.Rainis are staged at the Art Theatre mostly, but those by R.Blaumanis have won the favour of the National Theatre. Similarly, the plays by A.Upīts, whose contribution to the development of Latvian dramatic art is undeniable, are cherished there. Acting on the stages of these theatres a new generation of actors and directors gains experience and acquires stagecraft to become a legendary one despite of the disasterous year of 1940 and the looming tragedy.

The forceful annexation of Latvia to the USSR brought about great changes in the theatrical life. Following the instructions of the authorities, enthusiastic praising of Soviet way of living, its heroic past, promising and rosy future became an essential feature of the stagings of that time. In the 1950s there is a great demand for Soviet (mainly Russian) plays, moreover, the same plays are staged at several theatres simultaneously. On the whole, trivial and dull pieces of drama are put on. Likewise, the plays of Latvian writers-playwrights (V.Lācis, A.Grigulis) display lack of enduring value. In the 1950s and 1960s, staging world classical literature as well as contemporary repertoire, theatres start regaining their previous distinction. Tendency to classical realism is characteristic of the productions staged at the National Theatre. The production of R.Blaumanis' play *Skroderdienas Silmačos* (Tailors' Days in Silmači) in 1955 becomes quite a hit and has a long run. It seems to be the most popular play with Latvians, especially when performed on an open-air stage. At the same time the Art Theatre delivers performances — all-star casts — with H.Liepiņš, V.Artmane and E.Pāvuls starring.

In the mid-1960s, the relay of the outstanding directors A.Amtmanis-Briedītis and E.Smiļģis is taken over by A.Jaunušans, P.Pētersons and Ā.Šapiro, likewise that of older generation of actors — by U.Dumpis, Ģ.Jakovļevs and L.Ozoliņa. Stage designers of the younger generation prefer plain style, variform and many-faceted approach to stage-setting. They are in constant search for untraditional means of expression (lack of curtain-rise and fall, actors acting in the aisles among the audience). Besides, chamber halls ($\sim$100 — 400 seats) are made use of more widely. The Youth Theatre, staging philosophically sophisticated poetry dramatizations, has become the initiator of verse drama in Latvia. Professional theatres in the provinces (Liepāja Theatre and especially Valmiera Drama Theatre) are much inclined to staging of musicals. This tendency is taken over by Riga professional theatres quite successfully. In the 1970s and 1980s, theatres start losing their peculiar way of staging and performing — the so-called singing and dancing actor comes to the foreground; formely cherished and highly appreciated distinct articulation of every word and phrase has been neglected.

Nevertheless, in contrast to the singing and dancing stage life, there are stagings with strong and charismatic personality placed above everything. As the peculiarity of the Latvian theatre is harmonious ensemble, strange as it may seem, in such stagings the title-role usually is a brilliant masterpiece.

Both interesting and self-centered is the Puppet Theatre catering also for the tastes of grown-ups. In general it presents wonderfully staged plays created solely for puppet theatre.

Alongside with the professional theatres there are a lot of amateur companies, that operate under the guidance of professional directors. Despite of the lack of state subsidies several independent experimental companies have been set up recently (*Kabata*). Professional actors willingly participate in the performances staged there.

Nowadays Latvian theatre faces the most complicated problem — compatibility of enduring artistic value and the activities of national reawakening of the Latvian people.

BALLET. Latvian ballet had its beginnings only in the early 20th cent. Since the end of the 18th cent. Riga has been located in the middle of the art road between Western Europe and St. Petersburg. Here, on the way through, stopped and occasionally worked outstanding classic ballet masters L.Duport (1811), V.Reisinger (1854—59), K.Lanner (1859, 1968—69), M.Petipa (1860, 1863), L.Grahn (1862), V.Zucchi (1889), A.Pavlova (1908), O.Preobrajenska (1913—14), M. and V.Fokine (1915). The most extensive influence on the formation of Latvian classic ballet came from the Imperial Russian Ballet which, at the turn of the century and under the leadership of M.Petipa had become the best in the world.

Although M.Kauliņš and V.Komisārs can be considered the first professional Latvian ballet masters, the date of the birth of Latvian ballet is recognized as December 1, 1922, when the former ballet master of the St.Petersburg Maria Theatre, N.Sergejev, produced the first large-scale ballet at the Latvian National Opera — P.Hertel's *Veltīgā uzmanība* (Useless Attention). His work was continued by A.Fiodorova-Fokine, justifiably considered the founder of Latvian ballet who, while working in Riga as the principal ballet mistress and prima ballerina (1925—32) and while running her own studio (1925—37), staged all of the most outstanding classic ballets of that time and brought up the first distinguished generation of Latvian ballet dancers. H.Tangijeva-Birzniece, a soloist of the National Opera (1927—37) and the chief ballet mistress (1945—51, 1956—65), and A.Vilzaks, who headed the Latvian ballet from 1932 to 1934, also came from the St.Petersburg's school.

The most significant date in the history of Latvian ballet is May 9, 1935, when under the leadership of the premiere dancer and chief ballet master of the National Opera, O.Lēmanis, the first ballet performance of Latvian origin, *Mīlas uzvara* (The Triumph of Love) by J.Mediņš took place. O.Lēmanis was the leading Latvian ballet master until 1944, after which he worked as a teacher in the USA. During the post-war years, the Latvian ballet came under the powerful influence of the Moscow school from where came a string of soloists and teachers. The first academically educated Latvian choreographer, J.Čanga, who for his thesis produced the first ballet based on J.Rainis' play — Ā.Skulte's *Brīvības sakta* (The Brooch of Freedom, 1950), had graduated from the Moscow Institute of the Dramatic Arts. The work of J.Čanga in Riga Ballet (1950—61), together with that of H.Tangijeva-Birzniece, must be considered as the second (after O.Lēmanis) most productive period. The former and brilliant premiere dancer A.Lembergs held the position of the head of the Riga Ballet from 1968—85. Under his leadership, Latvian ballet once again entered the world of European culture, the traditions of the children's ballet were developed — A.Žilinskis *Sprīdītis* (Tom Thumb, 1968) and *Lolitas brīnumputns* (Lolita's Magic Bird, 1979), the tradition of the one-act ballet — G.Bizet/R.Szedrin's 'Carmen', J.Sibelius' 'Scaramouche' (1971), J.Karlson's *Uguni* (In the Fire, 1979). Since 1932, a government funded ballet school, the present-day School of Choreography, has existed in Riga; among its students must be noted the internationally recognized M.Barishnikov, A.Godunov, G.Markovsky.

The apex of Latvian ballet is closely connected with prima ballerinas E.Pfeifer-Frandsen (after WW II an outstanding ballet teacher in Western Europe), M.Griķe, A.Priede, V.Vilciņa, I.Ābele, Z.Errsa, L.Beiris, ballet dancers H.Plūcis (latter a notable ballet teacher in Western Europe), J.Grauds, A.Ozoliņš, H.Ritenbergs, V.Gelvāns, G.Gorbaņovs.

Classic ballet also existed at the Liepāja Opera (1922—50), where large-scale dance spectacles were staged. Since 1935 (with an interruption from 1940—68), the Riga Ballet Company has regularly visited Scandinavia, Italy, France, the Balkans, Latin America, Egypt, Israel and Southeast Asian countries.

CIRCUS. Circus came into being in Latvia in 1831, when a Vienna circus troupe delivered a guest-performance in Riga. Since Riga was considered a large cultural centre other companies from abroad followed to visit Riga regularly. A permanent circus building, in the arena of which performances are still held, was constructed in 1889. In 1899 the first professional Latvian circus artist began to perform at the Riga Circus, its programme was expanded by adding wrestling and championship tournaments in which K.Veilands-Šulcs, K.Buls and other celebrities of the time took part. The circus performers were predominantly from abroad, although the performances of Latvian circus artists (Bretini, Sanseti, Nortons, R.Cimze and others) were of world quality. During the 1920s—30s, the Latvian Circus Company often went on extensive tours abroad to visit the largest circuses of Russia and the USSR. After the incorporation of Latvia into the USSR, the Latvian Circus maintained its high performance technique and its professionally polished productions.

CINEMA. Cinematography has been known in Latvia since 1896, when the first movie seance took place. The first professional domestic movie was shot in 1910. The first films with live actors were produced in 1913 and 1914. During that time E.Tisē began his filming career; he would later become world-famous as the cameraman to S.Eisenstein, born in Riga.

Cinematography during the period of Latvia's independence, from 1920 to 1940, led an active life. Newsreels were shot regularly as well as documentaries and feature films were produced. Special note must be made of the work of E.Kraucis who, from 1929 to 1940, produced the weekly newsreels *Pēdējā brīdī* (At the Last Moment), *Latvijas hronika* (The Latvian Chronicle), and since 1934 *Latvijas skaņu hronika* (The Latvian Sound Chronicle), which provide a unique documentation about the events, society and eminent personalities of the time. International recognition was gained by J.R.Doreds, the only foreigner who managed to film Lenin's funeral illegally. During the 1920s, M.Lia and M.Leiko became movie stars well known throughout Europe. There were many daring attempts at establishing a truly industrial basis for the production of Latvian films, however, at that time, this was not realized.

The film industry was developed in Latvia after WW II, especially after 1961, when the Riga Film Studio was built. The studio annually produces up to 10 full-length feature films, puppet and animated films, documentaries, popular science and educational films, advertisements, as well as 48 newsreels. During the last years there have been several co-productions with Czecho-Slovakia, France and other countries. The studio is known for its excellent organization and the high professionalism of its staff. The most acclaim has gone to children's pictures (dir. G.Piesis, V.Brasla, L.Ločmele), films about the mentality of the Latvian people and its historical destinies (R.Kalniņš, A.Freimanis, J.Streičs), as well as detective movies and TV serials (A.Brenčs). International recognition has gone to A.Burovs' puppet and R.Stiebra's animated cartoons. These are characterized not only by their high professionalism, but also by their singular artistic solutions. Latvian documentary retrospectives have been shown at the International Film Festivals of Nyon and West Berlin, as well as received awards in Cannes and Oberhausen. The 1980s brought the Latvian documentaries to international attention, particularly through the films of H.Franks *Augstākā tiesa* (The Supreme Justice), J.Podnieks *Vai viegli būt jaunam?* (Is it Easy to Be Young?), *Hallo, vai jūs mūs dzirdat?* (Hallo, Do You Hear Us?) and I.Seleckis. Moreover, in 1990 the European top prize — 'Felix' — went to the Latvian documentary *Šķērsiela* (The Sidestreet) produced by I.Seleckis.

Another centre of film-making in Riga is Latvian TV (logo *Telefilma-Rīga*), which produces mainly documentaries and concert films. During the past few years the Riga Video Centre has become a noteworthy movie and video film production company with considerable international connections, under whose wing the international experimental and avant-guarde film forum *Arsenāls* has developed and grown. The superior level and potential of Latvian cinematography is assured by a well-trained staff and, although technically out-moded, a stable and strong production base.

ART PHOTOGRAPHY. The information about photography in Latvia is from 1839, the oldest recorded photograph being developed and printed around 1840 – 45. The first photo studios were opened by non-Latvians, mainly Germans: however, as early as the 1860s the photo laboratories owned by Latvians opened their doors and by the end of the 19th cent. there was an intensive activity among Latvian photo artists. The prosperity of photography in Latvia at the beginning of the 20th cent. is closely tied to the general flourishing of photography in Western Europe and Russia. The founder of Latvian professional art photography is M.Buclers through the artistic aspirations of who the development of the photo industry and the professional training of photographers was furthered. J.Rieksts, J.Balodis and R.Johansons opened their workshops. The first photo exhibition in Riga was held in 1902, in 1906 the Latvian Photo Artists Society was set up laying the foundation for the growing Latvian art photography. Gradually art photography gained popularity in Latvia; but during the 1920s and 1930s it won international recognition (V.Rīdzenieks, R.Johansons, J.Rieksts, E.Gaiķis). It must be noted that in 1938 Latvia began to produce the world-famous miniature camera *VEF-Minox*. The high level of picture-taking technique in Latvian art photography was preserved after Latvia was incorporated into the USSR. At the end of the 1960s, Latvian photographers strengthened their international authority by taking the first serious steps in art photography (G.Binde, J.Gleizds). The multi-faceted palette of Latvian art photography of today — the portraits, landscapes, still lifes, genre, nudes, commentary — ensures its internationally recognized level with the development of many photo studios that are led by the best professional photographers.

LIBRARIES. In the Latvian territory libraries originated as early as the 13th cent. Until the Reformation (16th cent.) they were attached to churches, monasteries and were intended for the use of the clergy. One of the first public libraries in Europe was founded in Riga in 1524 (now the Fundamental Library of the Latvian Academy of Sciences). From the 2nd half of the 18th cent. to the middle of the 19th cent., libraries grew in size and an extensive system of libraries was developed, to which the Neo-Latvians gave an essential push by setting up the first Latvian library in 1848, and in 1885, when they laid the foundation for the National (J.Misiņš') Library. By the beginning of the 20th cent., Latvia had libraries possessed by various societies as well as free, public libraries. Since the Republic of Latvia (1918 – 40) considered libraries to be a part of the educational system, there existed libraries attached to government, city authorities, associations, organizations, municipalities, and private libraries. After the occupation of Latvia in 1940, all libraries were nationalized and handed over to the state and its various departments. So-called 'spec-funds' (closed to the public) were developed where publications of and by the 'ideological enemy' were kept. Such funds existed until 1989.

Today Latvian libraries, after 50 years of the government's 'surplus' policy in its relationship towards culture, have suffered severely and arrived in a crisis situation: the number of libraries is on a steady decrease, the existing ones are over-crowded, most of the buildings are in poor condition, the salaries of their employees are among the lowest. Hope can be gleaned from the cultural politics of the newly elected Latvian government, as proved the construction of a new National Library (arch. G.Birkerts, USA).

ARCHIVES. The history of archives in Latvia dates from the 13th cent. (Archives of the Order of Livonia). The records of the 16th — 18th cent. were concentrated mainly in city archives, and those of country estates and circuits, a large part being destroyed during various historical upheavals. In 1919, the Republic of Latvia began setting up the State Archives of History, where material in regards to the Latvian territory, with the exception of Riga (its archives being founded in 1882), was collected. The occupants of Latvia (1940) reorganized the work and administration of the archives in accordance with those of the USSR State Archives, thus providing an opportunity for the collections to be transferred freely in various directions, something that happened quite often. Research within the archives was based mainly on the history of the Latvian revolutionary movement, the Great Patriotic War (WW II) and the Latvian CP, because the notorious 'spec-funds' existed as late as 1989. Today the archives of Latvia are taking an active part in making the true history of the Latvian people.

MUSEUMS, GALLERIES. The first museum presented to the town council and based on the collection of N.Himzel, was founded in Riga in 1773, but the next museum opened in the provinces (Jelgava, 1818). The first building constructed solely for a museum (today State Museum of Fine Arts) was begun in 1903. The Republic of Latvia paid special attention to the collection of historical and ethnographic material and the development of museums of regional studies, as well as to the establishment of museums of various societies. The construction and development of a new type of museum — the Open-Air Museum of Ethnography, was begun in 1924. The first memorial museum (dedicated to brothers Kaudzītes) was established in 1929.

The occupation of Latvia (1940) had a severe influence on the work of the Latvian museums during their later period. As late as 1989, it was forbidden to show almost any material from the museums' collections concerning the period of Latvia's independence, especially those showing its achievements. Scholars within the Latvian museums, being enthusiasts and even fanatics as far as their work was concerned, have managed throughout these years and despite the well-known state 'surplus' policy in its relationship toward culture, to do serious scientific research and to develop interesting, independent exhibitions and shows. During the 1980s, the number of exhibition halls in Riga has increased (*Latvija, Arsenāls*), interesting international exhibitions have been held, in the late 1980s the number of commercial galleries (*Ars Longa*) and commercial shows increased, non-traditional art galleries were established, the opportunities for young artists, especially representing avant-guarde, to exhibit abroad (Germany, USA) expanded.

PUBLISHING. The first book recorded was brought out in the territory of Latvia between 1225 — 27; however, the first book in the Latvian language did not appear until 1525 (in Germany). The first printing press (N.Mollīns, 1588) in Latvia revolutionized book-printing. Until the middle of the 18th cent. almost all books published in Latvian were of religious nature, only in 1766 the first book of fiction was published. The print-shops grew into large firms with a high technical level. The quality of the books improved, the finish tended to be in luxurious Baroque style. During the 2nd half of the 19th cent., as the development of the Latvian national intelligentsia (I.Alunāns, K.Stālbergs, E.Zīslaks) and literature took place, so did that of the national publishing establishments; its true golden age is closely connected to the period of independent Latvia (1918 — 40). During this period a generally high level of publication was attained, especially in the field of graphic arts (S.Vidbergs, R.Suta, N.Strunke, O.Ābelīte, J.Plēpis); thanks to these traditions the graphics of our books are still interesting and are in wide demand, even though the general situation in the publishing field at present is in dire shape. Especially out-moded is the printing equipment which can guarantee neither the quality nor quantity of its publications. During 1989, 1,927 books (total of 16,800,000 copies) were published, of these 990 books (total of 13,000,000 copies) were printed in Latvian.

THE PRESS. Short historical survey of Latvian printed periodicals is as follows: the first newspaper was published in 1680 in the German language; the first Latvian newspaper came out in Estonia, in 1768, but the first literary magazine in Latvian started its existence in Jelgava in 1881. At the end of the 19th cent., commercial publications flourished, the competition became keen and many publications lasted only a year or two. In 1886 the Latvian progressive intelligentsia launched the newspaper *Dienas Lapa* (Daily Page), which was closed in 1897, but its editors (P.Stučka, J.Rainis) were sent into exile; this publication marked the beginnings of the Marxist press in Latvia.

During the period of independence (1918 — 40), many literary magazines, the publications of the various political parties and groups, new writers' magazines and illustrated magazines were put out not only in Latvian, but also in the Russian, Polish and German languages. After the incorporation of Latvia into the SU, the entire press came under the CPSU and Latvian CP control. A monopoly, the Publishing House of the Latvian CP Central Committee, was established, periodicals were subjected to strict censorship. Only in 1988 did the first 'informal' (i.e., independent) publications began to appear, of which the most popular is *Atmoda* (Awakening), a newspaper of the LPF. At the beginning of 1990, the party press monopoly was broken up, thus press caters for all political views and wide range of interests. The leading Latvian periodicals are newspapers *Literatūra un Māksla* (Literature and Art), *Latvijas Jaunatne* (Latvian Youth), *Diena* (Day), monthlies *Avots* (Spring), *Zinātne un Mēs* (Science and Ourselves), *Veselība* (Health), *Sieviete* (Woman). In 1989, more than 290 newspapers and magazines were published, with a circulation of 516,100,000 (of these 183 publications with a circulation of 344,300,000 in Latv.).

RADIO, TV, NEWS AGENCIES. The first radio broadcast in Latvia was beamed to listeners on March 28, 1924, in Riga, but official broadcasting began on November 1, 1925. Since 1946, Radio Latvia has been a member of OIRT. In 1955 broadcasts in ultra-short wave length were begun, since 1967 there have been stereophonic broadcasts, since 1983 — 3 radio broadcast programmes were offered. At present Radio Latvia broadcasts 2 programmes, for a total broadcast time of 30 hours daily. It broadcasts in the Latvian and Russian languages, as well as in Swedish and English (range — 262.4m and 50.5m bands). There are also weekly broadcasts for minority audiences in Estonian, Lithuanian, Polish, Armenian, Ukrainian, etc.

LATVIAN TV began broadcasting in November, 1954. The television film department of Riga TV (*Telefilma-Riga*) has been in existence since 1957. Since 1962, Latvian TV is a member of 'Intervision'. Colour broadcasts began in 1968, since 1974 Latvian TV owns a mobile colour TV studio. In 1987, a new TV and radio complex was built and put into operation (the height of antenna — 368 m). Latvian TV broadcasts on 1 channel, for approximately 11 hours daily. Latvian TV collaborates with Germany (ZDF), Great Britain (BBC, MTV), USA (CNN) and television stations in Poland, France and Finland; recently it has become a member of the European culture programme 'Alise'.

THE LATVIAN NEWS AGENCY (*LETA*) was founded in 1920; it supplies the radio, TV and press with world news mainly, as well as provides material for use abroad. There are co-operative agreements with the agencies *Baltija*, 'Reuters', TASS.

RELIGION AND CHURCH

The foundation of Latvian Church is connected with the adoption of Christianity. The local tribes got acquainted with two Christianity systems: the Eastern (Russian Ortodox) and the Western (Roman Catholicism). Peaceful Christianizing from the East proved the existence of common features between the Latvian loose religious structure and that of the Slavs. The Western Christianity, which developed under the influence of the Latin school of jurisdiction was characterized by a rigid religious structure. It was the cause of its incoherence with the Latvian culture. The asynchronism of historical development in Europe and Latvia was about 1,000 years. It was the reason of great difficulties in the perception of refined religious culture. As a result patrimonial relations between the missionaries and prosalites developed, which included patrimonial rights and the economic subjection of the inhabitants to the missionaries of Christianity.

Archeological data bear evidence that the beginnings of the Latvian Church are connected with the expansion of orthodoxy in the 9 — 12th cent. According to *Heinrici Chronicon Livoniae*, orthodoxy was widespread in such Russian tributary states as Tālava and those on the River Daugava (Jersika, Koknese).

The Christianizing of Latvian tribes before the 13th cent. from the West had little effect. Historical data concerning the period are poor. The Augustinian monk Meinhard of Bremen is considered to be the founder of the Latvian Church. In fact Bishop Albert laid the foundation of the Latvian Church and state. Two formally independent bishoprics, namely, that of Zemgale (1225 — 51) and Kurzeme (Piltene; 1234 — 1583) were formed in the 13th cent.

In 1255 Pope Innocentius IV confirmed the Archbishopric of Riga, but the real power of the church was split between the bishop and the Livonian Order. In 1526 all Livonian bishops admitted the supreme direction of the Master of the Order — Plettenberg.

In the 1520s, the Reformation began in Latvia. Its leaders were A.Knopke and S.Tegetmeyer. The Reformation centres were in towns, mainly in Riga. In the countryside it developed slowly. After the decay of the State of the Livonian Order in 1561 and its surrender to Stefan Batory in 1562 the Counter-Reformation developed. Its most prominent representatives were E.Tolgsdorff, P.Skarga, P.Canisius.

Since the division of Livonia in 1562, territorial churches in Latvia started their development. In Vidzeme, since its subjection to Sweden, the Lutheran Church was established; Latgale's connection to Poland facilitated the foundation of the Catholic Church.

In Kurzeme and Zemgale the Lutheran Church with a catholic enclave consolidated. Swedish King Gustav II Adolph, having captured Riga, expelled the catholics from Vidzeme and Riga, according to the General Privilege of 1621. At the same time energetic elimination of paganism developed in Vidzeme's countryside. One of the most celebrated personalities of the time was E.Glück, who translated the Bible into Latvian. The New Testament was published in 1685, printing of the Old Testament was started in 1689. Swedish King Charles XI provided money for the publication of the Bible.

Latgale's Catholic Church was under the influence of Poland.The Jesuits and the catholic priests expelled from Riga (1621) and Cēsis (1625) moved to Latgale. The Board of the Livonian Bishopric was restored in 1679, its chair was situated in Dünaburg (Daugavpils). Since 1626, the Jesuit Board headed by E. Elger functioned there. In 1694 a Dominican mission was founded at Pasiene. The Theological Seminary was opened in Krāslava in 1757. The rule of the Russians over Vidzeme and

Riga (since 1710) and the joining of Latgale (1772) and Kurzeme (1795) the Russian Empire brought about changes in the Latvian Church. It was considerably reduced and put under the control of St.Petersburg's Synod. The most outstanding representatives of the church were A.Gräwen (1717) and J.Baumann (1747 – 59).

In the 19th cent., the established church in Lutheran areas and the catholic nonconformity in Catholic regions consolidated due to the Polish uprise of 1861 – 64 against Russia. Latgale's Bishopric was closed and the rule of the church was taken over by the Archbishop of Mogilev. The schools and cloisters were shut. The most distinguished representatives of the Catholic Church were K.Skrinda and N.Rancāns.

Since 1738, a movement of the Brethren Unities (Herrnhuters) began. It facilitated the development of Latvian culture. In the 19th cent., it came to an end. The most famous representatives of the movement were P.Škesteris (1702 – 87), J.Balodis (1788 – 1870).

Many members of the Brethren Unities adopted orthodoxy in the 19th cent. Since 1885 the Latvian orthodox converts suffered persecution by the government of Russia for their striving to return to the Lutheran Church.

In 1918 the Catholic Bishopric of Riga was restored. The first bishop of Latvian catholics A.Springovičs was nominated by Pope XI in 1922. A theological higher educational establishment was founded in Aglona (1920). In 1924 it was moved to Riga.

The first Synod of the independent Latvian Lutheran Church took place in 1922 with Bishop K.Irbe presiding. The Theological Faculty was founded at the University of Latvia.

Since 1940, the Latvian Church suffered persecution due to the occupation of Latvia by the USSR. The Evangelical Lutheran Church was headed by Archbishop G.Türs and Archbishop J.Matulis; the Catholic Church — by Bishop P.Strods and Cardinal J.Vaivods.

In 1989 revival of the Latvian Church was to be seen. The persecutions came to an end. The Constitution of the Evangelical Lutheran Church (1922) as well as the Theological Faculty was renewed. K.Gailītis was democratically elected Archbishop.

The Orthodox Church in Latvia as an institution exists since its joining to Russia in the 18th cent. It mainly unites the Russian members. The Orthodox Church is controlled by the Moscow Patriarchate. It is headed by a Metropolitan appointed from Russia.

LIVING STANDARD AND SOCIAL WELFARE

Living standard of the people in the Republic have not improved in the last years in spite of the fact that money incomes have grown greatly. Money deposits of the population amounted to 3,588,000,000 roubles in 1989 (average 1,781 roubles per person).

Average Monthly Earnings (in roubles)

	1980	1985	1988	1989
Workers and employees including the employed:	171	196	227	250
in material production	179	214[x]	243	267
in non-material sphere	147	166[x]	184	203
Rural collective farm members	152	213	243	264
Fishery collective farm members	—	279	329	378
Cooperative workers	—	—	408	526

[x] In 1986.

Inflation rates keep going up. In 1986 – 89 index of retail prices which reflects fluctuations in average consumer prices and service tariffs went up by 18% (visible inflation). The demand for goods and services outrunning the supply measured 1,800,000,000 roubles or 34% (invisible inflation). Inflation level in the consumption sector rose to 52%. Average prices in 1989 went up by 5.2%. Fruit and vegetable prices jumped 1.7 times, leather footwear by 42%, potatoes — by 39%, rubber footwear, confectionery and printed matter — by 15%.

Average Retail Prices (Base: 1985 = 100)

Date	All commodities	Foodstuffs	Consumer goods
1986	105.4	108.9	102.5
1987	110.0	117.9	103.9
1988	114.6	122.0	108.8
1989	120.6	125.3	116.7

Per Capita Industrial Output in 1989

Foodstuffs (kg)		Consumer goods	
Meat (including 1 st category by-products)	94.8	Knitwear	16 u.
Sausages	22.8	Socks and stockings	29 p.
Fish and fish preparations	204.1	Footwear	4 p.
Butter	17.4	Washing machines	23^x
Whole-milk products converted		Radio receivers	55^x
into milk	214.9	Electric coffee mills	32^x
Fat cheese	9.3	Chinaware	12 u.
Fruit juice (conv. jars)	19.4	Detergents	0.8 kg

^{x} Per 100 inhabitants.

Annual Per Capita Consumption of Foodstuffs (kg)

	1980	1985	1989
Meat and meat preparations	76	85	85
Milk and dairy produce	403	455	457
Eggs (pieces)	259	295	282
Sugar	46.3	46.8	43.6
Fish and fish preparations	23.4	23.8	23.0
Vegetable oil	8.8	8.8	8.0
Potatoes	128	122	118
Fruit and berries	72	80	74

Principal Commodities (per 1,000 inhabitants, by the end of the year)

	1980	1985	1989
Watches and clocks	2,358	2,507	2,677
Radio receivers	298	373	420
TV sets	308	373	409
Tape recorders	102	157	180
Cameras	176	188	190
Refrigerators and freezers	371	397	398
Washing machines	260	260	265
Vacuum cleaners	145	183	220
Cars	62	79	94
Motorcycles and scooters	45	57	58
Bicycles and mopeds	194	232	271
Sewing machines	189	193	193

265,000,000 roubles (3.6% of the national income) in 1989 were allotted from the Budget to health service in Latvia. 202 hospitals with 39,300 hospital beds (147 beds per 10,000 persons), 385 medical establishments providing examination and treatment, and 288 women and children's follow-up centres and polyclinics were at the disposal of the population in 1989. 13,400 doctors and 31,800 paramedical personnel worked in the Republic's medical institutions in 1989, the ratio being 50 and 119 per each 10,000 persons respectively. Further improvement of health service in the Republic depends greatly on up-to-date technology capable to provide efficient treatment.

At the end of 1990 the Republic had 38 stadiums (including the Central Daugava Stadium with 17,000 seats), 670 gyms, 22 swimming-pools (two of these being 50 m in length).

Principal Diseases Afflicting Population

	1980	1985	1989	1989 per 100,000 persons
Enteric Fever and Paratyphoid A,B,C	77	25	5	0.2
Bacillary Dysentery	2,390	3,832	1,200	45
Scarlet Fever	1,628	2,017	1,715	64
Whooping Cough	86	138	109	4
Chicken-Pox	10,474	11,972	12,859	482
Measles	1,549	200	17	1
Hepatitis, infectious	14,065	5,637	7,883	295
Flu and infectious diseases of respiratory organs	807,000	855,000	420,000	15,724
Malignant Tumors (1st inference)	6,360	7,119	7,154	268

In 1989 there were 631,000 retired people including 478,000 old-age pensioners in Latvia. Average pensions in 1989 amounted to 38% for workers and employees and 29% for farmers of the average monthly earnings.

Average Monthly Pensions (end of the year, in roubles)

	1980	1985	1989
Pensions payed out on the basis of the Law on State Pensions	63.6	89.2	84.4
Old-age pensions	69.5	89.2	100.4

Housing construction in the Republic is slow and does not meet the heavy demand for housing, especially in areas of economic prosperity. 42.9% of all capital investment went to the construction, remodelling and renovation of industrial enterprises while just 13.7% were allocated to housing in 1989. At the beginning of 1990, 165,000 families (i.e., every fifth family in the Republic) were registered for rehousing or receiving a new flat. 8% of the existing housing stock in the Republic are in worn-out and damaged state and yet approximately 200,000 people are compelled to live in such conditions.

Available Housing (end of the year)

	1980	1985	1989
Total floorspace (million sq km)	43.1	48.5	52.3
average space per person (sq m)	17.1	18.6	19.4
Urban housing (million sq km)	27.2	30.5	33.2
average space per person (sq m)	15.7	16.7	17.5
Countryside housing (million sq km)	15.9	17.9	19.1
average space per person (sq m)	20.1	22.9	24.5

The inhabitants of the Republic received 819,000,000 roubles worth of services in 1989 (305 roubles per person). 24% of this sum or 73.1 roubles per person went to the public catering services. On the territory of Latvia in 1989, 3,109 service houses and shops operated and offered services to the population. 1,291 of them provided services in the towns and cities, and 1,818 in the rural areas. The demand for services is outrunning the supply by 50% in the cities and by 60% in the countryside. Dressmaking and repair (19.5%), house-building and repair (19.4%), including installation of gas, car service and repair (19.1%) rank among the most widely demanded services in 1989.

USEFUL INFORMATION FOR A VISITOR

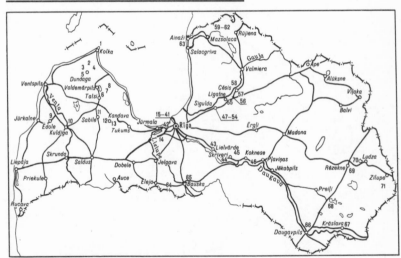

A FEW RECOMMENDATIONS TO TRAVELLERS IN LATVIA

Latvia is a beautiful country with many interesting historical and architectural monuments, various museums as well as picturesque spots and other places of interest. You can make a leisurely journey over Latvia by car or by boat, on bicycle or on foot comparatively inexpensively and spend a quiet evening by a camp-fire in a nice lonely place. The roads are rather good as well as public transport services.

Being northerners Latvians are even-tempered, restrained and hospitable as a rule. Their national dishes are mild and never strongly spiced. The peculiarities of dishes including bread vary in different regions. Latvia can boast of many excellent masters of applied arts and the display of their works especially with ethnographical motives can be a source of delight to visitors.

Nevertheless, travellers who are used to Western life standards may face some difficulties. The number of people who can speak a foreign language (English, German, French) is rather small. Service may be quite a problem sometimes. One has to bear in mind that supply of medicine, soap, diapers and other toilet articles is insufficient.

Distance Between the Largest Cities and Towns (km; highway)

	Alūk-sne	Dau-gavpils	Jel-gava	Kul-dīga	Lie-pāja	Riga	Rē-zekne	Sigul-da	Val-miera	Vents-pils
Ainaži	204	329	172	307	359	115	298	117	87	345
Alūksne	–	221	263	395	449	204	129	151	118	433
Bauska	259	192	45	181	221	66	230	119	187	220
Cēsis	123	206	151	283	337	92	199	38	30	321
Daugavpils	221	–	232	368	412	229	90	216	236	407
Jelgava	263	232	–	137	186	42	264	113	181	175
Jēkabpils	145	90	164	301	350	143	100	126	148	339
Jūrmala	262	264	55	126	208	24	276	112	180	160
Krāslava	215	45	274	411	455	267	86	249	272	449
Kuldīga	395	368	137	–	90	164	401	245	312	55
Liepāja	449	412	186	90	–	223	451	299	367	125
Mazsalaca	163	281	226	357	412	171	238	108	45	395
Riga	204	229	42	164	223	–	244	53	122	202
Rēzekne	129	90	264	401	451	244	–	226	193	439
Sabile	347	327	96	47	137	123	359	206	282	86
Saldus	347	316	84	53	102	121	348	197	265	108
Sigulda	151	216	113	245	299	53	226	–	63	283
Talsi	361	335	103	56	146	130	367	211	278	78
Valmiera	118	236	181	312	367	122	193	63	–	350
Ventspils	433	407	175	55	125	202	439	283	350	–

RIGA

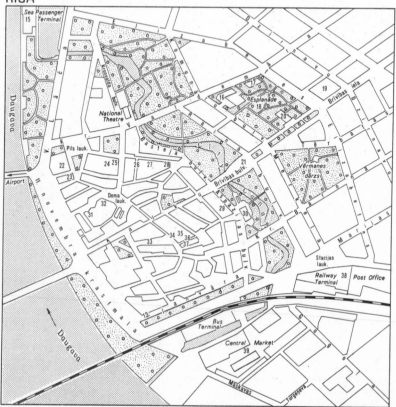

TELEPHONE DIRECTORY

EMERGENCIES (same tel. nrs used throughout Latvia)

Fire	01	Gas leakage	04
Police	02	Telegraph	06
Ambulance	03	Directory inquiries	09

GENERAL INFORMATION

Everyday services	009	Sea passenger terminal	329 882
Passenger taxies	334 041 − 049	River port	612 019
Freight taxies	225 551	Transport police	333 476
Trains	007	Lost property office	219 635, 283 504
Home delivery of tickets	226 022	Hotels	222 802, 224 546
	233 480	Bureau of tourism	221 727
Railway luggage	232 145	Travel agency INTOURIST	211 781, 213 141
Buses	213 611	Pharmacies, drugstores	285 927, 222 281
Home delivery of tickets	220 044	Inter-city telephone connections	282 222
Airline agency	223 175	Inter-city long distance	8 − 12
Airport RIGA	223 175, 223 305	International long	
Home delivery of tickets	226 495	distance	8 − 194, 287 344

CITY CODES (from Riga 8 − ..)

Moscow 095   Leningrad 812   Tallinn 0142   Vilnius 0122

Aizkraukle	251	Jelgava	230	Rēzekne	246
Alūksne	243	Krāslava	256	Saldus	238
Balvi	245	Kuldīga	233	Talsi	232
Bauska	239	Liepāja	234	Tukums	231
Cēsis	241	Limbaži	240	Valka	247
Daugavpils	254	Ludza	257	Valmiera	242
Dobele	237	Madona	248	Ventspils	236
Gulbene	244	Ogre	250		
Jēkabpils	252	Preiļi	253		

International telephone code to Latvia 7 − 013, to Riga 7 − 0132

ADDRESSES

HOTELS

BALTIJA Raiņa bulv. 33, tel. 227 461; **DAUGAVA** Kuģu 24, tel. 612 112; **19 LATVIJA** Elizabetes 55, tel. 212 503; **METROPOLE** Aspazijas bulv. 36/38, tel. 216 184; **RĪDZENE** Endrupa 1, tel. 324 433; **29 RĪGA** Aspazijas bulv. 2, tel. 216 000

RESTAURANTS

ASTORIJA Audēju 16, open 12 − 24, l.hr. 17 − 18; **KAUKĀZS** Merķeļa 8, 12 − 24, l.hr. 18 − 19; **19 LATVIJA** (hotel; several dining rooms, bars, variety show at 20.30 daily) Elizabetes 55; **METROPOLE** Aspazijas bulv. 36/38, 12 − 23.30, l.hr. 17 − 18; **29 RĪGA** Aspazijas bulv. 22, 13.30 − 22.30, l.hr. 16 − 18; **SENĀ RĪGA** 12 − 23.30, l.hr. 17 − 18; **SELGA** A.Čaka 55, 12 − 23.30, l.hr. 17 − 18; **SZCZECIN** Maskavas 264, 12 − 24, l.hr. 17 − 18; **TALLINN** Kr. Valdemāra 27/29, 12 − 24, l.hr. 17 − 18

CASINO Kaļķu 24, 16 − 04

CAFÈS

AINAVA Kronvalda bulv. 1, Mon − Fri 8 − 20, Sat, Sun 10 − 20; **BALTĀ ROZE** Laipu 1, Mon − Fri 10 − 22, Sat, Sun 12 − 22, l.hr. 15.30 − 17; **LUNA** Basteja bulv. 18, Mon − Sat 11 − 23, Sun 12 − 23, l.hr. 18 − 19; **LEŅINGRADA** Raiņa bulv. 25, 12 − 24, l.hr. 18 − 19; **MALVĪNE** (cocktails) Brīvības 101, 10 − 22; **MOŽUMS** Šķūņu 19, 11 − 23; **NĪCA** Brīvības 70, Mon − Fri 7.30 − 20, Sat, Sun 9 − 20, l.hr. 15 − 16; **PŪT, VĒJIŅI** Jauniela 18/22, Mon − Sat 11 − 23, Sun 13 − 23, l.hr. 17 − 18; **RĪDZENE** Skārņu 9, 10 − 22, l.hr. 16 − 17; **ROSTOCK** Tērbatas 13, 12 − 23, l.hr. 17 − 18; **SIGULDA** Brīvības bulv. 21, 7.30 − 21, l.hr. 16 − 16.30; **TRĪSPADSMIT KRĒSLI** Jauniela 11, 10 − 22, l.hr. 15 − 16; **VECRĪGA** Vaļņu 18, Mon − Fri 7 − 22, Sat, Sun 9 − 23, l.hr. 16 − 17; **VIDZEME** Lielgabalu 2a, 10 − 22, l.hr. 17 − 18; **JEVER** (hard currency Beerkeller) Kaļķu 6, 11 − 03

MUSEUMS

32 MUSEUM OF RIGA DOME Doma lauk. 1, Tue – Fri 13 – 17, Sat 10 – 14; **17 STATE MUSEUM OF FINE ARTS** Kr.Valdemāra 10a, Mon, Wed, Thur, Fri 12 – 18, Sat, Sun 11 – 18; **22 MUSEUM OF THE HISTORY OF LATVIA** Pils lauk. 3, Wed, Fri 13 – 19, Thur, Sat, Sun 11 – 17; **31 MUSEUM OF THE HISTORY OF RIGA AND NAVIGATION** Palasta 4, Wed, Sat 13 – 19, Thur, Fri, Sun 11 – 17; **22 MUSEUM OF FOREIGN ART** Pils lauk. 3, Tue, Thur, Sat, Sun 11 – 17, Wed, Fri 13 – 17; **LATVIAN CULTURE MUSEUM 'DAUDERI'** Tvaika 44, Wed – Sun 11 – 17; **28 WAR MUSEUM** Smilšu 20, Mon, Wed, Thur 10 – 17, Sat, Sun 11 – 18; **41 OPEN-AIR MUSEUM OF ETHNOGRA-PHY** Brīvības 440, Mon – Sun 10 – 17; **MUSEUM FOR HISTORY OF MEDICINE** L.Paegles 1, Wed – Fri 12 – 17.30, Sat, Sun 11 – 16.30; **MUSEUM OF FIRE-FIGHTING** Hanzas 5, Wed – Sun 10 – 17; **MOTOR MUSEUM** S.Eizenšteina 6, Tue – Sun 10 – 20

EXHIBITION HALLS

19 LATVIJA Brīvības 31, Tue – Sun 12 – 18; **ARSENĀLS** Torņu 1/3, Tue, Fri 12 – 18, Sat, Sun 11 – 18; **ĶĪPSALA** (ceramics) Balasta dambis 34, Wed – Sun 12 – 18; **36 JĀŅASĒTA** Jāņa sēta 7, 10 – 19; **JOURNALISTS' (REUTHERN'S) HOUSE** Mārstaļu 2, Tue – Sat 12 – 19

ART GALLERIES

ARS LONGA R.Vāgnera 4, Tue – Sun 11 – 17; **KOLONNA** Šķūņu 16, Tue – Fri 10 – 18, Sat 10 – 15; **22 SCULPTORS' HOUSE** Pils lauk. 3, Tue – Sun 11 – 18; **ARCHITECTS' HOUSE** Torņu 11, Mon – Fri 10 – 17; **ARTISTS' HOUSE** 11. novembra krastmala 35, Wed – Sun 11 – 18; **PHOTO-GRAPHERS' HOUSE** Mārstaļu 6, Tue – Sun 12 – 19

THEATRES

30 NATIONAL OPERA Aspazijas bulv. 3; **OPERETTA THEATRE** Brīvības 96; **NATIONAL THEATRE** Kronvalda 2; **ART (DAILES) THEATRE** Brīvības 75; **RUSSIAN DRAMA THEATRE** Kaļķu 16; **YOUTH THEATRE** Lāčplēša 37 (Latv.), Lāčplēša 25 (Russ.); **PUPPET THEATRE** Kr.Barona 16/18; **CIRCUS** Merķeļa 4

ZOO Meža prosp. 1, open 10 – 16, in season 10 – 20

CONCERT HALLS

32 DOME CATHEDRAL (organ music) Doma lauk. 1; **PHILHARMONIC** Amatu 6; **ACADEMY OF MUSIC** Kr.Barona 1; **RICHARD WAGNER CONCERT HALL** R.Vāgnera 4; **AVE SOL** Citadeles 7

CHURCHES

Lutheran: **32 DOME CATHEDRAL** Doma lauk. 1; **37 CHURCH OF ST.JOHN** Jāņa 7; **OLD CHURCH OF ST.GERTRUDE** Ģertrūdes 8; **NEW CHURCH OF ST.GERTRUDE** Brīvības 119; **CHURCH OF ST.PAUL** A.Deglava 1; **CHURCH OF CROSS** Ropažu 120; **CHURCH OF JESUS** Odesas 18
Catholic: **24 CATHEDRAL OF ST.JACOB** Klostera 2; **CHURCH OF ST.MARY MAGDALENE** Klostera 2; **23 CHURCH OF MATER DOLOROSA** L.Pils 5
Orthodox: **ORTHODOX CATHEDRAL** Kr.Barona 126; **ST.ALEXANDER NEVSKY CHURCH** Brīvības 56; **CHURCH OF ANNUNCIATION OF THE MOTHER OF GOD** Gogoļa 9
Others: **GREBENSCHIKOV'S CHURCH OF THE RUSSIAN OLD BELIEVERS** Krasta 73; **BALTIC UNION OF THE 7TH DAY ADVENTISTS** J.Kupalas 9; **UNION OF THE LATVIAN BAPTIST CONGREGATIONS** Matīsa 50b; **THE SYNAGOGUE** Peitavas 6/8

LIBRARIES

NATIONAL LIBRARY Kr.Barona 14, Mon – Fri 9 – 21, Sat, Sun 10 – 17, tel. 287 608; **FUNDAMEN-TAL LIBRARY OF THE ACADEMY OF SCIENCES** Lielvārdes 24, Mon – Fri 10 – 20, Sat 10 – 18, tel. 552 084; **J.MISIŅŠ LIBRARY** Skolas 3, Mon – Fri 10 – 20, Sat 10 – 18, tel. 289 540

RIGA CITY COUNCIL Kr.Valdemāra 3, tel. 321 230

MONEY EXCHANGE

BANK Kr.Valdemāra 2a, tel. 325 385, open 9.30 – 12.30; **29 HOTEL 'RĪGA'** Aspazijas bulv. 2, tel. 216 074, 9 – 18, l.hr. 12 – 13; **19 HOTEL 'LATVIJA'** Elizabetes 55, tel. 212 351, 9 – 20, l.hr. 13 – 14

SHOPPING

CENTRAL DEPARTMENT STORE Audēju 16, open Food store 9 – 21, Consumer goods Mon – Sat 10 – 20; **19 DZINTARKRASTS** (consumer goods for hard currency) Brīvības 31, 9 – 18, l.hr. 13 – 14; **BĒRNU PASAULE** (Children's World) Matīsa 25, Mon – Fri 10 – 20, Sat 10 – 18

WATCHES. JEWELRY

ROTA Kaļķu 15; **DIMANTS** Brīvības 66; **TIK-TAK** Kaļķu 4, Mon — Fri 10 — 19, Sat 10 — 17

FOLK ART. SOUVENIRS. AMBER. KNITTINGS. TEXTILES. WICKERWORK. EARTHENWARE

SAKTA Brīvības bulv. 32, Mon — Fri 10 — 20, Sat 9 — 18; Vaļņu 25, Mon — Fri 10 — 19, Sat 10 — 18, l.hr. 14 — 15; Aspazijas bulv. 30, Mon — Fri 10 — 19, Sat, Sun 9 — 17; Brīvības 52, Mon — Fri 10 — 19, l.hr. 14 — 15; Grēcinieku 20, Brīvības 84, Tue — Fri 10 — 19, Sat 10 — 17, l.hr. 14 — 15; Kaļķu 15, Mon — Fri 10 — 19, Sat 10 — 17

BOOKSHOPS

CENTRAL Aspazijas bulv. 24, Mon — Fri 10 — 19, Sat 10 — 17, l.hr. 14 — 15; **NIANSE** (art, photography, etc.) Kr.Barona 31, Mon — Fri 10 — 19, Sat 10 — 18, l.hr. 14 — 15; **GLOBUSS** (foreign literature) Aspazijas bulv. 26, Mon — Fri 10 — 19, Sat 10 — 17, l.hr. 14 — 15; **ZINĀTNISKĀ GRĀMATA** (science, medicine, history, language) Stabu 15, Mon — Fri 10 — 19, Sat 10 — 18, l.hr. 14 — 15; **MUSIC SHOP** Kr.Barona 3, Mon — Fri 10 — 19, l.hr. 14 — 15; **CENTRAL SECOND-HAND BOOKSHOP** Brīvības 46, Tue, Thur, Sat 9 — 18, l.hr. 13 — 14, Wed 11 — 20, l.hr. 15 — 16; **SECOND-HAND BOOKSHOP** (foreign literature) Tērbatas 5, Mon — Fri 9 — 18, l.hr. 13 — 14; **DAINA** (books for hard currency) Elizabetes 63, 9 — 18, l.hr. 13 — 14

PERFUMERY: LELDE A.Čaka 58, Mon — Fri 10 — 19, Sat 10 — 17, l.hr. 14 — 15; **DZINTARS** Kr.Barona 3, Mon — Fri 9 — 20, Sat 10 — 18, l.hr. 14 — 15

MARKETS: 39 CENTRAL MARKET Nēģu 7; **VIDZEME MARKET** Brīvības 90; **ĀGENSKALNS MARKET** L.Laicena 64, Tue — Sat 8 — 17, Sun, Mon 8 — 15

RECORDS: SONĀTE Elizabetes 77, Tue — Sat 11 — 20, l.hr. 14 — 15; Vaļņu 26, Mon — Fri 10 — 20, Sat 10 — 19

SPORTS HALLS AND CENTRES Kr.Barona 75, tel. 272 408; Kr.Barona 107, tel. 270 586; Maskavas 160, tel. 241 770; Ķīpsalas 5, tel. 616 989

MEDICAL SERVICE

EYE TREATMENT IN EMERGENCIES: HOSPITAL No 7 P.Dauges 2, tel. 536 339; **EMERGENCY DENTAL SERVICE** Stabu 9, tel. 274 546; **ACCIDENTS** Bruņinieku 8, tel. 296 734; Ģimnastikas 1, tel. 622 168; **ALL-NIGHT DRUGSTORES** Audēju 20; Brīvības 74; Elizabetes 21a; Brīvības 211; **HOMEOPATH'S SHOP** Vaļņu 26, tel. 223 434, Mon 12 — 19, Tue — Fri 8 — 21, Sat 9 — 16

SERVICE

DRYCLEANING Kr.Barona 52, Mon — Fri 8 — 20, Sat 8 — 16; Satekles 5/7, Mon — Fri 8 — 20, Sat 8 — 15; **RENTAL CENTRE** J.Kupalas 1, Mon, Thur 11 — 19, l.hr. 15 — 16, Tue, Fri 9 — 17, l.hr. 13 — 14; **BATHS** Mārstaļu 17, Tallinas 71, Wed — Sun 8 — 22; **HAIRDRESSER'S 'FANTĀZIJA'** Kr.Barona 36; **RĪGAS MODES** Brīvības 49/53, Mon — Sat 7 — 22, Sun 8 — 16; **LUKSS** Brīvības 40, Tue — Fri 7 — 21, Mon, Sat 7 — 19; **BARBER'S** Kr.Barona 24/26, Mon — Sat 7 — 22, Sun 8 — 16; **SHOE REPAIR** Marijas 30, Mon, Tue, Thur, Fri 8 — 20, Wed 8 — 16, Sat 8 — 18; Dzirnavu 78/80, Mon, Wed, Fri 8 — 15, Tue, Thur 11 — 19; **WATCH REPAIR** Marijas 3, Mon — Fri 9 — 19, Sat 8 — 15, l.hr. 14 — 15; **PHOTO AND CINE CAMERA REPAIR** Dzirnavu 2, Tue — Sat 11 — 20, l.hr. 14 — 15; **NOTARY ASSISTANCE** Raiņa bulv. 1, Mon, Tue, Fri 8 — 17, Wed, Thur 12 — 20, Sat 9 — 15, tel. 325 751, 325 746; Brīvības 133, Mon, Wed, Fri 14 — 20, Tue, Thur 8 — 14, tel. 371 510; **LEGAL ADVICE** Kr.Barona 36, Mon, Wed, Fri 10 — 20, Tue 8 — 18, Thur 9 — 18, tel. 289 859, 223 671; Miera 5, Mon 10 — 20, Tue, Thur 9 — 19, Wed 9 — 18, Fri 8 — 17, tel. 377 437; **38 POST OFFICE** Stacijas lauk., Mon — Fri 8 — 20, Sat 8 — 18, Sun 10 — 16, tel. 211 443; **CENTRAL POST OFFICE. TELEPHONE. TELEX** Brīvības bulv. 21, tel. 333 285; **TELEFAX** Brīvības bulv. 19, tel. 331 222

PUBLIC TRANSPORT

BUS TERMINAL Prāgas 1, tel. 213 611; **38 RAILWAY TERMINAL** Stacijas lauk., tel. 232 134; **AIRPORT** Skulte, tel. 207 009, 207 988, **CENTRAL AGENCY** Raiņa bulv. 11, tel. 223 175

CAR FILLING AND SERVICE STATIONS

Miera 3, tel. 377 319; Skaistkalnes 1, tel. 627 632; Pērnavas 78, tel. 273 715; Sporta 9, tel. 331 964; M.Nometņu 32, tel. 613 826; Uriekstes 3, tel. 382 433; Rumbula, tel. 255 017; Vienības gatve 117, tel. 613 258; Brīvības 386/388, tel. 551 806

ONE-DAY ROUTE USING PUBLIC TRANSPORT (see map p. 116)

There are two main landmarks in the city — the Daugava River and Brīvības Street traversing the city on the right bank. Being the main thoroughfare it has its name changed several times. Before the WW I the street bore the name of the tsar of Russia — Alexander Street. During the German occupation in the WW II it was renamed Hitler Strasse, in the post-war period until quite recently — Lenin Street. Foreign tourists usually put up in the hotels *Latvija* (**19**) and *Rīga* (**29**) situated along Brīvības Street. Not far from the hotels you will find the Railway Terminal and Post Office (**38**), Central Market (**39**) and Sea Passenger Terminal (**15**). The park opposite the hotel *Latvija* called *Esplanāde* (**18**) extends in the direction of the Old City. There you can have a look at the Monument to Rainis and sculptural portraits of the Latvian revolutionaries — victims of the notorious year of 1937 in the SU. The State Museum of Fine Arts (**17**) and Academy of Arts (**16**) are situated a little further to the right.

Let us walk along Brīvības bld. towards the Daugava. To the right rises the Orthodox Cathedral (**20**). Continuing our way we come to the Monument to Freedom (**21**), the most famous landmark of Riga. This monumental ensemble was moulded by the sculptor K.Zāle from 1931 to 1935. The central figure is holding in her upraised hands three stars symbolizing Latvia's three ethnographical regions. Over the City Canal to the left stands the National Opera House (**30**). Further away across the Canal the Old City begins. Let us proceed approximately 200 m then turn to the left into Skārņu Street. In the former St.George's Church (**34**) you can visit recently opened Museum of Applied Arts. After crossing *Konventa sēta* (Convent Yard, **35**) we come to Kalēju Street, turn to the right and passing through the former City Gate enter *Jāņasēta* (St.John's Courtyard, **36**) where we can have a look at a fragment of the old Fortification Wall with loop-holes and restored wooden gallery. Returning through *Jāņasēta* (it houses a small exhibition hall) to Skārņu Street on the left we pass the Lutheran Church of St.John (**37**). Its foundation was laid in the 13th cent. and in the course of time it has been destroyed and rebuilt many times. The church just opposite is the former St.Peter's (**33**), at present a spacious exhibition hall. This church was first mentioned in 1265 and has also been damaged by recurrent storms and fire. By the end of the 15th cent., a 137 m high wooden steeple was erected and till the WW II it was considered the highest wooden structure in the world. During warfare in 1941, the tower caught heavy fire and burnt down. In 1973 the tower underwent renovation and this time a 123 m high steel structure was set up. Tourists can enjoy vast panoramic views of Riga from 57 m and 71 m high observation platforms.

Let us visit another prominent edifice in Riga — the Dome Cathedral (**32**). Its construction began in the 13 th cent. and it also has been rebuilt several times. The cathedral organ ranks among the best in the world. You can have a look at exhibits in the inner patio of the cathedral. The adjoining former monastery houses the Museum of the History of Riga and Navigation (**31**).

The next place of interest is the Riga Castle (**22**) dating back to the 14th cent. Up to the 16th cent., it has been the residence of the Master of the Livonian Order. Today the Castle houses three museums featuring various exhibitions. The neighbouring Catholic Church of *Mater Dolorosa* (**23**) displays the style of early Classicism.

Along the narrow Old City streets we come to the building of the Supreme Council of the Republic of Latvia (**25**). It was built in the 19th cent. as the House of Vidzeme Knighthood. The Catholic Cathedral of St.Jacob (**24**) stands just opposite.

Trokšņa Street takes us back to Brīvības bld. To the right we see *Zviedru vārti* (Swedish Gate, **26**), a little further the renovated City Fortification Wall (**27**) and *Pulvertornis* (Powder Tower, **28**) which is the only tower of the medieval fortification system preserved unchanged to the present day. The height of walls is 26 m, thickness 3 m. The adjoining red brick building is the War Museum and Art Gallery.

In the north-eastern part of the city there is one of the most outstanding monuments of war memorial architecture — *Brāļu kapi* (Brethren Cemetery, **40**). K.Zāle, the author of the Monument to Freedom, worked at this ensemble from 1924 till 1936. The Rainis Cemetery is to the left, to the right — *Meža kapi* (Forest Cemetery). We recommend you to visit these places because of many outstanding works of art among the Latvian memorial sculpture. You can also get acquainted with the Latvian traditional care for their burial places.

In the eastern part of the city the main attractor is the Open-Air Museum of Ethnography (**41**) on the bank of Lake Jugla. Here you see samples of Latvian rural architecture of the previous centuries.

Not far from Riga along the seashore stretches the searesort Jūrmala (**42**) famous for its sandy beaches. It is a good place to rest in summer. One can try to restore health with mudbaths and healing waters in any of the numerous sanatoriums.

THE RING ROAD OF RIGA

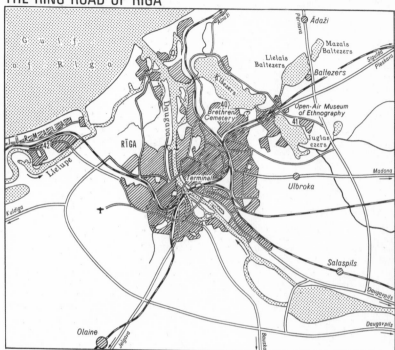

JŪRMALA

GENERAL INFORMATION

EMERGENCY telephone nrs see p. 117 RIGA. Telephone Directory
Long distance telephone connections . . . . Lienes 6/8, tel. 620 12
Bulduru prosp. 29, tel. 530 27
Kauguri, Talsu šos., tel. 362 25
Ķemeri, Tukuma 30, tel. 655 60
Taxies 616 60
Lost property office 471 57
Bureau of excursions . . . . Majori, Jomas 56, tel. 471 14, 473 42

ADDRESSES

HOTELS

JAUNĶEMERI Ventspils 6, tel. (6)365 75; **JŪRMALA** Jomas 47/49, tel. (7)613 41; **JŪRMALA** branch hotel in Lielupe, Viļņu 3, tel. (6)511 57; **MAJORI** Jomas 29, tel. (7)613 80; **PUMPURI** (summer hotel) Upes 2, tel. (7)675 54; **VAIVARI** (summer hotel) Atbalss 1, tel.(6)363 92

RESTAURANTS

Here and further only summer working hrs are given
BURA Lielupe, Vikingu 3, open 13 – 24; **JŪRA** Majori, Turaidas 3, 12 – 24; **JŪRAS PĒRLE** Bulduri, Vienības prosp. 2, 13 – 01; **JŪRMALA** Majori, Jomas 47/49, 13 – 24; **KAUGURI** Kauguri, Talsu šos. 39, 12 – 24; **ĶEMERI** Ķemeri, Tukuma 21, 11 – 24; **LAIVAS** Lielupe, Tīklu 1, 12 – 23; **LIDO** Majori, Turaidas 8, 13 – 01; **MIEZĪTIS** Majori, Konkordijas 13, 13 – 23; **ORIENTS** Majori, Jomas 86, 12 – 24; **PIE PATVĀRA** Dzintari, Dzintaru prosp. 32, 12 – 24

BARS

BALZĀMS Dzintari, Dzintaru prosp. 58, open 14 – 23; **BOULINGS** (cocktails) Dzintari, Dzintaru prosp. 32, 12 – 24; **BURA** Lielupe, Vikingu 3, 12 – 24; **DAILE** Dzintari, Dzintaru prosp. 32, 14 – 23;

JŪRAS PĒRLE Bulduri, Vienības prosp. 2, 17 – 24; **JŪRMALA** Majori, Jomas 47/49, 14 – 24; **KABŪRA** Pumpuri, Piejūras 1, 17 – 01; **OLIMPISKAIS** Lielupe, Padomju prosp. 18, 11 – 22; **ORIENTS** Majori, Jomas 86, 13 – 23; **SENCIS** (Beerkeller) Majori, Jomas 33, 12 – 24

CAFĖS

AERO Majori, Jomas 35, open 12 – 23; **BULDURI** Bulduri, Meža prosp. 27, 12 – 23; **DUBULTI** Dubulti, Muzeja 8/10, 12 – 24; **JOMA** Majori, Jomas 54, Wed – Mon 12 – 24; **SĀRTĀS BURAS** Kauguri, Talsu šos. 31, 11 – 22; **SEPTIŅAS MĀSIŅAS** Majori, Jomas 37, 12 – 24

SUMMER CONCERT HALL Dzintari, Turaidas 1; **EXHIBITION HALL** Dzintari, Turaidas 11, tel. 644 63, in season 12 – 19, Tue closed

SHOPS. SOUVENIRS. PRESENTS Dzintari, Turaidas 10/2, Tue – Sat 10 – 19, l.hr. 14 – 15; Majori, Jomas 46, Tue – Sat 10 – 19, l.hr. 14 – 15; Majori, Jomas 31, Tue – Sat 9 – 18, l.hr. 13 – 14

HOSPITALS Kosmonautu 36/38, tel. 324 82; 327 51; Dzintaru prosp. 16, tel. 620 82; Vienības prosp. 19/21, tel. 525 48

SERVICE

HAIRDRESSER'S. BARBER'S Bulduri, Bulduru prosp. 31, Mon – Sat 7 – 21, Sun 7 – 15; Dubulti, Slokas 20, Mon – Sat 8 – 21, Sun 8 – 15; **SHOE REPAIR** Bulduri, Bulduru prosp. 23, Tue – Fri 10 – 19, Sat 9 – 18, l.hr. 14 – 15; Majori, Jomas 66, Mon – Fri 10 – 19, l.hr. 14 – 15

KURZEME

THE ROUTE COVERS 600 KM AND TAKES 2 – 3 DAYS TRAVELLING BY CAR (see map p. 115)

The starting point of our journey is the Vanšu Bridge taking us across the Daugava. At the city borderline take the left road by-passing Jūrmala. Further along the road there are places where heavy fighting took place during the WW I. Latvian Riflemen broke the exceptionally strongly fortified German positions in *Ložmetējkalns* (Gun Hill, **14**) without the support of artillery fire thus demonstrating unprecedented heroism. Common soldiers graves are on both sides of the road.

Let us follow the route in the direction of Kuldīga and 20 km behind Tukums turn to the left. Now the road is running along the right side of the River Abava via Kandava (**13**) and Sabile. A lovely view to the dried-up river bed of Abava opens from Kandava, the parking place (**12**) 12 km further from Kandava and *Vīna kalns* (Wine Hill, **11**) in Sabile. Wine Hill in Sabile is registered in the Guinness Book of World Records as the northernmost spot where vine is cultivated in open air. In the Middle Ages wine was produced and exported to Western Europe. 4 km from Sabile you will find a small Abava waterfall – a nice place for rest.

The road continues to Kuldīga (**10**). The waterfall on the River Venta at Kuldīga called *Ventas Rumba* is one of the widest in Europe (110 m; with a total drop of 2 m). The Old Town in Kuldīga is rich in architectural monuments of the 16th and 17th cent.

Let us proceed to Ēdole (**9**). The Ēdole Castle dating back to the 13th cent. is mentioned in many old tales. Legend has it that the lord of the manor had two sons one of whom killed his brother in a quarrel. Day after day the murdered brother's blood appeared on the wall therefore a fireplace was built in that wall. Some people say that the place is haunted even today.

The easiest way to get to another beautiful Kurzeme town Talsi (**6**) is to return back via Kuldīga and Sabile. Talsi is situated in a lovely place among hillocks and lakes and has preserved many medieval buildings including a church. 15 km northeast from Talsi and 5 km from Vandzene lies a boulder (**7**) weighing 400 t which was placed on a hillock in bygone times. Its surface has been processed in a peculiar way and an enormous spatial sign can be observed from a bird's eye view.

Nogale (**8**) has been a hunters castle in olden times. Now it is going to be transformed into a museum. The estate park is characterized by unusual acoustic phenomena. If a few people are speaking or singing in the brick-layed grotto listeners on the opposite bank of the lake hear a performance of a big choir. In another place the echo comes down as if from heaven.

The road goes further in the direction of Dundaga. The Dundaga Castle (**5**) was erected in the 13th cent. It is reflected in folk tales and legends one of which says that the sister of baron Maidel intruded upon gnomes in their wedding and for punishment was immured alive in the walls. Some people believe that she has the habit of showing herself in the nights of full moon.

Pay attention to sound marvels at the entrance of the castle tower – your voices reverberate from above the tower. An oak-tree estimated 800 years of age grows in the park. 6 km further north from Dundaga lies a 2 m high stone pillar – *Āžu stāvakmens* (Goat Stone, **3**). Being an object of worship of the ancient Balts it shows traces of inscriptions and signs.

Proceeding northwards we come to the Slītere Precipice at Vidale (**2**). This striking geological formation (length 15 km, height 35 m) is reproduced on the map in the form of a rather precise fragment of circumference. From here the territory of the Slītere Nature Reserve begins. It is open to visitors with special permits.

Further in the direction of Kolka you can stop at *Upsīšu akmens* (Upsīšu Stone, **4**). This huge egg-shaped boulder with traces of ancient inscriptions is 5 m long and weighs about 12 t. Despite the neighbouring boggy surface the boulder has not sunk into the ground but lies like an enormous egg because of two stone pillows beneath it. Let us continue our journey to the Cape of Kolka (**1**). It is the borderline between the Baltic Sea and the Gulf of Riga. A place can be found where you can stand with your feet in two different seas. There are remains of an old lighthouse on the beach. The road back to Riga runs along the Kurzeme seashore through fishermen's villages. The surrounding landscape is quiet and charming. Here and there trees have part of their roots washed by seawater.

KULDĪGA

HOTEL' KURSA' Pilsētas lauk. 6, tel. 224 30, 243 42

RESTAURANT. CAFĒS. BARS

VENTA Pils lauk. 1, Tue — Fri, Sun 12 — 22, Mon, Sat 12 — 24; **KURSA** Pils lauk. 6, open 7.30 — 21; **LADA** Ēdoles 36, Tue — Sat 9 — 17; **STABURADZE** Liepājas 8, 10 — 22; **VĀVERĪTE** Baznīcas 32, 8 — 20; **VĒJIŅŠ** Mucenieku 1, 9 — 19; **BĀRS** Liepājas 8, 9 — 19; **EKSPRESBĀRS** Liepājas 18, 8.30 — 19.30

OTHER

HOSPITAL Liepājas 37, tel. 225 86; **POST OFFICE** Liepājas 34, tel. 226 84, open 8 — 18; **BUS TERMINAL** Stacijas 2, tel. 220 61; **CAR SERVICE** Ēdoles 36, tel. 225 58, Tue — Sat 9 — 17; **CAR FILLING** Graudu 5, tel. 222 53

TALSI

HOTEL Kareivju 16, tel. 226 89, 212 84

RESTAURANT. CAFĒS

KURZEME Brīvības 17a, open 12 — 24, l.hr. 18 — 19; **MĀRA** Lielā 16, Mon — Sat 7.30 — 19.30, l.hr. 14.30 — 15.30; **STŪRĪTIS** Mīlenbaha 6/8, Mon — Sat 7.30 — 19, l.hr. 13.30 — 14.30, Sun 8 — 17; **PIE EZERA** Kareivju 16, 11 — 22, l.hr. 17 — 18

OTHER

BUREAU OF EXCURSIONS Kareivju 16; **MUSEUM OF ARTS AND REGIONAL STUDIES** Rožu 7, tel. 227 70, Tue — Sun 12 — 18; **ART GALLERY** Lielā 31 — 3, Tue — Fri 10 — 17, Sat 10 — 14; **HOSPITAL** Ruģēna 7, tel. 227 91; **DEPARTMENT STORE** Brīvības 17a, Mon — Fri 9 — 19, l.hr. 14 — 15, Sat 9 — 14; **FOOD STORE 'KURZEMĪTE'** Kr. Valdemāra 50, Mon — Fri 9 — 19, l.hr. 15 — 16, Sat 8 — 15; **SOUVENIRS SHOP 'ROTA'** Lielā 18, Mon — Fri 9 — 19, l.hr. 14 — 15, Sat 9 — 14; **MARKET** Ezera 7, Tue — Sun 7 — 15, in season Tue — Sat 8 — 16; **DRUGSTORES** Ruģēna 7, Mon — Sat 8 — 20, Sun 8 — 14; Lielā 24, Mon — Fri 8 — 20; **POST OFFICE** Lielā 4/6, Mon — Fri 8 — 18, Sat 8 — 15; **BUS TERMINAL** Dundagas 15, tel. 221 05; **CAR SERVICE** Laidze, 'Krūzas' tel. 163 68; **CAR FILLING** Dundagas 24, tel. 248 31

ZEMGALE

ONE-DAY ROUTE USING SERVICES OF THE EXCURSION BUREAU (see map p. 115)

The most important sightseeing attraction is the magnificent Rundāle Palace (**64**) built in the 18th cent. There are interesting exhibitions in the palace. A visit to Rundāle is particularly advantageous to tourists travelling in the direction of Lithuania. The road continues through Bauska (**65**) where a medieval stone castle is being reconstructed.

BAUSKA

HOTEL Slimnīcas 7, tel. 247 05, 238 04

RESTAURANT. CAFĒS

PILSKALNS Brīvības bulv. 2, open 12 — 24; **BAUSKA** Slimnīcas 7, 8 — 20, l.hr. 16 — 17; **GLIEMEZĪTIS** Kalna 7, 9 — 20, l.hr. 15 — 16; **MŪSA** Rātslaukums 1, Mon — Thur 11 — 21, Fri — Sun 11 — 24

OTHER

BUREAU OF EXCURSIONS Slimnīcas 7, tel. 229 07; **MUSEUM OF ARTS AND REGIONAL STUDIES** Kalna 6, tel. 221 97, Wed — Sun 9 — 17; **BAUSKA CASTLE** Brīvības bulv. 2a, Wed — Sun 10 — 17; **DEPARTMENT STORE** Kalna 7, Mon — Fri 9 — 19, l.hr. 13 — 14; **MARKET** Rūpniecības 11, open 8 — 17 (Sun, Mon closed in winter); **HOSPITAL** Slimnīcas 2, tel. 231 53; **DRUGSTORE** Dārza 7, Mon — Fri 8 — 21, Sat, Sun 9 — 16; **POST OFFICE** Slimnīcas 9, tel. 222 68, Mon — Fri 8 — 19, l.hr. 14 — 15, Sat 8 — 16; **BUS TERMINAL** Slimnīcas 11, tel. 224 77, 5 — 22; **CAR FILLING** Code, tel. 222 65, Mon — Sat 6 — 23

LATGALE

A ROUTE OF 2 OR 3 DAYS USING SERVICES OF THE EXCURSION BUREAU (see map p. 115)
The road to Latgale runs along the right bank of the Daugava. We advise you to halt at Lielvārde (**43**) for a short rest and have a look at the local museum, the church and visit the castle mound. Not far from Skrīveri on the right side of the road there is a dendrologic park (**44**) planted by baron von Sievers in the 19th cent. Turning to the left into a country road 7 km from Skrīveri you come across *Meļķitaru akmens* (Meļķitaru Stone, **45**), a 3 m high boulder with a big hollow on top for gathering water. Our ancestors ascribed this water wonderful healing properties and held the stone in high esteem. Another boulder — *Velna akmens* (Devil's Stone, **46**) is located 4 km from Koknese on the right side. Legend has it that carrying this stone Devil tore it asunder. This is also an ancient place of worship. From here and further along the road wonderful views open to the Daugava.
Let us continue our way to Krāslava (**67**) via Daugavpils (**66**) and visit the Catholic Church of Krāslava. The road runs further to the spiritual centre of the Catholic Latgale — the Basilica of Aglona (**68**). Great multitudes of people attend the annual church festival in Aglona on August 15. Latgale excels in colourful scenery especially in the vicinity of Lake Rāzna, the road to Ezernieki and many other places. Latgale is called the 'Land of Blue Lakes' the waters of which are still pure and comparatively unpolluted. If you still have time we suggest a visit to the provincial towns Rēzekne (**69**) and Ludza (**70**). Along the eastern border of Latvia stretches a hilly elevation from which, especially from the close vicinity of the Catholic Pasiene Church (**71**), a superb panoramic view opens to the distant plains of Russia.

KRĀSLAVA

HOTEL 'KRĀSLAVA' Raiņa 35, tel. 214 49; **RESTAURANT. BAR. CAFĒS** Maskavas 92, Mon, Tue, Thur, Sat 12 — 23, Wed, Fri, Sun 12 — 24, l.hr. 18 — 19; Baznīcas 1, open 12 — 23, l.hr. 17 — 18; Smorugova 7, 8 — 20, l.hr. 15 — 16; Maskavas 131, 9 — 21, l.hr. 15 — 16; **MEDICAL AID** Maskavas 215, tel. 03; **DRUGSTORE** Smorugova 8, tel. 238 75, Mon — Fri 8 — 22, Sat, Sun 10 — 18; **BUS TERMINAL** Maskavas 129, tel. 234 00; **CAR SERVICE** Vasarnieku 92, tel. 213 28

RĒZEKNE

HOTEL 'LATGALE' Brīvības 2, tel. 221 80, 241 78; **RESTAURANT. CAFĒS 'LATGALE'** Brīvības 2, open 7.30 — 24; **LIRA** Ļeņina 109, 7.30 — 23; **RĒZNA** Ļeņina 100, 11 — 23; **BUREAU OF EXCURSIONS** Brīvības 3, tel. 235 29, Mon — Fri 8 — 17; **MUSEUM FOR THE HISTORY AND CULTURE OF LATGALE** Ļeņina 102, tel. 224 64, Tue — Sun 10 — 17; **ART GALLERY** Ļeņina 84, tel. 232 39; **DEPARTMENT STORE** Latgales 20, Mon — Sat 9 — 19; **MARKET** Liepājas 16, 7.30 — 17; **HOSPITAL** 18. novembra 41, tel. 221 00, 229 97; **DRUGSTORES** Dārzu 2, open 8 — 21; Ļeņina 117, Mon — Sat 8 — 20; **POST OFFICE** Ļeņina 81/5, tel. 07, 223 18, 10 — 20; **BUS TERMINAL** Latgales 17, tel. 231 82; **CAR FILLING** Varoņu 6; **PARKING** Dārzu 10; Blaumaņa 7; (technical help tel. 322 98)

LUDZA

HOTEL Stacijas 42, tel. 224 90; **RESTAURANT** Stacijas 30, 8 — 22; **MUSEUM OF REGIONAL STUDIES** Kuļņeva 2, tel. 239 31, 9 — 16; **DEPARTMENT STORE** Stacijas 30, 10 — 19; **HOSPITAL** Raiņa 43, tel. 221 11, 237 37; **DRUGSTORE** Latgales 114, tel. 238 52, 8 — 22; **POST OFFICE** Latgales 110/19, tel. 07; **BUS TERMINAL** Kr. Barona 45/14, tel. 226 83; **CAR FILLING** Latgales 255, tel. 230 09

VIDZEME

A ROUTE OF 2 OR 3 DAYS USING PUBLIC OR PRIVATE TRANSPORT

Let us drive along the Pskov motorway up to Sigulda. The River Gauja has carved deep in the primeval valley in Sigulda showing peculiar sandstone bluffs. A rope-way connects both banks of the Gauja Valley. There are a few sandstone caves (**47-50**) on the both banks of the river. In the distance on the right bank rises the partly restored Turaida Castle (**51**), now the Museum for Regional Studies. Near by is the Garden of Sculpture dedicated to the Latvian Father of *Dainas* (collector and publisher of Latvian folksongs Kr. Barons). Here is also the grave of the legendary Rose of Turaida (**52**), a monument to true love and faithfulness. The maiden Maija known as the Rose of Turaida chose death rather than infidelity to her beloved. From *Gleznotāju kalns* (Painters Hill, **53**), a hill on the left bank, you will enjoy a superb panorama opening to the Gauja Primeval Valley (**54**) and surrounding territory. Near Sigulda a new bobsleigh centre was built in 1986.

Let us leave Sigulda for Līgatne. In the Līgatne Recreation and Research Park (**55**) from special observation places tourists can watch elk, deer, auroch, wild boar in open-air enclosures, have a horse-back ride or special car drives along the most colourful landscapes.

Tourists can choose one of the two roads running from Līgatne to Cēsis. If we take the highway along the Gauja we come to an outstanding sandstone cliff behind the Amata tributary — the 16 m high *Zvārtas iezis* (Zvārta Rock, **56**). This road is possibly not so good but the scenery alongside it is more attractive. The other road to Cēsis is the Pskov motorway. In this case we advise you to choose the old motorway via Āraiši and have a look at the unique Mid-Lake Settlement (**57**) of the 9th cent. in Lake Āraiši which is undergoing renovation and study now.

In Cēsis a part of the Old Town, the Lutheran church and fragments of the stone castle (**58**) are preserved. Our next stop is Valmiera with a 13th cent. Lutheran church.

The road runs further via Matīši to Mazsalaca where you will see a 13th cent. Lutheran church and the picturesque banks of the River Salaca in the vicinity of Mazsalaca. The beautiful landscapes attract many tourists, besides there are a few ritual places of the ancient Balts. In olden times *Vilkaču priede* (Werewolf Pine, **59**) was believed capable of turning a man into werewolf in the nights of full moon simply by creeping through its roots after murmuring the 'magic words'.

On *Sapņu kāpnes* (Stairs of Dreams, **60**) young boys and girls can make sure if they are well matched in temper. There is also *Velna ala* (Devil's Cave, **61**) and *Velna kancele* (Devil's Pulpit) reflected in many legends and tales. A spring flows out of the of sand rock — the Devil's Cave. The waters of this spring are said to have healing qualities. Still further lies a red sandstone cliff *Skaņaiskalns* (Sound Hill, **62**) characterized by queer acoustic phenomena. The echo is reflected not from the cliff but comes as if from heaven retarded and more powerful than the original sound. Stepping back about 50 m from the bank a place can be found on the terrace which notably amplifies a singing voice. The most interesting trick can be demonstrated if the participants of the trip divided in two groups stand at certain places on the bank. In this case one hears not the echo of his own voice but that of the other group reverberating from above to the cliff. The echo is retarded and amplified. Similar sound marvels can be observed on the sandrock on the left bank of the Salaca.

The way back to Riga runs along the seashore through Ainaži. Between Ainaži and Salacgrīva instead of the sandy beach there are meadows (**63**) stretching far into the sea.

SIGULDA

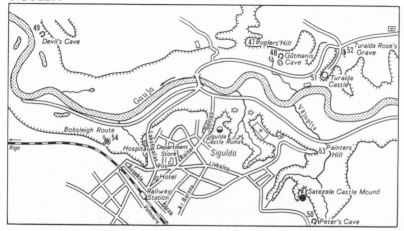

HOTEL Pils 6; **RESTAURANT 'GAUJA'** L. Paegles 3, open 12 – 24, l.hr. 18 – 19; **BUREAU OF EXCURSIONS** Pils 8; **MUSEUM OF REGIONAL STUDIES** Turaidas pils, 10 – 17; **DEPARTMENT STORE** L. Paegles 3, Mon – Fri 10 – 18, l.hr. 14 – 15, Sat 9 – 14; **HOSPITAL** Lakstīgalas 3; **DRUGSTORE** Pils 3, Mon – Fri 8 – 21, Sat, Sun 9 – 16; **POST OFFICE** Pils 2, Mon – Fri 8 – 18, Sat 8 – 14; **BUS TERMINAL** Raiņa 3, 5 – 22

DISTANCE BETWEEN LĪGATNE AND CĒSIS

LĪGATNE

GAUJA NATIONAL PARK Līgatne 'Pauguri', tel. 533 23, 533 24, in season 8 – 20; **HOSPITAL** Komjaunatnes 7, tel. 531 74; **DRUGSTORE** Komjaunatnes 3, Mon – Fri 8 – 16; **POST OFFICE** tel. 532 40, Mon – Sat 8 – 15

CĒSIS

HOTEL' TĒRVETE' Vienības lauk. 1, tel. 223 92

CAFÈS. BARS

CĒSIS Rīgas 10, open 7 – 21, l.hr. 15 – 16; **LAUMA** Rīgas 53, 10 – 22, l.hr. 15 – 16; **CĪRULĪŠI** Cīrulīšu 28, 9 – 21, l.hr. 15 – 16; **PIE RAUNAS VĀRTIEM** Rīgas 1/3, Mon 11 – 18, Tue – Sun 11 – 23, l.hr. 16 – 17; **TĒRVETE** Vienības lauk. 1, 8 – 22, l.hr. 15 – 16; **UGUNTIŅA** Raunas 12, 8 – 21; **VALNIS** Rīgas 49,10 – 22; **PIE KURMĪŠA** Valdemāra 13, Mon 11 – 20, Tue – Sun 11 – 22, l.hr. 16 – 17; **SULU BĀRS** (juices) Rīgas 25, Mon 9 – 18, Tue – Sun 9 – 20, l.hr. 14 – 15.30

OTHER

BUREAU OF EXCURSIONS Uzvaras 3, tel. 222 46; **MUSEUM OF REGIONAL HISTORY AND ARTS** Pils 9, tel. 226 15, Tue — Sun 10 — 17; **DEPARTMENT STORE** Vienības lauk. 2, Tue — Sat 9 — 18; **SOUVENIRS SHOP 'ROTA'** Rīgas 16, Tue — Sat 9 — 18, l.hr. 14 — 15; **HOSPITAL** Beverīnas 11, tel. 223 71; **DRUGSTORES** Rīgas 7, Mon — Fri 9 — 20, Sat 9 — 16; Rīgas 19a, Tue — Sun 9 — 19; **POST OFFICE** Raunas 14, tel. 227 72, long distance connections 227 21; **BUS TERMINAL** Uzvaras bulv. 26, tel. 236 13; **CAR SERVICE** Lapsu 36, tel. 229 00; Priekuļu 7, tel. 236 21

VALMIERA

HOTEL 'GAUJA' Tērbatas 2, tel. 221 65

RESTAURANT. CAFÈS. BAR

GAUJA Rīgas 4, open 12 — 23; **GAUJA** Tērbatas 2, 9 — 18.30; **SAULE** Rīgas 10, 9 — 21; **SPORTS** Rīgas 43, 9 — 21; **SAKTA** Rīgas 19, Mon — Fri 10 — 19;

OTHER

MUSEUM OF REGIONAL STUDIES Varoņu lauk. 3, Mon — Fri 12 — 18, Sat, Sun 11 — 18; **ART GALLERY** Rīgas 33, tel. 320 11; **DEPARTMENT STORE** Rīgas 4, Mon — Fri 10 — 19, Sat 9 — 14; **MARKET** Tērbatas 8a, Tue, Thur, Sat 7 — 15; **HOSPITAL** Jumaras 195, tel. 03; **DRUGSTORE** Rīgas 30, Mon — Sat 8 — 21; **BUS TERMINAL** tel. 226 56; **CAR FILLING** Kocēni, 'Ābelītes', tel. 555 98 (8th km Valmiera — Inčukalns motorway)

MAZSALACA

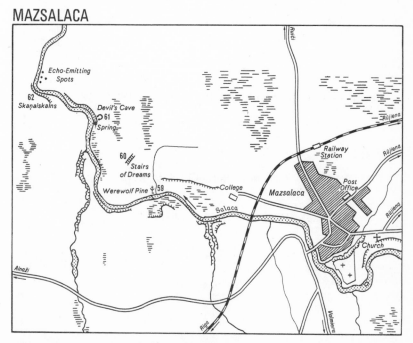

HOTEL Rīgas 17, tel. 512 35; **CAFÈ 'AURA'** Rūjienas 31, Mon — Fri 11 — 19; **MEDICAL AID** Brīvības bulv. 4, tel. 513 13; **DRUGSTORE** Rīgas 11, tel. 510 31; **CAR FILLING** Baznīcas 24, tel. 517 67, Mon — Fri 12 — 19, Sat 9 — 16

GOVERNMENT

SUPREME COUNCIL: Jēkaba 11, Rīga 226811, PDP
Chairman — Anatolijs Gorbunovs . . . . tel. 322 938; fax 211 611
1st Deputy Chairman — Dainis Īvāns . . . . tel. 323 142
Deputy Chairman — Andrejs Krastiņš 322 892
Secretary — Imants Daudišs 322 941
Press Centre . . . . tel. 326 093, 323 322; fax 211 077

STANDING COMMISSIONS OF THE SUPREME COUNCIL

Commission on Laws and Bills — Aivars Endziņš . . . . tel. 322 895
Commission on Economy — Ojārs Kehris 284 301
Commission on Agriculture and Forestry — Voldemārs Strīķis 323 716
Commission on Industry — Ģirts Krūmiņš 325 041
Commission on Architecture, Construction, Power, Transport and Computer Science —
Ojārs Blumbergs 323 354
Commission on Maritime Affairs — Vladimirs Einiņš 325 221
Commission on Trade and Service — Alfrēds Čepānis 323 745
Commission for Environmenal Protection — Oļegs Batarevskis 323 916
Commission on Health and Social Welfare — Ivars Krastiņš 614 440
Commission on Education, Science and Culture — Pēteris Laķis 323 918
Commission on Self-Government and Social Affairs — Jānis Škapars . . . 325 029
Commission on Human Rights and National Problems — Andrejs Panteļejevs . . 325 868
Commission on Defence and Interior Affairs — Tālavs Jundzis 325 924
Foreign Affairs Commission — Mavriks Vulfsons 331 516
Commission on Budget — Valentīna Zeile 323 810
Mandatory and Ethics Commission — Māris Budovskis 326 095

COUNCIL OF MINISTERS: Brīvības bulv. 36, Rīga 226170, PDP
Chairman — Ivars Godmanis . . . . tel. 332 232; fax 286 598
1st Deputy Chairman — Ilmārs Bišers . . . . tel. 285 223
Deputy Chairman — Arnis Kalniņš 282 828
Minister of Government Affairs — Kārlis Līcis 280 700
Information Service . . . . tel. 280 445; fax 280 469

DIPLOMATIC REPRESENTATION OF THE COUNCIL OF MINISTERS TO THE USSR:
Chapligina 3, Moscow 103062, USSR
The Authorized Representative of the Republic of Latvia — Jānis Peters . . tel. 925 27 03
925 27 07

MINISTRIES

MINISTRY OF ARCHITECTURE AND CONSTRUCTION: Raiņa bulv. 7, Rīga 226800, PDP
Minister — Aivars Prūsis 223 070
Department of External Affairs 227 643

MINISTRY OF FOREIGN AFFAIRS: Pils 11, Rīga 226800, PDP
Minister — Jānis Jurkāns 220 079
Consular Department 223 043

MINISTRY OF ECONOMY: Brīvības bulv. 36, Rīga 226919, PDP
Minister — Jānis Āboltiņš 288 444
Department for Foreign Economic Relations 287 995

MINISTRY OF POWER: Smilšu 1, Rīga 226904, PDP
Minister — Auseklis Lazdiņš 224 444
Department of External Affairs 223 532

MINISTRY OF FINANCE: Smilšu 1, Rīga 226919, PDP
Minister — Elmārs Siliņš 226 672
Department of External Affairs 211 752

MINISTRY OF THE INTERIOR: Raiņa bulv. 6, Rīga 226181, PDP
Minister — Aloizs Vaznis 287 260
Department of Foreigners' Registration and Visa Section 373 828

MINISTRY OF CULTURE: L. Paegles 2, Rīga 226310, PDP
Minister — Raimonds Pauls 224 772
Department of External Affairs 224 419

MINISTRY OF AGRICULTURE: Republikas lauk. 2, Rīga 226168, PDP
Minister — Dainis Ģēģeris 325 107
Department of External Affairs 325 695

MINISTRY OF MATERIAL RESOURCES: Kr. Valdemāra 26, Rīga 226329, PDP
Minister — Edgars Zausājevs 286 489
Department of External Affairs 277 271

MINISTRY OF FORESTRY: Smilšu 1, Rīga 226909, PDP
Minister — Kārlis Banis 228 873

MINISTRY OF INDUSTRY: Smilšu 1, Rīga 226918, PDP
Minister — Jānis Oherins 227 344
Department of Foreign Trade 225 085

MINISTRY OF COMMUNICATIONS: Elizabetes 41/43, Rīga 226153, PDP
Minister — Pēteris Videnieks 332 550
Department of External Affairs 332 785

MINISTRY OF TRANSPORT: Brīvības 58, Rīga 226806, PDP
Minister — Jānis Janovskis 226 922
Department of External Affairs and Computer Science 325 143

MINISTRY OF SOCIAL WELFARE: E.Veidenbauma 25, Rīga 226305, PDP
Minister — Uldis Gundars 286 720

MINISTRY OF EDUCATION: Vaļņu 2, Rīga 226050, PDP
Minister — Andris Piebalgs 222 415
Department of External Affairs 228 482

MINISTRY OF JUSTICE: Brīvības bulv. 34, Rīga 226173, PDP
Minister — Viktors Skudra 282 607

MINISTRY OF TRADE: Smilšu 1, Rīga 226917, PDP
Minister — Armands Plaudis 224 282
Department of External Affairs 223 050

MINISTRY OF PUBLIC HEALTH: Skolas 28, Rīga 226331, PDP
Minister — Edvīns Platkājis 271 713
Department of External Affairs 274 974

MINISTRY OF FISHERIES: Smilšu 6, Rīga 226176, PDP
Minister — Gunārs Zakss 322 498

STATE DEPARTMENTS AND COMMITTEES

COMMITTEE FOR TELEVISION AND RADIO BROADCASTING: Doma lauk. 8, Rīga 226935, PDP
Chairman — Rišards Labanovskis 226 304
Department of External Affairs 200 016

COMMITTEE FOR ENVIRONMENTAL PROTECTION: Peldu 25, Rīga 226282, PDP
Chairman — Indulis Emsis 223 612
Department of External Affairs 228 159

STATE SECURITY COMMITTEE: Brīvības 61, Rīga 226467, PDP
Chairman — Edmunds Johansons 270 779

STATE COMMITTEE FOR STATISTICS: Lāčplēša 1, Rīga 226301, PDP
Chairman — Gunārs Baltiņš 270 126

DEPARTMENT OF EXTERNAL ECONOMIC AFFAIRS: Brīvības bulv. 36, Rīga 226170, PDP
Director-General — Māris Gailis 288 656

MUNICIPAL DEPARTMENT: Brīvības bulv. 36, Rīga 226170, PDP
Director — Jānis Salenieks 282 488

DEPARTMENT OF RELIGIOUS MATTERS: Elizabetes 57, Rīga 226050
Head — Arnolds Kublinskis 288 879

COMMITTEE FOR PHYSICAL CULTURE AND SPORTS: Tērbatas 4, Rīga 226723, PDP
Chairwoman — Daina Šveica 284 206

CENTRAL BOARD OF ARCHIVES: Šķūņu 11, Rīga 226050
Head — Jānis Šneiders 212 539

DEPARTMENT OF CUSTOMS: Basteja bulv. 14, Rīga 226050
Director — Aivars Saliņš 226 246

SUPREME COURT: Brīvības bulv. 34, Rīga 226616, PDP
Chairman — Gvido Zemribo 289 434

PROSECUTOR'S OFFICE: Komunāru bulv. 6, Rīga 226050
Prosecutor General — Jānis Skrastiņš 320 085

STATE ARBITRATION: M. Jaunā 5, Rīga 226164, PDP
Head Arbitrator — Gvido Narkevičs 228 190

REPRESENTATIVES OF FOREIGN STATES IN LATVIA

DENMARK
INSTITUTE OF DANISH CULTURE: Kr.Barona 12, Rīga 226400, PDP
Director — Rikke Helms 289 994

SWEDEN
DIPLOMATIC REPRESENTATIVES OF THE CONSULTATE OF SWEDEN: Lāčplēša 13, Rīga 226050
Consul — Lars Fredens 286 276

BUSINESS DIRECTORY

INDUSTRIES AND ORGANIZATIONS

METALLURGY & HEAVY MACHINERY

LATVIJAS KŪDRA, peat processing ent. F. 1988. Offer: peat, peat products, sapropel, peat excavation machines. Demand: peat processing machines and equipm., partners for joint venture. Dir-Gen. Valentīns Čabuškins. *Add.* Smilšu 1, Rīga 226918; tel. 226 731.

RIGA CARRIAGE BUILDING PLANT. F. 1895. Offer: railway rolling stock (electric and diesel suburban trains — EMUs and DMUs). Demand: modern equipm. and technol. Dir-Gen. Valentīns Savins. *Add.* Brīvības 201, Rīga 226098; tel. 365 440, 365 447; telex 161124 RAIL SU; fax 555 219.

RIGA DIESEL PLANT. F. 1949. Offer: diesel engines, diesel generators, mowing-machines, household utensils, cold punching details. Demand: technol. equipm., computer aided manufacturing systems, consumer goods, means of transportation. Dir Andrejs Krasovskis. *Add.* Ganības dambis 40, Rīga 226005; tel. 391 662; telex 161198 SELGA SU; fax 381 402.

RIGA PLANT OF STEEL CONSTRUCTIONS. F. 1968. Proposed cooperation: establishing joint venture for the prod. and trade of hydraulic motorlifts. Dir Mihails Rožanskis. *Add.* Katlakalna 9, Rīga 226073; tel. 245 095; telex 161337 STAĻ SU.

MACHINERY & ELECTRICAL ENGINEERING

ALFA, electronic equipm. ent. F. 1972. Proposed cooperation: establishing joint venture for prod. of electronic equipm. and special test equipm. and measuring instruments. Dir-Gen. Jurijs Osokins. *Add.* Brīvības 372, Rīga 226037; tel. 553 075, 552 995.

DAUGAVPILS CHAIN BELT PLANT. F. 1949. Offer: roll-drive chains (step 12,7 mm; 15,875 mm); single-lined, double-lined platechains (step 15,875 mm), children's tricycles. Demand: advanced equipm. for prod. of 082 ISO 606 — 82, 081 ISO 606 — 82 roll-drive chains. Dir Aleksandrs Karevs. *Add.* Višķu 17, Daugavpils 228400; tel. 220 57, 430 07.

JAUDA, cooperative electric equipm. firm. F. 1961. Offer: establishing joint venture for prod. of lighting equipm., low tension electric equipm. for wood processing, details of carbon steel sheet remnants. Demand: technol. and equipm. for prod. of highly qualitative output, export-import operations. Dir Alfreds Bimbiruls. *Add.* Krustpils 119, Rīga 226065; tel. 245 287, 244 167.

KOMPRESORS, food refrigeration equipm. ent. F. 1946. Offer: refrigeration equipm., freon-drying filters, juice coolers, water cooling equipm., electric ice-cream freezers (for domestic use). Demand: partners for joint prod. of refrigerating equipm. Dir-Gen. Aldis Zicmanis. *Add.* Starta 1, Rīga 226026; tel. 378 066, 377 113.

KOMUNAĻNIKS, machine-building ent. F. 1944. Offer: nonstandard metal constr. Demand: partners for joint prod. of central heating installations, progressive technol. for building hangars, cooperation in prod. of sewage treatment machinery, etc. Dir Ivans Kraže. *Add.* Antenas 3, Rīga 226004; tel. 613 512; telex 161100 PTB SU (for KOMUNALNIKS); fax 629 138.

LIEPĀJA, hardware plant. F. 1940. Offer: prams, toys, shoppers. Demand: partners for joint venture, advanced technol., equipm. Dir Andris Ločmelis. *Add.* Avotu 10, Liepāja 229700; tel. 235 44.

RADIOTEHNIKA, radio ind. ent. F. 1928. Offer: acoustic systems, amplifiers and other audio-equipm. Demand: advanced technol. equipm. for wood and metal processing and treating plastics, electronic measuring instruments, partners for joint venture. Dir-Gen. Vladimirs Martinsons. **Add.** Popova 3, Rīga 226067; tel. 418 088, 459 201.

RAF, minibus plant. F. 1954. Offer: minibuses RAF – 2203, RAF – 22031, specialized minibuses. Demand: spare parts and accessories for minibuses. Dir Viktors Boserts. **Add.** Aviācijas 18, Jelgava 229600; tel. 202 43.

SIDRABE, vacuum coating firm. F. 1962. Proposed cooperation: vacuum coating equipm. and technol., establishing of joint venture. Dir Alfrēds Čolokjans. **Add.** Krustpils 17, Rīga 226073; tel. 249 859, 249 806.

STRAUME, electric household appliances ent. F. 1891. Offer: electric household appliances, electronic, mech., plastic toys. Demand: electric motors to produce ordinary electric equipm., partners for joint venture. Dir-Gen. Anatolijs Šabalovs. **Add.** E.Tēlmaņa 2, Rīga 226004; tel. 627 010; fax 627 997.

VALMIERA FIRE-FIGHTING EQUIPMENT PLANT. F. 1944. Offer: powder and foam fire extinguishers, metal petrol cans, modular fire extinguishers. Demand: establishing joint venture for produce of extinguishing equipm. and consumer goods, training of specialists for computer aided manufacturing systems. Dir Gunārs Lasmanis. **Add.** L.Laicena 2, Valmiera 228600; tel. 233 49; telex 161153 ATOM SU; fax 257 70.

VEF, electrical eng. company. F. 1919. Offer: telephones, exchanges, portable radios, cassette recorders; design; joint venture partnership. Demand: research in marketing opportunities to establish trade relations abroad, advanced technol. and principles of labour division. Dir-Gen. Ivars Bražis. **Add.** Brīvības 214, Rīga 226039; tel. 567 208; telex 161138 STYK SU; fax 567 208.

CHEMICAL INDUSTRIES

DZINTARS, racing-boat plant. F. 1955. Offer: racing boats, (rowing, canoeing), touring boats, different articles of fiberglass. Demand: advanced technol. and materials raising quality of prod., partners for joint venture. Dir Valdis Selga. **Add.** Slokas 64, Jūrmala 229070; tel. 691 32.

LĪVĀNI EXPERIMENTAL BIOCHEMICAL PLANT. F. 1971. Offer: forage lysine concentrate. Demand: equipm. for obtaining crystalline lysine (separators for crystal drying, packing equipm.), gas purification devices after fermentation. Dir Atis Sedvalds. **Add.** Celtniecības 8, Līvāni 228264; tel. 445 08, 440 97.

ĶĪMISKĀ ŠĶIEDRA, chem. fibre ent. F. 1964. Offer: tech. cord thread (9,35 dtx; 1,870 dtx), granulate 'Polyamid 6.' Demand: technol. equipm., chem. goods. Dir Jānis Ambainis. **Add.** Višķu 21, Daugavpils 228400; tel. 492 25, 493 03.

PLASTICS PROCESSING PLANT. F. 1966. Offer: plastic consumer goods, pipes (PVC, PE).

Demand: plastics processing equipm., raw materials, dyeing pigments for raw materials. Dir Ārijs Ruņģis. **Add.** Rīgas raj., Olaine 229014; tel. 964 501.

VALMIERA GLASS FIBRE PLANT. F. 1963. Offer: glass fibre products (fabrics for ind. application, tapes, non-woven materials, etc.), glass beads. Demand: joint venture partnership for producing fiberglass thermal insulating boards, roofing materials. Dir Inārs Poļaks. **Add.** Gagarina 1, Valmiera 228600; tel. 211 31, 223 21.

WOOD PROCESSING & FURNITURE

BALTIJA, wood-working ent. F. 1880. Offer: furniture (chairs, tabourets, sectionals, wall units), matches. Demand: tech. equipm., accessories, fittings for the prod. of chairs, wardrobes, matches. Dir Āris Grāmatiņš. **Add.** Jaunā 52/54, Liepāja 229700; tel. 239 62, 244 43.

BOLDERĀJA WOOD-WORKING PLANT. F. 1968. Offer: fibreboard, chipboard, laminated chipboard, expanded polyurethane plastic board, laminated plastic film, plastic edge, millboard, wood waste. Demand: machinery and spare parts, raw materials, machine-tools, means of transport, lifting and conveying machines. Dir Juris Čakstiņš. **Add.** Guberņciema 7, Rīga 226016; tel. 430 147.

GAUJA, furniture ent. F. 1976 . Offer: furniture design and prod. for living rooms and public premises. Demand: technol. equipm. for the prod. of high-quality furniture fittings. Dir Romāns Kumerovs. **Add.** Rūpniecības 52, Rīga 226200; tel. 381 476.

LATVIJAS KOKS, wood-working assoc. F. 1990. Offer: wood-working prod. (furniture, chipboard, fibreboard, plywood, matches). Demand: information on the latest technol., materials and machinery in wood-working ind., purchase of materials and machinery. Pres. Juris Biķis. **Add.** Smilšu 1, Rīga 226918, PDP; tel. 221 672.

RĪGA, furniture ent. F. 1974. Offer: establishing of joint venture, furniture and souvenir products for export. Demand: technol. equipm., finishing materials, semifinished products. Dir-Gen. Vasilijs Feoktistovs. **Add.** Ganību dambis 30a, Rīga 226005; tel. 381 828.

RT-MĪLGRĀVIS, wood-working plant. F. 1988. Offer: dressed timber, plywood, kitchen furniture, board games, wood waste. Demand: tech. equipm. for timber dressing and for the prod. of kitchen furniture, finishing materials (plastics, weather-proof lacquers), sanitary technics for kitchen furniture. Dir-Gen. Pēteris Rizga. **Add.** Meldru 3, Rīga 226015; tel. 340 787; telex 161111 LES SU.

SMILTENE, plant of household utensils and garden implements. F. 1979. Offer: pedal-operated dustbins, clothes-hangers, garden implements, garden cottages, metallic constr. (sheds, etc.). Demand: technol. equipm. for drying wood and compressing chips of wood waste. Dir Jevgeņijs Metlāns. **Add.** Pils 9, Smiltene 228675; tel. 726 32.

VALMIERA FURNITURE PLANT. F. 1960. Proposed cooperation: business contacts with firm 'Linon' (USA). Dir Modris Meļķis. **Add.** Purva 10, Valmiera 228600; tel. 221 56, 224 25.

VENEER PLANT. F. 1975. Offer: plywood, laminated arch and its products. Demand: technol. and equipm. for wood-working and plywood prod. Dir-Gen. Juris Biķis. **Add.** Bauskas 59, Rīga 226004; tel. 620 857; telex 161153 WEST SU.

VULKĀNS, wood-working plant. F. 1878. Offer: boards for furniture and wooden blocks for parquet, plywood for packing-cases, carpentry boards. Demand: technol. equipm. for chipboard processing (20,000 cu m p.a.), equipm. for veneer and furniture prod., machinery for saw-mill mechanization. Dir Aivars Brunovskis. **Add.** Jelgavas 45, Kuldīga 229500; tel. 226 05; telex 161810 VENTA SU.

PAPER & PRINTING

LATVIJAS KARTE, cartography and geodesy ent. F. 1946. Offer: issue of cartographic prod. to order. Demand: printing equipm. and materials, partners for joint venture, consumer goods. Dir-Gen. Jurijs Kuznecovs. **Add.** O.Vācieša 43, Rīga 226004; tel. 611 186.

LIEPĀJA PAPER FACTORY. F. 1898. Offer: paper labels. Demand: materials (paper, glue, printing ink) for label prod. Dir Jānis Vecvagars. **Add.** Pļavu 17, Liepāja 229700; tel. 246 05.

LĪGATNE PAPER FACTORY. F. 1815. Offer: writing paper, book cover paper, drawing paper, water-colour paper, album paper, cigarette manufacturing paper, crepe paper, thin typing and printing paper, note-paper, note-books, copy-books, etc. Demand: raw materials, advanced equipm. Dir Ilmārs Norītis. **Add.** Pilsoņu 1, Līgatne 228510; tel. 533 30, 533 60.

POLIGRĀFISTS, printing ent. F. 1980. Proposed cooperation: establishing joint venture for prod. of printed matter for foreign firms. Dir-Gen. Felicijans Čers. **Add.** Kr.Valdemāra 6, Rīga 226177; tel. 325 759.

RANKA CARDBOARD FACTORY. F. 1898. Offer: waste paper. Demand: cardboard glueing and processing equipm., fine-quality paper making machines. Dir Jānis Stūriška. **Add.** Krustakmens, Gulbenes raj., Ranka 228718; tel. 444 84.

ROTA, printing-house. F. 1944. Proposed cooperation: establishing joint venture for prod. of printed matter. Dir Nikolajs Pešins. **Add.** Blaumaņa 38/40, Rīga 226424, PDP; tel. 285 545.

SLOKA CELLULOSE AND PAPER FACTORY. F. 1895. Offer: different sorts of tech. paper — paper for punch-cards, ice-cream holders, book covers. Demand: establishing joint venture for installation of advanced equipm., spare parts for paper machines, vacuum pumps, centrifugal pumps, electrical equipm., test equipm. and measuring instruments. Dir Mihails Piskuns. **Add.** Fabrikas 2, Jūrmala 229070; tel. 324 69, 322 22; telex 168318 MORE SU.

BUILDING MATERIALS & CONSTRUCTION

BROCĒNI CEMENT AND SLATE WORKS. F. 1938. Offer: cement, ceramic tiles, crumbled limestone, limestone dust. Demand: capital investment and equipm. for increase of prod. and its quality. Dir Juris Reisons. **Add.** Saldus raj., Brocēni 229451; tel. 652 16, 652 12; fax 650 67.

BŪVMATERIĀLI, building materials and constr. ent. F. 1964. Offer: silica bricks, reinforced products. Demand: prod. equipm. Dir-Gen. Vladimirs Rodins. **Add.** Montētāju 7, Daugavpils 228400; tel. 315 15.

DOLOMĪTS, building materials ent. F. 1981. Offer: dolomite dust, nonmetal materials for splinter and gravel foundations and road surfacing. Dir-Gen. Galaktions Radionovs. **Add.** a.k. 59, Jēkabpils 228200; tel. 319 85.

GRANĪTS, nonmetal materials processing ent. F. 1964. Dir Anatolijs Gimelfarbs. **Add.** Miera 75/77, Rīga 226013; tel. 371 104.

JĒKABPILS BUILDING MATERIALS AND CONSTRUCTION WORKS. F. 1963. Offer: concrete pipes, building blocks, reinforced products. Demand: technol. for prod. of lightweight concrete. Dir Vjačeslavs Semeņenko. **Add.** Zīlānu 68, Jēkabpils 228200; tel. 313 71.

KALNCIEMS BUILDING MATERIALS ENTERPRISE. F. 1946. Offer: tech. textile fabrics for tennis-court surfacing (sewn through), ceramic bricks, thermal insulating material (mineral wool), polymer concrete prod. Demand: dye-staff for chem. fibres, machinery for the prod. of non-woven textile fabrics, consumer goods. Dir Vladimirs Starovoitovs. **Add.** Komjaunatnes 12, Kalnciems, Jelgavas raj. 229616; tel. 693 21.

LATVIJAS CELTNIEKS, constr. and building materials ent. F. 1990. Proposed cooperation: establishing joint venture, joint stock companies, cooperation in the field of constr. and building materials technol., gypsum-concrete output, wall materials, concrete roofing sheets. Chair. Jānis Lancers. **Add.** Rūpniecības 27, Rīga 226903, PDP; tel. 321 751, 321 739.

LAUKCELTNIEKS, constr. ent. F. 1963. Proposed cooperation: establishing joint venture for prod. of building materials, purchase of equipm. and know-how for prod. of building materials. Chair. Voldemārs Prūsis. **Add.** Grēcinieku 22/24, Rīga 226047; tel. 212 391.

LIEPĀJA LINOLEUM PLANT. F. 1886. Proposed cooperation: purchase of equipm. for prod. of linoleum. Dir Ivans Zaharovs. **Add.** Sarkanarmijas 5/7/9, Liepāja 229700; tel. 246 74.

LĪVĀNI BUILDING MATERIALS AND CONSTRUCTION WORKS. F. 1971. Offer: coarse and fine aggregate, wall tiles, lightweight concrete blocks. Dir Viktors Šilovs. **Add.** Celtniecības 1, Līvāni 228264; tel. 444 94.

LODE, building materials prod. ent. F. 1963. Offer: ceramic and facing bricks for trimming, fire bricks, roof tiles (4 sorts). Demand: spare parts for prod. equipm. of ceramic building products. Dir Jānis Slesars. *Add.* Cēsu raj., Liepa 228552; tel. 952 46.

RIGA ASPHALT-CONCRETE PLANT. F. 1968. Offer: concrete and reinforced concrete, wood briquettes, plastic and rubber granules. Demand: technol. equipm. and its spare parts, consumer goods. Dir Jānis Bertrands. *Add.* Granīta 13, Rīga 226065; tel. 248 828; fax 248 833.

RIGA BUILDING MATERIALS ENTERPRISE. F. 1979. Offer: earthenware, ceramic tiles for interior design. Demand: advanced technol. for prod. of siliceous bricks, equipm. for pressing concrete blocks. Dir-Gen. Anatolijs Nužnijs. *Add.* Platā 14, Rīga 226016; tel. 433 619; telex 161364 KAMIN SU.

SARKANDAUGAVA, glass plant. F. 1882. Offer: sheet glass, window glass. Demand: equipm. for sheet glass prod. Dir Pjotrs Geraščenkovs. *Add.* Sliežu 6, Rīga 226005; tel. 392 419.

TAUMA, building ent. F. 1989. Proposed co-operation: contracting of building maintenance services to facilitate tourism and recreation ind. in W-Latvia. Exec. Dir Jānis Muižnieks. *Add.* K.Paldiņa 7, Talsi 229550; tel. 222 24.

VANGAŽI, building materials and constr. ent. F. 1959. Dir Ņikita Kozlovs. *Add.* Rīgas raj., Vangaži 229036; tel. 995 500.

GLASS, PORCELAIN & JEWELRY

LATVIJAS KERAMIKA, ceramics plant. F. 1963. Proposed cooperation: sale of pottery, earthenware; setting up joint venture for manufacturing lighting fixtures, furnace equipm. Dir-Gen. Jānis Gasparenoks. *Add.* Rīgas 67, Jelgava 229600; tel. 228 68.

LATVIJAS STIKLS, glassware plant. F. 1884. Offer: perfume bottles, bottles, domestic glassware, ind. glassware. Demand: glass treating equipm. (cutting, polishing, decorating), glassware manufacturing equipm. Dir-Gen. Dmitrijs Laļkovs. *Add.* Daugavgrīvas 77, Rīga 226007; tel. 459 145.

LĪVĀNI GLASSWARE FACTORY. F. 1887. Offer: glassware, crystal glassware (glasses, vases, etc.), optical fibres. Demand: business associates for joint venture and application of new technol. Dir Jevgeņijs Skreivers. *Add.* Zaļā 23, Līvāni 228264; tel. 444 40; telex 161100 PKP SU (for LIVANI 323425 LEN).

RIGA JEWELRY FACTORY. F. 1963. Dir Viktors Čeļubejevs. *Add.* Līčupes 1, Rīga 226012; tel. 272 790.

RIGA PORCELAIN FACTORY. F. 1841. Offer: chinaware, dinner sets, coffee sets. Demand: technol. equipm., commodity goods. Dir Aleksejs Jeļinskis. *Add.* Maskavas 257, Rīga 226019; tel. 145 003; fax 145 003.

TEXTILES, KNITWEAR & DRESSMAKING

BĒRNU APĢĒRBS, children's clothes factory. F. 1944. Dir Rūdolfs Bojārs. *Add.* Kr. Barona 59/61, Rīga 226001; tel. 279 344.

LATVIJA, sewing firm. F. 1963. Offer: ready-made clothes; manufacturing of clothing on imported fine-quality machines. Demand: spare parts for sewing machines, consumer goods. Dir-Gen. Pjotrs Ņefjodovs. *Add.* Zilupes 7, Rīga 226019; tel. 143 817, 143 864.

LATVIJAS LINI, linen ent. F. 1889. Offer: gray flax fibres, bed clothes, table cloths, materials. Demand: technol. equipm. for assembling of spinning-mill and trimming-mill, assembly-shop for trimming. Dir-Gen. Staņislavs Špakovskis. *Add.* Lapskalna 18, Jelgava 229600; tel. 239 34.

LIELUPE, factory of decorative haberdashery. F. 1969. Offer: workforce for joint venture; sewn goods (bed linen, etc.). Demand: technol. equipm. for trimming and cutting out. Dir Aleksandrs Fetisovs. *Add.* Uzvaras 69, Jelgava 229600; tel. 272 74.

LAUMA, textile and haberdashery ware ent. F. 1971. Offer: undergarment for women (brassieres), laced goods and laced trimmed textiles, elasticated fabrics, ribbons. Demand: business associates for joint venture. Dir-Gen. Zigrīda Rusiņa. *Add.* Ziemeļu 19, Liepāja 229700; tel. 410 91; telex 161818 LAUMA SU; fax 410 90.

RIGA FASHION HOUSE. F. 1949. Proposed cooperation: exchange of experience and goods, creation of joint pattern coll., establishing joint venture for prod. and sale of sewn and knitted articles, fancy goods, footwear; launching and sale of a joint fashion journal; part. in int. fashion shows, sale of pattern coll. Art Dir Ingrīda Pumpure. *Add.* Brīvības 68, Rīga 226050; tel. 273 312.

RĪGAS AUDUMS, textile ent. F. 1925. Offer: synthetic silk fabrics, textile haberdashery, metallic thread. Demand: technol. equipm. (finishing) and chemicals for textile ind.; associates for joint venture. Dir-Gen. Andris Bruģētājs. *Add.* Salamandras 1, Rīga 226024, tel. 521 395.

RĪGAS FILCS, headgear factory. F. 1912. Offer: semifinished, ready-made goods. Demand: tech. equipm. Dir Andrejs Kokarevičs. *Add.* Lienes 28, Rīga 226009; tel. 270 648.

SAIVA, sewing and textile firm. F. 1968. Offer: knitted outerwear (for children and adults), gloves, sports clothes, sewn clothing articles. Demand: associates for joint venture, raw materials (woollen yarn, worsted), technol. equipm. Dir-Gen. Pāvels Kukels. *Add.* Teātra 31, Jūrmala 229070; tel. 647 98, 648 70.

SARKANAIS RĪTS, knitwear firm. F. 1924. Offer: knitted fabrics and knitwear, sewing to order. Demand: technol. equipm. (knitting, trimming, sewing, cutting out, packing and marking of goods), trimming materials, associates for joint venture. Dir-Gen. Vladimirs Sazonovs. *Add.* Valentīnas 3/5, Rīga 226046; tel. 611 540.

LEATHER & FOOTWEAR

KOSMOSS, hide processing ent. F. 1963. Offer: raw hide, semifinished goods. Demand: hide processing and tanning machinery. Dir-Gen. Edvards Savičs. *Add.* Kr. Valdemāra 114, Rīga 226013; tel. 374 518.

RĪGAS APAVI, ent. producing footwear to order. F. 1969. Dir Leonīds Meļehovs. *Add.* Vārnu 5, Rīga 226009; tel. 279 533, 297 081.

SARKANAIS KVADRĀTS, rubber footwear and ind. rubber products ent. F. 1924. Offer: setting up joint venture; footwear exports. Demand: rubber processing plant and equipm. for prod. of footwear and ind. rubber products. Dir-Gen. Vladimirs Korolišins. *Add.* Maskavas 322, Rīga 226063; tel. 252 251; fax 252 008.

SOMDARIS, leathern goods ent. F. 1940. Offer: imitation and genuin leathern goods. Demand: accessories, leathers; technol. equipm. Dir Valerijs Fokins. *Add.* Brīvības 109, Rīga 226483, PDP; tel. 370 058.

VENĒCIJA, footwear producing ent. F. 1991. Proposed cooperation: joint venture partnership. Dir-Gen. Sergejs Murasins. *Add.* Bauskas 16, Rīga 226004; tel. 629 572.

FOOD PRODUCTS

ALDARIS, beer brewing ent. F. 1865. Offer: light beer (*Aldaris, Senču, Speciālais*), dark beer (*Porteris*). Demand: technol. equipm.; starting a specialized shop. Dir-Gen. Vitālijs Gavrilovs. *Add.* Tvaika 44, Rīga 226005; tel. 391 652; telex 161143 AGRO SU; fax 391 011.

CĒSIS BREWERY. F. 1878. Offer: beer, mineral water, nonalcoholic drinks. Demand: installations and technol. equipm. for beverage ind. Dir Vitālijs Butāns. *Add.* Lenču 11, Cēsis 228500; tel. 224 23.

DZINTARS, cosmetics and perfumery ent. F. 1849. Offer: cosmetics, perfumes, cosmetic raw materials. Demand: technol. equipm. Dir Iļja Gerčikovs. *Add.* Mālu 30, Rīga 226058; tel. 621 625; fax 622 683.

JELGAVA SUGAR PROCESSING FACTORY. F. 1926. Offer: filtration precipitants, spare parts for packaging machinery (firm 'Hesser', Germany), container handling equipm. Dir Jurijs Semencovs. *Add.* Cukura 22, Jelgava 229600; tel. 238 85.

LAIMA, chocolate confectionery factory. F. 1870. Offer: chocolate confectionery of natural ingredients (cocoa), 534 items. Demand: partners for joint venture; packaging materials; natural ingredients; machinery. Dir Elmārs Gozītis. *Add.* Miera 22, Rīga 226486; tel. 379 690, 372 282; fax 379 690.

LATVIJAS BALZAMS, beverage ent. F. 1900. Offer: 'Riga Black Balsam', vodka (*Kristāldzidrais*). Demand: establishing joint venture for export of the produce. Dir-Gen. Leons Dukulis. *Add.* A.Čaka 160, Rīga 226012; tel. 277 231, 272 693.

LATVIJAS LABĪBA, assoc. of grain processing ent. F. 1990. Proposed cooperation: setting up joint venture for dried food prod.; wheat import, improvement of flour processing technol. Pres. Jevgeņijs Lukašenoks. *Add.* Dzirnavu 87/89, Rīga 226728, PDP; tel. 285 715, 285 679; fax 285 949.

RĒZEKNE CANNED MILK FACTORY. F. 1957. Offer: canned milk, cheeses, casein, whey powder. Demand: milk processing equipm. and spare parts, lab. equipm., measuring instruments, means of transportation, consumer goods. Dir-Gen. Pēteris Upenieks. *Add.* Ļeņina 155/1, Rēzekne 228100; tel. 324 54, 329 75.

RĪGA, nonalcoholic beverage factory. F. 1815. Offer: fruit syrop, fruit wine, calvados *Dzintarlāse* (Amberdrop). Demand: pasteurizers of bottled beer, water softening plant. Dir Ilmārs Lindenbergs. *Add.* Bruņinieku 2, Rīga 226450; tel. 273 217.

RIGA FRESH AND CANNED MEAT FACTORY. F. 1922. Proposed cooperation: business contacts with allied firms in Western Europe, imports of meat processing equipm. (livestock slaughter, cutting, mincing, sausage casing, meat cannery). Dir-Gen. Arnolds Keiviss. *Add.* Atlasa 7, Rīga 226026; tel. 552 152, 379 995.

RIGA WINE AND CHAMPAGNE FACTORY. F. 1952. Offer: champagne, fine wine. Demand: installations and technol. equipm. for beverage ind. Dir Jurijs Posmetnijs. *Add.* A.Barbisa 7, Rīga 226488, PDP; tel. 373 676, 378 714.

VĀRPA, brewery. F. 1865. Proposed cooperation: setting up joint venture for flash-pasteurization of canned beer, nonalcoholic drinks, produce of malt; high quality seed purchase (barley, hop). Dir Aleksandrs Seļeznovs. *Add.* Maskavas 231, Rīga 226019; tel. 241 222, 143 503.

AGRICULTURE & FISHERIES

ASSOCIATION OF FISHERY COLLECTIVE FARMS. F. 1947. Proposed cooperation: joint coordination of Latv. vessels in far distant sea fisheries, barter dealings (fish prod. for fish processing tech. equipm., technol., spare parts for ships, radio-nautical equipm., etc.). Chair. Andris Ūķis. *Add.* Jauniela 13, Rīga 226900; tel. 213 859; telex 161160 NORD SU; fax 212 151.

AUDA, fishery farm. F. 1947. Proposed cooperation: export of preserved fish. Chair. Broņislavs Salītis. *Add.* Audupes 15/17, Rīga 226030; tel. 347 101, 341 420; fax 347 477.

BANGA, fishery collective farm. F. 1947. Offer: frozen salmon, sprat and pilchard in oil,sardine and mackerel in tomato sauce, sprat, pilchard and herring in special brine, food paste *Surimi*. Chair. of the Bd Gunārs Trukšāns. *Add.* Ostas 7, Roja, Talsu raj. 229564; tel. 691 71, 691 38; telex 161817 BANGA SU.

DAUGAVA, agrofirm. F. 1945. Offer: paper wood, endocrine by-products, cattle and pig hides. Demand: machinery for agric., tech. equipm. for food processing. Dir-Gen. Ludis Skosta. *Add.* Susējas 11, Sala, Jēkabpils raj. 228222; tel. 631 86; telex 161194 SELIA SU; fax 316 60.

IECAVA, poultry ent. F. 1973. Offer: eggs, egg powder, poultry farming prod.; manure. Demand: tech. equipm. for egg and poultry processing and egg sizing. Dir Vilis Dubrovskis. *Add.* Bauskas raj., Iecava 229313; tel. 410 04; telex 161100 TSKP SU 8922 LOIA.

ĶEKAVA, agrofirm. F. 1949. Proposed cooperation: establishing joint venture for processing of agric. prod.; technol. and tech. equipm. for fur-farming. Chair. of the Bd Māris Šops. *Add*. Rīgas raj., Ķekava 229023; tel. 937 751, 937 174.

ĶEKAVA, poultry ent. F. 1964. Offer: poultry preparations, eggs, by-products; manure. Demand: poultry processing equipm. Dir Mārtiņš Skuja. *Add*. Ķekava, Rīgas raj. 229023; tel. 936 340; fax 936 500.

LĀČPLĒSIS, agrofirm. F. 1948. Proposed cooperation: export of beekeeping products, preserved food and vegetables, fruit and berry juice concentrates, the fur business (mink, fox), barter dealings. Chair. of the Bd Žanis Holšteins. *Add*. Lielvārde, Ogres raj. 228321; tel. 531 31, 544 05; fax 545 40.

LATVIAN FUR-FARMING ENTERPRISE. F. 1976. Offer: furs. Demand: equipm., med. for fur-farming. Dir-Gen. Andris Upenieks. *Add*. M.Juglas 3, Rīga 226077; tel. 532 183.

LATVIJAS PUTNKOPĪBA UN ZIVKOPĪBA, poultry and fishery assoc. F. 1966. Offer: poultry, powdered eggs; fish preparations; manure. Demand: process plant for food ind. Dir-Gen. Andrejs Grasis. *Add*. Republikas lauk. 2, Rīga 226168; tel. 321 939; fax 321 939.

RĪGA, vegetable growing ent. F. 1964. Offer: growing of hybrid vegetable seeds, fresh vegetables. Demand: the latest technol. and tech. equipm. for hot-houses. Dir Māris Gailītis. *Add*. Biķernieku 121, Ulbroka 229030; tel. 551 402; fax 598 783.

SARKANĀ BĀKA, fishery collective farm. F. 1946. Proposed cooperation: establishing joint venture for fish processing, export of marine products. Chair. of the Bd Arvīds Buks. *Add*. Loču 1, Ventspils 229910; tel. 243 35; telex 161815 BAKA SU; fax 212 19 BAKA SU.

TURĪBA, agrofirm. F. 1949. Offer: thoroughbred horses; starch; sweets. Demand: farm machinery; building materials, high-bred cattle. Dir-Gen Romualds Kavinskis. *Add*. Riebiņi, Preiļu raj. 228273; tel. 567 38.

UZVARA, agrofirm. F. 1947. Offer: apple-juice concentrate; timber; thoroughbred horses; tourism. Demand: food processing equipm., technol. Dir-Gen. Māris Ikaunieks. *Add*. Uzvara, Bauskas raj. 229307; tel. 562 85, Rīga 210 686; telex 161116 SVT SU.

TRADE & INTERMEDIARY ORGANIZATIONS

FORUMS, youth centre. F. 1988. Proposed cooperation: establishing joint venture in wood-working, metal-working, trade, promotion of foreign tourism and cultural events, consultations on legal and econ. problems, cooperation in the field of computer technol. Dir-Gen. Gunārs Slavinskis. *Add*. Basteja bulv. 12, a.k. 43, Rīga 226350; tel. 223 003, 212 068; telex 161186 FORUM SU; fax 213 578.

INTERLATVIJA, foreign trade assoc. F. 1987. Proposed cooperation: intermediation in export and import operations, establishing of joint ventures, cooperation in the field of advertising, cultural activities, foreign tourism and constr.

work. *Add*. Komunāru bulv. 1, Rīga 226010; tel. 333 602, 333 340; telex 161149 INLA SU.

LAMA, audio and visual marketing assoc. F. 1990. Proposed cooperation: selling, exchange and duplication of audiograms and videograms of Latv. TV and Radio, part. in European and world TV and radio markets, festivals, comp., screenings, organizing of joint prod. in Latvia. Dir Inese Vitkus. *Add*. Zaķusalas krastmala 3, Rīga 226018; tel. 200 688; telex 161188 VIDEO SU; fax 200 025.

LATVIJAS DĀRZEŅI, vegetable trade assoc. F. 1989. Offer: selling and buying of fruit (citric), vegetables and other agric. prod. and processed prod. in large quantities. Demand: the latest technol. and tech. equipm. for processing and packing. Dir-Gen. Antons Andžāns. *Add*. Nēģu 16, Rīga 226521; tel. 228 522; fax 210 611.

LATVIJAS GRĀMATA, book trade assoc. F. 1944. Proposed cooperation: establishing joint venture in the Baltic States. Dir Zaiga Siņicka. *Add*. Aspazijas bulv. 24, Rīga 226253, PDP; tel. 223 639.

LATVIJAS REKLĀMA, advertising firm. F. 1955. Proposed cooperation: advertising, organizing of conferences, symposiums and exh. Dir Jānis Rozīte. *Add*. Šķūņu 16, Rīga 226050; tel. 227 001, 226 438.

TRANSPORT & COMMUNICATIONS

CEĻU AUTOTEHNIĶIS, motor vehicles repair ent. F. 1944. Offer: trailer and refrigerator repair, foreign-made car repair. Demand: spare parts. Dir-Gen. Aleksandrs Gončarovs. *Add*. Margrietas 7, Rīga 226046; tel. 615 052.

CIVIL AVIATION DEPARTMENT. F. 1944. Proposed cooperation: charter transportation of cargoes to Europe and Far Eastern c., regular passenger and charter routes to Helsinki, Stockholm, Copenhagen, Frankfurt, Vienna, Sofia, Belgrade, Athens, New York. Chair. Anatolijs Belaičuks. *Add*. Pils lauk. 4, Rīga 226050; tel. 225 560; telex 161168 VZLET SU RIXAP SU.

LATINTERAUTO, motor transport assoc. F. 1981. Proposed cooperation: links with foreign expeditionary firms in the field of cargo transport to the Baltics and the USSR. Dir-Gen. Igors Popovs. *Add*. Uriekstes 3, Rīga 226005; tel. 383 044; fax 383 939.

LATVIJAS AUTOMOTOSERVISS, motor vehicles service ent. F. 1967. Proposed cooperation: business contacts with the allied firms in Sweden, Germany, France (repair, tech. services and provision of spare parts). Dir-Gen. Jevgeņijs Ivanovs. *Add*. Vagonu 35, Rīga 226009; tel. 599 454.

LATVIJAS SAKARNIEKS, communications assoc. F. 1988. Proposed cooperation: provide communications for private persons and state institutions, prod. of tech. equipm. for communications. Dir-Gen. Andris Jautrums. *Add*. Dzirnavu 16, Rīga 226010; tel. 332 622; fax 325 359.

RIGA CENTRAL POST OFFICE. F. 1632. Proposed cooperation: trading with postage-stamps, postcards and seal coll., advertis-

ing, direct agreements on post transportation and postal service. Head Aivars Droiskis. *Add.* Brīvības bulv. 21, Rīga 226000, PDP; tel. 224155; telex 161176 PTB SU; fax 331920.
RIGA FISHING SEAPORT. F. 1949. Chief Georgs Ševčuks. *Add.* Atlantijas 27, Rīga 226020; tel. 349201.
RIGA MOTOR DEPOT, Latv. Union of Consumers' Soc. F. 1948. Dir Jānis Gavars. *Add.* Bukaišu 3, Rīga 226004; tel. 620323, 620549.

FINANCIAL INSTITUTIONS

BALTIJA, Riga interregional cooperative bank. F. 1988. Proposed cooperation: training of experts in foreign banks, conference convening for European commercial banks. Chair. of the Bd Aleksandra Stecjuna. *Add.* Aspazijas bulv. 34, Rīga 226250; tel. 225024, 213444.
BANK OF THE REPUBLIC OF LATVIA. F. 1922. Chair. of the Bd Alfrēds Bergs-Bergmanis. *Add.* Kr. Valdemāra 2a, Rīga 226022; tel. 323863, 325266; fax 325486.
LATVIAN SAVINGS BANK. F. 1987. Proposed cooperation: establishing joint banks and their depts in Latvia, opening of joint accounts, providing financial services for foreigners in hard currency and roubles, establishing of joint venture. Chair. of the Bd Eduards Gross. *Add.* Palasta 1, Rīga 226929, PDP; tel. 222871, 228285.
RIGA COMMERCIAL BANK. F. 1989. Proposed cooperation: establishing of contacts with the largest European banks. Chair. of the Bd Vladimirs Kuļiks. *Add.* Smilšu 6, Rīga 226800, PDP; tel. 323967; telex 161112 BARK SU; fax 210080.

SCIENTIFIC & RESEARCH INSTITUTES

BALTIC ZONAL STATION FOR MACHINE TESTING. F. 1911. Proposed cooperation: import of machine testing devices and tech. systems, joint machine testing. Dir Jurijs Agafonovs. *Add.* Dārza 12, Priekuļi 228550; tel. 22612; telex 161102 ANITA SU.
BOTANICAL GARDEN, Latv. Acad. of Sci. F. 1956. Proposed cooperation: trade with seed stock of rare varieties and species of woody plants, local cultivars, forms and clones of ornamental plants, breeding of new resistant, winterhardy and productive black currant, blueberry, edible honeysuckle, sea-buckthorn, breeding and cultivation technol. of greenhouse flowers, seed prod. of annual flowers. Dir Andris Zvirgzds. *Add.* Rīgas 46, Salaspils — 1, 229021; tel. 947131.
BOTANICAL GARDEN, Latv. Univ. F. 1922. Proposed cooperation: exchange of seed stock and catalogues with allied inst. abroad. Dir Ādolfs Zorgevics. *Add.* Kandavas 2, Rīga 226083; tel. 450852.
HYDROMETEOROLOGICAL DEPARTMENT. F. 1940. Proposed cooperation: invest. of air pollution and radiation, hydrochem. and hydrobiol. study of the Baltic Sea and river system entering the Gulf of Riga, environment monitor-

ing system. Head Pēteris Bērziņš. *Add.* Kr.Valdemāra 19, Rīga 226010; tel. 332702, 332829.
INSTITUTE OF BIOLOGY, Latv. Acad. of Sci. F. 1951. Proposed cooperation: developing of the theoretical basis for increasing the productivity of agric. and farm animals; research of ecological processes, rational use of natural resources. Dir Gunārs Andrušaitis. *Add.* Miera 3, Salaspils 229021; tel. 947364.
INSTITUTE OF ECONOMICS, Latv. Acad. of Sci. F. 1946. Proposed cooperation: working out models for nat. econ. (specialization, structures policy, finance, scientific information, etc.) under conditions of econ. independence of Latvia. Dir Jānis Janovs. *Add.* Turgeņeva 19, Rīga 226524, PDP; tel. 222830.
INSTITUTE OF ELECTRONICS AND COMPUTER SCIENCE, Latv. Acad. of Sci. F. 1960. Proposed cooperation: joint research in computer sci. with related inst. in USA, Germany, England, Belgium. Dir Eduards Jakubaitis. *Add.* Akadēmijas 14, Rīga 226006; tel. 554500; telex 161127 ESTI SU.
INSTITUTE OF HISTORY, Latv. Acad. of Sci. F. 1936. Proposed cooperation: joint research on the following themes: city development in the region of the Baltic Sea, nat. and pol. movements (2nd half of 19th cent. — 1st half of 20th cent.), anthropology of ancient and contemporary inhabitants of the Baltics; Latvia — an econ. and cultural bridge between Eastern and W-Europe. Dir Indulis Ronis. *Add.* Turgeņeva 19, Rīga 226524, PDP; tel. 223715.
INSTITUTE OF INORGANIC CHEMISTRY, Latv. Acad. of Sci. F. 1946. Proposed cooperation: developing of new methods of concentration, extraction and determination of various elements, technol. of obtaining ultrafine powders and materials on their basis, electrochem. coatings. Dir Tālis Millers. *Add.* Miera 34, Salaspils 229021; tel. 946633; fax 940795.
INSTITUTE OF LANGUAGE AND LITERATURE, Latv. Acad. of Sci. F. 1946. Proposed cooperation: research in the Latv. lg., hist. of lit. and culture. Dir Viktors Hausmanis. *Add.* Turgeņeva 19, Rīga 226524, PDP; tel. 212872.
INSTITUTE OF MATHEMATICS AND COMPUTER SCIENCE, Latv. Univ. F. 1959. Proposed cooperation: joint research in theoretical computer sci., development of software tools for rapid prototyping of communication systems, etc.; development of pedag. software and intergraded courses for natural sci., theoretical research in the field of the theory of nonlinear boundary value problems, development of mathematical models, new numerical methods and packages of applied computer programs. Dir Nikolajs Ustinovs. *Add.* Raiņa bulv. 29, Rīga 226250, PDP; tel. 213425; telex 161172 TEMA SU; fax 225039.
INSTITUTE OF MICROBIOLOGY, Latv. Acad. of Sci. F. 1946. Proposed cooperation: joint venture partnership, drawing up joint projects, research in virus diagnostics and control of immunomodulators, bioconversion of organic matter, microbiol. synthesis, joint design of

biotechnol. apparatuses. Dir Rita Kukaine. **Add.** A.Kirhenšteina 1, Rīga 226067; tel. 426 197; telex 161193 KOLBA SU.

INSTITUTE OF MOLECULAR BIOLOGY, Latv. Acad. of Sci. F. 1990. Proposed cooperation: joint research in genome structure and org., molecular immunology, protein antigenic determinants, their structural org. and interaction with antibodies, molecular genetics of the plant cells. Dir Elmārs Grēns. **Add.** Krustpils 53, Rīga 226065; tel. 245 566; fax 331 920 RIGA POST LATVIA pn 430 GREN.

INSTITUTE OF ORGANIC SYNTHESIS, Latv. Acad. of Sci. F. 1957. Proposed cooperation: synthesis of med. substances (cancerolytic, virustatic, heart and blood-vascular diseases-preventive); computer prognostication methods of biol. activity of chem. substances; invest. of ultrahigh discerning quality of Si^{29} in nuclear magnetic resonance spectrum. Dir Edmunds Lukevics. **Add.** Aizkraukles 21, Rīga 226006; tel. 551 822; telex 161174 DUGA SU.

INSTITUTE OF PHILOSOPHY AND SOCIOLOGY, Latv. Acad. of Sci. F. 1991. Proposed cooperation: joint research in phil. anthropology, hist. of phil. and public opinion formation, Western phil., sociology. Dir Maija Kūle. **Add.** Meistaru 10, Rīga 226940, PDP; tel. 216 793.

INSTITUTE OF PHYSICAL ENERGETICS, Latv. Acad. of Sci. F. 1946. Proposed cooperation: tackling of problems in the fields of power eng., phys. and eng. of semiconductors, power semiconductor electronics, nondestructive testing methods, thermal phys., electrical machines, heat supply systems using alternative energy resources. Dir Juris Ekmanis. **Add.** Aizkraukles 21, Rīga 226006; tel. 552 011; telex 161127 ESTI SU; fax 551 394.

INSTITUTE OF PHYSICS, Latv. Acad. of Sci. F. 1946. Proposed cooperation: joint research in the fields of nuclear, radiation, solid state phys., ecology, magnetic hydrodynamics and its practical applying (energetics, metallurgy, metal casting, noncontact measuring apparatuses). Dir Jurijs Mihailovs. **Add.** Miera 32, Salaspils — 1, 229021; tel. 947 582, 947 188.

INSTITUTE OF POLYMER MECHANICS, Latv. Acad. of Sci. F. 1963. Proposed cooperation: research on further development of the theory of deformation and fracture of polymer and composite materials, methods of calculation and optimization of composite materials and manufactured structures; methods and devices for nondestructive testing of phys. and mech. properties in materials, diagnostics and prediction of load bearing capacity of structures under various operating conditions. Dir Imants Matīss. **Add.** Aizkraukles 23, Rīga 226006; tel. 551 145; fax 551 149.

INSTITUTE OF SOLID STATE PHYSICS, Latv. Univ. F. 1978. Proposed cooperation: joint research in the fields of phys. of ionic crystals, glass, ferroelectrics, electrochromic material phys. and solid state ionics, crystal growth, development of methods and tech. means for automatization of solid state research, automatization of educ. personnel training. Dir Andrejs Siliņš. **Add.** Ķengaraga 8, Rīga 226063; tel. 262 933; telex 161172 TEMA SU; fax 225 039.

INSTITUTE OF WOOD CHEMISTRY, Latv. Acad. of Sci. F. 1946. Proposed cooperation: conclusion of contracts on applied research work in the following fields: novel fire retardants and wood preservatives, veterinary preparations and animal feeds, med. agents, methods for furfural prod., heat resistant plastics, chem. modification of wood, reduction of formaldehyde emission. Dir Uldis Viesturs. **Add.** Akadēmijas 27, Rīga 226006; tel. 553 063; fax 555 983.

LATVIAN ACADEMY OF SCIENCES. F. 1946. 31 Full Mem., 47 Corr. Mems, 20 Foreign Mems, 16 Hon. Mems; 3 depts (Phys. and Tech. Sci.; Chem. and Biol. Sci.; Social Sci. and Humanities); 15 research inst. Pres. Jānis Lielpēteris. **Add.** Turgeņeva 19, Rīga 226524, PDP; tel. 225 361; fax 228 784.

RADIOASTROPHYSICAL OBSERVATORY, Latv. Acad. of Sci. F. 1946. Proposed cooperation: research in late-type star spectrum and solar radioemission. Dir Artūrs Balkavs. **Add.** Turgeņeva 19, Rīga 226524, PDP; tel. 226 796, 226 006.

RAŽĪBA, agric. research assoc. F. 1864. Proposed cooperation: research on chem. and phys. properties of soil, chem. analysis of plants and water, working out of recommendations, trade in fertilizers, purchase of analytic apparatuses. Chair. Antons Skromanis. **Add.** Struktoru 14a, Rīga 226039; tel. 552 996; telex 161143 AGRO SU.

RESEARCH INSTITUTE OF ECONOMICS AND AGROINDUSTRIAL COMPLEX. F. 1988. Proposed cooperation: drawing up joint projects for solving econ. and management problems of agroind. complex, exchange of information on agric. policy (price calculation methods, private ownership experience, etc.). Dir Inesis Feifers. **Add.** Struktoru 14, Rīga 226039; tel. 552 909; fax 273 787.

SIGRA, animal husbandry and veterinary research assoc. F. 1986. Offer: breeding stock, fine wool, furs (fox, mink), peas, rape, the latest methodology of livestock treatment and nutrition. Demand: agric. research lit. on livestock breeding, veterinary med., rural econ.; pat., lic.; breeding stock, agric. machinery, veterinary instruments, tech. equipm. for lab. and research. Dir-Gen. Aleksandrs Jemeļjanovs. **Add.** Institūta 1, Sigulda 229050; tel. 976 313, 976 307; telex 161143 AGRO SU.

SILAVA, forestry research inst. F. 1976. Proposed cooperation: exchange of experts, maintenance of commercial ties, establishing of joint venture (forestry, wood-working, machine-building and computer sci.). Dir-Gen. Imants Ieviņš. **Add.** Rīgas 111, Salaspils 229021; tel. 942 555, 947 833; telex 161171 SILA SU.

STARS, agric. machinery prod. and research assoc. F. 1986. Proposed cooperation: establishing joint venture for the prod. of agric. machinery and its components, organizing of foreign machinery exh. in Latvia, intermediary actions in trade and testing of agric. machinery in Latvia. Dir-Gen. Edgars Lāčgalvis. **Add.** Institūta 1, Ulbroka 229030; tel. 910 902, 910 709; telex 161100 PKP SU SPA STARS AT 1880 BOREC.

PLANNERS & DESIGNERS

AGROPROJEKTS, inst. of rural arch. and design. F. 1966. Proposed cooperation: joint research in the field of improving design technol., introducing of automatic design systems, establishing of joint venture, design services, topographical survey, geological and hydrogeological research. Dir Monvids Ēriks Kalsers. **Add.** Maskavas 40/42, Rīga 226504, PDP; tel. 213 067.

INSTITUTE FOR RESTORATION. F. 1951. Proposed cooperation: exchange of experience, holding of joint conferences, seminars, popularizing of Latv. cultural heritage, cooperation in solving problems of preserving and restoring cultural monuments. Dir Jānis Bokta. **Add.** M.Pils 19, Rīga 226050; tel. 224 735.

KOMUNĀLPROJEKTS, inst. of commercial and ind. design. F. 1965. Proposed cooperation: establishing joint ventures with French, Danish and Dutch firms. Dir Aloizs Ameļko. **Add.** Brīvības 148a, Rīga 226012; tel. 377 515, 376 715.

LATESA, ind. design and constr. assoc. F. 1961. Proposed cooperation: part. in int. exh., joint design and prod. of electric equipm., lines, substations. Head Ventis Jugāns. **Add.** Kr.Valdemāra 31, Rīga 226010; tel. 321 101; telex 161198 SELGA SU; fax 416 635.

ORBĪTA, bureau of radio design. F. 1960. Proposed cooperation: concluding of contracts, establishing joint venture for working out tech. documentation (audio systems, equipm. of radio communications) on demand of interested firms, adapting of programme packages provided by firms to the SU tech. equipm., establishing joint stock for organizing exchange of experience and consultative services. Dir Juris Čerkovskis. **Add.** Kr.Valdemāra 139, Rīga 226013; tel. 376 848, 373 844.

PILSĒTPROJEKTS, inst. of urban arch. and design. F. 1945. Proposed cooperation: establishing joint venture (applying automatic design systems) for designing dwelling-houses, public buildings, transport, tech. constr., communications. Chair of the Bd Andris Purviņš. **Add.** Kr.Valdemāra 38, Rīga 226306; tel. 270 130.

RIGA CENTRAL ARCHITECTURE BOARD. F. 1878. Proposed cooperation: joint solving of problems concerning urban, public building and residential arch., protection of hist. and cultural monuments, environmental planning, exchange of exh. (arch. and urban setting), information on arch. Head Gunārs Asaris. **Add.** Amatu 4, Rīga 226900, PDP; tel. 225 995; fax 223 902 RIGA ARCHI.

TIRDZNIECĪBAS PROJEKTS, inst. for trade distribution and design. F. 1960. Proposed cooperation: working out of new technol. for ind. warehouses, automatization of public eating-houses in ind. ent., design and advertising services. Dir Georgs Uļjanovs. **Add.** Raiņa bulv. 25, Rīga 226050; tel. 229 323.

ZEMESPROJEKTS, inst. for land planning and reclamation design. F. 1961. Proposed cooperation: drawing of maps and charts applying advanced research methods in land monitoring. Dir Valdis Niedre. **Add.** Jēkaba 10/12, Rīga 226800; tel. 222 634.

EDUCATIONAL INSTITUTIONS

UNIVERSITY OF LATVIA. F. 1919. 13 faculties, teaching staff of 850; 13,000 students. Proposed cooperation: student and teacher exchange, joint scientific research, holding of conferences. Rector Juris Zaķis. **Add.** Raiņa bulv. 19, Rīga 226098; tel. 228 928; telex 161172 TEMA SU; fax 225 039.

RIGA TECHNICAL UNIVERSITY. F. 1862. 10 faculties, teaching staff of 1,000; 13,000 students. Proposed cooperation: developing of new tech. projects and technol., exchange of students, undergraduates and teachers. Rector Egons Lavendelis. **Add.** Kaļķu 1, Rīga 226355; tel. and fax 225 885.

LATVIAN ACADEMY OF MEDICINE. F. 1950. 4 faculties, teaching staff of 399; 2,530 students. Proposed cooperation: student and teacher exchange, joint scientific research. Rector Vladislavs Korzāns. **Add.** Dzirciema 16, Rīga 226007; tel. 459 752.

LATVIAN ACADEMY OF AGRICULTURE. F. 1939. 9 faculties, teaching staff of 467; 6,167 students. Proposed cooperation: student and teacher exchange, joint scientific research, developing of new tech. projects. Rector Imants Gronskis. **Add.** Lielā 2, Jelgava 229600; tel. 225 84.

RIGA CIVIL AVIATION ENGINEERING INSTITUTE. F. 1960. 4 faculties, teaching staff of 460; 4,100 students. Proposed cooperation: joint training of radio and flight eng., research applying advanced aviation and radioelectronic technol. Rector Vladimirs Hodakovskis. **Add.** Lomonosova 1, Rīga 226019; tel. 242 197; telex 161473 KRILO SU.

LATVIAN ACADEMY OF MUSIC. F. 1919. 4 faculties, teaching staff of 240; 895 students. Proposed cooperation: exchange of students and teachers in the field of music perf., composition, theatrical art, stage perf. programmes and recitals; joint research work. Rector Juris Karlsons. **Add.** Kr.Barona 1, Rīga 226050; tel. 228 684; telex 161172 TEMA SU LVK.

LATVIAN ACADEMY OF ARTS. F. 1919. 5 faculties, teaching staff of 84; 350 students. Proposed cooperation: exchange of students and teachers, exh. (incl. commercial). Rector Indulis Zariņš. **Add.** Komunāru bulv. 13, Rīga 226185; tel. 332 202, 334 192.

DAUGAVPILS PEDAGOGICAL INSTITUTE. F. 1952. 5 faculties, teaching staff of 210; 2,846 students. Proposed cooperation: student and teacher exchange. Rector Oļegs Roždestvenskis. **Add.** 5. augusta 13, Daugavpils 228400; tel. 221 80.

LIEPĀJA PEDAGOGICAL INSTITUTE. F. 1954. 3 faculties, teaching staff of 141; 1,400 students. Proposed cooperation: student and teacher exchange, joint research programmes. Rector Kārlis Dobelis. *Add.* Lielā 14, Liepāja 229700; tel. 240 11, 235 68.

LATVIAN INSTITUTE OF PHYSICAL CULTURE. F. 1921. Teaching staff of 122; 1,250 students. Proposed cooperation: student and teacher exchange, joint holding of sports contests. Rector Uldis Grāvītis. *Add.* Brīvības 333, Rīga 226037; tel. 520 595, 520 156; telex 161172 TEMA SU.

PUBLIC HEALTH & SOCIAL WELFARE

ANTI-NARCOTICS DISPENSARY. F. 1977. Proposed cooperation: exchange of experience pertaining preventive measures and treatment of alcoholism, drug addiction and toxicomania. Head Physician Jānis Strazdiņš. *Add.* Aptiekas 7/9, Rīga 226005; tel. 391 074; fax 392 076.

ANTI-TUBERCULOSIS DISPENSARY. F. 1947. Proposed cooperation: joint exploration of tuberculosis prophylaxis and epidemiology; approbation of up-to-date diagnostic facilities, preparations and methods; exchange of experience for med. staff. Head Physician Voldemārs Saulīte. *Add.* Grēcinieku 8, Rīga 226047; tel. 223 022, 225 406.

BUREAU OF PATHOLOGICAL ANATOMY. F. 1984. Proposed cooperation: continuous exploration of the following: the determinants of patho-biol. arteriosclerosis in young people (under the leadership of WHO); comparison of arteriosclerosis epidemiology of the aortas and coronary arteries in the inhabitants of Riga (Latvia), Malmes (Sweden), Prague (Czecho-Slovakia). Chair. Vladimirs Volkovs. *Add.* P.Dauges 2, Rīga 226038; tel. 536 091, 536 070.

CENTRE OF ORTHOPAEDIC PROSTHESES. F. 1934. Proposed cooperation: export of artificial limbs, wheelchairs, vehicles; increased their prod. in assoc. with allied firms abroad. Dir Kārlis Krūmiņš. *Add.* Pērnavas 62, Rīga 226009; tel. 599 903.

CHILDREN'S CLINICAL HOSPITAL. F. 1899. Proposed cooperation: exchange of experience for physicians and nurses; org. of joint symposiums and exploration of med. problems; approbation of med. preparations. Head Physician Ivars Uldis Lamsters. *Add.* Vienības gatve 45, Rīga 226004; tel. 612 277.

DISPENSARY OF REMEDIAL PHYSICAL ACTIVITY. F. 1950. Proposed cooperation: exchange of experience for physicians; org. of joint symposiums. Head Physician Rūdolfs Keizers. *Add.* Brīvības 73, Rīga 226001; tel. 279 163, 272 510.

INSTITUTE OF TRAUMATOLOGY AND ORTHOPAEDICS. F. 1946. Proposed cooperation: joint exploration of biomech. of man's locomotor apparatus, application of advanced composite materials in traumatology and orthopaedics (artificial limbs, external fixation). Dir Viktors Kalnbērzs. *Add.* Duntes 12/22, Rīga 226005; tel. 392 348; fax 392 623.

KIDNEY TRANSPLANTATION CENTRE. F. 1973. Proposed cooperation: exchange of organs for transplantation with assoc. 'Eurotransplant' (Netherlands); joint research in transplantation of pancreas; treatment of renal diseases by means of kidney transplantation. Head Rafails Rozentāls. *Add.* Dzirciema 16, Rīga 226007; tel. 614 210, 613 152 ; fax 614 210.

LATVA, state insurance company. F. 1940. Proposed cooperation: negotiate, conclude, carry out contracts with foreign companies (W- Europe). Chair. Jānis Medens. *Add.* Vaļņu 1, Rīga 226912; tel. 212 341, 220 376; fax 210 134.

LATVIAN INSTITUTE OF CARDIOLOGY. F. 1977. Proposed cooperation: exchange of experience for med. staff, clinic trials of new drugs and treatment methods of cardiovascular diseases; part. in scientific programmes in the field of cardiology and cardiovascular physiology; establishing of personal contacts among scientists. Dir Vilnis Dzērve-Tāluts. *Add.* Pilsoņu 13, Rīga 226002; tel. 615 094, 617 772.

LATVIAN KIDNEY FUND. F. 1989. Proposed cooperation: exchange of organs for transplantation with assoc. 'Eurotransplant' (Netherlands); joint research in transplantation of pancreas. Pres. Rafails Rozentāls. *Add.* Pilsoņu 13, Rīga 226002; tel. 616 091, 613 152; fax 614 210.

ONCOLOGICAL DISPENSARY. F. 1939. Proposed cooperation: trials of new hormonal preparations; joint research in early diagnosis and treatment of malignant breast tumor; training of med. staff and exchange of experience. Head Physician Māris Siliņš. *Add.* P.Dauges 4, Rīga 226079 ; tel. 536 820.

P.STRADIŅŠ REPUBLICAN CLINICAL HOSPITAL. F. 1910. Proposed cooperation: application of reflex therapy in ophthalmology ; treatment of blood circulation pathology and neuroglioma, sensorineural diminished hearing; myocardial infarction; pancreatitis; inherited cardiovascular disease; implantation of artificial cardiac valves; surgical treatment of gastric and oesophagus disorders, transplantation of kidneys and pancreas. Head Physician Henriks Runds. *Add.* Pilsoņu 13, Rīga 226002; tel. 611 198.

REPUBLICAN DIAGNOSIS CENTRE. F. 1989. Proposed cooperation: diagnosis making for microsurgical treatment of eye. Head Physician Jānis Ducmanis. *Add.* Viļakas 8, Rīga 226003; tel. 227 331.

RESEARCH INSTITUTE OF CLINICAL MEDICINE. F. 1946. Proposed cooperation: joint research in scientific and clinical cytodiagnosis, cancerogenesis, early diagnosis of cancer, differential induction of cancer cells, identification of nucleic acids, diagnosis of gastric diseases. Dir Velta Bramberga. *Add.* O.Vācieša 4, Rīga 226004; tel. 612 038.

RIGA MATERNITY HOUSE No 1. F. 1945. Proposed cooperation: establishing joint venture for navel string and placenta processing; application of sodium hypochlorite in detoxification. Head Physician Anita Caune. *Add.* Miera 45, Rīga 226013; tel. 370 355.

RIGA MENTAL HOSPITAL. F. 1824. Proposed cooperation: exchange and training of phychologists and psychiatrists, joint research in the field of psychiatrics. Head Physician Zuzanna Sočneva. *Add.* Tvaika 2, Rīga 226005; tel. 392 378.

POLITICAL PARTIES & ORGANIZATIONS

INTER-FRONT OF THE WORKING PEOPLE OF THE LATVIAN SSR. F. 1988; membership obscure. Chair. Anatolijs Aleksejevs. *Add.*Smilšu 12, Rīga 226050; tel. 223 280

LATVIAN COMMUNIST PARTY. F. 1904; membership obscure; Latv. SC — 59 seats. 1st Sec. Alfrēds Rubiks. *Add.* Elizabetes 2, Rīga 226190, PDP; tel. 321166.

LATVIAN DEMOCRATIC LABOUR PARTY. F. 1990; 20,000 mems; Latv. SC — 10 seats. Proposed cooperation: exchange of information with SDP abroad, exchange of experience on management of affairs, organizing of joint activities. Chair. Ivars Ķezbers. *Add.* R. Blaumaņa 5a, Rīga 226050; tel. 280 845.

LATVIAN PARTY OF THE GREENS. F. 1990; 300 mems; Latv. SC — 7 seats. Proposed cooperation: exchange of information on environmental protection problems. Co-Chair. Oļegs Batarevskis. *Add.* tel. Rīga 323 916.

LATVIAN NATIONAL INDEPENDENCE MOVEMENT. F. 1988; 11,200 mems; Latv. SC — 20 seats. Proposed cooperation: contacts with Latv. org. abroad. Chair. Visvaldis Lācis. *Add.* Ģertrūdes 19/21 — 1, Rīga 226050; tel. and fax 272 220.

LATVIAN POPULAR FRONT. F. 1988; 175,000 mems; Latv. SC — 137 seats. Proposed cooperation: exchange of management experience, training of experts abroad, establishing of independent press system, part. in the work of int. org. as observers, etc. Chair. Romualds Ražuks. *Add.* Vecpilsētas 13/15, Rīga 226050; tel. 212 286, 229 340; telex 161177 LTF SU; fax 213 978.

LATVIAN SOCIAL DEMOCRATIC WORKERS' PARTY. F. 1904; ref. in 1989; 740 mems; Latv. SC — 5 seats. Chair. Uldis Bērziņš. *Add.* (h) Avotu 11 — 32, Rīga 226011; tel. 287 783.

VOLUNTARY ORGANIZATIONS

ASSOCIATION OF FREE TRADE UNIONS. F. 1990. Proposed cooperation: training of experts, exchange of tourists, obtaining of tech. equipm. for physically disabled workers. Chair. Andris Siliņš. *Add.* Bruņinieku 29/31, Rīga 226453, PDP; tel. 270 351, 270 465.

ASSOCIATION OF RED CROSS CHARITY NURSES. F. 1922. Proposed cooperation: exchange of experience, training of nurses abroad. Pres. Lūcija Lapiņa. *Add.* J. Asara 3, Rīga 226009; tel. 279 596.

DĒKLA, assoc. of large Latv. families world-wide. F. 1989. Proposed cooperation: establishing groups in support of the assoc., facilitating extensive exchange relations of children's tourism, invest. of the Latv. lg., culture and ethics. Chair., Riga soc., Andrejs Zvirbulis. *Add.* (h) Dzirnavu 115 — 17, Rīga 226011; tel. 289 763.

ENVIRONMENTAL PROTECTION CLUB. F. 1987. Proposed cooperation: contacts with allied org., institutions, green movements, especially in the sphere of protection of the Baltic Sea. Pres. Arvīds Ulme. *Add.* Kalnciema 30, Rīga 226046; tel. 612 850.

LATVIA AND THE LATVIANS WORLD-WIDE, scientific assoc. F. 1989. Proposed cooperation: exchange of information on the activities and achievements of Latv. and persons connected with Latvia and Latv. in various c. of the world, preparing of scientific and other publ. on the subject in Latvia and abroad. Chair. Jānis Stradiņš. *Add.* Meistaru 10 — 327, Rīga 226050; tel. 216 990.

LATVIAN CHILDREN'S FUND. F. 1987. Proposed cooperation: establishing of joint venture (prod. of rehabilitation apparatuses for handicapped children, ecologically pure products, children's clothes), joint publ. house, exchange of information and med. experience. Pres. Andris Bērziņš. *Add.* Brīvības 85, Rīga 226450; tel. 271 662.

LATVIAN CULTURE FUND. F. 1987. Proposed cooperation: holding comp., seminars, conferences on cultural hist., camps for tackling ecological problems, art exh.; scholarship sponsoring to foreigners for culture studies, facilitating return of cultural heritage to Latvia. Chair. Imants Ziedonis. *Add.* Basteja bulv. 12, Rīga 226900; tel. 228 449, 227 230.

LATVIAN SCIENTISTS' UNION. F. 1988. Chair. Elmārs Grēns. *Add.* Raiņa bulv. 19, Rīga 226098; tel. 245 566, 212 969; telex 161172 TEMA SU; fax 225 039.

LATVIAN UNION OF CONSUMERS' SOCIETIES. F. 1944. Chair. of the Bd Ivars Strautiņš. *Add.* Tērbatas 14, Rīga 226726, PDP; tel. 281 510; telex 161187 LATKO SU; fax 281 665.

RED CROSS SOCIETY. F. 1918. Chair. Uldis Laucis. *Add.* Skolas 28, Rīga 226300; tel. 275 635; fax 276 445.

SOCIETY OF THE BLIND. F. 1926. Proposed cooperation: social rehabilitation of the blind, brush prod. from local and imported materials, assembling of simple and medium complexity apparatuses. Chair. of Cent. Bd Genrihs Lebedeks. *Add.* Pāles 14, K — 1, Rīga 226024; tel. 532 607.

SOCIETY OF THE DEAF. F. 1945. Proposed cooperation: contacts with soc. of the deaf abroad in the field of culture, sport and rehabilitation. Chair. of the Bd Jānis Liepa. *Add.* Jāņa sēta 5, Rīga 226350, PDP; tel. 212 485, 224 021.

VOLUNTEER FIREMEN'S SOCIETY. F. 1865. Proposed cooperation: contacts in the sphere of fire combat with German and Austrian firemen. Chair. of the Bd Jānis Kleinbergs. *Add.* J. Asara 13, Rīga 226009; tel. 598 798.

CULTURAL INSTITUTIONS

MUSEUMS

MOTOR MUSEUM, joint stock company *Mežciems*. F. 1989. Proposed cooperation: exchange of antique specimens of motor cars and exh. Chair. Viktors Kulbergs. *Add.* S. Eizenšteina 6, Rīga 226079; tel. 537 140, 552 777; telex 161170 MOTO SU; fax 538 695.

MUSEUM FOR THE HISTORY OF MEDICINE. F. 1957. Proposed cooperation: holding of int. exh. Dir Kārlis Arons. *Add.* L. Paegles 1, Rīga 226300, PDP; tel. 222 914, 222 656; fax 216 903.

MUSEUM OF BOXING HISTORY. F. 1971. Proposed cooperation: exchange of exh. Dir Ilgonis Urstiņš. *Add.* Induļa 2, Rīga 226059; tel. 599 135.

MUSEUM OF FIRE-FIGHTING. F. 1978. Proposed cooperation: exchange of scientific personnel, coll., professional lit. Dir Velta Žerdiņa. *Add.* Hanzas 5, Rīga 226045; tel. 333 306, 331 891.

MUSEUM OF FOREIGN ART. F. 1773. Proposed cooperation: exchange of experts, org. of joint exh., exchange of coll., holding of int. seminars. Dir Mārīte Lapiņa. *Add.* Pils lauk. 3, Rīga 226844; tel. 228 776, 226 476.

MUSEUM OF THE HISTORY OF LATVIA. F. 1869. Proposed cooperation: exchange of museum personnel, holding of joint exh., exchange of exh., joint publ. Dir Ināra Baumane. *Add.* Pils lauk. 3, Rīga 226050; tel. 223 004.

MUSEUM OF THE HISTORY OF RIGA AND NAVIGATION. F. 1773. Proposed cooperation: exchange of experience among the scientific staff, coll., museum pieces, professional lit., cooperation with ICOM and foreign assoc. and centres of museographic training; joint publ. Dir Klāra Radziņa. *Add.* Palasta 4, Rīga 226050; tel. 211 358.

OPEN-AIR MUSEUM OF ETHNOGRAPHY. F. 1924. Proposed cooperation: setting up of a summer camp and organizing of field expeditions for museum personnel to acquire skills of primitive tool handling. Dir Juris Indāns. *Add.* Brīvības 440, Rīga 226056; tel. 994 510, 994 178.

RUNDĀLE PALACE MUSEUM. F. 1964. Proposed cooperation: holding of exh., joint publ. on studies of the hist. of Latvia (13 – 19th cent.), tracing of museum pieces in museums and coll. abroad, exchange of izographic and archive records pertaining to the monuments of Latv. arch. and art. Dir Imants Lancmanis. *Add.* Bauskas raj., Rundāle 229326; tel. 622 72, Rīga 331 920.

STATE MUSEUM OF FINE ARTS. F. 1905. Proposed cooperation: exchange of coll. Dir Māra Lāce. *Add.* Kr. Valdemāra 10a, Rīga 226342; tel. 325 021.

VENTSPILS MUSEUM OF HISTORY AND ARTS. F. 1928. Proposed cooperation: exchange of coll., museum pieces, commercial exh. of applied arts. Dir Spodra Bērziņa. *Add.* Akmeņu 3, Ventspils 229910; tel. 220 31.

WAR MUSEUM. F. 1919. Proposed cooperation: exchange of exh. (hist. of military eng., sci.). Dir Aija Fleija. *Add.* Smilšu 20, Rīga 226900; tel. 228 147, 228 112.

LIBRARIES

INSTITUTE OF BIBLIOGRAPHY. F. 1940. Proposed cooperation: supplying UNESCO with statistical data on Latv. press, cooperation with Latv. cultural centres abroad in compilation of nat. bibliography, joint research with IFLA in the sphere of methodology and automation of bibliography. Dir Laimdota Prūse. *Add.* Anglikāņu 5, Rīga 226816, PDP; tel. 225 135.

LIBRARY FOR TECHNICAL RESEARCH. F. 1949. Proposed cooperation: exchange of lit., purchasing of books, information on latest achievements in sci., technol., econ. in Latvia. Dir Agnese Buholte. *Add.* Šķūņu 17, Rīga 226930; tel. 227 310.

LIBRARY FOR THE BLIND. F. 1962. Proposed cooperation: obtaining of books recorded in Latv., lit. pertaining to life of the visually impaired abroad (in Engl., Ger.). Dir Tamāra Melberga. *Add.* Juglas 14, Rīga 226024; tel. 531 748.

MEDICAL LIBRARY. F. 1945. Proposed cooperation: exchange relations with firms 'SWETS and ZEITLINGER GmbH','ELSEVIER Science Publishers BV' concerning supply of foreign med. periodicals, publ. on med. by Latv. authors in exile, bibliographical information, catalogues of annual serials. Dir Raisa Kazankina. *Add.* Šarlotes 1, Rīga 226328, PDP; tel. 373 646.

NATIONAL LIBRARY. F. 1919. Proposed cooperation: training of staff, exchange of library materials, scientific and bibliographical information, exh. Dir Andris Vilks. *Add.* Kr. Barona 14, Rīga 226437; tel. 280 851.

THEATRES, CINEMAS

ART THEATRE. F. 1920. Halls of 1,032 and 400 seats. Guest perf. in European c. and USA. Chief Dir Kārlis Auškāps. *Add.* Brīvības 75, Rīga 226705, PDP; tel. 279 474, 270 424.

CINEMATOGRAPHERS' HOUSE. F. 1962. Dir Jānis Šulcs. *Add.* A. Čaka 67/69, Rīga 226001; tel. 297 010, 297 030; fax 277 300.

CIRCUS. F. 1888. Hall of 1,000 seats. Guest perf. in Greece and Bulgaria. Chief Dir and Man. Gunārs Katkēvičs. *Add.* Merķeļa 4, Rīga 226050; tel. 213 479, 224 366.

LATVIJAS KINO, cinematography assoc. F. 1988. Proposed cooperation: joint film prod. of all genres (feature films, animated cartoons, documentaries), hiring of tech. equipm. and professional stuntmen to foreign film studios, exchange of film programmes. Dir-Gen. Rihards Piks. *Add.* Šmerļa 3, Rīga 226037; tel. 520 411, telex 161116 SVT LATVIJAS KINO; fax 520 701.

NATIONAL OPERA. F. 1919. Hall of 1,235 seats. Guest perf. in Western Europe, Asia and South America. Artistic Dir Kārlis Zariņš, Chief Conductor Rihards Glāzups. *Add.* Aspazijas bulv. 3, Rīga 226251, PDP; tel. 223 817, 224 325; telex 161155 INTA SU; fax 551 542.

NATIONAL THEATRE. F. 1919. Halls of 1,028 and 100 seats. Guest perf. in European c. and USA. Chief Dir Oļģerts Kroders. *Add.* Kronvalda bulv. 2, Rīga 226829, PDP; tel. 332 828, 322 759.

PUPPET THEATRE. F. 1944. Latv. and Russ. companies. Hall of 300 seats. Guest perf. in European and Near Eastern c. Artistic Dir Tīna Hercberga. *Add.* Kr. Barona 16/18, Rīga 226011; tel. 285 415, 285 418.

RUSSIAN DRAMA THEATRE. F. 1883. Hall of 800 seats. Chief Dir Leonīds Beļavskis. *Add.* Kaļķu 16, Rīga 226050; tel. 224 660.

YOUTH THEATRE. F. 1941. Latv. and Russ. companies. Halls of 635 and 510 seats. Guest perf. in European c. Chief Dir Ādolfs Šapiro. *Add.* Lāčplēša 37, Rīga 226716; tel. 287 558, 223 379.

PERFORMING UNITS

AVE SOL, chamber choir. F. 1969. Prize winner of int. comp., concert tours in 16 c., 14 records. Dir Imants Kokars. *Add.* J. Alunāna 2, Rīga 226300, PDP; tel. 224 625.

DZIEDONIS, male choir. F. 1924. Prize winner of int. comp., concert tours in 10 c., 4 records. Dir Roberts Liepiņš, Vilmārs Vasulis. *Add.* Lāčplēša 43/45, Rīga 226011; tel. 288 715.

DZINTARS, female choir. F. 1947. Prize winner of int. comp., concert tours in 9 c., 6 records. Dir Ausma Derkēvica. *Add.* Kaļķu 11a, Rīga 226350, PDP; tel. 223 618, 213 497.

LATVIJA, academic state choir. F. 1942. Concert tours in 9 c., numerous records. Dir Imants Cepītis. *Add.* Kaļķu 11a, Rīga 226350, PDP; tel. 223 839, 223 618.

NATIONAL SYMPHONY ORCHESTRA. F. 1926. Concert tours in European c., numerous records. Chief Conductor Pauls Megi. *Add.* Amatu 6, Rīga 226050; tel. 224 850.

RĪGAS PANTOMĪMA, dumb show ensemble. F. 1956. Guest perf. in Western European c. and USA. Artistic Dir Roberts Ligers. *Add.* Ropažu 1, Rīga 226039; tel. 553 273, 378 683.

SHOWIMPEX, concert firm. F. 1989. Proposed cooperation: concert tour org. for musicians and various performing units. Man., Artistic Dir Zigmārs Liepiņš. *Add.* Ģertrūdes 37, Rīga 226011; tel. 276 002, 276 614.

SINDI PUTNU DĀRZS, chamber choir. F. 1986. Prize winner of int. comp., concert tours in 7 c. Dir Ivars Bērziņš. *Add.* Brīvības 85, Rīga 226450; tel. 278 712.

CRAFTS

DAIĻRADE, applied arts and souvenir mfrs assoc. F. 1971. Offer: hand-made articles of amber, wood, leather, flax; earthenware, clothes, haberdashery, jewelry; joint venture partnership. Demand: woodworking, knitting, sewing, leather processing equipm. Dir-Gen. Valdis Grimze. *Add.* Čiekurkalna 1. garā līnija 11, Rīga 226026; tel. 551 740, 551 820; telex 161149 INLA SU (for DAIĻRADE).

PHOTO FUND, Latv. Photo Artists' Soc. F. 1990. Proposed cooperation: establishing joint venture for printing, publ., prod. and sale of photographic materials and photographic equipm., photo advertising. Dir-Gen. Aivars Āķis. *Add.* Mārstaļu 6, Rīga 226050; tel. 210 327.

RIGA MUSICAL INSTRUMENTS FACTORY. F. 1958. Proposed cooperation: export or barter of musical instruments (pianos, citterns, metal-lophones, percussion instruments, musical toys). Dir Ēriks Kudrjavcevs. *Add.* Maskavas 250, Rīga 226063; tel. 253 852, 259 444.

RĪGAS FOTO, photo and pawnbroker's service ent. F. 1944. Proposed cooperation:establishing joint venture in the field of photography. Dir Nikolajs Jegorovs. *Add.* Kr. Valdemāra 36, Rīga 226300, PDP; tel. 270 556, 275 009.

CREATIVE SOCIETIES

LATVIAN ARCHITECTS' UNION. F. 1924. Proposed cooperation: concluding contracts for multilateral professional contacts with related soc. in Nordic and mid-European c. Chair. of the Bd Edvīns Vecumnieks. *Add.* Torņa 11, Rīga 226800, PDP; tel. 226 701, 212 802.

LATVIAN ARTISTS' UNION. F. 1941. Proposed cooperation: Latv. art exh. (incl. commercial), exh. of works by contemporary Latv. artists abroad, part. in int. exh., auctions. Chair. of the Bd Džemma Skulme. *Add.* Kr. Barona 12, Rīga 226400; tel. 287 626; telex 161115 GAMMA SU (for ARTISTS' UNION).

LATVIAN CINEMATOGRAPHERS' UNION. F. 1962. Proposed cooperation: holding of int. symposiums, film festivals, conferences; contacts with related org. worldwide; engaging in the activities of int. org. Chair. of the Bd Ivars Seleckis. *Add.* Brīvības 85, Rīga 226250, PDP; tel. 272 715.

LATVIAN COMPOSERS' UNION. F. 1944. Proposed cooperation: concluding of contracts with composers' soc. abroad, exchange of scores, music recordings, information on music life, mutual representation of composers. Chair. of the Bd Juris Karlsons. *Add.* Kr. Barona 12, Rīga 226440, PDP; tel. 287 447.

LATVIAN DESIGNERS' UNION. F. 1988. Proposed cooperation: contacts with int. designers' assoc. ICSID for the purpose of joining it. Chair. Gunārs Glūdiņš. *Add.* Tirgoņu 10, Rīga 226050; tel. 212 559; telex 161 172 TEMA SU LDC.

LATVIAN JOURNALISTS' UNION. F. 1957. Proposed cooperation: exchange of journalists, publ. abroad. Chair. Aivars Baumanis. *Add.* Basteja bulv. 4, Rīga 226050; tel. 211 433.

LATVIAN PHOTO ARTISTS' SOCIETY. F. 1989. Proposed cooperation: creative contacts with foreign photography artists, photographers, photogalleries, publ. houses, etc. Pres. Aivars Āķis. *Add.* Centrs, a.k. 137, Rīga 226098; tel. 210 327.

LATVIAN THEATRE PEOPLE'S SOCIETY. F. 1987. Proposed cooperation: maintenance of cultural contacts with centres of ITI in order to join ITI. Chair. of the Bd Ģirts Jakovļevs. *Add.*

E. Smiļģa 37/39, Rīga 226002; tel. 615169, 610498; fax 210368.

LATVIAN WRITERS' UNION. F. 1940. Proposed cooperation: concluding of contracts for cooperation with related soc. in Nordic and mid-European c. Chair. of the Bd Imants Auziņš. *Add.* Kr. Barona 12, Rīga 226400, PDP; tel. 287629.

CHURCHES & RELIGIOUS ORGANIZATIONS

CONSISTORY OF THE LATVIAN EVANGELICAL LUTHERAN CHURCH. F. 1920. Proposed cooperation: in the fields of educ., part. in int. ecclesiastical org., exchange of delegations. Archbishop Kārlis Gailītis. *Add.* Lāčplēša 4 — 4, Rīga 226010; tel. 334194, 334362; fax 334194.

CURIA OF THE ROMAN CATHOLIC CHURCH METROPOLIS. F. 1918. Metropolitan Jānis Pujāts *Add.* M. Pils 2a, Rīga 226047; tel. 227226.

DIEVTURI, community of Latv. ancient religion. F. 1926. Leader Eduards Detlavs. *Add.* (h) Dārza 36a — 53, Rīga 226083; tel. 450797.

HEBREW RELIGIOUS COMMUNITY OF RIGA (Synagogue). F. 1764. Head Mihails Arons. *Add.* Peitavas 6/8, Rīga 226050; tel. 224549.

LATVIAN EPARCHY OF THE ORTHODOX CHURCH. F. 1850. Bishop Aleksandrs (Kudrjašovs). *Add.* M.Pils 11, Rīga 226050; tel. 228324.

LATVIAN OLD BELIEVERS POMOR CHURCH. F. 1760. Head of the Cent. Council Ivans Miroļubovs. *Add.* Krasta 73, Rīga 226003; tel. 222981.

ROMAN CATHOLIC THEOLOGICAL SEMINARY OF RIGA METROPOLIS. F. 1920. Teaching staff of 8; 97 students. Rector Vilhelms Ņukšs. *Add.* Kijevas 16, Rīga 226003; tel. and fax 229641.

UNION OF THE SEVENTH DAY ADVENTISTS IN LATVIA. F. 1920. Proposed cooperation: exchange of information and experience; exchange of musicians and concert perf.; printing of religious lit. Chair. Viktors Geide. *Add.* J. Kupalas 9 — 1, Rīga 226010; tel. 321050.

UNION OF THE LATVIAN BAPTIST CHURCH. F. 1860. Bishop Jānis Eisāns. *Add.* Matīsa 50b, Rīga 226009; tel. 271312.

PERIODICALS

Due to the subversive activities and occupation of Riga Press House (joint stock company) by a special forces unit of the USSR Interior Ministry (Black Berets) on January 2, 1991, the editorial boards of the principal periodicals issued in Latvia have established temporary offices elsewhere. That accounts both for the reduced circulations and poor quality of printing as well as absence of permanent addresses of the editorial boards. The telephone numbers given in the directory are temporary.

ATMODA (Awakening). F. 1988; in Latv., Russ. and Engl.; LPF newspaper. Proposed cooperation: exchange of information, establishing joint venture (publ. house). E-in-C Elita Veidemane. *Add.* Vecpilsētas 13/15, Rīga 226250; tel. 210452; fax 213978.

DAMBRETE (Draughts). F. 1959; in Latv. and Russ.; popular draughts magazine. Proposed cooperation: exchange of publ., picture service; sharing of experience. E-in-C Vladimirs Vigmans. *Add.* Centrs, a.k. 55, Rīga 226098; tel. 224148, 225629.

DĀRZS UN DRAVA (Garden and Apiary). F. 1958; in Latv.; horticultural journal. Proposed cooperation: advertising (flower growing, beekeeping prod.). E-in-C Jānis Rukšāns. *Add.* Centrs, a.k. 441, Rīga 226001.

DAUGAVA. F. 1988; in Russ.; lit. journal. E-in-C Vladilens Dozorcevs. *Add.* tel. Rīga 321015 (h).

DIENA (Day). F. 1990; in Latv. and Russ.; social pol. newspaper. E-in-C Viktors Daugmalis. *Add.* Smilšu 1/3, Rīga 226900, PDP; tel. 210820, 220019; fax 228826.

GRĀMATA (Book). F. 1958; in Latv.; lit. and phil. journal. E-in-C Leons Briedis. *Add.* Aspazijas bulv. 24, Rīga 226050; tel. 226763.

KAROGS (Banner). F. 1940; in Latv.; lit. journal; publ. house since 1990. E-in-C Māra Zālīte. *Add.* tel. Rīga 289875.

LAUKU AVĪZE (Country Newspaper). F. 1987; in Latv.; popular agric. newspaper. Ed. Voldemārs Krustiņš. *Add.* tel. Rīga 327616, 327639.

LITERATŪRA UN MĀKSLA (Literature and Art). F. 1945; in Latv.; arts newspaper; publ. house since 1990. Proposed cooperation: establishing joint venture on the basis of *Literatūra un Māksla* and Latv. Assoc. of Fishery Farms for joint publ. and sale of books, printed matter; waste paper processing. E-in-C Māris Čaklais. *Add.* tel. Rīga 211748, 222453.

MĀKSLA (Art). F. 1959; in Latv.; ill. arts journal. Proposed cooperation: exchange of experience, joint publ. of articles, ill., photos; arrangement of visits to artists studios and attendance of cultural events (perf., etc.) to the visitors of allied professions during the stay in Riga. E-in-C Ēvalds Strods. *Add.* tel. Rīga 321812.

RĪGAS MODES (Riga Fashions). F. 1948; in Latv. and Russ.; ill. fashion journal. Proposed cooperation: advertising (wide circ. in USSR). E-in-C Rita Muceniece. *Add.* Kaļķu 24, Rīga 226436; tel. 213791.

SPORTS (Sports). F. 1955; in Latv.; popular sports newspaper. Proposed cooperation: exchange of information with related periodicals abroad. Ed. Egils Jurisons. *Add.* tel. Rīga 299511; fax 284412.

SVĒTDIENAS RĪTS (Holy Morning). F. 1920; in Latv.; newspaper of the Latv. Evangelical Lutheran Church. E-in-C Aida Prēdele. *Add.* Lāčplēša 4 — 4, Rīga 226010; tel. 334264.

ŠAHS (Chess). F. 1959; in Latv. and Russ.; popular chess magazine. E-in-C Aivars Ģipslis. *Add.* a.k. 241, Rīga 226050; tel. 286864, 284266.

ZĪLĪTE (Blue Titmouse). F. 1958; in Latv.; ill. magazine for 5 — 10 year-olds. E-in-C Daina Oliņa. *Add.* tel. Rīga 225810.

PUBLISHERS

AVOTS, popular publrs. F. 1980. Proposed cooperation: joint publ. on hist., phil., religion; books for gen. readership, dictionaries, calendars, placards, photoalbums. Dir Kārlis Skruzis. *Add.* Aspazijas bulv. 24, Rīga 226050; tel. 225 824, 211 394.

LATVIAN ENCYCLOPAEDIA PUBLISHERS. F. 1963. Proposed cooperation: providing of encyclopaedic references and wide-spectrum information on Latvia against contract; joint venture partnership, publ. opportunities. E-in-C Andris Vilks. *Add.* Maskavas 68, Rīga 226018; tel. 220 150.

SPRĪDĪTIS, children's publrs. F. 1989. Offer: joint venture partnership for publ. of children's lit., distribution and sale abroad. Demand: printing equipm. and paper. Dir Jāzeps Osmanis. *Add.* Aldaru 2/4, Rīga 226800; tel. 224 921, 225 672.

VIEDA, ecological publrs. F. 1989. Dir-Gen. Aivars Garda. *Add.* Odesas 17, Rīga 226018; tel. 223 497.

ZINĀTNE, scientific and scholarly publrs. F. 1951. Proposed cooperation: exchange and sale of scientific publ. in Latv., Russ., Engl. and Ger. abroad; transl. of Latv. authors into foreign lgs by contract with foreign partners. Dir Ivars Riekstiņš. *Add.* Turgeņeva 19, Rīga 226530; tel. 212 797.

ZVAIGZNE, textbooks publrs. F. 1966. Proposed cooperation: publ. in Latvia works of the Latv. authors residing abroad; distribution and sale of the textbooks to the Latvians abroad. Dir Guntars Vītoliņš. *Add.* Kr. Valdemāra 105, Rīga 226013; tel. 372 396, 371 348.

NEWS AGENCIES

LETA, news agency. F. 1920. Proposed cooperation: exchange of information with the news agencies of Nordic states, Reuters agency; picture service to AP. Dir Aivars Baumanis. *Add.* Palasta 10, Rīga 226947, PDP; tel. 223 462; telex 161132 LETA SU; fax 224 502.

BALTIC NEWS SERVICE. F. 1990. Proposed cooperation: exchange of first-hand information and news reports (on Latvia, Baltic States) with mass media and state inst. (pol., econ., scientific aspects). Dir Gints Vīns. *Add.* Smilšu 1/3, Rīga 226900, PDP; tel. 228 826, 212 858; telex 161101 DIENA SU; fax 228 826.

SPORTS & TOURISM ORGANIZATIONS

BIĶERNIEKI SPORTS CENTRE. F. 1966. Proposed cooperation: joint organizing of motor races (F — 4, F — 3, standard and sports cars, incl. European Champ. Cup stages in race-track; 125, 250, superbikes, F — 1 in race-track, speedway; go-kart races), hiring of sports centres for training and testing. Dir Eduards Kiope. *Add.* S. Eizenšteina 2, Rīga 226079; tel. 552 322; telex 161170 MOTO SU; fax 598 485.

CENTRAL TENNIS CLUB. F. 1968. Proposed cooperation: promotion and maintenance of training conditions (tennis courts, coaches). Dir Juris Trēziņš. *Add.* Baldones 7, Rīga 226046; tel. 612 604, 613 194.

CENTRAL YACHTING CLUB. F. 1946. Proposed cooperation: establishing joint venture for promotion and marketing of tourism. Dir Lauris Pavlovs. *Add.* Stūrmaņu 1a, Rīga 226016; tel. 433 344.

CHESS AND DRAUGHTS CLUB. F. 1944. Proposed cooperation: establishing contacts with chess and draughts clubs abroad, holding joint tournaments. Dir Kārlis Hauks. *Add.* Centrs, a.k. 100, Rīga 226098; tel. 213 313, 227 557.

LATVIAN OLYMPIC COMMITTEE. F. 1920. Proposed cooperation: contacts in all spheres of sport (incl. commerce). Pres. Vilnis Baltiņš. *Add.* Elizabetes 49, Rīga 226050; tel. 281 563, 280 269; fax 280 371.

MŪSA, sports centre. F. 1988. Proposed cooperation: joint holding of sports comp. (motor races), promotion of motor tourism and motor service. Dir Valdis Bensons. *Add.* Gailīšu pagasts, a.k. 47, Bauskas raj. 229307; tel. 230 32; telex 161116 SVT SU.

OPTIMISTS, sports club for invalids. F. 1985. Proposed cooperation: holding of joint comp., exchange of information and experience with sports org. for invalids abroad. Pres. Jānis Iluss. *Add.* Stabu 60, Rīga 226001; tel. 274 873, 270 528.

RIGA RECREATION PARKS ASSOCIATION. F. 1948. Proposed cooperation: import of recreation devices, equipm. for amusement parks. Dir Vilnis Grīviņš. *Add.* Meža prosp. 54, Rīga 22014; tel. 518 742, 557 490.

RIGA SPORTS PALACE. F. 1970. Proposed cooperation: exchange of experience with foreign sports centres. Dir Jevgeņijs Brands. *Add.* Kr. Barona 75, Rīga 226001; tel. 277 133; telex 161108 JET SU.

RIGA ZOO. F. 1912. Proposed cooperation: exchange of experience, trade and exchange of animals and tech. equipm. Dir Ilgvars Pūkainis. *Add.* Meža prosp. 1, Rīga 226014; tel. 518 409; telex 161172 TEMA SU.

SIGULDA, bobsleigh and sledging sports centre. F. 1986. Proposed cooperation: organizing of training camps, training of beginners, advertising, holding consultations on bobsleigh track maintenance, trade relations (sledges, bobsleds), arrangement of int. events. Dir Einars Fogelis. *Add.* Šveices 13, Sigulda 229050; tel. 973 813, 972 008; fax 972 006.

SWIMMING POOL, Riga Tech. Univ. F. 1989. Proposed cooperation: joint constr. of hotel and sports centres, promotion of foreign tourists and sportsmen (groups of swimmers) with leisure and recreational facilities (swimming pool, trainers, saunas, café). Dir Juris Briņķis. *Add.* Ķīpsalas 5, Rīga 226048; tel. 616 989; telex 161172 TEMA SU.

TECHNICAL SPORTS MOTOR CLUB. F. 1944. Proposed cooperation: exchange of sportsmen and delegations of sports officials, part. in motor sports comp. of various levels. Chief Valdis Mežulis. *Add.* Akas 4, Rīga 226050; tel. 280 629, 289 348.

VALTER'S BASKETBALL SCHOOL. F. 1988. Dir and Coach Valdis Valters. *Add.* Kr. Barona 122/2 — 35, Rīga 226012; tel. 245 376, 270 396 (h); telex 161155 INTA SU; fax 551 542.

WHO'S WHO

ĀBOLTIŅŠ, Jānis, Min. of Econ., 1990 − ; b. 1943; grad. Latv. Acad. of Agric., wood technol.; CSc. (Econ.); research in agric. econ. **Add.** Brīvības bulv. 36, Rīga 226169; tel. 288 444.

AGAFONOVS, Jurijs, Dir, Baltic Zonal Station for Machine Testing, 1981 − ; b. 1935; grad. Latv. Acad. of Agric., eng. (mech.); CSc. (Eng.); in the station since 1961. **Add.** Dārza 12, Priekuļi 228550; tel. 226 12, 306 30.

AKMENTIŅŠ, Roberts, Dean, Theol. Faculty of Latv. Univ., 1990 − ; b. 1910; grad. Latv. Univ., theologian; ThD, Prof.; Rector, Theol. Sem. of Latv. Evangelical Lutheran Church, 1980 − 90; research in psychology and ethics of religion. **Add.** (h) Pudiķa 14 − 3, Rīga 226006; tel. 555 974.

ĀĶIS, Aivars, Pres., Latv. Photo Artists' Soc., 1989 − ; Dir-Gen., Latv. Photo Fund, 1990 − ; b. 1934; grad. pedag. inst.; Artistic Dir, photo studio *Rīga*, 1975 − ; part. in int. exh.; one-man shows in Paris, Munich, Prague, Istanbul; works at French Photography Museum in Bièvres; AFIAP, 1977, EFIAP, 1988. **Add.** Mārstaļu 6, Rīga 226050; tel. 210 327.

ALEKSEJEVS, Anatolijs, Chair., Inter-Front of the Working People of the Latvian SSR, 1990 − ; b. 1935; grad. Riga Tech. Univ., eng. (civil); Latv. SC Deputy. **Add.** Smilšu 12, Rīga, 226050; tel. 223 280.

ALKSNIS, Andrejs, astronomer; b. 1928; grad. Moscow Univ.; CSc. (Math. & Phys.); at Radioastrophysical Observatory, 1953 − ; research in interstellar absorption and star distribution in the direction of Cepheus constellation, photometric properties of carbon stars; publ. in Engl. **Add.** Baldone, Riekstukalns, a.k. 11, Rīgas raj. 229025; tel. 932 088.

ALKSNIS, Arnolds, spec. in polymer chem.; b. 1932; grad. Latv. Univ.; DSc. (Eng.); at Inst. of Wood Chem., 1959 − , Research Dir, 1987 − ; research in synthesis of oligoesters and polyesters from wood decomposition products; pat. in USA, Japan, Germany, Poland; publ. in USA. **Add.** Akadēmijas 27, Rīga 226006; tel. 553 134.

AMBAINIS, Jānis, Dir, chem. fibre ent. *Ķīmiskā šķiedra*, 1980 − ; b. 1931; grad. Latv. Univ., chem. **Add.** Višku 21, Daugavpils 228400; tel. 493 03.

AMEĻKO, Aloizs, Dir, inst. of commercial and ind. design *Komunālprojekts*, 1978 − ; b. 1930; grad. Latv. Univ., eng. (civil). **Add.** Brīvības 148a, Rīga 226012; tel. 377 515.

ANDREJEVS, Georgs, anaesthesiologist; b. 1932; grad. Latv. Acad. of Med.; DSc. (Med.), Prof.; perfected general anaesthesia and artificial lung mask ('LEFORA', reg. in USA, Great Britain, Germany, Norway, Denmark); publ. in Engl.; Latv. SC Deputy. **Add.** Pilsoņu 13, Rīga 226002; tel. 613 855, 536 516.

ANDRUŠAITIS, Gunārs, Dir, Inst. of Biol., 1970 − ; b. 1930; grad. Latv. Univ., hydrobiol.; CSc. (Biol.), Corr. Mem., Latv. Acad. of Sci.; at Inst. of Biol. since 1957; research in ichtiology,

ecology, nature protection; mem. of several int. org. **Add.** Miera 3, Salaspils 229021; tel. 947 364.

ANDŽĀNS, Antons, Dir-Gen., vegetable trade assoc. *Latvijas dārzeņi*, 1989 − ; b. 1936; grad. Moscow Nat. Econ. Inst.; CSc. (Econ.). **Add.** Nēģu 16, Rīga 226521; tel. 228 522.

ANŠEĻĒVIČS, Jūlijs, internist; b. 1931; grad. Latv. Acad. of Med.; DSc. (Med.), Prof., Corr. Mem., Latv. Acad. of Sci.; research in urgent therapy, pathogenesis, diagnosis and treatment of myocardial ischemia, hypertension, pulmonary diseases, gastric secretion, clinical pharmacotherapy; publ. in Germany, Austria. **Add.** Bruņinieku 5, Rīga 226001; tel. 366 355.

APALS, Jānis, archeologist; b. 1930; grad. Latv. Univ.; at Inst. of Hist., 1959 − ; research in Latv. hydroarcheological monuments, leader of archeological expeditions of burial-mounds and underwater structures, incl. study and reconstr. of Āraiši Mid-Lake-Settlement. **Add.** Meistaru 10, Rīga 226524, PDP; tel. 216 769.

APKALNS, Ilmārs, photographer; b. 1931; author of photography series, expressive works; applies montage; 650 exh., 250 prizes; FIAP gold medallist, 1972, gold medal, Paris, 1971, Thailand, 1972, Malaysia, 1974; one-man shows in USSR, Germany; AFIAP, 1975, EFIAP, 1988. **Add.** a.k. 63, Rīga 226001; tel. 617 569.

ARONS, Kārlis, Dir, Museum for the Hist. of Med., 1974 − ; b. 1933; grad. Latv. Acad. of Med.; CSc. (Med.); lecturer, Latv. Acad. of Med.; research in popular med. **Add.** L.Paegles 1, Rīga 226300, PDP; tel. 222 914.

ARONS, Mihails, Head, Hebrew Religious Community of Riga, 1983 − ; b. 1922. **Add.** Peitavas 6/8, Rīga 226050; tel. 224 549.

ASARIS, Gunārs, Head, Riga Cent. Arch. Bd, Head Arch. of Riga, 1971 − ; arch.; b. 1934; grad. Riga Tech. Univ.; Full Mem., USSR Acad. of Arts; creatively synthesized monumental arch. and sculpture; co-author of Riga Masterplan (up to the year of 2005); Chair., Bd of Latv. Arch. Union, 1979 − 89. **Add.** Amatu 4, Rīga 226050; tel. 225 995.

AUŠKĀPS, Kārlis, Chief Dir, Art Theatre, 1987 − ; b. 1947; grad. Latv. Acad. of Med., Latv. Acad. of Music; actor, Art Theatre, 1974 − , stage dir, 1977 − . **Add.** Brīvības 75, Rīga 226705; tel. 279 474.

AUZIŅŠ, Imants, Chair., Bd of Latv. Writers' Union, 1989 − ; poet; b. 1937; grad. Latv. Univ.; 16 poetry coll., selections, essays, lit. criticism; renderings of Russ. (M.Lermontov, A.Blok, J.Vinokurov), Ukr. (M.Rylsky), Lith. (S.Nēris), Czech (V.Nezval) poetry; poems rendered into Russ., Lith., Ukr., Engl., Hung., Georgian. **Add.** Kr.Barona 12, Rīga 226400, PDP; tel. 287 629.

BANIS, Kārlis, Min. of Forestry, 1990 − ; b. 1941; grad. Latv. Acad. of Agric.; worked at forestry ent., 1982 − 90. **Add.** Smilšu 1, Rīga 226050; tel. 288 873.

BANKOVSKIS, Juris, spec. in analytical chem.; b. 1927; grad. Latv. Univ.; DSc. (Chem.), Prof., Acad., Latv. Acad. of Sci.; at Inst. of Inorganic Chem., 1948 — ; research in chem. of coordinate compounds, types of chem. bonds, synthesis, study, application of newly developed organic compounds; Mem., IUPAC. *Add.* Miera 34, Salaspils 229021; tel. 946 652.

BALDERIS, Helmuts, hockey player; b. 1952; Olympic silver medallist, 1980, world and European champ., 1978, 1979, 1983; thrice European Cup winner; best forward, world champ., 1977; coach in Japan, 1985 — 89; USA 'Minnesota North Stars' player, 1989 — 90; player of German team, 1991 — .

BALKAVS, Arturs, Dir, Radioastrophysical Observatory, 1969 — ; b. 1933; grad. Latv. Univ., phys.; CSc. (Phys. & Math.); author of the method for the restoration of genuine radiobrightness of radioactive sources if observations are carried out by radiointerferometer; publ. in Engl. *Add.* Turgeņeva 19, Rīga 226524, PDP; tel. 226 796.

BALTIŅŠ, Gunārs, Chair., State Cttee for Statistics, 1970 — ; b. 1930; grad. Latv. Univ. *Add.* Lāčplēša 1, Rīga 226301, PDP; tel. 270 126.

BALTIŅŠ, Vilnis, Pres., Latv. Olympic Cttee, 1988 — ; b. 1942; world champ., rowing, 1966. *Add.* Elizabetes 49, Rīga 226050; tel. 281 563.

BARKĀNS, Georgs, textile artist, arch.; b. 1925; grad. Latv. Univ., studied at Latv. Acad. of Arts; makes large-size tapestries for public interiors, classical Gobelin tapestries, small-size tapestries, batiks, collages; concerned with Latv. ancient hist., displays strong nat. colouring; part. in int. exh. *Add.* Mākslinieku savienība, Kr.Barona 12, Rīga 226440, PDP; tel. 287 591.

BĀRZDIŅŠ, Jānis, spec. in computer sci.; b. 1937; grad. Latv. Univ.; DSc. (Phys. & Math.), Prof., Corr. Mem., Latv. Acad. of Sci.; at Inst. of Math. and Computer Sci., 1965 — ; research in theory of automatic program synthesis, automatic check generation, author of several complex program systems; 70 research papers, monographs in Engl., Russ., Pol. *Add.* Raiņa bulv. 29, Rīga 226250; tel. 224 152.

BATAREVSKIS, Oļegs, Mem., SC Presidium, Chair., Commn for Environmental Protection, 1990 — ; Co-Chair., Latv. Party of the Greens, 1990 — ; b. 1951; grad. Latv. Univ., lawyer; Latv. SC Deputy. *Add.* Jēkaba 11, Rīga 226811, PDP; tel. 323 916.

BAUMANE, Ināra, Dir, Museum of the Hist. of Latvia, 1987 — ; b. 1940; grad. Latv. Univ., hist.; in the museum since 1979. *Add.* Pils lauk. 3, Rīga 226050; tel. 227 429.

BAUMANIS, Aivars, Dir, news agency *LETA*, 1990 — ; Chair., Latv. Journalists' Union, 1990 — ; b. 1937; grad. Latv. Univ., lawyer; in journalism since 1971; Head, Latv. dept of news agency APN, 1988 — 90. *Add.* Palasta 10, Rīga 226947, PDP; tel. 223 462.

BAUMANIS, Andris, violinist; b. 1951; grad. Moscow Conservatoire; prize winner, J.Sibelius comp., 1975; part. of folk music group *Daina*;

perf. in Italy, Austria, Finland, Bulgaria. *Add.* (h) Skolas 30 — 11, Rīga 226001; tel. 277 912.

BAUMANIS, Kārlis, sculptor; b. 1916; grad. Latv. Acad. of Arts; outstanding medallist; makes portraits, figurative and abstract compositions, monuments; uses granite, marble, bronze; works in Paris, Antwerp, Helsinki, Wrocław museums. *Add.* (h) Zalves 113, Rīga 226017.

BAUMAŅI, Biruta, b. 1956, and **Juris**, b. 1955; performers of ballroom dances; prize winners of European tournaments, USSR champ.; professional dancers since 1986. *Add.* Dejas asociācija, Brīvības 85, Rīga 226450; tel. 278 712.

BAUMS, Aldis, spec. in computer technol.; b. 1932; grad. Latv. Univ.; at Inst. of Electronics and Computer Sci., 1960 — ; research in microprocessor systems. *Add.* Akadēmijas 14, Rīga 226006; tel. 552 606.

BAUŠĶENIEKS, Auseklis, painter; b. 1910; grad. Latv. Acad. of Arts; satirist, genre painter, criticizes everyday occurences, societal virtues; works in private coll. in USA, Germany, Great Britain. *Add.* (h) Jaunsaules 7a — 39, Rīga 226083; tel. 453 330.

BEIRIS, Lita, prima ballerina, Nat. Opera; b. 1952; grad. Riga Choreography Sch.; bronze medal winner, Varna int. comp., 1980. *Add.* Aspazijas bulv. 3, Rīga 226251, PDP; tel. 222 823.

BEĶERS, Mārtiņš, spec. in tech. microbiol. and biotechnol.; b. 1928; grad. Latv. Acad. of Agric.; DSc. (Eng.), Prof., Acad., Latv. Acad. of Sci.; Research Dir, Inst. of Microbiol., 1962 — ; research in anabiosis of microorganisms, biosynthesis of active compounds (ferments, lysine, levan); publ. in USA, Germany. *Add.* A.Kirhenšteina 1, Rīga 226067; tel. 426 198.

BELAIČUKS, Anatolijs, Head, Civil Aviation Dept, 1990 — ; b. 1939; grad. Riga Civil Aviation Eng. Inst.; CSc. (Eng.); research in the field of constr. fatique. *Add.* Pils lauk. 4, Rīga 226050; tel. 225 560.

BELS, Alberts, writer; b. 1938; grad. Moscow Higher Courses of Scriptwriters; 9 novels, 3 short story coll.; depicts relations between individual and soc.; transl. in Russ., several European lgs; Latv. SC Deputy. *Add.* Rakstnieku savienība, Kr.Barona 12, Rīga 226011; tel. 287 629.

BELŠEVICA, Vizma, poetess; b. 1931; grad. M.Gorky Inst. of Lit. in Moscow; Hon. Mem., Latv. Acad. of Sci.; 8 poetry books, 2 short story coll., one play, film scripts; transl. in Sw., Russ., Byeloruss., Arm.; renderings from Engl. (W.Shakespeare, E.Hemingway, M.Twain, T.S.Eliot, J.K.Jerome), Russ. and other lgs. *Add.* (h) Kr.Valdemāra 145/1 — 8, Rīga 226013; tel. 361 239.

BEĻAVSKIS, Leonīds, Chief Dir, Russian Drama Theatre, 1964 — 75, 1988 — ; b. 1927; grad. Leningrad Inst. of Theatre, Music and Cinematography. *Add.* Kaļķu 16, Rīga 226050; tel. 227 336.

BĒMS, Romis, painter and art scholar; b. 1927; grad. I.Repin Inst. of Arts in Leningrad;

CSc. (Arts), Prof., Hon. Mem., Latv. Acad. of Sci.; paints water colours; exh. in European c., USA; research on Latv. art of 18th−19th cent. *Add.* Komunāru bulv. 13, Rīga 226050; tel. 332 202.

▪ **BENSONS, Valdis**, Dir, sports centre *Mūsa*, 1990−; b. 1961; grad. Riga Tech. Univ., eng. (mech.). *Add.* Gailīšu pagasts, Bauskas raj. 229307; tel. 230 32.

▪ **BERGS-BERGMANIS, Alfrēds**, Chair., Bd, Bank of the Rep. of Latvia, 1988−; b. 1929; grad. Latv. Univ., econ.; Man., USSR State Bank's Latv. Dept, 1972−88. *Add.* Kr.Valdemāra 2a, Rīga 226022; tel. 323 863.

▪ **BERKLAVS, Eduards**, politician; b. 1914; Vice-Chair., CM, 1954−56, 1958−59; groundlessly accused of nationalism, exiled to Russia, 1959−68; Chair., Latv. Nat. Indep. Movement, 1990−91; Mem., LPF CBd; Latv. SC Deputy.*Add.* (h) Brīvības 90−55, Rīga 226001; tel. 270 940.

▪ **BERTRANDS, Jānis**, Dir, Riga Asphalt-Concrete Plant, 1986−; b. 1941; grad. Riga Tech. Univ., eng. (mech.); in the plant since 1971. *Add.* Granīta 13, Rīga 226065; tel. 248 833.

▪ **BĒRZIŅA, Spodra**, Dir, Ventspils Museum of Hist. and Arts, 1984−; b. 1956; grad. Latv. Univ., hist. *Add.* Akmeņu 3, Ventspils 229910; tel. 220 31.

▪ **BĒRZIŅŠ, Andris**, Pres., Latv. Children's Fund, 1989−; b. 1955; grad. Latv. Univ., philol.; Sec., Cent. Cttee of Latv. YCL, 1985−89. *Add.* Brīvības 85, Rīga 226450; tel. 271 662.

▪ **BĒRZIŅŠ, Ansis**, animated film dir, scriptwriter; b. 1940; grad. Latv. Acad. of Arts, art hist.; at Latv. TV, 1961−88, Riga Film Studio, 1988−; main prize, TV film festival in Poland, 1978 for musical film 'A Sad Story about Carrie'; *Add.* Šmerļa 3, Rīga 226037; tel. 529 053.

▪ **BĒRZIŅŠ, Boriss**, painter; b. 1930; grad. Latv. Acad. of Arts, teacher of it; Corr. Mem., USSR Acad. of Arts; paints figurative works, still-lifes, landscapes; has peculiarly subdued manner, superb colourist and draftsman; twice-prize-winner at Bredford drawing exh. *Add.* (h) Jaunsaules 7a−59, Rīga 226083; tel. 458 284.

▪ **BĒRZIŅŠ, Ivars**, choral dir; b. 1954; grad. Latv. Acad. of Music, lecturer of it; Dir, chamber choir *Sindi putnu dārzs*, 1986−; Chief Conductor, Latv. Song Festival, 1990. *Add.* (h) Maskavas 303−4, Rīga 226063; tel. 253 559.

▪ **BĒRZIŅŠ, Pēteris**, Head, Hydrometeorological Dept, 1984−; b. 1935; grad. Latv. Acad. of Agric., eng. (hydrol.). *Add.* Kr.Valdemāra 19, Rīga 226010; tel. 332 829.

▪ **BĒRZIŅŠ, Uldis**, Chair., Latv. SDWP, 1990−; poet, translator; b. 1944; grad. Leningrad Univ.; 3 poetry coll.; renderings from Turk., Iranian, Semitic, Indo-European lgs; poems transl. in Engl., Ger., Pol., Russ. *Add.* (h) Avotu 11−32, Rīga 226011; tel. 287 783.

▪ **BĒRZIŅŠ, Viesturs**, textile artist; b. 1954; grad. Latv. Acad. of Arts; author of tapestry, applied graphic works, posters, animated cartoons; exh. in Finland, France, Denmark, Germany. *Add.* (h) M. Monētu 2−1, Rīga 226050; tel. 214 797.

▪ **BIĶIS, Juris**, Pres., wood-working assoc. *Latvijas koks*, 1990−; Dir-Gen., Veneer Plant, 1981−; b. 1940; grad. Latv. Acad. of Agric., wood technol. *Add.* tel. Rīga 221 672, 627 850, 620 857.

▪ **BIĶIS, Teofils**, pianist; b. 1952; grad. Moscow Conservatoire; teacher, Novosibirsk Conservatoire, 1975−90; Head, Dept, Latv. Acad. of Music, 1990−; first prize winner, Viana da Motta comp. in Lisbon, 1975; perf. in Czecho-Slovakia, Portugal. *Add.* (h) Merķeļa 5−5, Rīga 226050; tel. 229 161.

▪ **BILZONIS, Zigurds**, photographer; b. 1946; grad. Latv. Acad. of Music; poetic, colourful works; employs isohelium; author of portraits; 350 int. exh., 24 awards; FIAP gold medallist, 1981, 1984, gold medal in Belgium, 1979, 1990; works at French Photography Museum in Bièvres; AFIAP, 1979, EFIAP, 1988. *Add.* (h) Rostokas 16−29, Rīga 226029; tel. 205 255.

▪ **BILINSKIS, Ivars**, spec. in computer technol.; b. 1934; grad. North-Western Polytech. Inst. in Leningrad; DSc. (Eng.), Prof., Acad., Latv. Acad. of Sci., Acad.-Sec., Dept of Phys. and Tech. Sci.; at Inst. of Electronics and Computer Sci., 1962−, Research Dir, 1976−; research in randomization of signal discrete processing; 52 lic. and pat.; publ. in USA, Netherlands, Czecho-Slovakia, France, Germany, Spain. *Add.* Turgeņeva 19, Rīga 226524; tel. 528 936, 233 633.

▪ **BIMBIRULS, Alfreds**, Dir, cooperative electric equipm. firm *Jauda*, 1988−; b. 1948; grad. Riga Tech. Univ., eng. (mech.); chief mech., 1971−81. *Add.* Krustpils 119, Rīga 226065; tel. 242 632.

▪ **BINDE, Gunārs**, photographer; b. 1933; takes portraits, landscapes, nudes, still-lifes; part. in int. exh. (gold medallist in Argentina, 1965, Grand Prix in Belgium, 1967); one-man shows in Austria, Bulgaria, Czecho-Slovakia, Poland, Germany, USSR; title holder of many nat. photo assoc.; author of photography films, documentaries; AFIAP, 1975. *Add.* (h) a.k. 82, Rīga 226011; tel. 589 758.

▪ **BIRZE, Miervaldis**, writer; b. 1921; grad. Latv. Univ., physician; Hon. Mem., Latv. Acad. of Sci.; works devoted to anti-fascist theme (inmate of a German concentration camp during the WW II), laws of conscience, moral responsibility; author of humorous and satirical stories, essays, memories, dramas, comedies, journalism. *Add.* (h) Gaujas 85, Cēsis 228500; tel. 228 68.

▪ **BIŠERS, Ilmārs**, 1st Dep. Chair., CM, 1990−; b. 1930; grad. Latv. Univ., lawyer; DSc. (Law), Prof.; worked at Prosecutor's offices, headed Law Dept at CM; invest. in admin. law and state admin.; USSR People's Deputy. *Add.* Brīvības bulv. 36, Rīga 226170, PDP; tel. 285 223.

▪ **BLINKENA, Aina**, Latv. linguist; b. 1929; grad. Latv. Univ.; DSc. (Philol.), Corr. Mem., Latv. Acad. of Sci.; at Inst. of Lg. and Lit., 1953−; research on grammar, punctuation, terminology, lg. standards, Chair., Terminology Commn. *Add.* Turgeņeva 19, Rīga 226524, PDP; tel. 226 345.

BLUMBERGS, Ilmārs, stage designer; b. 1943; grad. Latv. Acad. of Arts; more than 60 sets for theatrical prod.; exh. in Prague, Novi Sada; has paintings, graphic works, book ill., posters; prize winner at numerous exh. of stage designs, posters, graphic arts; works in Hamburg, Bochum, Pori, Moscow, Chamaliéres museums. *Add.* (h) Ieriķu 66 – 241, Rīga 226059; tel. 562 576.

BLUMBERGS, Ojārs, Mem., SC Presidium, Chair., Commn on Arch., Constr., Power, Transport and Computer Sci., 1990 – ; b. 1934; grad. Latv. Univ., econ.; Mem., LPF Council; Latv. SC Deputy. *Add.* Jēkaba 11, Rīga 226811, PDP; tel. 323 354.

BLŪMS, Elmārs, physicist; b. 1936; grad. Latv. Univ.; DSc. (Eng.), Prof., Corr. Mem., Latv. Acad. of Sci.; at Inst. of Phys., 1968 – ; research in interaction of magnetic field with liquid metals, magnetic fluids, electrolytic solutions, application of magnetic colloids; several inv.; publ. in USA, Great Britain, Netherlands, Japan, Singapore. *Add.* Miera 32, Salaspils 229021; tel. 946 744.

BĻUGERS, Anatolijs, spec. in infectious diseases; b. 1926; grad. Moscow Inst. of Med. No 2; DSc. (Med.), Prof., Acad., Latv. Acad. of Sci.; research in biochem., morphology, immunology and chemotherapy of hepatic and infective diseases, congenital pigmentary hepatosis; suggested classification of jaundice disorders. *Add.* Dzirciema 16, Rīga 226007; tel. 459 467.

BOIKO, Mārtiņš, musicologist; b. 1960; grad. Latv. Acad. of Music, teacher of it; writes on musical aesthetics and ethnomusicology. *Add.* Kr.Barona 1, Rīga 226050, PDP; tel. 223 520.

BOJĀRS, Juris, law scholar; b. 1938; grad. Latv. Univ.; DSc. (Law), Prof.; Dir, Inst. of Int. Relations, Latv. Univ., 1991 – ; research in legal aspects of citizenship, human rigts, self-determination of nations, int. law; USSR People's Deputy, Latv. SC Deputy. *Add.* Raiņa bulv. 19, Rīga 226010; tel. 228 857, 210 347.

BOJĀRS, Rūdolfs, Dir, children's clothes factory *Bērnu apģērbs*, 1983 – ; b. 1945; grad. Riga Tech. Univ., eng. *Add.* Kr.Barona 59/61, Rīga 226001; tel. 279 344.

BOKTA, Jānis, Dir, Inst. for Restoration, 1981 – ; b. 1949; grad. Riga Tech. Univ., eng. (civil); in the inst. since 1973. *Add.* M. Pils 19, Rīga 226050; tel. 224 735.

BONDARENKO, Josifs, Pastor, Evangelical Christians and Baptists of Riga Church of the Cross, 1981 – ; b. 1936; expelled from Odessa Shipbuilding Inst. for his religious activity, in confinement, 1962 – 81; leader, Mission of Evangelization and Mercy of the Cross, 1988 – . *Add.* Ropažu 120, Rīga 226037; tel. 994 579.

BOSERTS, Viktors, Dir, minibus plant *RAF*, 1987 – ; b. 1948; grad. Kazan Aviation Inst., eng.; worked in Omsk motorplant. *Add.* Aviācijas 18, Jelgava 229604; tel. 202 43.

BRAMBERGA, Velta, Dir, Research Inst. of Clinical Med., 1971 – ; b. 1921; grad. Latv. Univ., oncologist; CSc. (Med.), Hon. Dr, Latv. Acad. of Sci.; lecturer, Latv. Acad. of Med.; at

the inst. since 1950; USSR leading spec. in scientific and clinical cytodiagnosis; worked out method of cytologic diagnosis of cancer; more than 130 scientific papers, 8 inv. *Add.* O.Vācieša 4, Rīga 226004; tel. 612 038.

BRANDS, Jevgeņijs, Dir, Riga Sports Palace, 1973 – ; b. 1922. *Add.* Kr.Barona 75, Rīga 226001; tel. 277 133.

BRAUNS, Uldis, film dir, cameraman; b. 1932; grad. Moscow Inst. of Cinematography; at Riga Film Studio, 1959 – ; one of Riga poetical documentary sch. founders; made also feature films. *Add.* Brīvības 85, Rīga 226250, PDP; tel. 272 715, 422 466 (h).

BRAUNS, Valdis, photographer; b. 1945; focuses on human emotional experience and natural occurences; winner of medals at numerous int. exh.; AFIAP, 1979, EFIAP, 1990. *Add.* Fotomākslinieku savienība, Mārstaļu 6, Rīga 226050; tel. 210 327.

BRAŽIS, Ivars, Dir-Gen., electrical eng. company *VEF*, 1987 – ; b. 1933; grad. Riga Tech. Univ., eng. (machine-building); in the ent. since 1951. *Add.* Brīvības 214, Rīga 226039; tel. 270 618.

BRENČS, Aloizs, Artistic Dir, detective film studio *Dekrim*, 1990 – ; film dir; b. 1929; grad. Latv. Acad. of Music, Refresher Courses in Moscow; at Riga Film Studio, 1953 – ; made documentary films (till 1965); directed criminal and detective films; TV serials 'The Long Way in the Dunes', 'The Zītars Family'. *Add.* Šmerļa 3, Rīga 226037; tel. 529 919, 520 330.

BRESIS, Vilnis Edvīns, Chair., Latv. Farmers' Assoc., 1990 – , b. 1938; grad. Latv. Acad. of Agric., agron.; Min. of Agric., 1986 – 1988; Chair., CM, 1988 – 90; USSR People's Deputy, Latv. SC Deputy. *Add.* Republikas lauk. 2, Rīga 226168; tel. 321 425.

BREŽE, Andris, graphic artist, poet; b. 1958; grad. Latv. Acad. of Arts; artist with sharpened view on social problems; makes also installations; part. in int. exh. *Add.* Mākslinieku savienība, Kr.Barona 12, Rīga 226400, PDP; tel. 626 524 (h).

BRIEDIS, Leons, E-in-C, lit. and phil. journal *Grāmata*, 1989 – ; poet, translator; b. 1949; grad. Kishinyov Univ.; 10 poetry coll. (4 for children), essays, plays, treatises on culture, phil., mythology, lit. criticism; 16 books transl. or rendered, mainly from Romance lgs. *Add.* Aspazijas bulv. 24, Rīga 226050; tel. 226 763.

BRINKIS, Juris, Dir, Swimming Pool, Riga Tech. Univ., 1989 – ; b. 1942; grad. Riga Tech. Univ., eng. (mech.); CSc. (Eng.). *Add.* Ķīpsalas 5, Rīga 226048; tel. 616 989.

BRUĢĒTĀJS, Andris, Dir-Gen., textile ent. *Rīgas audums*, 1980 – ; b. 1944; grad. Riga Tech. Univ., chem. *Add.* Salamandras 1, Rīga 226024; tel. 521 350.

BRUNOVSKIS, Aivars, Dir, wood-working plant *Vulkāns*, 1985 – ; b. 1936; grad. Latv. Acad. of Agric., wood technol. *Add.* Jelgavas 45, Kuldīga 229500; tel. 226 05.

BUDOVSKIS, Māris, Mem., SC Presidium, Chair., Mandatory and Ethics Commn, 1990 – ; b. 1939; grad. Latv. Acad. of Med., psychiatrist,

LATVIA

psychologist; CSc. (Med.), Asst Prof., Latv. Inst. of Physical Culture; Mem., LPF Council, 1989 − 1990; Latv. SC Deputy. *Add.* Jēkaba 11, Rīga 226811, PDP; tel. 326 095.

- **BUHOLTE, Agnese**, Dir, Library for Tech. Research, 1985 − ; b. 1952; grad. Latv. Univ., bibliographer. *Add.* Šķūņu 17, Rīga 226930; tel. 227 310.
- **BUKS, Arvīds**, Chair., Bd of fishery collective farm *Sarkanā bāka*, 1990 − ; b. 1936; grad. Liepāja Naval Sch.; ship capt., 1971 − 90. *Add.* Loču 1, Ventspils 229910; tel. 243 35.
- **BULAVA, Larisa**, organist; b. 1950; grad. Latv. Acad. of Music; Asst Prof.; perfected in Leipzig; perf. German Baroque, romantic and contemporary music; part. of int. music festivals; perf. in Scandinavia, Germany, Poland. *Add.* (h) Ļermontova 3 − 9, Rīga 226002; tel. 616 266.
- **BUROVS, Arnolds**, animated cartoon film dir, stage designer; b. 1915; grad. Latv. Acad. of Music; at Riga Film Studio, 1964 − ; puppet and animated cartoon studio *Dauka*, 1988 − ; pioneer of puppet films in Latvia; more than 30 films based on Latv. and world lit. classics; holder of several All-Union festival prizes. *Add.* Šmerļa 3, Rīga 226037; tel. 520 770, 371 069 (h).
- **BUTĀNS, Vitālijs**, Dir, Cēsis Brewery, 1985 − ; b. 1947; grad. Riga Tech. Univ., eng. (mech.); chief eng., 1979 − 85. *Add.* Lenču 11, Cēsis 228500; tel. 224 23.
- **BUTKĒVIČS, Marians**, ballet-dancer, Nat. Opera; b. 1963; grad. Riga Choreography Sch. *Add.* Aspazijas bulv. 3, Rīga 226251, PDP; tel. 228 402.
- **CAKULS, Jānis**, Asst Bishop, Riga Archdiocese, 1991 − ; b. 1926. *Add.* M.Pils 2a, Rīga 226047; tel. 227 226.
- **CAUNE, Anita**, Head Physician, Riga Maternity House No 1, 1985 − ; b. 1930; grad. Latv. Acad. of Med., gynaecologist; CSc. (Med.); in admin. since 1970. *Add.* Miera 45, Rīga 226013; tel. 370 355, 374 545 (h).
- **CEPĪTIS, Imants**, choral dir; b. 1933; grad. Latv. Acad. of Music; Art. Dir, Acad. State Choir *Latvija*, 1969 − ; Dir, int. prize winner female choir *Dzintars*, 1959 − 89; Chief Conductor, Latv. Song Festivals, 1965 − 85. *Add.* (h) Jerjomenko 4 − 167, Rīga 226084; tel. 586 464.
- **CEPLĪTIS, Laimdots**, Latv. linguist lexicographer; b. 1930; grad. Latv. Univ.; DSc. (Philol.); at Inst. of Lg. and Lit., 1959 − ; research in phonetics, syntax, public oratory; contrib. to dictionary compilation. *Add.* Turgeņeva 19, Rīga 226524, PDP; tel. 227 853.
- **CIELĒNS, Uldis**, spec. in silicates technol. and plasma chem.; b. 1940; grad. Riga Tech. Univ.; CSc. (Eng.); at Inst. of Inorganic Chem., 1958 − ; research in plasma chem., technol. properties and usage of ultrafine powders; publ. in Bulgaria, Czecho-Slovakia, USA. *Add.* Meistaru 10, Rīga 226934; tel. 213 752.
- **CIHOVSKA, Skaidrīte**, ceramist; b. 1937; grad. Latv. Acad. of Arts; makes mainly wheel-thrown vessels, park ceramics; exh. in Faenza, Westerwald, Gdańsk (medal of approval, 1973).

Add. (h) S.Eizenšteina 51 − 35, Rīga 226079; tel. 538 208, 612 467.

- **CIMDIŅŠ, Pēteris**, ecologist, hydrobiol.; b. 1944; grad. Latv. Univ.; DSc. (Biol.); Research Dir, Inst. of Biol., 1989 − ; research in river ecology, community structure of zooplankton in rivers and lakes; publ. in Great Britain, Belgium, Bulgaria, Czecho-Slovakia. *Add.* Miera 3, Salaspils 229021; tel. 947 348.
- **CINTIŅŠ, Oļģerts**, organist, pianist, conductor; b. 1935; grad. Latv. Acad. of Music; musician, at Latv. Philharmonic, 1959 − ; Dir, Dome Church Choir, 1989 − ; perf. J.S.Bach and romantic organ music; perf. abroad (also in Notre-Dame de Paris). *Add.* (h) L.Laicena 58 − 2, Rīga 226002; tel. 616 464.
- **ČABUŠKINS, Valentīns**, Dir-Gen., peat processing ent. *Latvijas kūdra*, 1988 − ; b. 1932; grad. Moscow Peatery Inst. *Add.* Smilšu 1, Rīga 226918; tel. 226 731.
- **ČAKLAIS, Māris**, E-in-C, art newspaper *Literatūra un Māksla*, 1987 − ; poet; b. 1940; grad. Latv. Univ.; 15 poetry (also children), essay, lit. criticism coll.; renderings of M.Cvetayeva, V.Hlebnikov, R.M.Rilke, B.Brecht, etc.; poetry rendered into Russ. (6 coll.), Engl., Ukr., Arm., Lith. *Add.* tel. Rīga 211 748, 222 453.
- **ČAKSTIŅŠ, Juris**, Dir, Bolderāja Wood-Working Plant, 1986 − ; b. 1938; grad. Latv. Acad. of Agric., wood technol. *Add.* Guberņciema 7, Rīga 226016; tel. 430 147.
- **ČEĻUBEJEVS, Viktors**, Dir, Riga Jewelry Factory, 1985 − ; b. 1941; grad. Riga Civil Aviation Eng. Inst. *Add.* Līčupes 1, Rīga 226012; tel. 272 790.
- **ČEPĀNIS, Alfrēds**, Mem., SC Presidium, Chair., Commn on Trade and Services, 1990 − ; b. 1943; worked in CP apparat; Dep. Chair., CM, 1988 − 90; USSR People's Deputy, Latv. SC Deputy. *Add.* Jēkaba 11, Rīga 226811, PDP; tel. 323 745.
- **ČERKOVSKIS, Juris**, Dir, bureau of radio design *Orbīta*, 1979 − ; b. 1941; grad. Riga Tech. Univ., eng. (machine-building). *Add.* Kr.Valdemāra 139, Rīga 226013; tel. 376 848, 373 844.
- **ČERS, Felicijans**, Dir-Gen., printing ent. *Poligrāfists*, 1986 − ; b. 1931; grad. Moscow Tech. Sch. of Printing; in printing-offices since 1961. *Add.* Kr.Valdemāra 6, Rīga 226050; tel. 325 759.
- **ČIPĒNS, Gunārs**, spec. in bioorganic chem.; b. 1933; grad. Latv. Univ.; DSc. (Chem.), Prof., Acad., Latv. Acad. of Sci; at Inst. of Organic Chem., 1958 − ; research in peptides and protein structure and molecular biol., immunoregulation; worked out theory of signature, synthetized cyclic analogues of linear peptide hormones; publ. in USA, Japan, Germany, Switzerland. *Add.* Aizkraukles 21, Rīga 226006; tel. 551 507.
- **ČOLAKJANS, Alfrēds**, Dir, vacuum coating firm *Sidrabe*, 1967 − ; b. 1930; grad. Novocherkask Polytech. Inst., eng. (mech.). *Add.* Krustpils 17, Rīga 226073; tel. 249 806.
- **DĀLE, Ansis**, surfer; b. 1967; world champ. in 'Mistral' class, 1990, champ. of Sweden and

Cuba in 'Lechner' class, 1989. *Add.* (h) Poruka 16, Rīga 226014; tel. 519 429.

- **DAMBIS Pauls**, composer; b. 1936; grad. Latv. Acad. of Music; Prof.; author of symphonic, chamber music (violin concerto, piano concerto, 6 string quartets, etc.); choir songs perf. by numerous European chamber choirs, recordings in France, Italy, Germany, Canada; chamber music perf. in USA, Canada, European c. *Add.* Kr.Barona 1, Rīga 226050; tel. 377 514 (h).

- **DANILĀNS, Igors**, geologist; b. 1928; grad. Latv. Univ.; Head, Geol. Dept, 1989 — ; DSc. (Geol.); invest. in quarternary geol., paleogeogr., geomorphology. *Add.* Stendera 2, Rīga 226014; tel. 518 757.

- **DAUDIŠS, Imants**, Sec., SC, 1990 — ; b. 1945; grad. Ivanovo Inst. of Chem. Technol.; worked in Govt and CP apparat; Latv. SC Deputy. *Add.* Jēkaba 11, Rīga 226811, PDP; tel. 322 941.

- **DAUGMALIS, Viktors**, E-in-C, social pol. newspaper *Diena*, 1990 — ; b. 1953; grad. M.Gorky Inst. of Lit. in Moscow; journalist, critic, pol. columnist. *Add.* Smilšu 1/3, Rīga 226900; tel. 210 820.

- **DEMBO, Aleksandrs**, graphic artist; b. 1931; grad. Latv. Acad. of Arts; Prof.; mainly creates easel works, figurative compositions, associative structures, miniature landscapes; applies etching, colour lithography, pastel, gouache; one-man shows in Rostock, Ruse, Prague, Bratislava, České Budějovice, Venice, New Jersey; exh. in Tokyo, Lublin, Krakow, Bredford, Friedrichstadt, Berlin, Baghdad; works in Moscow, Leningrad, Sofia, Rostock, Ruse museums. *Add.* Komunāru bulv. 13, Rīga 226050; tel. 332 202.

- **DEŅISOVA, Raisa**, anthropologist; b. 1930; grad. Moscow Univ.; DSc. (Hist.); at Inst. of Hist., 1957 — , research in anthropogenesis of ancient European people — Balts and Finns. *Add.* Turgeņeva 19, Rīga 226524, PDP; tel. 216 783.

- **DERKĒVICA, Ausma**, choral dir; b. 1929; grad. Latv. Acad. of Music; Dir, Acad. State Choir *Latvija*, 1969 — 89, int. prize winner female choir *Dzintars*, 1959 — ; concerts in European c., USA; Chief Conductor of Latv. Song Festivals. *Add.* (h) J.Kupalas 20 — 7, Rīga 226010; tel. 332 426.

- **DETLAVS, Eduards**, leader, community of Latv. ancient religion *Dievturi*, 1988 — ; b. 1919; grad. Latv. Acad. of Arts, artist (ceramics). *Add.* (h) Dārza 36a — 53, Rīga 226083; tel. 450 797.

- **DĪMANS, Sergejs**, Chair., SC minority faction *Līdztiesība* (Equality), 1990 — ; b. 1951; grad. Latv. Univ., econ.; CSc. (Econ.); research in marketing; USSR Supreme Soviet consulting econ.; Latv. SC Deputy. *Add.* Jēkaba 11, Rīga 226811, PDP; tel. 323 368.

- **DIMITERS, Juris**, poster artist, painter, stage designer; paintress Dž.Skulme's son; b. 1947; grad. Latv. Acad. of Arts; makes portraits, still-lifes with inclination to conceptualism and surrealism, ironically analytical approach in posters; prize winner at poster shows, Lahti,

1981, 1983, 1989, Colorado, 1983, drawing exh. in Nuremberg, 1982; one-man shows in Berlin, Milan, Rome, Stockholm, Pittsburgh; works in museums of Germany, USA et al. *Add.* (h) Vidrižu 4 — 23, Rīga 226006; tel. 554 574.

- **DINĒVIČS, Jānis**, Chair., LPF faction at SC, 1990 — ; b. 1948; grad. Riga Tech. Univ., eng. (power); lecturer, Riga Tech. Univ.; Dep. Chair., LPF CBd; second Asst Chair., Latv. SDWP, 1989 — 90; Latv. SC Deputy. *Add.* Jēkaba 11, Rīga 226811, PDP; tel. 213 732.

- **DOBELIS, Kārlis**, Rector, Liepāja Pedag. Inst., 1990 — ; b. 1937; grad. Liepāja Pedag. Inst.; CSc. (Phys. & Math.); lecturer since 1966. *Add.* Lielā 14, Liepāja 229700; tel. 240 11.

- **DOZORCEVS, Vladilens**, E-in-C, Russ. lit. journal *Daugava*, 1988 — ; Russ. writer; b. 1939; grad. Latv. Univ.; author of poetry, prose, plays (staged also abroad), film scripts; Mem., LPF Council; Latv. SC Deputy. *Add.* Jēkaba 11, Rīga 226811, PDP; tel. 321 015 (h).

- **DRIPE, Jānis**, architect; b. 1953; grad. Riga Tech. Univ.; Dep. Chair., Bd of Latv. Arch. Union, 1982 — ; city designer (Aizpute, Jelgava); designer of individual houses in nat. romantic style. *Add.* Torņu 11, Rīga 226800, PDP; tel. 226 701.

- **DROISKIS, Aivars**, Head, Riga Cent. Post Office, 1989 — ; b. 1951; grad. Latv. Univ., econ.; at the post office since 1975. *Add.* Brīvības bulv. 21, Rīga 226000, PDP; tel. 224 155.

- **DUBROVSKIS, Vilis**, Dir, poultry ent. *Iecava*, 1988 — ; b. 1943; grad. Riga Tech. Univ., eng. (mech.) and Latv. Acad. of Agric., agriculturist; CSc. (Eng.). *Add.* Bauskas raj., Iecava 229313; tel. 410 04.

- **DUBURS, Gunārs**, spec. in organic chem.; b. 1934; grad. Latv. Univ.; DSc. (Chem.), Prof., Corr. Mem., Latv. Acad. of Sci.; at Inst. of Organic Synthesis, 1964 — , Research Dir, 1980 — ; research in heterocyclic chem., development of radioprotectors, membranoprotectors, antioxidants, new clinical drugs with cardiovascular activity; about 400 publ., 30 pat., also abroad. *Add.* Aizkraukles 21, Rīga 226006; tel. 551 232.

- **DUCMANIS, Jānis**, Head Physician, Rep. Diagnosis Centre, 1989 — ; b. 1946; grad. Latv. Acad. of Med., surgeon; in public health admin. since 1977. *Add.* Viļakas 8, Rīga 226003; tel. 227 331.

- **DUKULIS, Leons**, Dir-Gen., beverage ent. *Latvijas balzams*, 1978 — ; b. 1928; grad. Latv. Univ., hist. *Add.* A.Čaka 160, Rīga 226012; tel. 277 231.

- **DZELDE, Ģirts**, tennis player; b. 1963; winner of several ATP tournaments, part. of Wimbledon and French champ. *Add.* Sporta komiteja, Tērbatas 4, Rīga 226011, PDP; tel. 284 206.

- **DUMPE, Inese**, prima ballerina, Nat. Opera; b. 1959; grad. Riga Choreography Sch.; silver medal winner, Varna int. comp., 1976. *Add.* Aspazijas bulv. 3, Rīga 226251, PDP; tel. 222 823.

- **DZENIS, Valdemārs**, spec. in building; b. 1931; grad. Latv. Univ.; DSc. (Eng.), Prof.; research in supersonic effects upon materials (incl. biol.) and structures; publ. abroad. **Add.** Āzenes 16, Rīga 226355, PDP; tel. 612 654.

■ **DZĒRVE-TĀLUTS, Vilnis,** Dir, Inst. of Cardiology, 1990 — ; b. 1941; grad. Latv. Acad. of Med., physiologist; CSc. (Med.); at the inst. since 1977; research in physiology and pathology of cardiovascular systems; regulation of vascular tone in healthy persons and patients with pathology of metabolism and hypertension; author of original research into pathogenesis of hyperkinetic circ.; 5 inv.; publ. in European c. **Add.** Pilsoņu 13, Rīga 226002; tel. 615 094.

■ **EBERHARDS, Guntis,** physical geographer; b. 1936; grad. Latv. Univ.; DSc. (Geogr.), Prof.; studies in nature protection, geomorphology. **Add.** Alberta 10, Rīga 226010; tel. 336 373.

■ **EINIŅŠ, Vladimirs,** Mem., SC Presidium, Chair., Commn on Maritime Affairs, 1991 — ; b. 1936; grad. Liepāja Naval Sch., Vilnius Higher CPSU Sch.; worked at fishery farm, 1978 — 90; Latv. SC Deputy. **Add.** Jēkaba 11, Rīga 226811, PDP; tel. 325 221.

■ **EISĀNS, Jānis,** Bishop, Union of the Latv. Baptist Church, 1990 — ; b. 1929; grad. Latv. Acad. of Agric.; clergyman since 1976; Ed., Latv. Baptist magazine *Labā Vēsts* (Good News), 1990 — . **Add.** Matīsa 50b, Rīga 226009; tel. 271 312.

■ **EKMANIS, Juris,** physicist; b. 1941; grad. Latv. Univ.; DSc. (Phys. & Math.); at Inst. of Phys., 1961 — 87; Research Dir, Inst. of Phys. Energetics, 1987 — ; research in radiation damages in dielectric materials and semiconductors; spectroscopy and electron microscopy of condensed matter; optical and radiation recording materials; publ. USA, Italy, Netherlands, Germany. **Add.** Aizkraukles 21, Rīga 226006; tel. 551 373, 552 011.

■ **EMSIS, Indulis,** Chair., Cttee for Environmental Protection, 1990 — ; b. 1952; grad. Latv. Univ.; CSc. (Biol.); worked at research inst. of forestry, headed lab. of nature protection; Latv. SC Deputy. **Add.** Peldu 25, Rīga 226050; tel. 223 612.

■ **ENDZIŅŠ, Aivars,** Mem., SC Presidium, Chair., Commn on Laws and Bills, 1990 — ; b. 1940; grad. Latv. Univ., lawyer; CSc. (Law), Asst Prof.; research in state legislation and theory; Mem., LDLP Cent. Cttee; Latv. SC Deputy. **Add.** Jēkaba 11, Rīga 226811, PDP; tel. 322 895.

■ **ĒRENPREISS, Jānis Oļģerds,** spec. in histochem.; b. 1929; grad. Latv. Acad. of Med.; DSc. (Med.); at Research Inst. of Clinical Med., 1959 — ; research in cancerogenesis, properties of cancer cells, application of electron microscopy in early diagnosis of cancer, differential induction of cancer cells, identification of nucleic acids by electron microscopy; publ. in USA, Belgium, Poland, Czecho-Slovakia. **Add.** O.Vācieša 4, Rīga 226004; tel. 956 916, 956 835.

■ **ERENŠTREITS, Jānis,** choral dir; b. 1942; grad. Latv. Acad. of Music; Dir, Boys' Choir of E.Dārziņš Music Sch., 1969 — ; Chief Conductor, Latv. Song Festival, 1990. **Add.** Kalnciema 10/12, Rīga 226048; tel. 612 653.

■ **ERIŅŠ, Pēteris,** wood chemist; b. 1929; grad. Latv. Univ.; DSc. (Chem.); at Inst. of Wood Chem., 1957 — ; research in structure of wood-fibre and components, its decomposition under phys. and chem. effects; publ. in USA. **Add.** Akadēmijas 27, Rīga 226006; tel. 555 906.

■ **ERRSA, Zita,** prima ballerina, Nat. Opera; b. 1952; grad. Riga Choreography Sch.; silver medal winner, Varna int. comp., 1972. **Add.** Aspazijas bulv. 3, Rīga 226251, PDP; tel. 222 823.

■ **EZERA, Regīna,** writer; b. 1930; grad. Latv. Univ.; 6 novels, 10 short story coll.; tranquil, deeply psychological, implicit descriptions prevail; vivid countryside scenes, emotionally reflected unity of man and nature; works transl. in many lgs of Europe and USSR, also filmed; active lit. critic; Mem., Bd of USSR Writers' Union. **Add.** (h) Brieži, a.k. 5, Ķegums, Ogres raj. 228320.

■ **FEIFERIS, Inesis,** Dir, Research Inst. of Econ. and Agroind. Complex, 1988 — ; b. 1949; grad. Riga Tech. Univ.; research in econ. of agric. policy and development, producers cooperation, property relations, ways of econ. management. **Add.** Struktoru 14, Rīga 226039; tel. 552 909.

■ **FELDBERGS, Ojārs,** sculptor; b. 1947; grad. Latv. Acad. of Arts; works in monumental, memorial, decorative, small-form sculpture; uses granite, marble, wood, concrete; exh. in Germany, Canada; works in Moscow, Düsseldorf museums. **Add.** T.Zaļkalna 45a, Rīga 226058; tel. 622 335.

■ **FEOKTISTOVS, Vasilijs,** Dir-Gen., furniture ent. *Rīga,* 1974 — ; b. 1932; grad. Moscow Technol. Inst., econ.; in furniture ind. since 1964. **Add.** Ganību dambis 30a, Rīga 226005; tel. 381 828.

■ **FETISOVS, Aleksandrs,** Dir, factory of decorative haberdashery *Lielupe,* 1988 — ; b. 1952; grad. Latv. Acad. of Agric., eng. (mech.). **Add.** Uzvaras 69, Jelgava 229600; tel. 272 74.

■ **FLEIJA, Aija,** Dir, War Museum, 1990 — ; b. 1944; grad. Latv. Univ.; in the system of museums since 1969. **Add.** Smilšu 20, Rīga 226900; tel. 228 147.

■ **FOGELIS, Einars,** Dir, bobsleigh and sledging sports centre *Sigulda,* 1990 — ; b. 1960; grad. Riga Tech. Univ., eng. (power); in the centre since 1983. **Add.** Šveices 13, Sigulda 229050; tel. 973 813.

■ **FOKINS, Valerijs,** Dir, leathern goods ent. *Somdaris,* 1986 — ; b. 1940; grad. Kostrom Technol. Inst., eng. (technol.). **Add.** Brīvības 109, Rīga 226483, PDP; tel. 370 058.

■ **FRANCKEVIČA, Ligita,** sculptress; b. 1947; grad. Latv. Acad. of Arts; brilliant creator of small forms; author of medals, plaques; employs bronze; part. of int. exh. and symposiums. **Add.** Mākslinieku savienība, Kr.Barona 12, Rīga 226400, PDP; tel. 287 432.

■ **FRANKS, Hercs,** documentary film dir and scriptwriter; b. 1926; grad. Legal Inst.; worked as journalist; at Riga Film Studio, 1965 — ; main theme — fate of the man on sociohist. background; prize for film 'Life' in Oberhausen, 1973, 3 main awards for film 'Supreme Justice' in Nyon, 1987, award for film 'Once There Lived

Seven Simeons' in Leipzig, 1990. *Add.* Šmerļa 3, Rīga 226037; tel. 529 805.

▪ **FREIBERGS, Andris,** Chief Artist, Youth Theatre, 1973 – ; stage designer; b. 1938; grad. Latv. Acad. of Arts, lecturer of it; designed more than 100 sets for theatrical prod. in Latvia, Krakow, Berlin, Caracas; exh. in European c., Japan, recipient of int. awards, one-man show in Krakow. *Add.* Lāčplēša 37, Rīga 226716, PDP; tel. 282 945.

▪ **FREIMANIS, Jānis,** spec. in organic chem.; b. 1935; grad. Latv. Univ.; DSc. (Chem.), Prof., Corr. Mem., Latv. Acad. of Sci.; at Inst. of Organic Synthesis, 1958 – ; research in chem. of prostaglandin and similar bioregulators, amino acid compounds; more than 500 research papers, 29 lic.; Mem., LPF CBd; Latv. SC Deputy. *Add.* Aizkraukles 21, Rīga 226006; tel. 555 996, 555 919.

▪ **FREIVALDS, Rūsiņš Mārtiņš,** mathematician; b. 1942; grad. Latv. Univ.; DSc. (Phys. & Math.); at Inst. of Math. and Computer Sci., 1970 – , Research Dir, 1985 – ; studies algorithm theory, numerical methods theory. *Add.* Raiņa bulv. 29, Rīga 226050; tel. 226 997.

▪ **GAGAINE-SILTUMA, Astrīda,** leatherwork artist; b. 1945; grad. Tallinn Art Univ.; makes book bindings, boxes, wall decors, seat coverings, ornamental forms, figurative compositions, landscapes, fancy goods; exh. in Germany, Czecho-Slovakia, Poland, Denmark, Sweden, Jordan, USA, Canada. *Add.* (h) Artilērijas 44 – 3, Rīga 226009; tel. 292 443.

▪ **GAGAINIS, Juris,** metalwork artist; b. 1944; grad. Tallinn Art Univ.; teacher, Latv. Acad. of Arts; gem-stone jewelry, desing of functional ware, lighting fixtures, emblem designs; silver medal, int. jewelry exh., Jablonec, 1970, Grand Prix, enamel symposium, Ketchkemet, 1989; exh. in Budapest, Helsinki et al. *Add.* (h) Vērdiņu 12, Rīga 226055; tel. 469 456.

▪ **GAILIS, Māris,** Dir-Gen., External Econ. Affairs Dept, 1990 – ; b. 1951; grad. Riga Tech. Univ., eng. (mech.). *Add.* Brīvības bulv. 36, Rīga 226170, PDP; tel. 288 656.

▪ **GAILĪTIS, Kārlis,** Archbishop, Consistory of Latv. Evangelical Lutheran Church, 1989 – ; b. 1936; grad. Latv. Acad. of Agric., Theol. Sem.; ThM; clergyman since 1976. *Add.* Lāčplēša 4 – 4, Rīga 226010; tel. 334 362.

▪ **GAILĪTIS, Māris,** Dir, vegetable growing ent. *Rīga,* 1977 – ; b. 1937; grad. Moscow Acad. of Agric., agron.; CSc. (Agric.). *Add.* Biķernieku 121, Ulbroka 229030; tel. 551 402.

▪ **GALANTE, Inese,** singer (soprano); b. 1954; grad. Latv. Acad. of Music; soloist, Nat. Opera, 1982 – ; first prize winner, All-Union opera singers contest, 1986; perf. in European c., Canada. *Add.* (h) Ganību 4/6 – 11a, Rīga 226045; tel. 334 333.

▪ **GARDA, Aivars,** Dir-Gen., ecological publrs *Vieda,* 1989 – ; b. 1955; grad. Latv. Univ., econ. *Add.* Odesas 17, Rīga 226018; tel. 223 497.

▪ **GARKLĀVA, Ināra,** graphic artist; b. 1957; grad. Latv. Acad. of Arts, teacher of it; author of

easel-drawings (etchings) and book ill.; excels in metaphoric, allegoric, symbolic representation of the meaning, imaginative concepts close to Latv. folklore; exquisite sense of humour in children's book ill. *Add.* (h) VSKB, 6 – 75, Rīga 226076; tel. 620 043.

▪ **GASPARENOKS, Jānis,** Dir-Gen., ceramics plant *Latvijas keramika,* 1984 – ; b. 1949; grad. Riga Tech. Univ., eng. (mech.). *Add.* Rīgas 67, Jelgava 229600; tel. 228 68.

▪ **GAUDIŅŠ, Ernests,** otorhinolaryngologist; b. 1922; grad. Latv. Univ.; DSc. (Med.), Prof.; research in otology, hearing rehabilitation, pathogenesis of otorhinolaryngological diseases (metabolic and immunological disorders); publ. in Great Britain, Germany, Sweden, Italy, USA. *Add.* Pilsoņu 13, Rīga 226002; tel. 615 148.

▪ **GAVARS, Jānis,** Dir, Riga Motor Depot, 1989 – ; b. 1953; grad. Latv. Acad. of Agric., eng. (mech.). *Add.* Bukaišu 3, Rīga 226004; tel. 620 323.

▪ **GAVRILOVS, Vitālijs,** Dir-Gen., beer brewing ent. *Aldaris,* 1985 – ; b. 1947; grad. Riga Tech. Univ., econ. *Add.* Tvaika 44, Rīga 226005; tel. 391 652.

▪ **GEIDE, Viktors,** Chair., Union of Seventh Day Adventists in Latvia, 1989 – ; b. 1933; preacher since 1980. *Add.* J.Kupalas 9 – 1, Rīga 226010; tel. 321 050.

▪ **GERAŠČENKOVS, Pjotrs,** Dir, glass plant *Sarkandaugava,* 1990 – ; b. 1934; grad. All-Union Building Inst. in Moscow, eng. (mech.). *Add.* Sliežu 6, Rīga 226005; tel. 392 419.

▪ **GERČIKOVS, Iļja,** Dir-Gen., perfumery and cosmetics ent. *Dzintars,* 1981 – ; b. 1938; grad. Voronez Technol. Inst., eng. (mech.); CSc. (Econ.); Dir, 1974 – 81. *Add.* Mālu 30, Rīga 226058; tel. 621 625.

▪ **GIMELFARBS, Anatolijs,** Dir, nonmetal material processing ent. *Granīts,* 1986 – ; b. 1940; grad. Novocherkask Polytech. Inst., eng. (mining). *Add.* Miera 75/77, Rīga 226013; tel. 371 104.

▪ **GIRSKIS, Artūrs,** violinist; b. 1968; student, London Royal Music Acad.; prize winner, A. Kurchi Contest in Naples, 1988; perf. in Germany, South America. *Add.* (h) Dzelzavas 11 – 35, Rīga 226084; tel. 566 702.

▪ **GLĀZUPS, Rihards,** Chief Conductor, Nat. Opera, 1967 – 76, 1990 – ; b. 1920; grad. Latv. Acad. of Music; composer (ballet, organ music, choir, solo songs). *Add.* Aspazijas bulv. 3, Rīga 226261, PDP; tel. 229 391.

▪ **GLEIZDS, Jānis,** photographer; b. 1924; main themes – sports, still-life, nude; 600 exh.; more than 120 prizes; one-man shows in Luxemburg, Germany, Spain; works at French Photography Museum in Bièvres; AFIAP, 1979. *Add.* (h) P.Dauges 9 – 5, Rīga 226079; tel. 539 248.

▪ **GLŪDIŅŠ, Gunārs,** Chair., Bd of Latv. Designers' Union, 1988 – ; b. 1938; grad. Latv. Acad. of Arts, designer; Head, designers office of factory *Sarkanā zvaigzne;* design of motorcycles, mopeds, telephone apparatuses, radio sets; exh. in Belgium, Germany, Finland, Poland,

India. **Add.** Biķernieku 19, Rīga 226039; tel. 552 220.

GODMANIS, Ivars, Chair., CM of the Rep. of Latvia, 1990 − ; b. 1951; grad. Latv. Univ., phys.; CSc. (Phys. & Math.); lecturer, Latv. Univ., 1986 − 90; Dep. Chair., LPF CBd, 1989 − 90; Latv. SC Deputy. **Add.** Brīvības bulv. 36, Rīga 226170, PDP; tel. 332 232.

GONČAROVS, Aleksandrs, Dir-Gen., motor vehicles repair ent. *Ceļu autotehniķis,* 1988 − ; b. 1936; grad. Latv. Acad. of Agric., eng. (mech.). **Add.** Margrietas 7, Rīga 226046; tel. 615 052.

GORBAŅOVS, Genadijs, ballet premier, Nat. Opera; b. 1950; grad. Riga Choreography Sch.; silver medal winner, Varna int. comp., 1972. **Add.** Aspazijas bulv. 3, Rīga 226251, PDP; tel. 222 823.

GORBUNOVS, Anatolijs, Chair., SC of the Rep. of Latvia, 1990 − ; b. 1942; grad. Riga Tech. Univ., eng. (civil); worked in CP apparat, Sec., Latv. CP Cent. Cttee, 1985 − 88; Chair., SC Presidium, 1988 − 90; USSR People's Deputy, Latv. SC Deputy. **Add.** Jēkaba 11, Rīga 226811, PDP; tel. 322 938.

GOZĪTIS, Elmārs, Dir, chocolate confectionery factory *Laima,* 1987 − ; b. 1932; grad. Riga Tech. Univ., Polytech. Inst. in the Urals. **Add.** Miera 22, Rīga 226486; tel. 379 690.

GRĀMATIŅŠ, Āris, Dir, wood-working ent. *Baltija,* 1981 − ; b. 1943; grad. Latv. Acad. of Agric., wood technol. **Add.** Jaunā 52/54, Liepāja 229700; tel. 239 62, 244 43.

GRASIS, Andrejs, Dir-Gen., poultry and fishery assoc. *Latvijas putnkopība un zivkopība,* 1972 − ; b. 1935; grad. Latv. Acad. of Agric., agriculturist. **Add.** Republikas lauk. 2, Rīga 226168; tel. 321 939.

GRĀVĪTIS, Oļģerts, composer, musicologist; b. 1926; grad. Latv. Acad. of Music; CSc. (Arts), Prof.; USSR Composers' Union representative of Int. Musicologists Symposium Org., Berlin, 1984 − ; 3 operas, symphonic and vocal compositions, vocal chamber music; 8 books; active proponent of music. **Add.** Kr. Barona 1, Rīga 226050, PDP; tel. 223 520.

GRĀVĪTIS, Uldis, Rector, Latv. Inst. of Physical Culture, 1988 − ; b. 1942; grad. Latv. Inst. of Physical Culture; CSc. (Pedag.); rower, basketball player and coach; worked out practicing programmes for tall players; Vice-Rector, 1981 − 88. **Add.** Brīvības 333, Rīga 226037; tel. 520 595.

GRĒNS, Elmārs, Dir, Inst. of Molecular Biol., 1990 − ; spec. in organic chem. and molecular biol.; b. 1935; grad. Latv. Univ.; DSc. (Chem.), Prof., Acad., Latv. Acad. of Sci., Corr. Mem., USSR Acad. of Sci.; at Inst. of Organic Synthesis, 1958 − 90; founder and Pres., Latv. Scientists' Union, 1988 − ; research in molecular biol., cell eng. methods, precise biotechnol.; foreign pat. and publ. in Great Britain, France, Sweden, USA. **Add.** Krustpils 53, Rīga 226065; tel. 245 566.

GRIMZE, Valdis, Dir-Gen., applied arts and souvenirs mfrs assoc. *Daiļrade,* 1985 − ; b. 1946; grad. Riga Tech. Univ., eng. **Add.**

Čiekurkalna 1. garā līnija 11, Rīga 226026; tel. 551 740.

GRĪVIŅŠ, Vilnis, Dir, Riga Recreation Parks Assoc., 1988 − ; b. 1934; grad. Latv. Univ., eng. (mech.). **Add.** Meža prosp. 54, Rīga 226014; tel. 557 490.

GROMOVS, Valerijs, wood chem.; b. 1923; grad. Latv. Univ.; DSc. (Eng.), Prof., Corr. Mem., Latv. Acad. of Sci.; at Inst. of Wood Chem., 1952 − 86; research in submicroscopic structure of wood, delignification problems in original pulp prod. processes; pat. in USA, Canada, Finland; publ. in China, Czecho-Slovakia, Romania. **Add.** Akadēmijas 27, Rīga 226006; tel. 551 559.

GRONSKIS, Imants, Rector, Latv. Acad. of Agric., 1985 − ; b. 1932; grad. Latv. Acad. of Agric., spec. in horticulture; CSc. (Agric.), Prof., Hon. Dr, Latv. Acad. of Sci.; research in fruit tree plant-breeding, virus-free material for planting, cultivation of cherries, plums, raspberries, cranberries. **Add.** Lielā 2, Jelgava 229600; tel. 225 84.

GROSS, Eduards, Chair., Bd of Latv. Savings Bank, 1987 − ; b. 1936; grad. Vilnius Higher CPSU Sch. **Add.** Palasta 1, Rīga 226929, PDP; tel. 222 871.

GULBIS, Harijs, playwright; b. 1926; grad. Latv. Univ.; 12 plays (all staged), 2 novels; focuses on social problems, human relations; novels transl. in Czech, Pol., Ger., Russ., Ukr. **Add.** (h) Vesetas 8 − 1, Rīga 226013; tel. 371 102.

GUNDARS, Māris, architect, interior designer; b. 1936; grad. Riga Tech. Univ.; Chair., Bd of Latv. Art Fund, 1987 − ; designs fashionable interiors and private residences; author of interior designs for hotel *Rīdzene,* sanatoriums in Jūrmala. **Add.** (h) Jāņasēta 5 − 3, Rīga 226050; tel. 212 547.

GUNDARS, Uldis, Min. of Social Welfare, 1990 − ; b. 1936; grad. Riga Tech. Univ., eng. (civil); occupied leading posts at constr. and building materials ent.; 1st Dep. Min., 1986 − 1990. **Add.** E.Veidenbauma 25, Rīga 226305, PDP; tel. 286 720.

ĢĒĢERS, Dainis, Min. of Agric., 1988 − ; b. 1946; grad. Riga Tech. Univ., eng. (mech.); CSc. (Eng.); worked as agric. eng. **Add.** Republikas lauk. 2, Rīga 226168, PDP; tel. 325 107.

ĢELZIS, Kristaps, graphic artist, son of M.Ģelzis; b. 1962; grad. Latv. Acad. of Arts; author of easel-drawings, book ill., posters, record design, installations, part. in various actions; exh. in Germany, Norway. **Add.** (h) E.Veidenbauma 41/43 − 13, Rīga 226001; tel. 271 306.

ĢELZIS, Modris, architect; b. 1929; grad. Latv. Univ.; at urban design inst. *Pilsētprojekts,* 1955 − , Head, Design Office, 1990 − ; consciously works in the mainstream of contemporary arch.; designed mainly public buildings (Children's Hospital, Aeroflot Agency, Sea Passenger Terminal in Riga, Dzintari Concert-Hall in Jūrmala). **Add.** Kr.Valdemāra 38, Rīga 226306, PDP; tel. 271 508.

- **ĢIPSLIS, Aivars,** E-in-C, popular chess magazine *Šahs*, 1970 – ; b. 1937; int. grand master; European champ., 1970, world champ. among students, 1957 – 58; world champ. N.Gaprindashvili's coach, 1966 – 78. *Add.* Dzirnavu 59, Rīga 226050; tel. 284 266.

- **HARADŽANJANS, Rafi,** pianist, musicologist; b. 1944; grad. Leningrad Conservatoire; CSc. (Arts); teacher, Latv. Acad. of Music; piano duo together with Nora Novika (founders of this genre in Latvia), 1968 – ; perf. old music, classical compositions, music by Baltic composers, arranged compositions for piano duos; 12 records, 12 coll. of piano duets publ. in Leningrad; perf. abroad. *Add.* (h) Tērbatas 6/8 – 28a, Rīga 226011; tel. 284 543.

- **HAUKS, Kārlis,** Dir, Chess and Draughts Club, 1985 – ; b. 1942; grad. Latv. Inst. of Physical Culture; senior coach, selected track-and-field team of Latvia, 1968 – 83. *Add.* Basteja bulv. 16, Rīga 226050; tel. 213 313.

- **HAUSMANIS, Viktors,** Dir, Inst. of Lg. and Lit., 1984 – ; lit. and drama critic; b. 1931; grad. pedag. inst.; DSc. (Philol.), Prof., Acad., Latv. Acad. of Sci.; in the inst. since 1957; 14 monographs on Latv. playwrights, actors, stage dir; publ. in USA, Sweden, Finland. *Add.* Turgeņeva 19, Rīga 226524, PDP; tel. 212 872.

- **HEIFECS, Jevgeņijs,** spec. in tech. operation of aircraft radio-receiving equipm.; b. 1938; grad. Riga Civil Aviation Eng. Inst.; DSc. (Eng.), Prof.; research in electromagnetic interaction of radioelectric equipm., radio-frequency spectrum; pat. in Great Britain, Germany. *Add.* Lomonosova 1, Rīga 226019; tel. 240 264.

- **HEIMRĀTS, Rūdolfs,** textile artist; b. 1926; grad. Latv. Acad. of Arts; Prof., Full Mem., USSR Acad. of Arts; makes tapestry, batik; also ceramist; silver medallist in Erfurt, 1978, prize in Lodz, 1981, silver medal, USSR Acad. of Arts; 1971. *Add.* Komunāru bulv. 13, Rīga 226050; tel. 332 202.

- **HEINRIHSONE, Helena,** paintress; b. 1948; grad. Latv. Acad. of Arts; bold, provocative colours and lines give orderly structure to her works where emotions and moods dominate in most unusual ways; exh. in Finland, Germany, Austria, France, USA; works in Tretyakov Gallery, private coll. in France, Germany, USA. *Add.* (h) E.Veidenbauma 7 – 10, Rīga 226050; tel. 222 625.

- **HEINRIHSONS, Ivars,** painter; b. 1945; grad. Latv. Acad. of Arts, teacher of it; poetical, deeply emotional manner, visually balanced paintings strike with polarity; favours all shades of gray; exh. in France, Germany, Finland, Bulgaria, Yugoslavia, USA, Canada; works in Tretyakov Gallery, private coll. in France, Germany, USA, USSR. *Add.* (h) E.Veidenbauma 7 – 10, Rīga 226050; tel. 222 625.

- **HERCBERGA, Tīna,** Artistic Dir, Puppet Theatre, 1966 – 73, 1990 – ; b. 1921; grad. Latv. Acad. of Music; stage dir, Puppet Theatre, 1953 – ; stage prod. in Leningrad, Gdańsk. *Add.* Kr.Barona 16/18, Rīga 226011; tel. 285 355.

- **HODAKOVSKIS, Vladimirs,** Rector, Riga Civil Aviation Eng. Inst., 1988 – ; b. 1940; grad. Riga Civil Aviation Eng. Inst., spec. in radioelectronics; DSc. (Eng.), Prof.; research in radionavigation, perf. stability of radioequipm.; Latv. SC Deputy. *Add.* Lomonosova 1, Rīga 226019; tel. 242 197.

- **HOLŠTEINS, Žanis,** Chair., Bd of agrofirm *Lāčplēsis*, 1979 – ; b. 1926; grad. Latv. Acad. of Agric., agron. *Add.* Lielvārde, Ogres raj. 228321; tel. 544 05.

- **IEVIŅŠ, Imants,** Dir, forestry research inst. *Silava*, 1964 – ; b. 1928; grad. Latv. Acad. of Agric.; DSc. (Eng.), Prof.; research in complex mechanization problems of forestry, rational use of the obtained biomass; several inv. *Add.* Rīgas 111, Salaspils 229021; tel. 942 555.

- **IKAUNIEKS, Māris,** Dir-Gen., agrofirm *Uzvara*, 1990 – ; Pres., Assoc. of Sugar Beet Growers, 1990 – ; b. 1948; grad. Latv. Acad. of Agric., eng. (hydrotechnol.). *Add.* Uzvara, Bauskas raj. 229307; tel. 562 85.

- **ILTNERE, Ieva,** paintress; b. 1957; grad. Latv. Acad. of Arts; paints contemporary characters, attempts to find harmony of epochal collisions and her inner self; poetical, symbolic, allegoric works executed in serene pastel shades; exh. in Germany, Sweden, USA et al. *Add.* (h) Kaļķu 24 – 9, Rīga 226050; tel. 216 926.

- **ILUSS, Jānis,** Pres., sports club for invalids *Optimists*, 1985 – ; b. 1942. *Add.* Stabu 60, Rīga 226001; tel. 274 873, 270 528.

- **INDĀNS, Juris,** Dir, Open-Air Museum of Ethnography, 1989 – ; b. 1948; grad. Latv. Univ., hist.; in the museum since 1970. *Add.* Brīvības 440, Rīga 226056; tel. 994 178.

- **INDRĀNE, Ilze,** writer; b. 1927; author of 5 novels, 2 coll. of stories, miniatures, 3 plays, 10 children's books; describes Latv. countryside, peasants' illusions and their defeat in the years of Soviet rule, youth problems; transl. in Russ., Ukr., Est., Lith., Czech. *Add.* (h) Ērgļu 7 – 19, Madona 229220; tel. 237 19.

- **INKULIS, Andrejs,** Chair., Riga City Exec. Cttee of People's Deputies Council, 1990 – ; b. 1941; grad. Moscow Inst. of Nat. Econ., eng. (technol.). *Add.* Kr.Valdemāra 3, Rīga 226162, PDP; tel. 320 530.

- **IRBE, Artūrs,** hockey player; b. 1967; goal-keeper, Riga *Dinamo* team, 1987 – 91; world champ., 1989, 1990, European champ. 1989; world champ. best goal-keeper, 1990; USA 'Minnesota North Stars' player, 1991 – .

- **ĪVĀNS, Dainis,** 1st Dep. Chair., SC, 1990 – ; b. 1955; grad. Latv. Univ., philol.; worked as teacher, journalist, publicist; Chair., LPF CBd, 1988 – 90; USSR People's Deputy, Latv. SC Deputy. *Add.* Jēkaba 11, Rīga 226811, PDP; tel. 323 142.

- **IVANOVS, Jevgeņijs,** Dir-Gen., motor vehicles service ent. *Latvijas automotoserviss*, 1984 – ; b. 1942; grad. Moscow Automech. Inst., eng. (mech.). *Add.* Vagonu 35, Rīga 226009; tel. 599 454.

- **IVBULIS, Viktors,** lit. scholar; b. 1933; grad. Latv. Univ.; DSc. (Philol.), Prof.; research in Bengal lit., world lit. contacts. **Add.** Visvalža 4a, Rīga 226011; tel. 229 034.

- **IZJUMOVS, Samsons,** singer (baritone); b. 1950; grad. Latv. Acad. of Music; soloist, Nat. Opera, 1978 – ; winner, All-Union singers contest, 1979; perf. W-European and Russ. classical music in Italy, Finland, Germany. **Add.** (h) A.Čaka 33 – 4, Rīga 226011; tel. 285 243.

- **JAKOVĻEVS, Ģirts,** Chair., Bd of Latv. Theatre People's Union, 1987 – ; actor; b. 1940; grad. Latv. Acad. of Music; in Nat. Theatre since 1960; film actor. **Add.** Kronvalda bulv. 2, Rīga 226047; tel. 322 828.

- **JAKUBAITIS, Eduards,** Dir, Inst. of Electronics and Computer Sci., 1960 – ; Vice-Pres., Latv. Acad. of Sci.; spec. in cybernetics; b. 1924; grad. Rostov Inst. of Railway Transport; DSc. (Eng.), Acad., Latv. Acad. of Sci.; research in computer technol., supersensitive equipm., tech. cybernetics; publ. in USA, China, France, Czecho-Slovakia, Poland. **Add.** Akadēmijas 14, Rīga 226005; tel. 554 200.

- **JANOVS, Jānis,** Dir, Inst. of Econ., 1990 – ; b. 1936; grad. Latv. Univ., econ.; DSc. (Econ.); research on development of Latv. nat. econ. **Add.** Turgeņeva 19, Rīga 226524, PDP; tel. 222 830.

- **JANOVSKIS, Jānis,** Min. of Transport, 1987 – ; b. 1950; grad. Latv. Acad. of Agric., eng. (mech.); worked at research inst., motor transport ent. **Add.** Brīvības 58, Rīga 226806, PDP; tel. 226 922.

- **JANSONS, Haralds,** surgeon, children's orthopaedist, spec. in biomech.; b. 1934; grad. Latv. Acad. of Med.; DSc. (Med.), Prof.; at Inst. of Traumatology and Orthopaedics, 1959 – , Research Dir, 1978 – ; research in biomech. examination methods, artificial bones and joints, composite fixation materials, electrical stimulation methods; pat. and publ. in European c., USA, Japan; Mem., New York Acad. of Sci. **Add.** Duntes 12/22, Rīga 226005; tel. 393 000, 392 610.

- **JANSONS, Viesturs,** ballet premier, Nat. Opera; b. 1958; grad. Riga Choreography Sch. **Add.** Aspazijas bulv. 3, Rīga 226251, PDP; tel. 222 823.

- **JAUNZEMS, Pēteris,** photographer; b. 1938; makes salon photos, portraits, nude, landscapes; 600 int. exh., 11-times FIAP medallist, numerous other medal winner; works in museums abroad; founder and leader of Liepāja Photo Studio; AFIAP, 1988. **Add.** (h) Sakņu 18 – 16, Liepāja, 229700; tel. 415 27, 233 35.

- **JAUTRUMS, Andris,** Dir-Gen., communications assoc. *Latvijas sakarnieks,* 1988 – ; b. 1944; grad. Ilmenava Tech. Higher Sch., information processing expert. **Add.** Dzirnavu 16, Rīga 226010; tel. 332 622.

- **JEGOROVS, Nikolajs,**Dir, photo and pawnbroker's service ent. *Rīgas foto,* 1982 – ; b. 1931; grad. Inst. of Light Ind. in Moscow. **Add.** Kr.Valdemāra 36, Rīga 226300, PDP; tel. 270 556.

- **JEĻINSKIS, Aleksejs,** Dir, Riga Porcelain Factory, 1988 – ; b. 1944; grad. Kaunas Polytech. Inst., econ.; Dep. Min. of Light Ind.,

1983 – 88. **Add.** Maskavas 257, Rīga 226019; tel. 145 003.

- **JEMEĻJANOVS, Aleksandrs,** Dir-Gen., animal husbandry and veterinary research assoc. *Sigra,* 1986 – ; Dir, Animal Husbandry and Veterinary Research Inst., 1985 – ; b. 1938; grad. Latv. Acad. of Agric., veterinarian; DSc. (Agric.). **Add.** Institūta 1, Sigulda 229050; tel. 976 307.

- **JOHANSONS, Edmunds,** Chair., State Security Cttee, 1990 – ; b. 1936; grad. Vilnius Higher CPSU Sch., lawyer; Army Major-Gen.; in state security bodies since 1970. **Add.** Brīvības 61, Rīga 226001; tel. 270 779.

- **JUGĀNS, Ventis,** Head, ind. desing and constr. assoc. *LATESA,* 1987 – ; b. 1937; grad. Latv. Acad. of Agric., eng. (mech.). **Add.** Kr.Valdemāra 31, Rīga 226010; tel. 321 560.

- **JUNDZIS, Tālavs,** Mem., SC Presidium, Chair., Commn on Defence and Interior, 1990 – ; b. 1951; grad. Latv. Univ., lawyer; CSc. (Law); at Latv. Prosecutor's Office, 1976 – 88; Latv. SC Deputy. **Add.** Jēkaba 11, Rīga 226811, PDP; tel. 325 924.

- **JURISONS, Egils,** Ed., popular sports newspaper *Sports,* 1991 – ; b. 1947; grad. Latv. Univ., philol. **Add.** tel. Rīga 299 511.

- **JURKĀNS, Jānis,** Foreign Min., 1990 – ; b. 1946; grad. Latv. Univ., philol.; worked as teacher; Co-Chair., LPF External Affairs Division, 1989 – 90. **Add.** L.Pils 11, Rīga 226800, PDP; tel. 220 079.

- **KALĒJS, Aivars,** organist, composer; b. 1951; grad. Latv. Acad. of Music; perf. in Riga Dome Cathedral, 1977 – ; compositions for organ, piano, chamber groups, choir; part. in organ music festivals in Belgium, Italy, Germany, Poland, USA; perf. in Scandinavia, France; 10 solo records; publ. on Latv. organ hist. **Add.** (h) Vaidavas 13 – 72, Rīga 226084; tel. 595 416.

- **KALNBĒRZS, Viktors,** Dir, Inst. of Traumatology and Orthopaedics, 1959 – ; orthopaedic surgeon; b. 1928; grad. Latv. Acad. of Med.; DSc. (Med.), Prof., Acad., USSR Acad. of Med. Sci.; research in external fixations in traumatology and orthopaedics, endoprosthetics of major joints, plastic surgery (phalloendoprosthetics, mammaplasty); lic. and publ. in European c., USA, Japan; Full Mem., SICOT, holder of Brno Univ. gold medal, J.E.Purkyně hon. medal; Latv. SC Deputy. **Add.** Duntes 12/22, Rīga 226005; tel. 392 348.

- **KALNCIEMA, Aina,** pianist, harpsichord player; b. 1944; grad. Leningrad Conservatoire, mastered harpsichord playing at Moscow Conservatoire, perfected in Switzerland, Germany, Poland, Czecho-Slovakia; soloist, at Latv. Philharmonic, 1981 – ; repertoire incl. 16th – 18th cent. and contemporary music; perf. abroad. **Add.** (h) Teikas lauk. 8 – 3, Rīga 226006; tel. 536 538.

- **KALNCIEMA, Vita,** organist; b. 1959; grad. Latv. Acad. of Music; winner, All-Union organist comp., prize winner, int. comp. in Poland, 1989; part. of comp. in Sweden, Germany, Bulgaria. **Add.** (h) Lokomotīves 78 – 68, Rīga 226065; tel. 279 848.

- **KALNCIEMS, Agris,** water motorsportsman; b. 1965; acknowledged best in USSR, 1990; first prize winner in scooter comp. in West Germany and Poland's Grand Prix, 5th place in world champ., USSR champ., 1988. **Add.** Sporta komiteja, Tērbatas 4, Rīga 226011, PDP; tel. 284 206.
- **KALNIŅŠ, Arnis,** Dep. Chair., CM, 1989 — ; b. 1935; grad. Latv. Univ., econ.; DSc. (Econ.), Acad., Latv. Acad. of Sci.; research in distribution of labour force in agric., wages, income, prices, cooperative farming, agric. prod. complex; USSR People's Deputy. **Add.** Brīvības bulv. 36, Rīga 226170, PDP; tel. 282 828.
- **KALNIŅŠ, Imants,** composer; b. 1941; grad. Latv. Acad. of Music; 3 operas (incl. rock opera), 5 symphonies, concertos, oratorios, musicals, choir music, pop, theatrical and cinema music; symphonies perf. in USA, Germany, Greece, Finland, Czecho-Slovakia; Chair., Latv. Music Society, 1987 — ; Mem., LPF Council; Latv. SC Deputy. **Add.** Jēkaba 11, Rīga 226811, PDP; tel. 278 712.
- **KALNIŅŠ, Mārtiņš,** chemist, spec. in polymer technol.; b. 1939; grad. Riga Tech. Univ.; DSc. (Eng.), Prof.; research in polymer composite materials, their phys. and mech. properties; publ. abroad. **Add.** Āzenes 14/24, Rīga 226355, PDP; tel. 616 918.
- **KALNIŅŠ, Rolands,** Head, *Studija-3*, 1990 — ; film dir; b. 1922; at Riga Film Studio, 1947 — ; depicted hist. destiny of Latv. people through deeply personal position and attitudes of his film characters; some films banned till 1988. **Add.** (h) Līduma 2 — 67, Rīga 226079; tel. 537 996.
- **KALSERS, Monvids Ēriks,** Dir, inst. of rural arch. and design *Agroprojekts,* 1965 — ; b. 1931; grad. Latv. Univ., eng. (civil). **Add.** Maskavas 40/42, Rīga 226504, PDP; tel. 213 067.
- **KALSONS, Romualds,** composer; b. 1936; grad. Latv. Acad. of Music; Prof.; 4 symphonies, 5 instrumental concertos, one-part symphonic pieces, choir songs, 22 vocal cycles, children's songs, theatrical and cinema music; part. in festivals in Ruse, Warsaw, Helsinki. **Add.** (h) Āgenskalna 29 — 48, Rīga 226046; tel. 450 826.
- **KALVIŅŠ, Ivars,** spec. in organic chem.; b. 1947; grad. Latv. Univ.; DSc. (Chem.); at Inst. of Organic Chem., 1969 — , Research Dir, 1987 — ; research in heterocyclic compounds, synthesis of amino acid analogues, study of their chem. and biol. properties, development of new clinical drugs (antitumour immunomodulators), preparations for raising animal productivity; 30 pat.; publ. in USA, Germany, Belgium. **Add.** Aizkraukles 21, Rīga 226006; tel. 553 233.
- **KAPULERS, Pāvels,** acrobatics coach; b. 1939; grad. Latv. Inst. of Physical Culture; CSc. (Pedag.); trained 12 world champ.; coach, USSR nat. team, 1975 — . **Add.** (h) Brīvības 88 — 48, Rīga 226001; tel. 291 606.
- **KAREVS, Aleksandrs,** Dir, Daugavpils Chain Belt Plant, 1975 — ; b. 1936; grad. Leningrad Eng. Inst. of Railway Transport, eng. **Add.** Viškņu 17, Daugavpils 228400; tel. 430 07.
- **KĀRKLIŅŠ, Romans,** spec. in tech. microbiol.; b. 1928; grad. Latv. Univ.; DSc. (Chem.),

Prof., Acad., Latv. Acad. of Sci.; Dir, Experimental Factory of Biochem. Substances, 1982 — ; research in biotechnol. of organic acids, ecologically safe biotechnol., ind. selection of microorganisms, separation and purification of biosynthetic compounds; pat. in 10 European c., USA, Argentina, India; publ. in Japan, Germany. **Add.** Brīvības 222, Rīga 226039; tel. 551 974.

- **KARLSONS, Juris,** Rector, Latv. Acad. of Music, 1990 — ; Chair., Bd of Latv. Composers' Union, 1990 — ; b. 1948; grad. Latv. Acad. of Music; author of ballet, symphony, 2 piano concertos with orch., choir symphony, choir and solo cycles; works perf. in France, Austria, Netherlands, Germany, USA, Brasil. **Add.** Kr. Barona 1, Rīga 226050; tel. 228 684.
- **KATKĒVIČS, Gunārs,** Chief Dir, Man., Circus, 1989 — ; b. 1946; grad. A.Lunacharsky Inst. of Dramatic Art in Moscow; former air acrobat. **Add.** Merķeļa 4, Rīga 226050; tel. 213 479.
- **KAVINSKIS, Romualds,** Dir-Gen., agrofirm *Turība,* 1955 — ; b. 1928; grad. pedag. inst. **Add.** Riebiņi, Preiļu raj. 228273; tel. 567 38.
- **KAZANKINA, Raisa,** Dir, Medical Library, 1985 — ; b. 1942; grad. Saratov Med. Inst., internist. **Add.** Šarlotes 1, Rīga 226328, PDP; tel. 373 646.
- **KEHRIS, Ojārs,** Mem., SC Presidium, Chair., Commn on Econ., 1990 — ; b. 1956; grad. Latv. Univ., econ.; CSc. (Econ.); lecturer, Latv. Univ.; Latv. SC Deputy. **Add.** Brīvības bulv. 36, Rīga 226170, PDP; tel. 284 301.
- **KEIVIŠS, Arnolds,** Dir-Gen., Riga Fresh and Canned Meat Factory, 1984 — ; b. 1937; grad. Leningrad Inst. of Cooling Technol., eng. (mech.). **Add.** Atlasa 7, Rīga 226026; tel. 373 995, 552 152.
- **KEIZERS, Rūdolfs,** Head Physician, Dispensary of Remedial Physical Activity, 1976 — ; b. 1932; grad. Latv. Acad. of Med., surgeon. **Add.** Brīvības 73, Rīga 226001; tel. 279 163.
- **KIOPE, Eduards,** Dir, Biķernieki Sports Centre, 1966 — ; motorsportsman; b. 1929. **Add.** S.Eizenšteina 2, Rīga 226079; tel. 552 322.
- **KIRKE, Frančeska,** paintress; b. 1953; grad. Latv. Acad. of Arts; author of figurative paintings, often finds her characters in the Old Testament; attempts to show differing mental qualities; dramatic, grotesque approach; poster artist and book ill.; exh. in European c., USA. **Add.** (h) M.Altonovas 14 — 4, Rīga 226004; tel. 612 557.
- **KLEINBERGS, Jānis,** Chair., Bd of Volunteer Firemen's Soc., 1972 — ; b. 1940; grad. Riga Tech. Univ., econ. **Add.** J.Asara 13, Rīga 226009; tel. 598 798.
- **KLEINS, Mārtiņš,** cameraman; b. 1938; grad. Moscow Inst. of Cinematography; at Riga Film Studio, 1958 — ; *Studija-3,* 1990 — ; feature films on Latv. classical lit.; int. awards: Grand Prix at Buenos Aires Festival, 1988 with dir G.Piesis, gold medal at Giffoni Film Festival, 1987 for fairy film *Sprīdītis* (Tom Thumb), top prize at All-Union Children's Film Festival. **Add.** (h) Meža prosp. 10 — 2, Rīga 226041; tel. 519 112.

- **KLEMENTJEVS, Ivans,** canoe rower; b. 1960; Olympic champ., 1988, world champ., 1985, 1989, 1990, 11-times USSR champ. **Add.** (h) Kahovkas 5 — 81, Rīga 226082; tel. 246 004.
- **KLIŠĀNS, Arvīds,** French horn player; b. 1934; grad. Latv. Acad. of Music; Prof.; group leader, Nat. Symphony Orch.; prize winner, Prague Spring Festival, 1962; perf. in European c., USA, Mexico, Japan. **Add.** (h) Dzelzavas 79 — 64, Rīga 226081; tel. 570 306.
- **KLOTIŅŠ Arnolds,** musicologist; b. 1934; grad. Latv. Acad. of Music; CSc. (Arts); at Inst. of Lg. and Lit., 1982 — ; studies focus on cultural, hist. and aesthetic aspect; books on Latv. composers. **Add.** Turgeņeva 19, Rīga 226524, PDP; tel. 229 894.
- **KLUŠA, Vija Zaiga,** pharmacologist; b. 1940; grad. Latv. Acad. of Med.; DSc. (Med.); at Inst. of Organic Synthesis, 1964 — ; research in psychopharmacology of regulatory peptides (neuropeptides, psychoneuroimmunoregulators) and membrane-modulating compounds (calcium antagonists, agonists, etc.); publ. in USA, Germany, Bulgaria, Czecho-Slovakia, Poland. **Add.** Aizkraukles 21, Rīga 226006; tel. 245 576.
- **KĻAVA, Sigvards,** choral dir; b. 1962; grad. Latv. Acad. of Music; perfected in Stuttgart; Dir, Radio Choir, 1987 — , Latv. Univ. female choir *Minjona,* 1988 — , teachers' choir *Beverīna,* 1990 — ; Chief Conductor, Latv. Song Festival, 1990; winner of D.Shostakovich Young Conductors Contest, 1986; perf. in European c., USA, Canada. **Add.** Doma lauk. 8, Rīga 226935; tel. 206 601, 206 671.
- **KŅĒTS, Ivars,** spec. in material mech. and biomech.; b. 1938; grad. Riga Tech. Univ.; DSc. (Eng.), Prof.; Vice-Rector, Riga Tech. Univ.; Head, Biomech. and Ergonomics Research Centre; research in mech. behaviour of composite materials and their substitutes (deformation, fracture); mem. of int. org.; pat. and publ. abroad. **Add.** Kaļķu 1, Rīga 226355, PDP; tel. 225 918.
- **KOKAREVIČS, Andrejs,** Dir, headgear factory *Rīgas filcs,* 1985 — ; b. 1954; grad. Latv. Univ., econ. **Add.** Lienes 28, Rīga 226009; tel. 270 648.
- **KOKARS, Imants,** choral dir; b. 1921; grad. Latv. Acad. of Music; Prof.; Rector, 1977 — 90; Dir, int. prize winner chamber choir *Ave Sol,* 1969 — ; perf. in European c., USA, Canada, Argentina, Brasil, Philippines, Japan; Chief Conductor of Latv. Song Festivals. **Add.** (h) Vesetas 8 — 44, Rīga 226013; tel. 374 848.
- **KOLBERGS, Andris,** writer; b. 1938; writes psychological detective works; 8 novels (7 film versions), 8 scripts, stories, satires; transl. in Engl., Ger., Finn., Czech, Pol., Bulg., Russ., etc.; Pres., Assoc. of Detective and Pol. Genre of Latv. Writers' Union. **Add.** (h) Kr.Valdemāra 145 — 1 — 10, Rīga 226013; tel. 361 223.
- **KONDRATOVIČS, Rihards,** botanist; b. 1932; grad. Latv. Univ.; Vice-Rector, Research Dept of Latv. Univ.; DSc. (Biol.), Prof., Corr. Mem., Latv. Acad. of Sci.; research in rhododendron introduction and selection, plant morphology. **Add.** Raiņa bulv. 19, Rīga 226098; tel. 225 075.

- **KOROLIŠINS, Vladimirs,** Dir-Gen., rubber footwear and ind. rubber products ent. *Sarkanais kvadrāts,* 1990 — ; b. 1949; grad. Lvov Polytech. Inst., chem. (technol.); in the ent. since 1974. **Add.** Maskavas 322, Rīga 226063; tel. 252 257.
- **KORZĀNS, Vladislavs,** Rector, Latv. Acad. of Med., 1963 — ; b. 1931; grad. Latv. Acad. of Med., biochem.; DSc. (Med.), Prof.; research in biochem. of parenteral digestion and myocarditis. **Add.** Dzirciema 16, Rīga 226007; tel. 459 752.
- **KOZLOVS, Ņikita,** Dir, constr. and building materials ent. *Vangaži,* 1985 — ; b. 1947; grad. Riga Tech. Univ., eng. (civil). **Add.** Rīgas raj., Vangaži 229036; tel. 995 500.
- **KRASOVSKIS, Andrejs,** Dir, Riga Diesel Plant, 1985 — ; b. 1948; grad. Riga Tech. Univ., eng. (mech.). **Add.** Ganību dambis 40, Rīga 226005; tel. 391 662.
- **KRASTA, Marta,** metalwork artist, jewelry designer; b. 1953; grad. Latv. Acad. of Arts; employs metal, plastics, leather, enamel, amber; one-woman show in Berlin; exh. in Jablonec (hon. diploma), Erfurt, amber-work exh. in Düsseldorf, exh. 'Colour' in Japan. **Add.** (h) Kalēju 21 — 1, Rīga 226150; tel. 210 543.
- **KRASTIŅA, Sandra,** paintress; b. 1957; grad. Latv. Acad. of Arts; paints figurative compositions in oil; excels as colourist; exh. in 10 European c., USA, Canada, India; works in Tretyakov Gallery and Ludvig Coll. (Germany). **Add.** (h) Baldones 24 — 3, Rīga 226083; tel. 455 903.
- **KRASTIŅŠ, Andrejs,** Dep. Chair., SC, 1990 — ; b. 1951; grad. Latv. Univ., lawyer; worked as investigator, barrister; Mem., Latv. Barristers' Collegium; Latv. SC Deputy. **Add.** Jēkaba 11, Rīga 226811, PDP; tel. 322 892.
- **KRASTIŅŠ, Ivars,** Mem., SC Presidium, Chair., Commn on Health and Social Welfare, 1990 — ; b. 1955; grad. Latv. Acad. of Med., anaesthesiologist, reanimatologist; Pres., Latv. Doctors' Assoc., 1988 — 90; Latv. SC Deputy. **Add.** Jēkaba 11, Rīga 226811, PDP; tel. 614 440.
- **KRAUKLIS, Oļģerts,** architect, painter; b. 1931; grad. Latv. Univ.; at inst. of urban design, 1955 — 83; Head Artist, Latv. Art Fund, 1983 — ; designs public buildings in brick, author of interior designs, watercolours. **Add.** (h) Kr.Valdemāra 94 — 28, Rīga 226013; tel. 376 777.
- **KRAŽE, Ivans,** Dir, machine-building ent. *Komunalņiks,* 1990 — ; b. 1958; grad. Riga Tech. Univ., eng. (mech.). **Add.** Antenas 3, Rīga 226004; tel. 613 512.
- **KREITUSS, Aivars,** spec. in polymer chem., phys. and technol.; Chair., research prod. firm *Latvijas koks,* 1989 — ; b. 1945; grad. Latv. Univ.; CSc. (Chem.); at Inst. of Wood Chem., 1978 — ; research in mass transference processes in wood, composite materials, synthetic polymers, their structure and protection; publ. abroad. **Add.** Akadēmijas 27, Rīga 226006; tel. 553 707.
- **KRENBERGA, Dita,** flutist; b. 1968; student, Latv. Acad. of Music; perfected in Spain,

Switzerland; prize winner, Concertino Praha, 1980, Grand Prix winner, Maria Canals int. comp. in Barcelona , 1988; part. at Boston Symphony Orch. summer festival, 1989 — 90; perf. in Spain, Switzerland, Germany, France, Canada, USA; part. in films. *Add.* (h) Brīvības 162 — 117, Rīga 226012; tel. 364 704.

▪ **KRĒSLIŅŠ, Andris,** spec. in heating, ventilation and air conditioning; b. 1938; grad. Riga Tech. Univ.; DSc. (Eng.), Prof.; Vice-Pres., Latv. Scientists' Union; research in automatic control and econ. optimization of heating, ventilation, air conditioning systems, hist. of Latv. higher educ. establishments; publ. in Engl., Ger. *Add.* Āzenes 20, Rīga 226355, PDP; tel. 615 191, 612 118.

▪ **KRIEVS, Arvīds,** film dir; b. 1944; grad. Higher Course of Film Dir (G.Panfilov's Workshop); at Riga Film Studio, 1964 — ; makes strikingly vivid, expressive films, also documentaries. *Add.* (h) Vesetas 10 — 43, Rīga 226013; tel. 372 554.

▪ **KRODERS, Oļģerts,** Chief Dir, Nat. Theatre, 1989 — ; b. 1921; grad. Moscow Higher Stage Dir Course; stage dir, Valmiera and Liepāja theatres, 1959 — 89. *Add.* Kronvalda bulv. 2, Rīga 226829, PDP; tel. 222 340.

▪ **KROLLE, Izabella,** ceramist, b. 1938; grad. Latv. Acad. of Arts; works in monumental art (mosaic), park ceramics, sculptural forms, painting, graphic art; uses earthenware chamotte, acryl; exh. in Faenza, Gdańsk, Erfurt et al. *Add.* (h) Vaidavas 13 — 12, Rīga 226084; tel. 560 560, 612 467.

▪ **KROLLIS, Gunārs,** graphic artist; b. 1932; grad. Latv. Acad. of Arts; Prof.; works in easel painting, miniature graphics, watercolour; prefers linocut, lithography, etching; superb draftsman; one-man shows in Beirut, Damascus, Vienna, Graz, Ruse, Pori, Toronto, Moscow. *Add.* (h) Vaidavas 13 — 12, Rīga 226084; tel. 560 560, 332 202.

▪ **KRŪMIŅŠ, Andris,** physicist; b. 1943; grad. Latv. Univ.; at Inst. of Solid State Phys., 1976 — , Research Dir, 1985 — ; research in optoelectronics, nonconductors and semiconductors phys. *Add.* Ķengaraga 8, Rīga 226063; tel. 261 414.

▪ **KRŪMIŅŠ, Ģirts,** Mem., SC Presidium, Chair., Commn on Ind., 1990 — ; b. 1941; grad. Riga Tech. Univ., eng. (electromech.); worked in machine-building research inst. and ent.; Latv. SC Deputy. *Add.* Jēkaba 11, Rīga 226811, PDP; tel. 325 041, 325 925.

▪ **KRŪMIŅŠ, Kārlis,** Dir, Centre of Orthopaedic Prostheses, 1987 — ; b. 1945; grad. Riga Tech. Univ.; in Riga Prostheses Works, 1975 — 1987. *Add.* Pērnavas 62, Rīga 222009; tel. 599 903.

▪ **KRUSTIŅŠ, Voldemārs,** Ed., popular agric. newspaper *Lauku Avīze,* 1987 — ; b. 1932; grad. pedag. inst.; in journalism since 1958. *Add.* tel. Rīga 327 616.

▪ **KUBLINSKIS, Arnolds,** Head, Religious Matters Dept, 1989 — ; b. 1937; grad. Latv. Univ., geogr. *Add.* Elizabetes 57, Rīga 226050; tel. 288 879.

▪ **KUDRJAŠOVS, Aleksandrs,** Bishop, Latv. Eparchy of Orthodox Church, 1990 — ; grad. Daugavpils Pedag. Inst., Zagorsk Theol. Sem.; clergyman since 1982; contrib. to periodicals of Orthodox Church. *Add.* M.Pils 11, Rīga 226050; tel. 228 324.

▪ **KUDRJAVCEVS, Ēriks,** Dir, Riga Musical Instruments Factory, 1983 — ; b. 1943; grad. Riga Tech. Univ., econ. *Add.* Maskavas 250, Rīga 226063; tel. 253 852.

▪ **KUKAINE, Rita,** Dir, Inst. of Microbiol., 1962 — ; virologist; b. 1922; grad. Latv. Univ.; DSc. (Med.), Prof., Acad., Latv. Acad. of Sci.; research in preventive treatment of poliomyelitis, morphogenesis and biochem. properties of cancerigenic virus; supporter of immunologic treatment of livestock leucosis; USSR People's Deputy. *Add.* A.Kirhenšteina 1, Rīga 226067; tel. 426 197.

▪ **KUKELS, Pāvels,** Dir-Gen., sewing and textile firm *Saiva,* 1989 — ; b. 1944; grad. Latv. Univ.; CSc. (Econ.). *Add.* Teātra 31, Jūrmala 229070; tel. 647 98.

▪ **KŪLA, Dainis,** javelin thrower; b. 1959; Olympic champ., 1980, World Cup winner, 1981, bronze medallist, world champ., 1983, USSR Champ., 1981 — 84. *Add.* Sporta komiteja, Tērbatas 4, Rīga 226011, PDP; tel. 284 206.

▪ **KULBERGS, Viktors,** Chair., joint stock company *Mežciems,* 1990 — ; b. 1948; grad. Latv. Acad. of Agric., eng. (machine-building); Chair., Antique Automobiles' Club, 1974 — 84. *Add.* S.Eizenšteina 6, Rīga 226079; tel. 552 777.

▪ **KŪLE, Maija,** Dir, Inst. of Phil. and Sociology, 1991 — ; b. 1951; grad. Latv. Univ.; CSc. (Phil.); research in phenomenology and hermeneutics. *Add.* Meistaru 10, Rīga 226940, PDP; tel. 216 793.

▪ **KUĻIKS, Vladimirs,** Chair., Bd of Riga Commercial Bank, 1989 — ; b. 1952; grad. Latv. Univ., econ. *Add.* Smilšu 6, Rīga 226800, PDP; tel. 323 967.

▪ **KUMEROVS, Romāns,** Dir-Gen., furniture ent. *Gauja,* 1988 — ; b. 1937; grad. Latv. Acad. of Agric., eng. (wood-working). *Add.* Rūpniecības 52, Rīga 226200; tel. 381 476.

▪ **KUZMINS, Afanasijs,** sportsman, bullet shooter; b. 1947; Olympic champ., 1988, world champ. 1974, 1982, 1986, 1989, European champ. 1975, 1981, 1985, 1989. *Add.* Sporta komiteja, Tērbatas 4, Rīga 226011, PDP; tel. 284 206.

▪ **KUZŅECOVS, Jurijs,** Dir-Gen., cartography and geodesy ent. *Latvijas karte,* 1970 — ; b. 1936; grad. Moscow Inst. of Printing Ind. *Add.* O.Vācieša 43, Rīga 226004; tel. 611 186.

▪ **ĶEZBERS, Ivars,** Chair., LDLP, 1990 — ; b. 1944; grad. Latv. Univ., lawyer, spec. in pol. studies; CSc. (Hist.); active in journalism, diplomacy; leading posts in USSR and Latv. Cttee for TV and Radio Broadcasting; Min. of Culture; Sec., Latv. CP Cent. Cttee, 1988 — 90; USSR People's Deputy. *Add.* Blaumaņa 5a, Rīga 226700; tel. 280 845.

▪ **ĶIKUTS, Raimonds,** neurosurgeon; b. 1932; grad. Latv. Acad. of Med.; DSc. (Med.), Prof.; research in magnetobiol. effects and application of plastics in neurosurgery. *Add.* Duntes 12/22, Rīga 226005; tel. 392 302.

■ **KIMELE, Māra,** stage dir, indep. theatre *Kabata,* 1989 — ; b. 1943; grad. A.Lunacharsky Inst. of Dramatic Art in Moscow; drama teacher, Latv. Acad. of Music; at Valmiera Theatre, 1969 — 89. *Add.* (h) Bruņinieku 28 — 19, Rīga 226001; tel. 290 733.

■ **KIPURS, Jānis,** bobsleigh rider; b. 1958; Olympic champ. and bronze medallist, 1988, European champ., 1984, World Cup winner, 1988; medallist of several world and European champ. *Add.* (h) J.Vācieša 4 — 32, Rīga 226082; tel. 247 955.

■ **LABANOVSKIS, Rišards,** Chair., Cttee for TV and Radio Broadcasting, 1990 — ; b. 1940; grad. Latv. Univ., philol.; at the cttee since 1966. *Add.* Doma lauk. 8, Rīga 226050; tel. 226 304.

■ **LĀCE, Māra,** Dir, State Museum of Fine Arts, 1988 — ; b. 1954; grad. Latv. Acad. of Arts, art scholar. *Add.* Kr.Valdemāra 10a, Rīga 226342; tel. 325 802.

■ **LĀČGALVIS, Edgars,** Dir-Gen., agric. machinery prod. and research assoc. *Stars,* 1986 — ; Dir, Inst. of Mechanization and Electrification of Agric., 1966 — ; b. 1930; grad. Latv. Acad. of Agric., eng. (mech.); CSc. (Eng.); research in farm mechanization. *Add.* Institūta 1, Ulbroka 229030; tel. 910 902.

■ **LAZDIŅŠ, Auseklis,** Min. of Power, 1990 — ; b. 1935; grad. Latv. Univ., eng. (electrical equipm.); worked in research inst.; Chair., State Cttee for Fuel and Power, 1988 — 90. *Add.* Smilšu 1, Rīga 226904, PDP; tel. 224 444.

■ **LAKIS, Pēteris,** Mem., SC Presidium, Chair., Commn of Public Educ., Sci., Culture, 1990 — ; b. 1952; grad. Latv. Univ., phil.; CSc. (Phil.); lecturer, Latv. Univ.; Mem., LPF CBd; Latv. SC Deputy. *Add.* Jēkaba 11, Rīga 226811, PDP; tel. 323 918.

■ **LAĻKOVS, Dmitrijs,** Dir-Gen., glassware plant *Latvijas stikls,* 1974 — ; b. 1932; grad. Leningrad Technol. Inst. *Add.* Daugavgrīvas 77, Rīga 226007; tel. 459 145.

■ **LĀMS, Visvaldis,** writer; b. 1923; author of 10 novels; his characters are lonely, 'wrong' people, in conflict with their 'self' and soc. due to their peculiar nature or extraordinariness; transl. in Engl., Ger., Russ., Bulg., Czech, Slovak, Hung., Est., Lith. lgs. *Add.* Rakstnieku savienība, Kr.Barona 12, Rīga 226011; tel. 287 629.

■ **LAMSTERS, Ivars Uldis,** Head Physician, Children's Clinical Hosp., 1963 — ; b. 1937; grad. Latv. Acad. of Med., surgeon. *Add.* Vienības gatve 45, Rīga 226004; tel. 612 277.

■ **LANCERS, Jānis,** Chair., constr. and building materials ent. *Latvijas celtnieks,* 1990 — ; b. 1933; grad. Moscow Building Inst.; Dep. Min., Chair., State Building Cttee, 1980 — 90. *Add.* Rūpniecības 27, Rīga 226903; tel. 321 302.

■ **LANCMANIS, Imants,** Dir, Rundāle Palace Museum, 1976 — ; art scholar, painter; b. 1941; grad. Latv. Acad. of Arts; paints still-lifes, portrets; research in hist. of arch. (mainly Baroque period). *Add.* Bauskas raj., Rundāle 229326; tel. 622 72.

■ **LAPIŅA, Lūcija,** Pres., Assoc. of Red Cross Charity Nurses, 1990 — ; b. 1941; hospital head nurse in Riga. *Add.* J.Asara 3, Rīga 226009; tel. 279 596.

■ **LAPIŅA, Mārīte,** Dir, Museum of Foreign Art, 1989 — ; b. 1946; grad. Latv. Acad. of Arts, art scholar. *Add.* Pils lauk. 3, Rīga 226844; tel. 228 776.

■ **LASMANIS, Gunārs,** Dir, Valmiera Fire-Fighting Equipm. Plant, 1983 — ; b. 1941; grad. Riga Tech. Univ., eng. (mech.). *Add.* L.Laicena 2, Valmiera 228600; tel. 233 49.

■ **LAŠČONOVA, Natālija,** gymnast; b. 1973; Olympic champ., 1988, world champ., 1989, USSR champ., 1988 — 89. *Add.* Sporta komiteja, Tērbatas 4, Rīga 226011, PDP; tel. 284 206.

■ **LAUCIS, Uldis,** Chair., Red Cross Soc., 1986 — ; b. 1936; grad. Latv. Acad. of Med.; hosp. head physician till 1986; USSR People's Deputy. *Add.* Skolas 28, Rīga 226300; tel. 275 635.

■ **LAVENDELIS, Egons,** Rector, Riga Tech. Univ., 1985 — ; spec. in mech.; b. 1934; grad. Latv. Univ.; DSc. (Eng.), Prof., Acad., Latv. Acad. of Sci.; research in oscillation theory, mech. of superelastic materials, optimality of dynamic synthesis, automatic design methods; publ. in Germany, Poland, Czecho-Slovakia. *Add.* Kaļķu 1, Rīga 226355, PDP; tel. 225 885.

■ **LAZOVSKIS, Ilmārs,** internist; b. 1931; grad. Latv. Acad. of Med.; DSc. (Med.), Prof., Corr. Mem., Latv. Acad. of Sci.; research in internal, joint and kidney diseases. *Add.* Dzirciema 16, Rīga 226007; tel. 615 063.

■ **LEBEDEKS, Genrihs,** Chair., Cent. Bd, Soc. of the Blind, 1982 — ; b. 1941; grad. pedag. inst. *Add.* Pāles 14, K-1, Rīga 226024; tel. 532 607.

■ **LEIMANIS, Aivars,** ballet premier, Nat. Opera; b. 1958; grad. Riga Choreography Sch.; part. in films. *Add.* Aspazijas bulv. 3, Rīga 226251, PDP; tel. 222 823.

■ **LEVINS, Nikolajs,** spec. in aviation; b. 1927; grad. Riga Civil Aviation Eng. Inst.; DSc. (Eng.), Prof.; research in electric power problems of autonomous objects (planes, wind devices, emergency electric systems); pat. in USA, Great Britain, France, Italy, Germany. *Add.* Lomonosova 1, Rīga 226019; tel. 240 225.

■ **LĪCE, Anda,** leather-work artist; b. 1946; grad. Riga Sch. of Applied Arts; makes decors, book bindings, leather accessories, clothes; exh. in Germany, Denmark, Japan, Canada, Czecho-Slovakia. *Add.* (h) Ciedru 5a, Rīga 226015; tel. 349 400.

■ **LĪCIS, Kārlis,** Min. of Govt Affairs, 1990 — ; b. 1941; grad. Riga Tech. Univ., eng. (technol.); worked as Chair. of Riga City Exec. Cttee, Man. of Govt Affairs. *Add.* Brīvības bulv. 36, Rīga 226170, PDP; tel. 280 700.

■ **LĪDAKA, Marģers,** spec. in organic chem.; b. 1928; grad. Latv. Univ.; DSc. (Chem.), Acad., Latv. Acad. of Sci.; Acad.-Sec., Dept of Chem. and Biol. Sci.; at Inst. of Organic Synthesis, 1958 — ; research in chem. of bioorganic compounds and physiologically active substances, developed drugs with antitumour activity (Tio-TEFA, Cyclophosphan, etc.); pat. in Great Britain,

Germany, USA, Japan. **Add.** Aizkraukles 21, Rīga 226006; tel. 555 920.

- **LIELĀ, Dace,** paintress; b. 1957; grad. Latv. Acad. of Arts; creates figurative compositions, landscapes; adherent of classical tonal painting; exh. in Finland, France (gold medallist, 1984), Czecho-Slovakia (Grand Prix, biennial of socialist c., 1984), Bulgaria (first prize, int. young artists exh., 1985), Germany (main prize, Soviet-German young artists exh., 1986), USA. **Add.** (h) M.Monētu 2 – 1, Rīga 226050; tel. 214 797.

- **LIELAUSIS, Oļģerts,** physicist, b. 1930; grad. Latv. Univ.; DSc. (Eng.); at Inst. of Phys., 1955 – ; research in magnetohydrodynamics – new technol. applications of MHD processes. **Add.** Miera 32, Salaspils 229021; tel. 947 195.

- **LIELDIDŽA, Zane,** prima ballerina, Nat. Opera; b. 1959; grad. Riga Choreography Sch.; part. in films. **Add.** Aspazijas bulv. 3, Rīga 226251, PDP; tel. 222 823.

- **LIELPĒTERIS, Jānis,** Pres., Latv. Acad. of Sci., 1989 – ; phys., spec. in magnetohydrodynamics – ; b. 1931; grad. Latv. Univ.; DSc. (Eng.), Acad., Latv. Acad. of Sci.; at Inst. of Phys., 1955 – ; research in magneto-hydrodynamic processes in induction generators and devices, worked out new measuring technol. **Add.** Turgeņeva 19, Rīga 226524, PDP; tel. 225 361.

- **LIEPA, Jānis,** Chair., Bd, Soc. of the Deaf, 1976 – ; b. 1928; lawyer. **Add.** Jāņa sēta 5, Rīga 226350, PDP; tel. 212 485.

- **LIEPIŅŠ, Edvards,** spec. in organic chem. and magneto-nuclear resonance spectroscopy; b. 1944; grad. Latv. Univ.; DSc. (Chem.); at Inst. of Organic Synthesis, 1968 – ; research in structures of organic compounds with the help of multinuclear magnetic resonance method; publ. in Engl., Ger. **Add.** Aizkraukles 21, Rīga 226006; tel. 555 985.

- **LIEPIŅŠ, Roberts,** choral dir; b. 1952; grad. Latv. Acad. of Music; Dir, male choir *Dziedonis,* 1972 – , J.Mediņš Music Sch., 1987 – . **Add.** L.Paegles 13, Rīga 226276, PDP; tel. 332 058.

- **LIEPIŅŠ, Zigmārs,** Man., Artistic Dir, concert firm 'Showimpex', 1989 – ; b. 1952; grad. Latv. Acad. of Music, composer (rock opera, about 300 songs, theatre and cinema music); former artistic dir of pop groups. **Add.** Gertrūdes 37, Rīga 226011; tel. 276 002.

- **LIFŠICS, Tovijs,** conductor, violinist; b. 1928; grad. Lith. Conservatoire; teacher, Latv. Acad. of Music; Chief Conductor, Artistic Dir, perf. violinist, Latv. Philharmonic Chamber Orch., 1969 – ; perf. in European c., USA. **Add.** (h) Hospitāļu 1 – 84, Rīga 226013; tel. 361 341.

- **LIGERS, Roberts,** Artistic Dir, founder, dumb show group *Rīgas pantomīma,* 1956 – ; b. 1931; grad. Latv. Acad. of Music; worked as actor at Art Theatre; guest perf. in Germany, Finland, France, Austria. **Add.** (h) Brīvības 190 – 12, Rīga 226012; tel. 378 683.

- **LINDENBERGS, Ilmārs,** Dir, nonalcoholic beverage factory *Rīga,* 1970 – ; b. 1928; grad. Latv. Acad. of Agric., eng. (technol.). **Add.** Bruņinieku 2, Rīga 226450; tel. 273 217.

- **LOČMELIS, Andris,** Dir, hardware plant *Liepāja,* 1988 – ; b. 1949; grad. Riga Tech. Univ., eng. (electromech.); chief eng., 1980 – 1988. **Add.** Avotu 10, Liepāja 229700; tel. 235 44.

- **LOZE, Ilze,** archeologist; b. 1936; grad. Leningrad Univ.; CSc. (Hist.); at Inst. of Hist., 1959 – ; research in Stone Age archeology (Neolithic culture), ways of amber distribution; publ. in Poland, Czecho-Slovakia. **Add.** Turgeņeva 19, Rīga 226524, PDP; tel. 216 792.

- **LUKAŠEŅOKS, Jevgeņijs,** Pres., assoc. of grain processing ent. *Latvijas labība,* 1990 – ; b. 1946; grad. Voronez Technol. Inst.; CSc. (Eng.); in grain processing ent. since 1971. **Add.** Dzirnavu 87/89, Rīga 226728, PDP; tel. 285 715.

- **LUKEVICS, Edmunds,** Dir, Inst. of Organic Synthesis, 1983 – ; spec. in organic chem.; b. 1936; grad. Latv. Univ.; DSc. (Chem.), Prof., Acad., Latv. Acad. of Sci.; at inst. since 1958: research in synthesis of organic compounds (silicon, germanium), their chem., spectroscopic, biol. properties, heterocyclic compounds chem.; publ. in USA, Germany, Great Britain, Romania. **Add.** Aizkraukles 21, Rīga 226006; tel. 551 822, 553 355.

- **LŪSIS, Jānis,** javelin thrower; b. 1939; Olympic champ., 1968, silver medallist, 1972, bronze, 1964, European champ., 1962, 1966, 1969, 1971, 12-times USSR champ.; acknowledged all-times best javelin thrower (IAAF, 1987); coach in Madagascar, 1986 – 90. **Add.** Sporta komiteja, Tērbatas 4, Rīga 226011, PDP; tel. 284 206.

- **MARTINOVS, Sergejs,** singer (bass); b. 1952; grad. Latv. Acad. of Music, teacher of it; perfected in Italy; soloist, Nat. Opera, 1977 – ; played the parts of Boris Godunov, Basilio, Mephistopheles; prize winner of int. comp., 1983 – 86; perf. in Italy, France, Germany, Greece, Finland et al. **Add.** (h) Mārcienas 1 – 41, Rīga 226084; tel. 579 573.

- **MARTINSONE, Agnese,** violoncellist; b. 1967; grad. Latv. Acad. of Music; mem., Nat. Symphony Orch., 1988 – ; prize winner, Prague comp., 1983, Belgrad, 1990. **Add.** (h) Matīsa 44 – 27, Rīga 226001; tel. 296 769.

- **MARTINSONS, Pēteris,** ceramist; b. 1931; grad. Latv. Univ., arch.; teacher, Latv. Acad. of Arts; makes decorative vessels, figurative sculptural forms, monumental decorative ceramics; works in earthenware, faience, chamotte, stone, porcelain; part. and prize winner of many int. exh.; gold medallist, Faenza, 1972, 1975, 1976, 2nd prize, Gdańsk, 1973, gold medallist, Sopot, 1976, diplomas and prizes in Erfurt, Vallauris, Zagreb et al.; Hon. Mem., Geneva Int. Ceramics Acad. **Add.** Komunāru bulv. 13, Rīga 226050; tel. 332 202, 521 649 (h).

- **MARTINSONS, Vladimirs,** Dir-Gen., radio ind. ent. *Radiotehnika,* 1987 – ; b. 1936; grad. Moscow Higher Tech. Sch.; chief technol., chief eng., 1969 – 87. **Add.** Popova 3, Rīga 226067; tel. 418 088.

- **MATĪSS, Imants,** Dir, Inst. of Polymer Mech., 1988 – ; spec. in electronics; b. 1935; grad. Latv. Univ.; DSc. (Eng.), Prof., Corr. Mem., Latv. Acad. of Sci.; at inst. since 1958; research in non-destructive testing of phys. and mech. properties; pat. in USA, Great Britain, France, Denmark, Japan. *Add.* Aizkraukles 23, Rīga 226006; tel. 551 145.

■ **MAURIŅŠ, Artūrs**, botanist; b. 1924; grad. Latv. Acad. of Agric.; DSc. (Biol.), Prof.; invest. in tree introduction. *Add.* Kronvalda bulv. 4, Rīga 226200; tel. 322 852.

■ **MEDENS, Jānis**, Chair., state insurance company *Latva*, 1991 — ; b. 1952; grad. Latv. Univ., lawyer; at insurance company since 1980. *Add.* Vaļņu 1, Rīga 226912, PDP; tel. 220 376.

■ **MEGI, Pauls**, Chief Conductor, Nat. Symphony Orch., 1990 — ; conductor, opera house *Estonia*, 1984 — 90; b. 1953; grad. Tallinn and Moscow Conservatoires, violinist and trumpet player; perf. abroad. *Add.* Amatu 6, Rīga 226050; tel. 224 850.

■ **MELBERGA, Tamāra**, Dir, Library for the Blind, 1981 — ; b. 1948; grad. Latv. Univ., philol. *Add.* Juglas 14, Rīga 226024; tel. 531 748.

■ **MELLUMA, Aija**, geographer, spec. in environmental protection; b. 1935; grad. Latv. Univ.; DSc. (Geogr.), Corr. Mem., Latv. Acad. of Sci.; Head, Research Centre for Environmental Protection, 1990 — ; worked at Latv. Univ. and Inst. of Biol.; research in theory of protection and maintenance of environment through community part., worked out original principles for systematic approach to selection and protected area management; studies regional problems; author of several monographs. *Add.* Peldu 25, Rīga 226282; tel. 226 472.

■ **MEĻEHOVS, Leonīds**, Dir, ent. producing footwear to order *Rīgas apavi*, 1987 — ; b. 1953; grad. Riga Tech. Univ., econ. *Add.* Vārnu 5, Rīga 226009; tel. 279 533.

■ **MEĻĶIS, Modris**, Dir, Valmiera Furniture Plant, 1976 — ; b. 1942; grad. Latv. Acad. of Agric., eng. (wood-working). *Add.* Purva 10, Valmiera 228600; tel. 221 56.

■ **MENCE, Selga**, composer; b. 1953; grad. Latv. Acad. of Music; author of symphonic, instrumental, choir, vocal music; lucid emotionality, diatonic melodies, pleasing harmonies prevail; employs folklore, writes songs and arrangements for children. *Add.* (h) Kristapa 23 — 3, Rīga, 226046; tel. 624 040.

■ **METLĀNS, Jevgeņijs**, Dir, plant of household utensils and garden implements *Smiltene*, 1979 — ; b. 1948; grad. Riga Tech. Univ., eng. (machine-building). *Add.* Pils 9, Smiltene 228675; tel. 726 32.

■ **MEŽULIS, Valdis**, Chief, Tech. Sports Motor Club, 1988 — ; b. 1937; grad. Latv. Inst. of Physical Culture, coach; in club admin., 1981 — 1988. *Add.* Akas 4, Rīga 226050; tel. 280 629.

■ **MIGLINIEKS, Igors**, basketball player; b. 1964; Olympic and USSR champ., 1988; player of *VEF* team, 1980 — 85, 1989 — ; mem., USSR nat. team, 1982 — . *Add.* (h) Struktoru 5 — 3, Rīga 226039; tel. 551 617.

■ **MIHAILOVS, Jurijs**, Dir, Inst. of Phys., 1967 — ; spec. in thermophys.; b. 1927; grad. Latv. Univ.; DSc. (Eng.), Prof., Acad., Latv. Acad. of Sci.; research in theory of mass and heat transference under the impact of magnetic field,

processes in gases, variation methods of non-linear theory of mass and heat transfer; publ. in USA, Great Britain, China. *Add.* Miera 32, Salaspils 229021; tel. 947 188, 947 582.

■ **MIHAILOVSKIS, Vilhelms**, photographer; b. 1942; makes portraits of artists, documentary photos, photomontage; one-man shows in European c., Japan; winner of 5 FIAP gold, 4 silver medals; works in museums of Belgium, France, Switzerland; 2 photography albums; co-author of int. favoured documentary 'Supreme Justice'; AFIAP, 1976, EFIAP, 1979. *Add.* (h) Ilūkstes 12 — 39, Rīga 226082; tel. 247 906.

■ **MĪLBRETA, Anita**, ceramist; b. 1943; grad. Latv. Acad. of Arts; author of decorative vessel compositions, park ceramics, monumental decorative compositions for public buildings, small-form ceramics; overpaintings with nature motifs, sculptural painted forms; exh. in Germany, France, Czecho-Slovakia; prize winner, Faenza, 1978, 1985; works in Faenza museums. *Add.* (h) Alauksta 16 — 9, Rīga 226009; tel. 271 801, 241 153.

■ **MILLERS Tālis**, Dir, Inst. of Inorganic Chem., 1984 — ; spec. in silicates technol. and plasma chem.; b. 1929; grad. Latv. Univ.; CSc. (Eng.), Corr. Mem., Latv. Acad. of Sci; research in plasma chem. and technol. of inorganic compounds, prod. and properties of ultradisperse powders, synthesis and properties of new compounds; pat. in Germany, France, Hungary; publ. in Great Britain, Germany, Czecho-Slovakia, Bulgaria. *Add.* Miera 34, Salaspils 229021; tel. 946 633.

■ **MIROĻUBOVS, Ivans**, Head, Cent. Council of Latv. Old Believers' Pomor Church, 1989 — ; Dir, Old Believers' Theol. Sch., 1988 — ; clergyman, Grebenschikov's Church of Russian Old Believers in Riga, 1984 — ; b. 1956; grad. Riga Tech. Univ., Leningrad Orthodox Sem., Moscow Orthodox Acad.; clergyman since 1980. *Add.* Krasta 73, Rīga 226003; tel. 222 981.

■ **MITRĒVICS, Jānis**, painter; b. 1957; grad. Latv. Acad. of Arts; life, performance and game are intertwining in his paintings where motion simulates high concentration of energy; exh. in Austria, Denmark, Italy, Germany, USA, Korea et al. *Add.* (h) Kaļķu 24 — 9, Rīga 226050; tel. 216 926.

■ **MUCENIECE, Rita**, E-in-C, ill. fashion journal *Rīgas Modes*, 1979 — ; b. 1937; grad. Latv. Univ., journalist; fashion designer, Riga Fashion House, 1968 — 79. *Add.* Kaļķu 24, Rīga 226436; tel. 276 191.

■ **MUGURĒVIČS, Ēvalds**, archeologist; b. 1931; grad. Latv. Univ.; DSc. (Hist.), Prof., Corr. Mem., Latv. Acad. of Sci.; at Inst. of Hist., 1971 — ; research in Iron Age in Latvia, medieval archeology; mem. of int. org.; publ. in European c., Canada, USA. *Add.* Meistaru 10, Rīga 226047; tel. 216 794.

■ **MUIŽNIEKS, Jānis**, Exec. Dir, building ent. *Tauma*, 1990 — ; b. 1947; grad. Latv. Acad. of Agric., eng. (mech.). *Add.* K.Paldiņa 7, Talsi 229550; tel. 222 24.

■ **MURASINS, Sergejs**, Dir-Gen., footwear producing ent. *Venēcija*, 1991 — ; b. 1957; grad.

Riga Tech. Univ., eng. (technol.). *Add.* Bauskas 16, Rīga 226004; tel. 629 572.

■ **NARKEVIČS, Gvido**, Head Arbitrator of the Rep. of Latvia, 1968 — ; b. 1931; grad. Latv. Univ., lawyer. *Add.* M.Jaunā 5, Rīga 226164, PDP; tel. 228 190.

■ **NEILANDS, Ojārs**, spec. in organic chem.; b. 1932; grad. Latv. Univ.; DSc. (Chem.), Prof., Corr. Mem., Latv. Acad. of Sci.; research in molecular transference, organic synthesis with iodine organic compounds; synthesized organic semiconductors, metals and superconductors; worked out fundamental principles for molecular electronics of organic compounds. *Add.* Āzenes 14, Rīga 226048; tel. 614 582.

■ **NIEDRE, Valdis**, Dir, inst. for land planning and reclamation design *Zemesprojekts*, 1987 — ; b. 1946; grad. Latv. Acad. of Agric., eng. (land reclamation). *Add.* Jēkaba 10/12, Rīga 226800; tel. 222 634.

■ **NĪTIŅA, Daina**, Latv. linguist; b. 1942; grad. Latv. Univ.; DSc. (Philol.), Prof., Corr. Mem., Latv. Acad. of Sci.; research in gen. linguistics, morphology and lg. standards; worked out classification system of pronouns. *Add.* Jūrmalas gatve 74/76, Rīga 226029; tel. 427 465.

■ **NORĪTIS, Ilmārs**, Dir, Līgatne Paper Factory, 1968 — ; b. 1931; grad. Latv. Univ., chem.; in the factory since 1955. *Add.* Pilsoņu 1, Līgatne 228510; tel. 533 30, 533 60.

■ **NOVIKA, Nora**, pianist; b. 1941; grad. Latv. Acad. of Music, teacher of it; piano duo together with Rafi Haradžanjans (founders of this genre in Latvia); perf. old music, classical comp., music by Baltic composers; 12 records, 12 coll. of piano duets publ. in Leningrad; perf. abroad. *Add.* (h) Olava 22 — 1, Rīga 226014; tel. 519 473.

■ **NUŽNIJS, Anatolijs**, Dir-Gen., Riga Building Materials Ent., 1984 — ; b. 1937; grad. Kaliningrad Inst. of Fishery and Technol., eng. (mech.). *Add.* Platā 14, Rīga 226016; tel. 433 619.

■ **NEFJODOVS, Pjotrs**, Dir-Gen., sewing firm *Latvija*, 1983 — ; b. 1935; grad. Leningrad Inst. of Railway Transport Eng., eng. (power). *Add.* Zilupes 7, Rīga 226019; tel. 143 817.

■ **ŅUKŠS, Vilhelms**, Rector, Roman Catholic Theol. Sem. of Riga Metropolis, 1987 — ; b. 1938; grad. Pontifical Gregorian Univ. in Rome; Prof., Theol. Sem.; bishop; Asst Bishop of Riga and Liepāja Diocese; Ed., magazine of Latv. Catholic Community *Katoļu Dzeive* (Catholic Life). *Add.* Kijevas 16, Rīga 226003; tel. 229 641.

■ **OHERINS, Jānis**, Min. of Ind., 1990 — ; b. 1943; grad. Riga Tech. Univ., eng. (electromech.); Dep. Chair., CM, 1985 — 86; Sec., Latv. CP Cent. Cttee, 1986 — 90. *Add.* Smilšu 1, Rīga 226918, PDP; tel. 227 344.

■ **OLIŅA, Daina**, E-in-C, ill. magazine for 5 — 10-year-olds *Zīlīte*, 1987 — ; b. 1951; grad. Latv. Univ., journalist. *Add.* tel. Rīga 225 810.

■ **OSIS, Jānis Andris**, painter; b. 1943; grad. Latv. Acad. of Arts; Prof., Vice-Rector; author of easel paintings, monumental and figurative works, still-lifes; great silver medal winner at Brussels int. exh., prize winner in Turin; exh. in USA, Hungary. *Add.* Komunāru bulv. 13, Rīga 226050; tel. 332 202.

■ **OSMANIS, Jāzeps**, Dir, children's publrs *Sprīdītis*, 1989 — ; poet; b. 1932; grad. Latv. Univ.; CSc. (Philol.); in publ. business since 1955; 15 coll. of poems, compiler of 4 anthologies for children; transl. from Pol., Russ., Ger.; recipient of 2 Pol. lit. awards. *Add.* Aldaru 2/4, Rīga 226800; tel. 224 921.

■ **OSOKINS, Jurijs**, Dir-Gen., electronic equipm. ent. *Alfa*, 1989 — ; b. 1937; grad. Moscow Inst. of Energetics, nonconductor and semiconductor spec.; CSc. (Eng.); in the ent. since 1962. *Add.* Brīvības 372, Rīga 226037; tel. 553 075.

■ **OZOLIŅA, Diana**, violoncellist; b. 1959; grad. Latv. Acad. of Music; perfected in Moscow; soloist, Latv. Philharmonic, 1986 — ; winner, All-Union cello players comp., 1985; perf. chamber music; part. of string quartet; perf. in Sweden, Great Britain, Singapore. *Add.* (h) Brīvības 42, Ogre 228300; tel. 226 75.

■ **PANTEĻEJEVS, Andrejs**, Mem., SC Presidium, Chair., Commn on Human Rights and Nat. Problems, 1990 — ; b. 1961; grad. Latv. Univ., phys.; Mem., LPF Council; Latv. SC Deputy. *Add.* Jēkaba 11, Rīga 226811, PDP; tel. 325 868.

■ **PAULS, Raimonds**, Min. of Culture, 1989 — ; composer, pianist; b. 1936; grad. Latv. Acad. of Music; founder of Latv. popular music; author of jazz compositions, pop and choir songs, 2 musicals, one-act ballet, theatrical and cinema music; actively perf. till 1989; former conductor and artistic dir of orch. and pop groups, worked in Latv. Radio; USSR People's Deputy. *Add.* L.Paegles 2, Rīga 226310, PDP; tel. 224 772.

■ **PAULS-VĪGNERE, Edīte**, textile artist; R.Pauls' sister; b. 1939; grad. Latv. Acad. of Arts; employs classical tapestry-making technique, tests her own techniques; one-woman shows in Prague, Bratislava, Moscow; second prize winner, int. textile art exh., Erfurt, 1974, Lodz, 1975. *Add.* (h) Artilērijas 3 — 20, Rīga 226001; tel. 279 989.

■ **PAVELKO, Vitālijs**, spec. in aircraft and engine operation, math.; b. 1941; grad. Riga Civil Aviation Eng. Inst.; DSc. (Eng.), Prof.; research in aircraft safety; publ. in USA. *Add.* Lomonosova 1, Rīga 226019; tel. 240 216.

■ **PAVLOVS, Lauris**, Dir, Cent. Yachting Club, 1980 — ; b. 1946; yachting coach; in the yachting club since 1969. *Add.* Stūrmaņu 1a, Rīga 226016; tel. 433 344.

■ **PĀŽE, Ģirts**, clarinettist; b. 1947; grad. Latv. Acad. of Music; Asst Prof.; mem., Nat. Symphony Orch., 1973 — ; active perf., part. of wind quintet. *Add.* (h) J.Kupalas 12 — 7, Rīga 226010; tel. 322 070.

■ **PELNĒNS, Vilnis**, oboist; b. 1944; grad. Latv. Acad. of Music; Asst Prof.; group leader, Nat. Symphony Orch., 1973 — ; part. of wind quintet and chamber orch.; perf. abroad. *Add.* (h) Imantas 1/11 — 27, Rīga 226029; tel. 415 367.

■ **PEŠINS, Nikolajs**, Dir, printing-house *Rota*, 1982 — ; b. 1934; grad. Moscow Inst. of Printing.

Add. Blaumaņa 38/40, Rīga 226424, PDP; tel. 285 545.

■ **PETERS, Jānis**, Authorized Representative of the Rep. of Latvia in CM Diplomatic Representation to USSR, 1990 – ; poet; b. 1939; Hon. Mem., Latv. Acad. of Sci.; author of 6 coll. of poems, essays, lit. criticism, contrib. to periodicals; his main theme is awareness of nation's hist., destination, his manner is close to folksong intonations; Chair., Bd of Latv. Writers' Union, 1985 – 89; USSR People's Deputy. *Add*. Chapligina 3, Moscow 103062, USSR; tel. 925 27 07; Rakstnieku savienība, Kr.Barona 12, Rīga 226011; tel. 287 629.

■ **PĒTERSONS, Ingus**, singer (tenor); b. 1959; grad. Latv. Acad. of Music; perfected in London; soloist, Nat. Opera, 1985 – ; prize winner, P.Pears singers comp., 1990, Belvedere, 1989; perf. in Great Britain (incl. London Nat. Opera), Germany, Sweden. *Add*. Aspazijas bulv. 3, Rīga 226251; tel. 952 774 (h).

■ **PIEBALGS, Andris**, Min. of Educ., 1990 – ; b. 1957; grad. Latv. Univ., phys.; worked as teacher, dir of sch. *Add*. Vaļņu 2, Rīga 226050, PDP; tel. 222 415.

■ **PIESIS, Gunārs**, film dir; b. 1931; grad. Moscow Inst. of Cinematography; at Riga Film Studio, 1961 – ; made documentaries, feature films; screen versions of Latv. lit. classics; int. awards: Grand Prix at Buenos Aires Festival, 1988, gold medal at Giffoni Film Festival, 1987, for fairy film *Sprīdītis* (Tom Thumb). *Add*. Šmerļa 3, Rīga 226037; tel. 379 960 (h).

■ **PIKS, Rihards**, Dir-Gen., cinematography assoc. *Latvijas kino*, 1990 – ; b. 1941; grad. Inst. of Cinematography, Higher Courses for Film Dir in Moscow, cameraman, film dir; Dir, Riga Film Studio, 1987 – 90; dir of newsreels, documentaries, feature films. *Add*. Šmerļa 3, Rīga 226037; tel. 520 411.

■ **PINNIS, Rūdolfs**, painter; b. 1902; studied at Latv. Acad. of Arts; perfected in Italy, Paris; paints still-lifes, landscapes, abstract compositions in decorative manner; excellent master of colours; part. in many int. exh., one-man shows in Germany, France, Japan; works in Tretyakov Gallery, Cologne and Hamburg museums. *Add*. (h) Ieriķu 66 – 138, Rīga 226059; tel. 561 310.

■ **PIROGOVS, Vladimirs**, spec. in cybernetics; b. 1932; grad. Riga Military Sch. for Aviation Eng.; DSc. (Eng.), Corr. Mem., Latv. Acad. of Sci.; at Inst. of Electronics and Computer Sci., 1960 – ; research in development and facilities for the design of informational networks; publ. in USA. *Add*. Akadēmijas 14, Rīga 226006; tel. 523 139.

■ **PISKUNS, Mihails**, Dir, Sloka Cellulose and Paper Factory, 1989 – ; b. 1943; grad. Byeloruss. Tech. Inst., chem.; in the factory since 1966. *Add*. Fabrikas 2, Jūrmala 229070; tel. 322 22.

■ **PLAKIDIS, Pēteris**, composer; b. 1947; grad. Latv. Acad. of Music; Prof.; author of instrumental concertos (for piano and orch., group of soloists and orch., 2 oboes and chamber orch.), instrumental chamber music (for wind quintet, piano trio), cycles for voice, choir songs, cinema and theatrical music; perf. in Germany, USA, Bulgaria, Czecho-Slovakia, Hungary, Yugoslavia. *Add*. (h) Dzirnavu 45/47 – 7, Rīga 226010; tel. 282 136.

■ **PLATKĀJIS, Edvīns**, Min. of Public Health, 1989 – ; b. 1938; grad. Latv. Acad. of Med., children's surgeon; CSc. (Med.); Dep. Min., 1979 – 89; research in surgical treatment of chronic pulmonary diseases. *Add*. Skolas 28, Rīga 226331, PDP; tel. 271 713.

■ **PLAUDIS, Armands**, Min. of Trade, 1990 – ; b. 1956; grad. Latv. Univ., econ.; worked in trade research inst., CM. *Add*. Smilšu 1, Rīga 226917, PDP; tel. 224 282.

■ **PLOCIŅŠ, Kārlis**, model aircraft constructor; b. 1939; world champ., 1968, 1970, 1972, 1974, European champ., 1963; int. category judge; Mem., CIAM branch, 1982 – . *Add*. tel. Rīga 274 837.

■ **PLOTNIEKS, Andris**, law scholar, b. 1938; grad. Latv. Univ.; DSc. (Law), Prof., Corr. Mem., Latv. Acad. of Sci.; research in state law; USSR People's Deputy, Latv. SC Deputy. *Add*. Jēkaba 11, Rīga 226811, PDP; tel. 227 303, 322 895.

■ **PODNIEKS, Juris**, cameraman, film dir; b. 1950; grad. Moscow Inst. of Cinematography; at Riga Film Studio, 1967 – ; int. awards for films 'Is it Easy to be Young?'and Soviet-British co-production – documentary serial 'Hello, Do you Hear Us?' (Prix Italia – Int. TV and Radio Programme Comp., Palermo, 1990). *Add*. (h) Stabu 19 – 25, Rīga 226001; tel. 272 519.

■ **POIKĀNS, Ivars**, painter, graphic artist; b. 1952; grad. J.Rozentāls Art College; grotesque, irony, travesty prevail his manner of presentation, attempts to comprehend and depict incomprehensible; exh. in Sweden, Germany, Spain et al. *Add*. (h) Malienas 8, Rīga 226079; tel. 533 069.

■ **POLIS, Miervaldis**, painter; b. 1948; grad. Latv. Acad. of Arts; creates figurative paintings, landscapes, still-lifes, nudes; has developed precisely photographic style of his private visions; part. in various actions, founder of 'Egocentre' for the studies of natural egocentrism as basis for creativity; exh. in Germany, Austria, Great Britain, Finland, Canada, USA. *Add*. (h) Kristapa 16 – 82, Rīga 226046; tel. 624 877.

■ **POĻAKOVS, Aleksandrs**, singer (baritone); b. 1953; grad. Latv. Acad. of Music; perfected in Moscow Conservatoire; soloist, Nat. Opera, 1977 – 90, Moscow Bolshoi Theatre, 1983 – 1985; Latv. Philharmonic, 1990 – ; prize winner, M.Glinka singers comp., 1979; more than 40 parts in various operas (incl. 15 in the Bolshoi), 10 solo concert programmes, repertoire of more than 250 songs; perf. in European c., Peru. *Add*. (h) Hospitāļu 1 – 69, Rīga 226013; tel. 361 268.

■ **POĻAKS, Inārs**, Dir, Valmiera Glass Fibre Plant, 1984 – ; b. 1940; grad. Riga Tech. Univ., eng.; in the ent. since 1963. *Add*. Gagarina 1, Valmiera 228600; tel. 223 21, 211 31.

■ **POĻAKS, Jānis**, wood-carver; b. 1941; grad. Riga Sch. of Applied Arts; works in decorative wood-carving. *Add*. (h) A.Deglava 106/1 – 14, Rīga 226080; tel. 576 144, 280 251.

- **POPOVS, Igors**, Dir-Gen., motor transport assoc. *Latinterauto*, 1981 − ; b. 1937; eng. (mech.). *Add.* Uriekstes 3, Rīga 226005; tel. 383 044.
- **POSMETNIJS, Jurijs**, Dir, Riga Wine and Champagne Factory, 1983 − ; b. 1940; grad. Kaliningrad Inst. of Fishery and Technol.; eng. (mech.). *Add.* A.Barbisa 7, Rīga 226488; tel. 373 676.
- **PRĒDELE, Aida**, E-in-C, newspaper of the Latv. Evangelical Lutheran Church *Svētdienas Rīts*, 1988 − ; b. 1950; grad. Latv. Univ., journalist; studying at Theol. Faculty of Latv. Univ.; ordained asst clergywoman in 1991; in journalism since 1969; Mem., WCC, 1991 − . *Add.* Lāčplēša 4 − 4, Rīga 226010; tel. 334 264.
- **PRIEDE, Gunārs**, playwright; b. 1928; grad. Latv. Univ., arch.; more than 30 plays (staged in USSR, USA, Australia); lyrical and placid dramas, comedies at the early stage, sharply critical everyday topics lately; Sec., Bd of Latv. Writers' Union, 1974 − 84. *Add.* Kr.Barona 12, Rīga 226011; tel. 287 629.
- **PRIEDĪTE, Arvīds**, textile artist; b. 1946; grad. Latv. Acad. of Arts; makes tapestries, monumental textile compositions. *Add.* Mākslinieku savienība, Kr.Barona 12, Rīga 226400, PDP; tel. 287 432.
- **PROKOFJEVS, Pēteris**, spec. in nuclear phys.; b. 1925; grad. Latv. Univ.; DSc. (Phys. & Math.), Prof., Corr. Mem., Latv. Acad. of Sci.; at Inst. of Phys., 1950 − ; research in nuclear spectroscopy; publ. in periodicals abroad. *Add.* Miera 32, Salaspils 229021; tel. 947 438.
- **PROKOPENKO, Emanuels**, Senior Preacher, Latv. Evangelical Christian Parishes (Pentecosts), 1989 − ; b. 1944. *Add.* (h) Emburgas 1a, Jelgava 229600; tel. 282 39.
- **PRŪSE, Laimdota**, Dir, Inst. of Bibliography, 1988 − ; b. 1942; grad. Latv. Univ., philol.; in the field of bibliography since 1968. *Add.* Anglikāņu 5, Rīga 226816, PDP; tel. 225 135.
- **PRŪSIS, Aivars**, Min. of Arch. and Constr., 1990 − ; b. 1938; grad. Riga Tech. Univ., eng. (civil); worked as leading spec., dir of ind. ent. *Add.* Raiņa bulv. 7, Rīga 226800, PDP; tel. 223 070.
- **PRŪSIS, Voldemārs**, Chair., constr. ent. *Laukceltnieks*, 1990 − ; b. 1937; grad. Riga Tech. Univ. *Add.* Grēcinieku 22/24, Rīga 226047; tel. 212 391.
- **PUJĀTS, Jānis**, Metropolitan, Curia of the Roman Catholic Church Metropolis, 1991 − ; b. 1930; grad. Roman Catholic Theol. Sem. of Riga Metropolis; Prof.; ordained priest in 1951; Vicar-Gen., Riga Archdiocese, 1979 − 84; transl. of Catholic liturgical books. *Add.* M. Pils 2a, Rīga 226050; tel. 220 775.
- **PŪKAINIS, Ilgvars**, Dir, Riga Zoo, 1989 − ; b. 1939; grad. Latv. Acad. of Agric., eng. (mech.). *Add.* Meža prosp. 1, Rīga 226014; tel. 518 409.
- **PUMPĒNS, Pauls**, spec. in molecular biol.; b. 1947; grad. Latv. Univ.; DSc. (Biol.), Corr. Mem., Latv. Acad. of Sci.; at Inst. of Molecular Biol., 1990 − ; worked out fundamental principles for a new, original trend in protein and cell eng., development of which can open up new methods in synthesis of vaccinal and diagnosis preparations. *Add.* Krustpils 53, Rīga 226065; tel. 245 566.
- **PUMPURE, Ingrīda**, Art Dir, Riga Fashion House, 1985 − ; b. 1941; grad. Latv. Acad. of Arts; fashion designer since 1965. *Add.* Elizabetes 20, Rīga 226011; tel. 285 919.
- **PURMALE, Līga**, paintress; b. 1948, grad. Latv. Acad. of Arts; works devoted to nature phil.; early works photographic in quality, later composite landscapes with mist as central part of Latv. nature prevail; favours green, grayish, yellow colours; exh. in Germany, Austria, Poland, Canada, USA; works in Tretyakov Gallery, West Berlin, Hermitage, private coll. abroad. *Add.* (h) Kristapa 16 − 82, Rīga 226046; tel. 624 877.
- **PURVIŅŠ, Andris**, Dir, urban design inst. *Pilsētprojekts*, 1989 − ; arch.; b. 1940; grad. Riga Tech. Univ.; leading arch. of inst., 1965 − 88; designed mostly public buildings in Riga (TV Centre). *Add.* Kr.Valdemāra 38, Rīga 226306; tel. 210 130.
- **PUTNIŅŠ, Pauls**, playwright; b. 1937; grad. Latv. Acad. of Music, stage dir; 24 plays, among them dramas, comedies, melodramas, tragicomedies, children's plays; creation devoted to ethical, psychological, social problems of human soc.; staged in USSR theatres. *Add.* (h) Vesetas 8 − 32, Rīga 226013; tel. 375 557.
- **PUTRĀMS, Juris**, graphic artist; b. 1956; grad. Latv. Acad. of Arts; works executed in various techniques; author of applied and book graphic works, installations, exh. arrangements; also paints, makes posters; exh. in Norway, Germany, Poland, USA. *Add.* (h) Rēznas 10 − 1, Rīga 226019; tel. 244 009.
- **RAČEVSKIS, Edgars**, choral dir; b. 1936; grad. Latv. Acad. of Music; Prof.; Dir, int. prize winner (Debrecen, 1988; Tours, 1990) male choir *Gaudeamus*, 1959 − , Choir of Latv. Acad. of Music, 1990 − , TV and Radio Choir, 1963 − 1987; perf. in European c. *Add.* Kr.Barona 1, Rīga 226050; tel. 227 241.
- **RADIONOVS, Galaktions**, Dir-Gen., building materials ent. *Dolomīts*, 1984 − ; b. 1939; grad. Leningrad Building Eng. Inst. *Add.* a.k. 59, Jēkabpils 228200; tel. 319 85.
- **RADZIŅA, Klāra**, Dir, Museum of the Hist. of Riga and Navigation, 1987 −; b. 1942; grad. Latv. Univ., hist.; in the museum since 1970. *Add.* Palasta 4, Rīga 226050; tel. 211 358.
- **RAJA, Solveiga**, singer (soprano); b. 1944; grad. Leningrad Conservatoire; soloist, Nat. Opera, 1976 − ; sings the parts of Aida, Violett, Turandot, Tosca, Salome, Elizabeth, Leonora; perf. in European c.; USA, Canada. *Add.* (h) Kr.Valdemāra 76 − 2, Rīga 226013; tel. 361 477.
- **RAŽUKS, Romualds**, Chair., LPF CBd, 1990 − ; b. 1955; grad. Vilnius Univ., neurosurgeon; CSc. (Med.); worked in Latv. Acad. of Med.; Mem., LPF CBd, 1989 − 90. *Add.* Vecpilsētas 13/15, Rīga 226050; tel. 226 265, 212 285.
- **REISONS, Juris**, Dir, Broceni Cement and Slate Works, 1984 − ; b. 1949; grad. Riga Tech.

Univ., eng. (highway). *Add.* Saldus raj., Brocēni 229451; tel. 652 16.

■ **RIEKSTIŅŠ, Ivars**, Dir, scientific publrs *Zinātne*, 1984 — ; b. 1936; grad. Latv. Univ., philol.; Ed., Latvian Encyclopaedia Publrs, 1966 — 83. *Add.* Turgeņeva 19, Rīga 226530; tel. 212 797.

■ **RIKARDS, Rolands**, spec. in material mech.; b. 1942; grad. Riga Tech. Univ.; DSc. (Eng.), Prof.; research in problems of composite materials and structures; publ. abroad; Latv. SC Deputy. *Add.* Kaļķu 1, Rīga 226355, PDP; tel. 203 317.

■ **RIVKINS, Jevgeņijs**, pianist; b. 1956; grad. Moscow Conservatoire; soloist, Latv. Philharmonic, 1980 — ; teacher, Latv. Acad. of Music; prize winner, All-Union comp., 1977, P.Tchaikovsky int. comp., 1978, Munich int. music comp., 1985; perf. in European c., USA. *Add.* (h) Hospitāļu 1 — 57, Rīga 226013; tel. 361 686.

■ **RIZGA, Pēteris**, Dir-Gen., wood-working plant *RT-Milgrāvis*, 1990 — ; b. 1938; grad. Latv. Acad. of Agric., wood technol. *Add.* Meldru 3, Rīga 226015; tel. 340 787.

■ **ROCĒNS, Kārlis**, spec. in material mech. and wood technol.; b. 1939; grad. Riga Tech. Univ.; DSc. (Eng.), Prof.; research in phys. and mech. properties of wood and other composite materials, their calculation and optimization methods; publ. abroad. *Add.* Āzenes 16, Rīga 226355, PDP; tel. 616 984.

■ **RODINS, Vladimirs**, Dir-Gen., building materials ent. *Būvmateriāli*, 1988 — ; b. 1940; grad. Riga Tech. Univ., eng. (civil); in the ent. since 1964. *Add.* Montētāju 7, Daugavpils 228400; tel. 315 15.

■ **ROKPELNIS, Jānis**, poet, b. 1945; grad. Latv. Univ., studied psychology and phil. at Leningrad Univ.; 3 poetry books; grotesque, ironical poems, paradoxical situations, alienation, sceptical and aesthetical main heroes; rendered poetry by I.Annensky, A.Blok, M.Cvetayeva, meditations on art. *Add.* (h) Kr.Valdemāra 77 — 48, Rīga 226013; tel. 376 467.

■ **RONIS, Indulis**, Dir, Inst. of Hist., 1988 — ; b. 1943; grad. Latv. Univ., hist.; DSc. (Hist.), Corr. Mem., Latv. Acad. of Sci.; research in Latv. pol. hist. of the 1920s, hist. of pol. parties (liberal in particular). *Add.* Turgeņeva 19, Rīga 226524, PDP; tel. 223 715.

■ **ROZENTĀLS, Rafails**, Pres., Latv. Kidney Fund, 1989 — ; Head, Kidney Transplantation Centre, 1976 — ; b. 1937; grad. Latv. Acad. of Med., surgeon; DSc. (Med.), Prof.; research in artificial organs and transplantation; author of 12 inv. *Add.* Pilsoņu 13, Rīga 226002; tel. 614 210, 613 152, 619 091.

■ **ROZĪTE, Jānis**, Dir, advertising firm, *Latvijas reklāma*, 1986 — ; b. 1931; grad. Riga Tech. Univ., eng. (mech.). *Add.* Šķūņu 16, Rīga 226050; tel. 227 001, 226 438.

■ **ROŽANSKIS, Mihails**, Dir, Riga Plant of Steel Constr., 1983 — ; b. 1937; grad. Leningrad Inst. of Water Transport, eng. *Add.* Katlakalna 9, Rīga 226073; tel. 245 095.

■ **ROŽDESTVENSKIS, Oļegs**, Rector, Daugavpils Pedag. Inst., 1977 — ; b. 1934; grad. Dau-

gavpils Pedag. Inst.; CSc. (Hist.). *Add.* 5. augusta 13, Daugavpils 228400; tel. 221 80, 243 21.

■ **RUBIKS, Alfrēds**, 1st Sec., Latv. CP Cent. Cttee, 1990 — ; b. 1935; grad. Riga Tech. Univ., eng.; leading posts in YCL and CP; Chair., Riga City Exec. Cttee, 1984 — 90; USSR People's Deputy, Latv. SC Deputy. *Add.* Elizabetes 2, Rīga 226190, PDP; tel. 321 166.

■ **RUDZĪTE, Marta**, linguist; b. 1924; grad. Riga Pedag. Inst.; DSc. (Philol.), Prof.; research in Latv. dialectology, ethnolinguistics, toponymy, lg. contacts of Finno-Ugrian and Latv. lgs; Foreign Mem., Finno-Ugrian Soc., Modern Lg. Assoc. of America, other int. org. *Add.* Visvalža 4a, Rīga 226011; tel. 224 811.

■ **RUKŠĀNS, Jānis**, E-in-C, horticultural journal *Dārzs un Drava*, 1977 — ; b. 1946; grad. Latv. Acad. of Agric., agron.; flower grower, collector of bulbous plants (tulips, daffodils, crocuses). *Add.* Centrs, a.k. 441, Rīga 226001.

■ **RUNDS, Henriks**, Head Physician, P.Stradiņš Rep. Clinical Hosp., 1979 — ; traumatic and orthopaedic surgeon; b. 1933; grad. Latv. Acad. of Med.; Dir, Inst. of Traumatology and Orthopaedics, 1965 — 79; research in treatment of sports injuries. *Add.* Pilsoņu 13, Rīga 226002; tel. 611 198.

■ **RUŅĢIS, Ārijs**, Dir, Plastics Processing Plant, 1972 — ; b. 1936; grad. Riga Tech. Univ., eng. (mech.). *Add.* Rīgas raj., Olaine 229014; tel. 964 501.

■ **RUSIŅA, Zigrīda**, Dir-Gen., textile and haberdashery ware ent. *Lauma*, 1984 — ; b. 1943; grad. Riga Tech. Univ., eng.; in the ent. since 1969. *Add.* Ziemeļu 19, Liepāja 229700; tel. 410 91.

■ **SADOVSKA-GOLUBEVA, Zoja**, player of draughts, int. grand master; b. 1967; grad. Minsk Inst. of Physical Educ.; world champ., 1986, 1988, 1990, silver medallist, 1985, bronze 1989; USSR champ., 1988 — 90. *Add.* Sporta komiteja, Tērbatas 4, Rīga 226011, PDP; tel. 284 206.

■ **SALENIEKS, Jānis**, Dir, Municipal Dept, 1990 — ; b. 1948; grad. Latv. Univ., lawyer; worked in state judicial bodies. *Add.* Brīvības bulv. 36, Rīga 226050; tel. 282 488.

■ **SALIŅŠ, Aivars**, Dir, Dept of Customs, 1990 — ; b. 1944; grad. Latv. Univ., hist.; in customs offices since 1973. *Add.* Basteja bulv. 14, Rīga 226050; tel. 226 246.

■ **SALĪTIS, Broņislavs**, Chair., fishery farm *Auda*, 1991 — ; b. 1938; grad. Tech. Sch. of Food Ind.; Mem., SC Presidium, Chair., Commn on Maritime Affairs, 1990 — 91; Latv. SC Deputy. *Add.* Audupes 15/17, Rīga 226030; tel. 347 101, 325 221.

■ **SAULĪTE, Voldemārs**, Head Physician, Anti-Tuberculosis Dispensary, 1963 — ; b. 1928; grad. Latv. Acad. of Med., tuberculotherapist. *Add.* Grēcinieku 8, Rīga 226047; tel. 956 801, 223 022.

■ **SAVIČS, Edvards**, Dir-Gen., hide processing ent. *Kosmoss*, 1987 — ; b. 1954; grad. Moscow Acad. of Veterinary; in the ent. since 1979. *Add.* Kr.Valdemāra 114, Rīga 226013; tel. 374 518.

- **SAVINS, Valentins**, Dir-Gen., Riga Carriage Building Plant, 1985 — ; b. 1936; grad. Kharkov Polytech. Inst.; CSc. (Eng.). *Add.* Brīvības 201, Rīga 226039; tel. 275 327.
- **SAZONOVS, Vladimirs**, Dir-Gen., knitwear firm *Sarkanais rīts*, 1982 — ; b. 1950; grad. Riga Tech. Univ., eng. *Add.* Valentīnas 3/5, Rīga 226046; tel. 611 540.
- **SEDMALIS, Uldis**, chemist, spec. in silicates technol.; b. 1933; grad. Latv. Univ.; DSc. (Eng.), Prof., Corr. Mem., Latv. Acad. of Sci.; research in phys. and chem. properties of glass and crystal phosphates; publ. abroad. *Add.* Āzenes 14/24, Rīga 226355, PDP; tel. 610 066.
- **SEDVALDS, Atis**, Dir, Līvāni Experimental Biochem. Plant, 1970 — ; b. 1935; grad. Latv. Acad. of Agric., food spec. *Add.* Celtniecības 8, Līvāni 228264; tel. 445 08.
- **SELECKIS, Ivars**, Chair., Bd of Latv. Cinematographers' Union, 1987 — ; film dir and cameraman; b. 1934; grad. Moscow Inst. of Cinematography; at Riga Film Studio, 1958 — ; made documentaries and feature films; Grand Prix for documentary 'Side-Street' in Amsterdam and Yamagata Festival, 1989, 'Felix' prize, 1990. *Add.* Šmerļa 3, Rīga 226037; tel. 529 853.
- **SELGA, Valdis**, Dir, racing-boat plant *Dzintars*, 1988 — ; b. 1947; grad. Latv. Acad. of Agric., wood technol. *Add.* Slokas 64, Jūrmala 229070; tel. 691 32.
- **SELEZŅOVS, Aleksandrs**, Dir, brewery *Vārpa*, 1989 — ; b. 1948; grad. Leningrad Technol. Inst., eng. (mech.). *Add.* Maskavas 231, Rīga 226019; tel. 241 222.
- **SEĻIVANOVS, Pāvels**, volleyball player; b. 1952; grad. Riga Tech. Univ.; Olympic champ., 1980, silver medallist, 1976, world champ., 1978, 1982, European champ., 1975, 1977, 1979, 1983; player of Belgium team, 1988 — .
- **SEMENCOVS, Jurijs**, Dir, Jelgava Sugar Processing Factory, 1985 — ; b.1936; grad. Moscow Inst. of Food Ind.; in the factory since 1960. *Add.* Cukura 22, Jelgava 229600; tel. 238 85.
- **SEMJONOVA, Uļjana**, basketball player; b. 1952; grad. Latv. Inst. of Physical Culture; Olympic champ., 1976, 1980, world champ., 1971, 1975, 1983, European champ., 1968, 1970, 1972, 1974, 1976, 1978, 1980, 1981, 1983; European Cup winner with *TTT* team, 1968 — 75, 1977, 1981; mem., Riga *TTT* team, 1967 — 87, USSR nat. team, 1968 — 86, Span. club 'Madrid Tintoretto', 1987 — 88. *Add.* Elizabetes 49, Rīga 226050; tel. 288 613.
- **SEMONENKO, Vjačeslavs**, Dir, Jēkabpils Building Materials and Constr. Works, 1986 — ; b. 1950; grad. Kharkov Building Inst., eng. (mech.). *Add.* Zīlānu 68, Jēkabpils 228200; tel. 303 71.
- **SILIŅŠ, Andrejs**, Dir, Inst. of Solid State Phys., 1984 — ; b. 1940; grad. Moscow Univ.; DSc. (Phys. & Math.), Corr. Mem., Latv. Acad. of Sci.; research in optical glass phys., point defect spectroscopy, modelling in silicon dioxide, generation methods of defects, their interaction with properties of glass; publ. in USA, Canada, Germany, Netherlands; Mem., American Phys.

Soc. *Add.* Ķengaraga 8, Rīga 226063; tel. 262 933.
- **SILIŅŠ, Andris**, Chair., Assoc. of Free TU, 1990 — ; b. 1945; in TU admin. since 1978. *Add.* Bruņinieku 29/31, Rīga 226001; tel. 270 351.
- **SILIŅŠ, Edgars**, physicist; b. 1927; grad. Latv. Univ.; DSc. (Phys. & Math.), Prof., Corr. Mem., Latv. Acad. of Sci.; at Inst. of Phys. Energetics, 1968 — ; research in solid state phys., spectroscopy, phys. phenomena in organic molecular crystals; publ. in Great Britain, Germany, Switzerland, Japan. *Add.* Aizkraukles 21, Rīga 226006; tel. 558 640.
- **SILIŅŠ, Elmārs**, Min. of Finance, 1990 — ; b. 1937; grad. Higher CPSU Sch.; worked at regional finance offices and Min.; financial adviser of São Tomé and Prīncipe; Dep. Min., 1989 — 90. *Add.* Smilšu 1, Rīga 226916, PDP; tel. 226 672.
- **SILIŅŠ, Māris**, Head Physician, Oncological Dispensary, 1990 — ; b. 1943; grad. Latv. Acad. of Med., gynaecologist, socio-hygienist. *Add.* P.Dauges 4, Rīga 226079; tel. 536 820.
- **SĪLIS, Ilda**, leather-work artist; b. 1938; grad. Tallinn Art Univ.; makes large-size wall tapestries, book bindings, albums, boxes, fancy goods; exh. in European c., Canada, Japan, Egypt. *Add.* (h) Gaismas 10, Babīte, Rīgas raj. 229002; tel. 297 766.
- **SĪMANIS, Dāvis**, cameraman; b. 1942; grad. Moscow Inst. of Cinematography; at Riga Film Studio, 1961 — ; makes feature films, documentaries; visually expressive and perfected style. *Add.* (h) Ganību 7 — 29, Rīga 226010; tel. 322 993.
- **SIŅICKA, Zaiga**, Dir, book trade assoc. *Latvijas grāmata*, 1988 — ; b. 1935; grad. Latv. Univ., philol.; worked in publ. houses. *Add.* Aspazijas bulv. 24, Rīga 226253, PDP; tel. 223 639.
- **SKOSTA, Ludis**, Dir-Gen., agrofirm *Daugava*, 1962 — ; b. 1936; grad. Latv. Acad. of Agric., agron.; Latv. SC Deputy. *Add.* Sala, Jēkabpils raj. 228222; tel. 635 06, 319 06 (h).
- **SKRASTIŅŠ, Jānis**, Prosecutor-Gen. of the Rep. of Latvia, 1990 — ; b. 1949; grad. Latv. Univ., lawyer; in Prosecutor's Office since 1974. *Add.* Komunāru bulv. 6, Rīga 226010; tel. 320 085.
- **SKREIVERS, Jevgeņijs**, Dir, Līvāni Glassware Factory, 1982 — ; b. 1940; grad. polytech. sch., technol. (silica technol.); in the factory since 1963. *Add.* Zaļā 23, Līvāni 228264; tel. 444 40, 445 40.
- **SKROMANIS, Antons**, Chair., agric. research assoc. *Ražība*, 1983 — ; b. 1935; grad. Latv. Acad. of Agric., agron.; DSc. (Agric.). *Add.* Struktoru 14a, Rīga 226039; tel. 552 996.
- **SKRUZIS, Kārlis**, Dir, popular publrs *Avots*, 1980 — ; b. 1928; journalist; in the publ. business since 1968. *Add.* Aspazijas bulv. 24, Rīga 226050; tel. 211 394.
- **SKUDRA, Alberts**, spec. in composite materials mech.; b. 1925; grad. Latv. Univ.; DSc. (Eng.), Prof., Corr. Mem., Latv. Acad. of Sci.; research in theory of load-bearing capacity of composite materials and application of those in

manufactured structures; Mem., European Cttee for Concrete; publ. and pat. abroad. *Add.* Āzenes 16, Rīga 226355, PDP; tel. 612 762.

■ **SKUDRA, Viktors**, Min. of Justice, 1990 —; b. 1943; grad. Latv. Univ., lawyer; worked at Prosecutor's Office; Dep. Prosecutor, 1982 — 1987; USSR People's Deputy. *Add.* Brīvības bulv. 34, Rīga 226173, PDP; tel. 282 607.

■ **SKUJA, Mārtiņš**, Dir, poultry ent. Ķekava, 1971 —; b. 1935; grad. Latv. Acad. of Agric., veterinarian. *Add.* Ķekava, Rīgas raj. 229023; tel. 937 340.

■ **SKUJENIEKS, Knuts**, Chair., Latv. PEN Club Riga Branch, 1990 —; poet; b. 1936; grad. M.Gorky Inst. of Lit. in Moscow; 3 coll. of poems, lit. criticism; renderings from Slavic, Germanic, Romance lgs; folk-song renderings, articles on folklore; repressed and exiled to Mordovia, 1962 — 69. *Add.* (h) Dārzu 5 — 1, Salaspils 229021; tel. 947 525.

■ **SKUJIŅŠ, Zigmunds**, writer; b. 1926; describes interconnection of intimate life and social problems of the time, with man in the focus; transl. in 12 lgs (Russ., Engl., Bulg., Czech, Pol., Hung., etc.); 3 works screened. *Add.* (h) Vesetas 8 — 37, Rīga 226013; tel. 371 652.

■ **SKULME, Džemma**, Chair., Bd of Latv. Artists' Union, 1982 —; paintress, water-colourist; b. 1925; grad. Latv. Acad. of Arts; CSc. (Arts); paints figurative monumental compositions, employs ethnographic motifs; outstanding colourist; exh. in European c., USA, Canada; one-woman shows in Geneva, Bergamo, Milan, Rome, Stockholm; works in Moscow, Leningrad, German, USA museums; USSR People's Deputy. *Add.* Kr.Barona 12, Rīga 226014; tel. 287 626, 519 086 (h).

■ **SLAVINSKIS, Gunārs**, Dir-Gen., youth centre *Forums*, 1988 —; b. 1952; grad. Latv. Acad. of Music. *Add.* Basteja bulv. 12, a.k. 43, Rīga 226360; tel. 223 003.

■ **SLESARS, Jānis**, Dir, building materials prod. ent. *Lode*, 1984 —; b. 1949; grad. Riga Tech. Univ., eng. (machine-building). *Add.* Cēsu raj., Liepa 228552; tel. 952 46.

■ **SOČŅEVA, Zuzanna**, Head Physician, Riga Mental Hosp., 1953 —; b. 1925; grad. Latv. Acad. of Med., psychiatrist; CSc. (Med.); lecturer, Latv. Acad. of Med.; research in the development of psychiatrics in Latvia. *Add.* Tvaika 2, Rīga 226005; tel. 392 378.

■ **SPROĢIS, Jānis**, singer (tenor); b. 1944; grad. Latv. Acad. of Music; soloist, Nat. Opera, 1980 — 86; Latv. Philharmonic, 1986 —; more than 20 opera parts, 40 large-size musical compositions, chamber music; 24 records; perf. in European c., USA, Canada. *Add.* (h) Elizabetes 21a — 19, Rīga 226010; tel. 333 342.

■ **SPRŪDŽS, Uldis**, violinist; b. 1956; grad. Latv. Acad. of Music; first violin in string quartet (prize winner, Prague Spring Festival, 1988); prize winner, Prague int. comp., 1972; perf. in European c., USA, Canada, India; part. in USA, Bulgarian, Salzburg festivals. *Add.* (h) Ģertrūdes 51 — 11, Rīga 226011; tel. 289 065.

■ **STALTS, Dainis**, Chair., Latv. Folklore Soc., 1989 —; b. 1939; grad. Riga Sch. of Applied Arts; founder and leader, folk group *Skandinieki*, 1976 —; Head, Folklore Division of Open-Air Museum of Ethnography, 1981 —. *Add.* Brīvības 440, Rīga 229065; tel. 994 174 , 619 283 (h).

■ **STANKEVIČS, Aleksandrs**, painter, graphic artist; b. 1932; grad. Latv. Acad. of Arts; Prof.; creates landscapes, portraits, book ill., hist. genre. *Add.* Komunāru bulv. 13, Rīga 226185, PDP; tel. 332 202.

■ **STAROVOITOVS, Vladimirs**, Dir, Kalnciems Building Materials Ent., 1985 —; b. 1939; grad. All-Union Textile and Light Ind. Inst., eng. (mech.); in the ent. since 1964. *Add.* Komjaunatnes 12, Kalnciems, Jelgavas raj. 229616; tel. 693 21.

■ **STECJUNA, Aleksandra**, Chair., Bd of Riga interregional cooperative bank *Baltija*, 1988 —; b. 1944; grad. Moscow Inst. of Finance; CSc. (Econ.). *Add.* Aspazijas bulv. 34, Rīga 226250; tel. 225 024.

■ **STEPIŅŠ, Atis**, organist, pianist, composer; b. 1958; grad. Latv. Acad. of Music, teacher of it; perfected in Netherlands; prize winner, West Germany comp. of organists, 1989, Italy, 1990; writes mainly organ music; perf. in Europe. *Add.* Kr.Barona 1, Rīga 226050, PDP; tel. 341 024 (h).

■ **STIEBRA, Roze**, animated cartoon film dir, scriptwriter; b. 1942; grad. Leningrad Inst. of Theatre, Music and Cinematography; at Latv. TV, 1966 — 88, puppet and animated cartoon studio *Dauka*, 1988 —; films based on Latv. classical lit.; award for film 'Pocket' at Animated Film Festival, Ukraine, 1983, for 'Visible Verse' at All-Union *KROK* Festival, 1989. *Add.* Šmerļa 3, Rīga 226037; tel. 529 053.

■ **STONE, Sarmīte**, rower; b. 1963; world champ., 1982, 1983, Goodwill Games medallist, 1990, 5-times USSR champ. *Add.* (h) Viestura prospekts 37 — 59, Rīga 226005; tel. 397 475.

■ **STRADIŅŠ, Jānis**, spec. in physical chem., hist. of natural sci.; b. 1933; grad. Latv. Univ.; DSc. (Chem.), Prof., Acad., Latv. Acad. of Sci., Hon. Dr, Latv. Univ.; at Inst. of Organic Synthesis, 1957 —; research in electrochem. of organic compounds, polarography, hist. of Latv. med., phys., chem.; publ. in Germany, Great Britain, Italy, Switzerland, Finland, Japan; Pres., Assoc. of Baltic Sci., Hist. and Phil.; Chair., scientific assoc. 'Latvia and the Latvians World-wide'. *Add.* Aizkraukles 21, Rīga 226006; tel. 555 987.

■ **STRAUTIŅŠ, Ivars**, Chair., Bd, Latv. Union of Consumers' Soc., 1985 —; b. 1942; grad. Inst. of Commerce; USSR People's Deputy. *Add.* Tērbatas 14, Rīga 226726, PDP; tel. 281 510.

■ **STRAUTIŅŠ, Vilnis**, Dir, Nat. Symphony Orch., 1990 —; b. 1939; grad. Latv. Acad. of Music, flutist; Prof.; mem., Nat. Symphony Orch., 1969, 1978, 1984 —; part. of wind quintet; perf. in European c., Japan. *Add.* Amatu 6, Rīga 226350; tel. 224 850, 223 719.

■ **STRAUTMANIS, Ivars**, architect; b. 1932; grad. Latv. Univ.; DSc. (Arch.), Prof.; author of public and living houses, sports stadiums; co-author of Salaspils Memorial Ensemble; advocates of Modernism and Postmodernism in arch.; author of several monographs. *Add.* Āzenes 16, Rīga 226048; tel. 615 056.

■ **STRAZDIŅŠ, Jānis,** Head Physician, Anti-Narcotics Dispensary, 1977 — ; b. 1941; grad. Latv. Univ., psychiatrist. *Add.* Aptiekas 7/9, Rīga 226005; tel. 391 074.

■ **STRĪĶIS, Voldemārs,** Mem., SC Presidium, Chair., Commn on Agric. and Forestry, 1990 — ; b. 1936; grad. Latv. Acad. of Agric., agron.; CSc. (Econ.), Prof.; research in econ. of plant-growing; author of textbooks; Latv. SC Deputy. *Add.* Jēkaba 11, Rīga 226811, PDP; tel. 323 352.

■ **STRODS, Ēvalds,** E-in-C, ill. arts journal *Māksla,* 1985 — ; b. 1933; grad. Latv. Univ., lawyer. *Add.* tel. Rīga 321 812.

■ **STŪRIŠKA, Jānis,** Dir, Ranka Cardboard Factory, 1970 — ; b. 1938; grad. Riga Tech. Univ., eng. (electric equipm.). *Add.* Krustakmens, Gulbenes raj., Ranka 228718; tel. 444 84.

■ **ŠABALOVS, Anatolijs,** Dir-Gen., electric equipm. ent. *Straume,* 1986 — ; b. 1940; grad. Riga Tech. Univ., eng. (radio-design). *Add.* E.Tēlmaņa 2, Rīga 226004; tel. 627 010.

■ **ŠAPIRO, Ādolfs,** Chief Dir, Youth Theatre, 1964 — ; b. 1939; grad. Kharkov Theatre Inst.; combines deep psychological analysis and up-to-date means of expression in his prod.; staged prod. in Moscow, Minsk, Tallinn, Finland, Germany, Nicaragua, Venezuela; part. in B.Brecht's festivals; Pres., ASSITEJ, 1990 — ; Pres., USSR Branch of ASSITEJ; Head, USSR Studio for training stage dir for children and youth theatres. *Add.* Lāčplēša 37, Rīga 226716, PDP; tel. 222 651.

■ **ŠEVČUKS, Georgs,** Chief, Riga Fishing Seaport, 1990 — ; b. 1954; grad. Kaliningrad Fishery and Technol. Inst., econ.; in the port since 1974. *Add.* Atlantijas 27, Rīga 226020; tel. 341 477.

■ **ŠILOVS, Viktors,** Dir, Līvāni Building Materials and Constr. Works, 1987 — ; b. 1951; grad. Riga Tech. Univ., eng. (civil). *Add.* Celtniecības 1, Līvāni 228264; tel. 444 94.

■ **ŠKAPARS, Jānis,** Mem., SC Presidium, Chair., Commn on Self-Govt and Social Affairs, 1990 — ; b. 1927; grad. Latv. Univ., lawyer; E-in-C, art newspaper *Literatūra un Māksla,* 1969 — 85; Chair., LPF CBd, 1989 — 90; Latv. SC Deputy. *Add.* Jēkaba 11, Rīga 226811, PDP; tel. 213 759.

■ **ŠMIDKENA, Silvija,** ceramist; b. 1935; grad. Latv. Acad. of Arts; author of decorative ware groups, sculptural forms, monumental decorative ceramics; exh. in Faenza, Prague (silver medallist, 1962), Gdańsk (prize winner, 1973), Sopot, Erfurt, Westerwald, Nagoya; Vallauris Culture and Art Assoc. prize, 1978. *Add.* (h) Vaidavas 13 — 46, Rīga 226084; tel. 560 920, 612 467.

■ **ŠNEIDERS, Jānis,** Head, Cent. Bd of Archives, 1988 — ; b. 1931; grad. Moscow Inst. of Printing; worked in CPSU and state admin. bodies. *Add.* Šķūņu 11, Rīga 226047; tel. 212 539.

■ **ŠOPS, Māris,** Chair., Bd of agrofirm *Ķekava,* 1976 — ; b. 1950; grad. Latv. Univ., econ. *Add.* Rīgas raj., Ķekava 229023; tel. 937 174, 937 751.

■ **ŠPAKOVSKIS, Staņislavs,** Dir-Gen., linen ent. *Latvijas lini,* 1984 — ; b. 1936; grad. Leningrad Textile Inst., eng.; CSc. (Eng.). *Add.* Lapskalna 18, Jelgava 229600; tel. 239 34.

■ **ŠULCS, Jānis,** Dir, Cinematographers' House, 1982 — ; b. 1940; studied at Moscow Inst. of Cinematography; cameraman; at Riga Film Studio, 1958 — 84. *Add.* A.Čaka 67/69, Rīga 226001; tel. 297 010.

■ **ŠVARCS, Kurts,** physicist; b. 1930; grad. Latv. Univ.; DSc. (Phys. & Math.), Prof., Acad., Latv. Acad. of Sci.; at Inst. of Phys., 1961 — ; research in radiation-induced processes, dynamic holography and non-linear optical phenomena in inorganic matter (ionic crystals, amorphous semiconductors); 250 publ., 6 monographs (also in Engl., Ger.). *Add.* Miera 32, Salaspils 229021; tel. 947 642.

■ **ŠVEICA, Daina,** Chair., Cttee for Physical Culture and Sports, 1990 — ; b. 1939; grad. Riga Tech. Univ.; CSc. (Chem.); European champ., rowing, 1963 — 65, 1967; Pres., Latv. Olympic Acad., 1989 — ; Mem., FISA, 1971 — .*Add.* Tērbatas 4, Rīga 226011, PDP; tel. 284 206.

■ **TABAKA, Maija,** paintress; b. 1939; grad. Latv. Acad. of Arts; creates portraits and figurative compositions combining juxtaposed elements, pieces and details in a specific, original, surrealistic whole; won scholarship and worked in West Berlin, 1977; works in museums abroad. *Add.* Mākslinieku savienība, Kr.Barona 12, Rīga 226400, PDP; tel. 287 614.

■ **TĀLS, Mihails,** chess player, int. grand master; b. 1936; grad. Latv. Univ.; world champ., 1961, Chess Olympics champ., 1958, 1960, 1962, 1966, 1972, 1974, 1980, 1982, European champ., 1957, 1961, 1970, 1973, 1977, 1980, USSR champ., 1957, 1958, 1967, 1972, 1974, 1978; winner of more than 40 int. chess tournaments. *Add.* Šaha un dambretes klubs, Aspazijas bulv. 16, Rīga 226050; tel. 213 313.

■ **TAMUŽS, Vitauts,** spec. in material mech.; b. 1935; grad. Moscow Univ.; DSc. (Phys. & Math.), Prof., Corr. Mem., Latv. Acad. of Sci.; at Inst. of Polymer Mech., 1964 — ; research in mech. of solid, composite materials, fracture mech., fatigue, dynamics; publ. USA, Netherlands, Germany. *Add.* Aizkraukles 23, Rīga 226006; tel. 525 705.

■ **TARNOPOĻSKIS, Jurijs,** spec. in material mech.; b. 1929; grad. Latv. Univ.; DSc. (Eng.), Prof., Acad., Latv. Acad. of Sci.; Head, Lab. of Inst. of Polymer Mech., 1963 — ; research in parametres of composite material structures, properties of various composite materials, testing methods of composite material structures; mem. of int. org.; author of 8 monographs (4 publ. in USA), 12 inv.; pat. in Great Britain, France, Belgium, Italy, Finland. *Add.* Aizkraukles 23, Rīga 226006; tel. 525 797.

■ **TEIKMANIS, Andris,** Chair., Riga City People's Deputies Council, 1990 — ; b. 1959; grad. Latv. Univ., lawyer; worked as investigator, judge; Mem., LPF Council, 1988 — 90; Latv. SC Deputy. *Add.* Kr.Valdemāra 3, Rīga 226162, PDP; tel. 320 680.

■ **TERJOHINS, Edgars**, yachtsman; b. 1955; European champ., model group '470', 1979; 'Withbread' part. (Sept. 2,1989 — May 22,1990); in search for sponsors for a one-man round-the-world trip. **Add.** (h) Ganu 4—11a, Rīga 226010; tel. 331 460.

■ **TRĒZIŅŠ, Juris**, Dir, Cent. Tennis Club, 1987—; b. 1951; grad. Latv. Inst. of Physical Culture; ex-coach in tennis. **Add.** Baldones 7, Rīga 226046; tel. 612 604.

■ **TRUKŠĀNS, Gunārs**, Chair., Bd of fishery collective farm *Banga*, 1988—; b. 1949; grad. Kaliningrad Higher Sch. of Naval Eng.; in the farm since 1973. **Add.** Ostas 7, Roja, Talsu raj. 229564; tel. 691 71.

■ **UGRJUMOVS, Pēteris**, cyclist; b. 1961; Peace Cycle-Race winner for USSR team, 1984, 1985, 1988; mem., Italian team 'Alfa Lum', 1988—.

■ **ŌĶIS, Andris**, Chair., Assoc. of Fishery Collective Farms, 1990—; b. 1938; grad. Kaliningrad Fishery and Technol. Inst.; Vice-Chair., 1979—90. **Add.** Jauniela 13, Rīga 226900; tel. 213 859.

■ **ULME, Arvīds**, Pres., Environmental Protection Club, 1987—; b. 1947; studied at Latv. Acad. of Agric.; Latv. SC Deputy. **Add.** Kalnciema 30, Rīga 226046; tel. 612 850, 137 162(h).

■ **UĻJANOVS, Georgs**, Dir, inst. for trade distribution and design *Tirdzniecības projekts*, 1989—; b. 1947; grad. Latv. Univ., econ. **Add.** Raiņa bulv. 25, Rīga 226050; tel. 229 323.

■ **UPENIEKS, Andris**, Dir-Gen., Latv. Fur-Farming Ent., 1985—; b. 1932; grad. Latv. Acad. of Agric., agriculturist. **Add.** M.Juglas 3, Rīga 226077; tel. 532 183.

■ **UPENIEKS, Pēteris**, Dir-Gen., Rēzekne Canned Milk Factory, 1963—; b. 1932; grad. Latv. Acad. of Agric., eng. (technol.). **Add.** Ļeņina 155/1, Rēzekne 228100; tel. 329 75.

■ **URBĀNS, Uldis**, oboist; b. 1951; grad. Latv. Acad. of Music; mem., Nat. Symphony Orch., 1970—; part. of chamber groups; perf. in Europe, USA. **Add.** (h) Kr.Barona 92—6, Rīga 226001; tel. 278 684.

■ **URSTIŅŠ, Ilgonis**, Dir, Museum of Boxing Hist., 1987—; b. 1934; grad. Latv. Inst. of Physical Culture. **Add.** Induļa 2, Rīga 226059; tel. 599 135.

■ **USTINOVS, Nikolajs**, Dir, Research Inst. of Math. and Computer Sci., 1984—; b. 1946; grad. Latv. Univ., phys.; DSc. (Phys. & Math.), Prof.; research in math. modelling, computer sci. **Add.** Raiņa bulv. 29, Rīga 226250; tel. 213 425.

■ **UTĀNS, Juris**, painter; b. 1959; grad. Latv. Acad. of Arts; paints figurative compositions; works characterized by keen social approach and metaphoric rendering of reality, executed in oil, acryl, mixed, techiques; exh. in Germany, Czecho-Slovakia, Bulgaria, Sweden, USA, Korea. **Add.** (h) Rudzutaka 78—25, Rīga 226069; tel. 420 097.

■ **UTKINS, Vladimirs**, surgeon; b. 1932; grad. Moscow Inst. of Med. No 1; DSc. (Med.), Prof.; spec. in chest surgery; research in oesophageal disorders and surgery, postoperative stomach; publ. in USA, France, Germany. **Add.** Dzirciema 16, Rīga 225007; tel. 616 923.

■ **VALNERIS, Guntis**, draughts player; b. 1967; silver medallist, world champ., 1990; world champ. among juniors, 1984—86. **Add.** Sporta komiteja, Tērbatas 4, Rīga 226011, PDP; tel. 284 206.

■ **VALTERS, Valdis**, basketball player; b. 1957; grad. Riga Tech. Univ.; world champ., 1982, silver medallist, 1986, 1987, European champ., 1981, 1985; European top player, 1985; mem., *VEF* team, 1980—88; Dir and Coach of his private basketball sch., 1988—. **Add.** (h) Kr.Barona 122/2—35, Rīga 226012; tel. 270 396.

■ **VARSLAVĀNS, Alberts**, historian; b. 1929; grad. Latv. Univ.; DSc. (Hist.), Prof.; research in British policy in the Baltics, int. relations in East Europe between WWI and WWII. **Add.** Brīvības bulv. 32, Rīga 226050; tel. 283 734.

■ **VASKS, Pēteris**, composer; b. 1946; grad. Lith. Conservatoire, Latv. Acad. of Music; author of chamber music, symphonic compositions and choir songs; compositions excel in harmony, diatonic simplicity, natural symbols, conventional folk music methods merge well with complex, up-to-date means of expression; publ. in Italy, Germany, USA; perf. abroad. **Add.** Komponistu savienība, Kr.Barona 12, Rīga 226011; tel. 287 614.

■ **VAZNIS, Aloizs**, Interior Min., 1990—; b. 1934; grad. Latv. Univ., lawyer; worked as Chief of Criminal Invest. Dept and Man. Dept of Interior Min. **Add.** Raiņa bulv. 6, Rīga 226181, PDP; tel. 287 260.

■ **VĒBERS, Jānis**, law scholar; b. 1930; grad. Latv. Univ.; DSc. (Law), Prof., Corr. Mem., Latv. Acad. of Sci.; research in civil law, family law; part. in drafting laws of Latv. Rep. **Add.** Raiņa bulv. 19, Rīga 226098; tel. 224 721.

■ **VECUMNIEKS, Edvīns**, Chair., Bd of Latv. Arch. Union, 1989—; b. 1935; grad. Riga Tech. Univ.; leading spec., inst. *Komunālprojekts*, 1970—; designer of public buildings, interiors; initiator of int. style arch. in post-Stalin era. **Add.** Brīvības 148a, Rīga 226012; tel. 364 017, 226 701.

■ **VECVAGARS, Jānis**, Dir, Liepāja Paper Factory, 1990—; b. 1935; grad. Latv. Acad. of Agric., wood technol.; in woodworking ent. since 1960. **Add.** Pļavu 17, Liepāja 229700; tel. 246 05.

■ **VEDERŅIKOVS, Nikolajs**, spec. in wood chem. and technol.; b. 1937; grad. Riga Tech. Univ.; DSc. (Chem.), Corr. Mem., Latv. Acad. of Sci.; at Inst. of Wood Chem., 1959—, Dep. Dir, 1985—; research in chem. and mech. destruction of polysaccharides, synthesis of furfural; pat. in European c., USA, Japan; publ. in USA, Japan, Czecho-Slovakia. **Add.** Akadēmijas 27, Rīga 226006; tel. 553 760.

■ **VEIDEMANE, Elita**, E-in-C, LPF newspaper *Atmoda*, 1988—; b. 1955; grad. Latv. Univ., philol. **Add.** Vecpilsētas 13/15, Rīga 226250; tel. 210 452.

■ **VĒRPE, Edgars**, painter; b. 1958; grad. Latv. Acad. of Arts; paints figurative compositions, still-lifes in oil, pastel; representative of symbolism; part. of numerous exh. **Add.** (h) Baldones 24—3, Rīga 226083; tel. 455 903.

▪ **VIDENIEKS, Pēteris**, Min. of Communications, 1990 — ; b. 1940; grad. Riga Tech. Univ., eng. (radio-design); DSc. (Eng.), Acad., Latv. Acad. of Sci.; worked at *VEF* company as Dir of *VEF* Research Inst.; designed radio receivers, leading spec. in multifunctional microprocessor systems for telephones, recorders and equipm. *Add.* Elizabetes 41/43, Rīga 226153, PDP; tel. 332 550.

▪ **VIESTURS, Uldis**, Dir, Inst. of Wood Chem., 1986 — ; Vice-Pres., Latv. Acad. of Sci.; b. 1936; grad. Latv. Acad. of Agric., biotechnol.; DSc. (Eng.), Prof., Acad., Latv. Acad. of Sci.; at Inst. of Microbiol., 1964 — 86; research in regularities of microorganism growth and metabolite biosynthesis; creation of tech. systems providing biosynthetic processes and designed products obtained from cultural liquids; bioconversion of photosynthesized biomass; chem. and bioeng.; pat. in Czecho-Slovakia, Bulgaria, Germany, Yugoslavia; publ. in European c., USA. *Add.* Akadēmijas 27, Rīga 226006; tel. 553 063.

▪ **VIGMANS, Vladimirs**, E-in-C, popular draughts magazine *Dambrete*, 1990 — ; b. 1952; silver medallist of the world champ., draughts, 64 sq, 1985 — 86, 1989; coach, USSR nat. team, 1983, 1986. *Add.* Centrs, a.k. 55, Rīga 226088; tel. 224 148, 225 629.

▪ **VILDE, Raimonds**, volleyball player; b. 1962; Olympic silver medallist, 1988, European champ., 1985, USSR champ., 1984; player of Riga team *Radiotehniķis*, 1982 — . *Add.* Sporta komiteja, Tērbatas 4, Rīga 226011, PDP; tel. 284 206.

▪ **VILKS, Andris**, Dir, Nat. Library, 1989 — ; b. 1957; grad. Latv. Univ., bibliographer; at the library since 1978. *Add.* Kr.Barona 14, Rīga 226437, PDP; tel. 280 851.

▪ **VILKS, Andris**, E-in-C, Latv. Encyclopaedia Publrs, 1989 — ; b. 1945; grad. Latv. Univ., phil.; DSc. (Phil.); in the publ. house since 1983. *Add.* Maskavas 68, Rīga 226018; tel. 220 150.

▪ **VILKS, Ģirts**, rower; b. 1968; world champ., 1990; world champ. among juniors, 1986; winner, Lucerne Regatta and Seattle Goodwill Games, 1990. *Add.* Sporta komiteja, Tērbatas 4, Rīga 226011, PDP; tel. 284 206.

▪ **VILLERUŠA, Inta**, pianist; b. 1943; grad. Latv. Acad. of Music, teacher of it; exquisite, refined accompanist, prefers romantic music. *Add.* (h) Bruņinieku 28 — 11, Rīga 226001; tel. 270 313.

▪ **VILLERUŠS, Māris**, violoncellist; b. 1931; grad. Latv. Acad. of Music; Prof.; prize winner, P.Tchaikovsky and P. Casals int. comp.; perf. in Canada, Germany, Finland, Poland, Hungary. *Add.* (h) Bruņinieku 28 — 11, Rīga 226001; tel. 270 313.

▪ **VĪNS, Gints**, Dir, Baltic News Service, 1990 — ; b. 1966; studying at Leningrad Inst. of Theatre, Music and Cinematography. *Add.* Smilšu 1/3, Rīga 226900, PDP; tel. 228 826.

▪ **VITKUS, Inese**, Dir, audio and visual marketing assoc. *LAMA*, 1990 — ; b. 1946; grad. Latv. Univ., philol.; worked in radio and TV. *Add.* Zaķusalas krastmala 3, Rīga 226018; tel. 200 688.

▪ **VĪTOLIŅŠ, Guntars**, Dir, textbooks publrs *Zvaigzne*, 1986 — ; b. 1931; grad. Latv. Univ., biol.; in the publ. business since 1966. *Add.* Kr.Valdemāra 105, Rīga 226013; tel. 372 396.

▪ **VĪTOLIŅŠ, Viesturs**, Man., Artistic Dir, Latv. Philharmonic, 1989 — ; b. 1942; grad. Latv. Acad. of Music, music critic; radio musical programme dir, 1973 — 82. *Add.* Kaļķu 11a, Rīga 226350, PDP; tel. 223 618.

▪ **VIZULIS, Vilnis**, painter; b. 1952; grad. Latv. Acad. of Arts; representative of expressive romanticism; paintings, water colours, employs also wax emulsion techniques; works in private coll. in Europe, USA, Canada, Australia; exh. in Germany, Bulgaria, Poland et al. *Add.* (h) Kr.Valdemāra 23 — 18, Rīga 226010; tel. 336 143.

▪ **VOLKOLAKOVS, Jānis**, surgeon; b. 1931; grad. Latv. Acad. of Med.; DSc. (Med.), Prof.; research in heart, bloodvessels, oesophagus, gastroenteric fistular surgery; author of textbooks on surgery; publ. in USA, Italy; Mem., ICVS. *Add.* Dzirciema 16, Rīga 226007; tel. 615 024.

▪ **VOLKOVS, Vladimirs**, Chair., Bureau of Pathological Anatomy, 1984 — ; b. 1939; grad. Latv. Univ.; CSc. (Med.). *Add.* P.Dauges 2, Rīga 226038; tel. 536 091.

▪ **VULFSONS, Mavriks**, Mem., SC Presidium, Chair., Foreign Affairs Commn, 1990 — ; journalist, spec. in pol. studies; b. 1918; grad. Latv. Univ.; Prof.; lecturer, Latv. Acad. of Arts, 1963 — 89; Mem., LPF CBd; USSR People's Deputy, Latv. SC Deputy. *Add.* Jēkaba 11, Rīga 226811, PDP; tel. 331 516, 323 760 (h).

▪ **ZAHAROVS, Ivans**, Dir, Liepāja Linoleum Plant, 1987 — ; b. 1932; grad. Riga Tech. Univ., eng. (mech.); in the plant since 1948. *Add.* Sarkanarmijas 5/7/9, Liepāja 229700; tel. 246 74.

▪ **ZAKSS, Gunārs**, Min. of Fisheries, 1990 — ; b. 1934; grad. Kaliningrad Inst. of Fishery and Technol., econ.; worked as ship capt., occupied leading posts in fishery ent.; Chair., Latv. Assoc. of Fishery Farms, 1985 — 90. *Add.* Smilšu 6, Rīga 226176, PDP; tel. 322 498.

▪ **ZAĶIS, Juris**, Rector, Latv. Univ., 1987 — ; phys.; b. 1936; grad. Latv. Univ.; DSc. (Phys. & Math.), Prof., Acad., Latv. Acad. of Sci.; at Latv. Univ. since 1960; headed Semiconductors Research Lab. and Inst. of Solid State Phys.; research in structure and defects of amorphous and vitreous solids, methodology of natural sci.; publ. in USA, Germany, Netherlands; USSR People's Deputy. *Add.* Raiņa bulv. 19, Rīga 226098; tel. 228 928.

▪ **ZĀLĪTE, Māra**, E-in-C, lit. journal *Karogs*, 1989 — ; poetess; b. 1952; grad. Latv. Univ.; 5 coll. of poems, 3 plays, libretto for rock opera, contrib. to periodicals. *Add.* tel. Rīga 289 875.

▪ **ZARIŅA, Aija**, paintress; b. 1954; grad. Latv. Acad. of Arts; avant-gardist; paintings carry decorative, monumental expression; part. of int. exh. *Add.* Mākslinieku savienība, Kr.Barona 12, Rīga 226400, PDP; tel. 287 432.

▪ **ZARIŅŠ, Indulis**, Rector, Latv. Acad. of Arts, 1987 — ; painter; b. 1929; grad. Latv. Acad. of Arts; Prof., Full Mem., USSR Acad. of Arts; versatile genre painter, creates, portraits, landscapes, still-life compositions; works in oil, tempera, watercolour, pastel; outstanding colourist; one-man shows in Moscow, Helsinki, Berlin, Rostock, Sofia, Budapest, Prague, Stockholm; exh. in Paris, Metropolitan and Varese museums; coll. in Uffizi and Tretyakov Galleries; USSR People's Deputy. *Add.* Komunāru bulv. 13, Rīga 226050; tel. 334 192.

■ **ZARIŅŠ, Kārlis**, Artistic Dir, Nat. Opera, 1990 — ; singer (dramatic tenor); b. 1930; grad. Latv. Acad. of Music; Prof.; perfected in Bulgaria; solo part singer, Nat. Opera, 1960 — ; parts of Radames, Othello, Pincerton, Tannhäuser, Don José; chamber singer; perf. in European c. *Add.* Aspazijas bulv. 3, Rīga 226251, PDP; tel. 224 325, 212 100 (h).

■ **ZARIŅŠ, Marģeris**, composer, writer; b. 1910; studied at Latv. Acad. of Music; 5 operas, 2 musicals, oratorios, cantatas, instrumental concertos (for piano, organ), solo music, approx. 80 choir songs, theatrical and cinema music; 7 novels, several coll. of short stories; transl. in Engl., Ger., Bulg., Czech, Rom.; striking, colourful humour, irony, histrionic plots. *Add.* (h) Baložu 10 — 1, Rīga 226007; tel. 612 904.

■ **ZAUSĀJEVS, Edgars**, Min. of Material Resources, 1990 — ; b. 1945; grad. Leningrad Inst. of Electrotech. Communications, econ.; occupied leading posts in electrotech. ent.; Dep. Chair., State Cttee for Material Tech. Resources, 1987 — 90. *Add.* Kr.Valdemāra 26, Rīga 226329, PDP; tel. 286 489.

■ **ZEILE, Valentīna**, Mem., SC Presidium, Chair., Commn on Budget, 1990 — ; b. 1937; grad. Latv. Univ., econ.; CSc. (Econ.); lecturer, Latv. Univ.; research in regional econ., living standards and social sci.; Latv. SC Deputy. *Add.* Jēkaba 11, Rīga 226811, PDP; tel. 323 810.

■ **ZEMRĪBO, Gvido**, Chair., Supreme Court, 1985 — ; b. 1932; grad. Latv. Univ., lawyer; worked as barrister, State Arbitrator; Dep. Chair., Supreme Court, 1971 — 85. *Add.* Brīvības bulv. 34, Rīga 226161, PDP; tel. 289 434.

■ **ZEMZARIS, Imants**, composer; b. 1951; grad. Latv. Acad. of Music; writes mainly instrumental chamber music, for unconventional instrumental combinations; author of small-size compositions and theatrical music. *Add.* Komponistu savienība, Kr.Barona 12, Rīga 226011; tel. 287 614.

■ **ZICMANIS, Aldis**, Dir-Gen., food refrigeration equipm. ent. *Kompresors*, 1987 — ; b. 1939; grad. Leningrad Inst. of Electrotech. Communications, eng.; Dir, *VEF* company, 1976 — 87. *Add.* Starta 1, Rīga 226026; tel. 377 113, 378 466.

■ **ZIEDONIS, Imants**, Chair., Latv. Culture Fund, 1987 — ; poet; b. 1933; grad. Latv. Univ.; Hon. Mem., Latv. Acad. of Sci.; 14 coll. of poems, 3 epiphany coll., 7 coll. of fairy-tales, prose, contrib. to periodicals, scripts; rendering of poetry by A.Blok, A.Pushkin, G.Vieru; works transl. in Engl., Sw., Czech, Pol., Rom., 8 lgs of USSR; recipient H.C.Andersen's Award (diploma), J.Korczak's Medal; Latv. SC Deputy, 1990 — 91. *Add.* Basteja bulv. 12, Rīga 226047; tel. 225 575.

■ **ZIEMIŅŠ, Erlends**, ballet premier, Nat. Opera; b. 1964; grad. Riga Choreography Sch.; contracted USA, 1991 — . *Add.* Aspazijas bulv. 3, Rīga 226251, PDP; tel. 222 823.

■ **ZIKMANE, Lolita**, graphic artist; b. 1941; grad. Latv. Acad. of Arts; excellent etcher; deeply associative reproduction of nature, metaphoric compositions; exh. abroad. *Add.* Mākslinieku savienība, Kr.Barona 12, Rīga 226400, PDP; tel. 287 432.

■ **ZILGALVIS, Dzintars**, painter; b. 1956; grad. J.Rozentāls Art College; representative of anti-aesthetic expressionism, stands against over-appreciation of beauty. *Add.* (h) Madonas 27 — 56, Rīga 226084; tel. 582 097.

■ **ZILBERTS, Ventis**, pianist; b. 1947; grad. Latv. Acad. of Music; Head, Accompanist Dept; perf. in European c., USA, Canada. *Add.* (h) Jerjomenko 12 — 101, Rīga 226084; tel. 581 880.

■ **ZIRNIS, Jānis**, choral dir; b. 1944; grad. Latv. Acad. of Music, Asst Prof.; at Nat. Opera, 1987 — ; conductor, Students Symphony Orch. of Latv. Acad. of Music, 1990 — ; Dir, int. prize winner (Tallinn, 1988) female choir *Ausma*, 1968 — ; Chief Conductor, Latv. Song Festival, 1990; perf. in European c. *Add.* (h) Vidus prosp. 20 — 32, Ogre 228300; tel. Rīga 227 471, 222 823.

■ **ZORGEVICS, Ādolfs**, Dir, Botanical Garden, Latv. Univ., 1965 — ; b. 1925; grad. Leningrad Inst. of Agric., agron.; flower grower (gladioluses and lilies). *Add.* Kandavas 2, Rīga 226083; tel. 450 852.

■ **ZOZUĻA, Vera**, sledge driver; b. 1956; grad. Inst. of Physical Educ. in Moscow region; Olympic, 1980, world, 1978, 1980, European champ. 1976; World Cup winner, 1982; coach. *Add.* Sporta komiteja, Tērbatas 4, Rīga 226011, PDP; tel. 284 206.

■ **ZVIDRIŅŠ, Pēteris**, economist; b. 1943; grad. Latv. Univ.; DSc. (Econ.), Prof., Corr. Mem., Latv. Acad. of Sci.; research in problems of statistics, demography, manpower planning in Latvia, the Baltics, worldwide; co-author of long-term programme 'Population of Latvia'; author of more than 180 scientific works, textbooks on demographic problems; mem. of several int. assoc., org., unions; winner of USA prize 'The Population Council'. *Add.* Aspazijas bulv. 5, Rīga 226050; tel. 226 368, 226 303.

► **ZVIRBULIS, Andrejs**, Chair., Riga soc., assoc. of large Latv. families world-wide *Dēkla*, 1990 — ; b. 1950; grad. Ranka Forest Sch. *Add.* Dzirnavu 115 — 17, Rīga 226011; tel. 289 763.

■ **ZVIRGZDS, Andris**, Dir, Botanical Garden, Latv. Acad. of Sci., 1980 — ; b. 1928; grad. Latv. Acad. of Agric., dendrologist; CSc. (Biol.); research on introduction, acclimatization propagation, and seed plots of ornamental woody plants, design of parks in rural areas, vital and integral peculiarities of woody plants. *Add.* Rīgas 46, Salaspils — 1, 229021; tel. 947 131.

■ **ŽERDIŅA, Velta**, Dir, Fire-Fighting Museum, 1978 — ; b. 1936; grad. pedag. inst.; an organizer of the museum in 1972. *Add.* Hanzas 5, Rīga 226045; tel. 333 306.

REPUBLIC OF
LITHUANIA

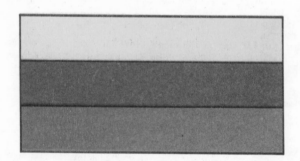

TAUTIŠKA GIESMĖ

(THE NATIONAL SONG)

Vincas KUDIRKAS

Lietuva, Tėvyne mūsų,
Tu didvyrių žeme,
Iš praeities Tavo sūnūs
Te stiprybę semia.

Tegul Tavo vaikai eina
Vien takais dorybės,
Tegul dirba Tavo naudai
Ir žmonių gėrybei.

Tegul saulė Lietuvoj
Tamsumus prašalina,
Ir šviesa, ir tiesa
Mūs žingsnius telydi.

Tegul meilė Lietuvos
Dega mūsų širdyse,
Vardan tos Lietuvos
Vienybė težydi.

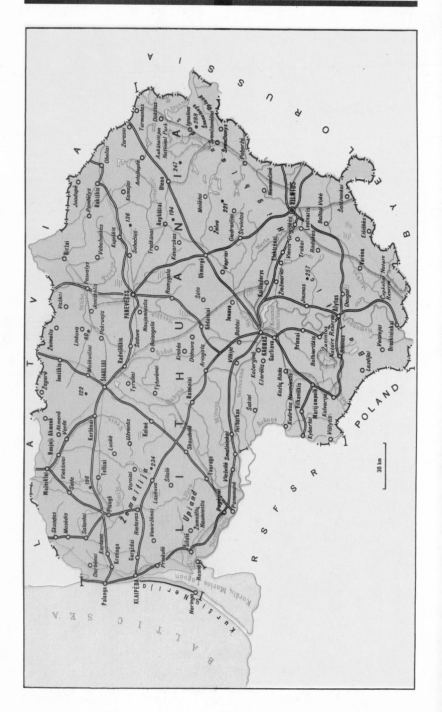

THE REPUBLIC OF LITHUANIA lies in the centre of Europe (the geometrical centre of the continent is in eastern Lithuania, near the village of Bernotai, 25 km north of Vilnius), on the eastern coast of the Baltic Sea (the length of the Lithuanian coastline is 99 km). The northernmost point of Lithuania is 56°27' and the southernmost 53°54' N; the westernmost point of Lithuania is 20°56' and easternmost 26°51' E. In the north Lithuania borders on Latvia (610 km of the borderline), in the east and south on Byelorussia (724 km), in the southwest on Poland (110 km) and the Kaliningrad region of the Russian Federation (303 km). The area of Lithuania (65,200 sq km) is larger than that of Belgium, Denmark, the Netherlands and Switzerland.

In 1990, Lithuania's population was 3,723,000. The official language is Lithuanian, the majority of believers are Roman Catholics. The administrative division of Lithuania includes 11 cities of national jurisdiction and 44 rural districts. The capital of Lithuania is Vilnius (592,500 inhabitants). Other major cities: Kaunas (430,000), Klaipėda (206,000), Šiauliai (148,000), Panevėžys (129,000). The state holiday is February 16, the Day of the Restoration of the Lithuanian State.

LANGUAGE

The Lithuanian language is spoken in Lithuania (its official language since 1989, spoken by more than 2,900,000 people) as well as in some other countries (mostly in the USA, Russia, Brazil, Latvia, Argentina, Canada, Kazakhstan, Poland, the Ukraine, Australia, Germany). It belongs to the Baltic group of the Indo-European language family and is closely related to the Latvian language. Lithuanian and Latvian languages split from the Eastern Proto-Baltic in the 5 — 7 cent. AD. The formation of standard Lithuanian, based on the southern subdialect of Western High Lithuanian dialect, was completed in the closing decades of the 19th cent. Lithuanian is a most archaic language. Of all the living Indo-European languages, it has retained the ancient sound system and numerous morphological peculiarities. Lithuanian is quite unique in the sense that it has a surprisingly large number of dialects (High Lithuanian, or *Aukštaičiai*, and Low Lithuanian, or *Žemaičiai* dialect) for such a small territory. Since the mid-20th cent., the dialects have been subject to assimilation, leading to extinction.

NATURE

RELIEF, HYDROGRAPHICAL NETWORK, CLIMATE. Lithuania lies on the western fringe of the East European Plain, in the middle and lower basin of the River Nemunas. The relief is a meridian-oriented alternation of lowland plains and hilly uplands. All the hilly uplands are accumulations of glacial drift. The plains lie 80 — 100 m below the uplands. Stretching along the Baltic coast is the Pajūrio Lowland. It is 15 — 20 km wide, up to 50 m of absolute height. To the east of it, lies the Žemaičiu Upland, Medvėgalis being the highest point (234 m). In the central part of Lithuania, the Middle Lowland runs from north to southwest (up to 100 km wide, 35 — 90 m of absolute height). In the south and east of Lithuania lie the Baltic Highlands (up to 282 m high). A sandy Southeastern Plain encircles the highlands in the southeast. Lying in the east of the country are small stretches of the Lithuanian-Byelorussian morainic uplands: the Švenčioniu Upland and the Medininku Upland. The latter boasts the highest point of Lithuania — Juozapinė Hill (294 m).

Lithuania has a dense, intricate network of rivers. In all, there are more than 29,900 watercourses over 250 m long, with a total length of 63,700 km. There are 758 rivers more than 10 km long, 18 of which are longer than 100 km (Nemunas — 937, Neris — 510, Venta — 350, Šešupė — 298, Šventoji — 246, Minija — 213). The rivers are of moderate turbidity. They stay frozen over for about 3 months yet during some winters they remain ice-free.

Lithuania lies in one of Europe's most abundant lake districts. There are 2,833 lakes exceeding 0.5 ha. They occupy an area of 876 sq km (1.5% of Lithuania's territory). About 1,600 lakes are smaller than 0.5 ha. The majority of lakes are in the north of the Baltic Highlands, in the Aukštaičiu Upland. Lithuania's largest (Drūkšiai, 44.8 sq km), deepest (Tauragnas, 60.5 m) and longest (Asveja, 21.9 km) lakes also lie in that area.

The climate of Lithuania is transitional between maritime and continental. The mean annual temperature is +6.1 °C, the average in January being −4.9 °C and in July +17 °C. The mean annual precipitation (75% in rain) varies from 540 mm (Middle Lowland) to 930 mm (southwest of the Žemaičiu Upland). Westerly winds prevail. Annually, there are 40−100 foggy days and 15−30 days with thunderstorms. During the colder season of the year, there are 10−15 days of freezing-rain and snowstorms. Thaws are frequent. The vegetation period lasts from 169 days in the east of Lithuania to 202 days in the west.

SOIL, FLORA AND FAUNA. Lithuanian soil makes a very diverse pattern. 35% of the territory are turfy podzols. 25% of the farmland is on sand, 33% on sandy loam, 34% on clay loam, 2% on clay and 6% on peat. The most fertile soil is in the Middle Lowland. Eroded soil accounts for 15.5% of the farmland.

Lithuania is located in the mixed forest subzone. There are over 2,000 species of higher plants (of which 1,200 grow by themselves). Woodlands (18,000 separate plots) cover 27.9% of Lithuania's territory. 38.1% of Lithuania's wooded area are pine forests, 20.7% spruce forests and 21.1% birch forests. There are tracts of white alder, black alder, aspen, while the ash and oak are very scarce. Southwestern Lithuania is the most densely wooded part of the country. Lithuanian forests are rich in mushrooms (chanterelle, boletus) and berries (bilberry, red whortleberry, bog whortleberry, cranberry).

Lithuania's wildlife is typical of coniferous and broadleaf deciduous woodlands, though arctic and steppe species also occur. There are 70 species of mammals, 293 of birds, 7 of reptiles, 11 of amphibians and 60 of fish. The hunt of the elk, red deer, roe, wild boar, fox, hare, badger, racoon dog, wolf, lynx, wild duck and some gallinaceous birds is permitted. The roach, bream, ruff and perch make up the bulk of the catch in the Kuršiu Lagoon, rivers and lakes.

GEOLOGY AND MINERAL RESOURCES. Lithuania's western part and the Baltic Sea shelf offer good prospects for oil extraction and the southeast of the country for mining iron ore and granite. There is limestone and clay (raw materials for the production of cement and lime) in the district of Akmené, clay (raw material for ceramics) in the districts of Ignalina, Kaunas and Tauragé, quartz sand (raw material for glass) in the district of Anykščiai. The richest deposits of sand used in house-building lie in the districts of Varéna and Raseiniai, while those of gravel used in ferroconcrete production and in road paving are found in the districts of Trakai, Jonava and Jurbarkas. There is dolomite in the district of Pakruojis, gypsum in the districts of Biržai and Pasvalys, chalk and chalky marl in the south and southwest of the country. Mineral water can be found at depths of 100 to 700 m all over Lithuania, and thermal water suitable for heating, in the west. The Baltic Sea coast, the districts of Zarasai, Ignalina, Utena, Molétai, Trakai and many others offer good recreational opportunities.

ECOLOGICAL SITUATION, NATURE CONSERVATION. The atmosphere in Lithuania is the purest in the south and most polluted in the northwest, the central part and the major cities. The clearest water is in the rivers Merkys, Šventoji, Stréva and Úla, while the Nevéžis, Nemunas, Neris and Múša are polluted heavily. The purest groundwater is in the south of Lithuania and the most polluted in the north. During the years of Soviet occupation certain attempts were made to improve the ecological situation: a Law on Nature Protection was adopted in 1959, nature reserves and preserves were established, water-purification systems were installed and the Lithuanian Red Data Book was drawn up in 1976. However, the complex environment protection project up to the year 2,000 was hardly being put into practice, leading to a deterioration of the ecological situation. Due to the self-will of the administration and various departments, even the landscape of nature reserves was polluted and damaged.

POPULATION

NATIONS, ETHNIC GROUPS, LINGUISTIC SITUATION. Lithuanians are the indigenous and predominant inhabitants. In 1989, their number was 2,924,000, with 65% living in towns. Nearly all speak Lithuanian. The believers are mostly Roman Catholics, there are also Evangelical Lutherans and Evangelical Reformists. Ethnographic and language peculiarities distinguish Žemaičiai and Aukštaičiai, the latter divided into Suvalkiečiai and Dzūkai. In language and origin, the Lithuanians belong to the Baltic group of the Indo-European family of nations.

Russians make up the second largest ethnic group in Lithuania (344,500). The Russians fall into local residents who inhabited Lithuania since ancient times and immigrants who arrived after WW II, the latter forming the majority. 90% of the Russians live in towns. Most of them speak Russian. The believers adhere to the Russian Orthodox Church or to the Old Faith.

The Polish population of Lithuania totals 258,000, most of them are local inhabitants Polonized in the 19th−20th cent.

The majority of the Poles live in south-eastern Lithuania, 58% in towns (chiefly in Vilnius). The majority of the local Poles speak a dialect of the Byelorussian language. After WW II, many Poles (esp. the younger generation) adopted Russian as their language. From 1945−58, 218,000 Poles and Polonized Lithuanians emigrated to Poland. The believers are Roman Catholics.

There are 63,200 Byelorussians in Lithuania, of which 85% live in towns (nearly 1/2 of them in Vilnius). They speak Byelorussian (40%), Russian or Polish. The believers are Russian Orthodox and Roman Catholics.

In 1989, the number of Jews was 12,300 (195,000 Jews were exterminated by the Nazis in 1941). The first Jewish settlers are believed to have come to Lithuania in the 12th cent. At present they live in the major cities. They speak Yiddish (36%) or Russian, for some the native language is Lithuanian. The believers are Judaists.

The Ukrainians of Lithuania (44,800) also live chiefly in towns. Many have become Russianized. The believers are Russian Orthodox or Roman Catholics.

The Latvian population of Lithuania is 4,200. They live in northern Lithuania. The majority speak Latvian, for some the native language is either Lithuanian or Russian. The believers are mostly Evangelical Lutherans.

Gypsies (2,700) mostly live in the major cities. The first settlers appeared in Lithuania in the 15th cent. Majority communicate in the Gypsy language. The believers are Roman Catholics or Russian Orthodox.

The German community is scattered throughout Lithuania (2,058). 56,000 Germans repatriated to Germany in 1940—41. The first settlers came in the 13th cent. They speak German (42%), Lithuanian, Russian. The believers are Evangelical Lutherans.

The predominant number of Tatars (5,135) live in Vilnius. They began settling in Lithuania in the 14th—15th cent. They speak Tatar (32%), Russian, Lithuanian, Polish. The believers are Sunni Muslims, some are Russian Orthodox.

The smallest ethnic group is Karaites (289) who settled in Lithuania in the 14th—15th cent. They live in Vilnius, Trakai, Panevėžys and speak Karaite (73%), Polish, Lithuanian, Russian. The believers are of the Karaite faith.

The number of Armenians, Uzbeks, Moldavians (Roumanians), Azerbaijanis in Lithuania is over 1,000 people each, while other nationalities are represented by several hundred. The majority of these are male inhabitants who settled in towns after WW II. The greater part of Russians, Byelorussians and Ukrainians have also come to Lithuania after the war.

DEMOGRAPHIC SITUATION. From 1940—58, Lithuania lost about 1 million people who were killed, exiled or left the country. The pre-war population level was reached in 1969 only. In 1990, the male and female population was 47.4% and 52.6% respectively. 57% of the inhabitants are of working age, while 24% are below and 19% above it. 30.2% are employed in industry, 17.6% in agriculture, 11.9% in construction, 9.8% in education, culture and arts. Those receiving scholarships, pensions and other kinds of state maintenance make up 20.2% of the population. The main source of income for the population is wages (the monthly average in 1989 being 244 roubles).

68.0% of men and 58.9% of women of marriageable age are married. Nearly 1/2 of men and women marry between 20 and 24 years of age. 33.5% of couples divorce. In 1989, single people made up 7.5% of the population. The predominant number of families have 1 or 2 children. The birth rate began to decline in 1961 and was 15.0‰ in 1989. 15.4% of babies in 1989 were born in ethnically mixed families. The death rate (slightly increasing since 1965) was 10.3‰, with 10.7‰ among babies up to one year of age. The natural increase was 4.8%. It is bigger in Byelorussian and Polish families. Due to deportations (~300,000 people) and Polish repatriation, the population of Lithuania decreased by 146,000 in the years 1950—57. Since 1958 the migration increase has been positive: in the period between 1958 and 1989 the mechanical increase was 237,000 people, the peak points being in 1988 (16,600) and in 1989 (16,300). Life expectancy in Lithuania is 72.4 years (67.7 for men and 76.6 for women in 1989). In Lithuania there are more than 500 people over 100 years of age.

Population and Its Density

	Total population ('000)	Density (persons per sq km)	Urban population, %
14th cent.	260	4	—
1528	330	5	—
1569	420	6	—
1650	960	15	—
1790	990	15	12
1857	1910	24	—
1897	2673	41	13
1914	2828	43	13
1923	2620	40	18
1940	3084	47	22
1950	2573	40	28
1959	2711	42	39
1970	3128	48	50
1979	3398	52	61
1989	3675	56	68

Population by Nationality (%)

	1857	1897	1923	1959	1970	1979	1989
Lithuanians	75.6	61.6	69.2	79.3	80.1	80.0	79.6
Russians	1.4	4.8	2.5	8.5	8.6	8.9	9.4
Poles	5.6	9.7	15.3	8.5	7.7	7.3	7.0
Byelorussians	0.3	4.7	0.4	1.1	1.5	1.7	1.7
Ukrainians	0.1	0.1	0.0	0.7	0.8	0.9	1.2
Jews	10.7	13.1	8.3	0.9	0.8	0.4	0.3
Latvians	1.0	1.3	0.6	0.2	0.1	0.1	0.1
Germans	5.1	4.4	3.4	0.4	0.1	0.1	0.1
Other nationalities	0.2	0.3	0.3	0.4	0.3	0.6	0.6

STATE STRUCTURE

The Republic of Lithuania is a sovereign democratic state expressing the common will and interests of its people. The foundations of the social system are enforced by the Provisional Fundamental Law (Constitution) of the Republic of Lithuania adopted on March 11, 1990, which also establishes the rights, freedoms and obligations (duties) of citizens. Under that law, sovereign state power is vested in the people of Lithuania and is exercised by the Supreme Council, the Government and the Court of the Republic of Lithuania.

THE SUPREME COUNCIL (SC) is the highest body of state power of the Republic of Lithuania. The SC is a one-chamber parliament which adopts and amends the Constitution, calls elections of deputies to all representative bodies of state power, establishes the order regulating the founding and the activities of state bodies and officials accountable to it, elects the Chairman of the SC, Deputy Chairmen and the Secretary, appoints the Prime Minister and other members of the Government and introduces changes in the Government, elects the Supreme Court and judges of district (city) courts, passes laws and decrees (which can also be adopted through a referendum), forms standing and special parliamentary commissions, and decides other major issues of national importance. The SC consists of 141 elected deputies. Accountable to the SC is the Presidium, comprising the Chairman of the SC, Deputy Chairmen, the Secretary and other members who are elected by the SC. The Chairman of the SC is the highest state official who represents the Republic of Lithuania in international relations. The Chairman is elected by the SC by secret ballot from deputies of SC for a period of 5 years, for a maximum of two consecutive terms.

THE GOVERNMENT is the highest authority of executive power. It comprises the Prime Minister, Deputy Prime Ministers and Ministers. Prime Minister is appointed by SC upon the recommendation of its Chairman, while the Deputy Prime Ministers and Ministers, upon the recommendation of the Prime Minister. The Government is responsible and accountable to the SC and, in the period between its sessions, to the Presidium of the SC. If the Government or a Minister receives a no-confidence vote by secret ballot from more than 1/2 of the total number of the SC deputies, the entire Government or the Minister has to resign. The Government adopts decisions and issues decrees compulsory for execution throughout Lithuania.

LOCAL SELF-GOVERNMENT is organized on the basis of the administrative-territorial division of Lithuania. Apylinkes (the smallest rural administrative units), urban-type settlements and district towns constitute the lower level of local self-government, while districts and cities form the upper level. Local self-government is representedly the municipal council elected by the local population for a period of 5 years on the basis of universal, equal and direct suffrage by secret ballot.

COURTS AND PROSECUTION. Justice is exercised exclusively by courts. The court system in Lithuania comprises the Supreme Court and district (city) courts made up of elected judges and assessors. Judges of district (city) courts and of the Supreme Court are elected by the SC for a term of 10 years. Assessors of local courts are elected by district (city) councils, assessors of the Supreme Court by the SC for a term of 5 years. Legal assistance is rendered by the Bar, while cases of business disputes are heard in the State Arbitration. Supreme legal supervision is exercised by the Prosecutor General of the Republic of Lithuania and by local prosecutors under his subordination. Prosecutor General and his deputies are appointed by the SC, local prosecutors by the Prosecutor General of the Republic of Lithuania.

POLITICAL PARTIES. The activity of parties is defined by the Provisional Fundamental Law (Article 5) and the Law on Political Parties. All political parties enjoy the freedom and independence of action. Their organizational structure is based exclusively on the territorial principle. The activity (branches) of political parties and organizations of other states in Lithuania is forbidden by law. Political parties are registered by the Ministry of Justice.

HISTORY

The earliest evidence of inhabitants on the present-day territory of Lithuania dates back to the 10th millennium BC. At the late 3rd — early 2nd millennium BC, people of cord-ware culture spread over a vast territory of Eastern Europe, between the Baltic Sea and the River Vistula in the west and the Moscow-Kursk line in the east. Merging with the indigenous population in the 2nd millennium BC, they gave rise to the Balts, an Indo-European ethnic group whose descendants are the present-day Lithuanian and Latvian nations and the now extinct Prussians.

The first mention of the name Lithuania in written sources dates back to the year 1009 AD. In the 1230s and '40s, Duke Mindaugas (died 1263) united the lands inhabited by the Lithuanians and, partically, the Samogitians, Yotvingians and Couronians into the Grand Duchy of Lithuania (GDL). The formation of the state was spurred up by the expansion into the Baltic lands of two German monastic military orders, the Order of the Knights of the Sword and the Teutonic Order. In 1251 Mindaugas adopted Catholic faith and on July 6, 1253, he was crowned the King of Lithuania. In 1261, however, his abdication followed.

Grand Duke Gediminas (ruled 1316 — 41) made two unsuccessful attempts to adopt Christianity and thus put an end to the political and cultural isolation of GDL from Western Europe. With that end in mind, he wrote letters to Pope John XXII and European cities where he maintained that the purpose of the Teutonic Order was to conquer lands rather than spread Christianity. Grand Duke Gediminas invited knights, merchants and artisans to come and settle down in Lithuania. His dynasty (the Gediminaičiai) ruled GDL until 1572. In the 13th — early 15th cent., the Lithuanian state expanded eastwards. During the rule of Grand Duke Algirdas (1345 — 77), its territory grew almost twice. At the same time, GDL continued its struggle against the Teutonic and Livonian Orders, achieving major victories at the Battles of Saulė (1236) and Durbė (1260). However, backed by the Pope and the Catholic West European countries, the Orders continued their aggression which greatly intensified in the 2nd half of the 14th cent. During the period Algirdas' brother, Kęstutis (Grand Duke in 1381 — 82) distinguished himself as the leader of the struggle against the Teutonic Order. The ongoing struggle, however, was the key reason underlying the 1385 Kreva Union signed by the Grand Duke of Lithuania Jogaila (ruled in 1377 — 81 and 1382 — 92) and the Queen of Poland Jadvyga. Jogaila (Jagiello) married Jadvyga in 1386 and became the King of Poland. One of the conditions of the Union was Lithuania's conversion to Christianity (1387) which intensified the economic and cultural development of the country, orientating it towards the Western world. The conversion invalidated the claims by the Teutonic Order and put an end to its wars against Lithuania.

Lithuania's independence under the union with Poland was restored by Grand Duke Vytautas. During his rule (1392 — 1430) GDL turned into one of the largest states in Europe, stretching over present-day Byelorussia, the greater part of the Ukraine and some West Russian lands (Smolensk). The united Polish-Lithuanian army, led by Jogaila and Vytautas defeated the Teutonic Order in the Battle of Tannenberg (Grünwald, or Žalgiris) in 1410. The victory put an end to the medieval drive of the Germans to the east (*Drang nach Osten*).

The 16th cent. witnessed a number of wars against the strengthening Russian state over the Russian, Ukrainian and Byelorussian lands ruled by GDL. The need for an ally in those wars, coupled with the wish of the middle and petty gentry to obtain more rights already granted to the Polish feudal lords, drew Lithuania closer to Poland. The Union of Lublin in 1569 united Poland and Lithuania into a commonwealth in which the highest power belonged to the Seim of the nobility and its elected King who was also the Grand Duke of Lithuania. The land reform carried out in the mid-16th cent., strengthened serfdom and yet promoted the development of agriculture owing to the introduction of a regular three-field rotation system.

The 16th cent. was marked by a more rapid development of agriculture, growth of towns, spread of ideas of humanism and the Reformation, book-printing, the emergence of Vilnius University and the Lithuanian Codes of Law (the Statutes of Lithuania) which stimulated the development of culture both in Lithuania and the neighbouring countries.

The rising domination of the big magnates, the 16 — 18th cent. wars against Russia and Sweden over Livonia, the Ukraine and Byelorussia, weakened the Polish-Lithuanian Republic. The end of the 18th cent. saw three divisions of the Commonwealth by Russia, Prussia and Austria. In 1795 most of Lithuania became part of the Russian Empire. Attempts were made to restore independence, however, the uprisals of 1794, 1830 — 31 and 1863 were suppressed and followed by a strengthening police regime, increasing Russification, closing down of Vilnius University in 1832 and the ban on the printing of Lithuanian books in the traditional Roman characters in 1864. Extra taxes were imposed on Catholic landowners and an increasing number of peasants became serfs. After the abolition of serfdom in 1861 market economy gradually took root in the country, Lithuanian farmers grew stronger contributing to the increase in the number of intellectuals of peasant descent which led to the growth of Lithuanian national movement. In the German-ruled Lithuania Minor (its greater part now belongs to the Kaliningrad region of the Russian Federation) Lithuanian publications were printed in large numbers and then smuggled into the Russian-ruled Lithuania. The most outstanding leaders of the national liberation movement were J.Basanavičius and V.Kudirka. The ban on the Lithuanian press was lifted in 1904.

During WW I, Lithuania was occupied by the German army in 1915. The occupation administration allowed to convene a Lithuanian Conference in Vilnius in September 1917. The Conference adopted a resolution demanding to restore the independent Lithuanian state and elected a standing body, the Lithuanian Council (Chair. A.Smetona). On February 16, 1918, the Council issued a decree on the restoration of independence. 1919 — 20 witnessed Lithuania's Independence War — against the Red Army (in the territory occupied by it, a Bolshevist provisional revolutionary government headed by V.Kapsukas was active in 1919), the Polish army (Lithuania failed to regain the Polish-occupied Vilnius region), and the Bermondt army (units of Russian and German troops under the command of the Germans).

On May 15, 1920, the Constituent Seim (parliament) of Lithuania began its work. The Constitution of Lithuania was adopted on August 1, 1922, declaring Lithuania a parliamentary republic. Following a military coup on December 17, 1926, leader of the Nationalist (*Tautininku*) party A.Smetona, became the President and gradually introduced an authoritarian regime. Between 1920 and 1923 the Republic of Lithuania was recognized by the major countries of the world. A decisive factor in favour of Lithuania's international recognition was the Moscow Treaty of July 12, 1920, by which Russia renounced all its previous claims to Lithuania and recognized its independence. In 1923 the region of Klaipėda (the northern part of-Lithuania Minor) was joined to Lithuania.

The major problem of Lithuania's foreign policy was the conflict over Vilnius. Lithuania did not recognize the occupation (1920) and annexation (1922) of Vilnius region by Poland due to which the relations between Lithuania and Poland were strained. On March 22, 1939, Germany forced Lithuania to surrender the Klaipėda region (the Nuremberg trials qualified the treaty as null and void). Lithuania's economic and social life was largely affected by a radical land reform in 1922 which reduced the number of estates considerably and contributed to the growth of small and middle farms and boosted agricultural production and exports, especially that of livestock. Industries adjusted themselves to a new market situation and developed new structures, the light and food industries emerging as the most successful.

The period between 1920 — 40 had a special significance to Lithuanian culture as it brought about the emergence of a comprehensive system of education (primary, secondary and higher) with Lithuanian as the language of instruction, the development of the press as well as literature, music, arts and theatre.

On August 23, 1939, Germany and the SU signed the so-called Molotov-Ribbentrop Pact, by which Lithuania was first in the sphere of influence of Germany and then, following the Soviet-German agreement of September 28, 1939, fell under the rule of the USSR. Soviet pressure and a complicated international situation forced Lithuania to sign an agreement with the USSR on October 10, 1939, by which Lithuania was given back the city of Vilnius and the part of Vilnius region seized by the Red Army during the Soviet — Polish war, however, in return 20,000-strong Soviet military bases were deployed on the territory of Lithuania.

On June 14, 1940, the Soviet government issued an ultimatum to Lithuania, demanding the formation of a new Lithuanian government and permission to station additional troops of the Red Army. The Lithuanian government succumbed to the Soviet demand. 100,000 Soviet troops moved into Lithuania on June 15. Arriving in Kaunas, the special envoy of the Soviet government V.Dekanozov began implementing a premeditated plan of Lithuania's incorporation into the SU, which included the following steps: on June 17, the so-called People's Government (Chair. J.Paleckis) was formed; on July 14 — 15, elections to the so-called People's Seim were held; although having no powers to this effect, the People's Seim proclaimed Lithuania a Soviet Socialist Republic on July 21, and passed a resolution on Lithuania's joining the SU; on August 3, the Lithuanian SSR officially became a union republic of the USSR. Structures of totalitarian rule were set up and Sovietization of the Lithuanian economy and culture began. Lithuanian state and public figures, employees and officers were arrested and exiled to Russia. During the mass deportation campaign of June 14 — 18, 1941 about 7,439 families (12,600 people) were deported to Siberia without any investigation or trial, and 3,600 people were imprisoned.

The outbreak of the war between Germany and the SU (June 22, 1941) was immediately followed by a Lithuanian uprisal against the Soviet occupation. On June 23, the rebels declared the restoration of Lithuania's independence on Radio Kaunas. In June 24 — August 5, the Provisional Lithuanian Government formed by the insurgents was active yet Germany did not recognize it. Lithuania became one of the general districts in the German occupational administrative unit, Ostland. Jews were deprived of civil rights and subjected to extermination; about 200,000 Lithuanian Jews were massacred by the Nazis and their collaborationists. People were repressed and taken for forced labour to Germany. Supporters of independence put up a resistance movement and succeeded in ruining the Nazi plans of recruiting Lithuanian young men to the German army. Soviet partisans were also active in Lithuania.

In 1944 the Red Army forced the Germans out of Lithuania, and Soviet order was re-established in the territory occupied by it. In 1944 — 47 Lithuania's Sovietization was headed by a special authority, the Lithuanian bureau of the all-Union CP (Bolshevik) Central Committee. The bureau mainly relied on the Soviet Unoin's military force and Communists sent into Lithuania (local Communists were few). Between 1945 — 53, campaigns of mass repressions and deportations were launched and an atmosphere of terror imposed. During the mass deportation campaigns of 1941 — 52 alone, 29,923 families were ex iled by administrative order to Siberia and other remote parts of the SU. According to official Soviet statistics, over 120,000 people were deported from Lithuania during the campaigns of 1941 — 52 (the total number of political prisoners and deportees is estimated to have reached the 300,000 mark). Lithuania's annexation, its intensive forced Sovietization and repressions gave rise to a resistance movement. Guerrilla warfare with the ultimate goal of independence continued in 1944 — 53. According to the estimates, there were several dozen thousand resistance fighters.

The 1950s — 70s in Lithuania were marked by intensive industrialization and economic integration into the SU. The old (light, food, timber-processing) industries expanded and new industries of machine-building, metal-working, electric power engineering, chemistry, petrochemistry and others emerged. Lithuanian industry was primarily developed to serve the interests of the SU, the needs of Lithuania, especially its ecological and social considerations, were ignored. The technical and technological level of most enterprises was behind the West European standards. The intensive industrialization stimulated Lithuania's urbanization. During 1959 — 89, the proportion of the urban population increased from 39% to 68%. In 1949 — 52 a speedy forced collectivization of agriculture was carried out, abolishing private ownership. Collective farms and soviet (state) farms were set up. Agricultural production declined, and the pre-war level of farming produce was reached in the late 50s only. Nevertheless, mechanization, electrification and chemicalization enabled the collective farmers to double the output. The intensification of agricultural production created additional ecological problems.

Throughout the Soviet period, the authorities of the USSR encouraged migration. Therefore, a lot of Russians and other Russian-speaking people settled down in Lithuania, especially in its cities and towns. Together with the local non-Lithuanian residents, they constituted about 20% of Lithuania's total population in 1990.

The 2nd half of the 20th cent. saw an increase in the number of all kind of schools, pupils and students, research institutions and scientists; specialists in various fields were trained who maintained the progress of culture. On the other hand, cultural life was subject to the dictatorship of the Soviet state and the CP. The creative work of scientists and artists was encumbered by absence of democratic freedoms and strict censorship. Even under such conditions, however, a number of significant works in literature and arts emerged. Lithuanian intellectuals opposed the oppression by both legal and illegal means, seeking to preserve the humanist and national values.

Up to the middle of 1988, all political, economical and cultural life was controlled by the CP. LCP (1st Sec. A.Snieckus, 1940 — 74) was integrated into the CP of the SU and obeyed the will of its leadership. In 1944 — 58, Lithuanians were a minority in the LCP (e. g., only 18% of the total membership in 1947). More Lithuanians began joining the LCP in mid-50s (in 1986, they made up about 70% of the party's 197,000-strong body). There were quite a few intellectuals among the party members and some of them took opportunities to alleviate the negative effects of Moscow's demands. In the meanwhile, especially during the N.Khrushchev thaw in the 1950s, the leadership of the LCP acquired limited independence in decision-making. Although following Moscow's instructions in the essence, it manoeuvred in order to somewhat reduce their negative effects on Lithuanian culture and economy.

The political and economic crisis that began in the SU in the mid-1980s involves Lithuania, too. The people of Lithuania, as well as of the other Baltic republics, offered active support to Gorbachev's programme of social and political reforms in the SU. In mid-1988, the Lithuanian Reform Movement *Sajūdis* (henceforth, *Sajūdis*) emerged under the leadership of the intellectuals. The movement declared a programme of democratic and national rights for the Lithuanian nation and, later, for the restoration of an independent Lithuanian state, thus winning a nation-wide popularity. On its demand, the Supreme Soviet of the Lithuanian SSR passed constitutional amendments on the supremacy of Lithuanian laws over the Soviet legislation, recognized to be null and void the 1940 decisions of the People's Seim on proclaiming Lithuania a Soviet Socialist Republic and its joining the USSR, legalized a multi-party system in the republic and adopted a number of other important decisions. A large number of LCP members also supported the ideas of *Sajūdis*. With the backing of the movement, A. Brazauskas was elected 1st Secretary of the Central Committee of the LCP in 1988. In December 1989, the LCP headed by A.Brazauskas split from the CP of the SU and became an independent party. In 1990, it renamed itself the Lithuanian DLP. A part of the members of the former LCP established, in 1989, a separate party — the LCP, which is part of the CPSU.

In 1990, *Sajūdis*-backed candidates won the elections to the Supreme Soviet of the Lithuanian SSR. By the act of March 11, 1990, the new SC (Chair. V.Landsbergis) proclaimed the restoration of the independence of the Republic of Lithuania, formed a new Cabinet of Ministers (Prime Minister K.Prunskienė, since January, 1991 — G.Vagnorius), adopted the Provisional Fundamental Law of the state and a number of by-laws. The leadership of the SU demanded to revoke the act of March 11 and began employing political and economic sanctions against Lithuania as well as demonstrating military force. Supporting the LCP attempt to take over the power Soviet troops occupied a number of buildings in Vilnius on January 11 — 13, 1991. In the course of the actions weapons were used against civilians, leaving 14 people killed and about 700 injured. During the national plebiscite of February 9, 1991, 90.5% of those who took part in the voting (76% of all eligible voters) voted in favour of an independent and democratic Lithuania. Lithuania's leadership is seeking Western diplomatic recognition of its independence, coordinating its policies with Estonia and Latvia which have also begun the restoration of their independence.

NATIONAL ECONOMY

Lithuania is an industrial agrarian state. In 1989 prices, its gross national product amounted to 24.3 billion roubles and national income, to 9.1 billion roubles. The value of all fixed assets (in comparable prices) in 1989 was 40.6 billion roubles (production assets accounted for 65.7 % of the sum, nonproduction assets, 34.3%). As of 1989, 1,544,500 workers and employees worked in national economy. With the integration of Lithuanian economy into the economic system of the USSR, it was developed according to the dictate of the centre and guided by the USSR strategic guidelines of economic development. The technological and engineering level of enterprises was lagging far behind the standards of Western Europe. Rapid industrialization was carried out along the lines of intensive development, accompanied by the manpower migration from other regions of the USSR as well as migration of rural population to towns. In 1989, 28,500 people moved into Lithuania from the USSR. In the period between 1959 — 90 urban population increased from 39% to 68%. In the course of the structural formation of Lithuanian industry and the selection of sites for new industrial objects the needs and interests of the Republic, its historic peculiarities and traditions, specifics of its resource base and ecological capacity were ignored.

In 1949 — 52 a forcible agricultural collectivization was carried out in Lithuania. Abolition of private ownership and establishment of collective farms ruined its production capacity. Its pre-war level was reached only by the end of the 1960s. Mechanization, electrification and chemicalization of agriculture in 1960 — 90 enabled the farmers to nearly double its output. Intensification of agricultural production, however, caused additional ecological problems. Great damage to Lithuanian economy was inflicted by the USSR economic blockade in 1990. Over a period of 10 months more than 1/2 of enterprises reduced their production, which caused losses amounting to 338 billion roubles. Less grain, potatoes, sugar beets and vegetables were grown on the farms, less fodder was stored as compared with 1989.

Gross National Product and National Income (%)

	GNP	National Income
Industry	56.3	35.9
Agriculture	22.9	29.6
Construction	10.0	13.4
Transport and communications	3.6	5.0
Trade, state purchases, material technical supplies and other branches	7.2	16.1
Total	100	100

Average Annual Number of Workers and Office Employees in 1989 ('000)

Industry (production workers)	507.3	Health services, sports and social welfare	110.3
Agriculture	121.5		
Transportation	93.8	Education	150.5
Communications	21.8	Culture	22.0
Construction	194.2	Arts	7.7
Trade, state purchases, material technical supplies	145.3	Science	36.7
		Management	22.1
		Total	1,544.5

As of 1989, industrial output (in wholesale prices of enterprises) amounted to 13.7 billion roubles (60% of which was made by output of means of production, 39.7% by production of consumer goods). The major part of industrial output in 1989 was constituted by machine-building and metal-working industry (25.7%), food-processing industry (21.9%) and light industry (20.8%). In 1989, 604 self-supporting enterprises operated in the sphere of industry; of these, 90 were production and scientific amalgamations. The average annual number of industrial workers is shown in the table below:

Average Annual Number of Industrial Workers ('000)

	1985	1988	1989
Power engineering	13.6	16.6	16.2
Fuel industry	5.0	4.8	5.8
Chemical and petrochemical industries	19.4	18.6	18.2
Machine building and metalworking	199.7	201.1	193.2
Forestry, wood-working, paper and pulp industries	41.9	42.3	41.4
Building materials	40.7	40.3	38.8
Light industry	103.1	99.0	97.4
Food processing	64.1	60.9	61.7
Total	525.8	524.2	509.2

POWER ENGINEERING AND FUEL INDUSTRY. Power engineering is based on imported fuel, with oil, natural gas and coal predominating. Power engineering was poorly developed before WW II. After the hostilities in 1944 there was not a single electric power station left. In 1945, the production of electricity made up 46% of the pre-war level. In 1951, Vilnius Thermal Power Station (48 MW) was put into operation; in 1959, Kaunas Hydroelectric Power Station, in 1962, Lithuanian Power Station (in Elektrėnai); later, thermal power stations in Kaunas and Mažeikiai. In 1983, Ignalina Nuclear Power Station was commissioned; and in 1984, Vilnius 3rd Thermal Power Station was completed. In 1989, industry consumed 52.0% of the total electric power; agriculture, 21.5%; construction, 1.6%; transportation, 1.5%. In 1980, Mažeikiai Oil Processing Plant was put into operation.

MACHINE BUILDING AND METALWORKING. The first machine-building and metalworking enterprises were established early in the 19th cent. in Klaipėda. In 1939, 135 machine-building and metalworking enterprises operated on the present-day territory of Lithuania, providing jobs for 4,558 workers and producing 4.8% of all industrial output. Their output included metal articles for household appliances and building equipment, such as nails, wire, sets of bindings, radiators. Agricultural implements and simple agricultural machines were also produced. After WW II machine-building and metalworking enterprises were geared to meet the industrial needs of the SU, turning out products which require highly skilled labour but little metal and electric power. Precision instruments, radio electronics and electrotechnical articles, machine tools, household appliances and equipment, agricultural machinery, shipbuilding and maintenance, spare parts for bicycles and cars, technological equipment for food-processing industry predominate.

CHEMICAL AND PETROCHEMICAL INDUSTRIES. Chemical enterprises appeared in Lithuania late in the 19th cent. They produced mainly varnishes, dyes and paints, various salts, acids, medicines and cosmetics. In 1939, 57 enterprises of chemical industry operated in Lithuania, with 2,058 workers. The development of chemical industry accelerated in the 1960s and 1970s, when Vilnius *Plasta* Plastics Plant, Kaunas Synthetic Fiber Plant, Kėdainiai Chemical Plant and Jonava Nitrogen Fertilizer Plant (since 1979, the production assoc. *Azotas*) emerged. At present the chemical industry produces mineral fertilizers (both nitric and phosphoric), sulphuric, nitric and phosphoric acids, methanol, chemical fibers, synthetic resins, synthetic washing detergents, varnishes, dyes and paints, household chemicals and other chemical products. The largest petrochemical enterprise is the Kaunas *Inkaras* Rubber Products.

FORESTRY, WOOD PRODUCTS, PAPER AND PULP INDUSTRIES. It is one of the oldest industries in Lithuania. The first factories of furniture, matches and timber articles were built in Kaunas and Vilnius in the 2nd half of the 19th cent. Sawmills producing output merely for their own needs as well as work-shops of carpentry and furniture-making prevailed in the period between 1919 — 40. In 1939, 308 enterprises of woodworking, pulp and paper industry operated in Lithuania, with a total of 5,912 workers. Intensive timber processing and recycling of industrial waste are being expanded. Chemical timber processing, production of furniture, pulp, paper, wood-fiber and wood-chip boards, joinery articles for building industry, cardboard and other packaging articles predominate.

BUILDING MATERIALS INDUSTRY. Up to the end of the 19th cent. building materials were usually produced at the construction site. In 1939, 67 enterprises of building materials were operating with 1,773 employees. They produced bricks, tiles, glazed tiles, lime, glass and drainage pipes.

At present the industry of building materials uses local resources mainly, such as clay, building and quartz sand, gravel, and dolomite. It produces cement, asbestos-cement sheets, plastic building materials and articles from polystyrene foam, glass and polystyrene dressing tiles, silicate bricks, mineral wool and its articles, precast ferroconcrete structures, window glass, bricks, drainage pipes. Large quarries of building materials are located in Vilnius, Petrašiūnai (Pakruojis district), Kalnėnai (Jurbarkas district), Rizgonys (Jonava district). Cement, glass, mineral wool, glass tiles, bricks and drainage pipes are exported.

LIGHT INDUSTRY. In the 18th — early 19th cent. light industry enterprises were usually on the !Ç(Çĺestates of large feudals. Early in the 19th cent. small artisan factories emerged, employing hired labour. The largest centres of leather footwear industry were Vilnius and Šiauliai. Textiles and knitwear industry underwent rapid development in 1919 — 40 due to protectionist duties levied on textiles, knitwear and needlework articles. In 1940, 340 light industry enterprises operated in Lithuania with a total of 14,000 employees.

At present textiles and knitwear are the main branches of light industry. Linen, cotton, silk fabrics, carpets, stockings and socks, underwear and outdoor knitwear are manufactured. The largest leather and footwear enterprises are *Lituanica*, *Elnias* and *Victoria*. Fur articles are produced in the enterprises *Vilkas* and Vilnius Furs Factory. The largest sewing factories are *Lelija*, *Baltija*, *Šatrija*. Soft man-made leather is produced at the Plungė Synthetic Leather Factory.

FOOD INDUSTRY. The first food industry enterprises appeared in the early 19th cent. In the period between 1919 — 40 nearly all food industry enterprises catered for the domestic market; meat and dairy products alone were exported.

At present this sector is dominated by meat, dairy, and fishing industries. Meat factories are in Kaunas, Vilnius, Klaipėda, Šiauliai, Panevėžys, Tauragė, Alytus, Utena. Dairy plants of Vilnius, Kaunas, Šiauliai, Panevėžys and Klaipėda include a number of smaller dairies and creameries in their respective areas. Klaipėda, with a fishing port, is the centre of fishing industry. The Republic also specializes in sugar, confectionery, bread, alcohol, beer, tobacco, canning industries and the production of vegetable oil.

MICROBIOLOGICAL INDUSTRY. Emerged in the 1970s — 1980s. The largest enterprises are Kèdainiai Biochemical Plant and Vilnius Enzymes Plant.

Output of Main Industrial Products

	1985	1988	1989
Power engineering and fuel industry			
Electric power (million kWh)	20,962	26,000	29,158
Chemical and petrochemical industries			
Inorganic fertilizers (active material; t)	747,000	791,000	632,000
Monohydrate of sulphuric acid (t)	440,000	430,000	512,000
Polymeric film (t)	16,700	22,400	22,000
Chemical fiber and yarn (t)	13,800	14,400	14,400
Linoleum (sq m)	1,102,000	1,266,000	1,624,000
Machine building and metal working			
Electric motors (u.)	6,221,000	7,453,000	7,659,000
Electric welding (u.)	71,800	74,900	76,900
Metal-cutting machine tools (u.)	28,300	13,400	13,300
Electric meters (u.)	3,301,000	3,631,000	3,612,000
Vitamin grass-meal units	2,452	2,022	1,302
Boilers (mWt)	1,035	984	835
Television sets (u.)	609,500	655,000	615,000
Tape recorders (u.)	237,900	176,100	186,600
Household refrigerators (u.)	310,300	345,000	350,200
Household vacuum-cleaners (u.)	146,100	165,500	185,800
Bicycles for teenagers (u.)	462,000	468,000	423,000
Forestry, wood products and paper and pulp industries			
Exported timber (cu m)	2,737,000	2,854,000	2,715,000
Sawn lumber (cu m)	934,000	1,006,000	938,000
Wood shaving slabs (cu m)	140,300	184,300	183,800
Wood fibre slabs (cu m)	26,933,000	28,923,000	27,622,000
Paper (t)	120,300	122,900	117,200
Cardboard (t)	145,200	146,100	138,900
Building materials			
Bricks (million u.)	1,250	1,381	1,462
Prefabricated concrete structures (cu m)	2,296,000	2,567,000	2,627,000
Asbestos-cement sheets (million u.)	106	114	114
Window glass (sq m)	4,021,000	4,093,000	4,172,000
Glass blocks (u.)	7,001,000	5,115,000	6,274,000
Light industry			
Textiles (million sq m)	222.0	225.9	217.7
Carpets (sq m)	6,736,000	6,917,000	6,953,000
Stockings and socks (million p.)	99.3	102.5	105.0
Knitted underwear (million u.)	45.4	44.1	44.1
Knitwear (million u.)	15.9	17.5	18.1
Footwear (million p.)	10.7	11.4	11.9
Needlework (million roubles)	367.7	373.1	414.4
Food processing			
Meat (t)	396,900	433,300	447,000
Sausages (t)	68,200	74,800	75,700
Butter (t)	71,800	77,900	77,500
Milk and milk products (t)	730,000	794,000	814,000
Canned foods (million standard containers)	326.5	405.1	423.4
Granulated sugar (t)	221,800	239,400	238,600
Fish and marine products (t)	458,500	425,400	417,900
Fish food products (without canned fish; t)	276,300	258,100	248,500
Confectionery (t)	79,200	89,900	91,400

AGRICULTURE. Two forms of nationalized ownership are still prevalent in agriculture: state farms and collective farms. Joint stock farming, however, is spreading on those farms and cooperative farming associations emerge. The Law on Farming adopted in July 1989, served as a basis for the emergence of individual farms. According to this law, the land is given to a farmer as his property without any right to sell, lease or pawn it. The size of such plots is 10 — 50 ha of farming land. All the

above forms of farming enjoy equal rights. Late in 1989 there were 835 collective farms (two of them fishery farms) and 275 state farms in Lithuania; 1,162 farmers managed farms on their own; 30% of all labour force of the national economy were engaged in agriculture. Agricultural farms occupied a total area of 4,625,600 ha; the area of collective farms was 3,273,500 ha, whereas that of state and other farms — 1,208,200 ha; individual farmers had about 20,695 ha, other users of land, such as industrial enterprises, boarding schools, etc. make up 443,600 ha. In all, there were 3,500,000 ha of farming land, arable land making 2,300,000 ha. The average rating of land indicating its economic value is 42. The best lands are in Central Lithuania (Kėdainiai district, 55.2 points), the worst, in Eastern Lithuania (Zarasai district, 28.0 points). The most important agricultural indices are shown in the table. Lithuanian agriculture specializes in animal husbandry. Late in 1989 its output made up 66% of the total output of collective and state farms. The total output of animal husbandry in 1985 — 89 in the farms of all categories increased by 7%, the increase in the public sector was 11%. Individual subsidiary plots accounted for 1/3 of the total production in the sector. In 1989 collective farmers' average monthly wage was 257 roubles, state farmers' — 243 roubles.
Lithuanian agriculture is supervised by the Ministry of Agriculture.

Land Use ('000 ha)

	1985	1988	1989
Areas for crops	2,348	2,326	2,292
Cereals	1,147	1,121	1,125
Fiber flax	34	29	28
Sugar beets	35	35	34
Potatoes	131	127	120
Vegetables	19	19	17

Gross Harvests and Annual Yields of Agricultural Crops

	Gross harvests ('000 t)			Annual yields (100 kg per ha)		
	1985	1988	1989	1985	1988	1989
Cereals	2,866	3,046	3,644	25.0	27.2	32.4
Fiber flax	14	14	15	4.0	4.8	5.5
Sugar beets	938	1,212	1,075	269	350	313
Potatoes	1,851	1,850	1,927	141	146	161
Vegetables	331	370	326	166	180	180

Horticulture

	1985	1988	1989
Area under gardens and berry shrubs (ha)	48,700	44,600	44,200
Gross harvest of fruit and berries (t)	183,000	127,100	253,300
Annual yields (100 kg per ha)	46.5	35.3	71.3

Livestock ('000 head)

	1985	1988	1990
Cattle	2,500	2,493	2,422
Cows	880	862	843
Swine	2,706	2,706	2,730
Sheep	101	86	65
Fowls	16,040	17,363	17,486

Livestock Products

	1986	1988	1989
Meat (slaughter weight; '000 t)	514	545	534
Milk ('000 t)	3,051	3,209	3,235
Eggs (million)	1,207	1,347	1,331
Wool (t)	200	189	160
Average of milk per cow (kg)	3,376	3,721	3,806

TRANSPORTATION. The main means of transportation in Lithuania are railway and motor-vehicle transport. In 1989 freight turnover by rail transport made 72.4%, motor-vehicle transport — 27.0% of the total freight turnover, rail transport passenger turnover — 26.1%, motor-vehicle (bus) transport — 55.8% of the total transport passenger turnover. The main railway trunk lines across Lithuania are Moscow — Minsk — Vilnius — Kaunas — Kaliningrad *(Königsberg)*, Leningrad — Vilnius – Grodno, Kaišiadorys – Šiauliai – Riga, Šiauliai – Klaipėda, Riga – Šiauliai – Kaliningrad. The main highways are Vilnius – Kaunas – Kryžkalnis – Klaipėda, Vilnius – Ukmergė – Panevėžys – Riga, Zarasai – Kaunas – Kaliningrad, Riga – Šiauliai – Sovietsk *(Tilsit),* Kaunas – Jurbarkas – Šilutė – Klaipėda. Sea routes link Klaipėda with 200 foreign ports. Railway sea ferry Klaipėda – Mukran (Germany) began operating in 1986. The largest airport is located in Vilnius, with minor airports in Kaunas, Palanga and Šiauliai. Passengers in urban districts are carried by buses, trolley-buses, and taxi-cabs. The main indices of transportation are shown in the table below:

	1985	1988	1989
Total length of roads			
(end of the year; km)			
railways	2,000	2,000	2,000
shipping routes	600	600	600
airlines	28,100	28,100	28,000
Freight haulage (million t)			
railway	33.3	34.0	32.7
sea	4.0	6.4	6.4
river	2.7	3.2	2.6
motor vehicles	329.3	364.2	348.3
total	**369.3**	**407.8**	**390.0**
Freight turnover (billion t-km)			
railway	20.9	22.6	21.8
sea (foreign routes; billion t-mile)	6.9	–	8.9
river	0.2	0.2	0.2
motor vehicles	7.4	8.1	8.1
Passenger conveyance (million)			
railway	32.5	34.0	30.6
river	3.5	4.1	4.1
buses	778.8	796.9	760.3
trolley-buses	272.7	291.7	288.2
air	0.7	0.9	0.9
total	**1,088.2**	**1,127.6**	**1,084.1**
Passenger traffic (million passenger-km)			
railway	3,417	3,665	3,470
river	19	21	22
bus	7,386	7,741	7,423
air	1,763	2,256	2,395
total	**12,585**	**13,683**	**13,310**

CULTURE

FOLKLORE. The major part of the Lithuanian folklore was created by peasants. The folklore reflects their work and social experience, family relations, ethics and practical wisdom.

The most archaic part of the surviving folklore consists of songs (*dainos*) created in the early feudal period. The most abundant and valuable folklore genre is made up of lyrical (work, calendar festivities, wedding) songs. Songs were created by women in the main. Especially old are threnodies and monophonic as well as polyphonic work and ritual songs (*sutartinės*). Lithuanian folk songs have both rigid and free rhythmic pattern with predominant textual or melodic element. Instrumental folk music was played solo or by instrumental groups. The folk musical instruments are *skrabalai* (cow bells), *dambrelis* (Jew's harp), *kanklės* (zither), *smuikas* (fiddle), *skudučiai* (panpipe), *lamzdelis* (recorder), *ragas* (horn), *daudytė* (long trumpet), *birbynė* (folk clarinet).

At present folk music is performed by ethnographic and folk music groups from villages and towns. A great number of folk songs have been harmonized by Lithuanian composers. Elements of folk music are characteristic of many professional compositions.

Narrative folklore is also abundant and original, some feature international plots and motifs. Lithuanian tales share common typological, historical and cultural features with Byelorussian and Russian folk tales.

The first records of Lithuanian folklore go back to the 16th – 17th cent. The first collection of songs was published by L.Rėza in 1825. A great deal of folklore was collected and published after WW II (*Lietuvių tautosaka* – Lithuanian Folklore, vols 1 – 5, 1962 – 68; *Lietuvių liaudies dainynas* – Lithuanian Book of Folk-Songs, vols 1 – 5, 1980 – 89). In the USA collections of Lithuanian fairytales 'The Evening Song' (1954) and 'Lithuanian Folk Tales' were published in English.

Folk architecture features dwelling houses (log cabins with hearths, *troba, pirkia, stuba),* farm buildings (granaries, animal sheds, threshing barns, hay barns), production buildings (mills, smithies, smoke-houses), public buildings (schools, inns, churches). Their predominant features are solid structure, simple plan (with regional differences), tectonic forms, moderate décor. Farmsteads consisted of buildings, a front yard, a vegetable garden and an orchard.

Folk art is dominated by articles of applied decorative character, such as bed-spreads, table-cloths, towels, sashes, woodworks and ceramics. Religious, work and everyday life themes prevailed in visual arts (wooden sculptures, paintings on wood and paper, woodcuts). Recently groups of wooden sculptures have gained popularity (Ablinga, Čiurlionis memorials).

EDUCATION. The late 14th — 15th cent. saw the emergence of the first parish schools in the Grand Duchy of Lithuania. In the 16th cent. the Reformation movement promoted the spread of education and book printing. In their efforts to Counter-Reformation the Jesuits established a collegium (a secondary school) in Vilnius in 1570. In 1579, it was reorganized into the first university of Lithuania (closed by the Russian authorities in 1832; reopened as a Polish university in 1919; from 1939, a Lithuanian university). Some 20 colleges were established by the Jesuits in the 17th cent. Besides, high schools were also established by the Evangelists, Lutherans, Evangelists Reformists, and the Catholic Piarist Order. In 1773, the Education Commission (a state body similar to modern ministries of education) set out to establish a secular education system. From the 19th cent., the language of tuition was Russian. Besides state schools, illegal elementary Lithuanian schools appeared. In the early 20th cent., the first legal schools with Lithuanian as the language of tuition appeared. In 1914, there were 1,620 elementary schools (incl. Jewish), 37 secondary schools and 45 incomplete secondary schools. In 1918 — 40 the education system of the Republic of Lithuania was based on the educational principles of Western Europe. In 1922, a law on compulsory secondary education was adopted. The year 1922 saw the foundation of the University of Vytautas Magnus in Kaunas, which was followed by the Academy of Agriculture, Veterinary Academy, and the Conservatoire. In 1938, there were 2,600 elementary schools, 98 gymnasiums (secondary schools) and progymnasiums (incomplete secondary schools), 25 secondary specialized schools and 7 higher schools. Alongside with Lithuanian schools Jewish schools and schools of other ethnic minorities functioned in the country. After Lithuania's annexation by the USSR in 1940 the Soviet education system was introduced. Jewish and German schools were closed. After WW II, the gymnasiums and progymnasiums were reorganized into secondary 11-year schools and incomplete secondary 7-year (later 8-year) schools, including the elementary course. Schools were enlarged, many elementary schools were merged with secondary schools. In 1978, compulsory secondary education was introduced. In 1950, the University of Vytautas Magnus was split into the Kaunas Polytechnic Institute (now Technological University) and Kaunas Medical Institute (now Academy). The Humanities had already been transferred to Vilnius University. Later a number of new higher schools were founded.

The following types of schools existed in Lithuania in 1990: elementary (1 to 4 forms), nine-year (1 to 9 forms) and secondary (1 to 12 forms). Tuition begins at the age of 6. In 1990, there were 789 elementary, 595 nine-year, 711 secondary, 109 professional-technical, 68 specialized secondary, and 16 higher schools (incl. Vilnius University, University of Vytautas Magnus, and Vilnius Technical University). Besides Lithuanian, there are Russian and Polish general education schools.

The year 1990 marked the beginning of a new national education system in the reestablished Republic of Lithuania. General education schools offer a course in religion. Various student organizations are being founded. Sunday schools were opened for Jews, Karaites, and other ethnic minorities.

SCIENCE. As a separate sphere of activity science in Lithuania began to develop in the 16th cent. To fight the ideas of Protestantism, the Jesuit Order was invited to Lithuania. In 1570 the Jesuits founded a college in Vilnius which was subsequently reorganized into an establishment of higher education in 1579 (*Alma academia et universitas Vilnensis*; now Vilnius University). Theology, scholastic philosophy and logic were taught there. In the 18th cent. new subjects of natural and social sciences were introduced and the research in the Lithuanian language was taken up. Exact and technical sciences advanced. In the 2nd half of the 18th cent. the ideas of Enlightenment began to spread and the attempts to secularize science were strengthened (in 1773 the Jesuit Order was abolished).

The Russian authorities closed Vilnius University for political reasons in 1832, and the Academy of Medicine and Surgery in 1842, thus leaving Lithuania without scientific institutions of its own. In 1907, however, the Lithuanian Scientific Society was founded which became the centre of the Lithuanian studies. The Society functioned up to 1940. In the period between 1918 — 40 scientific work was mainly carried out at the establishments of higher education, especially at Vytautas Magnus University in Kaunas. Significant selection research was done at the Agricultural Academy (by D. Rudzinskis). Scientists at the institutions of higher education investigated both fauna and flora, geological structure, mineral resources and their deposits as well as the health of the population in Lithuania. Prominent results were achieved in mathematical analysis, analytical chemistry, physics, electrochemistry, electric optics, construction statics and textile fiber. Specialists of the Lithuanian language (K. Büga and others), literature, folklore and Lithuanian history made a major contribution to the development of science in Lithuania. While working at Kaunas University, the Russian historian and philosopher L. Karsavin wrote a 5 volume History of European Culture. Philosopher V. Sezeman published works on logic and aesthetics, based mainly on the methodology of neo-Kantianism.

On January 16, 1941, the Academy of Sciences was founded in Lithuania following the model of the USSR scientific institutions. After WW II it was here that most of the scientists who chose to remain in Lithuania after 1944 continued to work; many of them were subjected to repressions. Many Lithuanian scientists emigrated to the West by the end of the war. The Soviet period saw the formation of a rather broad system of scientific institutions, while science was increasingly and continuously integrated into the science structure of the USSR. Many subdivisions of Soviet scientific institutions or their analogues were established. Quite a few Union ministries and departments had their scientific institutions in Lithuania and dictated the trends of investigations. In 1990, 46 scientific research institutes were functioning in Lithuania, 17 of them within the system of the Academy of Sciences. There were also 14 establishments of higher education. Altogether there were 15,400 scientists in the scientific research institutes in 1988 (7,128 scientists had scientific degrees in 1989). Scientists of the Academy of Sciences and higher schools were mainly involved in theoretical research work. Applied sciences were developed in departmental scientific-research institutes as well as in some institutes of the Academy of Sciences and higher schools. It was the USSR central offices that distributed means allotted for scientific research and approved the plans, problems and trends of scientific investigations drafted by scientific institutions. Naturally, the development of Lithuanian science was often predetermined by Soviet science programmes, priority was given to some studies in natural, exact and technical sciences which had little to do with the development of Lithuanian economy and culture. The situation in the humanities, especially in the studies of the Lithuanian language, was poor. The development of the Lithuanian science was limited by out-dated material technical facilities, loose ties with foreign scientific centres, centralization of management, subordination of social sciences to the ideology of the CP and to the dictate of governmental institutions. Given the adverse conditions, science in Lithuania has achieved considerable results. In the 1970s — 90s, the main trends in natural and technical sciences were probability theory and mathematical statistics, mathematical cybernetics, technical cybernetics and computer programming; theoretical and experimental nuclear and molecular spectroscopy; investigation of atmospheric pollution and the mechanism of its purification; study of Galaxy by means of multicoloured photometry; semiconductor physics and chemistry, design of devices and equipment; physical and technological problems of power engineering and galvanotechnics; biochemical and genetic fundamentals of cell functioning and synthesis of the active cell compounds; hereditary information and physiological-biochemical fundamentals of its realization in the process of plant growth and morphogenesis; laws of species, existence and productivity of zoofitocenoses and their rational use; current processes of physical and scientific fundamentals of Lithuanian natural environment protection; rational use of inland water resources and biological fundamentals of their productivity. Broad scientific research is carried out in the sphere of medicine (esp. in the pathology of blood-vessels) as well as in different spheres of agriculture. The main directions of social sciences are the following: increasing efficiency of social production, improvement of management and forecasting; history of the Lithuanian nation; the Lithuanian language, literature and folklore.

LITERATURE. The earliest writings of Lithuania are the 14th — 16th cent. chronicles in Old Slavonic and Latin. The 16th — 17th cent. fiction and publicist writings were in Latin and Polish. The first book published in Lithuanian was *Catechismusa Prasty Szadei* (1547) by M. Mažvydas. The late 16th cent. saw a translation of the Bible by J. Bretkūnas. The first major work of fiction was the poem *Metai* by K. Donelaitis (The Seasons, 1760 — 70) written in tonic hexametre, describing the nature and daily life of the serfs as well as the survival of the ethnic identity of Lithuanians in Lithuania Minor under the threat of Germanization.

In the early and mid-19th cent., the genre of poetry assumed a predominant position. An outstanding literary hallmark of the period was a lyrical romantic poem *Anykščių šilelis* (The Anykščiai Pine Forest, 1860 — 61) by A. Baranauskas. Literature of the late 19th — early 20th cent. was closely linked with the national liberation movement. The most outstanding poet of national rebirth was Maironis who laid foundations for modern Lithuanian poetry with his *Pavasario balsai* (Voices of Spring, 1895), a collection of lyrics expressing patriotic and romantic aspirations. The Lithuanian prose of the late 19th — early 20th cent. was dominated by realistic stories and novellas on peasants' daily life and morals (Žemaitė, J. Biliūnas, Vaižgantas, A. Vienuolis).

The first three decades of the 20th cent. were marked by a growing variety of literary genres and trends. Poetry gave expression to Symbolism with its philosophical reflections (V. Mykolaitis-Putinas, B. Sruoga), Futurism and Expressionism, with their youthful impetus, renewal and social protest (K. Binkis, K. Boruta, T. Tilvytis), Neoromanticism, with its dramatic emotionalism, lyrical subtlety and folk spirit (J. Aistis, A. Miškinis, S.Nėris). Characteristically pathetic and Christian in spirit was B. Brazdžionis' poetry, with its reminiscences of world culture. In the short stories realistic elements of daily life were combined with neoromantic ethics and search for a national character (V. Krėvė, J. Grušas). Impressionistic short stories and novels were written by I. Šeinius, K. Puida, and A. Vaičiulaitis, expressionistic short stories, by J. Savickis. The popular novel *Altorių šešėly* (In the Shadow of the Altars, 1932 — 33) by V. Mykolaitis-Putinas began the tradition of realistic psychological novel. Problems of the tragic destiny of Lithuania Minor under Germanization were highlighted in I. Simonaitytė's prose. Issues of social justice were raised in the short stories and novels by P. Cvirka and A. Venclova. Among other authors of realistic novels were Jonas Marcinkevičius, L. Dovydėnas, and J. Paukštelis. Historical tragedy dramas (plays) were written by V. Krėvė, B. Sruoga, and Vydūnas.

As the USSR occupied Lithuania for the second time in 1944, many writers fled to the West. Many refugees later settled in the USA. Many poets who resided in the USA (B. Brazdžionis, J. Aistis, K. Bradūnas, H. Nagys, et al.) continued the pre-war traditions, emphasizing man's link with the land of his forbears and the history of the nation. Some poets (H. Radauskas, A. Nyka-Nyliūnas, and A. Mackus) tended towards modernistic poetry and universal motifs. Novels on pre-war Lithuania and the life in exile were written by M. Katiliškis, A. Škėma, P. Andriušis, J. Jankus, V. Ramonas, B. Pūkelevičiūtė. The most distinguished playwrights were K. Ostrauskas, A. Landsbergis, the best known humourist, A. Gustaitis.

In the Soviet-occupied Lithuania the development of literature was deformed by ideological control and forceful imposition of the method of socialist realism requiring to extol Bolshevist policies and idealize reality. Of greater significance was the patriotic poetry by S. Nėris created during the war. The first post-war decade was especially detrimental to the development of literature. After 1956, the cultural atmosphere improved and poetry was the first to recover. Breaking away from the canons of socialist realism the 1960s – 1980s produced major poetic works representing a variety of styles (V. Mykolaitis-Putinas, E. Mieželaitis, J. Juškaitis, S. Geda, P. Širvys, J. Degutytė, J. Vaičiūnaitė, and M. Martinaitis). Politization of prose genre, especially the traditional epic and social writings, had left a negative impact that weakened their artistic appeal. Realistic social novels of epic character were written by J. Baltušis. J. Avyžius, V. Bubnys, V. Petkevičius, and R. Kašauskas. Subtle psychologism, lyricism and painful dramatic collisions marked the novellas and novels by M. Sluckis, R. Granauskas, V. Jasukaitytė, and R. Klimas; modern laconicism and skepticism represented by R. Lankauskas; lyrically ironical prose, by S. Šaltenis, J. Aputis, and R. Šavelis; intellectual psychologism, by B. Radzevičius, J. Mikelinskas, V. Martinkus, and R. Gavelis. S. T. Kondrotas resorts to allegoric images and paradoxes. Petras Dirgėla tends to historic and philosophical meditation. V. Sirijos-Gira is known for his adventure novels. The most famous dramatists are J. Grušas, K. Saja, Justinas Marcinkevičius, and J. Glinskis. The most distinguished humourist is V. Žilinskaitė.

The most outstanding pre-war literary critics were Vaižgantas, A. Jakštas, V. Mykolaitis-Putinas, B. Sruoga, and K. Korsakas; in the 1950s – 1980s, J. Lebedys, J. Lankutis, V. Zaborskaitė, V. Kubilius, A. Zalatorius, J. Girdzijauskas, and V. Daujotytė-Pakerienė.

ARCHITECTURE. The oldest architectural monuments of Lithuania are camp buildings (half sunken structures) from the late Paleolith and Mesolith. The 9th – 4th cent. BC saw the emergence of hill forts (Lithuanian *piliakalnis*) which later developed into settlements, forerunners of towns and cities. With the emergence of a centralized Lithuanian state in the 13th cent., wooden and stone enclosure fortresses were built (Vilnius, Kaunas, Medininkai), old settlements were enlarged and new ones constructed. At the turn of the 15th cent., the first Gothic buildings (Trakai Insular Castle, St. Anne's Church and the Church of the Bernardines in Vilnius, dwelling houses) and the earliest networks of streets (linear or radial) emerged. In mid-16th cent., the style of Renaissance found expression in the architecture of residential castles (Raudonė, Biržai) and churches (Siesikai, Simnas) as well as the layout of towns (a rectangular square in the centre with streets at the corners).

The style of Baroque (17th cent.) predominated in religious architecture (St. Peter and Paul's Church in Vilnius, Pažaislis Monastery). Baroque was superceded by Neoclassical architecture in the 2nd half of the 18th cent., establishing a rectangular town plan (Rokiškis, Rietavas) and producing a number of secular and religious monuments (Town Hall and Cathedral by L. Stuoka-Gucevičius in Vilnius) as well as palaces (Paežeriai, arch. M.Knakfus).

The early 20th cent. was marked by historicist tendencies (Neogothic, Neoclassical, *Art Nouveau*; Neoclassical bank in Kaunas, H.Songaila). During the period of independence Lithuanian architects were seeking for a national style (summer houses, schools, milk stations); elements of modern architecture evolved (Military Museum of Vytautas the Great, V.Dubeneckis, Chamber of Industry, Trade and Crafts, V.Landsbergis-Žemkalnis, both in Kaunas).

During the Soviet occupation (esp. in the immediately post-war years), the architectural environment changed considerably. WW II destroyed many Lithuanian towns and villages. Nationalization of private property led to the deterioration of buildings, especially in the old part of cities, many architectural monuments fell into decay (mostly churches and monasteries). Collectivization of agriculture changed the rural landscape (homesteads disappeared, numerous urban type settlements were built instead). Rapid industrialization facilitated urbanization and the construction of standardized cheap housing. In addition, uniform Soviet design norms and rules were adhered to, leading to the neglect of local conditions and architectural tradition, trends in the development of architecture, its forms and decór were centrally imposed. The prime goal was to rebuild cities and buildings destroyed by the war. Master plans (later corrected) for all Lithuania's cities were drawn, new industrial centres (Naujoji Akmenė, Elektrėnai) were constructed, large residential districts (Žirmūnai, Lazdynai, and Karoliniškės in Vilnius; Dainava and Šilainiai in Kaunas, Pempininkai in Klaipėda) and settlements of collective and state farms (Dainava, Juknaičiai) were built. Residential districts with public catering centres, schools, kindergartens were built according to standard designs (projects) from prefabricated sections (since 1959) or cast-on-site concrete (since 1980).

Attempts were made to alleviate the resulting monotony by loggias, balconies, partitions, texture and colour. Spatial structure was diversified by combinations of buildings of various height (from 5 to 20 storeys). Public buildings constructed according to individual designs enjoyed more originality due to free planning, plastic forms, original interiors, and better integration into the environment (arch. brothers Nasvytis, V.Čekanauskas, V.Brédikis, E.Chlomauskas, Z.Liandzbergis, G.Baravykas, N. Bučiūtė, A.Sprindys, G.Tiškus, E.Stasiulis, Č.Mazūras, E. Miliūnas). Recreational architecture also developed. Master plans for national parks, recreational zones and districts were drawn (chief arch. V.Stauskas). New sanatoriums, holiday homes, disease prevention centres, and tourist camps were built. Comprehensive restoration of the Old Towns of Vilnius, Kaunas, Klaipėda, and Kėdainiai and valuable arhitectural monuments began with the purpose to adapt them to contemporary needs.

FINE ARTS. The oldest art monuments are pottery, wooden, bone and amber artifacts from the Neolith. Following Lithuania's baptism, church art began spreading in the country. Manuscript miniatures of the Byzantine style (the Gospel of Laurušavas), Gothic sculptures (the so-called Madonna of Veliuona), specimens of wall-paintings (the fresco of the crypt of Vilnius Cathedral) were created in the 14th — 15th cent. In the 16th cent., Renaissance art, especially portraits, flourished (tombstone sculptures, medals, the painted portrait of Virgin Mary in the Chapel of the Aušros Gate in Vilnius, the first graphic portraits). In the 17th — 18th cent. (the Baroque period), art was dominated by sculpture and painting related to architecture, especially of church architecture (the sculpture and frescoes of St. Peter and Paul's Church in Vilnius, Pažaislis Church and Monastery). Articles of applied decorative art were manufactured at the textile mills of the nobility.

In the late 18th and early 19th cent., fine arts developed tendencies of the Enlightenment period (P.Smuglevičius, K.Jelskis) and of Romanticism, arising from the spirit of national liberation movement (J.Rustemas, J.Damelis). The trend of realism was steadily gaining strength (J.Rustemas, A. Remeris, J.Balzukevičius). At the turn of the 19th and 20th cent., the first departments of fine arts were established in Vilnius University (precursors of higher schools of fine arts) and its students put up their first art exhibitions. At the beginning of the 20th cent., the first Lithuanian Arts Society was set up (1907) which began setting up exhibitions of Lithuanian art (A.Žmuidzinavičius, K.Sklérius, A.Varnas, P.Kalpokas, P.Rimša, J.Zikaras). The most outstanding artist of the early 20th cent. was M.K.Čiurlionis whose works were based on Lithuanian folk art, on the principles of musical arrangement and ideas of neo-Romanticism, Symbolism and *Art Nouveau*.

The first three decades of the 20th cent. witnessed a growing number of stylistic trends and genres. The majority of artists gathered together around the Kaunas Art School founded in 1922 and participated in the activity of various groups (the Society of Independent Artists, founded in 1930; the *Ars*, 1932). Tendencies of Postimpressionism (J.Vienožinskis, V.Eidukevičius), Expressionism (A.Gudaitis, V.Vizgirda, A.Galdikas, A.Samuolis) and, occasionally, Cubism (S.Ušinskas, V.Kairiūk-štis) were manifested in painting. In sculpture, features of realism were often coupled with elements of academism, Impressionism (V.Grybas, J.Zikaras), Symbolism and *Art Nouveau* (P.Rimša), with emphasis on monumentalism, synthetism (J.Mikénas, B.Pundzius, R.Antinis) and expressiveness (M.Menčinskas). Graphic art fostered realistic and modernistic traditions (V.Petravičius, V.K.Jonynas, P.Augius). There was further development of stage design (S.Ušinskas, L.Truikys) and applied decorative art (L.Strolis, A.Tamošaitis).

WW II and the second Soviet occupation forced a certain part of Lithuanian artists to emigrate. In emigration, they held exhibitions (one of the biggest put up in New York in 1949), founded art galleries, schools, private studios and issued publications of art. The art by the Lithuanian émigrés reveals obvious links with the pre-war traditions of Lithuanian art (A.Varnas, V.Ignas, V.Kašuba), alongside with the influence of West European modernist art (A.Galdikas, K.Žoromskis, K.Varnelis, R.Viesulas, Ž.Mikšys, A.Mončys).

The artists, who remained in occupied Lithuania, were negatively affected by the exaggerated ideologization, the forcibly imposed method of socialist realism and the atmosphere of Stalin's cult. Politization, canonization and topicalization were especially distinct in the art of immediate post-war years. In that period, bigger achievements were made in portrait (J.Vienožinskis, A.Gudaitis) and landscape painting (A.Savickas, A.Petrulis), in book illustration (J.Kuzminskis, V.Jurkūnas, A.Kučas) and monumental sculpture (J.Mikénas, B.Pundzius). With changes in the cultural atmosphere, a new concept of the hero, object and space began taking shape in the late 50s. The trend was manifested in giving preference to ideas and emotions, emphatically revealed by means of monumentalized scenes, expressive forms and rich colours. There emerged obvious links with the world's stylistic trends. Expressiveness stands out as one of the most vivid stylistic features of Lithuanian painting. It takes various forms: dramatic (A.Savickas, A.Šaltenis), constructively rational (S.Džiaukštas, J.Švažas, V. Kisarauskas) or closely related to Lithuanian folk art (A.Gudaitis, A.Martinaitis, R.Bičiūnas). Works by some painters (A.Kuras, J.Daniliauskas, M.Skudutis, D.Kasčiūnaitė) display a tendency to improvization, use of metaphors and bonds with modernist art. In sculpture, the so-called austere style became apparent (L.Strioga, V.Vildžiūnas), specific types of symbolic (G.Jokūbonis, G.Karalius, S.Kuzma) and monumental sculpture (B.Vyšniauskas, S.Šarapovas, A.Ambraziūnas) developed, open-air expositions of decorative sculptures were put up (the Mažvydas Sculpture Park in Klaipėda, 1977). Symbolism and metaphor, relativeness and decorativeness of artistic expression are characteristic features of Lithuanian graphic arts: book illustrations (S.Krasauskas, V.Valius, V.Kalinauskas), prints (A.Makūnaité, P.Repšys, I.Guobiené, M.Vilutis, J.Stauskaité), posters

(J.Galkus, V.Kaušinis) and book-plates. Illustrations of children's books (A.Steponavičius, B.Žilytė) have gained international recognition.

Works of applied decorative art are especially popular in Lithuania; they combine functionalism, grace of form and, often, elements of fine arts. Articles of ceramics (A. Ličkutė, J.Adomonis, L.Šulgaitė, K.Karkaitė), textiles (J.Balčikonis, H.Švažienė, S.Giedrimienė), metal, leather, amber and glass are also created. Stained-glass (A.Stoškus, K.Morkūnas), fresco (S.Veiverytė, A.Kmieliauskas, P.Repšys) and mosaic are increasingly becoming component parts of architecture. Stage design, too, is further developed (J.Malinauskaitė, D.Mataitienė, A.Jacovskis).

MUSIC. The development of professional music in Lithuania follows the course of a similar development in Western and Central Europe, from medieval tradition, Renaissance, Baroque, Classicism, Romanticism to the stylistic trends of the 20th cent. From the 14th cent. onwards the development of both religious and secular music was promoted by the church as well as dynastic ties with European states, the union between Lithuania and Poland and the Magdeburg Law. Theatres and orchestras of Vilnius Lower Castle, cities' magistracies and schools staged operas, ballets, music parades and concerts. Many of Lithuania's musicians at that time were of Italian, Polish, German, Hungarian, Czech or French origins. Local musicians and performers were also active. Singing and organ schools functioned at churches and monasteries. Vilnius University also played an important role in the development of Lithuania's musical culture. In the 17th cent. the first books on music and music theory were published, thus laying the foundations for musicology in Lithuania. The late 19th – early 20th cent. saw the formation of national elements in music, such as Lithuanian themes and motifs of folklore. Composers wrote symphony, chamber and choir music. The first Lithuanian operas (in 1906) and musical comedies (by M.Petrauskas, 1905) were staged. Classical Romanticism marked the music by Č.Sasnauskas and J.Naujalis, while late Romanticism is characteristic of M.K.Čiurlionis' music. Many Lithuanian musicians graduated from the conservatoires in Warsaw, Leipzig, St. Petersburg and Moscow. At the time the traditions of Lithuanian church and secular music were also developing in Latvia, Russia, Germany, the USA, Great Britain.

In 1919 – 40 the development of professional music intensified: musicians were trained at state or private music schools; in 1933 Kaunas Conservatoire and in 1920 Kaunas Opera Theatre were established; various musical societies were also active. In 1924 the first all-Lithuania song festival was held in Kaunas, followed by similar festivals in 1928 and 1930. There were several symphony and chamber orchestras, choirs and soloists. Lithuanian folk music was collected and studied. Music of the period manifests elements of Neoromanticism, Impressionism and Expressionism as well as atonal and microtonic tendencies (J.Gruodis, V.Jakubėnas, J.Gaidelis, V.Bacevičius and J.Kačinskas). WW II and Soviet occupation (esp. its first two decades) distorted or even arrested the further development of music, especially church, choir and organ music. Many Lithuanians were deported to Soviet concentration camps, some emigrated to the West. Ideology had a restrictive effect on the freedom of musical expression. Until the 1960s, Romantic and Neoromantic trends prevailed (B.Dvarionas, A.Račiūnas, S.Vainiūnas, E.Balsys). The 1970s ushered in a greater diversity of styles. Modern systems of composition were linked with Lithuanian folk music systems and means of expression. The sphere of musicological subjects expanded, including analysis of Lithuanian classical heritage, folk music as well as contemporary works.

The Republic has a conservatoire with faculties in Klaipėda and Kaunas, 4 high music schools, 3 arts schools (in Vilnius, Kaunas and Klaipėda), 2 pedagogical music schools, 80 music schools for children, the State Opera and Ballet Theatre, Musical Theatres in Kaunas and Klaipėda, Symphony Orchestra of National Philharmonic Society and State Symphony Orchestra, Lithuanian Chamber Orchestra, Kaunas Chamber Orchestra, Chamber Orchestra *Ave musica*, Lithuanian String Quartet, Vilnius String Quartet, Čiurlionis String Quartet, Brass Quintet, *Musica Humana* and *Polifonija* Ensembles of ancient and contemporary music; a large number of choirs, jazz, variety and folk groups. Many Lithuanian soloists and companies are prize winners of international competitions.

Every five years national song festivals take place in Vilnius which is also venue for a variety of contests, e.g., Čiurlionis piano competition, Dvarionas young performers competition, festivals of chamber, organ, and folk music (*Baltica, Skamba skamba kankliai*); Šiauliai hosts festivals of old music, while jazz festivals are held in Birštonas and Panevėžys. Lithuanian composers, musicologists and performers in the USA, Canada, Germany, Latin America and Great Britain also contribute to the development of Lithuania's professional music. Active are the Chicago Lithuanian Opera (first perf. was staged in 1957) and the Archives of Lithuanian Musicology in Chicago.

THEATRE. Elements of theatre and puppet performance can be traced in ancient Lithuanian folk rituals, folk festivities and rites as well as in pagan worship and mythology. In 1570 – 1773 school theatres in Latin existed at Vilnius Jesuit College, Vilnius University and other schools, their performances containing elements of Renaissance, Baroque, Classical drama. In the late 16th – 18th cent. Lithuania hosted professional theatre groups from England and Italy. The first operas in Lithuania were staged by Marco Schacchi troupe at the Lower Castle Theatre in Vilnius in 1634 – 48. Drama, opera and ballet troupes in Vilnius were supported by the Grand Duke and the nobility. In 1785 the first public theatre of Lithuania was founded in Vilnius. In the 18th – early 19th cent. entrepreneurial theatre groups existed in Kaunas, Klaipėda and other towns.

Due to the ban on the Latin alphabet imposed by the tsarist regime in the late 19th cent., amateur theatre performances were staged in secret and were called *lietuviškieji vakarai* (Lithuanian evenings). They were a major contribution to Lithuanian national liberation movement and the emergence of professional national theatre. In 1899 the first public show, Keturakis' comedy *Amerika pirtyje* (America in the Bathhouse), was presented in Palanga. In the 1st half of the 20th cent. there were professional theatres in Kaunas, such as State Theatre (independent drama, opera and ballet troupes, 1925 — 40), *Vilkolakis* Theatre (1919 — 25), Youth Theatre (1931 — 35), Šiauliai (1931 — 35) and Klaipėda (1935 — 39) Theatres. Among stage directors were J.Vaičkus, A.Sutkus, B.Dauguvietis, R.Juknevičius. Original national dramas were written by V.Krėvė, B.Sruoga, P.Vaičiūnas. Lithuanian national theatre was influenced by the Russian and French theatre traditions. The period of independent Lithuania was too short to witness major national programmes in theatre development. Sovietization prevented the further development of Lithuanian theatre tradition, and yet during the period of Sovietization the theatre was a major factor in maintaining the ideals of humanism and ethnic consciousness. The most talented and honest dramatists, directors and actors opposed conformism, ideological constraints and falsehood. Some (J.Jurašas) preferred emigration to the West to betrayal of the ideals. Cultural resistence produced the greatest theatre achievements and the most outstanding stage directors of both senior and younger generations: J.Miltinis, J.Vaitkus, E.Nekrošius, G.Padegimas; dramatists J.Grušas, Justinas Marcinkevičius, K.Saja; many gifted actors.

Theatres	Founded
Lithuanian Opera and Ballet Theatre (Vilnius)	1920
Kaunas Drama Theatre	1920
Šiauliai Drama Theatre	1931
Klaipėda Drama Theatre	1935
Lithuanian Drama Theatre (Vilnius)	1940
Panevėžys Drama Theatre	1940
Kaunas Musical Theatre	1940
Russian Drama Theatre (Vilnius)	1946
Kaunas Puppet Theatre	1958
Lėlė Theatre (Vilnius)	1958
Youth Theatre (Vilnius)	1965
Klaipėda Musical Theatre	1987
Marijampolė Drama Theatre	1988

BALLET. Lithuanian ballet could be traced back to the 16th cent. Ballet troupes existed at the Lower Castle of Vilnius, at the manors of magnates and municipal theatres. For many years ballet schools and troupes were directed by foreigners who staged dances and ballet performances on the music by Italian or French composers. In the 19th cent. the art of ballet was outshone by opera and drama activities. Ballet reemerged in the 20th cent. after the restoration of Lithuania's independence. In 1921 O.Duboneckienė set up a ballet studio in Kaunas. In 1925 the choreographer P.Petrov staged Leo Delibes' 'Coppelia' at the State Theatre Studio and in 1928 he produced the first Lithuanian ballet 'The Lithuanian Rhapsody' (music by J.Karnavičius). The further development of Lithuanian ballet was influenced by the tradition of the Russian ballet school. Russian ballet stars like the solo dancer V.Nemčinova, choreographers N.Zverev, T.Vasilyev, G.Kiakštas, A.Obuchov, A.Fiodorova worked at the State Theatre. Among the soloists were J.Jovaišaitė, O.Malėjinaitė, M.Juozapaitytė, B.Kelbauskas (the first Lithuanian choreographer), H.Jagminas, P.Baravykas. In 1935, the Lithuanian ballet troupe was on tour in Monte Carlo and London.
In 1948 the Opera and Ballet Theatre was moved to Vilnius. The troupe included G.Sabaliauskaitė, T.Sventickaitė, H.Banys, H.Kunavičius, later joined L.Aškelovičiūtė, N.Antonova, S.Masaniova, R.Krugiškytė, R.Minderis, V.Kudžma. At present the theatre's ballet troupe consists of 80 dancers. N.Beredina, J.Valeikaitė, L.Bartusevičiūtė, P.Skirmantas, J.Katakinas, V.Chlebinskas, E.Smalakys perform leading parts in various ballets. The choreographers V.Grivickas, E.Bukaitis, V.Brazdylis, J.Smoriginas and several foreigners have staged performances by Western European, Russian and Lithuanian composers. The Lithuanian ballet troupes have produced 130 premieres, including 17 national ballet performances. The solo dancers or companies have toured Europe, North and South America, Asia, Africa, participated in various ballet festivals, and several dancers became prize winners of international competitions. Since 1948 the Kaunas Musical Theatre has been staging ballets as well. Dancers are trained at Vilnius Choreography School (since 1952) and Kaunas Naujalis Music School (since 1965) as well as choreography schools in Moscow, Leningrad.
CIRCUS. Elements of circus could be found in Lithuanian folk festivities, games. Popular were various acrobats, entertainers, animal trainers and beast tamers. From the 16th cent. onwards, bear shows grew in popularity. In the 17th — early 19th cent. there were the so-called Bear Academies in Smurgainys and Raudondvaris which provided trained bears for European circus companies. There were 2 permanent circus groups in Vilnius and Kaunas in the 2nd half of the 19th cent. which were famous for acrobats, equilibrists, wrestlers and athletes. Many small circus troupes emerged after WW I. Beginning with 1920 there were a number of professional itinerant and permanent circus troupes. On the initiative of J.Ramanauskas a professional circus troupe was founded in 1944 (since

1959 called *Vilnius*). The performances of acrobats, equilibrists, jugglers, animal trainers and clowns are noted for artistry and complexity. There are also six amateur circus companies in Lithuania.
CINEMA. The first film show in Lithuania took place in Vilnius in 1897. In the early 20th cent. production of documentaries began. In 1909 — 13, A.Račiūnas, a Lithuanian from the USA, filmed a number of scenes from the Lithuanian life. In 1909 V.Starevičius made the first ethnographic documentary 'At the Nemunas' in Kaunas and since 1910 produced animated (puppet) cartoons. From 1924 Lithuanian newsreels were shown on local screens, released on a regular basis from 1932. The joint stock film company *Akis* in Kaunas made the first feature films 'Doctor against his Own Will', 'The Soldier, Lithuania's Defender' and *Onytė ir Jonelis*, 1927 — 31.
In 1940 the Documentary Film Studio was established in Kaunas, renamed the Lith. Film Studio in 1946 and in 1949 moved over to Vilnius. It produces documentaries, popular science films, animated cartoons and feature pictures. Since 1962 TV films have been made; the company *Telefilmas*, opened in 1968, produces feature films.
In the period between 1945 — 90 film making was adversely affected by ideological censorship of the Soviet system. Up to the late 1960's, Lithuanian documentaries and scarce feature films were falsifications of history that could well serve as examples of dogmatic ideology. But in spite of centralization and administrative command system significant documentaries (directed by H.Šablevičius, R.Verba) and feature films emerged. Search for national self-expression led to the emergence of poetic films by A.Žebriūnas ('Living Heroes': 'The Last Shot', 'The Last Day of the Holidays', 'The Belle'). Significant efforts were made to offer an assessment of the historic past of Lithuania, the post-war resistance movement and bolshevik genocide in the films 'No One Wanted to Die' (dir. V.Žalakevičius), 'Staircase to the Sky' (R.Vabalas), 'Feelings' (A.Grikevičius and A.Dausa). Documentaries that emerged during the period of national revival and restoration of the independent Lithuanian Republic are noted for realism, emotionality and expressive form; feature films reflect a new freedom of approach, e.g., 'The Eternal Light' by A.Puipa. The most popular contemporary actors and actresses are G.Balandytė, N.Oželytė, R.Staliliūnaitė, R.Adomaitis, Donatas Banionis, J.Budraitis, A.Masiulis; cameramen J.Gricius, A.Mockus, J.Tomaševičius.
ART PHOTOGRAPHY. Elements of art photography can be traced back to the late 19th and early 20th cent. (photos by A.Straus, J.Czechowicz, S.Fleury, A.Jurašaitis). Significant in this respect is the creative activity of J.Bulhak at the beginning of the 20th cent. (separate works and albums of photography, books on photography techniques). The development of art photography intensified in the 1930s, with photo exhibitions set up, contests of ethnographic photography held and magazines on photography published. In 1933 the Lithuanian Amateur Photographers' Union was founded. The development of photography art was influenced by works and activity of B.Buračas, P.Karpavičius. The 1960s witnessed a specific boost in promoting the significance of art photography. In 1969, the Photography Art Society was founded (the National Association of Lith. Photographers of 1989). In 1976 — 77, the International Art Photography Federation conferred the title of Artists FIAP on 10 Lithuanian photographers. There is a gallery of art photography in Vilnius, the Photography Museum in Šiauliai and 5 photography galleries in other major towns. Several hundred photography exhibitions are put up every year. Significant works have been created by A.Sutkus, A.Kunčius, R.Rakauskas, A.Macijauskas, R.Požerskis, V.Šonta, A.Šeškus, R.Pačėsa, R.Budvytis, R.Balčytis.
LIBRARIES developed from private book collections in the 15 — 16th cent. The collection of Žygimantas Augustas was especially rich (4,000 vols, begun in 1543). It laid the foundations for the library of the Vilnius Jesuit Collegium (founded in 1570, later it became Vilnius University Library). In 1855, E. Tyszkiewicz (and others) founded a Museum of Antiques in Vilnius (functioned intermittently until WW I). At the beginning of the 20th cent., in Vilnius there was the Public Library (about 310,000 vols in 1914), Wrublewsky Library (about 80,000 vols), Library of the Lithuanian Learned Society (about 20,000 vols) and others. In independent Lithuania (1918 — 40), the largest library was the Central Library of Lithuania (founded in 1919 in Kaunas, transferred to Vilnius in 1963). Military Museum of Vytautas the Great was founded in Kaunas in 1921 and the M. K. Čiurlionis Art Gallery, the first art museum, in 1925.
During WW II, more than 20 public libraries were burnt and about 60 destroyed. In Vilnius the Nazis destroyed the Jewish Scientific Institute with a rich library and archives. More than 600,000 books published in the Republic of Lithuania and abroad were destroyed in 1944 — 51 by order of the authorities. Special restricted-access book depositories were formed in the major libraries to keep part of the books published in independent Lithuania, works by Lithuanian emigrees and other publications. Book stocks were mainly formed from publications issued in the SU. As of the 1980s, the major libraries began expanding links with Western countries and enriching their stocks with foreign publications (a considerable part of which was donated by Lithuanians in emigration). In 1989 — 90, when the restoration of Lithuania's independence began, restricted-access book stocks were opened to general readership. In 1990, there were over 200 cultural centres, 1,952 public libraries (of these 1,451 in the countryside), 46 museums and 15 state archives in Lithuania.
BOOK PRINTING. The first books in Lithuania (Vilnius) were published by F.Skorina in the early 16th cent. With Reformation book printing in Lithuanian began in Lithuania Minor. From the late 16th cent. books were published in the Grand Duchy of Lithuania (mostly in Vilnius). Especially active were the printing shops of Vilnius Academy (1586 — 1805, with interruptions) and the printing shops of the Orthodox Brotherhood of the Holy Spirit (1589 — 1660). In 1864 — 1904, the Russian authorities

imposed a ban on Lithuanian books in the Latin alphabet (the Cyrillic alphabet was allowed instead), due to which they were published abroad (in Eastern Prussia, the USA) and smuggled into Lithuania (in 1862 – 1904, 3,000 titles of books were published).

After the restoration of independence (1918), books were published by the Book Publishing Commission of the Ministry of Education, Kaunas University, publishing companies *Švyturys, Varpas, Dirva, Kultūra, Vaiva*, the Society of St. Casimir, publishing houses *Sakalas, Spaudos Fondas, Universitetas* and others. Over the period of 1918 – 40, they published about 20,000 books (titles) in Lithuanian.

After the annexation of Lithuania and WW II, publishing business was concentrated in the hands of state publishing houses. The most important are *Mintis, Mokslas, Šviesa, Vaga, Vyturys*, and the Encyclopaedia Publishers. Up to 1989, the state publishing houses totalled 1,500 – 2,000 books and brochures in 16 – 18 million copies (in Lithuanian 14 – 16 million copies) annually. With the adoption of the new law on publishing in 1989, numerous publishing houses of public organizations and cooperatives emerged; books are also published by private individuals (up to then this right belonged to state publishing houses only). In 1989, these publishing houses put out 2,000 books and brochures (3,320,000 copies), while the 8 state publishing houses published 862 books (20,400,000 copies). With the privatization of book printing, books are becoming more expensive, while their total editions are smaller.

THE PRESS. The first Lithuanian periodicals appeared in the early 19th cent. In the 19th – early 20th cent. (up to 1904), they were published in Eastern Prussia and the USA as the Russian authorities had banned printing in the Latin alphabet (1864 – 1904). In Lithuania they were distributed illegally. Especially important were the magazines *Aušra* (Morning) and *Varpas* (The Bell) that expressed the ideals of Lithuanian national movement.

In the Lithuanian Republic (1918 – 40), there were about 2,000 periodicals. When the SU occupied Lithuania in 1940 almost all of them were closed. Soviet censorship was imposed, all periodicals propagated communist ideology. In 1989, censorship was abolished, which created conditions for the development of free press. In 1990, 240 newspapers with a circulation of 4,500,000 and 43 magazines with a circulation of 2,600,000 were published.

RADIO, TV. Radio broadcasting from Kaunas began in 1926, from Vilnius in 1927. In 1990, the Lithuanian Radio broadcasts 2 national programmes on middle (Radio I on 400.5 m and 192.7 m, Radio II on 271 m) and ultra short waves, also programmes for foreign countries in English on short waves. The first TV programmes were broadcast in Vilnius in 1957. Since 1962, programme I of the USSR television has been relayed; since 1976, Soviet programme II. In 1990, Lithuanian TV broadcasted one national programme and the programme I and II of the USSR TV and Polish TV programme.

RELIGION AND CHURCH

The ancient Lithuanians worshipped objects and phenomena of nature and their ancestors. The cult of forests and fire was especially widespread. The sacred flame was kept burning in the shrines of the holy forests (shrine sites were found in Vilnius and Palanga).

Ancient Lithuanian religion was polytheistic. God of the bright daylight sky was often considered the supreme deity. More popular, however, was the god of thunder and lightning *Perkūnas* (Thunder), the guardian of wizards and sages *Velnias* (Devil). Also popular were the goddesses of forests and hunting *Medeina* and *Žvorūnė*.

By the end of the 12th cent., Christianity began to penetrate Lithuania. A considerable number of princes and noblemen adopted Greek Orthodox faith. In 1251, Grand Duke of Lithuania Mindaugas adopted Catholicism and received the royal crown. This period saw the construction of the first Catholic churches; monks, including Franciscans and Dominicans, settled down in Lithuania. In 1387, Catholicism was introduced in Aukštaitija.

With the spread of Reformation in the 1st half of the 16th cent., Calvinism, Lutheran faith and Arianism evolved in Lithuania. In the late 17th cent. Catholic Counter-Reformation won the battle, largely due to the efforts of the Jesuits. In the late 17th cent., due to the persecution of Old Believers in Russia, some of them settled in Lithuania. In the 18th cent. Lithuania was annexed to Russia. The Catholic Church, especially after 1863, was discriminated, monasteries were closed, many churches were given over to orthodox believers. From 1799 to 1915 Russian Orthodox faith was the official religion in Lithuania. During the period of Lithuanian Republic (1918 – 40), the Catholic Church regained its rights. In 1926, the Lithuanian Church Province was created under the direct subordination to the Pope. In 1927, the government of Lithuania and the Vatican signed the concordat. The state backed the churches of other religions, too.

Lithuania's occupation by the SU caused major losses to all churches (to a lesser degree, to the Russian Orthodox and Old Believers'). Many churches and all the Catholic monasteries were closed, repressive actions were taken against many clergymen, the publishing of religious literature was limited, it was prohibited to teach children catechism. In the 2nd half of 1988, when the Lithuanian Reform Movement *Sajūdis* emerged, the persecution of the church came to an end, the relations between the state and the church changed for the better. In 1990, Act of the Restitution of the Catholic Church was promulgated. In Lithuania there exist religious communities of 13 confessions (in 1990).

ROMAN CATHOLIC CHURCH. There are 668 congregations (parishes), 2 archdioceses (in Kaunas and Vilnius), 4 dioceses, or bishoprics (in Kaišiadorys, Panevėžys, Vilkaviškis, and Telšiai). Matters of local importance are settled by the Conference of Lithuanian bishops (Chair. — Cardinal V.Sladkevičius, Archbishop of Kaunas). Priests are trained at the Kaunas and Telšiai Seminaries. Monasteries are being reopened, including the Franciscans in Kretinga, Capuchins in Dotnuva, the convent of St. Casimir Sisters' in Pažaislis as well as the monasteries of Jesuits and Marian Fathers. In 1989, the Catholic organization *Caritas*, Lithuanian Catholic Teachers' Union, Catholic Action Centre, in 1990 Lithuanian Catholic Academy of Sciences. (transferred from abroad) resumed their activities. The magazines *Katalikų pasaulis* (The Catholic World), *Naujasis židinys* (The New Hearth), the newspaper *XXI amžius* (The 21st Age) are published.

RUSSIAN ORTHODOX CHURCH. There are 45 congregations governed by the archeparchy of Vilnius and of Lithuania (Archbishop — Chrizostom); the archeparchy is subject to the jurisdiction of the Moscow and All-Russia Patriarchate. There are 2 Russian Orthodox monasteries in Vilnius.

OLD BELIEVERS (THE OLD RITUALISTS). There are 51 religious congregations headed by the Supreme Pomorski Old Ritualists' Council in Vilnius (Chair. I.Yegorov). The magazine *Kitezh Grad* is published.

EVANGELICAL LUTHERAN CHURCH. There are 33 congregations governed by the Consistory of Evangelical Lutheran Church of Lithuania in Taurage (Bishop — J.Kalvanas). It is a member of the LWF since 1968. Together with the Evangelical Reformed Church it publishes the *Lietuvos evangelikų kelias* (The Road of the Lithuanian Evangelics).

EVANGELICAL REFORMED CHURCH. There are 8 congregations governed by the Consistory in Biržai (Chair. R.Moras).

Other confessions: Moslems (4 communities), Christians of Evangelical Faith (3 communities), Evangelical Christians-Baptists (3 congregations), Christians of Evangelical Faith in the Spirit of Apostles (2 communities), Seventh-day Adventists (2 communities), Judaists (2 communities), Krishnaites (2 communities), Karaites (1 community), Uniats (1 community).

LIVING STANDARD AND SOCIAL WELFARE

Of late the standards of living in Lithuania have been deteriorating although people's income is on the increase. In 1989 wages and salaries of workers and office employees averaged 244,2 roubles (in 1985, 190.0 roubles), wages of collective farmers 257.0 roubles (in 1985, 183.0 roubles). In 1989 the highest wages averaged 332,6 roubles (in housing construction), 270.5 roubles (management), 263.1 roubles (transportation) and 267.7 roubles (industrial enterprises). The lowest salaries were 151.1 roubles in cultural and 162.9 roubles in sports and social welfare institutions. Deposits in the Lithuanian Savings Bank reached 6,884,700,000 roubles towards the end of 1989 (individual deposits averaged 2,495 roubles). Other indices of standards of living are showed in the tables. The standards of living in Lithuania keep changing rapidly due to inflation (in 1989 the official purchasing power of the rouble fell by 10%) and the growth of state controlled retail princes for consumer goods. In 1980 — 89 state controlled retail prices for consumer goods increased by 13.0%, for foodstuffs, 24.1%, other wares, 4.1%. Price growth for sausages (24%), potatoes (27%) and vegetables (23%) was especially notable. Inadequate supply of commodities and services is a major cause of the price hike. The growing prices for material-technical resources and the purchasing prices for agricultural produce as well as the need to protect the domestic market caused the decision by the Lithuanian Government to increase the retail prices for foodstuffs by 2.8 times at the beginning of 1991. Many commodity prices (furniture, TV sets, refrigerators) have also gone up. Though compensations are paid, all this will inevitably have an adverse effect on the standards of living.

Consumer Goods Supply (end of the year; per 100 families)

	1980	1985	1988	1989
Watches	608	637	660	668
Radio sets	97	111	112	109
TV sets	75	93	104	107
Cameras	43	44	44	41
Refrigerators	86	91	91	91
Washing machines	64	64	66	70
Vacuum cleaners	36	48	57	60
Motor cycles and scooters	11	13	13	13
Bicycles, mopeds and motorized bicycles	72	80	84	84
Sewing machines	49	49	49	48
Tape recorders	21	34	42	44

Annual Consumption of Foodstuffs (kg per person)

	1980	1985	1988	1989
Meat and meat products (pure meat)	81	87	87	83
Milk and milk products (pure milk)	415	409	441	451
Eggs	253	285	319	316
Fish and marine products	16.7	17.8	19.4	18.6
Sugar	41.2	43.5	50.0	45.5
Oil	6.3	7.8	8.5	7.6
Potatoes	150	134	143	146
Vegetables, water-melons, melons, etc.	78	84	84	82
Fruits and berries (excluding processing into wine)	40	52	49	65
Grain products (bread, macaroni, flour, cereals, haricot, peas, etc.)	111	107	111	110

Output of Main Industrial Products (per person)

	1980	1985	1988	1989
Electric power (kWh)	3,398	5,844	7,080	7,867
Bicycles for teenagers (per '000 persons)	127	129	128	114
Paper (kg)	31	34	33	32
Fabrics (sq m)	58	62	61	59
Socks and stockings (p.)	26	28	28	28
Underwear and knitwear	18	17	17	17
Leather footwear (p.)	3.0	3.0	3.1	3.2
Rubber footwear (p.)	2.5	2.8	3.1	3.0
Meat (industrial products incl. subproducts of 1st category; kg)	91	111	118	121
Butter (kg)	15	20	21	21
Granulated sugar (kg)	62	62	65	64
Confectionery (kg)	20	22	24	25
Canned food (standard containers)	79	91	110	114

HEALTH CARE. For centuries folk medicine prevailed among Lithuanians. In the Middle Ages barbers practised as surgeons. The first professional physicians appeared in the early 15th cent. The first pharmacy was established in 1506 at the court of the Grand Duke in Vilnius. In about 1518 the first hospital (špitolė) was founded in Vilnius. The year 1781 saw the establishment of a medical faculty at Vilnius University. Until 1842 Vilnius University and the Academy of Medicine and Surgery had trained about 1,500 physicians. In the early 19th cent., Vilnius University clinical hospital was opened with the departments of therapy, surgery and obstetrics. In 1896 the average life expectancy was 32 years; mortality rate in Vilnius Land was 22.8, in Kaunas — 27.9 per 1,000 inhabitants.

The year 1922 witnessed the establishment of the medical faculty at the University of Lithuania. In 1922—40, 1,070 physicians, 547 dentists, and 229 pharmacists graduated from this faculty, 26 of them received doctoral degrees. Lithuanian medical terminology emerged; research was carried out in dietetics, allergy, rheumatism and trachoma epidemiology and treatment, organ transplantation. Advance in surgery was especially notable. In 1925 a law on patient social security (Ligonių kasos) was adopted. New hospitals in Alytus, Kėdainiai, Marijampolė, Mažeikiai, Panevėžys, Telšiai, Tauragė, University Clinical Hospital in Kaunas (1,200 beds) were built in 1922—40. As of 1939, there were 81 hospitals with 5,092 beds; 1,446 physicians, 686 dentists, 132 pharmacists, 327 pharmacist's assistants, and some 2,000 paramedical personnel. In 1940, there were 6.7 physicians and 30.0 hospital beds per 10,000 population; birth rate was 23.0, mortality rate — 13.0.

Following Lithuania's annexation by the SU in 1940, the local medical system was Sovietized. After WW II Lithuanian schools of cardiosurgery, cardiology, endocrinology, gastroenterology and rheumatology emerged. An integral system for cardiac ischemia treatment including prevention, early diagnosis, treatment and rehabilitation developed. Heart valve implantations, complicated surgical operations of inborn heart diseases are improved. In 1987, surgeons of the Cardiosurgery Clinic of Vilnius University made the first heart transplantation in Lithuania. Much has been achieved in surgical treatment of arrhythmia and in the field of electric heart stimulation, including research in heart rhythmology and creation of new electrocardic stimulators. Successful kidney transplantations number several hundred. Positive results have been achieved in extremity and finger replantation. Methods for treating rheumatism and diseases of the joints have been developed, experimental models for rheumatic process, cardiovascular insufficiency and muscle pathology have been suggested. Antiblastomic preparations have been synthesized. Electroröntgenography has been successfully introduced into clinical practice. As of 1989, there were 192 hospitals with 46,000 beds; 16,900 physicians, 45,500 paramedical personnel; birth rate was 15.1, mortality rate 10.3, natural increase of population 4.8 per 1,000 inhabitants.

	Number of physicians, paramedical personnel, and hospital beds per 100,000 persons		
	1985	1988	1989
Physicians of all specialities	42.4	45.1	45.7
Paramedical personnel	120.6	126.7	125.3
Hospital beds	123.7	124.8	125.8

SOCIAL WELFARE. The basis of social security is the national social security system. It comprises the compulsory (state) social insurance and social benefits provided by the state. The national social insurance covers all Lithuania's residents. It guarantees income security to people in the case of loss of work-related income or reduction of income due to old age, sickness or disability. To be entitled to social insurance pensions and benefits, a certain fixed work record is required. All individuals engaged in paid employment (employees), self-employed and owners of enterprises with a status of physical entity are insured according to the national social insurance scheme. Insurance is effected by both employers and employees. The national social insurance budget is independent from the budgets of the state or municipalities. Pensions and social benefits to individuals who are not covered by the national social insurance scheme due to the fact that they have not been insured or they have been insured for a shorter period than required by the national social security scheme are paid by the state from the Government funds. Social assistance benefits are paid from the municipality budget. By the end of 1989, old age pensions were paid to 839,000 pensioners, including 206,000 farmers (the average pension amounted to 85.4 roubles a month). Old age pensions are paid to men from the age of 60 with the work record of 25 years and to women from the age of 55 with the work record of 20 years. The disabled with no work record whatever are paid social benefits amounting to 35 roubles a month.

By the end of 1989, the housing floor space made 70,800,000 sq m, including 43,200,000 sq m of state and cooperative apartments and 27,600,000 sq m of private housing. 142,000 families and single people are still on the waiting lists (18% of all families).

By the end of 1989, there were 3,947 state-owned social service enterprises (in 1985 — 3,473) offering services for 275,100,000 roubles, 74.21 roubles per person (1985, 45.97 roubles per person). There were also social service cooperatives providing services for 43,900,000 roubles.

SPORTS. Sports movement and activities of sports organizations are coordinated by the Department for Physical Training and Sports. The sports facilities in 1987 included: 41 stadium, 8 indoor tracks, 3 horse-riding tracks, 55 swimming pools (43 of them indoor pools), 870 football, 585 handball, 4 motorball fields, 2,264 basketball, 1,872 volleyball, 132 tennis courts, 108 ice hockey rinks, 1,084 gymnasiums (140 of them specialized), 19 rowing centres, 1 underwater-swimming centre, 206 sports and health-building centres, 1 bicycle track, 100 grounds for figure driving, 17 karting race courses, 8 motorcycle racing tracks, 92 amateur radio stations, 529 shooting-ranges.

The largest sports facilities are: Vilnius *Žalgiris* Stadium (built in 1945; 15,000 seats), Klaipėda *Žalgiris* Stadium (1930; 15,000 seats), Stadium of Kaunas Sports Centre (1922, reconstructed in 1978; 12,000 seats), Stadium of Panevėžys Sports Centre (1965; 10,000 seats), Kaunas Sports Hall (1939; 4,900 seats), Vilnius Sports Palace (1971; 4,500 seats), Vilnius Track-and-field Centre (1976; 2,550 seats), Alytus Sports Palace (1977; 1,500 seats), Sports Stadium of Kaunas Synthetic Fibre Plant (1974; 1,250 seats), Trakai *Dinamo* Rowing Centre (1972), Kaunas Horse-Riding Manege (1978), Šiauliai Track-and-field Centre (1975), Klaipėda Bicycle Track (1979), Vilnius Aquatics Centre (1980).

Over 50 branches of sports are practised in Lithuania. Best results have been achieved by rowers, boxers, basketballers, track-and-field athletes, swimmers, handballers, table tennis-players. By 1990, the Lithuanian athletes had set 34 world, 15 European records. There were about 3,900 staff sports workers with higher education, about 30 international-class and about 1,100 national-class referees.

TOURISM. It is picturesque countryside as well as historical and cultural monuments that attract attention of foreign tourists to Lithuania. Such resorts as Palanga and Kuršių Nerija *(Kuriche Nehrung)* situated along the Baltic coast are famous for their clean beaches and natural sand dunes. Druskininkai and Birštonas are spas well-known for mineral waters and tranquility; the land of lakes, Zarasai is inimitable in its beauty. The first tourist institution was established in the late 19th cent. In 1935 the Lithuanian Tourist Society joined the International Union of Tourism.

Foreign tourism is coordinated by the Board for Foreign Tourism. In Vilnius the Board has a hotel 'Lietuva'. Domestic tourism is managed by the Lithuanian Council on Tourism. It includes 2 tourism and excursion associations, 3 tourist centres with hotels, 5 tourist homes, 13 travel and excursion bureaus. 28 tourist clubs function in the cities and districts of Lithuania. In 1989, Lithuania received 480,000 tourists from the USSR and 70,000 foreigners. Some 200,000 citizens of Lithuania travelled in the USSR and about 30,000 visited other countries.

Obsolete facilities as well as financial and administrative dependence on the USSR tourist institutions impeded the development of tourism during the past few decades. Foreign tourists were not allowed to visit many cities and historical sites; quite a few picturesque areas were declared military zones. In 1990, after the restoration of Lithuania's independence restrictions for foreigners were lifted; many private travel agencies emerged; comfortable motels are built in cooperation with foreign firms.

USEFUL INFORMATION FOR A VISITOR

LITHUANIAN PLACES OF INTEREST

1 Geographical centre of Europe (25 km from Vilnius) **2** Trakai Castle (14th — 15th cent.) **3** Trakų Vokės Estate (19th cent.) **4** Medininkai Castle (14th — 15th cent.) **5** Aukštadvaris Landscape Preserve **6** Street-village Zervynos (18th cent.) **7** M. K. Čiurlionis Road (ensemble of wooden sculptures along the road of Varėna — Druskininkai) **8** Remains of the Liškiava Castle (15th cent.) **9** Druskininkai. M. K. Čiurlionis Memorial Museum. Springs of mineral water **10** The Church of Simnas (16th — 18th cent.) **11** Lake Žuvintas, Nature Reserve **12** Punia Landscape and Historical Preserve **13** Birštonas. Mineral water. Museum of local lore **14** Rumšiškės Outdoor Country Life Museum **15** The Church of Zapyškis (16th cent.) **16** The Ensemble of Paežeriai Estate and park (18th — 19th cent.) **17** Veliuona. Landscape and Historical Preserve. **18.** Raudonė Castle (16th cent). **19** Panemunė Castle (17th — 18th cent.) **20** Rambynas Landscape Preserve **21** Fishermen village Minija **22** Ventės Ragas. Ornithological Station (birds are tagged) **23** Nida. T. Mann's House, Neringa Forest Park, dunes **24** Skomantai Hill-Fort **25** Palanga. Amber Museum **26** The Church of Kretinga (17th cent.) **27** Orvydai Absurdity Museum (village of Gargždelė) **28** Mosėdis Stone Museum **29** Žemaitija National Park (centre in Plateliai) **30** The Church of Žemaičių Kalvarija (15th cent.) **31** Botanical Gardens of Žemaičiai (in Kalnėnai) **32** Cathedral of Telšiai (18th cent.) **33** Šatrija Landscape Preserve **34** Medvėgalis Landscape and Historical Preserve **35** Baubliai (Village of Bijotai) **36** The Church and Chapel of Šiluva (18th cent.) **37** The Church of Tytuvėnai (17th — 18th cent.) **38** The Hill of Crosses (village of Jurgaičiai) **39** Kamanos Reserve **40** Biržai Castle (16th cent.) **41** Kėdainiai (the Old Town, 17th cent.) **42** The Church of Paberžė **43** Raguvėlė Country Estate (18th — 20th cent.) **44** Anykščiai. Museums of Lithuanian writers **45** Horse Museum (village of Niūronys) **46** The Anykščiai Pine Forest **47** Museum of Nature and Ethnography (village of Uoginai) **48** The Ensemble of Rokiškis Estate (19th cent.) **49** The Church of Rokiškis (19th cent.) **50** The Church of Stelmužė (17th — 18th cent.) **51** The Village of Šuminai (buildings of 19th — 20th cent.) **52** Aukštaitija National Park. The Church of Palūšė (18th cent.), Tourist Centre. The Mill of Ginučiai, Hill Forts, Ethnographic Village of Salos **53** Site of ancient castle in Dubingiai (15th — 16th cent.) **54** Kernavė Archeological and Historical Museum Preserve (12th — 13th cent.), burial mounds, hill forts (13th — 14th cent.)

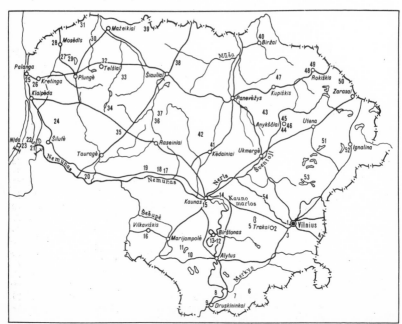

Distance Between the Largest Cities and Towns (km; highway)

	Alytus	Birštonas	Druskininkai	Kaunas	Klaipėda	Marijampolė	Nida	Palanga	Panevėžys	Šiauliai	Vilnius
Alytus	—	41	57	67	281	64	328	307	179	226	**105**
Anykščiai	178	154	235	111	288	173	335	280	61	143	**104**
Birštonas	41	—	81	43	257	49	304	283	161	202	**91**
Biržai	250	226	307	183	252	246	299	255	65	108	**204**
Druskininkai	57	81	—	124	338	90	385	364	236	283	**150**
Ignalina	215	201	260	175	367	238	414	380	149	233	**110**
Kaunas	67	43	124	—	214	63	261	240	118	159	**104**
Kėdainiai	123	99	180	56	206	119	253	215	62	105	**128**
Klaipėda	281	257	338	214	—	236	47	26	225	145	**316**
Lazdijai	47	85	49	104	289	48	336	292	216	242	**152**
Marijampolė	64	49	90	63	236	—	283	251	175	201	**140**
Mažeikiai	307	283	353	240	111	232	158	109	163	81	**303**
Molėtai	167	153	212	113	297	176	344	307	103	187	**62**
Nida	328	304	385	261	47	283	—	73	272	192	**363**
Palanga	307	283	364	240	26	251	73	—	229	145	**342**
Panevėžys	179	161	236	118	225	175	272	229	—	82	**138**
Raseiniai	153	129	205	86	134	115	181	160	121	77	**186**
Šiauliai	226	202	283	159	145	201	192	145	82	—	**222**
Telšiai	260	233	298	190	79	208	126	70	150	68	**290**
Trakai	80	64	132	83	293	113	340	319	150	227	**27**
Utena	200	177	245	134	326	197	373	327	98	184	**95**
Vilnius	**105**	**91**	**150**	**104**	**316**	**140**	**363**	**342**	**138**	**222**	—
Zarasai	250	227	295	184	379	285	426	381	152	234	**145**

TELEPHONE AND TELEFAX CODES FROM EUROPE TO LITHUANIA

Alytus . . . . 012 – 35	Marijampolė . . 012 – 43	Telšiai . . . . 012 – 94
Anykščiai . . . 012 – 51	Mažeikiai . . . 012 – 93	Ukmergė . . 012 – 11
Elektrėnai . . . 012 – 37	Palanga . . . 012 – 36	Utena . . . . 012 – 39
Jonava . . . 012 – 19	Panevėžys . . 012 – 54	Varėna . . . . 012 – 60
Jurbarkas . . . 012 – 48	Pabradė . . . 012 – 17	Vilkaviškis . . 012 – 42
Kaunas . . . 012 – 7	Plungė . . . . 012 – 18	Vilnius . . . . 012 – 2
Klaipėda . . 012 – 61	Raseiniai . . 012 – 28	
Lazdijai . . 012 – 68	Šiauliai . . . . 012 – 14	

CODES FROM LITHUANIA TO EUROPE

Berlin . . .8 – 10372	Lvov . . . . .8 – 0322	Prague . . .8 – 10422
Kaliningrad . .8 – 01122	Moscow . . .8 – 095	Riga . . . .8 – 0132
Kiev . . .8 – 044	Minsk . . . .8 – 0172	Tallinn . . .8 – 0142
Leningrad . .8 – 812		

CODES IN LITHUANIA

Alytus . . . 8 – 235	Kretinga . . . 8 – 258	Sniečkus . . 8 – 266
Anykščiai . . 8 – 251	Kupiškis . . . 8 – 231	Šakiai . . . 8 – 247
Birštonas . . 8 – 210	Lazdijai . . . 8 – 268	Šalčininkai . 8 – 250
Biržai . . . 8 – 220	Mažeikiai . . 8 – 293	Šiauliai . . . 8 – 214
Druskininkai . 8 – 233	Molėtai . . . 8 – 230	Šilalė . . . 8 – 269
Elektrėnai . . 8 – 237	Naujoji Akmenė . 8 – 295	Šilutė . . . 8 – 241
Gargždai . . 8 – 240	Nida . . . 8 – 259	Širvintos . . 8 – 232
Ignalina . . . 8 – 229	Pakruojis . . 8 – 291	Švenčionys . . 8 – 217
Jonava . . . 8 – 219	Palanga . . 8 – 236	Tauragė . . 8 – 246
Joniškis . . . 8 – 296	Panevėžys . . 8 – 254	Telšiai . . . 8 – 294
Jurbarkas . . 9 – 248	Pasvalys . . 8 – 271	Trakai . . . 8 – 238
Kaišiadorys . 8 – 256	Plungė . . . 8 – 218	Ukmergė . . 8 – 211
Kapsukas . . 8 – 243	Prienai . . . 8 – 249	Utena . . . 8 – 239
Kaunas . . . 8 – 27	Radviliškis . . 8 – 292	Varėna . . . 8 – 260
Kėdainiai . . 8 – 257	Raseiniai . . 8 – 228	Vilkaviškis . . 8 – 242
Kelmė . . . 8 – 297	Rokiškis . . . 8 – 278	Zarasai . . . 8 – 270
Klaipėda . . 8 – 261	Skuodas . . . 8 -- 216	

VILNIUS

TELEPHONE DIRECTORY

EMERGENCIES (same tel. nrs used throughout Lithuania)

Fire	01	Inquiry	05
Police	02	Telegraph	06
Ambulance	03	Call ordering desk	07
Gas leakage	04	Information	09

GENERAL INFORMATION

Post office	616 759	Advance booking	752 585
City Information	652 632	Check room	662 776
Trains		Taxis	772 929
Inquiry desk	630 086	River port	612 972
Advance booking	623 044	Chemist's	616 250
Booking office	626 956	Customs	264 653
Inter-city shipments	632 226	Bank (currency exchange)	224 790
Buses		Hotel 'Lietuva'	736 015
Inquiry desk	660 481	Notary assistance	612 079
Advance booking	630 977	Legal advice	619 313
Booking office	635 293	Excursion bureau	754 130
Inter-city shipments	638 293	Tugging of motor transport	458 564, 640 854
Airport		Lost property	624 606
Inquiry desk	630 201	Traffic police	619 230

ADDRESSES

HOTELS

56 ASTORIJA Didžiosios 35, tel. 629 914; **DRAUGYSTĖ** Čiurlionio 84, tel. 662 711; **64 GINTARAS** Sodų 14, tel. 634 496; **1 LIETUVA** Ukmergės 20, tel. 736 070; **43 NARUTIS** Pilies 24, tel. 622 882; **12 NERINGA** Gedimino pr. 23, tel. 610 516; **SKRYDIS** Rodūnios kelias 8 (airport), tel. 669 467; **SPORTAS** Bistryčios 13, tel. 748 453; **2 TURISTAS** Ukmergės 14, tel. 733 002; **15 VILNIUS** Gedimino pr. 20, tel. 623 665

RESTAURANTS. CAFĖS. BARS

AIRPORT (restaurant), tel. 662 476; **AKIMIRKA** Gedimino pr. 31, tel. 617 417; **37 ALUMNATAS** Universiteto 4, tel. 612 043; **51 AMATININKŲ UŽEIGA** Stiklių 2, tel. 626 506; **56 ASTORIJA** Didžiosios 35, tel. 224 043; **34 BOČIŲ** Šv. Ignoto 3, tel. 623 772; **13 DAINAVA** Vienuolio 4, tel. 617 481; **DRAUGYSTĖ** Čiurlionio 84, tel. 661 651; **ERFURTAS** Architektų 19, tel. 444 542; **64 GINTARAS** Sodų 14, tel. 635 370; **LAZDYNAI** Architektų 152, tel. 447 995; **1 LIETUVA** Ukmergės 20, tel. 736 431; **LITERATŲ SVETAINĖ** Gedimino pr. 1, tel. 611 889; **50 LOKYS** Stiklių 8, tel. 629 046; **MEDININKAI** Aušros vartų 6, tel. 614 019; **MĖTA** Gedimino pr. 39, tel. 624 128; **12 NERINGA** Gedimino pr. 23, tel. 617 456; **NYKŠTUKAS** Pamėnkalnio 14, tel. 610 735; **17 PALANGA** Vilniaus 10/16, tel. 620 186; **PAPARTIS** Erfurto 31/43, tel. 449 635; **66 RAILWAY TERMINAL** Geležinkelio 16, tel. 613 606; **RŪDININKAI** (beer) Rūdininkų 14, tel. 624 668; **RŪTA** Gedimino pr. 37, tel. 626 904; **38 SENASIS RŪSYS** Šv. Ignoto 16, tel. 611 137; **47 STIKLIAI** Žydų 7, tel. 627 971; **ŠALTINĖLIS** Žirmūnų 106, tel. 771 636; **TAURO RAGAS** (beer) Jasinskio 36, tel. 628 925; **TRAKAI** Trakų 3, tel. 227 260; **15 VILNIUS** Gedimino pr. 20, tel. 616 197; **ŽARIJA** Gedimino pr. 45, tel. 626 903; **ŽEMAIČIŲ ALINĖ** (beer) Vokiečių 24, tel. 616 573; **ŽIRMŪNAI** Žirmūnų 67, tel. 779 939

THEATRES. CONCERT HALLS

PALACE OF CULTURE AND SPORTS OF THE MINISTRY OF THE INTERIOR Sporto 21, tel. 751 030; **22 LITHUANIAN ACADEMIC DRAMA THEATRE** Gedimino pr. 4, tel. 629 771; **14 LITHUANIAN ACADEMIC OPERA AND BALLET THEATRE** Vienuolio 1, tel. 620 727; **59 NATIONAL PHILHARMONIC** Didžioji 45, tel. 627 165; **36 PALACE OF ART WORKERS** Daukanto a. 3/8, tel. 616 969; **57 PUPPET THEATRE** Arklių 5, tel. 628 678; **30 RUSSIAN DRAMA THEATRE** Basanavičiaus 13, tel. 620 552; **SCIENTISTS' PALACE** Turistų 49, tel. 770 073; **SMALL BAROQUE HALL** Daukanto a. 1, tel. 619 926; **28 TRADE UNION CULTURE PALACE** Mykolaičio-Putino 5, tel. 635 620; **58 YOUTH THEATRE** Arklių 5, tel. 616 126

MUSEUMS. EXHIBITION HALLS

VERKIAI EXHIBITION HALL Turistų 49, Wed, Sat, Sun 11 – 18, tel. 776 156; **53 ART EXHIBITION CENTRE** Vokiečių 2, daily 11 – 19, tel. 623 954; **63 ARTILLERY BASTION** Išganytojo 20/18, Mon, Wed – Sun 11 – 19, tel. 612 149; **54 ART MUSEUM** Didžioji 31, Tue – Sun 12 – 18, tel. 628 679; **27 CASTLE MUSEUM** Pilies kalnas, May – Sept, Mon, Wed – Sun 9 – 20, Oct – Apr, Mon, Wed – Sun 11 – 17, tel. 617 453; **FOLK ART EXHIBITION** Rūdininkų 22/21, Tue – Sun 12 – 18, tel. 617 414; **EXHIBITION OF LITHUANIAN ART** Goštauto 32/1, Tue – Sun 13 – 19, tel. 619 058; **EXHIBITION CENTRE** Laisvės pr. 5, Tue – Sun 10 – 18, tel. 451 800; **MEMORIAL MUSEUM OF WRITERS** Antakalnio 2, Wed – Sun 11 – 18, tel. 629 969; **V.MYKOLAITIS-PUTINAS MEMORIAL MUSEUM** Tauro 10 – 3, Wed – Sun 11 – 18, tel. 624 480; **26 MUSEUM OF APPLIED ARTS** Arsenalo 3, Mon, Tue, Thur – Sun 11 – 19, tel. 628 080; **MUSEUM OF ARCHITECTURE** Volano 13, Mon, Wed – Sun 11 – 19, tel. 610 456; **25 MUSEUM OF HISTORY AND ETHNOGRAPHY** Vrublevskio 1, Mon, Wed – Sun 11 – 19, tel. 629 421; **PANERIAI MUSEUM** Aukštieji Paneriai, Agrastų 15, Mon, Wed – Sun 11 – 18, tel. 641 847; **A. PUSHKIN MEMORIAL MUSEUM** Subačiaus 124, Wed – Sun 11 – 19, tel. 690 080; **JEWISH MUSEUM** Pamėnkalnio 8e, tel. 620 730

ARCHITECTURAL MONUMENTS

27 REMAINS OF THE UPPER AND THE LOWER CASTLE Pilies kalnas; **35 ST. IGNATIUS' CHURCH** Šv. Ignoto 6; **33 ST. CATHERINE'S CHURCH** Vilniaus 30; **CHURCH OF HOLY TRINITY** (Orthodox) **AND BASILIAN MONASTERY** Aušros vartų 49; **55 ST. CASIMIR'S CHURCH** Didžioji 34; **CHURCH OF BONI FRATRES** Daukanto a. 1; **36 PALACE OF BISHOPS** (Palace of Art Workers) Daukanto a. 3/8; **SS. JAMES AND PHILLIP'S CHURCH** Lukiškių a. 10; **RADVILŲ PALACE** Liejyklos 2; **RASOS CEMETERY** Rasų g.; **MISSIONARY CHURCH AND MONASTERY** Subačiaus 24; **BERNARDINE MONASTERY** Malūnų 3; **FRANCISCAN CHURCH** Trakų 9; **39 THE OLD VILNIUS UNIVERSITY PALACE** Universiteto 3; **37 ALUMNATAS** Universiteto 4; **VERKIAI ARCHITECTURAL ENSEMBLE** Verkių 77; **ST. GEORGE'S CHURCH** Sirvydo 4; **42 DWELLING HOUSES** (late 16th cent.) Pilies 12; **44 ST. MICHAEL'S CHURCH** Volano/Maironio g.; **62 AUŠROS GATE** Aušros vartų g. 12

CHURCHES

Catholic: **23 CATHEDRAL SQUARE** (of SS. Stanislas and Ladislas) Katedros a.; **46 ST. ANNE'S AND BERNARDINE CHURCHES** Maironio 8; **DOMINICAN CHURCH** Dominikonų 8; **40 ST. JOHN'S CHURCH** Šv. Jono 12; **52 ST. NICHOLAS' CHURCH** Šv. Mikalojaus 16; **7 SS. PETER AND PAUL'S CHURCH** Antakalnio 1/1; **4 ST. RAPHAEL'S CHURCH** Upės 4; **61 ST. THERESA'S CHURCH** Aušros vartų 12

Orthodox : **60 CHURCH OF THE HOLY GHOST** Aušros vartų 8; **ST. NICHOLAS' CHURCH** Didžioji 12; **48 CHURCH OF DORMITION OF THE HOLY VIRGIN** Maironio 12; **29 SS. MICHAEL'S AND KONSTANTIN'S CHURCH** Basanavičiaus 27

Lutheran: **49 EVANGELICAL LUTHERAN CHURCH** Vokiečių 18/12

Reformed: **32 EVANGELICAL REFORMED CHURCH** Pylimo 18

Other: **CHURCH OF RUSSIAN OLD BELIEVERS** Naujininkų 24; **THE SYNAGOGUE** Pylimo 39

LIBRARIES

24 CENTRAL LIBRARY OF THE ACADEMY OF SCIENCES Žygimantų 2/8, tel. 623 678; **28 LIBRARY OF TRADE UNIONS** Mykolaičio-Putino 5, tel. 610 613; **A. MICKEVIČIUS PUBLIC LIBRARY** Trakų 10, tel. 616 023; **9 NATIONAL M.MAŽVYDAS LIBRARY** Gedimino pr. 51, tel. 616 818; **35 REPUBLICAN SCIENTIFIC TECHNICAL LIBRARY** Šv. Ignoto 6, tel. 618 758; **39 VILNIUS UNIVERSITY LIBRARY** Universiteto 3, tel. 612 747; **VILNIUS CENTRAL LIBRARY** Žirmūnų 6, tel. 732 158

HIGHER SCHOOLS

45 ART ACADEMY Maironio 6, tel. 613 004; **MANAGEMENT ACADEMY** Pylimo 4, tel. 623 142; **PEDAGOGICAL INSTITUTE** Studentų 39, tel. 738 281; **11 CONSERVATOIRE** Gedimino pr. 42, tel. 612 691; **39 VILNIUS UNIVERSITY** Universiteto 3, tel. 623 779; **TECHNICAL UNIVERSITY** Saulėtekio al. 11, tel. 769 600 ; **POLICE ACADEMY** Ateities 20, tel. 779 424

ADMINISTRATION

8 SUPREME COUNCIL Gedimino pr. 53, tel. 628 986; **10 GOVERNMENT** Tumo-Vaižganto 2, tel. 622 101; **18 CITY COUNCIL AND GOVERNMENT** Gedimino pr. 9, tel. 628 626, 620 160

BANKS AND MONEY EXCHANGE

20 BANK FOR FOREIGN ECONOMIC AFFAIRS Totorių 2/8, tel. 224 790; **21 LITHUANIAN BANK** Gedimino 6, tel. 224 015; **SAVINGS BANK** Vilniaus 16, tel. 618 409; **1 HOTEL 'LIETUVA'** Ukmergės 20

SHOPPING

AIDAS (radio wares) Vilniaus 9/2, tel. 620 995; **CAR SPARE PARTS** Jasinskio 51, tel. 616 342; **3 CENTRAL DEPARTMENT STORE** Ukmergės 16, tel. 730 559; **CURIOSITY SHOP** Dominikonų 14, 16, tel. 624 071; **DAILĖ** (articles of art) Gedimino pr. 1, tel. 613 827; Pamėnkalnio 5/13, tel. 624 552; Vokiečių 2, tel. 619 516; **GRAŽINA** (haberdashery) Gedimino pr. 7, tel. 617 328; **HOUSEHOLD ARTICLES** Gedimino pr. 49a, tel. 628 657; **HUNTING AND FISHING ACCESSORIES** Vilniaus 4/35, tel. 622 446; **JEWELRY** Gedimino pr. 2, tel. 620 671; **KIRTIMAI** (bicycles, motor cycles), Eišiškių pl. 8, tel. 630 611; **MAKE HIMSELF** Viršuliškių 42, tel. 427 774; **MUSICAL INSTRUMENTS** Gedimino pr. 33, tel. 613 102; **OPTIKA** (optician) Gedimino pr. 3a, tel. 629 926; **PERFUMERY** Jogailos 8, tel. 623 550; **PHOTOACCESSORIES** Totorių 12, tel. 625 870; **RECORDS** Tilto 13/15, tel. 620 168; Vilniaus 17, tel. 620 168; **SOUVENIRS** Gedimino pr. 3a, tel. 610 017; **SPORTSWARE** Gedimino pr. 26, tel. 614 175; **STATIONERY** Vienuolio 14, tel. 610 509; **VAIVA** (haberdashery, knitwear) Gedimino pr. 44, tel. 626 153; **16 VILNIUS DEPARTMENT STORE** Gedimino pr. 18, tel. 616 891

HARD CURRENCY SHOPS

Konarskio 17, tel. 652 845; **MERKURIJUS** Laisvės pr. 31, tel. 268 833; **41 VILBARA** Pilies 2/1, tel. 610 750

GROCERY SHOPS

Antakalnio 44, tel. 741 873; Architektų 19, tel. 442 431; Architektų 152, tel. 446 111; Čiurlionio 82, tel. 632 647; Gedimino pr. 4/35, tel. 623 126; Gedimino pr. 24, tel. 621 549; Gedimino pr. 64, tel. 625 195; Pylimo 21, tel. 612 427; Pylimo 43, tel. 617 678; Savanorių pr. 31, tel. 633 569; Šeškinės 22, tel. 426 254; Šeškinės 33, tel. 415 172; Tuskulėnų 66, tel. 731 597; Viršuliškių 30, tel. 410 228; Žirmūnų 2, tel. 351 961; Žirmūnų 67, tel. 771 778; Žvaigždžių 29, tel. 424 292

MARKETS

CENTRAL MARKET Pylimo 58/1, tel. 625 536; **GARIŪNŲ MARKET** Gariūnų g.; **KALVARIJŲ MARKET** Kalvarijų 61, tel. 750 345

SPORTS

DARBO REZERVAI STADIUM Čiurlionio 112, tel. 639 879; **DINAMO STADIUM** Kosciuškos 7, tel. 628 761; **LOKOMOTYVAS STADIUM** Liepkalnio 5, tel. 655 402; **6 SPORT PALACE** Rinktinės 1, tel. 358 942; **WATER SPORT CENTRE** Erfurto 13, tel. 269 041; **5 ŽALGIRIS STADIUM** Rinktinės 3/11, tel. 357 946

MEDICAL SERVICE

HOSPITAL, DENTAL CLINIC Antakalnio 124, tel. 746 134, 742 590; **DENTAL CLINIC** Vilniaus 25, tel. 618 281; **EMERGENCY HOSPITAL** Lukiškių a. 10, tel. 624 483; **DRUG STORES** Gedimino pr. 27, tel. 610 135; Basanavičiaus 41, tel. 633 868

PETROL STATIONS Gariūnai, tel. 640 781; Pramonės 25a, tel. 672 787; Apkasų 18, tel. 750 300; Savanorių pr. 119, tel. 631 011; Valakampių 3, tel. 768 522; **CAR SERVICE** Eišiškių pl. 34, tel. 632 379; Kirtimų 41a, tel. 641 810; **LADA** Eišiškių pl. 8, tel. 660 764; Plytinės 27, tel. 762 987; Savanorių pr. 217, tel. 632 678; **TECHNICAL AID** tel. 458 564, 640 554; Ukmergės 156a, tel. 753 442; **PAID CAR PARKS** Birbynių g., tel. 619 775; **INQUIRY OFFICE** tel. 640 851; Kraševskio g., tel. 738 233; Viršuliškių g., tel. 422 836

DAILY SERVICE

DRY CLEANING Architektų 19, tel. 441 993; Savanorių pr. 43, tel. 638 358; Slucko 3/6, tel. 754 286; **REPAIR OF DOMESTIC APPLIANCES** Žalgirio 108, tel. 358 815; **BATHS** Juozapavičiaus 3, tel. 733 195; Vivulskio 18, tel. 638 422; **HAIRDRESSER'S** Gedimino pr. 36, tel. 624 979; Gedimino pr. 11, tel. 629 024; Ukmergės 12, tel. 732 329; **BARBER'S** Gedimino pr. 3a, tel. 618 525; Gedimino pr. 43, tel. 627 578; Kalvarijų 23, tel. 750 819; **HAIRDRESSER'S AND BARBER'S** Juozapavičiaus 3, tel. 751 651; Kalvarijų 59, tel. 570 744; Konarskio 21, tel. 652 909; **RENTING CENTRES** Antakalnio 69, tel. 741 908; Architektų 152, tel. 446 592; Juozapavičiaus 10, tel. 353 858; Ševčenkos 18, tel. 633 891; Vilniaus 180/1, tel. 671 819; Žirmūnų 106a, tel. 773 954

TRANSPORT AND COMMUNICATIONS

AIRPORT, tel. 630 201; **65 BUS TERMINAL** Sodų 22, tel. 660 481, 660 482, 660 483; **FREIGHT STATION** Panerių 56, tel. 630 748; **66 RAILWAY TERMINAL** Geležinkelio 16, tel. 630 086, 630 087; **19 CENTRAL POST OFFICE** Gedimino pr. 7, tel. 616 614; **31 TELEGRAPH, TELEPHONE** Vilniaus 33/2, tel. 625 634

KAUNAS

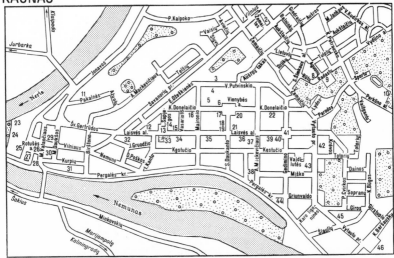

GENERAL INFORMATION

Post office	226 220	Chemist's	225 170
Address bureau	223 183	Bank (currency exchange)	200 480
Service bureau	221 288	Hotel inquiries	220 180
Everyday services	227 530	Shops	229 274
Trains		Notary assistance	226 727
Inquiry desk	221 093	Legal advice	225 138
Advance booking	227 166	Service bureau for foreign	
Buses		tourists	204 289
Inquiry desk	227 942	Excursion bureau	220 532
Booking office	204 368	Tugging of motor transport	718 922
Advance booking	204 391	Lost property	
Airport (in Karmėlava)		Taxis	260 582
Inquiry desk	228 176	Trolley-buses	740 625
Booking office	229 706	Buses	770 755
Taxis	777 775, 777 777	Inter-city buses	225 543
Wharf	261 348	Translation-typing bureau	203 357
Man-made lake wharf	750 392	Traffic police	228 112

ADDRESSES

HOTELS

43 BALTIJA Vytauto pr. 71, tel. 223 639, 228 785; **18 LIETUVA** Daukanto 21, tel. 205 992, 209 828; **39 BRANCH OF HOTEL LIETUVA** Laisvės al. 35, tel. 221 791; **15 NEMUNAS** Laisvės al. 88, tel. 223 102; **22 NERIS** Donelaičio 27, tel. 204 224

RESTAURANTS. CAFÈS. BARS

ARCHITEKTŲ Donelaičio 62, tel. 205 253; **43 BALTIJA** Vytauto pr. 71, tel. 293 244; **BIALYSTOKAS** Vytauto pr. 56, tel. 205 898; **30 GILDIJA** Rotušės a. 2, tel. 220 148, 220 003; **KALNIEČIAI** Savanorių pr. 375, tel. 259 343; **8 KAUKAS** Šimkaus al. 2, tel. 730 190; **19 METROPOLIS** Laisvės al. 68, tel. 204 427; **36 TULPE** Laisvės al. 49, tel. 221 736; **UGNĖ** Rotušės a. 23, tel. 208 634; **VAKARAS** Vasario 16-osios 1, tel. 227 666; **1 ŽALIAS KALNAS** Savanorių pr. 111, tel. 223 375

THEATRES. CONCERT HALLS

37 BRANCH OF THE NATIONAL PHILHARMONIC Sapiegos 5, tel. 228 478; **35 DRAMA THEATRE** Laisvės al. 71, tel. 224 064, 203 821; **33 MUSICAL THEATRE** Laisvės al. 91, tel. 200 933; **PANTOMIME THEATRE-SCHOOL** Ožeškienės 12, tel. 225 668; **34 PUPPET THEATRE** Laisvės al. 87a, tel. 209 893

MUSEUMS. EXHIBITION HALLS

CERAMICS MUSEUM Rotušės a. 15, Tue – Sun 12 – 18, tel. 203 572; **COMPOSER J.GRUODIS MEMORIAL MUSEUM** Salako 18, tel. 732 498; **P.CVIRKA MEMORIAL MUSEUM** Donelaičio 13, Wed – Mon 11 – 19, tel. 206 488; **4 M.K.ČIURLIONIS ART GALLERY** Putvinskio 55, Tue – Sun 12 – 18, tel. 205 205; **GALLERY AL** (private) Vilniaus 22, daily 12 – 19, tel. 202 655; **GALLERY OF PHOTOGRAPHY** Vilniaus 4, daily 11 – 19, tel. 202 674; **41 GALLERY OF SCULPTURE AND STAINED-GLASS** Nepriklausomybės a. 14, Tue – Sun 12 – 18, tel. 226 676; **25 LITERARY MUSEUM** Rotušės a. 13, Wed – Sat 11 – 19, Sun 11 – 17, tel. 201 284; **MUSEUM OF THE 9TH FORT** Žemaičių pl. 73, Tue – Sun 12 – 18, tel. 260 574; **S.NĖRIS MEMORIAL MUSEUM** Vilnelės 7, Wed – Mon 11 – 19, tel. 737 334; **PAŽAISLIS ARCHITECTURAL ENSEMBLE** Kauno jūros pr. 31, Wed – Sun 12 – 17, tel. 755 319; **K.PETRAUSKAS MEMORIAL MUSEUM** Petrausko 31, Wed – Sun 12 – 18, tel. 733 371; **7 PICTURE GALLERY** Donelaičio 16, daily 12 – 18, tel. 200 231; **5 MILITARY MUSEUM OF VYTAUTAS THE GREAT** Donelaičio 64, Wed – Mon 10 – 18, tel. 222 756; **12 ZOOLOGICAL MUSEUM** Laisvės al. 106, Tue – Sun 12 – 18, tel. 200 302; **40 A.ŽILINSKAS ART GALLERY** Nepriklausomybės a. 12, Tue – Sun 12 – 18, tel. 227 513, 207 203; **A.ŽMUIDZINAVIČIUS'S EXPOSITIONS** Putvinskio 64, Tue – Sun 12 – 18, tel. 203 514

ARCHITECTURAL MONUMENTS

6 FREEDOM MONUMENT Donelaičio g.; **27 PERKŪNAS HOUSE** Aleksoto 6; **PAŽAISLIS ARCHITECTURAL ENSEMBLE** Kauno jūros pr. 31; **32 ST. GERTRUDE'S CHURCH** Laisvės al.; **11 ST. NICHOLAS' CHURCH** Pakalnės 8; **24 ST. GEORGE'S CHURCH AND MONASTERY** Papilio 7; **23 KAUNAS CASTLE** Trakų g.; **26 ROTUŠE** (City Hall) Rotušės a.; **DOMINICAN CHURCH**, Vilniaus g.; **13 VYTAUTAS THE GREAT MONUMENT** Laisvės al.; **30 GILDIJA HOUSE**

Rotušės a. 2; **MAIRONIS' TOMBSTONE** (at the Cathedral); **MASALSKIS PALACE AND TRINITY CHURCH** Rotušės a. 22

CHURCHES

Catholic: **29 CATHEDRAL** (of SS. Peter and Paul's) Vilniaus 26; **ST. ANTHONY OF PADOVA CHURCH** Tvirtovės al. 11; **44 CARMELITE CHURCH** Gedimino 1; **JESUIT CHURCH** Rotušės a. 8; **ST. VINCENT CHURCH**, Kalantos 38; **SEMINARY CHURCH** Trakų 1; **CHURCH OF THE JESUS' HOLY HEART** Juozapavičiaus pr. 60a; **ST. JOSEPH'S CHURCH** Panerių 72; **28 VYTAUTAS THE GREAT CHURCH** Pergalės krantinė 1/3; **2 CHRIST'S RESURRECTION CHURCH** Aukštaičių 4 Other: **ORTHODOX CATHEDRAL** Giros 38; **3 EVANGELICAL LUTHERAN CHURCH** Pergalės krantinė; **SYNAGOGUE** Oželskienės g.

LIBRARIES

CENTRAL LIBRARY Laisvės al. 57, tel. 222 357; **9 PUBLIC LIBRARY** Radastų 14, tel. 226 142

HIGHER SCHOOLS

AGRICULTURE ACADEMY Noreikiškės, tel. 298 255; **PHYSICAL TRAINING INSTITUTE** Sporto 6, tel. 200 577; **VETERINARY ACADEMY** Tilžės 18, tel. 260 383; **38 MEDICAL ACADEMY** Mickevičiaus 9, tel. 226 110; **PRIEST SEMINARY** Trakų 1, tel. 221 428; **17 TECHNOLOGICAL UNIVERSITY** Donelaičio 73, tel. 227 044; **20 VYTAUTAS MAGNUS UNIVERSITY** Daukanto 28, tel. 206 753

ADMINISTRATION

14 CITY COUNCIL AND GOVERNMENT Laisvės al. 96, tel. 206 438, 226 958

BANKS:16 KAUNAS BRANCH OF THE LITHUANIAN BANK Maironio 25, tel. 200 480; **ŪKIO BANKAS** Gruodžio 9, tel. 203 651

SHOPPING

CURIOSITY SHOP Laisvės al. 33, tel. 205 879; **DAILĖ** (articles of art): Daukanto 17, tel. 222 785; Laisvės al. 31, tel. 224 664; Rotušės a. 27, tel. 229 916; **DOVANA** (gift shops): Vilniaus 15, tel. 222 981; Vilniaus 24, tel. 206 982; **JEWELLER'S** Laisvės al. 61, tel. 205 969; **GOODS FOR FOREIGN TOURISTS** Vilniaus 29; **MEDŽIOKLĖ IR ŽŪKLĖ** (articles of hunting and fishery) Krėvės 8a, tel. 791 488; **21 MERKURIJUS** (department store) Laisvės al. 60, tel. 203 202; **MOTOR-SHOP** Ateities 39, tel. 718 916; **NAŠLAITĖ** (flowers) Maironio 19, tel. 226 691; **OPTIKA** (optician) Laisvės al. 83, tel. 223 255; **RECORDS** Laisvės al. 77, tel. 204 710; **SOUVENIRS** Laisvės al. 90, tel. 229 882; **SPARE PARTS FOR CARS** Veiverių 47, tel. 298 898; **FURS** Laisvės al. 41, tel. 229 550; **POTTERY** Daukšos 28, tel. 201 914; **GROCERY 'CENTRAS'** Donelaičio g., tel. 204 325; **SKALSA** Laisvės al.; **VILNIUS** Kęstučio 55, tel. 229 924

MARKETS

ALEKSOTO Veiverių 47, tel. 295 464; **KOVO MARKET** Sartų 20, tel. 717 581; **VILIJAMPOLĖS MARKET** Griniaus 6, tel. 264 989; **ŽALIAKALNIO MARKET** Zanavykų 25, tel. 793 940

SPORTS

10 SPORTS HALL Perkūno al. 5, tel. 202 278, 201 470; **OUTDOOR STADIUM** Sporto 3, tel. 730 413; **SWIMMING POOLS** Stulginskio 176, tel. 740 900; Demokratų 34a, tel. 263 943; Partizanų, tel. 770 644; **ŽALGIRIS STADIUM** Baršausko 66, tel. 756 652

MEDICAL SERVICE

HOSPITAL 'RAUDONASIS KRYŽIUS' Mickevičiaus 4, tel. 226 671; **CLINICAL HOSPITAL** Laisvės al. 17, tel. 226 154; **EMERGENCY HOSPITAL** tel. 793 527; **DRUGSTORES** Laisvės al. 100, tel. 225 170

CAR SERVICE 'AUTOSERVISAS' Taikos pr. 151, tel. 712 378, 718 988; **PETROL STATIONS** Kęstučio 63, tel. 224 075; Savanorių pr., tel. 776 447; Taikos pr. 120, tel. 770 304; Utenos 4, tel. 731 750; Veiverių 47, tel. 295 976; **PAID CAR-PARKS** tel. 717 529 (superior); Partizanų g., tel. 778 914; Pramonės pr., tel. 777 450; Šiaurės pr., tel. 713 657

EVERYDAY SERVICES

RENTING CENTRES Rent of cultural goods and things of daily life, Vytauto pr. 37, tel. 207 410; Rent of radio receivers and tape-recorders, Savanorių pr. 225, tel. 730 583; **HAIRDRESSER'S AND**

BARBER'S Donelaičio 27 (Hotel 'Neris'), tel. 205 368; Daukanto 15, tel. 201 806; Rotušės a. 10, tel. 202 241; Vytauto pr. 37, tel. 221 737; **SHOE REPAIR** Demokratų 3, tel. 263 492; Gedimino 29, tel. 203 249; Laisvės al. 114, tel. 200 440; Mickevičiaus 27a, tel. 202 774; **LEATHER HABERDASHERY REPAIR** Vilniaus 44, Mon — Fri, Sun 10 — 13, 14 — 19, Sat 10 — 14

TRANSPORT AND COMMUNICATIONS

AIRPORT (agency) Požėlos 7/9, tel. 291 770; **45 BUS TERMINAL** Vytauto pr. 24, tel. 224 192; **46 RAILWAY STATION** Čiurlionio 16, tel. 221 093; **WHARF** Markso pr. 107, tel. 262 107; **CENTRAL POST OFFICE** Laisvės al. 102, tel. 226 220

KLAIPĖDA

GENERAL INFORMATION

Post office	137 30	Taxis	000, 192 58
Everyday services	502 08	Boat *Raketa*, booking office	144 88
Trains		Pier (ferry-boat)	122 24
Inquiry desk	146 14	Chemist's	142 81
Booking office	312 15	Bank (currency exchange)	598 79
Advance booking	936 56	Hotel	173 24
Buses		Notary assistance	157 34
Inquiry desk	148 63	Legal advice	135 73
Booking office	333 13	Excursion bureau	147 32
Advance booking	312 15	Tugging of motor transport	419 43
Airport		Stores	108 28
Inquiry desk	304 09	Traffic police	552 52
Booking office	304 09		

ADDRESSES

HOTELS

BALTIJA Janonio 4, tel. 149 67; **KLAIPĖDA** Naujo Sodo 1, tel. 199 60; **PAMARYS** Šaulių 28, tel. 199 43; **VĖTRUNGĖ** Taikos pr. 28, tel. 548 01; **VIKTORIJA** Šimkaus 12, tel. 136 70

RESTAURANTS. CAFĖS. BARS

BANGPŪTYS (bar) Kurpių 3, tel. 127 01; **DU GAIDELIAI** (children cafe) Mažvydo al. 8, tel. 133 09; **KLAIPĖDA** Naujo Sodo 1, tel. 126 37; **MERIDIANAS** Danės krantinė, tel. 168 51; **NEPTŪNAS** Pergalės 18, tel. 136 66; **REGATA** Danės krantinė 15, tel. 125 06; **SODŽIUS** Šilutės pl. 14a, tel. 947 94; **VĖTRUNGĖ** Taikos pr. 28, tel. 942 79; **VIKTORIJA** Šimkaus 12, tel.126 37; **ŽARDĖ** Taikos pr. 115, tel. 764 52; **ŽUVĖDRA** Kepėjų 10, tel. 156 67

THEATRES. CONCERT HALLS

CONSERVATOIRE CONCERT HALL Donelaičio 4, tel. 135 27; **DRAMA THEATRE** Teatro 2, tel. 125 89; **MUSICAL THEATRE** Danės krantinė 19, tel. 123 46

CINEMAS

BALTIJA Žvejų 3, tel. 167 28; **JŪRATĖ IR KASTYTIS** Taikos pr. 105, tel. 304 01; **ŠVYTURYS** Manto 27, tel. 175 53; **VAIDILA** Paryžiaus Komunos 4, tel. 529 87; **VAIVA** Manto 11, tel. 173 54; **ŽEMAITIJA** Manto 31, tel. 163 73

MUSEUMS. EXHIBITION HALLS

CLOCK MUSEUM Liepų 12, Tue — Sun 12 — 18, tel. 136 94; **EXHIBITION PALACE** Aukštoji 3/3a, Wed — Sun 11 — 19, tel. 118 77; **PICTURE GALLERY** Liepų 33, Wed — Sun 12 — 18, tel. 133 19; **LITHUANIA MINOR MUSEUM** Liepų 7, Tue — Sun 12 — 18, tel. 152 21; **SEA MUSEUM AND AQUARIUM** Smiltynė, Wed — Sun 11 — 19, tel. 911 33

CHURCHES

Catholic: **CHRIST KING CHURCH** Bokštų 10a, tel. 144 53; **PEACE QUEEN CHURCH** Rumpiškės g., tel. 168 10
Other: **EVANGELICAL CHURCH** Pylimo 2, tel. 156 51; **ORTHODOX CHURCH** Liepų 45a, tel. 155 10

LIBRARIES

CENTRAL LIBRARY Turgaus 8, tel. 152 32; **REPUBLICAN SCIENTIFIC AND TECHNICAL LIBRARY** Sukilėlių 11, tel. 598 36; **I.SIMONAITYTĖ PUBLIC LIBRARY** Manto 25, tel. 132 86

BANK Turgaus 1, tel. 598 79

ADMINISTRATION: CITY COUNCIL AND GOVERNMENT Liepų 13, tel. 137 95, 136 41

SHOPPING

AITVARAS (department store) Taikos pr. 39, tel. 504 18; **DAILĖ** (artistic articles) Turgaus 7, tel. 157 77; **DEBRECENAS** Taikos pr. 101, tel. 357 79; **DRAUGYSTĖ** (bookshop) Pilies 7, tel. 173 08; **GAUSA** (food store) Mažvydo al. 5, tel. 525 55; **JEWELRY** Tiltų 3, tel. 146 24; **MARGINIAI** (exhibition and sale-room) Sukilėlių 3, tel. 598 73; **PAJŪRIS** (department store) Turgaus 14, tel. 139 71; **SATURNAS** (household goods) Taikos pr. 5, tel. 168 68; **SOUVENIRS** Tiltų 26a, tel. 581 40; **ŠIAULIAI** Šilutės pl. 86, tel. 372 23; **ŽARDĖ** Taikos pr. 115, tel. 333 17

MARKETS Turgaus a. 5, tel. 155 72; Taikos pr. 80, tel. 759 01

SPORTS

BALTIJA STADIUM Dubysos g., tel. 994 43; **BICYCLE TRACK** 16-osios divizijos g., tel. 977 28; **LAWN-TENNIS COURTS** Mažvydo parkas, tel. 133 12; **TRACK-AND-FIELD MANEGE** Taikos pr. 50, tel. 941 10; **ŽALGIRIS SPORTS PALACE** Dariaus ir Girėno 10, tel. 977 99; **ŽALGIRIS STADIUM** Sportininkų 46, tel. 977 90

CAR SERVICE Mokyklos g., tel. 189 22; Šilutės pl., tel. 419 43; Tilžės g., tel. 562 74; Butkų Juzės g., tel. 122 76; **PETROL STATIONS** Tilžės pl., tel. 128 16; Kretingos pl., tel. 972 44; Jakai, tel. 122 88; Minijos g., tel. 743 44; **GAS STATION** tel. 588 56

EVERYDAY SERVICES

GRAŽINA (hairdresser's) Manto 20, tel. 135 25; **RASA** (hairdresser's) Šilutės pl. 73, tel. 408 59; **RENTING CENTRE** Kepėjų 1, tel. 159 02

TRANSPORT AND COMMUNICATIONS

AIRPORT Janonio 2, tel. 304 09; **BUS STATION** Butkų Juzės 9, tel. 333 13; **RAILWAY STATION** Taikos pr. 107, tel. 312 15; **CENTRAL POST OFFICE** Liepų 16, tel. 137 30; **CENTRAL TELEGRAPH** Liepų 16, tel. 160 75

OTHER PLACES OF INTEREST

CULTURE AND RECREATION PARK Manto 83; **REMAINS OF CASTLE AND FORTIFICATIONS** Žvejų 12; **REMAINS OF DEFENSIVE STRUCTURES** Pakalnės g.; **COMPLEX OF FACHWERK BUILDING AND WAREHOUSE** Aukštoji 3; **COMPLEX OF HOUSES AND WAREHOUSES** Tiltų 5, Kepėjų 14, Jūratės 3; **BUILDINGS OF THE OLD MARKET** Turgaus 4; **MAŽVYDAS SCULPTURE PARK**

ŠIAULIAI

GENERAL INFORMATION

Post office	306 20	Taxi	
Information bureau	336 51	Inquiry desk	400 04
Everyday services		Orders	422 01
Information	336 51	Chemist's	385 31
Food stores	547 74	Hotel	373 33
Commodity stores	500 62	Notary assistance	328 69
Trains		Legal advice	305 13
Inquiry desk	306 52	Excursion bureau	339 95
Advance booking	325 47	Tugging of motor transport	364 65
Check-room	944 41	Lost property	973 27
Buses	338 64	Traffic police	325 62
Airport	326 61		

ADDRESSES

HOTELS: ŠIAULIAI Draugystės pr. 25, tel. 373 33, branch hotel, Vytauto 74, tel. 329 33

RESTAURANTS. CAFÈS

ŠIAULIAI Draugystės pr. 25, tel. 366 73; **RAILWAY STATION** Dubijos 2, tel. 304 51; **JAUNYSTĖ** Draugystės pr. 14, tel. 347 47; **MINUTĖ** Vilniaus 174, tel. 314 69; **SODŽIUS** Stoties 3, tel. 318 67

THEATRES

DRAMA THEATRE Tilžės 155, tel. 329 40; **MAŽASIS THEATRE** Vilniaus 247, tel. 367 00

MUSEUMS. EXHIBITION HALLS

AUŠRA MUSEUM (history and ethnography) Aušros al. 47, Wed — Sun 11 — 18, tel. 387 22; the 2nd house — Vytauto 89, tel. 337 55; **BICYCLES MUSEUM** Vilniaus 139, Wed — Sun 11 — 19, tel. 337 88; **EXHIBITION PALACE** Vilniaus 245, Wed — Sun 11 — 19, tel. 304 34; **CATS' MUSEUM** Žuvininkų 18, Wed — Sun 11 — 17, tel. 389 14; **J. KRIKŠČIŪNAS-JOVARAS MEMORIAL MUSEUM** Vytauto 116, Tue — Fri 10 — 17, tel. 373 25; **MUSEUM OF PHOTOGRAPHY** Vilniaus 140, Thur — Mon 12 — 19, tel. 372 03

LIBRARIES

CITY CENTRAL LIBRARY (has 12 branches), Mon — Fri 9 — 18, tel. 282 02; **P.VIŠINSKIS PUBLIC LIBRARY** Aušros al. 62, Mon — Fri 10 — 21, Sun 11 — 18, tel. 315 31

CHURCHES

ST. GEORGE'S CHURCH Stoties g., tel. 307 68; **SS. PETER AND PAUL'S CHURCH** Pergalės a., tel. 306 28; **ORTHODOX CHURCH** Ežero g.

HIGHER SCHOOL: PEDAGOGICAL INSTITUTE Višinskio 25, tel. 336 73

ADMINISTRATION: CITY COUNCIL AND GOVERNMENT Vasario 16-osios 62, tel. 335 55, 334 44

SHOPPING

BOOKSHOP Vilniaus 213, tel. 315 57; **CURIOSITY SHOP** Tilžės 148, tel. 319 74; **DAĖNAI** (food shop) Karecko 13, tel. 500 46; **DAILĖ** (articles of art) Vilniaus 136, tel.346 81; **DEPARTMENT STORE** Vilniaus 206, tel. 349 44; **EGLĖ** (food shop) Varpo 27, tel. 367 03; **FLORIST'S** Vilniaus 221, tel. 317 76; **HOUSEHOLD SHOP** Vilniaus 204, tel. 364 32; **PHOTO** Tilžės 149, tel. 328 81; **RADIO** Vilniaus 206, tel. 345 35; **RECORDS** Tilžės 151, tel. 357 52; **SOUVENIRS** Vilniaus 134, tel. 344 73; **CAR SPARE PARTS** Dvaro 46, tel. 314 13; **SPORTSWARE** Draugystės pr. 2, tel. 366 63

MARKET Turgaus g., tel. 308 72

PETROL STATIONS Kosmonautų g., tel. 531 91; Kuršėnų pervaža, tel. 362 71; Bielskio 47, tel. 403 70; Tilžės 223, tel. 373 54; Vilniaus 12, tel. 365 75; Žemaitės g., tel. 554 09; **CAR SERVICE** Vilniaus 8, tel. 364 65; **PAID CAR PARKS** Daukanto g., tel. 339 90; Gardino 2, tel. 564 37; Knyvos g., tel. 570 10; Valančiaus-Vilniaus corner, tel. 339 90

RENTING CENTRES Vilniaus 168, tel. 386 33; Žiburkaus 16, tel. 580 24

OTHER PLACES OF INTEREST

CENTRAL POST OFFICE Aušros al. 42, tel. 306 20; **BUS STATION** Tilžės 109, tel. 338 64; **RAILWAY STATION** Dubijos 44, tel. 306 52; **AIRPORT** Meškuičiai, tel. 777 18; **THE HILL OF REBELS** Vilniaus g.; **THE SUN CLOCK** Aušros takas. In the vicinity of Šiauliai: **GINKŪNAI** (the manor-house of V.Zubov and school, cemeteries); **THE HILL OF CROSSES** (about 18 km in the direction of Meškuičiai); **THE MOUND OF SALDUVĖS**, the Aleksandrija Hill

PANEVĖŽYS

GENERAL INFORMATION

Post office	644 45	Taxis	666 56
City telephone information	641 65	Chemist's	686 51
Trains	636 15	Hotel	351 17
Buses		Notary assistance	327 71
Inquiry desk	636 33	Legal advice	622 97
Advance booking	685 84	Excursion bureau	667 43
Airport		Car service	331 13
Advance booking	332 98	Traffic police	611 83

ADDRESSES

HOTELS

NEVĖŽIS Laisvės a. 26, tel. 351 17; **RAMBYNAS** Respublikos 34, tel. 610 07; **UPYTĖ** Respublikos 38, tel. 667 47

RESTAURANTS. CAFĖS. BARS

AGUONĖLĖ Laisvės a. 15, tel. 338 09; **BIČIULIS** Marijonų 27, tel. 688 65; **GRILBARAS** Laisvės a. 4, tel. 686 55; **NEVĖŽIS** Laisvės a. 26, tel. 351 15; **PUŠYNAS** Tulpių 52, tel. 632 17; **SEKLYČIA** Laisvės a. 1, tel. 357 54; **STUMBRAS** Aukštaičių 4, tel. 354 84; **ŽARA** Dariaus ir Girėno 4, tel. 262 10; **ŽIOGELIS** (for children) Ukmergės 3, tel. 635 57; **BERŽELIS** Piniava, tel. 525 36; **KARČIAMA RUŽAVA** Molainiai, tel. 679 07

THEATRE: DRAMA THEATRE Laisvės a., tel. 628 37

MUSEUMS. EXHIBITION HALLS

ART GALLERY Respublikos 3, Wed — Sun 12 — 20; tel. 636 75; **MUSEUM OF REGIONAL STUDY** Vasario 16-osios 23, Tue — Sun 12 — 20, tel. 627 77; **FOLK ART MUSEUM** Respublikos 56

CHURCHES

Catholic: **CATHEDRAL** (Christ King) Katedros a. 12, tel. 331 41; **SS. PETER AND PAUL'S CHURCH** Smėlynės 10, tel. 631 75; **HOLY TRINITY CHURCH** Sodų 2, tel. 666 66 Other: **LUTHERAN CHURCH** Ukmergės 29, tel. 338 74; **ORTHODOX CHURCH** Tilvyčio 5; **CHURCH OF RUSSIAN OLD BELIEVERS** Mackevičiaus 10

LIBRARY

G.PETKEVIČAITĖ-BITĖ PUBLIC LIBRARY Respublikos 35, tel. 657 67

ADMINISTRATION

CITY COUNCIL AND GOVERNMENT Laisvės a. 20, tel. 640 74, 634 55

BANK Respublikos 56, tel. 610 35

SHOPPING

HUNTING AND FISHING ACCESSORIES Smėlynės 2a, tel. 631 53; **JEWELRY** Laisvės a. 24, tel. 676 65; **KLEVAS** (household goods) Respublikos 71, tel. 647 43; **MANUFACTURED GOODS** Basanavičiaus 3, tel. 329 70; **SPORTSWARE** Vilniaus 4, tel. 674 35; **ŠYPSENA** (haberdashery) Laisvės a. 24, tel. 676 65; Bookshops: **CENTRAL** Respublikos 21, tel. 689 63; **VILNIUS** Vilniaus 14, tel. 314 21; Food shops: **ŽARA** Dariaus ir Girėno 2, tel. 622 87; **KAUNAS** Smėlynės 49, tel. 608 69; **SKAISTKALNIS** Vilniaus 43, tel. 341 01; **STUMBRAS** Aukštaičių 4, tel. 320 59

MARKET Ukmergės 26, tel. 339 65

SPORTS

PALACE OF SPORT AND STADIUM Jakšto al. 1, tel. 638 97

CAR SERVICE 'AUTOSERVISAS' Velžio kelias 48, tel. 331 13; **CAR REFUELLING** Klaipėdos g., tel. 339 48; Velžio kelias, tel. 333 13; Smėlynės g., tel. 659 81; Ramygalos g., tel. 374 29; **PAID CAR PARKS** Bielinio g., tel. 655 35; Parko g., tel. 210 79; Pilėnų g., tel. 352 45; Kerbedžio g., tel. 634 23; Ateities g., tel. 620 17

EVERYDAY SERVICE

RENTING CENTRE Vasario 16-osios 11, tel. 689 61; **HAIRDRESSER'S, BARBER'S** Laisvės a. 26, tel. 357 25; Respublikos 28, tel. 654 23; Savanorių a. 13, tel. 689 97

TRANSPORT AND COMMUNICATIONS

BUS TERMINAL Savanorių a. 5, tel. 633 25; **RAILWAY TERMINAL** Stoties g., tel. 630 51; **CENTRAL POST OFFICE** Respublikos 60, tel. 644 45

OTHER PLACES OF INTEREST

EXCURSION BUREAU Respublikos 38, tel. 641 85; **UPYTĖS REGION COURT ARCHIVES PALACE** Kranto 21; **FLAX MUSEUM** (15 km outside Panevėžys)

DRUSKININKAI

GENERAL INFORMATION

Post office	521 11	Taxis	526 02
Trunk-call office	512 22	Chemist's	512 52
Everyday service	523 68	Bank (currency exchange)	532 96
Trains		Hotel	525 66
Inquiry desk	534 43	Notary assistance	523 57
Buses		Legal advice	522 17
Inquiry desk	513 33	Excursion bureau	534 34
Booking office	526 75	Cinemas	515 17
Airport	510 25	Traffic police	525 02

ADDRESSES

HOTEL: DRUSKININKAI Kudirkos 41, tel. 525 66

RESTAURANTS. CAFÈS. BARS

ALKA Veisiejų 13, tel. 528 49; **ASTRA** Vilniaus al. 10, tel. 533 35; **BEBENČIUKAS** Čiurlionio 103, tel. 535 14; **KADAGYS** (beer) Turistų 1, tel. 523 15; **KAŠTONAS** Čiurlionio 79, tel. 529 94; **NEMUNAS** Fonbergo 5, tel. 510 07; **TURISTAS** Taikos 12, tel. 538 05; **VAIVA** (cocktail bar) Veisiejų 3, tel. 523 16

MUSEUMS

M.K.ČIURLIONIS MEMORIAL MUSEUM Čiurlionio 41, Tue — Sun 12 — 18, tel. 527 55; **GIRIOS AIDAS** Čiurlionio 102, Tue — Sun 12 — 18, tel. 539 01

CHURCH: CATHOLIC CHURCH Druskininkų 26, tel. 535 54

LIBRARIES Vilniaus al. 5, tel. 526 82; Sporto 20, tel. 521 62

ADMINISTRATION

CITY COUNCIL Čiurlionio 73, tel. 553 55; **CITY GOVERNMENT** Vilniaus al. 18, tel. 512 33

BANK Kudirkos 31, tel. 534 54

SHOPPING

AMATININKAS (home made goods) Laisvės a. 3, tel. 512 21; **GLUOSNIS** (commission shop) Laisvės a. 5, tel. 524 78; **GULBĖ** (department store) Vilniaus a. 22, tel. 525 39; **RAIGARDAS** (department store) Čiurlionio 125, tel. 516 88; **FOOD SHOPS** Laisvės a. 2 (meat), Laisvės a. 3 (fish, greengrocery); Laisvės a. 4, Liepų 10, Veisiejų 41, Veisiejų 31, Merkinės 9, Vytauto 21, Čiurlionio 54, Čiurlionio 133, Vytauto 17, Vytauto 39

MARKET Čiurlionio 133a, tel. 520 38

CAR SERVICE Baravykų 5a, tel. 527 98; **PETROL STATION** Gardino 53, tel. 523 05; **TYRE RESTORATION** Nemuno 26, tel. 518 20; **CAR PARK** Žalioji g., tel. 523 87

EVERYDAY SERVICE

DRY CLEANING AND LAUNDRY Baravykų 5, tel. 529 86, 526 73; **EVERYDAY SERVICE SHOP** Veisiejų 32, tel. 511 38; **HAIRDRESSER'S AND BARBER'S** Vilniaus al. 8, tel. 525 28; **RENTING CENTRES** Vilniaus al. 8, tel. 526 67; Taikos 5, tel. 526 77

TRANSPORT AND COMMUNICATIONS

AIRPORT (booking office) Čiurlionio 2, tel. 510 25; **BUS TERMINAL** Gardino 1, tel. 513 33; **RAiLWAY TERMINAL** Gardino 3, tel. 534 43; **POST OFFICE** Kudirkos 41, tel. 521 11

OTHER PLACES OF INTEREST

HEALTH PALACE Dineikos 6, tel. 523 60; **MONUMENT TO M.K.ČIURLIONIS** Kudirkos g.; **REMEDIAL GYMNASTICS AND CLIMATOTHERAPY PARK** Sausoji g.; **ARTICLES OF ART** Druskonio 7, tel. 518 65; **CAMPING** Nemuno 26, tel. 525 77; **GUEST SERVICE SHOP** Dineikos 13, tel. 523 68; **REINGARDAS VALLEY; MINERAL WATER**

PALANGA

GENERAL INFORMATION

Post office	534 44	Chemist's	532 52
Trains inquiry desk	536 94	Bank	534 54
Buses		Notary assistance	327 71
Inquiry desk	533 33	Legal advice	534 66
Advance booking	538 31	Excursion bureau	531 19
Airport		Traffic police	571 27
Inquiry desk	530 31		
Advance booking	534 31		

ADDRESSES

HOTEL

PAJŪRIS Basanavičiaus 9, tel. 533 45

RESTAURANTS. CAFÈS. BARS

AUŠRINĖ Vytauto 98, tel. 520 69; **BALTIJA** Vytauto 98, tel. 520 69; **BANGA** Basanavičiaus 2, tel. 513 70; **BIRUTĖ** Vytauto 64, tel. 515 26; **GABIJA** Vytauto 40, tel. 519 11; **KLUMPĖ** Nėries 9, tel. 539 00; **MĖTA** Vytauto 98, tel. 572 04; **PAJŪRIS** Basanavičiaus 9, tel. 535 59; **VAKARIS** Vytauto 64, tel. 537 15; **VIRBALIŠKĖ** Klaipėdos pl. 62a, tel. 561 29

CONCERT HALLS

SUMMER CONCERT HALL Vytauto 43, tel. 522 10; **JAUNYSTĖ** (cinema) Basanavičiaus 16, tel. 528 31; **NAGLIS** (cinema) Vytauto 82, tel. 518 94

MUSEUMS. EXHIBITION HALLS

AMBER MUSEUM Vytauto 17, Tue—Sun 11—18, tel. 535 01; **EXHIBITION PAVILION** (in summer) Dariaus ir Girėno 13; **HISTORY MUSEUM** Vytauto 23a, daily 12—17, tel. 545 59

CHURCH

CHURCH OF ASSUMPTION OF THE BLESSED VIRGIN MARY Vytauto 51, tel. 561 86

LIBRARIES

CHILDREN LIBRARY Vytauto 155, tel. 515 79; **PALANGA I LIBRARY** Vytauto 55, tel. 535 32

ADMINISTRATION

CITY COUNCIL AND GOVERNMENT Vytauto 73, tel. 533 32, 532 33

BANK Jūratės 17, tel. 534 54

SHOPPING

ARTICLES FOR CULTURAL NEEDS Vytauto 66, tel. 537 11; **BOOKSHOP** Vytauto 84, tel. 511 83; **CHILDREN CLOTHES** Vytauto 98, tel. 531 86; **DAILE** (artistic articles) Vytauto 49, tel. 539 59; **FISH** Virbališkės takas 6, tel. 535 44; **FOOD STORE** Vytauto 98, tel. 522 31, Vytauto 160, tel. 528 89; **HABERDASHERY, KNITTED GOODS** Vytauto 96, tel. 536 45, 534 45; **LIAUDIES DAILĖ** (amateur art articles) Ražės 5, tel. 521 28; **MEAT** Vytauto 63, tel. 538 44; **READY-MADE CLOTHES** Vytauto 98, tel. 531 66; **ROPĖ** (vegetables) Virbališkės takas 6, tel. 530 34, **ROŽĖ** Virbališkės takas 10, tel. 517 36; **SOUVENIRS** Vytauto 63, tel. 575 14; **SPARTA** (footwear) Vytauto 66, tel. 542 37; **TEXTILES** Vytauto 67, tel. 539 45; **ŽIBUTĖ** (florist's) Vytauto 86, tel. 514 70

MARKET Beržų 12, tel. 532 13

SPORTS

CURATIVE COMPLEXES' POOL Vytauto 155, tel. 584 78; **REMEDIAL SWIMMING POOL** Nėries 44, tel. 526 96; **SPORTS GROUND** Dariaus ir Girėno g., **SPORTS HALL** Poželos 18; **STADIUM** Sporto 9; **TENNIS COURT** Gėlių a.

CAR REFUELLING Kretingos 9; **CAR REPAIR** Vytauto 106, tel. 524 91

EVERYDAY SERVICES

DRY CLEANING Poželos 8, tel. 520 34; **RENTING CENTRE** Smilčių 11, tel. 531 33; **STATE ENTERPRISE OF EVERYDAY SERVICE** Vytauto 106, tel. 538 32

TRANSPORT AND COMMUNICATIONS

AIRPORT (booking office) Vytauto 100, tel. 533 31; **BUS STATION** Jasinskio 1, tel. 533 33; **RAILWAY STATION** (booking office) Jasinskio 26, tel. 536 94; **AUTOMATIC INTER-CITY TELEPHONE CONNECTIONS** Biliūno 1, tel. 562 22; Vytauto 39, tel. 531 40; **COMMUNICATION SERVICE** Vytauto 53, tel. 534 44

OTHER PLACES OF INTEREST

BICYCLE TRACK (from Palanga to Šventoji); **BOTANICAL GARDENS** Vytauto 15, tel. 516 01; **CAMPING** Vytauto 8, tel. 535 33; **CAMPING** (in tents) Užkanavės, tel. 516 76; **RUNNING TRACK MYLIA** (from the Jūratė pool to Kunigiškiai); **BIRUTĖ HILL**; **SEA BRIDGE** Basanavičiaus g.; **SCULPTURES** *Jūratė ir Kastytis, Eglė — žalčių karalienė*

BIRŠTONAS

GENERAL INFORMATION

Trains		Out-patients' clinic	565 82
Booking office	560 09	Bank	566 39
Buses	563 33	Lodgement bureau	562 87
Airport		Legal advice	565 30
Booking office	565 62	Excursion bureau	569 28
Life-boat station	564 14	Traffic police	564 23
Chemist's	567 91		

ADDRESSES

HOTELS

NEMUNAS Algirdo 3, tel. 563 45; **TOURIST** Turistų 1, tel. 563 31

RESTAURANTS. CAFÈS

DRUSKUPIS Algirdo 17, tel. 567 81; **BIRUTĖ** Dariaus ir Girėno 32, tel. 563 57; **NIDA** Algirdo 1, tel. 569 96; **SEKLYČIA** Prienų 7, tel. 562 11; **VILNIS** Nemuno 3, tel. 566 17

OTHER PLACES OF INTEREST

HISTORICAL MUSEUM Vytauto 9, tel. 563 94; **LIBRARIES** Jaunimo 4, tel. 567 60; Birutės 4, tel. 566 15; **BOOKSHOP** Dariaus ir Girėno 4; **CATHOLIC CHURCH** Birutės 10; **ACADEMIC ROWING OLYMPIC STATION** Birutės 21; **BUS STATION** Vaižganto 20, tel. 563 33; **HANDICRAFT GOODS** Nemuno 5, tel. 567 38; **DAILY SERVICES** Dariaus ir Girėno 14, tel. 563 06; **MINERAL WATERS**

GOVERNMENT

SUPREME COUNCIL: Gedimino pr. 53, Vilnius 232026; tel. 628 986; telex 261138 LTINF SU; fax 614 544

Chairman — Vytautas Landsbergis . . . . tel. 628 986
Deputy Chairmen — Bronislovas Kuzmickas 627 533
       Kazimieras Motieka 621 654
       Česlovas Vytautas Stankevičius 615 680
Secretary — Liudvikas Sabutis 621 632

STANDING COMMITTEES OF THE SUPREME COUNCIL

Agrarian — Eimantas Grakauskas 224 708
Budget — Audrius Rudys 629 554
Civil Rights and Ethnic Affairs — Virgilijus Čepaitis 224 577
Economics — Kazimieras Antanavičius 226 061
Education, Science and Culture — Stanislovas Gediminas Ilgūnas 618 965
Foreign Affairs — Emanuelis Zingeris 628 729
Health Care and Social Affairs — Medardas Čobotas 224 995
Legal System — Jonas Prapiestis 615 687
Municipal Affairs — Stasys Kropas 224 998
Mandate and Ethics — Aloyzas Sakalas 226 164
National Defence and Internal Affairs — Jonas Liaučius 224 691
Nature Protection — Jonas Šimėnas 226 268
State Restoration — Gediminas Šerkšnys 613 855
Information Department 626 680

COUNCIL OF MINISTERS: Tumo-Vaižganto 2, Vilnius 232039; tel. 622 101; telex 261105 LTMT SU; fax 619 953

Prime Minister — Gediminas Vagnorius . . . . tel. 622 101
Deputy Prime Ministers — Zigmas Vaišvila 620 665
        Vytautas Pakalniškis 621 429
Press Bureau . . . . tel. 625 651; fax 613 464

MINISTRIES

MINISTRY OF AGRICULTURE: Gedimino pr. 19, Vilnius 232025
Minister — Rimvydas Raimondas Survila . . . . tel. 625 438

MINISTRY OF HOUSING AND URBAN DEVELOPMENT: Jakšto 4/9, Vilnius 232694
Minister — Algimantas Nasvytis 610 558

MINISTRY OF COMMUNICATIONS: Vilniaus 33, Vilnius 232008
Minister — Kostas Birulis 620 443

MINISTRY OF CULTURE AND EDUCATION: Volano 2/7, Vilnius 232691
Minister — Darius Kuolys 622 483

MINISTRY OF ECONOMICS: Gedimino pr. 38/2, Vilnius 232600
Minister — Albertas Šimėnas 622 416

MINISTRY OF ENERGY: Gedimino pr. 12, Vilnius 232600
Minister — Leonas Vaidotas Ašmantas 615 140

MINISTRY OF FINANCE: Šermukšnių 9, Vilnius 232600
Minister — Elvyra Kunevičienė 625 172

MINISTRY OF FOREIGN AFFAIRS: Akmenų 6, Vilnius 232600
Minister — Algirdas Saudargas 618 537

MINISTRY OF FORESTRY: Gedimino pr. 56, Vilnius 232 685
Minister — Vaidotas Antanaitis 626 864

MINISTRY OF HEALTH CARE: Gedimino pr. 27, Vilnius 232682
Minister — Juozas Olekas 621 625

MINISTRY OF THE INTERIOR: Šventaragio 2, Vilnius 232754
Minister — Marijonas Misiukonis 626 752

MINISTRY OF JUSTICE: Lentpjūvių 24, Vilnius 232755
Minister — Vytautas Pakalniškis 626 757

MINISTRY OF MATERIAL RESOURCES: Tumo-Vaižganto 8a/2, Vilnius 232640
Minister — Vilius Židonis 628 830

MINISTRY OF SOCIAL WELFARE: Vivulskio 11, Vilnius 232693
Minister — Algis Dobravolskas 651 236

MINISTRY OF TRADE: Gedimino pr. 30/1, Vilnius 232695
Minister — Albertas Ambraziejus Sinevičius 617 007

MINISTRY OF TRANSPORTATION: Gedimino pr. 17, Vilnius 232679
Minister — Jonas Biržiškis 621 445

DEPARTMENTS OF THE LITHUANIAN GOVERNMENT

DEPARTMENT OF THE ENVIRONMENT: Juozapavičiaus 9, Vilnius 232686
Director General — Evaldas Vėbra 355 868

DEPARTMENT OF STATE CONTROL: Pamėnkalnio 31, Vilnius 232669
State Controller — Kazimieras Uoka 621 646

DEPARTMENT OF CONSERVATION OF HISTORIC PROPERTIES: Upės 3, Vilnius 232005
Director General — Vytautas Zubovas 354 058

DEPARTMENT OF LABOUR SAFETY: Jakšto 1/25, Vilnius 232600
Director General — Jonas Šimkūnas 661 854

DEPARTMENT OF NATIONAL DEFENCE: Gynėjų 3, Vilnius 232710
Director General — Audrius Butkevičius 624 821

DEPARTMENT OF NATIONAL SECURITY: Tumo-Vaižganto 2, Vilnius 232039
Director General — 625 728

DEPARTMENT OF NATIONALITIES: Basanavičiaus 5, Vilnius 232683
Director General — Halina Kobeckaitė 613 049

DEPARTMENT OF PHYSICAL TRAINING AND SPORTS: Žemaitės 6, Vilnius 232600
Director General — Algirdas Raslanas 635 363

DEPARTMENT OF PRESS: Vrublevskio 6, Vilnius 232671
Director General — Pranas Damijonaitis 617 385

DEPARTMENT OF STANDARDIZATION AND QUALITY: Jakšto 1/25, Vilnius 232600
Director General — Valerijonas Sakalauskas 753 320

DEPARTMENT OF STATISTICS: Gedimino pr. 29, Vilnius 232746
Director General — 619 556

JUDICIAL SYSTEM

SUPREME COURT: Lentpjūvių 24, Vilnius 232725
Chairman — Mindaugas Lošys 610 560

STATE ARBITRATION: Gedimino pr. 39/1, Vilnius 232640
Chief Arbitrator — Aloyzas Marčiulionis 622 843

PROSECUTOR'S OFFICE: Smetonos 6, Vilnius 232709
Prosecutor General — Artūras Paulauskas 610 537

DEPARTMENT OF CUSTOMS: Jakšto 1/25, Vilnius 232600
Director General 226 424

STATES SERVICE

GEODESIC SERVICES: Konarskio 35, Vilnius 232600
Director — Zenonas Kumetaitis 634 642

GEOLOGICAL SERVICES: Konarskio 35, Vilnius 232600
Director — Gediminas Motūza-Matuzevičius 632 889

LITHUANIAN BOARD FOR HYDROMETEOROLOGY: Rudnios 6, Vilnius 232600
Head — Petras Korkutis 751 194

BUSINESS DIRECTORY

INDUSTRIES AND ORGANIZATIONS

POWER ENGINEERING & FUEL INDUSTRY

IGNALINA NUCLEAR POWER STATION. 2 reactors (f. 1983 and 1987) in action, capacity 1,500 MW each. Electric power supplied to Lithuania, Latvia and Byelorussia by 110 and 330 kV electric lines. Dir Anatolij Chromčenko. *Add.* Sniečkus 234741; tel. 311 31.

KAUNAS HYDROELECTRIC POWER STATION. 4 hydroturbines (f. 1959 and 1960), capacity 25,200 kW each. Total capacity 100.8 MW, produces 384 million kWh; electric power supplied to Lithuania. Dir Mykolas Mankevičius. *Add.* Masiulio 22, Kaunas 233014; tel. 529 11.

LITHUANIAN POWER STATION. Capacity 1,800 MW; 4 energy blocks (f. 1968) of 150 MW and 4 blocks (f. 1972) of 300 MW capacity. Fuel crude oil and natural gas. Output: 9 billion kWh electric and 860,000 GJ heating power. Supplies electricity for Lithuania and heating for the town of Elektrėnai. Dir Pranas Noreika. *Add.* Elektrėnai 234061; tel. 332 50.

MAŽEIKIAI OIL PROCESSING PLANT. F. 1980; 2,980 empl. Produces gasoline A-76, A-92, masut, gas-oil, liquified gas, constr. road bitumen, roof bitumen, sulphur; exports to Armenia, Latvia, Moldavia, Kaliningrad region (Russia). Dir Bronislavas Vainora. *Add.* Juodeikiu gyvenv., Mažeikiai 235500; tel. 522 39; telex 296050 VOLNA SU.

VILNIUS 3RD THERMAL POWER STATION. Includes: Vilnius Power Station No 2 (f.1958, reconstr. 1965–69; 28 MW; 2 turbine generators, 4 steam and 7 water boilers) and Vilnius Power Station No 3 (f. 1984 and 1986; 360 MW). Supplies electric power for Lithuania, heating for Vilnius. Annual capacity 1,800 million kWh electric and 11.3 million GJ heating power. Dir Rimvydas Rukšėnas. *Add.* Jačioniu 13, Vilnius 232053; tel. 649 359.

MACHINE BUILDING & METALWORKING

ASTRA, plant. F. 1929; 1,450 empl. Produces washing machines (70 and 120 l capacity), ironing presses, feather cleaning machines, dubbing presses, consumer goods (electric grills, electric radiators, wood processing machines, caps for preserves), spare parts. Dir Semion Bondarev. *Add.* Ulonu 33, Alytus 234580; tel. 521 76; fax 522 65.

ATRAMA, plant. F. 1940; 700 empl. Produces gas cylinders (50 l capacity), metal milk cans, water meters, hot water tanks with fast water heaters, tech. and med. oxygen. Seeks partners for prod. of hot and cold water meters, all types of fuel boilers, gas, electric and microwave ovens, automatic equipm. for gas boilers. Dir Stasys Gagas. *Add.* Raudondvario pl. 162, Kaunas 233021; tel. 260 801.

AURIDA, company. F. 1959; 3,800 empl. Produces autocompressors, vibrating bins, spare parts for agric. machinery, pig-iron castings, bicycle pumps, household compressors, water sprinklers, special order equipm. Dir-Gen. Augustinas Sutkus. *Add.* Pramonės 8, Panevėžys 235319; tel. 637 13; fax 229 51.

BANGA, Lith. television equipm. company. F. 1987; 18,000 empl. Subsidiaries: Kaunas TV-sets, Kaunas television equipm., Šiauliai TV-sets plants, Šiauliai Branch of Television Sci. Research Inst., int. marketing company and repair-constr. offices. Produces TV channel selectors, B/W and colour TV-sets, equipm. sets for TV-studios, movable TV-stations and applied television equipm.; exports B/W and colour TV sets, TV channel selectors, television equipm. Sponsor of Lith. Encyclopaedias. Dir-Gen. Leonas Jankauskas. *Add.* Draugystės 19, Kaunas 233031; tel. 756 777; telex 261147 BANGA SU.

EKRANAS, plant. F. 1962; 6,950 empl. Produces colour TV picture tubes 61LK5C, agric. devices (autostethoscopes, 3-phase engine protection equipm. FU2-M); exports to Bulgaria, Poland, Turkey. Dir Eimutis Žvybas. *Add.* Elektronikos 1, Panevėžys 235300; tel. 634 50; telex 287424 ZKE SU; fax 234 15.

ELFA, electrotech. ent. F. 1940; 5,200 empl. Produces asynchronous electric engines, electric household appliances (tape recorders, electrical grinders, vegetable choppers); exports to Romania, Yugoslavia, Germany, USSR. Sponsor of Lith. Encyclopaedias. Dir-Gen. Gintaras Saunoris. *Add.* Vytenio 50, Vilnius 232654; tel. 631 531; telex 261226 ELFA SU; fax 662 436.

FASA, packing equipm. company. F. 1960; 2,100 empl. Produces automated packing equipm. and lines for paste-food products, automated packing equipm. for dairy products, meat and groats products, polyethylene film welding equipm.; exports to 29 foreign c. (Hungary, Czecho-Slovakia, Greece, Finland, India). Dir-Gen. Jonas Šeškevičius. *Add.* Sporto 9, Marijampolė 234520; tel. 505 62; fax 504 69.

KAUNAS IRON WORKS. F. 1962; 1,840 empl. Produces cast-iron castings, ground for castings, mech. and thermic processing of castings, special-order equipm., model equipm., consumer goods (car pumps, oil injectors, spare parts). Sponsor of Lith. Encyclopaedias. Dir E. Majauskas. *Add.* Kalantos 39, Kaunas 233718; tel. 751 090.

KOORDINATĖ, machine-tools assoc. F. 1959; 2,600 empl. Produces co-ordinate lathe and grinding, electro-erosion and special machine-tools, linear and angular meters, consumer goods; exports 25% of prod. Dir-Gen. Arūnas Kairys. *Add.* Savanoriu pr. 192, Kaunas 233702; tel. 733 267; telex 269134 AUDRA SU; fax 731 669.

KYBARTAI COMMERCIAL EQUIPMENT PLANT. F. 1959; 690 empl. Produces bread-cutters, fish-cleaning machines, butter dispensers, dish washing tubs, tables for food preparing, cultural-household goods. Dir V. Baltutis. *Add.* Vištyčio 38, Kybartai 234290; tel. 581 50.

LIETKABELIS, plant. F. 1959; 1,186 empl. Produces enamel and lacquer coated copper wire; exports to USSR. Dir V. Šleinota. *Add.* Janonio 4, Panevėžys 235319; tel. 617 35; telex 287419 PLG SU.

MAŽEIKIAI COMPRESSOR PLANT. F. 1965; 3,230 empl. Produces compressors for household refrigerators, starting protective relays, electric household vegetable graters, plastic toys, wire holders for curtains; exports to USSR. Dir Vaclovas Radvilas. *Add.* Ventos 8, Mažeikiai 235500; tel. 655 37.

MAŽEIKIAI ELECTRICAL ENGINEERING PLANT. F. 1959; 1,600 empl. Produces low power electric engines. Dir Aldevinas Martinaitis. *Add.* Laisvės 216, Mažeikiai 235500; tel. and fax 324 48.

MODULIS, computer plant. F. 1960; 1,600 empl. Produces power sources and control units, transformers, filters, magnetic heads, bunched conductors and cables, consumer goods (lights for Christmas trees, photoflashes, sets of cutting tools, signalling lights); exports to USSR. Sponsor of Lith. Encyclopaedias. Dir Jonas Bendorius. *Add.* Arnionių 60, Pabradė 234710; tel. 545 92; fax 546 34.

NERIS, farm equipm. factory. F. 1958; 23,400 empl. Produces equipm. for vitamin-rich grass powder prod. equipm., sets for flaked combined forage prod.; exports to Bulgaria, Mongolia, USSR. Dir-Gen. Vytautas Šumakaris. *Add.* Pramonės 97, Vilnius 232048; tel. 670 023; telex 261256 CIKLON SU.

NUKLONAS, electronics factory. F. 1968; 3,200 empl. Produces integrated circuits (television, logical, memory and name/analogical), household appliances; exports to 19 c. Includes a special design-technol. bureau. Dir Vytautas Slanina. *Add.* Architektų 1, Šiauliai 235419; tel. 522 35; telex 296426 META SU; fax 535 04.

SIRIJUS, scientific ind. company. F. 1931; 1,820 empl. Produces alkaline batteries and elements for electronical, electrotech. and household equipm.; exports to USSR, E-European c. Sponsor of Lith. Encyclopaedias. Dir Petras Kravtas. *Add.* Artojų 7, Klaipėda 235799; tel. 127 57; telex 278118.

SNAIGĖ, refrigerator plant. F. 1964; 3,200 empl. Produces household refrigerators *Snaigė 5, Snaigė 15, Snaigė 15E, Snaigė 117, Snaigė 122*; exports to Poland, Hungary, Netherlands, Greece, Spain. Dir-Gen. Antanas Andriulionis. *Add.* Pramonės 6, Alytus 234580; tel. 575 80; telex 269849 ALITA SU; fax 576 12.

SPORTINĖ AVIACIJA, design and constr. bureau. F. 1969; 390 empl. Produces gliders, trailers for glider transportation, electronic variometers, superlight aircrafts. Dir Aleksandras Jonušas. *Add.* Pociūnai, Prienų raj. 234340; tel. 515 75; fax 530 39.

TAURAS, television plant. F. 1961; 6,000 empl. Produces colour TV sets *Tauras-51ST 311D, 61ST 311D, 42ST 402D, 51ST 402D, 37ST 402D, 37ST 402D; Šilelis-42ST 401D, 32ST 401D*, TV equipm. (blocks for TV studies, TV-cinema equipm., mobile TV stations for TV-centres and correspondent posts, equipm.

blocks for mobile TV stations), exports to USSR, E-European c. Dir Raimundas Virbickas. *Add.* Pramonės 15, Šiauliai 235419; tel. 522 20; telex 296126 EKRANAS SU; fax 273 44.

VAIRAS, cycle engine factory. F. 1948; 2,950 empl. Produces bicycles for teenagers *Ereliukas 171-831, Kregždutė 172-841, Rambynas 175-821*, moped engines, castings; exports to Cuba, Hungary, Bulgaria, Mongolia. Dir Steponas Bytautas. *Add.* Tilžės 74, Šiauliai 235419; tel. 521 34.

VENTA, scientific ind. company. F. 1970; 2,180 empl. Produces integrated circuits; exports to USSR, Bulgaria, Romania, Czecho-Slovakia, Poland, Germany, Cuba, Mongolia, Syria, Libya. Sponsor of Lith. Encyclopaedias. Dir-Gen. Kazimieras Juozas Klimašauskas. *Add.* Ateities 10, Vilnius 232057; tel. 775 939; telex 261169 VENTA SU.

VILNIUS DRILL PLANT. F. 1957; 1,600 empl. Produces spiral drills with cylindrical (0,35 − 0,45 mm diameter) and conical (0,4 − 2 mm diameter) shafts; exports to 25 foreign c. Dir Petras Ramanauskas. *Add.* Muitinės 10, Vilnius 232647; tel. 633 774; telex 261126 GUA SU; fax 261 065.

VILNIUS ELECTRICAL MEASUREMENT DEVICES FACTORY. F. 1949; 3,751 empl. Produces one-phase household electric meters, information systems for electric metering, electro-panels, car battery circuit breakers, auto testers, car antennas; exports to 10 c. Sponsor of Lith. Encyclopaedias. Dir Vincas Babilius. *Add.* Aukštaičių 7, Vilnius 232600; tel. 628 415; telex 261159 TEKS SU.

VILNIUS ELECTRICAL WELDING EQUIPMENT COMPANY. F. 1953; 3,600 empl. Produces welding equipm., welding generators, welding transformers, rectifiers, household vacuum cleaners, electric toasters; exports to 28 c. Dir-Gen. Ivan Makmak. *Add.* Konarskio 57, Vilnius 232653; tel. 632 941; fax 634 775.

VILNIUS FUEL OUTFIT COMPANY. F. 1959; 7,110 empl. Subsidiaries in various regions of USSR. Produces fuel outfit for diesel engines (pumps, sprinklers, injectors), consumer goods, spare parts for cars, furniture parts, steel molds; exports to 28 c. Dir-Gen. Algirdas Didžiulis. *Add.* Kalvarijų 143, Vilnius 232650; tel. 776 261; telex 261161 ALMAZ SU; fax 776 569.

VINGIS, radio component company. F. 1959; 6,672 empl. Produces deflection systems and transformers for B/W and colour TV sets, special technol. equipm., consumer goods. Dir-Gen. Algirdas Linartas. *Add.* Savanorių 176, Vilnius 232646; tel. 653 884.

WESTERN SHIPREPAIR YARD. F. 1969; 3,000 empl. Produces machinery, spare parts for agric. equipm., iron rings, fish products, special order products; repairs ships. Dir Man. Boris Trofimov. *Add.* Minijos 180, Klaipėda 235816; tel. 356 31; telex 278125 WEST SU.

ŽALGIRIS, machine-tools plant. F. 1947; 1,636 empl. Produces metal-cutting machines, milling machines, special machine-tools, machines with digital program control, manufacturing centres, cast-iron castings, forged semiproducts, consumer goods (umbrellas, serving tables, household baskets); exports to 20 c. Dir Jurijus Sivickis. *Add.* Pramonės 141, Vilnius 232048; tel. 671 476; telex 261145 DIODAS SU.

CHEMICAL & PETROCHEMICAL INDUSTRIES

ALYTUS CHEMICAL PLANT. F. 1936; 300 empl. Produces polishes, ingredients for paints and lacquers, car care products, shoe polish, rosin; exports to Switzerland, Cuba, Angola. Dir Albinas Varpukevičius. *Add.* Sakų 3, Alytus 234580; tel. 525 75.

AZOTAS, chem. fertilizer company. F. 1965; 4,210 empl. Produces ammonia, ammonium nitrate, carbamide, ammonia water, carbamide formaldehyde resins, methanol, liquefied carbon dioxide, dry ice; exports to Poland, Hungary, Great Britain. Dir-Gen. Bronislavas Lubys. *Add.* Taurosto 26, Jonava 235000; tel. 566 21; telex 304152 AZOTAS SU.

INKARAS, rubber products factory. F. 1933; 2,370 empl. Produces rubber and polymeric footwear, tech. rubber products, parts for radiotech., electrotech., printing, textile ind. and constr., parts for motor vehicles and agric. machinery, rubber, glue. Dir K.Šeputis. *Add.* Raudondvario pl. 127, Kaunas 233021; tel. 260 520; telex 269121 SLED SU.

KAUNAS SYNTHETIC FIBER PLANT. F. 1965; 2,000 empl. Produces acetate, triacetate yarn of various linear density, textured yarn of various linear density, knitted fabric, fibre; exports to Germany, Poland, Yugoslavia. Dir Algimantas Anužis. *Add.* Pramonės 4, Kaunas 233711; tel. 750 023; telex 269804 MARS SU; fax 750 165.

KĖDAINIAI CHEMICAL PLANT. F. 1963; 1,680 empl. Produces sulphuric acid, amophos fertilizer, granulated superphosphate, granulated superphosphate with boron aluminum fluoride, microelement fertilizers *Žaluma.* Dir Kazys Pilkauskas. *Add.* Juodkiškio 32, Kėdainiai 235030; tel. 522 73; fax 532 41.

LIETUVOS BUITINĖ CHEMIJA, firm. F. 1970; 2,040 empl. Produces synthetic washing detergents, car cleaning and care means, paints, solvents, glues, aerosols, cosmetic products. Sponsor of Lith. Encyclopaedias. Dir-Gen. Vytautas Milinavičius. *Add.* Kirtimų 47, Vilnius 232028; tel. 640 760; telex 261250 BLESK SU; fax 641 413.

PLASTA, plant. F. 1960; 2,378 empl. Produces polyethylene films and tubes, plastic products; exports to Cuba, Mongolia, Nigeria, Finland, USSR, Vietnam. Dir Algirdas Griškevičius. *Add.* Savanorių pr. 180, Vilnius 232644; tel. 631 558; fax 639 876.

VILNIUS POLYMER PRODUCTS PLANT. F. 1965; 330 empl. Produces multilayer polyvinyl chloride linoleum, polyvinyl chloride linoleum with thermoinsulation basis EX-X and EKP-X, various types of glues, hermetic liquid AG-41, rubber surfaces for livestock farms, *Gervolent* air-tight bands, plastic ventilation lattice, cylinders for electrical installations, folding floor-bands, thin borders for bathtubs. Sponsor of Lith. Encyclopaedias. Dir-Gen. Aloyzas Daublys. *Add.* Kirtimų 45, Vilnius 232028; tel. 640 943.

FORESTRY, WOOD PRODUCTS, PAPER & PULP INDUSTRIES

ALYTUS EXPERIMENTAL HOME-BUILDING FACTORY. F. 1979; 3,690 empl. Produces assembled dwelling houses, wood fiber slabs, saw timber, doors and window frames, mineral insulation, parquet-boards; exports to Bulgaria, Yemen, USA, Mongolia, Finland, USSR, Germany. Dir Bronislovas Janonis. *Add.* Naujoji 124, Alytus 234580; tel. 574 96; telex 304005 STRELA SU; fax 349 95.

AŽUOLAS, furniture factory. F. 1889; 646 empl. Produces living room furniture sets *Meda* and *Bitė*, folding beds, rocking chairs, soft parts for furniture; exports to Netherlands. Dir-Gen. Pavel Burak. *Add.* Juozapavičiaus 6, Vilnius 232600; tel. 357 425.

GRIGIŠKĖS, Lith.-American joint venture. F. 1922; 2,320 empl. Produces paper, cardboard, wood fiber slabs, teletype tape, one-layer filter material for cigarette filters; exports to Poland, Hungary, Yugoslavia, Pakistan, USA, Great Britain, Sweden, Finland, Denmark, Belgium, Germany, France, Greece, Morocco. Dir-Gen. Liudvikas Miškinis. *Add.* Grigiškės 234058; tel. 633 904; fax 651 486.

KAUNAS PAPER MILL. F. 1933; 1,170 empl. Produces paper for newspapers, magazines, writing, dielectric, electrographic-panchromatic, packaging paper; diazotype paper; magnetographic paper; polyvinyldenchloride-coated paper; corrective paper for typewriters, household goods; exports to Afghanistan, Belgium, Bulgaria, Czecho-Slovakia, Laos, Mongolia, Vietnam. Dir Rimvydas Daugėla. *Add.* Kalantos 34, Kaunas 233014; tel. 752 955; fax 757 044.

KAUNO BALDAI, furniture company. F. 1880; 2,790 empl. Produces living room furniture sets *Ema, Galvė, Jotulė, Žalgiris, Žilvytis*, shelves *Silvija, Nataša*, divan-beds, matresses; exports to France, Netherlands. Dir Steponas Arciškevičius. *Add.* Drobės 66, Kaunas 233002; tel. 740 687, 740 425.

KLAIPĖDA CARDBOARD PLANT. F. 1900; 2,000 empl. Produces art and conventional cardboard for boxes, packaging paper, fodder yeast, ligno sulphonates (preparations for reducing soil erosion); exports to USSR, Latvia, Estonia, Czecho-Slovakia, Great Britain, Turkey. Sponsor of Lith. Encyclopaedias. Dir Gytis Albrechtas. *Add.* Nemuno 2, Klaipėda 235802; tel. 146 43; fax 524 42.

KLAIPĖDA TIMBER COMPANY. F. 1899; 1,190 empl. Produces chip boards, plywood, planed veneer, glued furniture elements. Dir Antanas Tauras. *Add.* Liepų 68, Klaipėda 235799; tel. 122 12.

UKMERGĖ FURNITURE FACTORY. F. 1941; 960 empl. Produces writing tables, wardrobes, cabinets, furniture sets for youth; exports to Belgium, Great Britain, Austria. Dir Romualdas Macijauskas. *Add.* Vytauto 51, Ukmergė 234120; tel. 533 82.

VILNIUS, furniture factory. F. 1960; 2,462 empl. Produces living-room soft furniture sets *Voruta, Volungė, Aras*, cabinet units *Neris-3, Neris-4,*

Vilnius-4, bookshelves, cupboards, fuel brickets; exports to Netherlands, Belgium, France. Dir-Gen. Vaclovas Čepas. *Add.* Savanorių pr. 178, Vilnius 232600; tel. 653 273; fax 633 395.

PRINTING INDUSTRY

AUŠRA (Dawn), printing house. F. 1948; prints books, periodicals. Dir Ričardas Markovas. *Add.* Vytauto pr. 23, Kaunas 233000; tel. 226 457.
SPINDULYS, Lith.-American printing house. F. 1989; 670 empl. Produces polygraphic products, printing work. Dir Vincentas Vaičekauskas. *Add.* Gedimino 10, Kaunas 233000; tel. 221 547; telex 269806 BOOK SU.
VILTIS, printing house. F. 1789; 530 empl. Produces books and booklets, pictorial prod., newspapers. Dir Romaldas Pakulis. *Add.* Strazdelio 1, Vilnius 232600; tel. 628 632; fax 613 891 VILTIS.

BUILDING-MATERIALS INDUSTRY

AKMENĖS CEMENTAS, cement company. F. 1952; 2,500 empl. Produces portland cement, corrugated slate boards, asbestos-cement pipes; exports to Latvia, Byelorussia, Russia, Finland, Sweden. Dir Leopoldas Petravičius. *Add.* Naujoji Akmenė 235464; tel. 583 23; telex 296419 ACG SU.
DVARČIONYS, plant. F. 1888; 510 empl. Subsidiaries in Ukmergė and Družai. Produces ceramic wall and floor tiles, facing tiles, ceramic rugs, stove tiles, ceramic products for restoration work, IKAS binding agent, PM-86B film forming material, anticorrosion acid resistant paints, polymeric paints, CHV-161 paint; exports to foreign c. Dir-Gen. Juozas Raišelis. *Add.* Keramikų 2, Vilnius 232036; tel. 747 021; fax 747 061.
VILMETA, company. F. 1962; 680 empl. Subsidiary in Alytus. Produces metallic building structures, constr. equipm., trailer frames, pipe isolation; exports to foreign c. Dir-Gen. Genadij Gorochov. *Add.* Granito 10, Vilnius 232028; tel. 640 358; telex 261172 LMS SU; fax 640 002.

GLASS, PORCELAIN & JEWELRY

ALEKSOTAS, glass-works. F. 1927; 855 empl. Produces bottles, jars, frit, lamp shades, various consumer goods; exports to Latvia, Russia, Moldavia, Byelorussia, Poland. Dir Jurgis Mockevičius. *Add.* Suvalkiečių pl. 23, Kaunas 233010; tel. 295 754; telex 269258 PIRS SU.
AMBRA, company. F. 1989; 15 empl. Produces amber jewelry, amber articles of applied arts; exports to Germany, Italy, Japan. Pres. Šarūnas Davainis. *Add.* Latvių 7, Vilnius 232004; tel. 758 656, 750 278; fax 354 636.
JESIA, decorative ceramics plant. F. 1938; 1,390 empl. Produces china-ware, vases, decorative household ceramic products, parts for lighting fixtures, clay and porcelain souvenirs; exports to 7 c. Dir Leonas Timleris. *Add.* Chemijos pr. 29, Kaunas 233031; tel. 750 563; telex 269176 VAZA SU.

PANEVĖŽYS GLASS-WORKS. F. 1965; 1,100 empl. Produces window glass, glass blocks, black glass finish tiles, furniture glass, glass-cloth-base laminate; exports to Germany, Finland, Great Britain, Morocco. Sponsor of Lith. Encyclopaedias. Dir Stasys Stoškus. *Add.* Pramonės 10, Panevėžys 235319; tel. 637 47; telex 287421 PSF SU; fax 657 03.
ŪLA, company. F. 1968; 1,137 empl. Subsidiaries in Merkinė, Alytus, Palanga. Produces amber and silver jewelry, consumer goods of non-ferrous metal souvenirs; exports to Japan, Korea. Dir-Gen. Jonas Jonaitis. *Add.* Čiurlionio 135, Druskininkai 234690; tel. 537 27; fax 554 85.
VILNIUS GLASS-WORKS. F. 1920; 200 empl. Produces flower vases, fruit bowls, glasses, dishes for salad and herring; exports to Germany, USSR. Dir-Gen. Pranas Palunkiškis. *Add.* Pelesos 3, Vilnius 232600; tel. 663 009.

LIGHT INDUSTRY

AIDAS, state ent. F. 1964; 1,160 empl. Subsidiary in Daugėliškiai. Produces prams, toys, school desks, rocking chairs, flashlights, plastic products, isoprene, fuel filters for cars; exports prams, toys, flashlights. Dir Vincas Stelmokas. *Add.* Raudondvario pl. 164, Kaunas 233 021; tel. 260 262.
AKMENA, consumer goods factory. F. 1962; 4 branches; 620. empl. Produces special order furniture, overalls, ropes, constr. tow, wooden toys, visual teaching aids; exports to Great Britain, Finland, Canada, Japan, Denmark, Netherlands, Czecho-Slovakia. Dir Benediktas Raubickas. *Add.* Vytauto 19, Kretinga 235700; tel. 544 31; fax 515 31.
ALYTUS COTTON FABRIC FACTORY. F. 1968; 5,634 empl. Produces cotton yarn, ready made fabric of cotton and cotton-blend with synthetic fiber; exports to European, Asian and American c. Sponsor of Lith. Encyclopaedias. Dir Gintautas Andriuškevičius. *Add.* Pramonės 1, Alytus 234580; tel. 573 57; fax 355 66.
AUDA, knitwear company. F. 1975; 5,660 empl. Produces stockings, socks and panty-hose for children, knitwear and underwear for children and adults, curtains. Dir Algimantas Auškalnis. *Add.* Raudondvario pl. 93, Kaunas 233008; tel. 261 507; telex 269817 AUDA SU; fax 263 786.
AUDĖJAS, ent. F. 1956; 930 empl. Produces fabrics for soft furniture and car and plane interiors, cotton yarn; exports to Finland. Dir-Gen. Jonas Karčiauskas. *Add.* Zarasų 24/1, Vilnius 232600; tel. 627 477; telex 261115 AUD SU; fax 614 676.
AUDIMAS, knitwear factory. F. 1936; 950 empl. Produces knitwear for adults and children, underwear for adults and children, products of scrap material; exports to Great Britain, Greece, USSR. Dir R.S. Bakanas. *Add.* Raudondvario pl. 80, Kaunas 233008; tel. 260 889; telex 269112 PAUK SU.
BALTIJA, sewing company. F. 1972; 1,900 empl.; 8 branches. Produces shirts for men, clothes for women, corset articles and consumer

goods; exports to Germany. Dir-Gen. Raimundas Živatauskas. *Add.* Gaižiūnų 4, Kaunas 233009; tel. 774 258; telex 269866 MODEL SU.

DINAMO, sports goods factory. F. 1955; 540 empl. Produces skis, sleds, ping-pong and billiard tables, paddles, pommel and vaulting horses for gymnastics. Dir J.Satkūnas. *Add.* Taikos pr. 145, Kaunas 233036; tel. 773 33.

DOVANA, ent. F. 1967; 2,330 empl.; 8 depts. Produces textiles and knitwear, decorative figurines, cotton fabric, artificial flowers; exports to Japan, Germany, Ireland, Hungary, Poland, USSR. Dir-Gen. Bronius Vintys. *Add.* Sudervės 51, Vilnius 232050; tel. 458 844; telex 261158 MVSO SU; fax 458 858.

DROBĖ, wool company. F. 1920; 4,100 empl. Produces wool, wool-blend fabrics for suits and dresses. Dir-Gen. Vytenis Gubavičius. *Add.* Jonavos 60, Kaunas 233000; tel. 262 917; telex 269818 DROBĖ SU; fax 262 474.

ELNIAS, leather and footwear company. F. 1877; 2,870 empl. Produces hard and soft leather, footwear (for men, women and children); exports to Italy. Dir Sigitas Vilčiauskas. *Add.* Vilniaus 72, Šiauliai 235419; tel. 338 55; telex 296127 OB SU.

KASPINAS, textile company. F. 1939; 1,020 empl. Subsidiary in Skirsnemunė. Produces cotton fabrics, textile articles. Dir Vaclovas Pečatauskas. *Add.* Raudondvario pl. 76, Kaunas 233008; tel. 260 446.

KAUNAS COTTON SPINNING FACTORY. F. 1966; 850 empl. Produces cotton yarn, cotton wool, non-woven fabrics. Dir Jonas Kiudulas. *Add.* Draugystės 14, Kaunas 233031; tel. 751 204.

KAUNAS SPINNING FACTORY. F. 1922; 1,320 empl. Produces wool and wool-blend yarn. Dir Pranas Gedžius. *Add.* Drobės 62, Kaunas 233002; tel. 740 770; telex 269128 DROBĖ SU.

KAUNO AUDINIAI, joint stock company. F. 1930; 1,420 empl. Produces silk, fabrics; exports to Austria. Dir Edmundas Kokvaitis. *Add.* Griunvaldo 3/5, Kaunas 232697; tel. 226 484; telex 269853 ALFA SU; fax 228 323.

KELMĖ KNITWEAR FACTORY. F. 1963; 800 empl. Subsidiaries in Tytuvėnai and Užventis. Produces tracksuits, cotton underwear for men and children, knitted fabric of cotton, cotton-synthetic and wool-blend yarn; exports to Czecho-Slovakia. Dir A. Neverdauskas. *Add.* Mažūnai, Kelmės rj. 235470; tel. 512 71.

KOTON, stockings factory. F. 1925; 1,200 empl. Produces panty-hose for children and women, socks and stockings, high elasticity children panty-hose. Sponsor of Lith. Encyclopaedias. Dir Gediminas Žemaitaitis. *Add.* Ukrainiečių 4, Kaunas 233002; tel. 740 889.

LELIJA, sewing company. F. 1947; 3,955 empl. Produces overcoats and suits for women, suits for men; exports to Switzerland and France. Dir-Gen. Genė Zaveckienė. *Add.* Panerių 43, Vilnius 232600; tel. 630 761; fax 661 577.

LENTVARIS CARPET FACTORY. F. 1957; 1,180 empl. Produces jacquard carpets, sewed carpets. Dir Liucija Talačkienė. *Add.* Klevų al. 46, Lentvaris, Trakų rj. 234200; tel. 581 56.

LINAS, flax company. F. 1975; 3,900 empl. Subsidiaries Plungė *Linu audiniai* factory, Panevėžys Flax Plant, Biržai *Siūlas* factory. Produces linen and linen-blend fabric for table-cloths, bed-sheets, curtains, as well as tech. fabrics, non-woven fabrics and sewed articles; exports to Austria, Italy, Denmark, Sweden, Germany, Singapore, Finland. Dir-Gen. Antanas Dubauskas. *Add.* Kerbedžio 23, Panevėžys 235319; tel. 614 87; telex 287412 PLK SU; fax 226 07.

LITEKSAS, weaving factory. F. 1927; 1,260 empl. Produces wool and wool-blend fabric for coats and dresses. Dir-Gen. Virgilijus Varža. *Add.* Draugystės 16, Kaunas 233031; tel. 753 477; fax 752 910.

LITUANICA, footwear company. F. 1934; 2,334 empl. Produces footwear for men (shoes, boots, high boots, sandals, slippers for men and women). Dir-Gen. Antanas Songaila. *Add.* Jonavos 3, Kaunas 233000; tel. 227 330; telex 269825 PUGA SU; fax 209 638.

MASTIS, knitwear company. F. 1981; 3,750 empl.; 7 branches. Produces outdoor knitwear, gloves (wool, wool-blend, cotton), jumpers (wool, wool-blend and combined yarn), sweaters (wool), jackets, suits. Dir K. Standžys. *Add.* Pramonės 11, Telšiai 235610; tel. 533 41; fax 541 54.

NERINGA, commercial company. F. 1946; 1,750 empl.; Lith.-British joint venture 'Wemblay-Neringa'. Produces toys, household goods; exports abroad. Dir-Gen. Algimantas Matulevičius. *Add.* Daugėliškio 32, Vilnius 232600; tel. 750 822; telex 261122 GSN SU; fax 352 595.

PLUNGĖ SYNTHETIC LEATHER PLANT. F. 1971; 904 empl. Produces soft synthetic leather, linoleum; exports to USSR. Dir Egidijus Bulavas. *Add.* Pramonės pr. 4, Plungė 235640; tel. 532 01; telex 278005 KOŽA SU.

SPARTA, knitwear and stockings factory. F. 1945; 1,860 empl. Produces socks for men, stockings for women, panty-hose for women, knitted underwear, knitwear for children; exports to Poland, Cuba, Mongolia, Finland, USSR, Hungary. Dir-Gen. Petras Zenonas Janavičius. *Add.* Švitrigailos 32, Vilnius 232006; tel. 632 261.

ŠATRIJA, sewing company. F. 1955; 1,475 empl. Produces pants, suits, skirts, jackets, tracksuits of Bolognia-fabric; exports to Russia, Kazakhstan. Dir-Gen. Jonas Stravinskas. *Add.* Pergalės 5, Raseiniai 234400; tel. 522 97; telex 304504 ŠATRIJA SU.

ŠIAULIAI NON-WOVEN FABRIC FACTORY. F. 1963; 410 empl. Produces non-woven fabrics; knitted-sewed sheet wadding, half-wool yarn, recycled wool and fiber; exports to Poland. Dir Leonas Karpalavičius. *Add.* Basanavičiaus 103c, Šiauliai 235402; tel. 410 11; fax 406 88.

ŠILKAS, textile factory. F. 1956; 3,000 empl. Produces silk fabrics for dresses, linings, sportswear, haberdashery ind., velvet, synthetic fur for outdoor clothes, footwear, toys, non-woven fabrics; exports to Austria. Dir-Gen. Jurgis Keliuotis. *Add.* Neries kr. 16, Kaunas 233713; tel. 264 235; fax 261 293.

TRINYČIAI, company. F. 1923; 1,300 empl. Produces cotton yarn. Dir-Gen. Romualdas Komisoraitis. **Add.** Bangu 22, Klaipėda 235800; tel. 122 28; fax 188 04.

UTENOS TRIKOTAŽAS, company. F. 1967; 3,000 empl. Produces cotton and synthetic knitted underwear and knitwear for men, women, children. Dir-Gen. Nijolė Dumbliauskienė. **Add.** Basanavičiaus 122, Utena 234910; tel. 514 45; telex 303842 LIPA 1 SU; fax 693 58.

VERPSTAS, knitwear factory. F. 1926; 1,840 empl. Produces knitwear (jumpers, jackets, dresses, suits); exports to Germany. Dir-Gen. Aldona Mikšienė. **Add.** Traku 43, Šiauliai 235400; tel. 335 23; fax 339 40.

VILKAS, fur company. F. 1932; 1,600 empl. Produces sheep-skin coats, astrakhan, mink and fox coats and jackets for women, sheep-skin and mink caps; exports to Yugoslavia, Hungary. Dir-Gen. Vaclovas Kliunka. **Add.** Raudondvario pl. 101, Kaunas 233008; tel. 261 576; telex 269829 AVIS SU.

VILKAVIŠKIS SEWING FACTORY. F. 1955; 810 empl. Produces pants (for men, women and children), clothes for new-born babies. Dir Juozas Rudaitis. **Add.** Vytauto 4, Vilkaviškis 234270; tel. 525 02; telex 304104 SVEJA SU.

VILNIUS FUR FACTORY. F. 1964; 1,610 empl. Processes rabbit, fox, mink, musk-rat and astrakhan hides; produces fur coats for men and women, short overcoats for men, caps, gloves; exports abroad. Dir-Gen. Juozas Macevičius. **Add.** Paupio 28, Vilnius 232600; tel. 627 803.

FOOD INDUSTRY

ALYTUS SOFT DRINKS AND CHAMPAGNE FACTORY. F. 1963; 600 empl. Produces wine, champagne, concentrated juice, dry apple extract, soft drinks, mineral water; exports to Austria, Denmark, Czecho-Slovakia, Cyprus, Finland, Hungary, Germany. Sponsor of Lith. Encyclopaedias. Dir Juozas Daukšys. **Add.** Miškininku 17, Alytus 234580; tel. 523 37; telex 269841 NEMUS SU; fax 544 67.

GUBERNIJA, soft drinks and beer factory. F. 1786; 240 empl. Produces beer, soft drinks; exports to Russia. Dir Vytautas Urbonas. **Add.** Dvaro 179, Šiauliai 235419; tel. 402 50.

KAUNAS CONFECTIONERY FACTORY. F. 1921; 1,090 empl. Produces chocolates, candies with and without chocolate glazing, toffees, dragee, marmalade-pastille products, crackers; exports to Poland, Hungary, Afghanistan, USSR. Dir Lionginas Turauskas. **Add.** Taikos pr. 88, Kaunas 233031; tel. 750 589; telex 269132 KAKAO SU; fax 705 827.

KLAIPĖDA MEAT PLANT. F. 1966; 2,440 empl. Produces meat (with the 1 st category subproducts), sausages, canned meat, meat semiproducts; exports to Czecho-Slovakia, France, Italy, Finland, Sweden, USSR, Hungary, Germany. Dir-Gen. Valdas Trinkūnas. **Add.** Šilutės pl. 79, Klaipėda 235799; tel. 412 00; telex 278139 DUB SU.

PANEVĖŽYS MEAT PLANT. F. 1931; 1,490 empl. Branches in Pasvalys, Pakruojis, Biržai.

Produces meat, sausage products, smoked meat, canned meat, sub-products (fats, entrails, hides); exports to Cuba, Netherlands, France, Germany. Dir Pranciškus Raškauskas. **Add.** Smėlynės 85, Panevėžys 235319; tel. 619 23; telex 287411 PMK SU.

PAVENČIAI SUGAR PLANT. F. 1935; 850 empl. Produces granulated and granulated refined sugar of sugar beets and semi-manufactured canes. Sponsor of Lith. Encyclopaedias. Dir Jurgis Ignotas. **Add.** Ventos 79, Kuršėnai 235420; tel. 344 59; telex 296882 LIAUDA SU; fax 718 42.

PERGALĖ, confectionery factory. F. 1952; 910 empl. Produces confectionery (sweets, chocolates, packaged sweets, biscuits), chewing gum. Dir Algirdas Miltenis. **Add.** Stirnu 25, Vilnius 232600; tel. 751 311.

RŪTA, confectionery plant. F. 1976; 1,020 empl. Produces caramel, sweets, caramel syrup, extract; exports to Mongolia, USSR. Dir Antanas Buitkus. **Add.** Tilžės 133, Šiauliai 235419; tel. 304 22; telex 296116.

ŠVYTURYS, soft drinks and beer factory. F. 1784; 270 empl. Produces beer, soft drinks, malt liquors. Dir Algirdas Stanaitis. **Add.** Kuliu vartai 7, Klaipėda 235799; tel. 139 04; fax 135 96.

TAURAS, soft drinks and beer factory. F. 1945. Subsidiary in Raudondvaris. Produces beer, soft drinks, enzymes, mineral water. Dir-Gen. Vytautas Kazakevičius. **Add.** Dainavos 11/2, Vilnius 232649; tel. 627 526; fax 223 754.

UTENA SOFT DRINKS AND MALT LIQUOR FACTORY. F. 1977; 790 empl. Produces beer, soft drinks, malt, polyethylene boxes, performs constr. works; offers transportation service; sells prod. waste; exports to USSR, Australia, Poland. Sponsor of Lith. Encyclopaedias. Dir Gediminas Jackevičius. **Add.** Pramonės 12, Utena 234910; tel. 527 87; telex 261157 UNGK SU.

MICROBIOLOGICAL INDUSTRY

KAUNAS ENDOCRINAL PREPARATIONS FACTORY. F. 1969; 650 empl. Produces preparations applied in cases of cardiovascular diseases, eye drops, preparations for regulation and treatment of endocrinal system (Insulin, Calcitrin, Somatotrophin, Pituitrin, Hypotocin, Lactin, Korticotrophin, Thyrotropin), preparation of lyophilized gall, Lyobil, radioimmunological kits for hormone detection in human blood. Sponsor of Lith. Encyclopaedias. Dir Henrikas Dūdėnas. **Add.** Veiveriu 134, Kaunas 233010; tel. 227 432; telex 269254.

SANITAS, pharmaceutical pilot plant. F. 1922; 910 empl. Produces medications in ampules and packages, extracts from med. herbs, honey products, biopolymeric prolonged action forms for med. transdermal systems; exports to Bulgaria, Czecho-Slovakia, Laos, Mongolia, Romania, Hungary, Vietnam. Dir Jonas Makauskas. **Add.** Vytauto pr. 3, Kaunas 233000; tel. and fax 226 725.

VILNIUS ENZYMES PREPARATIONS PLANT. F. 1970; 530 empl. Produces enzyme products

(Amilosubtilinum, Protosubtilinum, Lysosubtilinum, Lysocinum, Maltavamorinum) for agric., leather and fur ind., beer making, poultry farms and veterinary service; Puthidoilum for reduction of environment pollution by oil and its products, α-amilasium for med. purposes. Dir Ignas Kiudulas. **Add.** Fermentu 8, Vilnius 232028; tel. 640 835; fax 641 104.

TRADE & INTERMEDIARY ORGANIZATIONS

BALTIA-UNION, int. company. F. 1989; 70 empl. Includes firms: *Agro Lietuva* (manufacturing-commercial), *Baltia-Hermis* (commercial), *Baltia-Trans, Baltia-Vita*. Services: cargo transportation by cars, car service, prod. and sale of agric. and ind. products and building materials, tourism, hotel, camping constr. and utilization, commercial mediation. Dir-Gen. Antanas Bakaitis. **Add.** Birutės 56, Vilnius 232004; tel. 357 373, 354 241; telex 261162 ALKA SU; fax 353 736.
ELITA, interbranch assoc. F. 1990; 4 founders. Cultivates buckthorn, produces sea buckthorn, oil, wine and tea. Chair. Jonas Grigonis. **Add.** POB 625, Vilnius 232012; tel. 779 330.
LITIMPEKS, Lith. foreign trade company. F. 1987; 50 empl. Chooses partners for exports-imports, organizes commercial talks, drafts contracts, organizes shipment of goods, deals with financial accounts, customs declarations and customs fees, commercial activities in arts, sports, tourism and hunting, organizes commercial fairs in Lithuania and establishment of joint ventures. Dir-Gen. Justinas Antanaitis. **Add.** Verkiu 37, Vilnius 232600; tel. 352 544; telex 261148 LIET SU; fax 614 194.
VILBARA, Lith.-Ger. joint venture. F. 1989. Sells for hard currency Ger., Japanese and other foreign goods such as cars, audio and video equipm., souvenirs, food and other consumer goods. Dir Gediminas Daubaras. **Add.** Pilies 2/1, Vilnius 232001; tel. 610 750; telex 261177 VILBA SU; fax 614 160.

FINANCE

AGRICULTURAL BANK OF LITHUANIA. F. 1990. Chair. of the Bd Pranas Viliūnas. **Add.** Totoriu 4, Vilnius 232629; tel. 628 842.
BANK OF LITHUANIA. F. 1990. Chair. of the Bd Vilius Baldišis. **Add.** Gedimino pr. 6, Vilnius 232629; tel. 224 015; fax 221 501.
ŪKIO BANKAS, commercial bank. F. 1989; grants credits and carries out settlements, marketing, factoring, leasing operations among ent., org., population. Chair. of the Bd Valdemaras Būtėnas. **Add.** Gruodžio 9, Kaunas 233000; tel. 203 651; fax 204 296.
JOINT-STOCK INNOVATION BANK OF LITHUANIA. F. 1988; branch in Kaunas; grants loans, accepts deposits, assists in seeking out partners for commercial activity and selling prod. in Lithuania and abroad, takes part in foundation of new ent. and their activity. Dir Artūras Balkevičius. **Add.** Šv. Stepono 27, Vilnius 232006; tel. 261 826; telex 261114 LCO SU; fax 661 550.

LITHUANIAN BANK FOR FOREIGN ECONOMIC AFFAIRS. F. 1988; carries out int. settlements, runs personal currency accounts, grants credits. Chair. of the Bd Danutė Tučkienė. **Add.** Totoriu 2/8, Vilnius 232629; tel. 224 790; telex 261123 LUB SU.
SPAUDOS BANKAS, commercial bank. F. 1990; grants credits, secures large dividents for shareholders, part. in the activities of ent., intermediates in selling prod., creates programmes of currency operations. Chair. Julius Niedvaras. **Add.** Vrublevskio 6, Vilnius 232671; tel. 610 723.
SAVINGS BANK OF LITHUANIA. F. 1988. Chair. of the Bd Kostas Jakutis. **Add.** Vilniaus 16, Vilnius 232736; tel. 618 409.

SCIENTIFIC & RESEARCH INSTITUTES

INSTITUTE OF BIOCHEMISTRY. F. 1967; 10 lab. and experimental facilities. Research in biochem. and genetic basis of cell functioning, synthesis of active combinations of cells. Dir Juozas Kulys. **Add.** Mokslininku 12, Vilnius 232021; tel. 776 933.
INSTITUTE OF BOTANY. F. 1959; 12 lab., 2 sectors and experimental base, herbarium ($\sim$ 86,500 samples). Research in the regularities of the Lith. flora and vegetation evolution, their importance to landscape, algal and higher fungi, natural and anthropogenic rhythms of various ecosystems, regularities of inherited information realization in the processes of morphogenesis of plants. Part. of int. programmes 'Man and Biosphere', etc. Dir Romas Pakalnis. **Add.** Turistu 47, Vilnius 232021; tel. 777 462; fax 618 464.
INSTITUTE OF CHEMISTRY AND CHEMICAL TECHNOLOGIES. F. 1941; 18 scientific lab., experimental facilities, post-graduate courses. Research in the problems of theoretical phys. chem., electrochem. and galvanotechnol. Part. of various int. programmes. A number of technol. of galvanic processes designed at the Inst. are used in Lith. and foreign plants. Dir Romanas Višomirskis. **Add.** Goštauto 9, Vilnius 232600; tel. 611 543.
INSTITUTE OF CULTURE AND ARTS. F. 1990. Research in the development of Lith. culture and its relations with the cultures of other nations, Lith. art hist. and its originality, preservation problems of cultural values, culture of nat. minorities in Lithuania; carries out a common programme with Poles, Czechs. Dir Algirdas Gaižutis. **Add.** Tilto 4, Vilnius 232001; tel. 613 646.
INSTITUTE OF ECOLOGY. F. 1959; 14 lab., experimental aquarium and vivarium; expedition bases in Ventė, Rusnė, Obelų Ragas. Research in animal behaviour, regularities in the functioning of ecosystems, populations, communities; works out means of forecasting and rationing of the anthropogenic influence as well as ecological foundations of regional environment protection, has worked out practical measures for the protection of land and water animals, as well as for the protection of water ecosystems, for the efficient use of sources and regulation of animal

behaviour. Part. of int. complex programmes ('Influence of Power Eng. on Natural Environment', 'Monitoring of the Baltic Basin'). Publ. 'Pheromones', *Ekologija* (Ecology), *Acta Hydrobiologica Lituanica*, *Acta Parasitologica Lituanica*, *Acta Entomologica Lituanica*, *Šiluminė energetika ir aplinka* (Thermal Energy and Environment), *Vabzdžių chemorecepcija* (Chemoreception of Insects). Dir Juozas Virbickas. *Add.* Akademijos 2, Vilnius 232600; tel. 359 275.

INSTITUTE OF ECONOMICS. F. 1941. Research in prod. efficiency, improvement of management and forecasting, coordination of econ. research. Dir Eduardas Vilkas. *Add.* Goštauto 11, Vilnius 232600; tel. 623 502.

INSTITUTE OF GEOGRAPHY. F. 1990; 3 lab., movable facilities in Neringa. Research in regularities of natural-geographic processes on Lith. territory and South-East Baltic region, development of landscape optimization and structures of public areas. Part. of int. programme 'Man and Biosphere'. Dir Gediminas Pauliukevičius. *Add.* Akademijos 2, Vilnius 232600; tel. 776 967.

INSTITUTE OF IMMUNOLOGY. F. 1990; 5 lab., 2 sectors, experiment facilities. Research in cellular, genetic and molecular mechanisms of immunity functioning, prepares biotechnol. of immunostimulators, diagnosticums and vaccines. Takes part in the following int. programmes: 'Leucoses of People', 'Animals and Birds'; 'Structure and Function of Immune System Molecular Elements'. Sponsor of Lith. Encyclopaedias. Dir Vytas Tamošiūnas. *Add.* Mokslininkų 12, Vilnius 232021; tel. 359 192.

INSTITUTE OF LITHUANIAN AGRARIAN ECONOMY. F. 1990. Research in agrarian policies, pricing system, taxation, market analysis, agric. reform, rural sociology, improvement of econ. relations in agroservice and processing ind. Prepares forecasts of agric. and social evolution of the countryside. Maintains scientific ties with the univ. of Cambridge, Giessen, Iowa, Finn. Inst. of Agric. Econ. Dir Bronislavas Kužulis. *Add.* Kudirkos 18, Vilnius 232009; tel. 614 526.

INSTITUTE OF LITHUANIAN HISTORY. F. 1941. Research in the hist. of Lith., archeology, ethnography, hist. of sci. and technol. Dir Vytautas Merkys. *Add.* Kosciuškos 30, Vilnius 232600; tel. 614 436.

INSTITUTE OF MATHEMATICS AND INFORMATION TECHNOLOGY. F. 1977; 17 divisions and lab., computer centre. Research in theory of probabilities and math. statistics, differential equations and numerical methods of their solution, math. logics and theory of algorithms, identification of random processes, data analysis, multiextreme optimization, math. modelling of systems, programming technol., instrumental systems and intellectual packages of programs, data bases and expert systems, sch. information technol., computerization of Lith. lg. studies. Holds int. conferences in the theory of probabilities and math. statistics. Sponsor of Lith. Encyclopaedias. Dir Vytautas Statulevičius. *Add.* Akademijos 4, Vilnius 232600; tel. 359 209; telex 261131 IMC SU.

INSTITUTE OF THE LITHUANIAN LANGUAGE. F. 1941. Card indexes: the Lith. lg. vocabulary (~ 4 million words), index of proper names (>1.5 million), index of Lith. dialects (>1 million). Research in linguistics. Publ. *Lietuvių k. žodynas* (Dictionary of the Lith. Lg.), *Lietuvių k. atlasas* (Atlas of the Lith. Lg.), periodicals *Lietuvių kalbotyros klausimai* (Problems of Lith. Linguistics), *Kalbos kultūra* (Culture of Lg.). Dir Aleksandras Vanagas. *Add.* Antakalnio 6, Vilnius 232055; tel. 624 726.

INSTITUTE OF THE LITHUANIAN LITERATURE AND FOLKLORE. F. 1941; scientific library with a set of manuscripts ($<90,000$ items), a set of folklore manuscripts (>1 million records). Research in folklore, lit. issues a continued publ. *Literatūra ir kalba* (Lit. and Lg.), journal *Lituanistica*. Dir Jonas Lankutis. *Add.* Antakalnio 6, Vilnius 232055; tel. 621 946.

INSTITUTE OF THEORETICAL PHYSICS AND ASTRONOMY. F. 1990; 5 research divisions, astrophysical observatories in Molėtai district and Uzbekistan. Research in the theory of multiparticle systems, its application in the studies of atoms, their nuclei, molecules, plasma spectroscopy and kinetics, the problems of phys. and evolution of stars and interstar matter. Takes part in int. programmes with scientific inst. of USA, Sweden, Spain, Great Britain. Dir Zenonas Rudzikas. *Add.* Goštauto 12, Vilnius 232600; tel. 620 939.

INSTITUTE OF PHILOSOPHY, SOCIOLOGY AND LAW. F. 1977; 8 depts. Research in hist. of Lith. phil., ethics, law, information on soc. sci. Dir Arvydas Matulionis. *Add.* Saltoniškių 58, Vilnius 232600; tel. 752 455.

INSTITUTE OF PHYSICAL AND ENGINEERING PROBLEMS OF ENERGY RESEARCH. F. 1956; 14 research lab. and 3 service units. Research fields: heat transfer and fluid dynamics, thermal phys., refractory phys., ceramic and polymer eng., large power system control, forecasting development and optimization of energy and fuel market in Lithuania, thermal and hydrological problems in large cooling ponds of thermal and nuclear power plants, computation systems for experiments in thermal phys., renewable energy resources (sun and wind energy, bio-gas, heat pumps, heat engines operating on Stirling cycle, electric energy and heat demand management, efficiency increasing in heat energy prod., distribution and consumption, as well as in bio-gas utilization). Takes part in int. cooperation programmes with the scientific inst. of USA, Great Britain, Sweden, Yugoslavia, Poland, Czecho-Slovakia, Yemen, Germany. Dir Jurgis Vilemas. *Add.* Metalo 4, Kaunas 233684; tel. 757 304; telex 269822 ERGAS SU.

INSTITUTE OF PHYSICS. F. 1977; 3 research complexes: spectroscopy and optics with 8 lab., ecology with 8 lab., laser eng. and technol. with 4 lab. and experimental prod. Research in experimental spectroscopy and nonlinear optics, atmospheric phys. and environmental protection, laser eng. and technol. Takes part in int. programmes EMEP, EUROTRAC, WMOGO$_3$OS.

Sponsor of Lith. Encyclopaedias. Dir Remigijus Baltramiejūnas. **Add**. Goštauto 12, Vilnius 232600; tel. 612 610.

INSTITUTE OF SEMICONDUCTOR PHYSICS. F. 1967. Research in characteristics of semiconductors and semiconductor structures in electrical field, movement of magnetoplasmic waves in semiconductors, electrical, optical and photoelectrical properties of thin pellicles. Dir Steponas Ašmontas. **Add**. Goštauto 11, Vilnius 232600; tel. 619 759.

LITHUANIAN INSTITUTE OF AGRICULTURE. F. 1956; branches in Vokė and Vėžaičiai, 8 experimental stations. Research in soils of Lithuania, their utilization and improvement, new kinds of field plants and determination of their agrotechnics, meadows and pastures, their rational utilization and supervision. Part. of the int. programme 'Man and Biosphere'. Dir Rimantas Dapkus. **Add**. Dotnuva-Akademija, Kėdainių rj. 235052; tel. 526 57.

LITHUANIAN INSTITUTE OF LIVESTOCK BREEDING. F. 1990; centre of livestock breeding in Lithuania; experimental farms in Baisogala, Šeduva, Vėriškiai. Research in fodder improvement, technol. of fodder preparation, cattle feeding, reproduction, breeding and selection, specialization and concentration of livestock breeding. Dir Antanas Kairys. **Add**. Žebenkos 12, Baisogala 235125; tel. 536 08.

VOKĖ'S BRANCH OF AGRICULTURAL INSTITUTE. F. 1956. Works in soils, agric., fertilization, plant selection, herbs and grasses, seed-breeding, ecology of weeds, specialized crop rotation, phenology. Worked out methods of cartography and bonitation of Lith. soils, prepared maps of soils, developed new varieties of plants (lupines *Lupinus*, seradella *Ornithopus*, esparcet *Onobrychis*, potatoes, perennial grasses). Prepared plant growing technol. for light soil, carries on seed-breeding of meristem potatoes. Dir Justinas Lazauskas. **Add**. Traku, Vokė, Vilniaus rj. 234002; tel. 629 775.

EDUCATIONAL INSTITUTIONS

KAUNAS MEDICAL ACADEMY (Kaunas Medical Institute until 1990). F. 1950; 5 faculties; central scientific-research lab. with 15 lab., 2,900 students. Trains physicians, dentists, pharmacists. Extended non-infectious diseases prevention centre of WHO. Neurosurgery, traumatology, eye-microsurgery, infectious diseases, pulmonology, mother and child care centres. Med. technol. pat. research. Rector Vilius Grabauskas. **Add**. Mickevičiaus 9, Kaunas 233000; tel. 226 110; telex 269268 RASA SU; fax 220 733.

KAUNAS TECHNOLOGICAL UNIVERSITY (Kaunas Polytechnic Institute until 1990). F. 1950; 14 faculties; 4 research lab.; 14,000 students. Trains 46 types of eng.: biotechnol., chem. technol., food ind., leather processing and textiles, information technol., electromech., energy, mech., microelectronics, process management, radiotechnol., robot technol., constr. materials, sociology, ultrasound and vibration tech-

nol. Sponsor of Lith. Encyclopaedias. Rector Vladislavas Domarkas. **Add**. Donelaičio 73, Kaunas 233006; tel. 227 044.

LITHUANIAN AGRICULTURE ACADEMY. F. 1924; 8 faculties; 42 depts, dendrology park, experimental farm ($\sim$5,000 ha), greenhouses (6.5 ha covered area); 7,000 students. Trains agric. spec. in 9 areas incl. forestry. Research in hydroreclamation, rape selection and processing, storage of agric. produce, forest ecology, ecologically clean agric. Rector Rimantas Urbonas. **Add**. Noreikiškės, Kaunas-Akademija 234324; tel. 298 255; fax 296 531.

LITHUANIAN CONSERVATOIRE. F. 1933; 7 faculties; 10 lab.; 2,000 students. Trains musicians, composers, music critics and teachers, concert masters, producers, actors, chorus leaders, choreography teachers, employees for community centres. Rector Vytautas Laurušas. **Add**. Gedimino pr. 42, Vilnius 232001; tel. 612 691; telex 261078 FLEITA SU.

LITHUANIAN PHYSICAL TRAINING INSTITUTE. F. 1945; 2 faculties; 1,340 students. Trains specialists of physical training. Research in physical development, training of highly skilled sportsmen and sports spec., changes in the adaptation of nervous and muscles systems of sportsmen and individuals who do not engage in sports. Rector Valerijus Jasiūnas. **Add**. Sporto 6, Kaunas 233029; tel. 200 577.

LITHUANIAN POLICE ACADEMY. F. 1990; trains workers for Lith. police, awards degrees of bachelor and master. Rector Alvydas Pumputis. **Add**. Ateities 20, Vilnius 232057; tel. 779 424.

LITHUANIAN VETERINARY ACADEMY. F. 1936; 4 faculties; veterinary clinics, experimental farm; 2,500 students. Trains veterinarians and zoo-eng. Research in diagnostics of animal diseases diagnosis, improvement of med. treatment and prevention, rational feeding of animals, improvement of cattle and poultry productivity and breeding characteristics. Sponsor of Lith. Encyclopaedias. Rector Rimantas Karazija. **Add**. Tilžės 18, Kaunas 233022; tel. 260 383; fax 261 417.

ŠIAULIAI PEDAGOGICAL INSTITUTE. F. 1948; 6 faculties; 7,100 students. Trains teachers in 12 areas, kindergarten nurses, music teachers. Research in child teaching, defectology, functional lg. interaction, Lith. lg. and lit. Rector Vytautas Bendikas. **Add**. Višinskio 25, Šiauliai 235419; tel. 336 73.

VILNIUS ART ACADEMY (Vilnius Arts Institute until 1990). F. 1951; 3 faculties; 17 depts; 800 students. Trains garment designers, painters, sculptors, graphic artists, ceramicists; textile, glass, china and ind. artists; art critics, restoration spec., landscape arch., interior designers, drawing teachers. Rector Vytautas Brėdikis. **Add**. Maironio 6, Vilnius 232600; tel. 611 012; telex 619966.

VILNIUS PEDAGOGICAL INSTITUTE. F. 1935; 9 faculties; 43 depts; 6,400 students. Trains 20 types of teachers. Research in teaching and educ., professional guidance, inst. of higher learning, pedag. Rector Saulius Razma. **Add**. Studentų 39, Vilnius 232034; tel. 738 281.

VILNIUS TECHNICAL UNIVERSITY (Vilnius Civil Eng. Inst. until 1990). F. 1969; 5 faculties; 3 centres of sci. and studies, 7 scientific lab.; 6,000 students. Trains eng. in 18 fields. Research in urban sociology, urban planning, arch., constr. materials, design, technol., communications eng., mech., machinery, mech. of solid bodies, geodesy, environment protection, marketing, management, ind. automation, radiotechnol. Rector Edmundas Kazimieras Zavadskas. *Add.* Saulėtekio al. 11, Vilnius 232054; tel. 769 600.

VILNIUS UNIVERSITY. F. 1579; 14 faculties; 108 depts; 38 scientific-research lab.; Botanical Gardens; sci. centres of laser research and computing; 100 training lab.; Sci. Museum; 15,200 students. Trains spec. in 31 areas, with majoring in 100 fields. Research in semiconductor phys., molecular acoustics, spectroscopy of atoms and molecules, stimulants of plant and animal growth, heart and blood-vessel surgery, med. synthesis and research, pathology of digestion organs, hist. of Lith. phil., development and structure of Baltic lgs, development of Lith. lit. Scientific ties with Prague, Krakow, Greifswald, Debrecen, Brazzaville, Addis Ababa, Erfurt, Frankfurt am Main and other univ. and acad. Rector Rolandas Pavilionis. *Add.* Universiteto 3, Vilnius 232734; tel. 623 779.

VYTAUTAS MAGNUS UNIVERSITY. F. 1922; ref. 1989; 8 faculties; 600 students. Trains spec. in humanities, theol., econ., information technol., biol., phys., math., arts research, psychology, cultural anthropology. Research in information technol., management, humanities, phys. Rector Algirdas Avižienis. *Add.* Daukanto 28, Kaunas 233000; tel. 206 753.

POLITICAL PARTIES

LIETUVIŲ TAUTININKŲ SĄJUNGA (Lithuanian Nationalist Union). F. 1924, ref. 1989; 480 mems; 11 divisions; publ. *Viltis.* Chair. Rimantas Smetona. *Add.* Gedimino pr. 22, Vilnius 232600; tel. 624 935.

LITHUANIAN CHRISTIAN DEMOCRATIC PARTY. F. 1904, ref. 1989; 4,000 mems; 45 divisions; publ. *Apžvalga.* Chair. Egidijus Klumbys. *Add.* Aukštaičiu̇ 6, Kaunas 233000; tel. 741 621.

LITHUANIAN CHRISTIAN DEMOCRATIC UNION. F. 1904, ref. 1989; 300 mems; 7 divisions; publ. newspaper *Nepriklausoma Lietuva,* magazine *Lietuvos sargas;* Mem., Christian Dem. Union Int. Chair. Viktoras Petkus. *Add.* Pylimo 35 – 8, Vilnius 232001; tel. and fax 624 008.

LITHUANIAN DEMOCRATIC LABOUR PARTY. F. 1990; 18,000 mems; 57 divisions; publ. *Tiesa.* Chair. Algirdas Mykolas Brazauskas. *Add.* Radvilaitės 1, Vilnius 232000; tel. 612 625.

LITHUANIAN DEMOCRATIC PARTY. F. 1902; ref. 1989; 1,300 mems; 30 divisions; publ. *Vasario 16-oji, Tribūna.* Chair. Saulius Pečeliūnas. *Add.* Gedimino pr. 34 – 9, Vilnius 232001; tel. 626 033.

LITHUANIAN GREEN PARTY. F. 1989; 300 mems; 20 divisions; publ. *Pusiausvyra.* Heads

Irena Ignatavičienė, Romualdas Juknys, Zigmas Vaišvila. *Add.* Radvilaitės 1, Vilnius 232600; tel. 611 764.

LITHUANIAN HUMANISM PARTY. F. 1989; 1,000 mems; 12 divisions. Chair. Vytautas Kazlauskas. *Add.* Mykolaičio-Putino 5, Vilnius 232009; tel. 619 164.

LITHUANIAN LIBERAL UNION. F. 1990; 500 mems; 10 divisions. Chair. Vytautas Radžvilas. *Add.* Maironio 6, Vilnius 232600; tel. 629 468.

LITHUANIAN SOCIAL DEMOCRATIC PARTY. F. 1896, ref. 1989; 1,000 mems; 31 division; publ. *Lietuvos žinios;* Mem. of Socialist International. Chair. Aloyzas Sakalas. *Add.* Basanavičiaus 16/5, Vilnius 232009; tel. 652 311; fax 652 157.

NEPRIKLAUSOMYBĖS PARTIJA (Independence Party). F. 1990; 1,000 mems; 5 divisions; publ. *Kovo 11.* Chair. Virgilijus Čepaitis. *Add.* Vilniaus 39, Vilnius 232600; tel. 221 529.

POLITICAL ORGANIZATIONS

LIETUVOS LAISVĖS LYGA (Lith. Liberty League). F. 1981, legal status since 1988; strongly advocates secession of Lithuania from the USSR; publ. *Laisvės šauklys.* Leader Antanas Terleckas. *Add.* Nemenčinės pl. 68, Vilnius 232016; tel. 764 841.

LITHUANIAN EXILES UNION. F. 1989; ~ 120,000 mems; 54 branches; unites the Lith. citizens, deported by the Soviet power to the USSR, and their family mems; publ. a newspaper *Tremtinys;* Pres. of the Union Balys Gajauskas, Chair. of the Council Antanas Lukša. *Add.* Donelaičio 70b, Kaunas 233000; tel. 206 735.

LITHUANIAN HELSINKI GROUP. F. 1976; 26 mems; movement for human rights. *Add.* Pylimo 35 – 8, Vilnius 232001; tel. and fax 624 008.

LITHUANIAN POLITICAL PRISONERS UNION. F. 1990; 12 branches; unites citizens of Lithuania, who were persecuted by the Soviet power for their pol. views; directing body is Presidium. *Add.* Šermukšniu̇ 3, Vilnius 232000; tel. 614 675.

SĄJŪDIS (Lithuanian Reform Movement). F. 1988; divisions in all regions and cities; advocates secession from the USSR. Chair. Juozas Tumelis. *Add.* Gedimino pr. 1, Vilnius 232001; tel. 224 881; telex 261111 SIA SU; fax 224 890.

YEDINSTWO (Unity). F. 1988; a movement for socialism, which advocates remaining of Lithuania within the USSR, membering mostly not Lith. speaking people.

VOLUNTARY ORGANIZATIONS

ASSOCIATION OF LITHUANIAN AUTOMOBILISTS. F. 1974; 74,000 mems; 42 clubs; organizes conferences, sport comp., int. motor tourism; there are sch. for training amateur car drivers; publ. *Rieduva.* Chair. Marius Pagirys. *Add.* Lvovo 9, Vilnius 232005; tel. 351 273; fax 358 919.

BISHOP M.VALANČIUS SOMBRIETY MOVEMENT. F. 1988; 44 town and district councils; 2,500 mems; publ. newspaper *Blaivioji Lietuva.*

Chair. Juozas Končys. *Add.* POB 2007, Vilnius 232012; tel. 757 359.

CHILDREN FUND OF LITHUANIA. F. 1988. Supports poor children materially, helps seriously ill children, grants stipends to gifted children. Chair. Juozas Nekrošius. *Add.* Žygimantų 12, Vilnius 232600; tel. 627 180.

ETHOS, soc. for ethical culture. F. 1989; 6 branches; 800 mems; publ. magazine *Dora.* Chair. Vincentas Žemaitis. *Add.* Sėlių 1/46, Vilnius 232600; tel. 755 912.

LITHUANIAN ABSTINENT SOCIETY. F. 1988; 43 branches; 25,000 mems; publ. newspaper *Blaivybė aušra.* Chair. Algirdas Mikalkevičius. *Add.* Vrublevskio 6, Vilnius 232600; tel. 629 958.

LITHUANIAN CONFEDERATION OF FREE TRADE UNIONS. F. 1990; 1,100,100 mems; 20 affiliated mems; publ. newspaper *Pozicija,* magazine *Darbas ir poilsis;* Chair. Marijonas Visakavičius. *Add.* Gynėjų 3, Vilnius 232710; tel. 615 260; fax 226 106.

LITHUANIAN CONSUMERS ASSOCIATION. F. 1989; 14 divisions; defends interests of consumers, informs and consults them; mem., Int. Warsaw Consumers Assoc. Pres. Algirdas Kvedaravičius. *Add.* Gedimino pr. 3, Vilnius 232600; tel. 616 134; telex 261141 LMA SU; fax 618 464.

LITHUANIAN CULTURE FUND. F. 1989; 48 assoc. and communities. Accumulates means for reconstr. and restoration of monuments, for perpetuation the memory of notable people. Publ. *Santara.* Chair. Jurgis Dvarionas. *Add.* Vienuolio 5/32, Vilnius 232600; tel. 617 634; fax 226 036.

LITHUANIAN DOG-FANCIERS UNION. F. 1988; 46 branches; 5,000 mems. Pres. Vytautas Klovas. *Add.* Rudens 33b, Vilnius 232040; tel. 696 735.

LITHUANIAN ESPERANTISTS UNION. F. 1919, ref. 1979; 300 mems; publ. *Litova stelo.* Chair. Laurynas Algimantas Skūpas. *Add.* Donelaičio 6, Kaunas 233000; tel. 208 503.

LITHUANIAN FARMERS' UNION. F. 1990; 44 branches; 4,500 mems. Chair. Jonas Čiulevičius. *Add.* Noreikiškės, Kauno rj. 234324; tel. 296 842.

LITHUANIAN FOLK ART ASSOCIATION. F. 1966; 2,500 mems; 6 divisions and sections in regional centres. Organizes exh. of folk art, conferences, creative campings; exh. and sales abroad. Chair. Žilvinas Bautrėnas. *Add.* Vytenio 13, Vilnius 232009; tel. 662 974.

LITHUANIAN GREEN MOVEMENT. F. 1988; 3,000 mems; in towns and districts there are clubs or groups; publ. the newspaper *Žalioji Lietuva;* it is directed by Co-ordination Council. *Add.* Kalvarijų 130 – 48, Vilnius 232048; tel. 765 609; fax 766 737.

LITHUANIAN INVALIDS SOCIETY. F. 1988; 200,000 mems. Chair. Jonas Mačiukevičius. *Add.* Jogailos 9/1, Vilnius 232001; tel. 226 727.

LITHUANIAN MANUFACTURERS ASSOCIATION. F. 1989; unites over 400 firms; 7 branches. Pres. Algimantas Matulevičius. *Add.* Trakų 9/1, Vilnius 232001; tel. 221 323.

LITHUANIAN BUSINESSMEN ASSOCIATION. F. 1989; 200 mems; represents interests of joint venture companies, private ent. and econ. assoc. Pres. Arvydas Barauskas. *Add.* Pylimo 4, Vilnius 232001; tel. 614 963.

LITHUANIAN PUBLISHERS ASSOCIATION. F. 1989; represents interests of book publrs. Pres. Juozas Vaitkus. *Add.* Algirdo 31, Vilnius 232600; tel. 660 665.

LITHUANIAN RED CROSS SOCIETY. F. 1940; 1,600,000 mems; 55 divisions; publ. *Bičiulystė.* Chair. Juozas Šapoka. *Add.* Gedimino pr. 3a, Vilnius 232600; tel. 619 923.

LITHUANIAN SOCIETY OF INVENTORS AND INNOVATORS. F. 1989; 5 councils; 100,000 mems; has 21 innovation firms. Chair. Kazys Baltrūnas. *Add.* Smetonos 11/2, Vilnius 232600; tel. 615 314.

ŽINIJA (Knowledge), lecturers soc. F. 1940; 55 district and city org.; 15,000 mems. Chair. Juras Požela. *Add.* Vilniaus 22, Vilnius 232698; tel. 618 337.

LITHUANIAN SOCIETY FOR STUDY OF LOCAL LORE. F. 1926, ref. 1961; 37,800 mems; 50 divisions; organizes comprehensive and local expeditions, exh., comp.; publ. *Kraštotyra.* Chair. Irena Seliukaitė. *Add.* Trakų 2, Vilnius 232001; tel. 622 476.

LITHUANIAN SOCIETY OF HUNTERS AND ANGLERS. F. 1920; ref. 1947; 89,000 mems; 45 divisions; rents hunting and fishing grounds. Chair. Jonas Vyšniauskas. *Add.* Stiklių 6/8, Vilnius 232024; tel. 626 735.

LITHUANIAN SOCIETY OF PHILATELISTS. F. 1967; 2,500 mems; 40 divisions; publ. *Lietuvos filatelistas.* Chair. Petras Rutkauskas. *Add.* Valančiaus 3, Vilnius 232009; tel. 650 149.

LITHUANIAN SOCIETY OF THE DEAF. F. 1944; 3,500 mems; 86 divisions; publ. newspaper *Akiratis.* Chair. Algirdas Jakaitis. *Add.* Šv. Kazimiero 3, Vilnius 232600; tel. 628 115.

LITHUANIAN UNION OF THE BLIND. F. 1944; 6,500 mems; 43 divisions; publ. *Mūsų žodis* (in Braille alphabet and in usual print). Chair. Juozas Dzidolikas. *Add.* Labdarių 7/11, Vilnius 232001; tel. 619 691.

LITHUANIAN WORKERS' UNION. F. 1988; 100,000 mems; 37 branches; publ. newspaper *Lietuvos darbininkas.* Chair. Aldona Balsienė. *Add.* Mykolaičio-Putino 5, Vilnius 232600; tel. 621 743; fax 625 092.

POLISH UNION. F. 1988; 16,000 mems; 7 depts; publ. *Magazyn Wilenski, Nasza gazeta.* Chair. Jan Sienkiewicz. *Add.* Didžioji 40, Vilnius 232601; tel. 223 388.

TĖVIŠKĖ (Motherland), Lith. soc. for relations with Lith. abroad. F. 1964; publ. *Gimtasis kraštas.* Chair. Vaclovas Sakalauskas. *Add.* Tilto skg. 8/2, Vilnius 232600; tel. 613 580; fax 624 092.

VOLUNTARY SOCIETIES

ALMA LATINA, Lith.-Latin American soc. F. 1989; 60 mems. Chair. Pranas Juozas Žilinskas. *Add.* Žirgo 1 – 1, Vilnius 232040; tel. 769 457.

LITHUANIAN-AMERICAN SOCIETY. F. 1938, ref. 1989; 200 mems. Chair. Edmundas Juškys. *Add.* Tumo-Vaižganto 9/1, Vilnius 232001; tel. 224 035.

LITHUANIAN-BRITISH SOCIETY. F. 1990; 70 mems. Chair. Algis Geniušas. *Add.* Universiteto 3, Vilnius 232734; tel. 618 784.

LITHUANIAN-DANISH SOCIETY. F. 1990; 100 mems. Chair. Albertas Steponavičius. *Add.* Birutės 56, Vilnius 232004.

LITHUANIAN-FINNISH SOCIETY. F. 1927; ref. 1990; 200 mems. Chair. Stasys Skrodenis. *Add.* Ukmergės 200 – 91, Vilnius 232010; tel. 469 522.

LITHUANIAN-FRENCH SOCIETY. F. 1989; 600 mems. Pres. Rolandas Pavilionis. *Add.* Universiteto 3, Vilnius 232734; tel. 623 779.

LITHUANIAN-GERMAN SOCIETY. F. 1989; 100 mems. Chair. Jonas Grigonis. *Add.* Universiteto 3, Vilnius 232734; tel. 611 687.

LITHUANIA – IBEROAMERICA, Lith.- Span. and Span. speaking c. soc. F. 1989; 50 mems. Chair. Romualdas Grigaliūnas. *Add.* Žuvinto 15 – 26, Kaunas 233031.

LITHUANIA – ISRAEL, soc. F. 1989; 300 mems. Chair. Česlovas Kudaba. *Add.* Blindžių 33 – 10, Vilnius 232004; tel. 382 624. Representative in Israel G.Alpern; tel. 5322 283.

LITHUANIAN-ITALIAN SOCIETY. F. 1989; 60 mems. Chair. Bronislovas Kuzmickas. *Add.* Basanavičiaus 18 – 57, Vilnius 232009; tel. 652 116.

LITHUANIAN-NORWEGIAN SOCIETY. F. 1990; 100 mems. Chair. Raimondas Rajeckas. *Add.* Universiteto 3, Vilnius 232734; tel. 626 701.

LITHUANIAN-SWEDISH SOCIETY. F. 1925, ref. 1989; 120 mems. Chair. Juozas Vidmantis Vaitkus. *Add.* Universiteto 3, Vilnius 232734; tel. 613 140.

LITHUANIAN-SWISS SOCIETY. F. 1932, ref. 1989; 150 mems. Chair. Marcelijus Martinaitis. *Add.* Universiteto 3, Vilnius 232734; tel. 611 076.

LIBRARIES

CENTRAL LIBRARY OF THE LITHUANIAN ACADEMY OF SCIENCES. F. 1941; 3,500,000 library u. (200,000 vols from the 11th – 16th cent.); exchanges printed matters with 730 foreign libraries and scientific inst. Dir Juozas Marcinkevičius. *Add.* Žygimantų 2/8, Vilnius 232632; tel. 629 537.

KAUNAS PUBLIC LIBRARY. F. 1950; 2,400,000 library u. (55,000 rare printings); exchanges printed matters with foreign libraries, scientific inst. Dir Alvydas Samėnas. *Add.* Radastų 14, Kaunas 233681; tel. 226 142; telex 269865 BIBLIOTEKA SU; fax 202 995 BIBLIOTEKA.

LITHUANIAN NATIONAL M.MAŽVYDAS LIBRARY. F. 1919; the biggest library of gen. type in Lithuania; 5,000,000 library u. (over 30,000 books from the 15th – 18th cent. and rare publ. from the 19th – 20th cent.); exchanges printed matters with 240 foreign libraries and org. Dir Vladas Bulavas. *Add.* Gedimino pr. 51, Vilnius 232635; tel. 629 023.

VILNIUS UNIVERSITY LIBRARY. F. 1570; the oldest library of gen. type in Europe; serves as a depository of UNO; 4,600,000 library u. (182,629 books from the 16th – 18th cent.); exchanges printed matters with 461 foreign libraries and scientific inst. Dir Birutė Butkevičienė. *Add.* Universiteto 3, Vilnius 232633; tel. 610 616.

CREATIVE UNIONS

LITHUANIAN ARCHITECTS' UNION. F. 1944; 970 mems; branches in Kaunas, Klaipėda, Šiauliai, Panevėžys. Chair. Juozas Vaškevičius. *Add.* Kalvarijų 1, Vilnius 232005; tel. 756 483.

NATIONAL ASSOCIATION OF LITHUANIAN PHOTOGRAPHERS. F. 1969; 230 mems. Chair. Laima Skeivienė. *Add.* Universiteto 4, Vilnius 232600; tel. 611 665.

LITHUANIAN ARTISTS' UNION. F. 1935; 960 mems; divisions in Kaunas, Klaipėda, Šiauliai, Panevėžys. Chair. Bronius Leonavičius. *Add.* Kosciuškos 28, Vilnius 232600; tel. 622 935.

LITHUANIAN CINEMATOGRAPHERS' UNION. F. 1958; 160 mems. Chair. Skirmantas Valiulis. *Add.* Kalvarijų 1, Vilnius 232005; tel. 731 204.

LITHUANIAN COMPOSERS' UNION. F. 1941; 130 mems; branches in Kaunas, Klaipėda; publ. *Gaida*, agency *LITUS*. Chair. Julius Andrejevas. *Add.* Mickevičiaus 29, Vilnius 232600; tel. 752 232.

LITHUANIAN DESIGNERS' UNION. F. 1990; 170 mems. Chair. Antanas Bielskis. *Add.* Juozapavičiaus 11, Vilnius 232600; tel. 351 916.

LITHUANIAN JOURNALISTS' UNION. F. 1957; 1,500 mems; publ. newspapers *Žurnalistų žinios*, *Ekspresas*. Chair. Rimgaudas Eilunavičius. *Add.* Vilniaus 35, Vilnius 232600; tel. 611 790.

LITHUANIAN SCIENTISTS' UNION. F. 1990; 1,100 mems; publ. newspaper *Mokslo Lietuva* and periodical for Engl. learners 'Step by Step'. Chair. Bronislovas Kuzmickas. *Add.* Gedimino pr. 14, Vilnius 232009; tel. 618 713.

LITHUANIAN THEATRE UNION. F. 1987; 1,000 mems; publ. magazine *Teatras*. Chair. Juozas Budraitis. *Add.* Gedimino pr. 1, Vilnius 232001; tel. 623 586.

LITHUANIAN WRITERS' UNION. F. 1940; 260 mems; division in Kaunas; publ. newspaper *Literatūra ir menas*, magazines *Metai*, *Nemunas*, *Vilnius* (Russ.). Chair. Vytautas Martinkus. *Add.* Rašytojų 6, Vilnius 232600; tel. 223 919.

CHURCHES & RELIGIOUS ORGANIZATIONS

ROMAN CATHOLIC CHURCH

CURIA OF DIOCESE OF KAIŠIADORYS. Apostolic Administrator Bishop Juozapas Matulaitis. *Add.* Gedimino 67, Kaišiadorys 234230; tel. 522 08.

CURIA OF ARCHDIOCESE OF KAUNAS. Roman Catholic Church Cardinal Archbishop of Kaunas Vincentas Sladkevičius. *Add.* Valančiaus 6, Kaunas 233000; tel. 222 197.

CURIA OF DIOCESE OF PANEVĖŽYS. Apostolic Administrator Bishop Juozas Preikšas. *Add.* Žemgulio 45, Panevėžys 235300; tel. 351 56.

CURIA OF DIOCESE OF TELŠIAI. Bishop of Telšiai Antanas Vaičius. *Add.* Spaudos 4, Telšiai 235610; tel. 511 67.

CURIA OF DIOCESE OF VILKAVIŠKIS. Apostolic Administrator Bishop Juozas Žemaitis. *Add.* Armino 6, Marijampolė 234520; tel. 566 75.

CURIA OF ARCHDIOCESE OF VILNIUS. Archbishop of Vilnius Julijonas Steponavičius. *Add.* Šv. Mikalojaus 4, Vilnius 232001; tel. 627 098.

KAUNAS INTERDIOCESAN PRIESTS SEMINARY. F. 1865; ~200 students. Trains Catholic priests. Rector Sigitas Tamkevičius SJ. *Add.* Traku 1, Kaunas 233000; tel. 221 428.

CARITAS, Lith. Catholic women's assoc. F. 1989; main task — restoration of a family, educ. of a man and social help for the poor, single people; publ. *Caritas.* Chair. Albina Pajarskaitė. *Add.* Vilniaus 29, Kaunas 233000; tel. 205 427.

OTHER CHURCHES

VILNIUS AND LITHUANIAN EPARCHY OF THE RUSSIAN ORTHODOX CHURCH. Archbishop Chrizostom (Martishkin). *Add.* Aušros vartu 2, Vilnius 232024; tel. 625 896.

LITHUANIAN OLD BELIEVERS POMOR CHURCH. Chair. of the Cent. Council Ivan Yegorov. *Add.* Naujininku 24, Vilnius 232030; tel. 752 068.

CONSISTORY OF THE LITHUANIAN EVANGELICAL LUTHERAN CHURCH. Bishop Jonas Kalvanas. *Add.* Laisvės 68, Tauragė 235900; tel. 523 45.

CONSISTORY OF THE LITHUANIAN EVANGELICAL REFORMED CHURCH. Chair. Reinholdas Moras. *Add.* Basanavičiaus 17, Biržai 235280; tel. 520 61.

DAILY NEWSPAPERS

ECHO LITVY (Echo of Lithuania). F. 1940; 5 a week; circ. 55,000; in Russ.; public pol.; publ. by the SC and CM. Ed.Vasilii Yemelyanov. *Add.* Laisvės pr. 60, Vilnius 232019; tel. 428 463.

KURIER WILENSKI (Vilnius Express). F. 1953; 5 a week; circ. 31,170; in Pol., public pol.; publ. by the SC and CM. Ed. Zbigniew Balcewicz. *Add.* Laisvės pr. 60, Vilnius 232019; tel. 427 901.

LIETUVOS AIDAS (Echo of Lithuania). F. 1917, ref. 1990; 5 a week; circ. 110,000; in Lith.; publ. by the Lith. State. E-in-C Saulius Stoma. *Add.* Gynėju 3, Vilnius 232710; tel. 615 208; fax 224 876.

LIETUVOS RYTAS (Lithuania's Morning). F. 1990; 5 a week; circ. 235,000; (weekly in Russ.); supplement for youth *Mes.* Ed. Gedvydas Varnauskas. *Add.* Gedimino pr. 12a, Vilnius 232001; tel. 622 680.

RESPUBLIKA (Republic). F. 1989; 5 a week; circ. 230,000; in Lith. (on Sat also in Russ.); indep.; E-in-C Vitas Tomkus. *Add.* Šventaragio 4, Vilnius 232600; tel. 223 112; fax 223 538.

TIESA (Truth). F. 1917; 5 a week; circ. 101,000; in Lith.; public pol.; publ. by the Lith. DLP. Ed.

Domas Šniukas. *Add.* Laisvės pr. 60, Vilnius 232019; tel. 429 788.

PERIODICALS

AITVARAS (Brownie). F. 1989; 2 a week; circ. 204,860; in Lith.; newspaper for children. Ed. Laima Drazdauskaitė. *Add.* Laisvės pr. 60, Vilnius 232019; tel. 429 462.

ATGIMIMAS (Rebirth). F. 1988; weekly; circ. 22,000; in Lith.; Dep. E-in-C Saulius Arvasevičius. *Add.* Žygimantu 26, Vilnius 232600; tel. 224 406; fax 224 531.

BIČIULYSTĖ (Friendship). F. 1990; weekly; circ. 15,000; in Lith.; newspaper for family. Ed. Robertas Grikevičius. *Add.* Gedimino pr. 14, Vilnius 232008; tel. 628 943.

DARBAS IR POILSIS (Work and Rest). F. 1969; monthly; circ. 24,900; in Lith.; magazine; publ. by the Lith. TU. E-in-C Juozas Šiupšinskas. *Add.* Klaipėdos 2/14, Vilnius 232600; tel. 625 624.

DIENOVIDIS (Midday). F. 1990; weekly; circ. 13,100; in Lith.; lit. and phil. Ed. Aldona Žemaitytė. *Add.* Pilies 23a, Vilnius 232001; tel. 221 911.

GENYS (Woodpecker). F. 1940; monthly; circ. 96,500; in Lith.; ill., for 5 — 10-year-olds. E-in-C Vytautas Račickas. *Add.* Pilies skg. 8, Vilnius 232600; tel. 616 334.

GIMTASIS KRAŠTAS (Native Land). F. 1967; weekly; circ. 102,400; in Lith.; publ. by the soc. for cultural relations with Lith. living abroad *Tėviškė.* E-in-C Algimantas Čekuolis. *Add.* Tilto skg. 8/2, Vilnius 232600; tel. 623 881; fax 222 727.

GIMTINĖ (Native Land). F. 1989; monthly; circ. 5,000; in Lith.; local lore newspaper. Ed. Kazimieras Račkauskas. *Add.* Bokšto 11, Vilnius 232024; tel. 226 136.

GIMTOJI KALBA (Native Language). F. 1933; monthly; circ. 8,000; in Lith.; publ. by the Soc. of the Lith. Lg. Ed. Aldonas Pupkis. *Add.* Žygimantu 12, Vilnius 232000; tel. 629 629.

JAUNIMO GRETOS (Ranks of Youth). F. 1944; monthly; circ. 110,000; ill., for youth; in Lith. E-in-C Kazys Žilėnas. *Add.* Bernardinu 8, Vilnius 232600; tel. 624 818.

KALBA VILNIUS (Vilnius Calling). F. 1956; weekly; circ. 105,500; in Lith.; TV and Radio programmes. E-in-C Algirdas Kratulis. *Add.* Konarskio 49, Vilnius 232674; tel. 661 022.

KATALIKŲ PASAULIS (Catholic World). F. 1989; fortnightly; circ. 39,600; in Lith.; publ. by the Publishing House of the Episcopalian Conference of the Lith. Catholic Church. E-in-C Vaclovas Aliulis. *Add.* Pylimo 27, Vilnius 232001; tel. 222 422.

KRANTAI (Banks). F. 1989; monthly; circ. 4,800; in Lith.; journal of Lith. Artists', Composers' and Theatre Unions. E-in-C Vaidotas Daunys. *Add.* POB 511, Vilnius 232000; tel. 617 585.

KULTŪROS BARAI (Domains of Culture). F. 1965; monthly; circ. 7,300; in Lith.; journal of the Min. of Culture and Educ. E-in-C Vilhelmas Chadzevičius. *Add.* Daukanto a. 3/8, Vilnius 232600; tel. 610 538.

LIETUVOS ŪKININKO PATARĖJAS (Lithuanian Farmers' Adviser). F. 1989; weekly; circ. 30,000; in Lith.; publ. by the Lith. Farmers' Union; supplements *Šeimininkė* (Housewife), *Jaunasis ūkininkas* (The Young Farmer). E-in-C Vytenis Neverdauskas. *Add.* Kęstučio 19, Kaunas 233000; tel. 223 452.

LIETUVOS ŪKIS (Lithuania's Economy). F. 1921; fortnightly; circ. 4,500; in Lith. (4 a year in Russ. and Engl.); econ. thought's magazine. E-in-C Liubomiras Viktoras Žeimantas. *Add.* Algirdo 31, Vilnius 232600; tel. 662 279.

LITERATŪRA IR MENAS (Literature and Art). F. 1946; weekly; circ. 19,200; in Lith.; publ. by the Lith. Writers' Union. E-in-C Vytautas Rubavičius. *Add.* Universiteto 4, Vilnius 232600; tel. 612 586.

MAGAZYN WILENSKY (Vilnius Journal). F. 1990; fortnightly; circ. 6,900; in Pol. E-in-C Michal Mackiewicz. *Add.* Didžioji 40, Vilnius 232601; tel. 223 388.

MAŽOJI LIETUVA (Lithuania Minor). F. 1932; weekly; circ. 23,600; in Lith.; newspaper of Klaipėda Land. Ed. Kęstutis Oginskas. *Add.* Manto 2, Klaipėda 235800; tel. 180 74.

METAI (Year). F. 1991; monthly; circ. 11,700; in Lith.; journal of Lith. Writers' Union. E-in-C Juozas Aputis. *Add.* Gedimino pr. 37, Vilnius 232600; tel. 617 344.

MOTERIS (Woman). F. 1952; monthly; circ. 350,000; in Lith.; ill. E-in-C Regina Paulauskienė. *Add.* Maironio 1, Vilnius 232600; tel. 610 169.

MŪSŲ GAMTA (Our Nature). F.1964; monthly; circ. 23,000; in Lith.; popular sci., nature preservation. E-in-C Rimantas Budrys. *Add.* Rudens 33b, Vilnius 232040; tel. 696 964.

MŪSŲ SODAI (Our Gardens). F. 1959; monthly; circ. 53,800; in Lith. Ed. Pranas Keibas. *Add.* Kalvarijų 62, Vilnius 232005; tel. 752 351.

NAUJASIS ŽIDINYS (New Hearth). F. 1991; monthly; circ. 10,000; in Lith.; religious and cultural magazine. E-in-C Petras Kimbrys. *Add.* Pylimo 27/14, Vilnius 232001; tel. 222 422; fax 222 122.

NEMUNAS. F. 1967; monthly; circ. 40,000; in Lith.; magazine of Lith. Writers' Union; popular, for youth. E-in-C Laimonas Inis. *Add.* Gedimino 45, Kaunas 233000; tel. 223 066.

PASAULIS (World). F. 1945; fortnightly; circ. 7,000; in Lith. and Russ.; public pol. E-in-C Romanas Miliauskas. *Add.* Bernardinų 8, Vilnius 232600; tel. 613 113.

PHEROMONES. F. 1990; 4 a yr; circ. 3,000; in Engl.; scientific; publ by the Lith. Acad. of Sci. Ed. Algirdas Skirkevičius. *Add.* Akademijos 2, Vilnius 232600; tel. 359 274.

POLITIKA (Politics). F. 1990; 3 a month; circ. 40,000; in Lith.; public pol. magazine. E-in-C Algimantas Semaška. *Add.* Maironio 1, Vilnius 232656; tel. 610 414.

POZICIJA (Point of View). F. 1990; weekly; circ. 16,500; in Lith.; publ. by the Lith. Assoc. of Human Rights Protection and Lith. TU. Ed. Vytautas Budnikas. *Add.* Mykolaičio-Putino 5, Vilnius 232600; tel. 637 843.

SOGLASIYE (Concord). F. 1988; weekly; circ. 10,000; in Russ. Ed. Liubov Thernaya. *Add.* Žygimantų 26, Vilnius 232600; tel. 224 415; fax 224 531.

SPORTAS (Sports). F. 1956; 3 a week; circ. 27,500; in Lith. E-in-C Aleksandras Krukauskas. *Add.* Gedimino pr. 37, Vilnius 232600; tel. 616 757.

ŠIAURĖS ATĖNAI (Northern Athens). F. 1989; weekly; circ. 20,200; in Lith. Ed. Saulius Šaltenis. *Add.* Strazdelio 1, Vilnius 232600; tel. 613 662; fax 613 891.

ŠLUOTA (Broom). F. 1934; fortnightly; circ. 70,000; in Lith.; satirical magazine. E-in-C Rytis Tilvytis. *Add.* Bernardinų 8/8, Vilnius 232722; tel. 613 171.

ŠVYTURYS (Beacon). F. 1949; fortnightly; circ. 109,800; in Lith.; pol., fiction. E-in-C Juozas Baušys. *Add.* Maironio 1, Vilnius 232600; tel. 627 488.

TĖVYNĖS ŠVIESA (Light of the Homeland). F. 1953; weekly; circ. 11,700; in Lith.; newspaper for teachers; publ. by the Min. of Culture and Educ. Ed. Juozas Subačius. *Add.* Antakalnio 31, Vilnius 232055; tel. 748 943.

TREMTINYS (Exile). F. 1988; fortnightly; circ. 15,000; in Lith.; publ. by the Lith. Union of Exiles. Ed. Vanda Poderytė. *Add.* Donelaičio 70b, Kaunas 233000; tel. 209 530.

TRIMITAS (Trumpet). F. 1920; fortnightly; circ. 4,000; in Lith.; publ. by the Lith. Union of Šauliai (Riflemen). Ed. Gediminas Jankus. *Add.* Laisvės al. 34, Kaunas 233000; tel. 228 432.

XXI AMŽIUS (21st Century). F. 1990; weekly; circ. 12,500; in Lith.; newspaper of Lith. Catholics, publ. by Ed. Bd. *Add.* Vilniaus 29, Kaunas 233000; tel. 209 683.

VALSTIEČIŲ LAIKRAŠTIS (Peasants' Newspaper). F. 1940; 3 a week; circ. 209,400; in Lith. Ed. Vladas Būtėnas. *Add.* Laisvės pr. 60, Vilnius 232019; tel. 429 942.

VILNIAUS LAIKRAŠTIS (Vilnius Newspaper). F. 1990; weekly; circ. 15,500; in Lith. E-in-C Linas Medelis. *Add.* Apkasų 23 − 59, Vilnius 232042; tel. 691 513.

ZNAD WILII (From Vilia). F. 1989; fortnightly; circ. 5,100; in Pol.; publ. by Czesław Okińczyc and Romuald Mieczkowski. *Add.* POB 1755, Vilnius 232019; tel. 650 463, 425 165.

ŽALIOJI LIETUVA (Green Lithuania). F. 1989; weekly; circ. 10,000; in Lith.; publ. by the Lith. Green Movement. Ed. Daina Karlonaitė. *Add.* Jakšto 9 − 127, Vilnius 232600; tel. 627 458.

Add. and circ. are given up to the events on January, 1991

PUBLISHERS

KATALIKŲ PASAULIS (Catholic World), publrs. F. 1990; publ. religious lit., periodicals. Dir Vaclovas Aliulis. *Add.* Pylimo 27, Vilnius 232001; tel. 222 422.

MINTIS (Idea), publrs. F. 1940; phil., hist., econ., reference books, vols of nat. retrospective bibliography, entertainment lit., art books, books on culture, pol., law, public thought of the

past. Dir Zigmas Maliukevičius; E-in-C Kęstutis Trečiakauskas. *Add*. Sierakausko 15, Vilnius 232600; tel. 632 943.
MOKSLAS (Science), publrs. F. 1975; natural and tech. sci., agric., med., hist., linguistics. Dir Zigmantas Pocius; E-in-C Vaidotas Januškis. *Add*. Žvaigždžių 23, Vilnius 232050; tel. 458 525.
ŠVIESA (Light), publrs. F. 1945; textbooks and pedag. lit. Dir Jonas Barcys; E-in-C Stanislovas Petrauskas. *Add*. Vytauto pr. 25, Kaunas 233000; tel. 741 634.
VAGA (Furrow), publrs. F. 1945; fiction, art criticism, theatre sci., art albums. Dir Algirdas Pekeliūnas; E-in-C Aleksandras Krasnovas. *Add*. Gedimino pr. 50, Vilnius 232600; tel. 626 443.
VALSTYBINĖ ENCIKLOPEDIJŲ LEIDYKLA (State Encyclopaedia Publrs). F. 1957; encyclo-

paedias, reference books. Dir-Gen. Mykolas Mikalajūnas. *Add*. Algirdo 31, Vilnius 232600; tel. 660 349.
VYTURYS (Lark), publrs. F. 1985; fiction, popular and toy books for children and youth, postcards; prod. mailed abroad. Dir Juozas Vaitkus; E-in-C Liudas Pilius. *Add*. Algirdo 31, Vilnius 232600; tel. 660 665; fax 263 449.

RADIO AND TV

LITHUANIAN RADIO AND TELEVISION. Dir-Gen. Skirmantas Valiulis. *Add*. Konarskio 49, Vilnius 232674; tel. 660 637.
RADIO VILNIUS. F. 1926; broadcasts in Lith., Russ., Pol. and Engl.
TV VILNIUS. F. 1957; broadcasts in Lith., Russ., Pol.

WHO'S WHO

• **ABIŠALA, Aleksandras Algirdas**, Min. of the Lith. Rep., 1991 — ; b. 1955; grad. Vilnius Univ., phys.; CSc. (Phys.&Math.); at Kaunas Radio Measuring Eng. Scientific Research Inst., 1981 — 90; was born in Russia in a family of pol. prisoners; Lith. SC Deputy. *Add*. Tumo-Vaižganto 2, Vilnius 232039; tel. 622 415.
• **ABUKEVIČIUS, Petras**, film dir, cameraman; b. 1928; grad. Moscow Inst. of Cinematography; Lith. Film Studio, 1957 — ; documentaries, popular sci. films to his scenarios on nature themes; silver medal for the film 'Black Storks, a Young Deer and Nida' (New York, 1980). *Add*. (h) Taikos 110 — 4, Vilnius 232017; tel. 462 568.
• **ADOMAITIS, Regimantas**, theatre and film actor; b. 1937; grad. Vilnius Univ. and Lith. Conservatoire; works at Vilnius Drama Theatre; acting notable for intellectuality, subtlety and irony; has worked with film studios of Lithuania, Italy, Hungary, Czecho-Slovakia, Bulgaria, Germany and USSR. *Add*. (h) Blindžių 31 — 1, Vilnius 232001; tel. 731 371.
• **ADOMONIS, Juozas**, ceramist; b. 1932; grad. Vilnius Art Acad.; teaches at it, 1962 — ; Prof.; author of decorative and household ceramics and books on applied decorative art. *Add*. (h) Krivių 41 — 28, Vilnius 232007; tel. 696 410.
• **ALBRECHTAS, Gytis**, Dir, Klaipėda Cardboard Plant, 1986 — ; b. 1940; grad. Vilnius Univ., eng.; Pres., Klaipėda Chamber of Commerce, 1990 — . *Add*. (h) Alksnynės 4a — 20, Klaipėda 235819; tel. 382 54.
• **ALEKSA, Jonas**, conductor; b. 1939; grad. Lith. Conservatoire; postgrad. Leningrad Conservatoire under E.Mravinsky; worked on probation in Vienna under H. Svarovsky; Doc.; lecturer, Lith. Conservatoire, 1965 — ; Chief Conductor, Lith. Opera and Ballet Theatre, 1975 — ; Chief Conductor of Lith. Song Festivals. *Add*. (h) Vilniaus 9/2 — 22, Vilnius 232000; tel. 611 192.
• **ALIULIS, Vaclovas**, E-in-C, magazine *Katalikų pasaulis*, 1989 — ; b. 1921; grad. Kaunas

Priest Sem.; ordained in 1944; Marian; licentiate of theol.; Chair., Liturgical Cttee of Lith. Bishops, 1979 — 90; Dir, publrs *Katalikų pasaulis*; ed. of transl. of the Holy Bible and Catholic lit. into Lith. *Add*. (h) Pavasario 36 — 1, Vilnius 232055; tel. 745 909.
• **AMBRAZAITYTĖ, Nijolė**, singer (mezzo-soprano); b. 1939; grad. Lith. Conservatoire; lectures at it, 1979 — ; Doc.; soloist, Lith. Opera and Ballet Theatre, 1966 — ; has toured W-European theatres, Chile, Cuba, Peru, Norway; part. in Enesku singing comp. in Bucharest (2nd prize, 1970); 1948 — 57 was deported with parents to Siberia; Lith. SC Deputy. *Add*. (h) Vienuolio 14 — 26, Vilnius 232001; tel. 620 741.
• **AMBRAZAS, Algirdas**, musicologist; b. 1934; grad. Lith. Conservatoire; lectures at it, 1965 — ; CSc. (Arts), Prof.; has written works on creations of Lith. composers of the 20th cent., monograph *Juozo Gruodžio gyvenimas ir kūryba* (Juozas Gruodis' Life and Creative Works, 1981); Head, ed. group of anthology *Muzika*. *Add*. (h) Kupalos 34 — 14, Vilnius 232004; tel. 351 838.
• **AMBRAZAS, Vytautas**, linguist (Lith. philol.); b. 1930; grad. Vilnius Pedag. Inst.; DSc. (Philol.); Inst. of Lith. Lg., 1953 — ; main works: *Lietuvių kalbos dalyvių istorinė sintaksė* (Hist. Syntax of Participles of the Lith. Lg., 1979), *Baltų kalbų istorinė sintaksė* (Hist. Syntax of the Baltic Lgs, 1990; in Russ.). *Add*. (h) Kražių 7 — 3, Vilnius 232001; tel. 620 261.
• **AMBRAZIENĖ-KOSTECKAJA, Ana**, track-and-field athlete; b. 1955; grad. Lith. Inst. of Physical Training; world 400 m hurdle race record holder (1983; 54.2 s); sport instructor, *Gintaras* club, 1988 — . *Add*. (h) Grybo 41 — 21, Vilnius 232040; tel. 741 665.
• **ANDREJEVAS, Julius**, Chair., Lith. Composers' Union, 1989 — ; composer, pianist; b. 1942; grad. Lith. Conservatoire; Doc.; lectures at Conservatoire, 1973 — ; major works: TV

opera *Liūdna pasaka* (A Sad Tale), cantata, concertos, chamber music; perf. piano and chamber music. *Add.* (h) Kupalos 34 — 2, Vilnius 232004; tel. 351 339.

■ **ANDRIUKAITIS, Vytenis**, physician; b. 1951; grad. Kaunas Med. Acad. and Vilnius Univ., physician, hist.; Vice-Chair., Lith. SDP; was born in a family of exiles in Yakutia; Lith. SC Deputy. *Add.* Basanavičiaus 16/5, Vilnius 232600; tel. 652 380.

■ **ANDRIUŠKEVIČIUS, Gintautas**, Dir, Alytus Cotton Fabric Factory, 1990 — ; b. 1945; grad. Kaunas Technol. Univ., econ.; at the factory since 1968. *Add.* (h) Naujoji 26 — 9, Alytus 234580; tel. 361 18.

■ **ANTANAITIS, Vaidotas**, Min. of Forestry, 1990 — ; b. 1928; grad. Leningrad Forest Technol. Acad., forestry eng.; DSc. (Agric.), Prof.; lecturer, Lith. Agric. Acad., 1960 — 90; works on forest surveying, stand increment, ecology; 16 books (some transl. into Ger., Chinese, Czech). *Add.* Gedimino pr. 56, Vilnius 232685; tel. 626 864.

■ **ANTANAVIČIUS, Juozas**, musicologist; b. 1940; grad. Lith. Conservatoire, postgrad. Leningrad Conservatoire; worked on probation in Vienna; CSc. (Arts), Prof.; lecturer, Lith. Conservatoire, 1969 — , Vice-Rector, 1982 — ; lectured at Havana Art Inst., 1977 — 79; has written works on specificity of Lith. music lg.; E-in-C, serial publ. *Menotyra*. *Add.* (h) Kupalos 34 — 5, Vilnius 232004; tel. 351 716.

■ **ANTANAVIČIUS, Kazimieras**, Chair., Econ. Cttee of SC, 1990 — ; b. 1937; grad. Kaunas Technol. Univ., econ.; DSc. (Econ.), Prof.; lecturer, Vilnius Tech. Univ., 1967 — 90; works on econ. and org. of constr.; 6 books; Chair., Lith. SDP, 1988 — 91; Lith. SC Deputy. *Add.* Gedimino pr. 53, Vilnius 232026; tel. 226 061.

■ **ANUŠKEVIČIUS, Jonas**, engineer (arch.); b. 1947; grad. Kaunas Technol. Univ.; since 1970 at design inst.; Dir, arch. design firm *A*, 1990 — ; co-author of educ., admin., recreational buildings; hon. prize, comp. in Finland, 1984. *Add.* (h) Stanevičiaus 88 — 12, Vilnius 232029; tel. 447 234.

■ **APANAVIČIŪTĖ, Gražina**, singer (soprano); b. 1940; grad. Lith. Conservatoire; lecturer at it, 1986 — ; soloist, Lith. Opera and Ballet Theatre, 1968 — ; has toured Europe, USA. *Add.* (h) Goštauto 34 — 32, Vilnius 232001; tel. 628 057.

■ **APUTIS, Juozas**, E-in-C, journal *Metai*, 1990 — ; writer; b. 1936; grad. Vilnius Univ.; moral responsibility, dissatisfaction with everyday life, complicated experiences of intellectual who feels his guilt, psychologism is noted for his works; coll. of short stories: *Horizonte bėga šernai* (Wild-Boars Running in the Horizon, 1970), *Sugrįžimas vakarėjančiais laukais* (Return Over the Evening Fields, 1977), *Keleivio novelės* (Wayfarer Story, 1985), book of tales *Tiltas per Žalpę* (Bridge over the Žalpė, 1980). *Add.* (h) Mildos 31 — 1, Vilnius 232055; tel. 353 526.

■ **ARCIŠKEVIČIUS, Steponas**, Dir, furniture co *Kauno Baldai*, 1967 — ; b. 1925; grad. Kaunas

Technol. Sch., technol. *Add.* (h) Algirdo 16 — 1, Kaunas 233009; tel. 730 997.

■ **AŠMANTAS, Leonas Vaidotas**, Min. of Energy, 1990 — ; b. 1939; grad. Moscow Inst. of Power Eng., eng. (atomic power); DSc. (Eng.), Doc.; Inst. of Phys. and Eng. Problems of Energy Research, 1969 — 90; 2 books (transl. into Engl.). *Add.* Gedimino pr. 12, Vilnius 232600; tel. 615 140.

■ **AŠMONTAS, Steponas**, Dir, Inst. of Semiconductors Phys., 1989 — ; b. 1945; grad. Tomsk Univ., phys.; DSc. (Phys.&Math.); research in the electro-gradient phenomena caused by hot charge carriers in homogeneous and nonhomogeneous semiconductors. Was exiled with parents to Siberia in 1948. *Add.* Goštauto 11, Vilnius 232600; tel. 778 588.

■ **AVIŽIENIS, Algirdas**, Rector, Vytautas Magnus Univ., 1990 — ; b. 1932; grad. Illinois Univ. (USA), computer spec.; PhD, Hon. Dr, Prof., Foreign Mem., Lith. Acad. of Sci.; taught at California Univ., 1982 — 90; headed constr. of self-diagnostic computer STAR; co-author of spaceship 'Apollo' computer systems; Dir, World Lith. Culture, Sci. and Educ. Centre. *Add.* Daukanto 28, Kaunas 233000; tel. 206 753.

■ **AVYŽIUS, Jonas**, writer; b. 1922; the novels *Kaimas kryžkelėje* (Village at the Crossroad, 1964), *Chameleono spalvos* (The Colours of the Chameleon, 1979), *Degimai* (1982) deal with the social and ethic problems; the most significant novel *Sodybų tuštėjimo metas* (The Lost Home, 1970 — 89) depicts the events of WW II and the post-war period, raises problems of the nation's fate, civil and moral responsibility of an individual; vivid characters, traditional epic narration mark his works; books transl. into Engl., Ger., Russ. and other lgs. *Add.* (h) Šeimyniškiu 36 — 13, Vilnius 232051; tel. 751 988.

■ **AŽUBALIS, Audrius**, journalist; b. 1958; grad. Vilnius Univ.; representative of the press, SC of Lithuania, 1990 — . *Add.* Gedimino pr. 53, Vilnius 232026; tel. 628 423.

■ **BAGDONAS, Albinas**, psychologist; b. 1941; grad. Moscow Univ.; CSc. (Biol.), Doc.; lecturer, Vilnius Univ., 1969 — ; Pres., Lith. Psychologists' Union, 1989 — ; books: *Eksperimentinė dėmesio psichologija* (Experimental Psychology of Attention, 1974), *Sensorinės sistemos* (Sensory Systems, 2 vols, 1977), *Pripratimas* (Habit, 1982; in Russ.), *Zoopsichologija* (Zoopsychology, 1983). *Add.* (h) Žaibo 1/42 — 27, Vilnius 232051; tel. 451 455.

■ **BAGDONAS, Vladas**, theatre and film actor; b. 1949; grad. Lith. Conservatoire; Lith. Youth Theatre, 1970 — ; expressive perf., wide range of roles, gives concerts as a singer. *Add.* (h) Stanevičiaus 66 — 32, Vilnius 232029; tel. 625 556 (off.).

■ **BAJORAS, Feliksas Romualdas**, composer; b. 1934; grad. Lith. Conservatoire; major works: opera *Dievo avinėlis* (Lamb of God), oratorio *Varpo kėlimas* (Hoisting of the Bell), 3 symphonies, chamber ensembles, incidental music; prize winner, Cazella composers comp. in Naples (1970) for variations for double bass and string quartet. **Add.** (h) Kupalos 34 — 11, Vilnius 232004.

- **BAKAITIS, Antanas,** Dir-Gen., *Baltica-Union* co, 1989 — ;b. 1946; grad. Lith. Agric. Acad., agron. **Add.** (h) Birutės 56, Vilnius 232004; tel. 228 333.
- **BALAKAUSKAS, Osvaldas,** composer; b. 1937; grad. Vilnius Pedag. Inst. and Kiev Conservatoire; lecturer, Lith. Conservatoire, 1985 — ; major works: ballet *Zodiak* (film), 'Macbeth', 2 symphonies, *Opera Strumentale* for symphony orch., *Passio Strumentale* for string quartet and symphony orch., 4 concertos, Ostrobothnian symphony for strings, vocal and chamber music (~40); Vice-Chair., Lith. Composers' Union. **Add.** (h) Kupalos 34 — 9, Vilnius 232004; tel. 354 435.
- **BALCEWICZ, Zbigniew,** Ed., newspaper *Kurier Wilenski*, 1988 — ; b. 1946; grad. Vilnius Univ., lawyer; Lith. SC Deputy. **Add.** (h) Basanavičiaus 18 — 10, Vilnius 232009; tel. 652 022.
- **BALČIKONIS, Juozas,** textile artist; b. 1924; grad. Kaunas Inst. of Applied and Decorative Arts; teacher, Vilnius Art Acad., 1951 — ; Prof.; author of thematic and decorative tapestries, batiks, decorative fabrics, designer of nat. costumes, compiler of textiles albums. **Add.** (h) Šilo 29 — 13, Vilnius 232055; tel. 749 718.
- **BALČIŪNIENĖ, Irena,** dentist, anthropologist; b. 1941; grad. Kaunas Med. Acad.; DSc. (Biol.), Prof.; lecturer, Vilnius Univ., 1973 — ; compiled odontological map of Lithuania, described hist. of Lith. odontological type; works on the epochal changes of pathology of the mastication apparatus of the Lith. inhabitants, on social and biol. influence upon caries and beginning of parodont diseases. **Add.** (h) Šiltnamių 2 — 1, Vilnius 232043; tel. 443 781.
- **BALČYTIS, Vytautas,** photographer; b. 1955; grad. Vilnius Tech. Univ.; photographs conceptual, minimalistic (views of Lith. towns); exh. abroad, winner of prizes. **Add.** (h) Taikos 134 — 33, Vilnius 232017; tel. 462 565.
- **BALDAUSKAS, Juozapas,** E-in-C, magazine *Mokslas ir gyvenimas*, 1975 — ; b. 1932; grad. Vilnius Univ., journalist; press worker, 1956 — . **Add.** Vilniaus 37, Vilnius 232600; tel. 618 329.
- **BALDIŠIS, Vilius,** Chair., Bd of the Bank of Lithuania, 1990 — ; b. 1961; grad. Vilnius Univ., econ.; lectured at it, 1986 — 90; Lith. SC Deputy. **Add.** Gedimino pr. 6, Vilnius 232629; tel. 224 015.
- **BALĖNAS, Kazimieras,** engineer (arch.); b. 1935; grad. Kaunas Technol. Univ.; Chief Arch. of designs, Design Inst. of City Constr., 1968 — ; co-author of housing projects and admin. buildings in Klaipėda and Vilnius. **Add.** (h) Vivulskio 6/15 — 30, Vilnius 232009; tel. 651 201.
- **BALKEVIČIUS, Artūras,** Dir, Joint-Stock Innovation Bank of Lithuania, 1988 — ; b. 1948; grad. Kaunas Technol. Univ., eng. (automatic); lectured at it, 1971 — 88. **Add.** Šv. Stepono 27, Vilnius 232006; tel. 260 336.
- **BALSIENĖ, Aldona,** Chair., Lith. Workers' Union, 1991 — ; b. 1955; grad. Vilnius Electromech. Tech. Sch.; Vilnius Calculating Machine Plant, 1975 — ; Sec. of this Union,

1988 — 90. **Add.** Mykolaičio-Putino 5, Vilnius 232600; tel. 621 743.

- **BALTRAMIEJŪNAS, Remigijus,** Dir, Inst. of Phys., 1989 — ; b. 1945; grad. Vilnius Univ., phys.; DSc. (Phys.&Math.), Prof.; research in multiphoton spectroscopy of semiconductors, electron-hole plasma, laser spectroscopy of excitons, hot electron quasiparticles in crystals, nonlinear optics in solid state. **Add.** (h) Rinktinės 19 — 128, Vilnius 232005; tel. 754 275.
- **BANIONIS, Donatas,** theatre and film actor; b. 1924; grad. Panevėžys Drama Theatre Studio; actor at it, 1940 — , Chief Dir, 1980 — ; has played nearly 100 theatre and 50 film roles; acts in film studios of Lithuania, *DEFA*, *Mosfilm*, *Lenfilm*, Bulgaria; a versatile actor; excellent in revealing psychology of his characters; prize at the Sorento Festival, 1972. **Add.** (h) Ukmergės 47a — 16, Panevėžys 235300; tel. 334 22.
- **BANSEVIČIUS, Ramutis,** engineer (mech.); b. 1939; grad. Kaunas Technol. Univ.; its lecturer, 1967 — ; DSc. (Eng.), Prof., Corr. Mem., Lith. Acad. of Sci.; research in the dynamics of precise mechanisms and robots; 250 inv. **Add.** (h) Januškevičiaus 31 — 40, Kaunas 233005; tel. 732 960.
- **BARANAUSKAS, Marijonas,** photographer; b. 1931; grad. Vilnius Univ., journalist; photographs noted for lyricism, optimistic approach; numerous exh. abroad, winner of prizes; albums *Vaikų pasaulis* (Children World, 1982), *Lietuvos žvejai* (Lith. Fishermen, 1984); AFIAP, 1976. **Add.** (h) Čiobiškio 31 — 13, Vilnius 232010; tel. 410 596.
- **BARAVYKAS, Gediminas,** Chief Arch. of Vilnius, 1987 — ; architect; b. 1940; grad. Vilnius Art Acad.; worked at Design Inst. of City Constr.; author of public buildings and memorials in Vilnius. **Add.** (h) Rudens 2 — 9, Vilnius 232007; tel. 745 560.
- **BARCYS, Jonas,** Dir, *Šviesa* publrs; 1980 — ; b. 1933; grad. Vilnius Pedag. Inst.; E-in-C of publrs, 1968 — 80; compiled readers for sch., transl. works of fiction. **Add.** Vytauto pr. 25, Kaunas 233000; tel. 741 634.
- **BAREIKIS, Vytautas,** physicist; b. 1937; grad. Vilnius Univ.; DSc. (Phys.&Math.), Prof.; Inst. of Semiconductor Phys., 1967 — ; research on the fluctuation phenomena in semiconductors in the strong electrical field. **Add.** (h) Kalvarijų 134 — 54, Vilnius 232042; tel. 768 407.
- **BARKAUSKAS, Vytautas,** composer; b. 1931; grad. Lith. Conservatoire; lectures at it, 1961 — ; Doc.; major works: opera *Legenda apie meilę* (A Legend about Love), 5 symphonies, symphonic triptych *Trys aspektai* (Three Aspects), oratorio *Viltis* (The Hope), 4 concertos, chamber music, incidental music. **Add.** Mickevičiaus 29, Vilnius 232600; tel. 752 811.
- **BARTULIS, Vidmantas,** composer; b. 1954; grad. Lith. Conservatoire; music section man., Kaunas Drama Theatre, 1983 — ; major works: requiem, mass, cantata *Sutemų giesmės* (Songs of Twilight), 2 symphonies, chamber music, incidental music. **Add.** (h) Gvardiečių 78 — 18, Kaunas 233043; tel. 725 749.

■ **BARTUSEVIČIŪTĖ-NOREIKIENĖ, Loreta,** ballet dancer; b. 1958; grad. M. K. Čiurlionis Art Sch., postgrad. course at Leningrad Maly Opera and Ballet Theatre; ballet soloist, prima ballerina, Lith. Opera and Ballet Theatre, 1977 − ; danced with the Moscow Bolshoi Theatre, Leningrad Kirov Opera and Ballet Theatre, toured European, Asian, S-American, African c. **Add.** (h) Šilo 54 − 3, Vilnius 232055; tel. 748 936.

■ **BARYSAS, Rolandas,** journalist; b. 1961; grad. Moscow Univ., int. journalist; in *ELTA* news agency, 1985 − , Dir, 1990 − ; publr, newspaper *Forumas.* **Add.** (h) Aguonų 18 − 11, Vilnius 232006; tel. 631 750.

■ **BAŠINSKAS, Justinas,** composer; b. 1923; grad. Lith. Conservatoire; major works: opera *Marti* (Daughter-in-Law), ballet *Užkeikti vienuoliai* (Accursed Monks), oratorio *Ąžuolas* (The Oak), 4 cantatas, 7 symphonies, concerto for flute, chamber music. **Add.** (h) Kupalos 34 − 6, Vilnius 232004; tel. 351 312.

■ **BAŠKAUSKAS, Liucija,** Vice-Rector, Vytautas Magnus Univ., 1990 − ; b. 1942; grad. California Univ. in Los Angeles, cultural anthropologist; PhD, Prof.; lectured at Northridge Univ., 1972 − 88; research in evolution of social culture, ethnic refugees; publ. monographies. **Add.** Daukanto 28, Kaunas 233000; telex 269857 VYTUN SU.

■ **BAUŠYS, Juozas,** E-in-C, magazine *Švyturys,* 1985 − ; b. 1939; grad. Vilnius Univ.; journalist; press worker, 1961 − ; scripts for documentaries. **Add.** Maironio 1, Vilnius 232600; tel. 627 488.

■ **BENDORIUS, Jonas,** Dir, computer plant *Modulis,* 1962 − ; b. 1935; grad. Kaunas Technol. Univ., eng. (mech.). **Add.** (h) Gamyklos 5 − 7, Pabradė 234710; tel. 543 04.

■ **BEREDINA, Neli,** ballet dancer; b. 1957; grad. Moscow Choreographic Sch.; soloist, prima ballerina, Lith. Opera and Ballet Theatre, 1975 − ; danced with Leningrad Maly Opera and Ballet Theatre, Moscow Bolshoi Theatre, toured European, Asian, African c. **Add.** (h) Šeškinės 35 − 43, Vilnius 232010; tel. 464 212.

■ **BERNOTAS, Stasys,** Dir, Inst. of Agric. Branch in Vėžaičiai, 1989 − ; b. 1957; grad. Lith. Agric. Acad., agron.; CSc. (Agric.); researches in agric. **Add.** Vėžaičiai, Klaipėdos rj. 235845; tel. 535 77.

■ **BIČIŪNAS, Rimas Zigmas,** painter; b. 1945; grad. Vilnius Art Acad.; paintings offer a unique interpretation of the traditions of Lith. folk painting, images of women, birds and flowers prevail; part. at exh. in Germany, Netherlands, Italy, Spain, Japan; paintings acquired by Moscow Tretyakov, Cologne Ludwig and other art galleries. **Add.** (h) Žeručio 24 − 60, Vilnius 232043; tel. 696 113.

■ **BIČKAUSKAS, Egidijus,** Permanent Representative in Moscow of the Govt of Lith. Rep., 1990 − ; b. 1955; grad. Vilnius Univ., lawyer; worked at Lith. Prosecutor's Office as an interrogator of special cases; Lith. SC Deputy. **Add.** Pisemskovo 10, Moscow 121069; tel. 291 26 43.

■ **BIELIAUSKAS, Alfonsas,** writer; b. 1923; grad. Vilnius Univ.; his novels *Rožės žydi raudonai* (Scarlet Roses are Blooming, 1959), *Kauno romanas* (Novel of Kaunas, 1966), *Tada, kai lijo* (At that Time When it was Raining, 1977) are noted for social themes, ethical collisions of heroes, based on pol. division, propagation of Soviet ideology, inner monologue. **Add.** (h) Švyturio 22 − 3, Vilnius 232040; tel. 741 484.

■ **BIELSKIS, Antanas Algimantas,** Chair., Lith. Designers' Union, 1989 − ; b. 1937; grad. Leningrad V. Muchina Higher Ind. Art Sch., designed; taught at Vilnius Art Acad., 1964 − 86; designed instruments, installations, system of visual communication. **Add.** (h) 16-osios divizijos 71 − 24, Klaipėda 235818.

■ **BIKELIS, Algimantas,** mathematician; b. 1937; grad. Vilnius Univ.; its lecturer, 1961 − ; DSc. (Phys.&Math.), Prof.; Vice-Rector of Univ., 1979 − 85; research in the theory of probabilities, asymptotic analysis of probability distribution of statistics and sum totals of independent random vectors. **Add.** (h) Vienuolio 6 − 26, Vilnius 232001; tel. 621 794.

■ **BINGELIS, Petras,** conductor; b. 1943; grad. Lith. Conservatoire; lectures at it, 1982 − ; worked on probation under K.Mazur and R.Lenter in Leipzig; chief conductor and artistic leader, Kaunas State Choir, 1969 − ; toured European c.; Chief Conductor of Lith. Song Festivals. **Add.** (h) Cvirkos 13 − 6, Kaunas 233000; tel. 234 433.

■ **BIRULIS, Kostas,** Min. of Communications, 1990 − ; b. 1925; grad. Kaunas Technol. Univ., eng.; worked at Min. of Communications, 1952 − . **Add.** Vilniaus 33, Vilnius 232008; tel. 620 443.

■ **BIRŽIŠKIS, Jonas,** Min. of Transportation, 1990 − ; b. 1932; grad. Irkutsk Mining and Metallurgical Inst., mining and road-building eng.; CSc. (Eng.); at *Granitas* production amalgamation of the road-building materials ind., 1959 − 90. **Add.** Gedimino pr. 17, Vilnius 232679; tel. 621 445.

■ **BLOŽĖ, Vytautas,** poet; b. 1930; coll. of poems *Iš tylinčios žemės* (From the Silent Earth, 1966), *Polifonijos* (Polyphonies, 1981), *Žmonės* (The People, 1984), a narrative poem-novel *Miko Kėdainiškio laiškai* (The Letters of Mikas Kėdainiškis, 1986); his works are marked by dramatic meditation on the contrasts of hist. and the present life, the problems of an individual and modernistic form. **Add.** (h) Liškiavos 31 − 30, Druskininkai 234690; tel. 453 25.

■ **BOLOTINAS, Adolfas,** physicist; b. 1925; grad. Vilnius Univ.; its lecturer, 1949 − ; DSc. (Phys.&Math.), Prof.; research in quantum mech. and group theory. **Add.** (h) Kupalos 10 − 2, Vilnius 232004; tel. 731 438.

■ **BONDAREVAS, Semionas,** Dir, plant *Astra,* 1987 − ; b. 1951; grad. Kaunas Technol. Univ., eng. (mech.). **Add.** (h) Statybininkų 9 − 21, Alytus 234580; tel. 305 69.

■ **BORUTA, Jonas Algimantas,** Roman Catholic priest; b. 1944; grad. Vilnius Univ.; CSc. (Phys.&Math.); priest, 1982 − ; Jesuit; Rector, St. Casimir's Church in Vilnius, 1990 − ; spiritual leader of students' union *Ateitininkai*. **Add.** (h) Dūkštų 12 — 92, Vilnius 232010; tel. 429 826.

■ **BRAZAUSKAS, Algirdas Mykolas,** Chair., Lith. DLP, 1990 — ; b. 1932; grad. Kaunas Technol. Univ., eng. (civil); CSc. (Econ.); 1st Dep. Chair., State Plan Cttee, 1966 — 77; Sec., Cent. Cttee, LCP, 1977 — 89, 1st Sec., 1989 — 90; Chair., Presidium of the Supreme Soviet of Lith. SSR, 1989 — 90; Dep. Prime Min. of Lith. Rep., 1990 — 91; Lith. SC Deputy. **Add.** Radvilaitės 1, Vilnius 232000; tel. 612 625.

■ **BRAZDYLIS, Vytautas,** ballet master; b. 1947; grad. Moscow Choreographic Sch., Leningrad Conservatoire; danced with Lith. Opera and Ballet Theatre, Head Ballet Master of this theatre, 1980 — ; producer of classical and Lith. ballets. **Add.** (h) Pervažos 14 — 2, Vilnius 232001; tel. 357 031.

■ **BRĖDIKIS, Jurgis,** cardiovascular surgeon; b. 1929; grad. Kaunas Med. Acad.; Chief of its cardiosurgery clinic, 1984 — ; DSc. (Med.), Prof., Acad., USSR Med. Acad. of Sci.; was first in the world to use laser for heart operations, introduced electrical stimulation of the heart into clinical practice, began to operate patients with heart rhythm disorders; designed a heart tone measuring device, electrodes for temporary electrical heart stimulation, electrical stimulators. **Add.** (h) Kęstučio 83 — 8, Kaunas 233000; tel. 730 355 (off.).

■ **BRĖDIKIS, Vytautas,** Rector, Vilnius Art Acad., 1988 — ; b. 1930; grad. this Acad.; its lecturer, 1965 — ; arch.; Prof.; co-author of Lazdynai residential area and various public buildings in Vilnius. **Add.** (h) Žirmūnų 55 — 4, Vilnius 232051; tel. 737 059.

■ **BRUVERIS, Jonas,** musicologist; b. 1939; grad. Lith. Conservatoire; postgrad. Leningrad Conservatoire; CSc. (Arts), Doc.; lecturer, Lith. Conservatoire, 1969 — ; lectured at Bratislava Univ., 1981 — 84; studies: book ed. *Čiurlioniui — 100* (Čiurlionis Centenary, 1977), works on music aesthetics and Lith. professional music of 20th cent. **Add.** (h) Subačiaus 8 — 18, Vilnius 232024; tel. 624 364.

■ **BUBNYS, Vytautas,** writer; b. 1932; grad. Vilnius Pedag. Inst.; a cycle of novels *Alkana žemė* (The Hungry Earth, 1971), *Po vasaros dangum* (Under Summer Sky, 1973), *Nesėtų rugių žydėjimas* (Flowering of the Unsown Rye, 1976), novels *Pilnaties valandą* (At the Hour of Full Moon, 1980), *Piemenėlių mišios* (Shepherds' Mass, 1988), *Atleisk mūsų kaltes* (Forgive Us Our Sins, 1989), tales for teenagers; works offer a realistic description of the dramatic events in the Lith. countryside during the war and the post-war period, social and psychological development of peasants, daily life of intellectuals, with considerable attention to family ethics. **Add.** (h) Švyturio 22 — 12, Vilnius 232040; tel. 741 570.

■ **BUČIŪTĖ, Elena Nijolė,** architect; b. 1930; grad. Vilnius Art Acad.; CSc. (Arch.), Prof.; Design Inst. of City Constr., 1953 — 75; lecturer, Vilnius Tech. Univ., 1976 — ; author of public buildings in Vilnius. **Add.** (h) Donelaičio 18 — 16, Vilnius 232009; tel. 630 332.

■ **BUDRAITIS, Juozas,** Pres., Lith. Theatre Union, 1990 — ; film and theatre actor; b. 1940; grad. Vilnius Univ. and Higher Course on Film-making in Moscow; manner is noted for restraint and inner expressiveness; has acted in film studios of Lithuania, *DEFA*, Czecho-Slovakia, Bulgaria, *Mosfilm*, *Lenfilm*, *Tallinnfilm*. **Add.** (h) Čiurlionio 16 — 2, Vilnius 232009; tel. 635 408.

■ **BUDRYS, Algirdas,** clarinettist; b. 1939; grad. Lith. Conservatoire, postgrad. Leningrad Conservatoire; worked on probation under J.Lanslo in Paris; Prof.; lecturer, Lith. Conservatoire, 1968 — ; lectured at Cairo Conservatoire, 1972 — 75; artistic leader and clarinettist of Brass Quintet of Lith. Nat. Philharmonic, 1965 — ; Mem., Int. Assoc. of Clarinettists; has toured Europe, Egypt, USA, Canada. **Add.** (h) Čiurlionio 6 — 18, Vilnius 232009; tel. 617 296.

■ **BUDRYS, Rimantas,** E-in-C, magazine *Mūsų gamta*, 1964 — ; b. 1930; grad. Vilnius Univ., journalist; travel sketches, books for children (in Engl., Ger.). **Add.** Rudens 33b, Vilnius 232040; tel. 696 964.

■ **BUDVYTIS, Alfonsas,** photographer; b. 1949; grad. Kaunas Med. Acad.; photographs conceptual, minimalistic (views of Lith. towns); personal exh. abroad, winner of prizes. **Add.** (h) Laisvės pr. 43 — 112, Vilnius 232044; tel. 458 086.

■ **BŪDVYTIS, Antanas,** agronomist; b. 1928; grad. Lith. Agric. Acad.; CSc. (Agric.), Corr Mem., USSR Agric. Acad. of Sci.; Inst. of Agric., 1954 — , Dir, 1966 — 89; research on labour org. **Add.** (h) Parko 8 — 4, Dotnuva-Akademija 235051; tel. 576 50.

■ **BUKAITIS, Elegijus,** ballet master; b. 1941; grad. A.Vaganova Dance Acad.; Head Ballet Master, Lith. Opera and Ballet Theatre, 1974 — 78; directs amateur dance groups, 1984 — ; producer of classical, Lith., and modern ballets. **Add.** (h) Sudervės 21 — 27, Vilnius 232044; tel. 447 902.

■ **BUMBLIAUSKAS, Alfredas,** historian; b. 1956; grad. Vilnius Univ.; lectures at univ., 1979 — ; CSc. (Hist.); works on Reformation, theoretical problems of the hist. of Lithuania; Dep. Chair., Sąjūdis Seim Council. **Add.** Universiteto 3, Vilnius 232734; tel. 612 772.

■ **BURAČAS, Antanas,** economist; b. 1939; grad. Vilnius Univ.; DSc. (Econ.), Prof., Acad., Lith. Acad. of Sci.; Inst. of Econ., 1975 — ; lectured at Vilnius Univ., 1968 — 86; works on metaecon., hist. of econ., theory of social reproduction and infra-structure, methodology of regional forecasting; some works publ. in Engl., Russ.; Chair., Assoc. of Lith. Sci. Hist. and Phil.; Lith. Assoc. of Human Rights Protection, 1990 — . **Add.** (h) Šilo 62 — 6, Vilnius 232055; tel. 749 649.

■ **BURAK, Pavel,** Dir, furniture factory *Ąžuolas*, 1984 — ; b. 1933; grad. Byeloruss. Forestry Tech. Inst., eng. (mech.). **Add.** (h) Antakalnio 32 — 5, Vilnius 232055; tel. 741 725.

■ **BUROKEVIČIUS, Mykolas,** 1st Sec., Cent. Cttee, LCP (CPSU), 1990 — ; b. 1927; grad.

Vilnius Pedag. Inst.; lectured at it, 1976 — 90; DSc. (Hist.), Prof.; research in the activity of CP in Lithuania, problems of intellectuals and culture; 6 books; Mem., Politbureau, CPSU Cent. Cttee. *Add.* Gedimino pr. 11, Vilnius 232001; tel. 615 310.

- **BŪTĖNAS, Valdemaras,** Chair., Bd of the commercial bank *Ūkio bankas,* 1989 — ; b. 1952; grad. Kaunas Technol. Univ., eng. (econ.). *Add.* Gruodžio 9, Kaunas 233000; tel. 203 651.

- **BUTKEVIČIUS, Audrius,** Dir-Gen., Dept of Nat. Defence, 1990 — ; b. 1960; grad. Kaunas Med. Acad., psycho-therapist, narcologist; worked at hosp., 1985 — 90; Lith. SC Deputy. *Add.* Gynėjų 3, Vilnius 232710; tel. 624 821.

- **BUTKUS, Viktoras,** Roman Catholic priest; b. 1923; grad. Kaunas Priest Sem.; Rector of this Sem., 1962 — 89; studied at Lateran Univ.; ThD, Prof. *Add.* (h) Muzikos 8, Kaunas 233019; tel. 226 068.

- **BUTVILA, Algimantas,** ceramist; b. 1943; grad. Vilnius Art Acad.; author of expressive decorative works of monumental, geometric shape. *Add.* (h) Šilo 29 — 25, Vilnius 232055; tel. 749 725.

- **BUTYRIN, Vitaly,** photographer; b. 1947; author of fantastic, allegoric, views (mainly photomontage); personal exh. abroad, winner of many prizes; album 'Photomontage — Photographic Arts' (Leipzig, 1987); AFIAP, 1976, EFIAP, 1988. *Add.* (h) Ukmergės 228 — 56, Vilnius 232010; tel. 417 067.

- **BYTAUTAS, Steponas,** Dir, cycle engine factory *Vairas,* 1986 — ; b. 1950; grad. Vilnius Tech. Univ., eng. (mech.). *Add.* (h) Vilniaus 116 — 1, Šiauliai 235400; tel. 337 04.

- **CHLOMAUSKAS, Eduardas,** engineer (arch.); b. 1927; grad. Kaunas Technol. Univ.; Chief Arch. of designs, Design Inst. of City Constr., 1960 — ; co-author of expressive med., sports, admin. buildings. *Add.* (h) Miglos 59 — 50, Vilnius 232034; tel. 757 409.

- **CHOMENTAUSKAS, Gintaras,** psychologist; b. 1957; grad. Vilnius Univ.; CSc. (Psychology), Doc.; lecturer, Vilnius Pedag. Inst., 1985 — ; books: *Šeimos piešimo metodikos taikymas vaiko psichologiniams tyrimams* (Application of Family Drawing Method for Psychological Research into Child, 1983), *Šeima vaiko požiūriu* (Family from the Point of View of Child, 1989; in Russ.). *Add.* (h) Raseinių 9 — 3, Vilnius 232009; tel. 652 882.

- **CHRIZOSTOM** (proper name Georgii Martishkin), Administrator of the Russian Orthodox Diocese of Vilnius and Lithuania, 1990 — ; b. 1935; grad. Moscow Theol. Sem.; archiereus, archbishop; since 1961 performs pastoral work; Administrator of dioceses in Russia, 1974 — 90; archimandrite of the Vilnius Holy Spirit Cloister. *Add.* Aušros vartų 8, Vilnius 232001; tel. 625 896.

- **CHROMČENKO, Anatolii,** Dir, Ignalina Nuclear Power Station, 1986 — ; b. 1932; grad. Ural Polytech. Inst., eng. (electric); at nuclear power stations since 1977. *Add.* (h) Olimpiados 7 — 33, Sniečkus 234761; tel. 317 88.

- **ČEKANAUSKAS, Vytautas,** architect; b. 1930; grad. Vilnius Art Acad.; Corr. Mem., USSR Art Acad.; Chief Arch. of designs, Design Inst. of City Constr., 1962 — 89; lecturer, Vilnius Art Acad., 1989 — ; co-author of Lazdynai residential area in Vilnius, rational public and admin. buildings of expressive plan and volume. *Add.* (h) Paco 13 — 9, Vilnius 232055; tel. 351 711.

- **ČEKUOLIS, Algimantas,** E-in-C, weekly *Gimtasis kraštas,* 1986 — ; journalist, writer; b. 1931; grad. M.Gorky Lit. Inst. in Moscow; worked on fishing-boats, was correspondent of APN in Canada, Portugal, Spain; author of stories, travel sketches. *Add.* (h) Raseinių 13 — 1, Vilnius 232009; tel. 623 881 (off.).

- **ČEPAITIS, Virgilijus,** Chair., Civil Rights and Ethnic Affairs Cttee of SC, 1990 — ; Chair., Lith. Indep. Party; b. 1937; grad. M.Gorky Lit. Inst. in Moscow; translator; transl. into Russ. prose works by famous Lith. authors, from Engl. into Lith. works by A.Milne, W. Saroyan, T.Williams; Sec.-in-Chief, *Sąjūdis* Seim Council, 1988 — 90; Lith. SC Deputy. *Add.* Gedimino pr. 53, Vilnius 232026; tel. 224 577.

- **ČERNIAUSKAS, Mindaugas,** Dir, Cttee of Int. Org. of Lithuania, 1990 — ; b. 1960; grad. Vilnius Univ., econ.; works in sphere of econ. relations with foreign c., 1982 — ; Pres., commercial chamber *Baltwest. Add.* Daukanto a. 3/8 — 13, Vilnius 232600; tel. 222 630.

- **ČESIŪNAS, Vladas,** rower; b. 1940; grad. Lith. Inst. of Physical Training; Olympic, 1972, world, 1973, 1974, 1975 champ.; coach, *Dinamo* sports soc., 1979 — . *Add.* (h) Vienuolio 14 — 19, Vilnius 232000; tel. 616 554.

- **ČETKAUSKAITĖ, Genovaitė,** ethnomusicologist; b. 1925; grad. Vilnius Pedag. Inst. and Lith. Conservatoire; CSc. (Arts); Lith. Conservatoire, 1961 — 84; invest. Lith. folk melodies; formulated principles of the classification of song melodies, compiled a typological catalogue of melodies; arranged coll. of songs and recordings. *Add.* (h) Antakalnio 88 — 32, Vilnius 232040; tel. 742 631.

- **ČIŽAS, Algirdas Eduardas,** engineer (constr.); b. 1929; grad. Kaunas Technol. Univ.; DSc. (Eng.), Prof.; lecturer, Vilnius Tech. Univ., 1963 — ; worked out theoretical and methodological basis for the simulation methods of optimum linear strengthening systems. *Add.* (h) Kalinausko 11 — 6, Vilnius 232009; tel. 617 393.

- **ČOBOTAS, Medardas,** Chair., Health Care and Social Affairs Cttee of SC, 1990 — ; b. 1928; grad. Vilnius Univ.; rheumatologist, gerontologist; CSc. (Med.), Doc.; Scientific Research Inst. of Experimental and Clinical Med., 1960 — 90; works on rheumatology, gerontology, sanitation and hygiene, disease prevention. Lith. SC Deputy. *Add.* Gedimino pr. 53, Vilnius 232026; tel. 224 995.

- **DAGYS, Raimundas,** physicist; b. 1930; grad. Vilnius Pedag. Inst.; DSc. (Phys.&Math.), Prof., Corr. Mem., Lith. Acad. of Sci.; Inst. of

Semiconductor Phys., 1967 — ; research in the math. methods of theoretical spectroscopy, electronic structure of crystals. *Add.* (h) Justiniškių 109 — 51, Vilnius 232017.

■ **DAINYS, Balys**, surgeon; b. 1941; grad. Vilnius Univ.; its lecturer, 1965 — ; Chief of its nephrological clinic, 1990 — ; DSc. (Med.), Prof.; made original experiments of kidney transplantation; in 1970 together with colleagues made first kidney transplantation in Lithuania, attached liver of another man to a patient for temporary use. *Add.* (h) Antakalnio 93 — 45, Vilnius 232040; tel. 768 520.

■ **DAMIJONAITIS, Pranas**, Dir-Gen., Dept of Press, 1990 — ; b. 1951; grad. Chemnitz Higher Tech. Sch. (in Germany), designing eng.; in printing and publishing ind. since 1975. *Add.* Vrublevskio 6, Vilnius 232671; tel. 617 385.

■ **DANYS, Jurgis**, Dir, Endocrinological Centre (Kaunas), 1978 — ; b. 1921; grad. Kaunas Univ., physician endocrinologist; DSc. (Med.), Prof.; introduced new methods of diagnostics and treatment of thyroid gland. *Add.* (h) Juro 22 — 6, Kaunas 233000; tel. 738 416.

■ **DAPKUS, Rimantas**, Dir, Inst. of Agric., 1989 — ; b. 1952; grad. Lith. Agric. Acad., agron.; CSc.(Agric.); at the Inst. since 1976; works on perennial grasses, seed growing, plant breeding. *Add.* (h) Ruokio 7 — 32, Dotnuva-Akademija 235051; tel. 573 24.

■ **DAUBARAS, Gediminas**, Dir, Lith.-Ger. joint venture *Vilbara*, 1990 — ; b. 1934; grad. Vilnius Univ., econ.; pol. prisoner, 1951 — 53. *Add.* Pilies 2/1, Vilnius 232001; tel. 610 750.

■ **DAUBLYS, Aloyzas**, Dir, Vilnius Polymer Products Plant, 1990 — ; b. 1944; grad. Vilnius Univ., econ.; at Min. of Building Materials, 1971 — 88. *Add.* (h) Kapsų 22 — 53, Vilnius 232038; tel. 695 339.

■ **DAUJOTYTĖ-PAKERIENĖ, Viktorija**, lit. critic; b. 1945; grad. Vilnius Univ.; DSc. (Lit.); monographs: *Jurgis Baltrušaitis* (1974), *Lietuvių filosofinė lyrika* (Lith. Philosophical Lyrics, 1977), *Tautos žodžio lemtys* (The Fortunes of the Nation's Tongue, 1990). *Add.* (h) Žirgo 1 — 12, Vilnius 232040; tel. 768 956.

■ **DAUKANTAS, Feliksas**, designer, jeweller; b. 1915; grad. Vilnius Art Acad.; teaches at this Acad., 1961 — ; author of leather, metal articles, amber jewelry. *Add.* (h) Jakšto 13 — 5, Vilnius 232001; tel. 624 946.

■ **DAUKŠYS, Juozas**, Dir, Alytus Soft Drinks and Champagne Factory, 1963 — ; b. 1931; grad. Vilnius Univ., econ. *Add.* (h) Užuovėjos 13, Alytus 234580; tel. 515 44.

■ **DAUNORAS, Vaclovas**, singer (bass); b. 1934; grad. Lith. Conservatoire; worked on probation in *La Scala* theatre in Milan; Prof.; lecturer, Lith. Conservatoire, 1968 — ; soloist, Lith. Opera and Ballet Theatre, 1960 — 86; has toured Europe, USA, Canada, Egypt; Tchaikovsky singing comp. (4th prize, 1966) and Toulouse singing comp. (Grand Prix, 1971). *Add.* (h) Vykinto 27 — 12, Vilnius 232004; tel. 738 187.

■ **DAUNYS, Vaidotas**, E-in-C, journal *Krantai*, 1989 — ; poet; b. 1958; grad. Vilnius Univ.*Add.* (h) Taikos 76 — 15, Vilnius 232017; tel. 461 391.

■ **DIČIUS, Vytautas**, architect; b. 1930; grad. Vilnius Art Acad.; Doc.; Design Inst. of City Constr., 1959 — 71; lecturer, Vilnius Tech. Univ., 1971 — ; author of educ., commercial, sports, recreational buildings in Kaunas, Palanga, Alytus. *Add.* (h) Didžioji 25 — 28, Vilnius 232001; tel. 627 991.

■ **DIDŽIULIS, Algirdas**, Dir-Gen., Vilnius fuel outfit co *Kuro aparatūra*, 1980 — ; b. 1926; grad. Kaunas Technol. Univ., eng. (electromech.); Dir, plant *Kuro aparatūra*, 1966 — 80. *Add.* (h) Akmenų 4 — 3, Vilnius 232600; tel. 650 282.

■ **DIGRYS, Leopoldas**, organist; b. 1934; grad. and postgrad. Moscow Conservatoire; worked on probation in Prague under J.Reinberger; Prof.; lecturer, Lith. Conservatoire, 1960 — ; toured European c. *Add.* (h) Blindžių 21 — 7, Vilnius 232004; tel. 351 450.

■ **DINEIKA, Arnas Karolis**, engineer (arch.); b. 1928; grad. Kaunas Technol. Univ.; Doc.; Leningrad Design Inst., 1952 — 72; lecturer, Vilnius Tech. Univ., 1974 — ; author of educ., sports buildings. *Add.* (h) Čiurlionio 5 — 5, Vilnius 232009; tel. 631 679.

■ **DIRGĖLA, Petras**, writer; b. 1947; novels *Šalavijų kalnas* (The Sage Mountain; co-author — his brother Povilas Dirgėla, 1977), *Kūlgrinda* (1985), *Joldijos jūra* (The Yoldia Sea, vols 1 — 2, 1987 — 88), *Amžių dienai dūzgianti giria* (The Buzzing Forest For the Day of Ages, 1988), short stories, essays; his works are dominated by phil. problems of an individual and the fate of the nation; the allegoric and romantic outlook upon the world. *Add.* (h) Tuskulėnų 60 — 6, Vilnius 232051; tel. 751 367.

■ **DOBRAVOLSKAS, Algis**, Min. of Social Welfare, 1990 — ; b. 1951; grad. Vilnius Univ.; CSc. (Econ.), Doc.; Inst. of Econ., 1982 — 89; 2 books on the development of social infra-structure. *Add.* Vivulskio 11, Vilnius 232693; tel. 651 236.

■ **DOBROVOLSKIS, Mykolas**, Roman Catholic priest, amateur artist; b. 1918; grad. Kaunas Priest Sem.; ordained in 1944; Capuchin (Father Stanislov); pastor in Paberžė, 1966 — 90; in 1990 ref. monastery in Dotnuva; author of roofed-pole crosses, collector of religious articles; pol. prisoner, 1948 — 57. *Add.* (h) Vytauto 64, Dotnuva 235050; tel. 499 06.

■ **DOBROVOLSKIS, Pranciškus**, chemist; b. 1941; grad. Vilnius Univ.; CSc. (Chem.); Vice-Dir, Inst. of Chem. and Chem. Technol., 1978 — ; research in zinc-, nickel- and copper-plating. *Add.* (h) Minties 7 — 2, Vilnius 232042; tel. 756 257.

■ **DOMARKAS, Juozas**, conductor; b. 1936; grad. Lith. Conservatoire; Doc.; Chief Conductor, Lith. Nat. Philharmonic Symphony Orch., 1964 — ; lectures at Lith. Conservatoire; has toured France, Germany, Finland, Norway, Turkey, Mexico. *Add.* (h) Jogailos 16 — 5, Vilnius 232001; tel. 625 610.

■ **DOMARKAS, Vladislavas**, Rector, Kaunas Technol. Univ., 1983 — ; b. 1939; grad. Kaunas Technol. Univ., eng. (radio); its lecturer, 1967 — ; DSc. (Eng.), Prof., Corr. Mem., Lith. Acad. of Sci.; research in the theory and creation of piezoelectric measuring converters; 50 inv. **Add.** (h) Slénio 33 — 7, Kaunas 233031; tel. 743 757.

- **DOVYDĖNAS, Algirdas**, stained-glass artist; b. 1944; grad. Vilnius Art Acad.; author of monumental and small-sized stained-glass panels, glass articles for interior decoration. **Add.** (h) Čiurlionio 13 — 4, Vilnius 232009; tel. 632 157.

- **DUBAUSKAS, Antanas**, Dir-Gen., flax co *Linas*, 1990 — ; b. 1945; grad. Kaunas Technol. Univ., eng. (mech.); Dep. Dir of *Linas*, 1986 — 90. **Add.** (h) Kniaudiškių 28 — 9, Panevėžys 235300; tel. 204 66.

- **DŪDĖNAS, Henrikas**, Dir-Gen., Kaunas Endocrine Products Factory, 1987 — ; b. 1933; grad. Kaunas Med. Acad., pharmacist; CSc. (Pharmacy), Doc.; Dir, Kaunas pharmaceutical pilot plant *Sanitas*, 1967 — 87. **Add.** (h) Putvinskio 32 — 4, Kaunas 233000; tel. 223 455.

- **DULEVIČIUS, Jonas**, engineer (mech.); b. 1935; grad. Moscow Inst. of Machine-Tools and Instruments; DSc. (Eng.), Prof.; lecturer, Kaunas Technol. Univ., 1970 — ; research in the sealing of hydraulic engine systems of flying vessels; 43 inv. **Add.** (h) Mickevičiaus 37, Kaunas 233000; tel. 206 610.

- **DUMČIUS, Arimantas**, cardiology surgeon; b. 1940; grad. Kaunas Med. Acad.; lectures at it, 1969 — ; DSc. (Med.), Prof.; was the first in Lith. to implant heart's musc le work helper, designed surgical instruments and heart electrodes; invest. principles of creation and application of biomech. heart; 1941 — 48 deported to Siberia with his parents. **Add.** (h) Urbšo 17 — 34, Kaunas 233043; tel. 779 844.

- **DUNDULIS, Bronius**, historian; b. 1909; grad. Kaunas Univ.; studied at Sorbonne Univ.; DSc. (Hist.), Prof.; lecturer, Vilnius Univ., 1941 — ; works on foreign policy of the Grand Duchy of Lithuania and Lithuania's situation during the Napoleonic wars; 12 books (*Napoleonas ir Lietuva 1812*, Napoleon and Lithuania 1812, 1940). **Add.** Universiteto 3, Vilnius 232734; tel. 623 997.

- **EIDINTAS, Alfonsas**, historian; b. 1952; grad. Vilnius Pedag. Inst.; lectured at this Inst., 1973 — 87; DSc. (Hist.), Doc.; Dep. Dir, Inst. of Lith. Hist., 1987 — ; works on Lith. emigration, pol. hist. of modern times, activities of the famous people; 4 monographs (*Antanas Smetona*, 1990). **Add.** Konarskio 40, Vilnius 232600; tel. 623 829.

- **EILUNAVIČIUS, Rimgaudas**, Chair., Lith. Journalists' Union, 1990 — ; b. 1938; educ. Kaunas Technol. Univ.; newspaper *Tiesa*, 1977 — 89. **Add.** Vilniaus 35, Vilnius 232600; tel. 661 790.

- **GAGAS, Stasys**, Dir, plant *Atrama*, 1973 — ; b. 1939; grad. Kaunas Technol. Univ., eng. (mech.). **Add.** (h) Daubos 16 — 8, Kaunas 233005; tel. 733 590.

- **GAIDAMONIENĖ, Dalija**, Dir, Inst. of Pulmonology, 1989 — ; b. 1938; grad. Kaunas Med. Acad., physician pulmonologist; DSc. (Med.), Prof.; research on the epidemiology of sarcoidosis in Lithuania, applied liver puncture for diagnosis of sarcoidosis. **Add.** (h) Ozo 30 — 63, Vilnius 232034; tel. 468 468.

- **GAIDYS, Povilas**, theatre dir, actor; b. 1937; grad. Lith. Conservatoire and Moscow A.Lunacharsky Inst. of Dramatic Art; Chief Dir, Klaipėda Drama Theatre, 1963 — ; plays are noted for subtle psychological insight. **Add.** (h) Mažvydo al. 13 — 10, Klaipėda 235800; tel. 139 88.

- **GAIŽUTIS, Algirdas**, Dir, Inst. of Culture and Art, 1990 — ; b. 1941; grad. Moscow Univ., phil.; DSc. (Phil.), Prof., Corr. Mem., Lith. Acad. of Sci.; Dep. Dir, Inst. of Hist., 1985 — 89; works on aesthetics, study of art and culture; 3 books. **Add.** Tilto 4, Vilnius 232001; tel. 613 646.

- **GAJAUSKAS, Balys**, Pres., Lith. Exiles Union, 1989 — ; b. 1926; part. in resistance movement; in 1948 was arrested and sentenced to 25 years imprisonment; in 1977 again sentenced to 10 years imprisonment; Int. Freedom and Peace Prize (1981, Houston); Lith. SC Deputy. **Add.** Gedimino pr. 53, Vilnius 232026; tel. 619 940.

- **GALKUS, Juozas**, graphic artist; b. 1932; grad. Vilnius Art Acad.; teaches at it, 1960 — ; Prof.; produced theatre, exh. and other posters, designed books. **Add.** (h) Šilo 29 — 11, Vilnius 232055; tel. 749 713.

- **GARASTAS, Vladas**, basketball coach, b. 1932; grad. Lith. Inst. of Physical Training; Chief Coach, Kaunas *Žalgiris* basketball team, 1979 — 89, USSR team, 1989 — 91; his team was a winner of Inter-continental Cup, 1986, and world and European prize-winner. **Add.** (h) Dujotiekio 7 — 21, Kaunas 233031; tel. 755 484.

- **GAUDRIMAS, Juozas**, musicologist; b. 1911; grad. Kaunas Conservatoire; DSc. (Arts), Prof., Acad., Lith. Acad. of Sci.; lecturer, Lith. Conservatoire, 1949 — ; studies: *Iš lietuvių muzikinės kultūros istorijos* (Hist. of Lith. Music Culture, vol. 1 — 2, 1958 — 64), *Tarybų Lietuvos kompozitoriai ir muzikologai* (Composers and Musicologists of Soviet Lithuania, 1988; Russ., 1978). **Add.** (h) Vasario 16-osios 16 — 8, Vilnius 232000; tel. 618 307.

- **GAVELIS, Ričardas**, writer; b. 1950; grad. Vilnius Univ.; coll. of stories *Įsibrovėliai* (The Invaders, 1982), *Nubaustieji* (The Punished, 1987), novels *Jauno žmogaus išpažintis* (The Confession of a Young Man, 1989), *Vilniaus pokeris* (The Poker of Vilnius, 1989); in his works the problem of ethical guilt, conscience of an individual is combined with the social and pol. circumstances; equivocation, irony and grotesque are characteristic of his writings. **Add.** (h) Laisvės pr. 43 — 46, Vilnius 232044.

- **GEDA, Sigitas**, poet; b. 1943; grad. Vilnius Univ.; verse coll. *Pėdos* (The Footsteps, 1966), *Mėnulio žiedai* (The Moon Blossoms, 1977), *Žalio gintaro vėriniai* (Necklaces of Green Amber, 1988), a narrative poem *Strazdas* (1967); rhymes, plays for children; motifs of the unity between nature and man based on mythical ideas, hist. and cultural themes, original metaphors, tendency to phil. reflection mark his poetry. **Add.** (h) Taikos 88 — 5, Vilnius 232017; tel. 420 134.

- **GEDŽIUS, Pranas**, Dir, Kaunas Spinning Factory, 1975 – ; b. 1934; grad. Kaunas Technol. Univ., eng. (mech.). *Add.* (h) Taikos pr. 82a – 48, Kaunas 233036; tel. 791 812.
- **GENIUŠAS, Algis Tomas**, Chair., Lith.-British Soc., 1990 – ; b. 1932; grad. Leningrad Univ., anglicist; DSc. (Philol.), Prof.; at Acad. of Sci., Dept of Foreign Lgs, 1980 – . *Add.* (h) Kalvarijų 172 – 81, Vilnius 232042; tel. 770 046.
- **GENIUŠIENĖ, Emma**, linguist (Baltic and Engl. philol.); b. 1938; grad. Leningrad Univ.; lecturer, Vilnius Univ., 1963 – ; DSc. (Philol.), Prof.; linguistic research in the syntax and semantics of Lith., Latv., Old Prussian, Engl.; linguistic typology, text linguistics. Major works: 'Reflexive Verbs in the Baltic Lgs and the Typology of Reflexives' (1983, in Russ.), 'The Typology of Reflexives' (1987, in Engl.). *Add.* (h) Žirmūnų 52 – 28, Vilnius 232051; tel. 734 810.
- **GENZELIS, Bronislovas**, philosopher; b. 1934; grad. Moscow Univ.; DSc. (Phil.), Prof.; lecturer, Vilnius Univ., 1964 – ; compiled reading book of hist. of phil. (4 books); Lith. SC Deputy. *Add.* (h) Smėlio 3 – 10, Vilnius 232055; tel. 744 898.
- **GIBAVIČIUS, Rimantas**, graphic artist; b. 1935; grad. Vilnius Art Acad.; its lecturer, 1960 – ; Prof.; author of plates, book ill., stage settings, frescoes. *Add.* (h) Literatų 9 – 21, Vilnius 232000; tel. 624 456 (off.).
- **GIRDENIS, Aleksas**, linguist (Baltic and Lith. philol.); b. 1937; grad. Vilnius Univ.; lecturer at it, 1962 – ; DSc. (Philol.), Prof.; has co-authored, with Z.Zinkevičius, a new classification of dialects of the Lith. lg. (publ. in 1966); research in phonetics, morphology, dialectology of the Lith. lg.; book *Fonologija* (Phonology, 1981), study on the versification of K.Donelaitis, 1991; Corr. Mem., Milan Linguistic Soc. *Add.* (h) Vileišio 12 – 47, Vilnius 232055; tel. 743 982.
- **GIRDZIJAUSKAITĖ, Audronė**, theatre and art critic; b. 1938; grad. Moscow A.Lunacharsky Inst. of Dramatic Art; works at Inst. of Culture and Art; monograph *Kazimiera Kymantaitė* (1983); notices, studies on theatre hist. *Add.* (h) Vaižganto 9 – 31, Vilnius 232001; tel. 618 191.
- **GIRDZIJAUSKAS, Juozapas**, lit. critic; b. 1935; grad. Vilnius Univ.; lecturer at it, 1962 – ; DSc. (Lit.), Prof.; promotes Lith. lit.; monographs *Lietuvių eilėdara. Silabinės-toninės sistemos susiformavimas* (Lith. Prosody. The Formation of the Syllabic-Tonic System, 1966), *Lietuvių eilėdara. XX a.* (Lith. Prosody. The 20th Cent., 1979). *Add.* (h) Kalvarijų 47 – 5, Vilnius 232045; tel. 610 897.
- **GLAVECKAS, Kęstutis**, economist; b. 1949; grad. Vilnius Univ.; lecturer at it, 1979 – ; DSc. (Econ.), Prof.; Sec., Cent. Cttee, LCP, 1989 – 90; Chair., Inst. of the Lith. Free Market; Lith. SC Deputy. *Add.* Saulėtekio al. 9, Vilnius 232054; tel. 768 997.
- **GRABAUSKAS, Vilius**, Rector, Kaunas Med. Acad., 1991 – ; b. 1942; grad. Kaunas Med. Acad., physician cardiologist; DSc. (Med.), Doc.; Head of Chronic Noninfectious Diseases Prevention Programme (WHO; Geneva),

1978 – 83, 1985 – 88; Vice-Pres., Lith. Physicians' Union; Dir, Cent. Scientific Research Lab. of Kaunas Med. Acad., 1988 – ; created Kaunas and Rotterdam Disease Prevention Programme. *Add.* (h) Gluosnių 13, Kulautuva 234321; tel. 543 254.
- **GRAKAUSKAS, Eimantas**, Chair., Agrarian Cttee of SC, 1990 – ; b. 1947; grad. Vilnius Univ., lawyer; CSc. (Law), Doc.; Head, Legal Dept of Min. of Agric., 1976 – 85; taught at Vilnius Univ., 1986 – 90; works on legal regulation of agric. activity; Lith. SC Deputy. *Add.* Gedimino pr. 53, Vilnius 232026; tel. 224 708.
- **GRANAUSKAS, Romualdas**, writer; b. 1938; coll. of stories *Duonos valgytojai* (The Bread-Eaters, 1975), novellas *Jaučio aukojimas* (The Offering of a Bull, 1975), *Gyvenimas po klevu* (Life Under the Maple Tree, 1988); characteristic of his works is the contraposition of the traditional ethic values and the present moral decline of the Lith. countryside. *Add.* (h) Gerosios Vilties 20 – 13, Vilnius 232015; tel. 638 771.
- **GRICIUS, Jonas**, cameraman; b. 1928; grad. Moscow Inst. of Cinematography; Lith. Film Studio, 1957 – , Dir, 1978 – 81; Chair., Lith. Cinematographers' Union, 1981 – 88; motion pictures are noted for natural approach and breadth of composition, visual expression; prize winner, int. film festivals in Carlovy Vary (1960), Venice (1964), Locarn (1965), Cannes (1966). *Add.* (h) Kaštonų 1 – 16, Vilnius 232001; tel. 619 163.
- **GRICIŪTĖ, Laima**, physician oncologist; b. 1926; grad. Kaunas Med. Acad.; DSc. (Med.), Prof.; Head, Experimental Lab. of Centre of Oncology, 1990 – ; Head, Environmental Cancerogens Dept of Int. Cancer Research Centre, 1974 – 80; Dir, Inst. of Oncology, 1982 – 90; created experimental models of the animal pulmonary cancer, studied the influence of new chem. preparations upon tumours. *Add.* (h) Kareivių 16 – 15, Vilnius 232000; tel. 775 868.
- **GRIGAS, Jonas**, physicist; b. 1938; grad. Vilnius Univ.; its lecturer, 1963 – ; DSc. (Phys.&Math.), Prof.; research in microwaves, solid state phys. (ferroelectricity) and phase transitions. *Add.* (h) Sruogos 36 – 24, Vilnius 232040; tel. 773 548.
- **GRIGAS, Kazys**, folklorist; b. 1924; grad. Vilnius Univ.; DSc. (Lit.); Inst. of Lith. Lit. and Folklore, 1954 – ; monograph *Lietuvių patarlės* (Lith. Sayings, 1976); compiled a comparative coll. of sayings *Patarlių paralelės* (Parallels of Sayings, 1987), coll. of Lith. folklore. Made up a systematic file of Lith. sayings (some 200,000 items). *Add.* (h) Čiurlionio 15 – 5, Vilnius 232009; tel. 632 260.
- **GRIGELIONIS, Bronius**, mathematician; b. 1935; grad. Vilnius Univ.; DSc. (Phys.&Math.), Prof., Acad., Lith. Acad. of Sci.; Inst. of Math. and Information Technol., 1959 – ; lecturer of Vilnius Univ.; research in theory and statistics of random processes. *Add.* (h) Vykinto 27 – 23, Vilnius 232004; tel. 751 789.
- **GRIKEVIČIUS, Almantas**, film dir; b. 1935; grad. Moscow Inst. of Cinematography; Lith.

Film Studio, 1964 − ; author of documentaries and feature films; Tours festival prize for the film 'The Sun Tales', 1966; San Remo festival prize for 'Feelings', 1969; Cannes Festival − 'The Fact', 1981. **Add.** (h) Kareivių 16 − 3, Vilnius 232012; tel. 776 944.

- **GRINBERGAS-GRINBERGS, Janis**, handball coach; b. 1925; grad. Latv. Inst. of Physical Culture; chief handball coach of Lith., 1953 − 88; coach of USSR handball women team, 1956 − 64, men, 1963 − 65, 1968 − 70; referee of int. rank; author of several books. **Add.** (h) Debesijos 8 − 8, Vilnius 232040; tel. 749 849.

- **GRIŠKEVIČIUS, Algirdas**, Dir, plant *Plasta*, 1971 − ; b. 1931; grad. Kaunas Technol. Univ., eng. **Add.** (h) Rūdninku 8 − 6, Vilnius 232024; tel. 611 676.

- **GUBAVIČIUS, Vytenis**, Dir-Gen., wool co *Drobė*, 1987 − ; b. 1951; grad. Kaunas Technol. Univ., eng. (econ.). **Add.** (h) Rasytės 42 − 16, Kaunas 233040; tel. 250 051.

- **GUČAS, Rimantas**, musicologist; b. 1942; grad. Lith. Conservatoire; established a studio of organ restoration at the Inst. of Conservation of Ancient Monuments and heads it, 1972 − ; this studio restored and reconstr. many organs of hist. significance, built new organs; compiles a hist. list of organs. **Add.** (h) Pušu 12 − 2, Vilnius 232004; tel. 753 357.

- **GUDAVIČIUS, Edvardas**, historian; b. 1929; grad. Kaunas Technol. and Vilnius Univ.; DSc. (Hist.), Doc.; Inst. of Lith. Hist., 1974 − ; lecturer, Vilnius Univ., 1975 − ; works on the medieval hist. of Lithuania, makes preparations for press of the Statutes of Lithuania; 5 books (*Kryžiaus karai Pabaltijyje ir Lietuva XIII a.*, Crusades in the Baltics in 13th cent., 1989). **Add.** Kosciuškos 30, Vilnius 232600; tel. 628 006.

- **GUDMONAS, Jonas**, graphic artist; b. 1941; grad. Vilnius Art Acad.; teaches at it, 1966 − ; Vice-Rector; author of pol., advertising and other posters. **Add.** (h) Žeručio 13 − 84, Vilnius 232043; tel. 447 539.

- **GUREVIČIUS, Arvydas**, jeweller; b. 1951; grad. Tallinn Art Univ.; autor of advertising signs, silver, ivory jewelry, enamel articles, drawings of original technique; exh. abroad. **Add.** (h) Taikos 20 − 51, Vilnius 232017; tel. 429 135.

- **IEŠMANTAS, Gintautas Vincas**, journalist; b. 1930; grad. Vilnius Pedag. Inst.; press worker, 1953 − ; in 1977 − 88 for contrib. in illegal press was imprisoned in Russia; Freedom Prize (1990, Denmark); Lith. SC Deputy. **Add.** Gedimino pr. 53, Vilnius 232026; tel. 629 084.

- **ILGŪNAS, Stanislovas Gediminas**, Chair., Educ., Sci. and Culture Cttee of SC, 1990 − ; b. 1936; grad. Vilnius Univ., journalist; part. of resistance movement, imprisoned in 1953 − 57, later persecuted; worked at constr. trust, 1962 − 90; works on the Lith. cultural figures of the 19th cent.; 2 books; Lith. SC Deputy. **Add.** Gedimino pr. 53, Vilnius 232026; tel. 618 965.

- **INIS, Laimonas**, E-in-C, magazine *Nemunas*, 1972 − ; b. 1938; grad. Vilnius Univ., journalist,

writer; has written some fiction books. **Add.** (h) Cvirkos 45 − 10, Kaunas 233000; tel. 226 474.

- **JACKEVIČIUS, Gediminas**, Dir, Utena Softs Drinks and Beer Factory, 1974 − ; b. 1942; grad. Kaunas Technol. Univ., eng. (mech.). **Add.** (h) Vilniaus 49a, Utena 234910; tel. 529 93.

- **JAKAITIENĖ, Evalda**, linguist (Lith. philol.); b. 1940; grad. Vilnius Univ.; lecturer at it, 1962 − ; DSc. (Philol.), Prof.; research in morphology, lexicology of modern Lith. lg. and lg. culture; publ. *Veiksmažodžių daryba. Priesagų vediniai* (Derivation of Verbs. Suffix Derivatives, 1973), *Lietuvių kalbos leksikologija* (Lexicology of the Lith. Lg., 1980), *Leksinė semantika* (Lexical Semantics, 1988). **Add.** (h) Čiurlionio 86 − 24, Vilnius 232009; tel. 662 507.

- **JAKUBAUSKAS, Feliksas**, textile artist; b. 1949; grad. Vilnius Art Acad. and Budapest Higher Sch. of Applied Art; artist, factory *Ramunė*, 1981 − ; author of tapestries of even, meticulous weave. **Add.** (h) Šv. Jono 7 − 2, Vilnius 232000; tel. 221 559.

- **JALOVECKAS, Romanas**, engineer (arch.); b. 1931; grad. Kaunas Technol. Univ.; Chief Arch., Restoration Trust of Cultural Monuments, 1970 − ; author of plans for renovation of old quarters of Vilnius, ecclesiastical and commercial buildings, co-founder of Nat. Heritage Museum. **Add.** (h) Žemaitės 7 − 56, Vilnius 232015; tel. 664 660.

- **JANKAUSKAS, Leonas**, Dir-Gen., Lith. TV equipm. co *Banga*, 1987 − ; b. 1941; grad. Kaunas Technol. Univ., eng. (mech.); Dir, Kaunas Radio Plant, 1980 − 87. **Add.** (h) Cvirkos 17 − 9, Kaunas 233000; tel. 227 198.

- **JANKAUSKAS, Vladislovas**, Dir-Gen., Dept of Statistics, 1990 − ; b. 1938; grad. Kaunas Technol. Univ., eng. (econ.); worked at Cent. Cttee, LCP, 1980 − 89. **Add.** Gedimino pr. 29, Vilnius 232746; tel. 619 556.

- **JANKEVIČIENĖ, Agota Algė**, arch. critic; b. 1930; grad. Kaunas Technol. Univ., CSc. (Arch.); Inst. of Constr. and Arch., 1956 − ; works on the Lith. professional and folk arch.; 2 monographs. **Add.** (h) Žuvinto 13 − 7, Kaunas 233031; tel. 243 972.

- **JANONIS, Bronislovas**, Dir, Alytus Experimental Home-Building Factory, 1982 − ; b. 1935; grad. Lith. Agric. Acad., eng. (forester). **Add.** (h) Kaštonu 50 − 21, Alytus 234580; tel. 318 60.

- **JANUŠAUSKAS, Algimantas Jonas**, mathematician; b. 1935; grad. Irkutsk Univ.; DSc. (Phys. & Math.); Novosibirsk Inst. of Math., 1963 − 87; Inst. of Math. and Informatics, 1987 − ; research in nonfreholmic boundary problems and theory of degenerating elliptical equations; was exiled with parents to the land of Altay (USSR) in 1941. **Add.** (h) Fabijoniškiu 90 − 59, Vilnius 232029.

- **JASIŪNAS, Valerijus**, Rector, Lith. Inst. of Physical Training, 1990 − ; Pres., Lith. Olympic Acad.; b. 1947; grad. it Lith. Inst. of Physical Training; CSc. (Pedag.), Doc.; teacher, researcher, 1973 − ; works on training and rehabilitation of sportsmen; **Add.** (h) Eidukevičiaus 35 − 34, Kaunas 233042; tel. 722 560.

- **JASUKAITYTĖ, Vidmantė**, writer; b. 1948; coll. of poems *Taip toli esu* (I Am So Far Away, 1979), *Saulės per daug* (Too Much Sun, 1986), books of novellas *Stebuklinga patvorių žolė* (The Miraculous Grass By the Fence, 1981), *Balandė, kuri lauks* (The Pigeon Who Will Wait, 1989), a novel about the post-war rural life *Po mūsų nebebus mūsų* (After Us There Will Be No Us, 1987, vol. 1); her works deal with the theme of man's ties with nature and hist., the fate of woman; romantic enthusiasm; Lith. SC Deputy. *Add.* (h) Gedimino pr. 45 — 6, Vilnius 232022; tel. 612 525.
- **JOKŪBONIS, Gediminas**, sculptor; b. 1927; grad. Vilnius Art Acad.; its lecturer, 1965 — ; Prof., Acad., USSR Art Acad.; author of memorial sculptures, monuments and tombstones, reliefs, sculptural portraits, medals. *Add.* (h) Kudirkos 4 — 3, Vilnius 232009; tel. 630 714.
- **JONAITIS, Jonas**, Dir-Gen., co *Ūla*, 1990 — ; b. 1944; grad. Kaunas Technol. Univ., eng. (electromech.). *Add.* (h) Partizanų 106 — 30, Kaunas 233009.
- **JUČAS, Mečislovas**, historian; b. 1926; grad. Vilnius Univ.; lecturer at it, 1958 — 66, 1972 — ; DSc. (Hist.), Prof.; at the Inst. of Lith. Hist., 1952 — 85; works on the medieval and modern hist. of Lithuania; 12 books (*Baudžiavos irimas Lietuvoje*, Decay of Serfdom in Lithuania, 1972; textbooks, coll. of hist. documents). *Add.* Universiteto 3, Vilnius 232734; tel. 623 997.
- **JUOZAPAITIS, Jurgis**, composer; b. 1942; grad. Lith. Conservatoire; major works: opera *Marių paukštė* (The Sea Bird), ballet *Andromeda*, 2 cantatas, 5 symphonies, symphonic poem *Vitražai* (Stained-glass Windows), chamber music. *Add.* (h) Kupalos 34 — 12, Vilnius 232004; tel. 352 585.
- **JUOZAITIS, Arvydas**, philosopher; b. 1956; grad. Vilnius Univ.; CSc. (Phil.); works at Inst. of Phil., Sociology and Law; prize winner in breast swimming (Montreal Olympic Games, 1976); Ed., newspaper *Sąjūdžio žinios*, 1988 — 89. *Add.* Saltoniškiu 58, Vilnius 232600; tel. 751 898.
- **JUOZAPAITIS, Vytautas**, composer; b. 1936; grad. Lith. Conservatoire; major works: opera *Čičinskas*, 2 oratorios, 3 symphonies, *Lietuviški šokiai* (Lith. Dances) for symphony orch., chamber music. *Add.* (h) Kupalos 34 — 18, Vilnius 232004; tel. 354 242.
- **JURĖNAITĖ, Raminta**, art scholar; b. 1953; grad. Vilnius Art Acad.; its lecturer, 1976 — ; CSc. (Arts); articles on modern Lith. and foreign art (mainly painting); set up Lith. art exh. in Austria, Norway. *Add.* (h) Pavasario 17 — 2, Vilnius 232055; tel. 610 557.
- **JURGINIS, Juozas**, historian; b. 1909; grad. Vilnius Univ.; lectured at it, 1950 — 72; DSc. (Hist.), Prof., Acad., Lith. Acad. of Sci.; Inst. of Lith. Hist., 1948 — ; works on the hist. of social econ. relations and culture; 21 book (*Baudžiavos įsigalėjimas Lietuvoje*, Strengthening of Serfdom in Lithuania, 1962); textbooks, coll. of hist. sources, a reader. *Add.* Kosciuškos 30, Vilnius 232600; tel. 741 502 (h).
- **JURŠĖNAS, Česlovas**, journalist; b. 1938; grad. Vilnius Univ.; works in periodicals, broad-casting; writes on int. problems; counsellor of the Govt of Lith. Rep.; Lith. SC Deputy. *Add.* Tumo-Vaižganto 2, Vilnius 232039; tel. 618 262.
- **JUŠKAITIS, Jonas**, poet; b. 1933; grad. Vilnius Univ.; coll. of poems *Ir aušros, ir žaros* (Both Dawns, And Evening-Glows, 1962), *Mėlyna žibutė apšvietė likimą* (The Blue Violet Has Lit Up the Fate, 1972), *Tolimos dainos* (The Far-Away Songs, 1981), *Dešimt žodžių jazmino žiedui* (Ten Words to the Jasmine Blossom, 1984), *Anapus gaiso* (Beyond the Glow, 1987), *Pučia vėjas į širdį* (The Wind Blows Into the Heart, 1990); he conveys the hist. of the native land by means of the situations of the human existence, extols spiritual virtues, tends to meditation and aestheticism; poems of religious motifs. *Add.* (h) Vytauto 6 — 8, Vilnius 232004; tel. 732 904.
- **JUŠKEVIČIUS, Pranciškus**, engineer (constr.); b. 1942; grad. Kaunas Technol. Univ.; CSc. (Arch.), Doc.; Vice-Rector, Vilnius Tech. Univ., 1990 — ; research in the urban communication systems, transport planning and urban development. *Add.* (h) Žvaigždžių 8 — 271, Vilnius 232050; tel. 447 870.
- **JUZELIŪNAS, Julius**, composer; b. 1916; grad. Kaunas Conservatoire; postgrad. Leningrad Conservatoire; DSc. (Arts), Prof.; lecturer, Lith. Conservatoire, 1952 — ; major works: operas *Sukilėliai* (The Insurgents), *Žaidimas* (A Game), ballet *Ant marių kranto* (On the Seashore), symphony-oratorio *Cantus Magnificat*, 5 symphonies, symphonic suite *Afrikietiški eskizai* (African Sketches), 4 concertos, chamber music; study *Akordo sandaros klausimai* (Problems of the Chord Structure, 1972); Chair., Research Centre of Bolshevism and Nazi Repressions in Lithuania. *Add.* (h) Birutės 11 — 4, Vilnius 232004; tel. 753 525.
- **KAIRYS, Antanas**, Dir, Inst. of Livestock Breeding and Veterinary, 1984 — ; b. 1934; grad. K.Timiriazev Agric. Acad. in Moscow, zootechnician; DSc. (Agric.), Prof., Corr. Mem., Lith. Acad. of Sci.; lectures at this Inst., 1960 — ; works on feed prod. and pig feeding. *Add.* Žebenkos 12, Baisogala, Radviliškio rj. 235125; tel. 536 08.
- **KALVANAS, Jonas Viktoras**, Chair., Consistory of the Lith. Evangelical Lutheran Church, 1976 — ; b. 1914; grad. Latv. Univ.; licentiate of theol.; bishop; since 1939 perf. pastoral work; ed. of the transl. into Lith. of the Little Catechism by M.Luther. *Add.* (h) Laisvės 68, Tauragė 235900; tel. 523 45.
- **KAMAITIS, Ipolitas Zenonas**, engineer (constr.); b. 1933; grad. Kaunas Technol. Univ.; CSc. (Eng.), Prof.; Vice-Rector, Vilnius Tech. Univ., 1990 — ; research in the reconstr., renovation, reinforcement and protection from corrosion of buildings and constr. *Add.* (h) Rinktinės 21 — 117, Vilnius 232051; tel. 758 677.
- **KAMINSKAS, Vytautas**, engineer (electrotech.); b. 1946; grad. Kaunas Technol. Univ.; DSc. (Eng.), Prof.; Vice-Rector, Vytautas Magnus Univ., 1990 — ; Dir, scientific centre *Informatika*, 1989 — ; research in computer modelling, diagnostics and management systems.

Add. (h) Pykuolio 84 — 2, Kaunas 233026; tel. 266198.

- **KAMUNTAVIČIUS, Gintautas Pranciškus,** physicist; b. 1942; grad. Vilnius Univ.; DSc. (Math. & Phys.); lecturer, Vytautas Magnus Univ., 1990 — ; research in the theory of a few body quantum systems, atom nuclei theory. **Add.** (h) Justiniškių 21 — 27, Vilnius 232056; tel. 410 607.

- **KANAPĖNAS, Rimantas,** engineer (mech.); b. 1941; grad. Kaunas Technol. Univ.; DSc. (Eng.); Dir, Laser Technol. Centre, 1989 — ; creates and introduces ecologically pure ind. laser technol., as well as portable med. laser magnetic equipm.; 120 inv. **Add.** (h) Jakšto 22 — 6, Vilnius 232009; tel. 224 524.

- **KANIAVA, Eduardas,** singer (bariton); b. 1937; grad. Lith. Conservatoire; lectures at it, 1979 — ; Prof.; worked on probation at Sofia Nat. Opera; soloist, Lith. Opera and Ballet Theatre, 1958 — ; toured Prague, Sofia, Havana, perf. concerts in European, Asia c., USA, Australia. **Add.** (h) Blindžių 19 — 1, Vilnius 232004; tel. 356 077.

- **KANOVIČ, Grigorij,** writer; b. 1929; grad. Vilnius Univ.; trilogy of novels *Žvakės vėjyje* (The Candles in the Wind, 1974 — 79), novels *Kvailių ašaros ir maldos* (The Tears and Prayers of the Fools, 1983), *Ir nėra vergams rojaus* (No Paradise For Slaves, 1989), *Ožiukas už du grašius* (The Kid for Two Pennies, 1989); his works depict the life of the Jewish community, the human fates during the periods of hist. changes; vivid details of everyday life and parabolic constr. mark his writings. **Add.** (h) Mildos 35 — 2, Vilnius 232055; tel. 744 245.

- **KARALIUS, Gediminas,** sculptor; b. 1942; grad. Vilnius Art Acad.; its lecturer, 1989 — ; author of decorative memorial and small-size sculptures, sculptural portraits, medals. **Add.** (h) Mėsinių 9 — 2, Vilnius 232024; tel. 622 786 (off.).

- **KARAŠKA, Arvydas,** ethnomusicologist; b. 1943; grad. Lith. Conservatoire; leads the folk ensemble *Kanklės,* 1988 — ; has written works on Lith. folklore, music instruments; reconstr. relic music instruments for museums in Moscow, Prague, Warsaw, Helsinki, Paris; Mem., Study Group on Music Archeology Research of the Int. Council for Traditional Music. **Add.** (h) Antakalnio 67 — 18, Vilnius 232040; tel. 741 617.

- **KARAZIJA, Rimantas,** Rector, Lith. Veterinary Acad., 1976 — ; b. 1936; grad. Lith. Veterinary Acad.; its lecturer, 1961 — ; CSc. (Veterinary), Prof.; works on the pathomorphological diagnostics and treatment of animals and poultry; 3 inv.; Chair., Lith. Union of Veterinary Surgeons. **Add.** (h) Demokratų 3 — 3, Kaunas 233026; tel. 260 847.

- **KAROSAS, Justinas,** philosopher; b. 1937; grad. Vilnius Univ.; lectures at it, 1963 — ; CSc. (Phil.), Doc.; book *Socializmas ir ideologija* (Socialism and Ideology, 1976). **Add.** (h) Debesijos 4 — 4, Vilnius 232055; tel. 749 143.

- **KARPALAVIČIUS, Leonas,** Dir, Šiauliai Non-woven Fabrics Plant, 1971 — ; b. 1932; grad. Vilnius Univ., econ.; Dir, textiles haberdash-

ery factory *Pakaita,* 1962 — 64; Dir, woollen cloth factory *Spartuolis,* 1964 — 71. **Add.** (h) Vytauto 98 — 4, Šiauliai 235400; tel. 388 58.

- **KARPAVIČIENĖ, Lilijana,** fashion designer; b. 1954; grad. Vilnius Art Acad.; teaches at it, 1990 — ; author of original design clothes, adorned with leather, guipure. **Add.** (h) Gelvonų 45 — 31, Vilnius 232010; tel. 467 255.

- **KASČIŪNAITĖ, Dalė,** painter, graphic artist; b. 1947; grad. Vilnius Art Acad.; abstractionist works of playful imagination and elegant design; one-person exh. in Bielefeld (Germany), Salzburg, Paris; works acquired by Moscow Tretyakov Gallery, numerous foreign collectors. **Add.** (h) Justiniškių 95 — 53, Vilnius 232056; tel. 426 711.

- **KAŠAUSKAS, Raimondas,** writer; b. 1934; grad. Vilnius Univ.; coll. of short stories and novellas *Suaugusiųjų žaidimai* (The Games of Grown-Ups, 1969), *Motociklininkai* (The Motorcyclists, 1973), *Mano motinos akys* (My Mother's Eyes, 1979), novels *Mažos mūsų nuodėmės* (Our Small Sins, 1975), *Gerumo kaina* (The Price of Goodness), *Vakaris vėjas* (The Western Wind, 1989), *Saulelė raudona* (The Sun Is Red, 1984); the author offers an epic description of the conflict between restless heroes and the environment, extols spiritual virtues exercised in everyday life. **Add.** (h) Švyturio 22 — 9, Vilnius 232040; tel. 741 673.

- **KAŠAUSKAS, Stasys,** journalist; b. 1943; grad. Vilnius Univ.; books on the social problems in the countryside, the crimes of Stalinism; Lith. SC Deputy. **Add.** (h) Lentupio 10 — 4, Vilnius 232400; tel. 741 410.

- **KATAKINAS, Jonas,** ballet dancer; b. 1950; grad. M.K.Čiurlionis Art Sch., postgrad. course at Leningrad Kirov Opera and Ballet Theatre; soloist, ballet premier, Lith. Opera and Ballet Theatre, 1970 — ; danced with the Moscow Bolshoi Theatre, toured European c. **Add.** (h) Dūkštų 8 — 53, Vilnius 232010; tel. 417 080.

- **KATILIUS, Raimondas,** violinist; b. 1947; grad. and postgrad. Moscow Conservatoire; Prof.; first violinist, String Quartet of Moscow Philharmonic; lecturer, Lith. Conservatoire, 1975 — ; has toured Europe, America, Africa and Asia; part. in String Quartets Comp. in Belgrad (1st prize, 1971), Bratislava (1st prize, 1972); prizes at Sibelius violinists comp. in Helsinki (1970) and Montreal (1972). **Add.** (h) Rudens 4 — 28, Vilnius 232040; tel. 744 043.

- **KATINAS, Vladas,** geologist; b. 1939; grad. Vilnius Univ.; CSc. (Geol. and Mineralogy); Inst. of Geol., 1962 — ; research in the formation of amber and its property; 2 books. **Add.** (h) Architektų 53 — 32, Vilnius 232049; tel. 440 608.

- **KAUKAITĖ, Giedrė,** singer (soprano); b. 1943; grad. Lith. Conservatoire; lectures at it, 1978 — ; Doc.; worked on probation at *La Scala* theatre in Milan under Genare Barra, at Int. Acad. *Mozarteum* in Salzburg under Paul Schilawsky; soloist, Lith. Opera and Ballet Theatre, 1968 — 78, Lith. Nat. Philharmonic, 1978 — ; has toured European c., USA; World Youth and Students Festival in Sofia (3rd prize, 1968); Glinka singing comp. (1st prize, 1977). **Add.**

(h) Tumo-Vaižganto 4 — 3, Vilnius 232001; tel. 625 793.

■ **KAVALIAUSKAS, Česlovas**, Roman Catholic priest; b. 1923; grad. Kaunas Priest Sem.; ordained in 1946; transl. the New Testament from Greek (1972, 1988); pol. prisoner, 1950 — 56. *Add.* (h) Bulikos 1, Jieznas 234362; tel. 571 91 (off.).

■ **KAVALIAUSKAS, Vilius**, journalist; b. 1951; grad. Vilnius Univ.; press worker since 1972; 'Moscow News' correspondent in USA, 1984 — 88. *Add.* (h) Blindžių 31 — 9, Vilnius 232004; tel. 750 595.

■ **KAZĖNAS, Zinas**, photographer; b. 1936; grad. photo studies in Daugavpils; colour photography of Lith. culture and arch., for advertisement, touristic publ., fashions; personal exh. abroad, winner of many prizes; Chair., Photo and advertisement studio *Zika*, 1991 — . *Add.* POB 1196, Vilnius 232001; tel. 410 221.

■ **KAZLAUSKAS, Vytautas**, Chair., Lith. Humanist Party; phil.; b. 1932; CSc. (Phil.), Doc.; lectured at Vilnius Art Acad., 1961 — 68; lecturer, Vilnius Conservatoire, 1962 — ; research on spiritual problems of an individual; 2 monographs (*Dvasios pasaulio grožis*, Beauty of Spiritual World, 1990). *Add.* Gedimino pr. 42, Vilnius 232001; tel. 623 462.

■ **KAŽDAILIS, Arvydas Stanislovas**, graphic artist; b. 1939; grad. Vilnius Art Acad.; teaches at Čiurlionis Art Sch., 1965 — ; author of book ill., prints, frescoes. *Add.* (h) Algirdo 26a — 5, Vilnius 232009; tel. 633 095.

■ **KAŽYS, Rimantas Jonas**, engineer (radio technol.); b. 1943; grad. Kaunas Technol. Univ.; its lecturer, 1970 — ; DSc. (Eng.), Prof.; research in acoustic measuring systems; 90 inv. *Add.* (h) Vasiliausko 39 — 12, Kaunas 233031; tel. 736 895.

■ **KELIUOTIS, Jurgis**, Dir, textile factory *Šilkas*, 1973 — ; b. 1935; grad. Kaunas Technol. Univ., eng. (mech.). *Add.* (h) Būgos 20 — 1, Kaunas 233000; tel. 220 706.

■ **KERBELYTĖ, Bronislava**, folklorist; b. 1935; grad. Moscow Univ.; DSc. (Lit.); Inst. of Lith. Lg., 1958 — ; research in the semantics and structure of narrative Lith. folklore; publ. study *Lietuvių liaudies padavimai* (Lith. Folk Legends, 1970), has filed a catalogue of narrative Lith. folklore (some 80,500 texts). *Add.* (h) Gerosios Vilties 6 — 58, Vilnius 232015; tel. 631 636.

■ **KIMTYS, Liudvikas**, physicist; b. 1940; grad. Vilnius Univ.; its lecturer, 1966 — ; DSc. (Chem.), Prof.; research in gen. phys. and molecular spectroscopy. *Add.* (h) Žirgo 3 — 22, Vilnius 232040; tel. 765 396.

■ **KISIELIUS, Kęstutis**, architect; b. 1952; grad. Vilnius Tech. Univ.; Design Inst. of City Constr., 1975 — ; author of sports, commercial, educ., cultural buildings. *Add.* (h) Gelvonų 23 — 18, Vilnius 232033.

■ **KITKAUSKAS, Napoleonas**, civil eng.; b. 1931; grad. Kaunas Technol. Univ.; CSc. (Arch.); pol. prisoner, 1947 — 54; at Monument Restoration Inst. since 1970, Chief Spec., 1978 — ; author of plans for renovation of cultural, ecclesiastical, ancient defence buildings in Vilnius; works on the restoration of Lith. defence and cultural arch. monuments. *Add.* (h) Ligoninės 4 — 3, Vilnius 232024; tel. 612 873.

■ **KIUDULAS, Ignas**, Dir, Vilnius Enzymes Preparations Plant, 1983 — ; b. 1944; grad. Vilnius Univ., microbiol.; at the plant since 1971. *Add.* (h) Baltupio 72 — 27, Vilnius 232057; tel. 779 702.

■ **KIUDULAS, Jonas**, Dir, stockings factory *Koton*, 1985 — ; b. 1942; grad. Kaunas Technol. Univ., eng. (econ.). *Add.* (h) Savanorių pr. 397 — 21, Kaunas 233702; tel. 712 247.

■ **KLIMAŠAUSKAS, Kazimieras Juozas**, Dir-Gen., scientific ind. co *Venta*, 1977 — ; b. 1938; grad. Vilnius Univ., phys.; DSc. (Eng.); at co since 1963. *Add.* (h) Vokiečių 14 — 2, Vilnius 232024; tel. 617 886.

■ **KLUMBYS, Egidijus**, Chair., Lith. Christian Dem. Party, 1990 — ; b. 1952; grad. Kaunas Med. Acad., neurosurgeon; CSc. (Med.); Head, Neurosurgery Lab., 1982 — 90; Lith. SC Deputy. *Add.* Gedimino pr. 53, Vilnius 232026; tel. 618 291.

■ **KMIELIAUSKAS, Antanas**, painter, graphic artist, sculptor; b. 1932; grad. Vilnius Art Acad.; teaches at this Acad., 1977 — ; author of portraits, frescoes, sculptures, gravestones, prints (most depict arch. monuments of Vilnius), ex libris; gold medal in San Vit contest, first prize in Beld contest (both in 1974); numerous works acquired by collectors in USA, Italy. *Add.* (h) Sibiro 28 — 2, Vilnius 232014; tel. 611 327.

■ **KOBECKAITĖ, Halina**, Dir-Gen., Dept of Nationalities, 1990 — ; b. 1939; grad. Vilnius Univ.; CSc. (Phil.), Doc.; lecturer, Vilnius Tech. Univ., 1971 — 89. *Add.* Basanavičiaus 5, Vilnius 232683; tel. 613 049.

■ **KOMISORAITIS, Romualdas**, Dir-Gen., co *Trinyčiai*, 1981 — ; b. 1937; grad. Kaunas Technol. Inst., eng. (mech.). *Add.* Igulos 24 — 55, Klaipėda 235818; tel. 178 47.

■ **KONTRIMAVIČIUS, Vytautas**, helminthologist; b. 1930; grad. Leningrad Veterinary Inst.; DSc. (Biol.), Acad., Lith. Acad. of Sci., Corr. Mem., USSR Acad. of Sci.; Dir, Inst. of Biol. Problems of the North (in Magadan), Far East Scientific Centre of the USSR Acad. of Sci., 1968 — 82; Acad.-Sec., Lith. Acad. of Sci., 1984 — ; works on helminth faunae, taxonomy, ecology, theory of parasitism; 5 monographs. *Add.* (h) Vienuolio 14 — 8, Vilnius 232001; tel. 616 155.

■ **KORKUTIS, Petras**, Head, Lith. Board for Hydrometeorology, 1989 — ; b. 1938; grad. Vilnius Univ., meteorologist; CSc. (Geogr.);. Head, Research and Control Centre on Natural Surroundings Pollution, 1980 — 89; publ. monograph *Atmosferos oro apsauga Lietuvoje* (Protection of Atmospheric Air in Lithuania, 1984; in Russ.). *Add.* Rudnios 6, Vilnius 232600; tel. 751 194.

■ **KRASNOVAS, Aleksandras**, lit. critic; b. 1948; grad. Vilnius Univ.; E-in-C, *Vaga* publrs, 1989 — ; a study *Vidinio monologo proza* (The Prose of the Inner Monologue, 1983). *Add.* (h) Architektų 51 — 55, Vilnius 232043; tel. 440 185.

- **KRAVTAS, Petras**, Dir, scientific ind. co *Sirijus*, 1987 — ; b. 1950; grad. Kaunas Technol. Univ., eng. (mech.). *Add.* (h) Kooperacijos 7 — 36, Klaipėda 235800; tel. 561 53.
- **KRIŠČIŪNAS, Kęstutis**, engineer (electromech.); b. 1944; grad. Kaunas Technol. Univ.; its lecturer, 1965 — , Vice-Rector, 1990 — ; DSc. (Eng.), Prof.; research in the automation of electric gears and ind. equipm., information ties between man and machine; 50 inv. *Add.* (h) Vitkausko 39 — 4, Kaunas 233031.
- **KROPAS, Stasys**, Chair., Municipal Affairs Cttee of SC, 1990 — ; b. 1953; grad. Vilnius Univ., financier; CSc. (Econ.), Doc.; lecturer, Vilnius Univ., 1977 — 88; works on financial system in ind. and transportation. Lith. SC Deputy. *Add.* Gedimino pr. 53, Vilnius 232026; tel. 224 998.
- **KROTKUS, Arūnas**, physicist; b. 1948; grad. Vilnius Univ.; DSc. (Phys. & Math.); Inst. of Semiconductors Phys., Vice-Dir, 1989 — ; research in picosecond optoelectronics, phenomena of hot electrons in semiconductors. *Add.* Požėlos 52, Vilnius 232600.
- **KRUKAUSKAS, Aleksandras**, E-in-C, newspaper *Sportas*, 1988 — ; b. 1939; grad. Lith. Veterinary Acad., zootechnician; press worker since 1960. *Add.* Gedimino pr. 37, Vilnius 232600; tel. 616 757.
- **KRŪMINIS, Bronislovas**, architect; b. 1928; grad. Vilnius Art Acad.; Chief Arch. of designs, Design Inst. of City Constr., 1961 — ; author of multi-storey cast concrete dwelling houses of serial prod. and hostels in Vilnius, Kaunas, Šiauliai, Klaipėda. *Add.* (h) Architektų 59 — 2, Vilnius 232049; tel. 770 805.
- **KRUTINIS, Vaclovas**, sculptor; b. 1948; grad. Vilnius Art Acad.; Sec., Lith. Artists' Union, 1987 — ; Dir, Fund of Lith. Artists' Union, 1989 — ; author of park and small-size sculptures, tombstones. *Add.* (h) Antakalnio 20 — 32, Vilnius 232055; tel. 744 037.
- **KUBILIUS, Jonas**, mathematician; b. 1921; grad. Vilnius Univ.; its lecturer, 1946 — , Rector, 1958 — 90; DSc. (Phys. & Math.), Prof., Acad., Lith. Acad. of Sci.; Hon. Dr, Greifswald, Latv., Prague Univ.; founder and head of the Lith. sch. of theory of probabilities and number theory; research in the theory of probabilities and probability digital theory; publ. in Engl., Russ. *Add.* (h) Kuosų 14, Vilnius 232055; tel. 748 989.
- **KUBILIUS, Vytautas**, lit. critic; b. 1928; grad. Vilnius Univ.; DSc.(Philol.); Inst. of Lith. Lit. and Folklore, 1955 — ; monographs about the works of S. Nėris (1968), K.Boruta (1980), I.Simonaitytė (1987), *XX a. lietuvių lyrika* (1987), Lyrics of the 20th Cent., 1982), *Lietuvių literatūra ir pasaulinės literatūros procesas* (Lith. Lit. and the Process of World Lit., 1983), *Žanrų kaita ir sintezė* (The Change and Synthesis of Genres, 1986). *Add.* (h) Mildos 31 — 15, Vilnius 232055; tel. 358 906.
- **KUDZYS, Antanas**, engineer (civil); b. 1925; grad. Kaunas Univ.; DSc. (Eng.), Prof., Acad., Lith. Acad. of Sci.; lecturer, Vilnius Tech. Univ., 1965 — ; Hon. Dr, Budapest Technol. Univ.; created the theory of reliability of ferro-concrete

buildings and constr. . *Add.* (h) Jūratės 15, Vilnius 232055; tel. 740 123.
- **KULIKAUSKIENĖ-VOLKAITĖ, Regina**, archeologist; b. 1916; grad. Vilnius Univ.; DSc. (Hist.), Prof., Corr. Mem., Lith. Acad. of Sci.; Inst. of Lith. Hist., 1962 — ; works on the ethnogenesis of Lithuanians, material culture of the 9th — 12th cent., development of social relations; 10 books (*Lietuvos archeologijos bruožai*, Outline of Lith. Archeology, 1961; co-author), albums. *Add.* (h) Kuosų 6, Vilnius 232055; tel. 741 656.
- **KULYS, Juozas**, Dir, Inst. of Biochem., 1985 — ; b. 1944; grad. Moscow Univ.; DSc. (Chem.), Prof., Corr. Mem., Lith. Acad. of Sci.; at the Inst. of Biochem. since 1971; initiator of the creation of biol. transformers for primary information, has created electrochem., optical and solid biosensors used for prod. of metabolic analysers; 4 monographs, 40 inv. *Add.* (h) Pašilaičių 16 — 75, Vilnius 232022; tel. 359 144 (off.).
- **KUNČIUS, Algimantas**, photographer; b. 1939; studied at Vilnius Univ. and Vilnius Pedag. Inst.; his photographs are noted for emotionality, fragmentary composition, distinct texture; personal exh. abroad, winner of many prizes; albums: *Senojo Vilniaus vaizdai* (Views of Old Vilnius, 1969), *Susitikimai* (Meetings, 1984); AFIAP, 1976. *Add.* (h) Kupalos 16 — 1, Vilnius 232000; tel. 750 846.
- **KUNEVIČIENĖ, Elvyra**, Min. of Finance, 1991 — ; b. 1939; grad. N.Voznesensky Financial and Econ. Inst. in Leningrad; CSc. (Econ.), Doc.; worked with Lith. Management Acad., 1975 — 91; works on finances and calculation. *Add.* Šermukšnių 9, Vilnius 232600; tel. 625 172.
- **KUOKŠTIS, Edmundas**, physicist; b. 1953; grad. Vilnius Univ.; DSc. (Phys.&Math.); lecturer, Vytautas Magnus Univ., 1990 — ; research in luminescence and optical properties of highly excited semiconductors, laser spectroscopy of condensed media. *Add.* (h) Nočios 4 — 23, Vilnius 232009; tel. 639 562.
- **KUOLYS, Darius**, Min. of Culture and Educ., 1990 — ; b. 1962; grad. Vilnius Univ., Lith. philol.; worked at Vilnius Univ., 1985 — 90; works on Lith. cultural hist. *Add.* Volano 2/7, Vilnius 232691; tel. 622 483.
- **KUPREVIČIUS, Giedrius**, composer; b. 1944; grad. Lith. Conservatoire; has written musicals, operas, rock oratorio, cantatas for choir and synthesizer, symphony, chamber music, compositions for carillon, incidental music; perf. concerts, plays the Kaunas Carillon, 1957 — . *Add.* (h) Rokiškio 12, Kaunas 233005; tel. 225 519.
- **KURAS, Algimantas**, painter; b. 1940; grad. Vilnius Art Acad.; Lith. Art Museum, 1967 — ; author of landscapes, still-lifes (mostly old things against the background of nature), assemblages. *Add.* (h) Žvaigždžių 1 — 28, Vilnius 232050; tel. 456 203.
- **KŪRIS, Pranas**, lawyer (int. law); b. 1938; grad. Vilnius Univ.; lectures at it, 1961 — ; DSc. (Law), Prof., Corr. Mem., Lith. Acad. of Sci.; in

1976 lectured at Paris Univ.; Min. of Justice, 1977–91; 5 books. *Add.* (h) Čiurlionio 6–9, Vilnius 232009; tel. 769 877 (off.).

- **KUTAVIČIUS, Bronius**, composer; b. 1932; grad. Lith. Conservatoire; lecturer, Čiurlionis Art Sch., 1975–, Lith. Conservatoire, 1984–; major works: opera for children *Kaulo senis ant Geležinio kalno* (Doddering Old Man on the Iron Mountain), opera-poem *Strazdas – žalias paukštis* (Thrush, the Green Bird), oratorios: *Panteistinė oratorija* (Pantheistic Oratorio), *Paskutinės pagonių apeigos* (The Last Pagan Rites), *Iš jotvingių akmens* (From the Jatvingian Stone), *Pasaulio medis* (Tree of the World), mystery *Magiškas sanskrito ratas* (A Vicious Circle of Sanskrit), *Dvylika vartų* (Twelve Gates) for chamber orch., chamber music. *Add.* (h) Kupalos 34 – 1, Vilnius 232004; tel. 356 464.
- **KUZMA, Stanislovas**, sculptor; b. 1947; grad. Vilnius Art Acad.; works (park, exterior, small-size sculptures in wood, bronze) emotional, of subtle, aestheticized forms. *Add.* (h) Krivių 41 – 2, Vilnius 232007; tel. 696 642.
- **KUZMICKAS, Bronislavas Juozas**, Dep. Chair., SC of Lith. Rep., 1990–; b. 1935; grad. Vilnius Univ., phil., hist.; DSc. (Phil.), Prof.; worked at Inst. of Phil., Sociology and Law, lectured at Vilnius higher sch., 1973–90; research in Catholic modernism, hist. of phil.; 7 books; Chair., Lith. Scientists' Union and Lith.-It. Soc.; Lith. SC Deputy. *Add.* Gedimino pr. 53, Vilnius 232026; tel. 627 533.
- **KUŽULIS, Bronislovas**, Dir, Inst. of Agrarian Econ., 1990–; b. 1938; grad. Lith. Veterinary Acad., econ.; CSc. (Econ.); at Inst. since 1973; works on the management and org. of agric. prod. *Add.* Sierakausko 18, Vilnius 232600; tel. 614 525.
- **KVEDARAVIČIUS, Algirdas**, Pres., Lith. Consumers Assoc., 1989–; b. 1938; grad. Kaunas Technol.Univ., eng. (mech.); worked at the Soc. of Inventors and Innovators, 1965 – 80. *Add.* Gedimino pr. 3, Vilnius 232600; tel. 616 134.
- **LANDSBERGIS, Vytautas**, Chair., SC of Lith. Rep., 1990 – ; b. 1932; grad. Lith. Conservatoire, musicologist; CSc. (Arts), Prof.; Hon. Dr, Loyola Chicago Univ.; taught at Lith. Conservatoire, 1975 – 90; works (8 monographs) on the hist. of Lith. music, mainly on the artist and composer M.K.Čiurlionis; Chair., *Sąjūdis* Seim Council, 1988 – 90; Lith. SC Deputy. *Add.* Gedimino pr. 53, Vilnius 232026; tel. 628 986.
- **LANKAUSKAS, Romualdas**, writer; b. 1932; coll. of short stories and novellas *Klajojantis smėlis* (The Moving Sand, 1960), *Šiaurės vitražai* (The Stained Glass Panels of the North, 1970), *Džiazo vežimas* (The Cart of the Jazz Band, 1971), novels *Vidury didelio lauko* (In the Midst of a Big Field, 1962), *Netikėtų išsipildymų valanda* (The Hour of Unexpected Fulfilments, 1975), *Projektas* (The Project, 1986), *Nė vienas nebus pagailėtas* (No One Will Be Spared, 1990); in his works the conflicts of intellectuals with the surrounding world, the phenomena of philistinism, the standardization of everyday life and mentality of contemporary soc. are dominant;

the style is laconic; books transl. into Pol., Russ., Est. and other lgs. *Add.* (h) Mildos 31 – 16, Vilnius 232055; tel. 358 909.

- **LANKUTIS, Jonas**, Dir, Inst. of Lith. Lit. and Folklore, 1984–; b. 1925; grad. Vilnius Univ., philol.; DSc. (Philol.), Acad., Lith. Acad. of Sci.; scientific works on the Lith. lit. of 20th cent., the drama, works of famous writers (studies on Justinas Marcinkevičius, 1977, in Russ., 1980, Juozas Grušas, 1981, Eduardas Mieželaitis, 1965, Vincas Mykolaitis-Putinas, 1961, 1973, 1986), monographs *Lietuvių dramaturgijos raida* (Development of Lith. Drama, 1974, 1976), author and ed. of *Lietuvių literatūros istorija* (Hist. of Lith. Lit., 1957 – 68, 4 vols, 1979 – 1982, 2 vols). *Add.* Antakalnio 6, Vilnius 232055; tel. 621 946.
- **LASAVICKAS, Sigitas**, architect; b. 1926; grad. Vilnius Art Acad.; Monument Preservation Inst., 1969 – ; author of plans for renovation of ecclesiastical, ancient defence buildings; co-author of master plan for the reconstr. of Old Vilnius. *Add.* (h) Ligoninės 4 – 13, Vilnius 232024.
- **LATĖNAS, Algirdas**, theatre and film actor; b. 1953; grad. Lith. Conservatoire; works at Youth Theatre. *Add.* Arklių 5, Vilnius 232001; tel. 626 732.
- **LATĖNAS, Faustas**, composer; b. 1956; grad. Vilnius Conservatoire; Man., Vilnius *Lėlė* theatre, 1990 – ; major works: symphonic picture *Nerimas* (Anxiety), oratorio *Rauda-atminimas* (Lamentation Memory), 2 cantatas, *Agnus Dei* for mixed choir, chamber music, incidental music (~70). *Add.* (h) Blindžių 33 – 9, Vilnius 232004; tel. 351 628.
- **LAUCEVIČIUS, Aleksandras**, physician cardiologist; b. 1950; grad. Vilnius Univ.; Head, Sector of Electrocardiogram and Ultra-sound, Cardiosurgery Clinic; DSc. (Med.), Prof.; pioneered echocardiography in Lithuania, promoted foundation of heart clinical electrophysiological service in Vilnius, lab. for heart non-invasion electrophysiological research, intracardial and electrophysiological research, ultra-sound diagnosis of heart diseases and echocardiography load. *Add.* (h) Oginskio 4 – 14, Vilnius 232040; tel. 768 329.
- **LAURUŠAS, Vytautas**, Rector, Lith. Conservatoire, 1983 – ; composer; b. 1930; grad. Lith. Conservatoire; lectures at it, 1961 – ; Prof.; Chair., Lith. Composers' Union, 1971 – 1989; Vice-Chair., Supreme Soviet of the Lith. SSR, 1980 – 90; major works: opera *Paklydę paukščiai* (Stray Birds), cantatas, concerto for voice, chamber music. *Add.* (h) Kupalos 38 – 2, Vilnius 232004; tel. 751 684.
- **LAZAUSKAS, Juozas**, Dir, Research Inst. of Agric., Vokė Branch, 1965 – ; b. 1931; grad. Lith. Agric. Acad., selectionist plant-grower; DSc. (Agric.), Prof., Acad., Lith. Acad. of Sci., Corr. Mem., USSR Acad. of Agric. Sci.; bred new varieties of bird's-foot, fodder lupin, potatoes, esparto grass; 5 monographs. *Add.* (h) Mildos 5 – 24, Vilnius 232055; tel. 744 198.
- **LAZUTKA, Stasys**, historian; b. 1923; grad. Vilnius Univ.; lectures at it, 1948 – 52, 1959 – ;

DSc. (Hist.); works on Lithuania's hist. of law, culture; 4 books (*I Lietuvos statutas — Didžiosios Lietuvos kunigaikštystės feodalinis kodeksas*, The 1st Statute of Lithuania — Feudal Code of the Grand Duchy of Lithuania, 1973; in Russ.), makes preparations for press of the Statutes of Lithuania. *Add.* Universiteto 3, Vilnius 232734; tel. 623 997.

▪ **LECKAS, Algimantas**, engineer (arch.); b. 1934; grad. Kaunas Technol. Univ.; Chief Arch. of designs, Design Inst. of City Constr., 1966 — ; author of original commercial, recreational, sports, med. buildings in Kaunas, Palanga; author of detailed residential area plans in various towns. *Add.* (h) Birutės 40b — 5, Vilnius 232004; tel. 730 667.

▪ **LEITAITĖ, Judita**, singer (mezzo-soprano); b. 1959; grad. Lith. Conservatoire; worked on probation under E.Schwarzkopf in Salzburg; soloist, Lith. Nat. Philharmonic, 1984 — ; has toured European c., USA; part. in Glinka singing comp. (2nd prize, 1989). *Add.* (h) Didžioji 45, Vilnius 232024; tel. 626 802.

▪ **LEONAVIČIUS, Bronius**, Chair., Lith. Artists' Union, 1987 — ; b. 1933; grad. Kaunas Žukas Art Sch., engraver; worked for publishing houses, 1969 — 86; author of book ill., posters. *Add.* (h) Pilies 26 — 11, Vilnius 232001; tel. 626 766.

▪ **LIANDZBERGIS, Zigmantas**, engineer (arch.); b. 1929; grad. Kaunas Technol. Univ.; Doc.; Chief Arch. of designs, Design Inst. of City Constr., 1964 — ; lecturer, Vilnius Tech. Univ., 1978 — ; co-author of original med., commercial, sports buildings and original interiors. *Add.* (h) Sėlių 64 — 1, Vilnius 232004; tel. 753 073.

▪ **LIAUČIUS, Jonas**, Chair., Nat. Defence and Internal Affairs Cttee of SC, 1991 — ; b. 1947; grad. Vilnius Univ., lawyer; worked as advocate in Panevėžys. Lith. SC Deputy. *Add.* Gedimino pr. 53, Vilnius 232026; tel. 224 691.

▪ **LOŠYS, Mindaugas**, Chair., Supreme Court of Lith. Rep., 1990 — ; b. 1939; grad. Vilnius Univ., lawyer; judge, Lith. Supreme Court, 1972 — 74; advocate, 1974 — . *Add.* Lentpjūvių 24, Vilnius 232725; tel. 610 560.

▪ **LUBYS, Bronislavas**, Dir-Gen., chemical fertilizer co *Azotas*, 1985 — ; b. 1938; grad. Kaunas Technol. Univ., eng. (technol.); CSc. (Chem.), Doc.; at the Jonava Nitrogen Fertilizer Plant, 1963 — 79; Lith. SC Deputy. *Add.* (h) Vilniaus 5 — 21, Jonava 235000; tel. 541 21.

▪ **LUKŠA, Antanas**, Chair., Lith. Exiles Union, 1990 — ; b. 1923; educ. Kaunas Univ., teacher; pol. prisoner, exile, 1947 — 57. *Add.* (h) Lauručiai, Prienų rj. 234340; tel. (8 — 249) 449 60.

▪ **LUKŠAS, Aleksandras**, Dir, Monument Restoration Inst., 1986 — ; b. 1941; grad. Kaunas Technol. Univ., eng. (arch.); at design inst. since 1966; designed some public and dwelling houses in Vilnius. *Add.* (h) Filaretų 42a — 53, Vilnius 232007; tel. 696 512.

▪ **LUKŠAS, Gytis**, film dir; b. 1946; grad. Moscow Inst. of Cinematography; Lith. Film Studio, 1970 — ; makes feature films. *Add.* (h) Pervažos 22 — 2, Vilnius 232001; tel. 357 048.

▪ **LUKŠIENĖ, Meilė**, historian of culture; b. 1913; grad. Kaunas Univ.; DSc. (Pedag.); Inst. of Pedag., 1959 — ; author of studies 'Traits of the Hist. of Lith. Educ. in Early XIX Cent.' (1970), 'Democratic Thought of Bringing up in Lithuania: 2nd Half of the XVIII Cent. — 1st Half of the XIX Cent.' (1985). *Add.* (h) Brolių 7 — 40, Vilnius 232038; tel. 266 948.

▪ **MACAITIS, Saulius**, film critic; b. 1940; grad. Moscow Inst. of Cinematography; Ed., magazine *Kinas*, 1974 — ; Inst. of Culture and Art, 1989 — ; book 'The 25 Houses', 1990; scenarios for documentaries. *Add.* (h) Žirmūnų 112 — 26, Vilnius 232012; tel. 770 620.

▪ **MACEVIČIUS, Juozas**, Dir-Gen., Vilnius Fur Factory, 1967 — ; b. 1932; grad. Kaunas Technol. Univ., eng. (technol.). *Add.* (h) Antakalnio 62 — 32, Vilnius 232055; tel. 744 521.

▪ **MACIJAUSKAS, Aleksandras**, photographer; b. 1938; photographs noted for grotesque elements, metaphors; personal exh. abroad, winner of many prizes; AFIAP, 1976. *Add.* (h) Taikos 63 — 56, Kaunas 233036; tel. 750 800.

▪ **MACIŪTĖ, Regina**, singer (soprano); b. 1946; grad. Lith. Conservatoire; lectures at it, 1988 — ; worked on probation in Sofia under J.Josifov and in Stuttgart Back Acad.; soloist, Lith. Nat. Philharmonic; has toured Europe, USA; Glinka singing comp. (4th prize, 1973). *Add.* (h) Viršuliškių 65 — 35, Vilnius 232056; tel. 410 652.

▪ **MAČIULIS, Algimantas**, architect; b. 1931; grad. Vilnius Art Acad.; teaches at it, 1971 — ; CSc. (Arts), Prof.; Chief Arch. of Vilnius, 1968 — 71; designer of large admin., cultural, public, sch. buildings and stores of complex composition (mainly in Vilnius) as well as interiors. *Add.* (h) Tuskulėnų 7 — 57, Vilnius 232051; tel. 733 734.

▪ **MAKAČINAS, Teisutis**, composer; b. 1938; grad. Lith. Conservatoire; teaches at Vilnius Tallat-Kelpša Secondary Music Sch., 1961 — ; major works: 2 cantatas, *Saulės poema* (Poem of the Sun) for mezzo-soprano, choir and symphony orch., *Trys šokiai* (Three Dances) and *Sinfonia giocosa* for chamber orch., chamber music. *Add.* (h) Kupalos 36 — 2, Vilnius 232004; tel. 753 242.

▪ **MAKARIŪNAS, Kęstutis**, physicist; b. 1932; grad. Vilnius Univ.; DSc. (Phys.&Math.); Inst. of Phys., 1959 — ; research in nuclear spectroscopy, application of its methods in solid state phys., influence of nuclear chem. environment on radioactive decay constants. *Add.* (h) Antakalnio 83 — 15, Vilnius 232040; tel. 744 925.

▪ **MAKAUSKAS, Jonas**, Dir, pharmaceutical plant *Sanitas*, 1987 — ; b. 1936; grad. Kaunas Med. Acad., pharmaceutist; in the plant since 1958. *Add.* (h) Borisos 6 — 16, Kaunas 233005; tel. 732 031.

▪ **MAKMAK, Ivan**, Dir-Gen., Vilnius Electric Welding Equipm. Prod. Assoc., 1975 — ; b. 1931; grad. Marijampolė Metallurgy Inst., eng. metallurgist; in the admin. since 1964. *Add.* (h) Vileišio 9 — 5, Vilnius 232055; tel. 743 464.

▪ **MALDONIS, Alfonsas**, poet; b. 1929; grad. Vilnius Univ.; Chair., Bd of the Lith. Writers'

Union, 1976 — 88; coll. of poems *Saulėti lietūs* (The Sunny Rains, 1962), *Auga medžiai* (The Trees Are Growing, 1965), *Rytas vakaras* (The Morning, the Evening, 1978), *Rugiaveidė* (The Rye-Face, 1982); concentrates on ethic problems, man's ties with nature, moral responsibility, the destiny of the native land; poems are distinguished for restrained emotion. *Add.* (h) Švyturio 22 — 13, Vilnius 232040; tel. 741 881.

▪ **MALIUKEVIČIUS, Zigmas**, Dir, *Mintis* publrs, 1984 — ; b. 1934; grad. Vilnius Univ., journalist. *Add.* (h) Grybo 13 — 23, Vilnius 232040; tel. 743 980.

▪ **MARCINKEVIČIUS, Algimantas**, cardiovascular surgeon; b. 1921; grad. Vilnius Univ.; its lecturer, 1947 — ; Head, Cardiosurgery Clinic, 1982 — 90; DSc. (Med.), Prof., Acad., Lith. Acad. of Sci. and USSR Med. Acad. of Sci.; founder of modern cardiosurgery and organ transplantations in Lithuania; was the first in Lithuania to perform surgical reconstr. of blood vessels, open heart operation using hypothermia and artificial circulation of blood; the first to create heart valve prosthesis, transplant kidney, reconstruct coronary heart arteries, resect aneurysm of thoracic aorta; in 1987 supervised the first heart transplantation; Pres., Lith. Physicians' Union. *Add.* (h) Oginskio 4 — 10, Vilnius 232040.

▪ **MARCINKEVIČIUS, Justinas**, poet; b. 1930; grad. Vilnius Univ.; Acad., Lith. Acad. of Sci.; verse coll. *Liepsnojantis krūmas* (The Burning Bush, 1968), *Gyvenimo švelnus prisiglaudimas* (Life Touched Me Softly, 1978), *Būk ir palaimink* (Be and Bless, 1980), *Vienintelė žemė* (The Only Land, 1984), the trilogy of poetic dramas *Mindaugas, Mažvydas, Katedra* (The Cathedral, 1969 — 76), a book of essays *Dienoraštis be datų* (The Diary Without Dates, 1981), narrative poems; in his works ethic humanist problems are combined with the hist. and cultural experience of the Lith. nation; typical of them is intimate meditation, restrained emotionality, phil. generalization. *Add.* (h) Mildos 33 — 6, Vilnius 232055; tel. 740 162.

▪ **MARČIULIONIS, Aloyzas**, Chief Arbitrator of Lith. Rep., 1990 — ; b. 1938; grad. Vilnius Univ., lawyer; Dep. Chief Arbitrator, 1983 — 90. *Add.* Gedimino 39/1, Vilnius 232640; tel. 622 843.

▪ **MARIŪNAS, Mečislovas**, engineer (mech.); b. 1940; grad. Kaunas Technol. Univ.; DSc. (Eng.), Prof.; lecturer, Vilnius Tech. Univ., 1984 — ; research in the dynamic transitional processes of magnetic heads, accuracy of variable step frictional gears and oscillation of rotor systems. *Add.* (h) Perkūno 6 — 260, Vilnius 232050; tel. 268 775.

▪ **MARKOVAS, Ričardas**, Dir, printing-house *Aušra*, 1972 — ; b. 1935; grad. Lvov Polygraphy Inst., eng. (econ.); at polygraphy ent. since 1951. *Add.* Vytauto pr. 23, Kaunas 233000; tel. 226 457.

▪ **MARTINAITIS, Aldevinas**, Dir, Mažeikiai Electrical Eng. Plant, 1990 — ; b. 1953; grad. Kaunas Technol. Univ., eng. (electromech.). *Add.* (h) Laisvės 226 — 3, Mažeikiai 235503; tel. 403 10.

▪ **MARTINAITIS, Algirdas**, composer; b. 1950; grad. Lith. Conservatoire; major works: cantatas *Karvelis, skrendantis vakarop* (The Dove Flying into Twilight), *Cantus ad Futurum* and *Muzikinė auka* (Musical Offering), concerto for choir, *Negrįžtantis koncertas* (Nonreturning Concerto) for chamber orch., chamber music, incidental music. *Add.* (h) Ševčenkos 18 — 25, Vilnius 232006; tel. 639 669.

▪ **MARTINAITIS, Marcelijus**, poet; b. 1936; grad. Vilnius Univ.; lectures at it, 1980 — ; coll. of poems *Saulės grąža* (The Return of the Sun, 1969), *Akių tamsoj, širdies šviesoj* (In the Heart's Light, 1974), *Toli nuo rugių* (Far-away from the Rye, 1982); reflects on the dramatic conflicts at the crossroads of nature and civilization, extols human values, resorts to folklore and mythological images; in a ballad-like coll. of poems *Kukučio baladės* (Ballads of Kukutis, 1977) recreates elements of the archaic spiritual experience of the people; essays, plays for puppet theatre. *Add.* (h) Vokiečių 15 — 20, 232024; tel. 221 520.

▪ **MARTINKUS, Vytautas**, Chair., Bd of the Lith. Writers' Union, 1989 — ; writer; b. 1943; grad. Kaunas Technol. Univ.; novels *Akmenys* (The Stones, 1972), *Medžioklė draustinyje* (The Hunt in a Reservation, 1983), *Neskęsta žvaigždė paukščio pėdoje* (The Star Does Not Sink in the Bird's Footstep, 1988), novellas; deal with the dramatic situations in this age of machinery; intellectuality, psychologism, conditionality mark his writings. *Add.* (h) Dominikonų 15 — 9, Vilnius 232024; tel. 613 975.

▪ **MASALSKIS, Valentinas**, theatre and film actor; b. 1954; grad. Lith. Conservatoire; actor, Kaunas Drama Theatre, 1976 — ; devotes much attention to resourcefulness finding new means of expression. *Add.* (h) Laisvės al. 71, Kaunas 233000; tel. 224 198.

▪ **MATULAITIS, Juozapas**, Roman Catholic bishop; b. 1936; grad. Kaunas Priest Sem.; ordained in 1964; Apostolic Administrator of the Diocese of Kaišiadorys, 1989 — . *Add.* Kęstučio 44, Kaišiadorys 234230; tel. 546 56.

▪ **MATULEVIČIUS, Algimantas**, Dir-Gen., commercial co *Neringa*, 1981 — ; b. 1948; grad. Vilnius Univ., econ.; CSc. (Econ.); Pres., Lith. Mfrs Assoc. *Add.* (h) Lentupio 8 — 9, Vilnius 232040; tel. 749 306.

▪ **MATULIS, Alfonsas**, Dir, Inst. of Experimental and Clinical Med., 1970 — ; b. 1927; grad. Vilnius Univ., physician rheumatologist; DSc. (Med.), Prof.; generalized distribution diagnostics and treatment of latent rheumatism, developed methods of treating rheumatism with immunoregulation remedies. *Add.* (h) Kęstučio 44, Vilnius 232009; tel. 614 878.

▪ **MATULIONIS, Arvydas**, Dir, Inst. of Phil., Sociology and Law, 1990 — ; b. 1946; grad. Kaunas Technol. Univ., radio constructor and technol.; DSc. (Phil.), Prof.; at Inst. since 1969; research in sociology (problems of youth, educ. and culture). *Add.* Saltoniškių 58, Vilnius 232600; tel. 752 455.

- **MAZŪRAS, Česlovas**, engineer (arch.); b. 1942; grad. Kaunas Technol. Univ.; Chief Arch. of designs, Design Inst. of City Constr., 1981 − ; designer of cultural, sch., admin., public buildings, multi-storeyed dwelling houses in Vilnius. **Add.** (h) Didlaukio 68 − 24, Vilnius 232057; tel. 779 831.

- **MAZŪRAS, Petras**, sculptor; b. 1949; grad. Vilnius Art Acad.; teaches at Čiurlionis Art. Sch. and (since 1990) at Vilnius Art Acad.; works mostly in granite and bronze, associative, expressive. **Add.** (h) Šilo 29 − 6, Vilnius 232055; tel. 749 709.

- **MAZŪRAS, Vitalis**, stage designer, producer; b. 1934; grad. Vilnius Art Acad.; Vilnius *Lėlė* theatre, 1969 − ; Chief Producer, 1971 − 79, 1988 − 89, Art Dir, 1989 − ; designer of original puppets, settings for drama theatres. Add. (h) Didžioji 25 − 15, Vilnius 232024; tel. 620 404.

- **MAŽIULIS, Vytautas**, linguist (Baltic philol.); b. 1926; grad. Vilnius Univ.; lectures at this Univ., 1955 − ; DSc. (Philol.), Prof., Acad., Lith. Acad. of Sci., Corr., Mainz (Germany) Acad. of Sci. and Lit.; Corr. Mem., Milan Linguistic Soc.; Ed., linguistic journal *Baltistica*; major works: *Baltų ir kitų indoeuropiečių kalbų santykiai (Deklinacija)* [Relations Between Lith. and Indo-European Lgs (Declination), 1970], *Prūsų kalbos paminklai* (Monuments of the Old Prussian Lg., 1966 − 81), *Prūsų kalbos etimologinis žodynas* (Etymological Dictionary of the Old Prussian Lg., 1988, vol. 1). **Add.** (h) Kalvarijų 276 − 27, Vilnius 232042; tel. 763 934.

- **MELNIKAS, Borisas**, Rector, Lith. Management Acad., 1990 − ; b. 1950; grad. Vilnius Tech. Univ. and Lith. Conservatoire; DSc. (Econ.), Prof.; works with Acad., 1977 − ; studies on investitions, sci. and technique progress, management. **Add.** (h) Mickevičiaus 9 − 12, Vilnius 232004; tel. 731 330.

- **MERKYS, Vytautas**, Dir, Inst. of Lith. Hist., 1987 − ; b. 1929; grad. Vilnius Univ.; DSc. (Hist.), Acad., Lith. Acad. of Sci.; at the Inst. since 1953; works on the socioecon., cultural hist. of Lithuania in the 19th cent., on the Lith. nat. movement, activities of the famous people. 11 books (*Lietuvos valstiečiai ir spauda XIX a. pab. − XX a. pr.*, Lith. Peasants and the Press in the Late 19th Cent. − the Early 20th Cent., 1982), textbooks, publ. of the famous hist. writings, hist. sources. **Add.** Kosciuškos 30, Vilnius 232600; tel. 614 436.

- **MICHELBERTAS, Mykolas**, archeologist; b. 1939; grad. Vilnius Univ.; lectures at this Univ., 1984 − ; DSc. (Hist.), Prof.; lectured at Vilnius Pedag. Inst. 1969 − 84; research on the archeological burial monuments of the 1st − 4th cent.; 4 books (*Lietuvos gyventojų prekybiniai ryšiai I − XIII a.*, Trade Ties of the Lith. Inhabitants in the 1st − 4th Cent., 1972), atlas. **Add.** Universiteto 3, Vilnius 232734; tel. 611 313.

- **MICHELEVIČIUS, Vladislovas**, Roman Catholic bishop; b. 1924; grad. Kaunas Priest Sem., studied in Rome; ordained in 1948; Asst Arcbishop of Kaunas, 1989 − ; teaches at the Kaunas Priest Sem. **Add.** Vilniaus 29, Kaunas 233000; tel. 227 672.

- **MICKIS, Algis**, pharmacologist; b. 1927; grad. Kaunas Univ.; DSc. (Med.), Prof., Corr. Mem., Lith. Acad. of Sci.; lecturer, Kaunas Med. Acad., 1956 − ; works on the influence of neurothropic substance upon high frequency components of electrocorticogram; introduced into practice research method of clinical electroencephalography. **Add.** (h) Jasaičio 3, Kaunas 233000; tel. 796 433.

- **MIECZKOWSKI, Romuald**, publr, newspaper *Znad Wilii*; b. 1950; grad. Vilnius Pedag. Inst., philol.; press worker, 1973 − . **Add.** (h) Laisvės pr. 44 − 63, Vilnius 232044; tel. 425 165.

- **MIEŽELAITIS, Eduardas**, poet; b. 1919; lyricism, melodious intonations are characteristic of his early works; poetic book *Žmogus* (The Man, 1962); books of poetry and essays *Lyriniai etiudai* (The Lyrical Etudes, 1964), *Čia Lietuva* (This Is Lithuania, 1968), *Iliuzijos bokštas* (The Tower of Illusion, 1973), *Mūza ir upėtakis* (The Muse and the Trout, 1984); the ethic phil. problems, motifs of world cultural hist., experiments with form mark his works; works for children; books transl. into Russ., Pol., Ger. and other lgs. **Add.** (h) Mickevičiaus 32 − 24, Vilnius 232004; tel. 752 911.

- **MIKALAJŪNAS, Mykolas**, Dir, State Encyclopaedia Publrs, 1989 − ; b. 1937; grad. Vilnius Univ., meteorologist; CSc. (Geogr.); Head, Lith. Bd for Hydrometeorology, 1976 − 89; works on applied meteorology. **Add.** (h) Krivių 25 − 7, Vilnius 232007; tel. 618 585.

- **MIKELINSKAS, Jonas**, writer; b. 1922; grad. Vilnius Univ.; stories, novellas, novels *Vandens nešėja* (The Water-Carrier, 1964), *Už horizonto − laisvė* (Is Freedom Behind the Horizon, 1978), *Kur lygūs laukai* (Where the Meadows Stretch Wide, 1981), *Juodųjų eglių šalis* (Country of the Black Spruce, 1988) depict the social and psychological conflicts of the post-war countryside, ethic collisions among intellectuals; the epic style, constructiveness and phil. tone are typical features of his writings. **Add.** (h) Mildos 31 − 6, Vilnius 232055; tel. 354 462.

- **MIKUTAVIČIUS, Ričardas**, Roman Catholic priest, poet, collectioner; b. 1935; grad. Kaunas Priest Sem.; ordained in 1958; licentiate of theol.; pastor of Vytautas the Great Church in Kaunas; coll. of poetry: *Kad Lietuva neišsivaikščiotų* (In Order Lithuania not Break Up, 1989, Chicago), *Poterių upė* (River of Prayers, 1990); coll. of paintings of 16th − 19th cent. **Add.** (h) Aleksoto 10 − 4, Kaunas 233000; tel. 222 371.

- **MILIAUSKAS, Romanas**, E-in-C, magazine *Pasaulis*, 1988 − ; b. 1947; grad. Vilnius Univ., journalist; CSc. (Phil.); writes on int. affairs and ethnic relations. **Add.** (h) Debesijos 520, Vilnius 232055; tel. 749 722.

- **MILINAVIČIUS, Vytautas**, Dir-Gen., prod. assoc. *Lietuvos buitinė chemija*, 1974 − ; b. 1932; grad. Moscow Light Ind. Technol. Inst., eng. (mech.). **Add.** (h) Mildos 5 − 16, Vilnius 232055; tel. 748 041.

- **MILIŪNAS, Eugenijus**, architect; b. 1952; grad. Vilnius Tech. Univ.; Design Inst. of City Constr. (Kaunas branch), 1975 — ; co-designer of large cultural, public buildings, stores (Žilinskas Art Gallery, Kalniečiai Commercial Centre) of original complex character. *Add.* (h) Valančiaus 5, Kaunas 234316, Garliava.

- **MILIUS, Vacys**, ethnographer; b. 1926; grad. Vilnius Univ.; CSc. (Hist.); Inst. of Lith. Hist., 1954 — ; works on food, instruments of labour, handicrafts of Lithuanians, on the hist. of Lith. ethnography; 4 books (*Lietuvių etnografijos bruožai*, Outline of Lith. Ethnography, 1964), atlases, bibliographies. *Add.* Kosciuškos 30, Vilnius 232600; tel. 629 410.

- **MILKEVIČIŪTĖ, Irena**, singer (soprano); b. 1947; grad. Lith. Conservatoire; worked on probation in *La Scala* theatre in Milan; soloist, Lith. Opera and Ballet Theatre, 1976 — ; toured Europe, Cuba, Philippines, Japan; Koday-Erkel singing comp. in Budapest (2nd prize, 1982), Madam Butterfly part performing comp. in Tokyo (2nd prize, 1986). *Add.* (h) Žalgirio 99 — 36, Vilnius 232005; tel. 730 105.

- **MINKEVIČIUS, Jokūbas**, philosopher; b. 1921; DSc. (Phil.), Prof., Acad., Lith. Acad. of Sci.; books: *Šiuolaikinė katalikybė ir jos filosofija* (Contemporary Catholicism and Its Phil. 1965; in Russ.), *Katalikybė ir nacija* (Catholicism and Nation, 1971; in Russ.), *XX amžiaus filosofijos panorama* (Panorama of Phil. of 20th Cent., 1981); Lith. SC Deputy. *Add.* (h) Vykinto 27 — 8, Vilnius 232004; tel. 738 073.

- **MISIUKONIS, Marijonas**, Min. of the Interior, 1989 — ; b. 1939; grad. Vilnius Univ., lawyer; Major-Gen.; worked at the State Security Cttee, 1962 — 84; Dep. Min. of the Interior, 1987 — 89. *Add.* Šventaragio 2, Vilnius 232754; tel. 626 752.

- **MOCKUS, Jonas**, engineer (cybernetic); b. 1931; grad. Kaunas Technol. Univ.; DSc. (Eng.), Prof., Acad., Lith. Acad. of Sci.; Inst. of Math. and Informatics, 1969 — ; research in the methods of optimization and their use in design. *Add.* (h) Architektų 28 — 57, Vilnius 232043; tel. 440 436.

- **MONTRIMAS, Edmundas**, physicist; b. 1933; grad. Vilnius Pedag. Inst.; DSc. (Phys.&Math.), Prof.; lecturer, Vilnius Univ., 1964; research in semiconductor phys., electrography and optoelectronics. *Add.* (h) Žirgo 1 — 25, Vilnius 232040; tel. 777 018.

- **MONTVILA, Vytautas**, composer; b. 1935; grad. Lith. Conservatoire; consultant at Lith. Composers' Union, 1975 — ; major works: cantatas *Čiurlionis* and *Vizijos* (The Visions), *Atgimimo simfonija* (Rebirth Symphony), cycle of poems *Šventinė poema* (The Festive Poem), *Chorai* (Choruses) and *Gotiška poema* (The Gothic Poem) for symphony orch., 2 concertos, chamber music. *Add.* (h) Karoliniškių 22 — 30, Vilnius 232044; tel. 455 743.

- **MORAS, Reinholdas**, Chair., Consistory of Lith. Evangelical Reformed Church, 1988 — ; b. 1958; educ. Theol. Sem. of Latv. Evangelical Lutheran Church. *Add.* (h) Basanavičiaus 17, Biržai 235280; tel. 520 61.

- **MORKŪNAS, Kazys**, stained-glass artist; b. 1924; grad. Vilnius Art Acad.; teaches at it, 1953 — ; Prof.; author of monumental stained-glass panels of complex technol. *Add.* (h) Krivių 41 — 26, Vilnius 232007; tel. 696 391.

- **MORKŪNIENĖ, Elena**, choreographer; b. 1929; grad. Lith. Inst. of Physical Training; CSc. (Hist.), Doc.; directs amateur dance groups, 1949 — ; teaches at the Vilnius Univ., 1957 — ; Head Ballet Master of the Lith. Song Festivals; author of 100 choreographical scenes and dances. *Add.* (h) Mildos 19a, Vilnius 232055; tel. 741 846.

- **MOTIEJŪNAITĖ, Lydija**, choreographer, spec. in theatre sci.; b. 1924; grad. D.Nasvytytė Modern Dance Sch., Vilnius Univ.; CSc. (Arts); ballet dancer with the Lith. theatres, 1944 — 67; instructor, children classical dance group *Liepsnelė*, 1967 — ; author of dance compositions and monographs (*M.Juozapaitytė*, 1969). *Add.* (h) Architektų 67 — 13, Vilnius 232049; tel. 457 944.

- **MOTIEKA, Kazimieras**, Dep. Chair., SC of Lith. Rep., 1990 — ; b. 1929; grad. Vilnius Univ., lawyer; worked at the Vilnius First Legal Advice Office, 1967 — 90; Lith. SC Deputy. *Add.* Gedimino pr. 53, Vilnius 232026; tel. 621 654.

- **MOTŪZA-MATUZEVIČIUS, Gediminas**, Dir, State Geol. Service, 1991 — ; b. 1946; grad. Vilnius Univ., geol.; CSc. (Geol. & Mineralogy); worked at the composite geol. expedition, 1973 — 84. *Add.* Konarskio 35, Vilnius 232600; tel. 632 889.

- **MULEVIČIUS, Leonas**, historian; b. 1927; grad. Vilnius Univ.; lectures at it, 1969 — ; DSc. (Hist.), Prof.; Inst. of Lith. Hist., 1958 — ; works on the Lith. socioecon. relations in the modern ages, on nat. movement, methods and terms of the hist. sci.; 4 books (*Lietuvos valstiečių judėjimas 1861 — 1914 m.*, The Movement of Lith. Peasants in 1861 — 1914, 1975), publ. of hist. sources. *Add.* Kosciuškos 30, Vilnius 232600; tel. 628 006

- **NAMAVIČIUS, Zenonas**, lawyer; b. 1943; grad. Vilnius Univ.; lectures at it, 1967 — , Vice-Rector, 1991 — ; CSc. (Law), Doc.; research in hist. of pol. theories, theory of state and law; Chair., Lith. Soc. of Jurists, 1989 — . *Add.* (h) Didlaukio 68 — 10, Vilnius 232057; tel. 774 386.

- **NARBUTAITĖ, Onutė**, composer; b. 1956; grad. Lith. Conservatoire; major works: symphony, 2 cantatas, chamber music. *Add.* (h) Kupalos 34 — 16, Vilnius 232004; tel. 351 919.

- **NARBUTIENĖ, Ona**, musicologist; b. 1930; grad. Lith. Conservatoire; teaches at Čiurlionis Art Sch., 1969 — ; Lith. Conservatoire, 1989 — ; was deported with parents to Siberia, 1949 — 55; monographs on Lith. composers and performers of the 20th cent.; compiled a book *Juozas Naujalis* (1968) and album *Juozas Gruodis* (1984). *Add.* (h) Kupalos 34 — 16, Vilnius 232004; tel. 351 919.

- **NASVYTIS, Algimantas**, Min. of Housing and Urban Development, 1990 — ; b. 1928; grad.

Vilnius Art Acad., artist arch.; Doc.; Chief Arch. of design, Design Inst. of City Constr., 1962 — 90; lectured at Vilnius Tech. Univ.; co-designer (with his brother Vytautas) of imposing public, admin. buildings, original interiors. Chief Artist of Lith. Song Festivals. **Add.** Jakšto 4/9, Vilnius 232694; tel. 610 558.

■ **NASVYTIS, Vytautas**, architect; b. 1928; grad. Vilnius Art Acad.; teaches at it, 1953 — ; Prof.; co-designer (with his brother Algimantas) of imposing public, admin. buildings and original interiors (Café *Neringa*, Hotel *Lietuva*). **Add.** (h) Šilo 56 — 1, Vilnius 232055; tel. 749 772.

■ **NAVICKAS, Vytas**, Min. of Economics, 1990 — 91; b. 1952; grad. Vilnius Univ., econ. (math.); CSc. (Econ.); Inst. of Econ., 1975 — 88. **Add.** Gedimino pr. 38/2, Vilnius 232600; tel. 622 416.

■ **NAVICKYTĖ-RAMANAUSKIENĖ, Lili**, ballet master, teacher; b. 1933; grad. Vilnius Univ., Moscow A. Lunacharsky Inst. of Dramatic Art; ballet dancer, Lith. Opera and Ballet Theatre, 1952 — 57; Dir, Vilnius Choreographic Sch., 1986 — . **Add.** (h) Žirmūnų 52 — 54, Vilnius 232051; tel. 737 253.

■ **NEKRAŠAS, Evaldas**, philosopher; b. 1945; grad. Vilnius Univ.; lectures at it, 1968 — ; DSc. (Phil.), Prof.; Pres., Lith. Soc. of Phil.; monographs *Loginis empirizmas ir mokslo metodologija* (Logical Empiricism and Sci. Methodology, 1979), *Tikimybinis žinojimas* (Probability Knowledge, 1987; in Russ.). **Add.** (h) Perkūno 10 — 32, Vilnius 232050; tel. 453 340.

■ **NEKROŠIUS, Eimuntas**, theatre dir, film actor; b. 1952; grad. Moscow A. Lunacharsky Inst. of Dramatic Art; Dir, Lith. Youth Theatre, 1980 — ; prod. noted for poetic metaphors. **Add.** (h) Didžioji 43 — 4, Vilnius 232000; tel. 622 727.

■ **NEMURA, Antanas**, engineer (cybernetic); b. 1927; grad. Kaunas Technol. Univ.; DSc. (Eng.), Prof., Corr. Mem., Lith. Acad. of Sci.; Head, Lab. for Adaptive Systems at the Inst. for Phys. and Eng. Problems of Energy Research; research in the identification and automatic regulation of systems. **Add.** (h) Taikos 37 — 51, Kaunas 233009; tel. 735 600.

■ **NOREIKA, Pranas**, Dir, Lith. Power Station, 1960 — ; b. 1927; grad. Kaunas Technol. Univ., eng. (electrotech.). **Add.** Elektrėnai 234061; tel. 332 50.

■ **NOREIKA, Virgilijus**, singer (tenor); b. 1935; grad. Lith. Conservatoire; lectures at it, 1976 — ; Prof.; worked on probation at *La Scala* theatre in Milan under Genare Barra; soloist, Lith. Opera and Ballet Theatre, 1957 — , Dir and artistic leader, 1975 — 90; has prepared over 40 opera parts; toured Milan, Paris, Berlin, Buenos-Aires, Moscow and other cities; World Youth and Students Festival in Moscow (1st prize, 1957). **Add.** (h) Šilo 54 — 3, Vilnius 232055; tel. 748 936.

■ **NORVAIŠA, Česlovas**, b. 1935, and **Jūratė**, b. 1935, ballroom dancers of extra class, married couple; head the ballroom dance ensemble *Sūkurys*, 1974 — ; dance teachers of USSR team, 1979 — , Bulgaria team (1980, 1982, 1984); have made original dance compositions; top prizes at

Gintarinė pora int. comp. in Kaunas (1968, 1971) and news of world comp. in Klaxon, Great Britain (1968). **Add.** (h) Kiškių takas 20 — 1, Kaunas 233000; tel. 245 730.

■ **OLEKAS, Juozas**, Min. of Health Care, 1990 — ; b. 1955; grad. Vilnius Univ., microsurgeon; CSc. (Med.); worked at Vilnius Univ., 1985 — 90; Dep. Pres., Lith. Union of Physicians. **Add.** Gedimino pr. 27, Vilnius 232682; tel. 621 625.

■ **OKIŃCZYC, Czesław**, publr, newspaper *Znad Wilii;* b. 1955; grad. Vilnius Univ., lawyer; advocate in Vilnius, 1982 — 90; Lith. SC Deputy. **Add.** POB 1755, Vilnius 232019; tel. 650 463 (h).

■ **ONAITYTĖ, Jūratė**, theatre and film actor; b. 1954; grad. Lith. Conservatoire; Kaunas Drama Theatre, 1976 — ; noted for subtle portrayal of inner world of her heroines. **Add.** (h) Vilniaus 14 — 1, Kaunas 233000; tel. 208 595.

■ **OZOLAS, Romualdas**, philosopher, journalist; b. 1939; grad. Vilnius Univ.; lectured at it, 1973 — 89; Dep. E-in-C, publrs *Mintis*, 1980 — 89; E-in-C, newspaper *Atgimimas*, 1989 — 90; Dep. Prime Min. of Lith. Rep., 1990 — 91; Dep. Chair., *Sąjūdis* Seim Council, 1988 — 90; Lith. SC Deputy. **Add.** Gedimino pr. 53, Vilnius 232026; tel. 224 691.

■ **OŽELYTĖ, Nijolė**, film actress; b. 1954; grad. Lith. Conservatoire; plays in the cinema and TV films, 1974 — ; perf. expressive, sensitive; Lith. SC Deputy. **Add.** (h) Taikos 87 — 49, Vilnius 232017; tel. 427 508.

■ **PADEGIMAS, Gytis**, theatre dir; b. 1952; grad. Moscow A.Lunacharsky Inst. of Dramatic Art; Chief Dir, Šiauliai Drama Theatre; prod. are noted for emotional appeal and expressiveness. **Add.** (h) Cvirkos 13 — 15, Kaunas 233000; tel. 221 472.

■ **PAGIRYS, Marius**, Pres., Assoc. of Lith. Automobilists, 1989 — ; b. 1933; grad. Vilnius Univ., philol.; Ed., E-in-C, publrs *Mintis*, 1957 — 89. **Add.** (h) Kalinausko 8/11, Vilnius 232009; tel. 652 356.

■ **PAJARSKAITĖ, Albina**, Chair., Catholic union *Caritas*, 1989 — ; Ed., magazine *Caritas*, 1989 — ; b. 1927; grad. Vilnius Univ.; CSc. (Agric.); works on soil erosion and structure of top-soil. **Add.** (h) Savanorių 287a — 44, Kaunas 233009; tel. 773 903.

■ **PAKALNIS, Romas**, Dir, Inst. of Botany, 1989 — ; b. 1941; grad. Lith. Agric. Acad., forest ecologist; CSc. (Biol.); at the Inst. since 1970; created original sch. of landscape ecology; works on ecological botany, nature protection; 4 monographs. **Add.** (h) Žaibo 10 — 27, Vilnius 232044; tel. 452 010.

■ **PAKALNIŠKIS, Vytautas**, Dep. Prime Min. of Lith. Rep., Min. of Justice, 1991 — ; b. 1944; grad. Vilnius Univ., lawyer; lectures at it, 1972 — ; CSc. (Law), Doc.; works on civil and lodging law; 1 textbook, 3 books (with others). **Add.** Tumo-Vaižganto 2, Vilnius 232039; tel. 621 429.

■ **PAKULIS, Romaldas**, Dir, printing-house *Viltis*, 1987 — ; b. 1950; grad. Vilnius Univ., econ.; Dir, Klaipėda printing-house *Rytas*,

1977 — 87. **Add.** Strazdelio 1, Vilnius 232000; tel. 628 632.

▪ **PALECKIS, Justas Vincas**, journalist, diplomat; b. 1942; grad. Vilnius Univ.; Dep. Chair., Lith. DLP, 1990 — ; 1969 — 82 in diplomatic service in Switzerland, Germany, USSR Min. of Foreign Affairs; Sec., Cent. Cttee, LCP, 1989 — 90; Lith. SC Deputy. **Add.** Radvilaitės 1, Vilnius 232000; tel. 615 410.

▪ **PALIONIS, Jonas**, linguist (Lith. philol.); b. 1924; grad. Vilnius Univ.; lectures at it, 1951 — ; DSc. (Philol.), Prof.; major works: *Lietuvių literatūrinė kalba XVI — XVII a.* (Lith. Lit. Lg. in the XVI — XVII Cent., 1967), *Lietuvių literatūrinės kalbos istorija* (Hist. of Lith. Lit. Lg., 1979). **Add.** (h) Lukiškių a. 9/1, Vilnius 232001; tel. 617 455.

▪ **PALUNKIŠKIS, Pranas**, Dir, Vilnius Glass Works, 1984 — ; b. 1946; grad. Kaunas Technol. Univ., eng. (technol.). **Add.** (h) Savanorių pr. 56 — 2, Vilnius 232015; tel. 667 679.

▪ **PARČIAUSKAS, Vytautas**, Dir, Design Inst. of City Constr., 1990 — ; b. 1934; grad. Kaunas Technol. Univ., eng. (arch.); Chief Arch., Design Inst. of City Constr., 1977 — 90; supervised renovation works at hist. centres of Vilnius and Klaipėda, designed stores in Kaunas as well as original interiors. **Add.** (h) Blindžių 33 — 3, Vilnius 232004; tel. 351 330.

▪ **PAŠKAUSKAS, Pranciškus**, Dir, Panevėžys Meat Plant, 1983 — ; b. 1931; grad. Vilnius Univ., econ. **Add.** (h) Danutės 13 — 16, Panevėžys 235319; tel. 317 52.

▪ **PAULAUSKAS, Artūras**, Prosecutor Gen. of Lith. Rep., 1990 — ; b. 1953; grad. Vilnius Univ., lawyer; worked as an interrogator, prosecutor, 1976 — 89, Dep. Prosecutor of the Rep., 1989 — 90. **Add.** Smetonos 6, Vilnius 232709; tel. 610 537.

▪ **PAULAUSKAS, Vygantas**, mathematician; b. 1944; grad. Vilnius Univ.; its lecturer; DSc. (Phys.&Math.), Prof., Corr. Mem., Lith. Acad. of Sci.; research in the asymptotic analysis of elements of random infinite-dimension Banach spaces. **Add.** (h) Dubingių 15, Vilnius 232042; tel. 733 355.

▪ **PAULAUSKIENĖ, Aldona**, linguist (Lith. philol.); b. 1935; grad. Vilnius Univ.; lectures at it, 1964 — ; DSc. (Philol.), Prof.; major works: *Dabartinės lietuvių kalbos veiksmažodis* (The Verb of Modern Lith. Lg., 1971), *Gramatinės lietuvių kalbos veiksmažodžio kategorijos* (Grammatical Categories of the Verb in the Lith. Lg., 1979), *Lietuvių kalbos morfologijos apybraiža* (Outline of Morphology of the Lith. Lg., 1983). **Add.** (h) Sruogos 8, Vilnius 232040; tel. 768 287.

▪ **PAULAUSKIENĖ, Regina**, E-in-C, magazine *Moteris*, 1986 — ; b. 1944; grad. Vilnius Pedag. Inst.; press worker since 1970. **Add.** Maironio 1, Vilnius 232600; tel. 610 169.

▪ **PAUPARAS, Povilas**, Man., Information Dept, SC of Lith. Rep., 1990 — ; b. 1953; grad. Kaunas Technol. Univ., eng. (automatic); Dep. Shop Man., Vilnius Calculating Machine Plant, 1987 — 90. **Add.** Gedimino pr. 53, Vilnius 232026; tel. 626 680.

▪ **PAVILIONIS, Rolandas**, Rector, Vilnius Univ., 1991 — ; b. 1944; grad. Vilnius Univ.; lectures at it, 1968 — ; DSc. (Phil.), Prof., Corr. Mem., Lith. Acad. of Sci.; works on logic, lg. phil. and semantics; Chair., soc. Lithuania — France. **Add.** Universiteto 3, Vilnius 232734; tel. 623 779.

▪ **PAŽŪSIS, Lionginas**, linguist (Engl. philol.), translator; b. 1940; grad. Vilnius Univ.; lectures at it, 1962 — ; CSc. (Philol.), Doc.; publ. writings on N-American Lith. lg., transl. the Lith. poetry into Engl.: anthology *Gintaro vėrinys* (Beads of Amber, 1979); coll. of poems by Justinas Marcinkevičius *Tokia yra meilė* (Such is Love, 1983). **Add.** (h) Žirmūnų 20 — 113, Vilnius 232051; tel. 755 153.

▪ **PEČATAUSKAS, Vaclovas**, Dir, textile co *Kaspinas*, 1984 — ; b. 1938; grad. Vilnius Univ., econ.; at stockings factory *Koton*, 1960 — 84. **Add.** (h) Laisvės al. 98 — 38, Kaunas 233000; tel. 206 885.

▪ **PEČELIŪNAS , Saulius**, Chair., Lith. Dem. Party; b. 1956; grad. Vilnius Tech. Univ., road-building eng.; Design Inst. of City Constr., 1979 — 90; Lith. SC Deputy. **Add.** Gedimino pr. 53, Vilnius 232026; tel. 628 708.

▪ **PEMPĖ, Kęstutis**, architect; b. 1949; grad. Vilnius Tech. Univ.; Chief Arch. of designs, Design Inst. of City Constr., 1984 — ; designer of commercial, med., admin. buildings. **Add.** (h) Paberžės 26 — 3, Vilnius 232010; tel. 463 460.

▪ **PETKEVIČIUS, Vytautas**, writer; b. 1930; grad. Moscow Univ.; the novel *Apie duoną, meilę ir šautuvą* (Of Bread, Love and Rifle, 1967) is an attempt to give an impartial description of the post-war Soviet activists who fought with Lith. partisans; social novels about officials, scientists, hist. novel of the family chronicle type *Paskutinis atgailos amžius* (The Last Cent. of Repentance, 1986); stories for children, polemic publ. works on subjects of ecology, ethics. **Add.** (h) Mildos 31 — 11, Vilnius 232055; tel. 352 200.

▪ **PETRAVIČIUS, Leopoldas**, Dir, cement co *Akmenės cementas*, 1962 — ; b. 1927; grad. Kaunas Technol. Univ., eng. (technol.). **Add.** (h) Gedimino 19, Naujoji Akmenė 235464; tel. 515 56.

▪ **PETKUS, Viktoras**, Chair., Lith. Christian Dem. Union, 1990 — ; b. 1930; for pol. activity he was imprisoned for 25 years by the Soviet authorities, signatory of Lith. Helsinki Group; Chair., Lith. Indep. Union; Hon. Chair., Lith. Assoc. of Human Rights Protection. **Add.** (h) Pylimo 35 — 8, Vilnius 232001; tel. 624 008.

▪ **PYRAGAS, Kazimieras**, physicist; b. 1938; grad. Kazan Univ.; DSc. (Phys.&Math.), Prof.; lecturer, Vilnius Pedag. Inst., 1981 — ; research in the problems of motion stability, relativistic gravitation theory, stochastic processes in astrophys. **Add.** (h) Šeškinės 11 — 49, Vilnius 232019; tel. 758 501 (off.).

▪ **PISKARSKAS, Algis**, physicist; b. 1942; grad. Moscow Univ.; DSc. (Phys.&Math.), Prof., Corr. Mem., Lith. Acad. of Sci.; lecturer, Vilnius Univ., 1969 — ; research in quantum electronics, nonlinear optics, laser spectroscopy, biophys. **Add.** (h) Žirgo 1 — 10, Vilnius 232040; tel. 768 846.

- **POCIUS, Zigmantas**, Dir, publrs *Mokslas*, 1991 — ; b. 1935; grad. Vilnius Univ., philol.; worked with the editorial board of encyclopaedias, 1964 — 84, Dep. E-in-C, 1989 — 90. **Add.** (h) Žaibo 10 — 30, Vilnius 232050; tel. 459 343.

- **POLIS, Juozas**, photographer; b. 1920; quality colour photography, mostly landscapes, townscapes and seascapes; personal exh. abroad; album *Atgimstanti Lietuva* (The Rebirth of Lithuania, 1989). **Add.** (h) Basanavičiaus 36/2 — 5, Vilnius 232009; tel. 634 091.

- **POŠKAITIS, Kazys**, choreographer; b. 1922; grad. Vilnius Univ.; Doc.; Lith. Folk-Culture Centre, 1954 — ; teaches at Lith. Conservatoire; Head Ballet Master of Lith. Song Festivals; described some of Lith. dances; books: *Šokis dainų šventėje* (Dance at a Song Festival , 1980), *Lietuvių šokio kelias į sceną* (The Road of Lith. Dance to the Stage, 1985). **Add.** (h) Antakalnio 45 — 18, Vilnius 232055; tel. 741 078.

- **POŽELA, Juras**, Pres., Lith. Acad. of Sci., 1984 — ; b. 1925; grad. Moscow Univ.; DSc. (Phys.&Math.), Prof., Acad., Lith. and USSR Acad. of Sci.; Inst. of Phys. of Semiconductors, 1967 — ; research in solid state plasma, phys. of hot electrons in semiconductors, generation and amplification of superhigh frequency oscillations in semiconductors under the conditions of cumulative ionization. **Add.** (h) Paco 7/2 — 7, Vilnius 232055; tel. 614 010 (off.).

- **POŽERSKIS, Romualdas**, photographer; b. 1951; photographs noted for emotional tension, subtle psychology; personal exh. abroad, winner of many prizes; album *Atlaidai* (Church Festivals, USA, 1990). **Add.** (h) Mapų 8 — 2, Kaunas 233000; tel. 204 045.

- **PRAGARAUSKAS, Henrikas**, mathematician; b. 1947; grad. Kaunas Technol. Univ.; DSc. (Phys.&Math.); Inst. of Math. and Information Technol., 1971 — ; research in optimum control theory of random processes and nonlinear integral-differential equations. **Add.** (h) Ozo 17 — 1, Vilnius 232056; tel. 417 847.

- **PRAPIESTIS, Jonas**, Chair., Legal System Cttee of SC, 1990 — ; b. 1952; grad. Vilnius Univ., lawyer; lectured at it, 1982 — 90; CSc. (Law); works on criminal law and punitive justice; Lith. SC Deputy. **Add.** Gedimino pr. 53, Vilnius 232026; tel. 615 687.

- **PRAŠKEVIČIUS, Antanas**, biochemist; b. 1934; grad. Kaunas Med. Acad.; DSc. (Biol.), Prof., Acad., Lith. Acad. of Sci.; Rector, Kaunas Med. Acad., 1984 — 91; works on ischemia sensitive components of mitochondria respiration chain, disturbance mechanisms of polyenzime system of fat acids oxidation, causes and consequences of disturbance of mitochondria energetic function. **Add.** (h) Kęstučio 55 — 4, Kaunas 233000; tel. 229 827.

- **PREIKŠAS, Juozas**, Roman Catholic bishop, b. 1926; grad. Kaunas Priest Sem.; lectured at it, 1954 — 66; ordained in 1951; licentiate of theol.; Apostolic Administrator of the Diocese of Panevėžys, 1989 — ; Chair., Liturgical Cttee of Lith.

Bishops, 1991 — . **Add.** Žemgulio 45, Panevėžys 235300; tel. 329 30.

- **PRUDNIKOV, Vladimir**, singer (bass); b. 1949; grad. Lith. Conservatoire; lectures at it, 1979 — ; soloist, Lith. Opera and Ballet Theatre; toured Paris, Palermo an other European cities; Maria Callas singing comp. in Athens (2nd prize, 1981). **Add.** (h) Vokiečių 10 — 4, Vilnius 232001; tel. 616 808.

- **PRUNSKIENĖ, Kazimiera Danutė**, economist; b. 1943; grad. Vilnius Univ.; lectured at it, 1965 — 85; DSc. (Econ.), Prof.; Dep. Chair., CM of the Lith. SSR, 1989 — 90; Prime Min. of Lith. Rep., 1990 — 91; book on econ., food ind.; Lith. SC Deputy. **Add.** Gedimino pr. 53, Vilnius 232026; tel. 626 477.

- **PUIPA, Algimantas**, film dir; b. 1951; grad. Moscow Inst. of Cinematography; Lith. Film Studio, 1974 — ; noted for feature films, documentaries, screen scripts for documentaries; Grand Prix at San Remo festival for the film 'The Eternal Light', 1990. **Add.** (h) Justiniškių 36 — 10, Vilnius 232017; tel. 228 434.

- **PUMPUTIS, Alvydas**, Rector, Lith. Police Acad., 1990 — ; b. 1950; grad. Vilnius Univ.; CSc. (Law), Doc.; research in realization of constitutional standards, org. of local admin. **Add.** (h) Ozo 30 — 59, Vilnius 232010; tel. 466 118.

- **PUTELIS, Vidmantas**, Dir, news agency *ELTA*, 1991 — ; b. 1934; grad. Vilnius Univ., journalist; radio journalist, 1974 — 91. **Add.** Gedimino pr. 21/2, Vilnius 232750; tel. 613 667.

- **RAČICKAS, Vytautas**, writer; b. 1952; grad. Vilnius Univ.; E-in-C, children magazine *Genys*, 1989 — ; books for children (novella *Zuika padūkėlis*, Zuika the Wild, 1985) are distinguished by their lyricism, humour. **Add.** (h) Šaltinių 10 — 1, Vilnius 232006; tel. 661 908.

- **RADVILAS, Vaclovas**, Dir, Mažeikiai Compressors Plant, 1976 — ; b. 1942; grad. Kaunas Technol. Univ., eng. (mech.). **Add.** (h) Vaižganto 10 — 10, Mažeikiai 235500; tel. 535 60.

- **RADŽVILAS, Vytautas**, Chair., Lith. Liberal Union, 1990 — ; b. 1958; grad. Vilnius Univ.; lectured at it, 1984 — 89; psychologist; CSc. (Phil.), Doc.; lecturer, Vilnius Art Acad., 1989 — . **Add.** (h) Šilo 40a — 1, Vilnius 232055; tel. 749 761.

- **RAGULSKIS, Kazimieras**, engineer (mech.); b. 1926; grad. Kaunas Technol. Univ.; DSc. (Eng.), Prof., Acad., Lith. Acad. of Sci., Corr. Mem., USSR Acad. of Sci.; Head, Scientific Centre of Vibrotechnol., 1988 — ; E-in-C, periodical 'Vibrotechnology'; created precise vibromech.; author and co-author of 1,500 inv. and pat. **Add.** (h) Donelaičio 17 — 2, Kaunas 233000; tel. 224 029.

- **RAJECKAS, Raimundas**, Vice-Pres., Lith. Acad. of Sci., 1989 — ; b. 1937; grad. Kaunas Technol. Univ., econ. (technol.); DSc. (Econ.), Prof., Acad. Lith. Acad. of Sci.; lecturer, Vilnius Univ., 1968 — ; an initiator of the scientific trend of econ. cybernetics in Lithuania; works on methods and models of econ. prognosis (also in Russ., Pol.). **Add.** (h) Juozapavičiaus 8 — 36, Vilnius 232005; tel. 754 095.

- **RAJECKAS, Valentinas**, engineer (technol.); b. 1930; grad. Kaunas Technol. Univ.; its lecturer, 1962 — ; DSc. (Eng.), Prof., Corr. Mem., Lith. Acad. of Sci.; research in leather footwear stuffs and technol.; 28 inv. *Add.* (h) Darželio 19 — 1, Kaunas 233009; tel. 717 974.

- **RAKAUSKAS, Romualdas**, photographer; b. 1941; grad. Vilnius Univ., journalist; at magazine *Nemunas* editorial office, 1967 — ; photographs subtle and expressive, conveying relations between man and nature; exh. abroad, winner of many prizes; albums *Naujoji Lietuvos architektūra* (Lith. New Arch., 1984), *Žydėjimas* (Florescence, 1986), AFIAP, 1976. *Add.* (h) Urbšo 26 — 34, Kaunas 233043; tel. 713 690.

- **RAMANAUSKAS, Petras**, Dir, Vilnius Drill Plant, 1963 — ; b. 1932; grad. Kaunas Technol. Univ., eng. (mech.). *Add.* (h) Kudirkos 6/9 — 17, Vilnius 232009; tel. 637 983.

- **RAMUNIS, Gytis**, architect; b. 1950; grad. Vilnius Art Acad.; Chief Arch. of designs, Design Inst. of City Constr., 1986 — ; co-designer of original admin., commercial, sch. buildings. *Add.* (h) Karoliniškių 13 — 172, Vilnius 232044; tel. 452 436.

- **RASLANAS, Algirdas**, Dir-Gen., Dept of Physical Training and Sports, 1990 — ; b. 1956; grad. Lith. Inst. of Physical Training; lectured at it, 1980 — 90; CSc. (Pedag.); worked as a coach. *Add.* Žemaitės 6, Vilnius 232600; tel. 635 363.

- **RAUBICKAS, Benediktas**, Dir, consumer goods factory *Akmena*, 1974 — ; b. 1932; grad. Kaunas Sch. of Econ., econ. *Add.* (h) Žemaičių 8 — 3, Kretinga 235700; tel. 523 85.

- **RAZMA, Liudvikas Saulius**, Rector, Vilnius Pedag. Inst., 1989 — ; b. 1938; grad. Vilnius Univ.; CSc. (Econ.), Doc.; lecturer at Vilnius Pedag. Inst., 1963 — 72; persecuted for his views, fired from Inst.; Lith. SC Deputy. *Add.* (h) Oginskio 4 — 1, Vilnius 232040; tel. 738 281 (off.).

- **REKAŠIUS, Antanas**, composer; b. 1928; grad. Lith. Conservatoire; major works: opera-oratorio *Šviesos baladė* (The Ballad of Light), 6 ballets (*Gęstantis kryžius*, The Smouldering Cross; *Aistros*, Passions; *Idėja*, The Idea; *Amžinai gyvi*, Alive Forever), 7 symphonies, 2 *Autokoliažai* (Auto-Collages) for symphony orch., concertos, chamber music. *Add.* (h) Kupalos 38 — 1, Vilnius 232004; tel. 753 131.

- **REPŠYS, Petras**, graphic artist; b. 1940; grad. Vilnius Art Acad.; teaches at it, 1989 — ; author of prints, book ill., medals and a frescoe at the Centre of Lith. Studies of Vilnius Univ. *Add.* (h) Kalvarijų 142 — 54, Vilnius 232042; tel. 766 156.

- **RIMANTIENĖ, Rimutė**, archeologist; b. 1920; grad. Vilnius Univ.; DSc. (Hist.); works at Inst. of Lith. Hist.; works on Stone and Bronze Ages in Lithuania; 7 books (*Akmens amžius Lietuvoje*, The Stone Age in Lithuania, 1984), albums, atlases. *Add.* (h) Bendroji 12, Vilnius 232040; tel. 764 515.

- **RINKEVIČIUS, Gintaras**, conductor; b. 1960; grad. Leningrad Conservatoire; postgrad. Moscow Conservatoire under J.Simonov, conductor, Lith. Nat. Philharmonic Symphony

Orch., 1980 — 88; Chief Conductor, Lith. State Symphony Orch.; has toured many European c.; Int. Herbert fon Karajan conducting comp. in Berlin (3rd prize, 1984 — 85); Int. In memoriam Janos Ferenscik comp. in Budapest (2nd prize and special prize, 1986). *Add.* (h) Naugarduko 12 — 2, Vilnius 232006; tel. 262 747.

- **RUBACKYTĖ, Mūza**, pianist; b. 1955; grad. under J.Flier and postgrad. Moscow Conservatoire under M.Voskresensky; worked on probation in Paris; Doc.; lectures at Lith. Conservatoire, 1978 — , and Paris Second Conservatoire, 1990 — ; has toured Europe, Argentina; Int. Liszt and Bartok pianists comp. in Budapest (2nd prize, 1981); piano comp. Great Masters of French Music in Paris (Grand Prix, 1990). *Add.* (h) Vokiečių 16 — 13, Vilnius 232001; tel. 220 280.

- **RUBAVIČIUS, Vytautas**, E-in-C, newspaper *Literatūra ir menas*, 1990 — ; poet; b. 1952; grad. Vilnius Univ., phil. *Add.* (h) Totorių 5 — 13, Vilnius 232001; tel. 625 593.

- **RUDAITIS, Juozas**, Dir, Vilkaviškis Sewing Factory, 1971 — ; b. 1943; grad. Kaunas Technol. Univ., eng. (mech.). *Add.* (h) Lauko 26 — 34, Vilkaviškis 234270; tel. 517 79.

- **RUDYS, Audrius**, Chair., Budget Cttee of SC, 1990 — ; b. 1951; grad. Vilnius Univ.; lectures at it, 1974 — ; financier; CSc. (Econ.), Doc.; works on the reform of financial system in the agrarian sector. Lith. SC Deputy. *Add.* Gedimino pr. 53, Vilnius 232026; tel. 629 554.

- **RUDZIKAS, Zenonas**, Dir, Inst. of Theoretical Phys. and Astronomy, 1990 — ; b. 1940; grad. Vilnius Univ., phys.; DSc. (Phys. & Math.), Prof., Corr. Mem., Lith. Acad. of Sci.; research in many-electron atoms and the theory of their spectrum. *Add.* (h) Mickevičiaus 13 — 15, Vilnius 232004; tel. 756 386.

- **RUKŠĖNAS, Rimvydas**, Dir, Vilnius 3rd Thermal Power Station, 1983 — ; b. 1941; grad. Moscow N.Bauman Higher Tech. Sch., spec. in turbine prod.; in energy system since 1965. *Add.* (h) Varpų 3 — 13, Vilnius 232007; tel. 696 177.

- **RUZGAITĖ, Aliodija**, spec. in theatre sci.; b. 1923; grad. Ballet Studio of Kaunas State Theatre, Kaunas Univ., Moscow A. Lunacharsky Inst. of Dramatic Art; ballet dancer with Lith. Opera and Ballet Theatre, 1942 — 66; teaches at Vilnius Choreographic Sch., 1966 — ; books: *Choreografijos menas* (Art of Choreography), 1960), *Lietuviško baleto kelias* (Road of Lith. Ballet, 1964). *Add.* (h) Vokiečių 5 — 3, Vilnius 232024; tel. 624 983.

- **SABALIAUSKAS, Algirdas**, linguist (Lith. philol.); b. 1929; grad. Vilnius Univ.; Inst. of Lith. Lg., 1953 — ; DSc. (Philol.); monographs: *Lietuvių kalbos tyrinėjimo istorija* (Hist. of the Lith. Lg. Research, 1979 — 82, vol. 2), *Lietuvių kalbos leksika* (Lexics of the Lith. Lg., 1990), books for gen. public: *Žodžiai atgyja* (Words Revive, 1967; 1973 in Engl.), *Mes baltai* (We Are the Balts, 1986). *Add.* (h) Žirmūnų 76 — 81, Vilnius 232051; tel. 773 808.

- **SABONIS, Arvydas**, basketball player; b. 1964; player of Kaunas *Žalgiris* team, 1982 — ; USSR basketball team, 1982 — 89; has been playing in Spain, 1989—; world, 1982, Olympic, 1988, European, 1985, champ.; best European basketball player, 1984, 1985, 1988. **Add.** (h) Vasiliausko 20—38, Kaunas 233031; tel. 772 233.

- **SABUTIS, Liudvikas**, Sec., SC of Lith. Rep., 1989—; b. 1939; grad. Vilnius Univ., lawyer; councillor of justice; at the Prosecutor's Office, 1974—89; Public Prosecutor of Rep., 1987—1989. Lith. SC Deputy. **Add.** Gedimino pr. 53, Vilnius 232026; tel. 621 632.

- **SADŪNAITĖ, Nijolė**, a nun; b. 1938; grad. secondary sch. in Anykščiai; imprisoned and exiled to Siberia for preparation and propagation of 'Lith. Catholic Church Chronicle'; publ. *KGB akiratyje* (In the Horizon of KGB, 1985, Chicago; transl. in 8 lgs), *Gerojo Dievo globoje* (Under the Guardianship of God, 1989, Chicago). **Add.** (h) Architektų 27—2, Vilnius 232043; tel. 444 112.

- **SAJA, Kazys**, writer; b. 1932; grad. Vilnius Pedag. Inst.; many dramatic works of various genres; comedies and dramas that ridicule moral vices of rural and narrow-minded people, ethical tragicomedies of parabolic structure (*Mamutų medžioklė*, Mammoth Hunt, 1968), folk style plays; his dramas are noted for its bold exposure of social problems, folk humour; Lith. SC Deputy. **Add.** (h) Antakalnio 8—28, Vilnius 232055; tel. 614 579.

- **SAKALAS, Aloyzas**, Chair., Mandate and Ethics Cttee of SC, 1990—; Chair., Lith. SDP, 1991—; b. 1931; grad. Kaunas Technol. Univ., phys.; DSc. (Phys. & Math.), Prof.; lecturer, Vilnius Univ., 1963—; works on phys. characteristics of semiconductor combination; 16 inv; Lith. SC Deputy. **Add.** Gedimino pr. 53, Vilnius 232026; tel. 226 164.

- **SAKALAUSKAS, Tomas**, journalist; b. 1932; grad. Vilnius Univ., works at the editorial office of the magazine *Švyturys*, 1962—; monographs on the famous Lith. artists J.Miltinis (1981), B.Grincevičiūtė (1982), V.Eidukevičius (1987), A.Gudaitis (1990). **Add.** (h) Ozo 30—54, Vilnius 232010; tel. 466 703.

- **SAKALAUSKAS, Vaclovas**, Chair., Lith. soc. for relations with Lithuanians abroad *Tėviškė*, 1986—; b. 1938; grad. Vilnius Univ., lawyer; on diplomatic service in Uganda, USA, 1977—86. **Add.** (h) Blindžių 31—7, Vilnius 232004; tel. 352 032.

- **SAKALAUSKAS, Valerijonas**, Dir-Gen., Dept of Standardization and Quality, 1990—; b. 1934; grad. Kaunas Technol. Univ., eng. (mech.); Dep. Min., Min. of Local Ind., 1978—90. **Add.** Jakšto 1/25, Vilnius 232600; tel. 753 320.

- **SAPAGOVAS, Mifodijus**, mathematician; b. 1939; grad. Vilnius Univ.; DSc. (Phys. & Math.), Corr. Mem., Lith. Acad. of Sci.; Inst. of Math. and Information Technol., 1961—, Dep. Dir, 1967—; research in solution of nonlinear differential equations, usage of math. methods and computers in phys. and technol. **Add.** (h) Tuskulėnų 7—65, Vilnius 232051; tel. 756 248.

- **SASNAUSKAS, Kęstutis**, engineer (technol.); b. 1923; grad. Kaunas Univ.; DSc. (Eng.),

Prof.; lecturer, Kaunas Technol. Univ., 1950—; research in the synthesis and use of calcium hydrosilicates, improvement of technol. of autoclave silicate articles. **Add.** (h) Vitkausko 26—38, Kaunas 233000; tel. 759 652.

- **SAUDARGAS, Algirdas**, Min. of Foreign Affairs, 1990—; b. 1948; grad. Kaunas Med. Acad., biophys.; lectured at it; Dep. Chair., Lith. Christian Dem. Party. Lith. SC Deputy. **Add.** Akmenų 6, Vilnius 232600; tel. 618 537.

- **SAUKA, Donatas**, lit. historian, folklorist; b. 1929; grad. Vilnius Univ.; lectures at it, 1956—; DSc. (Lit.), Prof.; books: *Salomėjos Nėries kūryba 1921—40* (Works by Salomėja Nėris from 1921—40, 1957), *Tautosakos savitumas ir vertė* (Originality and Artistic Value of Folklore, 1970), *Lietuvių tautosaka* (The Lith. Folklore, 1982; 1986 in Russ.), *Žemaitės stebuklas* (The Miracle of Žemaitė, 1988), book of essays *Noriu suprasti* (I Want to Understand, 1991). **Add.** (h) Ozo 3—24, Vilnius 232056; tel. 410 937.

- **SAUKA, Leonardas**, folklorist; b. 1931; grad. Vilnius Univ.; DSc. (Lit.), Prof., Corr. Mem., Lith. Acad. of Sci.; Inst. of Lith. Lit. and Folklore, 1957—; books: *Lietuvių vestuvinės dainos* (The Lith. Wedding Songs, 1968), *Lietuvių folkloro eilėtyros istorijos ir teorijos klausimai* (Problems on the Hist. and Theory of the Lith. Folklore Study of Verse, 1974), *Lietuvių liaudies dainų eilėdara* (Versification of Lith. Folk Songs, 1978), *Tikra ir netikra liaudies kūryba* (Authentic and Non-Authentic Folk Art, 1983). **Add.** (h) Peteliškių 12—57, Vilnius 232007; tel. 696 987.

- **SAUNORIS, Gintaras**, Dir-Gen., electric-tech. ent. *Elfa*, 1988—; b. 1945; grad. Kaunas Technol. Univ., eng. (electrical); at *Elfa* since 1963. **Add.** (h) Viršuliškių 87—121, Vilnius 232056; tel. 410 430.

- **SAVICKAS, Augustinas**, painter; b. 1919; grad. Vilnius Art Acad.; teaches at it, 1951—72, 1985—; CSc. (Arts), Prof., Corr. Mem., USSR Art Acad.; monumental works of generalized forms and rich colours; author of books on art hist. and autobiographies; paintings acquired by Moscow Tretyakov, Cologne Ludwig art galleries. **Add.** (h) Nočios 4—4, Vilnius 232009; tel. 639 851.

- **SEMAŠKA, Algimantas**, E-in-C, magazine *Politika*, 1990—; b. 1941; grad. Vilnius Univ., journalist; press worker, 1960—; books for tourists on Lithuania (in Ger.). **Add.** Maironio 1, Vilnius 232656; tel. 610 414.

- **SIENKIEWICZ, Jan**, Chair., Polish Union, 1988—; b. 1956; grad. Minsk Inst. of Foreign Lgs, philol. (Engl. and Ger. philol.); press worker, 1978—. **Add.** (h) Konarskio 20—3, Vilnius 232009; tel. 650 659.

- **SIMANAVIČIUS, Žibartas**, engineer (arch.); b. 1930; grad. Kaunas Technol. Univ.; Inst. of Monument Restoration, 1953—90; designed renovation of defence works, admin. buildings, dwelling houses, also original interiors. **Add.** (h) Rūdninkų 6—4, Vilnius 232024; tel. 624 387.

- **SINEVIČIUS, Albertas Ambraziejus**, Min. of Trade, 1990—; b. 1943; grad. Kaunas Technol. Univ., eng. (mech.); worked in light ind., 1967—90, Dep. Min., Min. of Light Ind.,

1987 – 90. **Add.** Gedimino pr. 30/1, Vilnius 232695; tel. 617 007.

▪ **SIRIJOS, Gira Vytautas**, writer; b. 1911; grad. Vilnius Univ., physician; prior to WW II wrote modern poetry; gained popularity due to recent adventure and love novels dealing with urban life *Adomas nori būti žmogumi* (Adam wants to Be a Man, 1959), *Raudonmedžio rojus* (Mahogany Paradise, 1972), *Voratinkliai draikės be vėjo* (Gossamers Floated in Calm Air, 1975), *Kanarėlės* (Canaries, 1983), *Paskutinis sekmadienis* (The Last Sunday, 1990). **Add.** (h) Švyturio 22 – 10, Vilnius 232040; tel. 743 802.

▪ **SIRVYDIS, Vytautas**, cardiovascular surgeon; b. 1935; grad. Vilnius Univ.; its lecturer, 1964 – ; DSc. (Med.), Prof.; Head, Cardiosurgery Clinic, 1990 – ; improved method of contrasting angiography, many inborn heart disease operations, introduced into practice heart valve prostheses and coronary reconstr., co-perf. the first reconstr. operations of abdominal aorta and kidney artery in Lithuania and Lithuania's first heart operation using the artificial circulation of blood; in 1987, together with others perf. the first heart transplantation in Lithuania. **Add.** (h) Architektų 89 – 48, Vilnius 232049; tel. 449 758.

▪ **SKEIVIENĖ, Laima**, Pres., Nat. Assoc. of Lith. Photographers, 1990 – ; b. 1953; grad. Vilnius Univ., philol.; photography and art critic; compiler of photography books and exh. **Add.** (h) Musninkų 2 – 34, Vilnius 232010; tel. 411 492.

▪ **SKIRKEVIČIUS, Algirdas**, E-in-C, magazine 'Pheromones', 1990 – ; b. 1939; grad. Lith. Agric. Acad.; DSc. (Biol.), Prof., Corr. Mem., Lith. Acad. of Sci.; Inst. of Ecology, 1969 – , Dep. Dir, 1990 – ; research in the pheromonine communication of the insects; 2 books. **Add.** (h) Architektų 212 – 24, Vilnius 232049; tel. 443 476.

▪ **SKIRMANTAS, Petras**, ballet dancer; b. 1957; grad. M.K. Čiurlionis Art Sch., postgrad. course at Leningrad Maly Opera and Ballet Theatre; soloist, ballet premier, Lith. Opera and Ballet Theatre, 1974 – ; leading dancer; danced with Leningrad Kirov Opera and Ballet Theatre, Moscow Bolshoi Theatre, toured European, Asian, African c., USA. **Add.** (h) Ukmergės 186 – 15, Vilnius 232010; tel. 422 456.

▪ **SKVARNAVIČIUS, Gediminas**, film dir; b. 1933; grad. Leningrad Univ.; Lith. Film Studio, 1960 – ; author of many film essays; noted for humour and irony. **Add.** (h) Kalvarijų 126 – 6, Vilnius 232042; tel. 765 419.

▪ **SLADKEVIČIUS, Vincentas**, Roman Catholic Cardinal; b. 1920; grad. Theol. Faculty of Kaunas Univ.; ordained in 1944; after he was concecrated bishop the Soviet authorities for a period of 1959 – 82 did not allow to enter upon his duties and exiled him to the Biržai district; Apostolic Administrator of the Diocese of Kaišiadorys, 1982 – 88; Chair., College of Ordinaries of the Lith. Dioceses, 1988 – ; Archbishop of Kaunas, 1989 – . **Add.** Valančiaus 6, Kaunas 233000; tel. 226 132.

▪ **SLUCKIS, Mykolas**, writer; b. 1928; grad. Vilnius Univ.; his coll. of stories are notable for their more tender attitude, emotionality as compared with the politicized prose of the post-war period; the most important novels *Laiptai į dangų* (Stairway to the Sky, 1963), *Adomo obuolys* (Adam's Apple, 1966), *Saulė vakarop* (The Sun Towards Evening, 1976), *Medžliepis* (The Maple, 1986) revive the traditions of the lyrical romantic style in the Lith. prose; in his works civic problems are combined with subtle psychologism; books transl. into Ger., Russ., Czech, Hung. and other lgs. **Add.** (h) Švyturio 22 – 10, Vilnius 232040; tel. 744 418.

▪ **SMETONA, Rimantas**, Chair., Lith. Nationalist Union, 1990 – ; b. 1944; grad. Leningrad Theatre, Music and Cinematography Inst., TV dir; works at Lith. TV, 1972 – ; Ed., newspaper *Viltis.* **Add.** Gedimino pr. 22, Vilnius 232600; tel. 624 935.

▪ **SMORIGIN, Yury**, ballet dancer; b. 1955; grad. M.K.Čiurlionis Art Sch., Leningrad Conservatoire; postgrad. course at Dresden Paluca Modern Dance Sch.; soloist ballet premier, Lith. Opera and Ballet Theatre, 1977 – , ballet master, 1987 – . **Add.** (h) Vokiečių 13 – 9, Vilnius 232024; tel. 618 617 (off.).

▪ **SONDECKIS, Saulius**, conductor; b. 1928; grad. Lith. Conservatoire; postgrad. Moscow Conservatoire; Prof.; conductor, Čiurlionis Art Sch. Orch., 1955 – ; founder and conductor of Lith. Chamber Orch., 1960 – ; lecturer, Lith. Conservatoire, 1957 – ; has toured many European c., USA, Canada, Cuba, Japan; a judge at Int. Karajan (1978), E. Anserme (1984) and Tchaikovsky (1986) comp.; Čiurlionis Art Sch. Orch. was awarded the 1st prize and gold medal at Karajan Fund Comp. in Berlin (1976). **Add.** (h) Šeimyniškių 30 – 1, Vilnius 232051; tel. 752 558.

▪ **SPRINDYS, Algimantas**, engineer (arch.); b. 1928; grad. Kaunas Technol. Univ.; Chief Arch. of designs, Design Inst. of City Constr., 1965 – 76; Kaunas Chief Arch., 1976 – 90; designer of original admin., commercial buildings, housing developments and interiors for stores. **Add.** (h) Cvirkos 35 – 20, Kaunas 233000; tel. 222 425.

▪ **STAČIOKAS, Stasys**, lawyer; b. 1937; grad. Vilnius Univ.; lectures at it, 1973 – ; CSc. (Law), Doc.; Dir, Inst. of Forensic Expertise, 1973 – 91; research in the theory of state and law, constitutional (state) law, land law, activities of state bodies, crime prevention. **Add.** (h) Žirmūnų 129 – 52, Vilnius 232012; tel. 775 466.

▪ **STALILIŪNAITĖ, Rūta**, theatre and film actress; b. 1938; grad. Lith. Conservatoire; works at Kaunas Drama Theatre; a versatile actress, noted for a subtle psychological manner. **Add.** (h) Kęstučio 87 – 1, Kaunas 233000; tel. 228 077.

▪ **STANIŠKIS, Jurgis Kazimieras**, engineer (electromech.); b. 1943; grad. Kaunas Technol. Univ.; its lecturer, 1965 – ; DSc. (Eng.), Prof.; research in the modelling of biotechnol. processes, automation and management; 136 inv. **Add.** (h) Plieno 1 – 11, Kaunas 233035; tel. 743 160.

▪ **STANKEVIČIUS, Česlovas Vytautas**, Dep. Chair., SC of Lith. Rep., 1990 – ; b. 1937; grad.

Kaunas Technol. Univ., eng. (civil); Chief Eng. of designs, Kaunas Design Inst. of City Constr., 1974 – 90. Lith. SC Deputy. *Add.* Gedimino pr. 53, Vilnius 232026; tel. 615 680.

▪ **STAPULIONIS, Algimantas**, engineer (arch.); b. 1924; grad. Kaunas Technol. Univ.; Chief Arch., state ent. *Guoba*, 1971 – 88; Sec., Designers' Union, 1988 – ; designer of interiors, furniture for mass prod. for public, educ. buildings and homes. *Add.* (h) Sėlių 39/2 – 5, Vilnius 232004; tel. 753 546.

▪ **STASIULEVIČIUS, Aloyzas**, painter; b. 1931; grad. Vilnius Art Acad.; taught at it, 1976 – 79; author of urban landscapes (mainly Vilnius), still-lifes; works have been acquired by Moscow Tretyakov, Cologne Ludwig art galleries. *Add.* (h) Architektų 25 – 58, Vilnius 232043; tel. 442 527.

▪ **STASIULIS, Edmundas**, architect; b. 1943; grad. Vilnius Art Acad.; Design Inst. of City Constr., 1972 – ; designer of original sports, admin., sch. buildings in Vilnius. *Add.* (h) Justiniškių 23 – 15, Vilnius 232056; tel. 416 382.

▪ **STATULEVIČIUS, Vytautas**, Vice-Pres., Lith. Acad. of Sci., 1985 – ; Dir, Inst. of Math. and Information Technol.; b. 1929; grad. Vilnius Univ., math.; DSc. (Phys. & Math.), Prof., Acad., Lith. Acad. of Sci; at the Inst. since 1957; Dir, World Lith. Culture, Sci. and Educ. Centre, 1989 – . E-in-C, journal *Tikimybių teorija ir jos taikymas* (Probability Theory and its Application); research in limit theorems and asymptotic analysis of probability theory. *Add.* (h) Oginskio 4 – 7, Vilnius 232040; tel. 768 775.

▪ **STAUSKAS, Vladas**, engineer (arch.); b. 1932; grad. Kaunas Technol. Univ.; DSc. (Arch.), Prof.; Inst. of Constr. and Arch., 1968 – ; designer of admin. buildings in Kaunas, recreational and dwelling houses in Nida, Pervalka, Palanga; co-author of master plans for health resorts, author of blueprints for nature protection and recreational system; 2 monographs. *Add.* (h) Ivanausko 104 – 54, Kaunas 233030; tel. 771 136.

▪ **STEPONAVIČIUS, Julijonas**, Roman Catholic archbishop; b. 1911; grad. Kaunas Priest Sem.; ordained in 1935; ThM; Apostolic Administrator of the Archdiocese of Vilnius and the Diocese of Panevėžys, 1958 – 61; in 1961 the Soviet Govt removed him from this office and exiled to Žagarė; Archbishop ordinary of Vilnius, 1989 – . *Add.* Šv. Mikalojaus 4, Vilnius 232001; tel. 626 177.

▪ **STIRBYS, Petras**, cardiovascular surgeon; b. 1948; grad. Kaunas Med. Acad.; its lecturer, 1983 – , Vice-Rector, 1989 – ; DSc. (Med.), Prof., Mem., New York Acad. of Sci.; created electrode implants and their int. code, set of instruments for implantation of electrocardiac stimulation systems, device for modelling of surgical seams, improved methods of electric heart stimulation. *Add.* (h) Signalo 4 – 7, Kaunas 233043; tel. 718 869.

▪ **STOMA, Saulius**, E-in-C, newspaper *Lietuvos aidas*, 1990 – ; b. 1954; grad. Vilnius Tech. Univ., arch.; press worker, 1979 – ; Ed., weekly

Šiaurės Atėnai, 1989 – 90. *Add.* Gynėjų 3, Vilnius 232710; tel. 610 544.

▪ **STONKUS, Stanislovas**, basketball player; b. 1931; grad. Lith. Inst. of Physical Training; its Rector, 1978 – 90; DSc. (Pedag.), Prof.; coach of int. class; Pres., Lith. Basketball Federation; European champ., 1957; books about basketball. *Add.* (h) Laisvės al. 110 – 8, Kaunas 233000; tel. 225 403.

▪ **STOŠKUS, Algimantas**, stained-glass artist; b. 1925; grad. Kaunas Applied and Decorative Art Inst.; lecturer, Vilnius Art Acad., 1951 – ; Prof.; author of spatial and kinetic stained-glass panels from thin and thick glass. *Add.* (h) Krivių 41 – 7, Vilnius 232007; tel. 696 377.

▪ **STOŠKUS, Krescencijus**, philosopher; b. 1938; grad. Vilnius Univ.; lectures at it, 1964 – ; CSc. (Phil.), Doc.; works on ethics, aesthetics, theory of culture, semiotics. *Add.* Universiteto 3, Vilnius 232734; tel. 625 053.

▪ **STRAIŽYS, Vytautas**, astrophysicist; b. 1936; grad. Vilnius Univ.; DSc. (Phys. & Math.), Prof.; Inst. of Theoretical Phys. and Astronomy, 1961 – ; research in multicolour-photometry of stars; classification of stars, structure of the Galaxy; author of Vilnius astro-photometric system. *Add.* (h) Architektų 25 – 18, Vilnius 232043; tel. 442 531.

▪ **STRAVINSKAS, Povilas**, pianist; b. 1950; grad. Moscow Conservatoire; teaches at Lith. Conservatoire, 1976 – ; soloist, Lith. Nat. Philharmonic, 1976 – ; toured European c., USA; since 1990 gives concerts and lectures at New York Univ. *Add.* 735 Anderson Hill Rd., Purchase, New York 10577 – 1400 USA.

▪ **STREČEN-MAŽEIKAITĖ, Sigita**, handball player; b. 1958; Olympic, 1980, world, 1982 champ.; mem., Vilnius *Eglė* team, 1970 – 89, USSR team, 1977 – 86; left for Germany, 1989 – . *Add.* (h) Didlaukio 39 – 53, Vilnius 232057; tel. 764 799.

▪ **STRIELKŪNAS, Jonas**, poet; b. 1939; coll. of poems *Vėjas rugiuos* (The Wind in the Rye, 1971), *Varpo kėlimas* (The Raising of a Bell, 1978), *Po tylinčiom žvaigždėm* (Under the Silent Stars, 1982), *Lapkričio medus* (November Honey, 1985), *Tamsūs buvo žiedai* (The Blossoms Were Dark, 1990); patriotic motifs of man's link with the native land prevail in his poetry; the link with the motherland is the criterion of ethic values, the foundation of the existence of a man; his poetry is distinguished for its melodious intonations, characteristic of the Lith. lyrics, natural simplicity, calm contemplation, tendency to speak about the tangible surrounding world. *Add.* (h) Rinktinės 19 – 117, Vilnius 232051; tel. 750 152.

▪ **STUNDŽIA, Bonifacas**, linguist (Baltic philol.); b. 1952; grad. Vilnius Univ.; lectures at it, 1976 – ; CSc. (Philol.), Doc., Corr. Mem., Milan Linguistic Soc.; research in the hist. morphology of the Baltic lgs, accentology, Lith. dialectology, hist. of Lith. linguistics. *Add.* (h) Taikos 18 – 72, Vilnius 232017; tel. 426 262.

▪ **SUBAČIUS, Juozas**, Ed., newspaper *Tėvynės šviesa*, 1987 – ; b. 1939; grad. Vilnius Univ.,

philol.; press worker, 1971 — . **Add.** Antakalnio 31, Vilnius 232055; tel. 748 943.
- **SURGAILIS, Donatas**, mathematician;
b. 1943; grad. Vilnius Univ.; DSc. (Phys.
& Math.), Corr. Mem., Lith. Acad. of Sci.; Inst. of
Math. and Information Technol., 1973 — ; research in the theory of automodelling and
Markov fields with the Est. math. T.Arak
investigated the new class of polygonal Markov
fields with a finite set of states. **Add.** (h) Slyvų
4 — 3, Vilnius 232001; tel. 624 759.
- **SURGAILIS, Leopoldas**, painter; b. 1928;
grad. Vilnius Art Acad.; taught at it, 1960 — 82;
his works (many of them based on mythology)
are a unique interpretation of Lith. folk tradition, with elements of grotesque; paintings
acquired by Moscow Tretyakov, Cologne Ludwig
art galleries. **Add.** (h) Pylimo 11 — 5, Vilnius
232001; tel. 618 837.
- **SURVILA, Rimvydas Raimundas**, Min. of
Agric., 1991 — ; b. 1939; grad. Lith. Agric. Acad.,
zootechnician; works on the technol. of animal
produce; Head Zootechnician, Vievis Poultry
Farm; Lith. SC Deputy. **Add.** Gedimino pr. 19,
Vilnius 232025; tel. 625 438.
- **SUTKUS, Augustinas**, Dir-Gen., co *Aurida*,
1982 — ; b. 1948; grad. Kaunas Technol. Univ.,
eng. (mech.). **Add.** (h) Laisvės al. 25 — 14,
Panevėžys 235300; tel. 641 44.
- **SUTKUS, Antanas**, photographer; b. 1939;
studied at Vilnius Univ.; Chair., Bd of Lith.
Photography Art Soc., 1969 — 74, 1980 — 90;
photographs noted for expressive composition,
emotionality, psychologism; personal exh. abroad, winner of many prizes; albums *Neringa*
(1982), *Daina Lietuvai* (Songs for Lithuania,
1984) and others; AFIAP, 1976. **Add.** (h) Šeimyniškių 38 — 7, Vilnius 232051; tel. 731 155.
- **SVARINSKAS, Alfonsas**, Roman Catholic
priest; b. 1925; studied at Kaunas Priest Sem.;
ordained in 1956; Monsignor; Chancellor, Curia
of Kaunas Archdiocese, 1990 — ; has a reputation for sermons, anti-alcoholic actions; leader
of Catholic Action Centre; pol. prisoner,
1946 — 56, 1958 — 64, 1983 — 88. **Add.** (h) Druskininkų 4 — 2, Kaunas 233000; tel. 226 266.
- **SVENTICKAS, Valentinas**, lit. critic;
b. 1948; grad. Vilnius Univ.; at publrs *Vaga*,
1979 — 84; Sec., Bd of the Lith. Writers' Union,
1986 — ; a study *Alfonso Maldonio lyrika* (Lyrics
of Alfonsas Maldonis, 1982), coll. of articles on
the Lith. poetry *Eilėraščio keliais* (Along the
Roads of the Poem, 1978). **Add.** (h) Mildos
33 — 3, Vilnius 232055; tel. 741 680.
- **ŠABLEVIČIUS, Henrikas**, film dir; b. 1930;
grad. Vilnius Drama Theatre Studio; Lith. Film
Studio, 1971 — ; author of nearly 30 film essays
and feature films, awarded prizes for the film
'Living Heroes' (Karlovy Vary, 1960) and 'A
Man, Going Home' (Oberhausen, 1987). **Add.** (h)
Kalvarijų 182 — 46, Vilnius 232042; tel. 773 668.
- **ŠALTENIS, Arvydas**, painter; b. 1944; grad.
Vilnius Art Acad.; teaches at it, 1975 — 81,
1989 — ; Sec., Lith. Artists' Union; author of
expressionist figure compositions, landscapes,
portraits. **Add.** (h) Architektų 101 — 13, Vilnius
232049; tel. 445 027.

- **ŠALTENIS, Saulius**, writer; b. 1945; novellas *Riešutų duona* (Hazelnut Bread, 1972),
Duokiškis (1977), a novel *Kalės vaikai* (Sons-
of-a-Bitch, 1989); plays, short stories, film
scripts; scenes of everyday life of the pre-war
village and town, irony, humour, paradoxes are
typical features of his works; Ed., weekly
Šiaurės Atėnai; Lith. SC Deputy. **Add.** (h) Mildos 31 — 10, Vilnius 232055; tel. 358 908.
- **ŠAVELIS, Rimantas**, writer; b. 1942; grad.
Vilnius Univ., studied in Moscow; a novel *Dievo
avinėlis* (Lamb of God, 1974), a novella *Amžinoji
šviesa* (The Eternal Light, 1987); writes on the
post-war countryside, the fate of an individual
during the pol. conflicts and hist. perturbations;
intricate plot, paradoxical situations, irony;
short stories, film scripts, TV scenarios. **Add.**
(h) Vokiečių 15 — 27, Vilnius 232024; tel.
613 130.
- **ŠEIBOKAS, Justinas**, architect; b. 1929;
grad. Vilnius Art Acad.; Chief Arch. of designs,
Design Inst. of City Constr., 1965 — ; designer
of original admin. buildings and interiors;
co-author of reconstr. plan for the Old Town of
Vilnius. **Add.** (h) Žirmūnų 26 — 7, Vilnius
232051; tel. 769 305.
- **ŠENDEROV, Anatolij**, composer; b. 1945;
grad. Lith. Conservatoire; worked on probation
at Tel-Aviv Music Acad.; major works: ballets
Mergaitė ir mirtis (A Girl and Death), 'Maria
Stewart', 3 symphonies, vocal-symphonic poems
Varpai (The Bells), *Ikaras* (Icarus), 2 cantatas,
Dvi Sulamitos giesmės (Two Songs of Shulamith)
for soprano and piano. **Add.** (h) Taikos
203 — 16, Vilnius 232017; tel. 461 202.
- **ŠERKŠNYS, Gediminas**, Chair., State Restoration Cttee of SC, 1990 — ; b. 1948; grad.
Kaunas Med. Acad., biophys.; CSc. (Eng.);
worked at Z.Januškevičius Inst. of Physiology
and Pathology of the Cardiovascular System,
1980 — 89. Lith. SC Deputy. **Add.** Gedimino
pr. 53, Vilnius 232026; tel. 613 855.
- **ŠEŠELGIS, Kazys**, engineer (arch.); b. 1915;
grad. Kaunas Univ.; DSc. (Arch.), Prof.; lecturer
of Kaunas and Vilnius higher sch., 1950 — ;
co-author of reconstr. plan for the Old Town of
Vilnius, author of a comprehensive population
plan which was used as basis for regional
planning; master plans of Lith. towns; works on
town planning, folk arch. district planning. **Add.**
(h) Vykinto 27 — 13, Vilnius 232004; tel.
730 017.
- **ŠILEIKA, Algirdas**, physicist; b. 1932; grad.
Vilnius Univ.; DSc. (Phys. & Math.), Prof., Acad.,
Lith. Acad. of Sci.; Inst. of Semiconductor Phys.,
1967 — ; research in optical properties of semiconductors, phys. fundamentals of modulative
spectroscopy methods, use of these methods in
the studies of energy band structure of complicated and anisotropic semiconductors. **Add.**
Požėlos 52, Vilnius 232600; tel. 749 768 (h).
- **ŠILGALIS, Henrikas Kęstutis**, Dir, assoc.
Architprojektas, 1987 — ; b. 1944; grad. Kaunas
Univ., eng. (arch.); designer of a collective farm
settlement in Latvia, community centres and
reconstr. of the monument of Three Crosses in

Vilnius. **Add.** (h) Architektų 111−14, Vilnius 232043; tel. 443 975.

- **ŠILINIS, Rimantas**, film dir; b. 1937; grad. Vilnius Univ.; Lith. Film Studio, 1965−; documentaries, scenarios on themes of man and nature, moral problems, portraits of cultural figures. **Add.** (h) Tuskulėnų 26−40, Vilnius 232051; tel. 758 192.
- **ŠILINSKAS, Romualdas**, architect; b. 1934; grad. Vilnius Art Acad.; Chief Arch. of designs, design technol. trust *Orgstatyba*, 1983−90; co-designed (with his wife Aušra) original med., recreational, commercial buildings of complex composition in Palanga, Druskininkai, Birštonas. **Add.** (h) Smėlio 29−42, Vilnius 232055; tel. 743 911.
- **ŠIMĖNAS, Albertas**, Min. of Econ., May 1991−; b. 1950; grad. Vilnius Univ., econ. (math.); CSc. (Econ.); lecturer at Vilnius Tech. Univ., 1984−89; Prime Min. of Lith. Rep., January 10−14, 1991; Lith. SC Deputy. **Add.** Gedimino pr. 38/2, Vilnius 232600; tel. 622 416.
- **ŠIMĖNAS, Jonas**, Chair., Nature Protection Cttee of SC, 1990−; b. 1953; grad. Vilnius Univ., hydrogeol.; worked at Lith. Geol. Dept, 1978−89; works on Lith. econ. zone of Baltic shelf, compiled a complete set of its geol. maps. Lith. SC Deputy. **Add.** Gedimino pr. 53, Vilnius 232026; tel. 624 077.
- **ŠIMKŪNAS, Jonas**, Dir-Gen., Dept of Labour Safety, 1990−; b. 1942; grad. Vilnius Tech. Univ., eng. (electronics); worked at the electricity supply service and municipal services, 1976−90. **Add.** Jakšto 1/25, Vilnius 232600; tel. 624 478.
- **ŠINKUS, Algimantas**, Dir-Gen., Lith. Fishing Ind. Prod. Assoc., 1988−; b. 1940; grad. Murmansk Higher Navigation Eng. Sch., eng. (mech.). **Add.** (h) Nemuno 32, Klaipėda 235800; tel. 107 21.
- **ŠIUPŠINSKAS, Juozas**, E-in-C, magazine *Darbas ir poilsis*, 1969−; journalist; b. 1933; writes on tourism; Mem., FIJET. **Add.** (h) Architektų 164−30, Vilnius 232049; tel. 449 900.
- **ŠLIOGERIS, Arvydas**, philosopher; b. 1944; grad. Kaunas Technol. Univ.; DSc. (Phil.), Prof.; lecturer, Vilnius Univ., 1973−; books: *Žmogaus pasaulis ir egzistencinis mąstymas* (Man's World and Existential Thinking, 1985), *Daiktas ir menas* (Object and Art, 1988), *Būtis ir pasaulis* (Being and the World, 1990). **Add.** (h) Sudervės 5−94, Vilnius 232051; tel. 456 064.
- **ŠNIUKAS, Domas**, Ed., newspaper *Tiesa*, 1990−; b. 1932; grad. Vilnius Univ., journalist; press worker, 1954−; correspondent of newspaper *Pravda*, 1974−89; Chair., Radio and TV Cttee, 1989−90; Chair., Lith. Journalists' Union, 1988−90; publicistic books on Lithuania. **Add.** (h) Šilo 60−6, Vilnius 232055; tel. 749 757.
- **ŠONTA, Virgilijus**, photographer; b. 1952; grad. Kaunas Technol. Univ.; photographs expressive, aesthetic, depicting natural forms; personal exh. abroad, winner of many prizes. **Add.** (h) Kemerno 3−1, Kaunas 233002; tel. 749 607.

- **ŠUGUROV, Viktor**, physicist; b. 1928; grad. Vilnius Univ.; its lecturer, 1953−; DSc. (Phys. & Math.), Prof.; research in the simulation of characteristics of atoms, molecules and nuclei, gyromagnetic electrodynamics and electronics. **Add.** (h) Švyturio 25−6, Vilnius 232040; tel. 740 319.
- **ŠVAŽIENĖ, Marytė**, textile artist; b. 1930; grad. Vilnius Art Acad.; author of decorative carpets, plane and spatial tapestry. **Add.** (h) Jogailos 12−26, Vilnius 232001; tel. 624 160.
- **TALAČKIENĖ, Liucija**, Dir, Lentvaris Carpet Factory, 1987−; b. 1938; grad. Vilnius Univ., econ.; in the factory since 1962. **Add.** (h) Lelijų 3−2, Lentvaris 234200; tel. 584 10.
- **TAMKEVIČIUS, Sigitas**, Rector, Kaunas Interdiocesan Priest Sem., 1990−; grad. from this Sem.; ordained in 1962; Jesuit; Roman Catholic bishop, May 1991; conscience prisoner in Russ., 1983−88. **Add.** Trakų 1, Kaunas 233000; tel. 221 428.
- **TAMONIS, Matas**, engineer (thermal technol.); b. 1938; grad. Kaunas Technol. Univ.; DSc. (Eng.), Prof.; Inst. for Phys. and Eng. Problems of Energy Research, 1959−; research in thermal technol. and thermal phys. **Add.** (h) Taikos 62−106, Kaunas 233031; tel. 736 453.
- **TAMOŠIŪNAS, Vytas**, Dir, Inst. of Immunology, 1990−; b. 1942; grad. Lith. Veterinary Acad.; DSc. (Biol.), Prof.; worked at Inst. of Biochem., 1966−90; works on the influence of retrovirus upon organism immunosystem, its functioning in organism cells and molecules under leukemia and virus infection, problems of immunotechnol.; 2 monographs. **Add.** (h) Architektų 132−104, Vilnius 232049; tel. 449 003.
- **TAMULEVIČIŪTĖ, Dalia**, theatre dir, teacher; b. 1940; grad. Moscow A. Lunacharsky Inst. of Dramatic Art; Chief Dir, Vilnius Youth Theatre, 1971−88; lecturer, Lith. Conservatoire, 1989−; realistic manner; elements of wit and parabole prevail in *mise en scène*. **Add.** (h) Žirmūnų 12−23, Vilnius 232051; tel. 763 742.
- **TAPINAS, Laimonas**, film critic, journalist; b. 1944; grad. Vilnius Univ.; advanced studies at Sorbonne; CSc. (Arts); Doc.; lecturer, Vilnius Univ., 1984−; books: 'At the Fair of Illusions', 1983; 'Lithuanian Filmmakers', 1986 (1988, Engl., Ger.). **Add.** (h) Tuskulėnų 18−2, Vilnius 232051; tel. 758 390.
- **TAURAGIS, Adeodatas**, musicologist; b. 1936; grad. Lith. Conservatoire; postgrad. Moscow Conservatoire; Doc., lecturer, Lith. Conservatoire, 1962−; works on foreign and Lith. music hist.; books: 'Benjamin Britten' (Russ., 1965), 'Lithuanian Music: Past and Present' (Engl. 1971, Ger. 1972). **Add.** (h) Ukmergės 186−31, Vilnius 232010; tel. 466 500.
- **TAURAS, Antanas**, Dir, Klaipėda Timber Company, 1987−; b. 1943; grad. Vilnius Univ., econ.; in timber-processing ind. since 1964. **Add.** (h) 16-osios divizijos 43−46, Klaipėda 235818; tel. 558 23.
- **TAUTAVIČIUS, Adolfas**, archeologist; b. 1925; grad. Vilnius Univ.; CSc. (Hist.); Inst. of Lith. Hist., 1946−; research on the Lith. archeological monuments of 5th−14th cent.;

8 books (*Lietuvos archeologijos bruožai*, Outline of Lith. Archeology, 1961), atlases. **Add.** Kosciuškos 30, Vilnius 232600; tel. 625 630.

■ **TELKSNYS, Adolfas Laimutis**, cybernetics spec.; b. 1930; grad. Kaunas Technol. Univ.; DSc. (Eng.), Prof., Corr. Mem., Lith. Acad. of Sci.; Inst. of Math. and Information Technol., 1965 — ; Pres., Lith. Assoc. of Information Technol., 1990 — ; research in the theory of recognition of random processes and automation of recognition, eng. and med. diagnostics. **Add.** (h) Gedimino pr. 49a — 39, Vilnius 232001; tel. 617 004.

■ **THERNAYA, Liubov**, Ed., newspaper *Soglasije*, 1989 — ; b. 1941; grad. Moscow Polygraphic Inst., journalist; Ed., publrs *Mintis*, 1968 — 89. **Add.** (h) Savanorių pr. 32 — 6, Vilnius 232015; tel. 668 203.

■ **TYLA, Antanas**, historian; b. 1929; grad. Vilnius Univ.; DSc. (Hist.); Inst. of Lith. Hist., 1958 — ; works on the medieval and modern social, econ., and pol. relations, cultural and nat. movements of Lithuania; 7 books (*Lietuva ir Livonija XVI a. pab. — XVII a. pr.*, Lithuania and Livonia in the Late 14th — Early 17th Cent., 1986), has prepared for press a coll. of hist. sources, documents. **Add.** Kosciuškos 30, Vilnius 232600; tel. 628 715.

■ **TILVYTIS, Rytis**, E-in-C, magazine *Šluota*, 1990 — ; b. 1933; grad. Vilnius Univ., journalist; press worker, 1956 — . **Add.** Bernardinų 8/8, Vilnius 232722; tel. 613 171.

■ **TIŠKUS, Gytis**, engineer (arch.); b. 1934; grad. Kaunas Technol. Univ.; Chief Arch. of designs, Design Inst. of City Constr. (Klaipėda branch), 1966 — ; designer of original and monumental housing developments, shopping and public centres, commercial, admin. buildings. **Add.** (h) Taikos 97 — 22, Klaipėda 235815; tel. 106 49.

■ **TOMKUS, Vitas**, E-in-C, daily *Respublika*, 1989 — ; b. 1956; grad. Vilnius Univ., journalist; worked in the magazine *Šluota*, 1980 — 89; a book on the stagnation times *Taranas* (Battering-ram, 1989). **Add.** Šventaragio 4, Vilnius 232600; tel. 233 424.

■ **TRILUPAITIENĖ, Jūratė**, musicologist; b. 1943; grad. Lith. Conservatoire; CSc. (Arts); Culture and Art Inst., 1988 — ; studies on Lith. musical culture of the 15th — 18th cent.; coll. of organ tabulatures of the 17th cent. in the library of Lith. Acad. of Sci. **Add.** (h) Šilo 5 — 21, Vilnius 232055; tel. 742 239.

■ **TRIMAKAITĖ, Sigita**, singer (soprano); b. 1959; grad. Lith. Conservatoire; soloist, Lith. Nat. Philharmonic, 1985 — ; has toured several European c., USA, Canada; Glinka singing comp. (3rd prize, 1984), Maria Callas singing comp. in Athens (1st prize, 1987). **Add.** (h) Ozo 15 — 72, Vilnius 232056; tel. 417 987.

■ **TRIPONIS, Vytautas**, angiosurgeon; b. 1938; grad. Vilnius Univ.; lectures at it, 1962 — ; Head, Blood-vessels Surgery Centre; DSc. (Med.), Prof.; created and introduced into clinical practice the method of electric angiosurgery; perf. Lithuania's first operation on the small arteries of the skin, reconstr. of visceral aorta branches, replaced a cut off hand and arm, created method for renewal of the function of old vessel prosthesis. **Add.** (h) Žirgo 1 — 4, Vilnius 232040; tel. 764 273.

■ **TROFIMOV, Boris**, Dir-Man., Western Ship-repair Yard, 1985 — ; b. 1940; grad. Odessa Nautical Eng. Inst., eng. (shipbuilding and repair); at the shipyard *Baltija*, 1965 — 85. **Add.** (h) Debreceno 37 — 5, Klaipėda 235819; tel. 343 07.

■ **TRUSKA, Liudas**, historian; b. 1937; grad. Vilnius Univ.; lectured at it, 1966 — 88; CSc. (Hist.), Doc.; lecturer, Vilnius Pedag. Inst., 1988 — ; works on the agrarian relations in feudal Lithuania, on modern pol. hist.; 3 books. **Add.** Studentų 39, Vilnius 232034; tel. 452 344.

■ **TUČKIENĖ, Danutė**, Chair., Bank for Foreign Econ. Affairs of Lithuania, 1988 — ; b. 1935; grad. Vilnius Univ., econ.; at Lith. banks since 1956. **Add.** Totorių 2/8, Vilnius 232629; tel. 224 790.

■ **TUMELIS, Juozas**, Chair., *Sąjūdis* Seim Council, 1990 — ; b. 1938; grad. Vilnius Univ., hist.; at M. Mažvydas Nat. Library, 1979 — ; research in hist. of Lith. culture. **Add.** Gedimino pr. 1, Vilnius 232001; tel. 224 912.

■ **TUMINAS, Rimas**, theatre dir; b. 1952; grad. Lith. Conservatoire and Moscow A.Lunacharsky Inst. of Dramatic Art; artistic leader of Vilnius Small Theatre; prize winner at Toronto-Montreal Festival (1990). **Add.** Gedimino pr. 4, Vilnius 232000; tel. 629 832.

■ **TUNAITIS, Juozas**, Roman Catholic auxiliary bishop of Vilnius; b. 1928; grad. Kaunas Priest Sem.; ordained in 1954; Monsignor; at Curia of the Archdiocese of Vilnius, 1980 — . **Add.** Šv. Mikalojaus 4, Vilnius 232001; tel. 627 098.

■ **TURAUSKAS, Lionginas**, Dir, Kaunas Confectionery Factory, 1969 — ; b. 1939; grad. Vilnius Univ., econ. **Add.** (h) Vasiliausko 8 — 47, Kaunas 233028; tel. 733 416.

■ **UMARAS, Gintautas**, cyclist; b. 1963; twice (individual and team pursuit race) Olympic champ., 1988, twice world champ., 1987, individual pursuit race world record-holder, 1984, 1985, 1986, 1987. **Add.** (h) Krėvės pr. 14a — 60, Kaunas 233036; tel. 774 500.

■ **UMBRASAS, Algimantas**, architect; b. 1929; grad. Vilnius Art Acad.; Chief Arch. of designs, Design Inst. of City Constr., 1962 — ; designed renovation of defensive, ecclesiastical buildings. **Add.** (h) Pilies 12 — 9, Vilnius 232001; tel. 623 204.

■ **UOKA, Kazimieras**, State Controller, 1990 — ; b. 1951; grad. Vilnius Univ.; worked at Kaunas Constr. Assemblage Trust; Hon. Chair., Lith. Workers' Union; Lith. SC Deputy. **Add.** Pamėnkalnio 31, Vilnius 232669; tel. 621 646.

■ **URBAITIS, Mindaugas**, composer; b. 1952; grad. Lith. Conservatoire; lectures at it, 1977 — ; major works: concerto piccolo for symphony orch., compositions for 3 — 5 oboes, Bach-variationen for 4 violins, various music. **Add.** (h) Dūkštų 5 — 97, Vilnius 232010; tel. 413 231.

■ **URBANAVIČIUS, Vytautas**, archeologist; b. 1935; grad. Vilnius Univ.; CSc. (Hist.); Inst. of Lith. Hist., 1965 — ; research in burial grounds, settlements, ancient ritual places; by way of plastic reconstr. he has recreated ~200 graphic and ~30 sculptural images of the Lithuania's people of various periods (among them that of Kristijonas Donelaitis); 1 book, 25 scientific films. *Add.* Kosciuškos 30, Vilnius 232600; tel. 625 630.

▪ **URBONAS, Rimantas**, Rector, Lith. Agric. Acad., 1989 — ; b. 1935; grad. Lith. Agric. Acad.; lectures at it, 1966 — ; eng. (hydrotech.); CSc. (Eng.), Doc.; works on pressure land reclamation. *Add.* (h) Akademijos gyvenvietė 9 — 9, Kaunas-Akademija 234324; tel. 296 567.

▪ **URBUTIS, Vincas**, linguist (Baltic philol.); b. 1929; grad. Vilnius Univ.; lectures at it, 1954 — ; DSc. (Philol.), Prof.; research in etymology; books: *Žodžių darybos teorija* (Theory of Word Derivation, 1978), *Baltų etimologijos etiudai* (Sketches of Baltic Etymology, 1981). *Add.* (h) Pylimo 11 — 3, Vilnius 232001; tel. 625 286.

▪ **VABALAS, Raimondas**, film dir; b. 1937; grad. Moscow Inst. of Cinematography; scenario writer; Lith. Film Studio, 1960 — ; feature films, documentaries, TV films; interested in socio-psychological problems. *Add.* (h) Aušros vartų 2 — 6, Vilnius 232024; tel. 220 642.

▪ **VAGNORIUS, Gediminas**, Prime Min. of Lith. Rep., 1991 — ; b. 1957; grad. Vilnius Tech. Univ., eng. (econ.); CSc. (Econ.); scientific worker, Inst. of Econ., 1988 — 90; Lith. SC Deputy. *Add.* Tumo-Vaižganto 2, Vilnius 232039; tel. 622 101.

▪ **VAICEKAUSKAS, Julius**, photographer; b. 1939; grad. Vilnius Univ., journalist; B/W photography of Lith. nature, countryside and people, personal exh. abroad, winner of many prizes; AFIAP, 1977. *Add.* (h) Vytauto 6, Perloja 234650.

▪ **VAIČEKAUSKAS, Vincentas**, Dir, printing-house *Spindulys*, 1980 — ; b. 1938; grad. Moscow Polygraphy Inst., eng. (mech.); at polygraphy ent. since 1961. *Add.* Gedimino 10, Kaunas 233000; tel. 266 243.

▪ **VAIČIUS, Antanas**, Roman Catholic bishop; b. 1926; grad. Kaunas Priest Sem.; ordained in 1951; Apostolic Administrator of the Diocese of Telšiai, 1982 — 89, bishop ordinary, 1989 — ; Dep. Chair., College of Ordinaries of the Lith. Dioceses. *Add.* Spaudos 4, Telšiai 235610; tel. 513 94.

▪ **VAINAUSKAS, Gedvydas**, Ed., newspaper *Lietuvos rytas*, 1990 — ; b. 1955; grad. Vilnius Univ., journalist; at the newspaper since 1977; publicistic books. *Add.* Gedimino pr. 12a, Vilnius 232001; tel. 622 680.

▪ **VAINORA, Bronislovas**, Dir, Mažeikiai Oil Processing Plant, 1984 — ; b. 1944; grad. Azerbaijan Oil and Chem. Inst., oil and gas technol.; was deported with parents to Siberia, 1948. *Add.* (h) Valstiečių 42, Mažeikiai 235500; tel. 332 99.

▪ **VAINTRAUBAS, Saliamonas**, journalist; b. 1922; grad. Vilnius Univ.; press worker, 1940 — ; *ELTA* news agency reviewer, 1972 — ; books on sports. *Add.* (h) Žvaigždžių 38 — 119, Vilnius 232050; tel. 454 959.

▪ **VAIŠVILA, Zigmas**, Dep. Prime Min. of Lith. Rep., 1991 — ; b. 1956; grad. Vilnius Univ., phys.; CSc. (Phys. & Math.); Inst. of Phys., 1979 — 88; works on atom nucleus theory, problems of ecology; Head, Lith. Green Party; Lith. SC Deputy. *Add.* Tumo-Vaižganto 2, Vilnius 232039; tel. 620 665.

▪ **VAITEKŪNAS, Povilas Ričardas**, painter; b. 1940; grad. Vilnius Art Acad.; teaches at it, 1989 — ; author of original figure compositions, landscapes, still-lifes. *Add.* (h) Gedimino 43 — 18, Vilnius 232001; tel. 621 828.

▪ **VAITYS, Leonardas**, engineer (arch.); b. 1943; grad. Kaunas Technol. Univ.; Design Inst. of Communal Services, 1968 — , Chief Arch., 1987 — ; designer of admin., cultural, shopping centres. *Add.* (h) Tuskulėnų 38 — 14, Vilnius 232051; tel. 755 233.

▪ **VAITKEVIČIUS, Juozas**, teacher; b. 1928; grad. Vilnius Pedag. Inst.; DSc. (Pedag.), Prof.; lecturer, Vilnius Univ., 1980 — ; monographs *Mokymo procesas* (The Process of Teaching, 1985), *Socialinės pedagogikos bruožai* (The Outline of Social Pedagogics, 1988). *Add.* (h) Vileišio 19 — 129, Vilnius 232055; tel. 750 435.

▪ **VAITKUS, Jonas**, theatre dir; b. 1944; grad. Leningrad Inst. of Theatre, Music and Cinematography; Chief Dir, Kaunas Drama Theatre, 1978 — 88; lecturer, Lith. Conservatoire, 1981 — ; interested in the psychological relationship between individual and soc. *Add.* Gedimino pr. 42, Vilnius 232001; tel. 612 691.

▪ **VAITKUS, Juozas**, Dir, publrs *Vyturys*, 1984 — ; b. 1934; grad. Vilnius Univ., philol.; E-in-C, publrs *Mintis*, 1968 — 75, *Mokslas*, 1975 — 84; author of travel sketches, translator of fiction into Lith.; Pres., Lith. Publrs Assoc., 1989 — . *Add.* Algirdo 31, Vilnius 232600; tel. 660 665.

▪ **VAITKUS, Juozas Vidmantis**, physicist; b. 1941; grad. Vilnius Univ.; its lecturer, 1967 — ; DSc. (Phys.&Math.), Prof., Corr. Mem., Lith. Acad. of Sci.; research in the band structure of solid state, defects and nonequilibrium electric and optic phenomena in highly excited semiconductors.; Chair., Lith.-Sw. Soc. *Add.* (h) Žirgo 1 — 23, Vilnius 232040; tel. 768 877.

▪ **VALEIKA, Laimutis**, linguist (Engl. philol.); b. 1937; grad. Vilnius Univ.; lectures at it, 1962 — ; DSc. (Philol.), Prof.; major works: *Žodžių tvarka lietuvių ir anglų kalbose* (Word Order in the Lith. and Engl. Lgs, 1974), 'Transposition in the Lith. and Engl. Lgs (1980, in Russ.), 'Introduction to Linguistic Analysis and Synthesis of the Text' (1985, in Engl.). *Add.* (h) Didlaukio 64 — 24, Vilnius 232057; tel. 614 146 (off.).

▪ **VALEIKAITĖ, Jolanta**, ballet dancer; b. 1963; grad. M. K. Čiurlionis Art Sch.; prima ballerina, Lith. Opera and Ballet Theatre; danced with Moscow Bolshoi Theatre, toured European, American, Asian, African c.; prize winner of int. ballet comp. in Moscow (1980, 1988), Varna, Paris (1988). *Add.* (h) Tverečiaus 7 — 14, Vilnius 232040; tel. 745 337.

- **VALIULIS, Algirdas Vaclovas**, engineer (mech.); b. 1943; grad. Kaunas Technol. Univ.; CSc. (Eng.), Doc.; Vice-Rector, Vilnius Tech. Univ., 1990 — ; research in the prod. of resistant alloyed cast iron, metal welding, thermal processing, soldering. *Add.* (h) Antakalnio 91 — 36, Vilnius 232040; tel. 768 460.
- **VALIULIS, Skirmantas**, Dir-Gen., Lith. Radio and TV, 1990 — ; b. 1938; grad. Vilnius Univ., film critic; Chair., Lith. Cinematography Union. *Add.* (h) Jurginų 4 — 1, Vilnius 232048; tel. 677 550.
- **VALIUS, Vytautas**, graphic artist, painter; b. 1930; grad. Vilnius Art Acad.; its lecturer, 1965 — 71; author of book ill., cycles of prints, thematic compositions, settings for theatre prod. *Add.* (h) Klinikų 17/40 — 4, Vilnius 232055; tel. 740 508.
- **VALKŪNAS, Leonas**, physicist; b. 1949; grad. Vilnius Univ.; DSc. (Phys. & Math.); employed at the Inst. of Theoretical Phys. and Astronomy; research in the interaction of laser radiation and organic molecular structures and solid state. *Add.* (h) Bagramiano 1 — 50, Vilnius 232029; tel. 626 106.
- **VALUCKAS, Konstantinas**, Dir, Lith. Oncology Centre, 1990 — ; b. 1943; grad. Kaunas Med. Acad.; physician radiologist; DSc. (Med.); senior scientific worker, Inst. of Oncology, 1972 — 88; created diagnostics method of prostate tumours, improved methods of electroröntgenoskenography. *Add.* (h) Karoliniškių 9 — 30, Vilnius 232044; tel. 451 862.
- **VANAGAS, Aleksandras**, Dir, Inst. of the Lith. Lg., 1990 — ; b. 1934; grad. Vilnius Univ., linguist (Lith. philol.); at the Inst. since 1959; DSc. (Philol.), Corr. Mem., Lith. Acad. of Sci.; Mem., Int. Cttee of Onomastics Sci.; books: *Lietuvos TSR hidronimų daryba* (The Formation of Lith. SSR Hydronyms, 1970), *Lietuvių hidronimų semantika* (The Semantics of Lith. Hydronyms, 1981), *Lietuvių hidronimų etimologinis žodynas* (The Etymological Dictionary of Lith. Hydronyms, 1981), *Lietuvių pavardžių žodynas* (The Dictionary of Lith. Surnames, co-authored with others, 1985 — 88, vol. 2). *Add.* (h) Architektų 109 — 87, Vilnius 232049; tel. 443 849.
- **VANAGAS, Jurgis**, engineer (arch.); b. 1933; grad. Kaunas Technol. Univ.; DSc. (Arch.), Prof.; lecturer, Vilnius Tech. Univ., 1980 — ; author of master plans of 4 Lith. towns, interior designs; Hon. Mem., Int. People's Ecological Assoc. *Add.* (h) Vileišio 15 — 30, Vilnius 232055; tel. 748 084.
- **VARPUKEVIČIUS, Albinas**, Dir, Alytus Chem. Plant, 1987 — ; b. 1943; grad. Kaunas Technol. Univ., eng. (mech.). *Add.* (h) Vingio 19 — 45, Alytus 234580; tel. 334 36.
- **VASILIAUSKAS, Kazimieras**, Roman Catholic priest; b. 1922; grad. Kaunas Priest Sem.; ordained in 1946; Monsignor; priest of Vilnius Archcathedral, 1989 — ; pol. prisoner, 1949 — 1969. *Add.* (h) Pylimo 6 — 7, Vilnius 232001; tel. 619 297.
- **VAŠKEVIČIUS, Juozas**, Chair., Lith. Arch. Union, 1990 — ; b. 1924; grad. Kaunas Technol.

Univ., eng. (arch.); Chief Arch. of designs, Design Inst. of City Constr., 1962 — 90; designer of dwelling houses; master plans of some Lith. towns, general plan for Greater Palanga. *Add.* (h) Debesijos 3 — 36, Vilnius 232040; tel. 749 332.
- **VĖBRA, Evaldas**, Dir-Gen., Dept of Environment, 1990 — ; b. 1932; grad. Lith. Pedag. Inst.; CSc. (Phys.&Math.); Inst. of Phys., 1962 — 90. *Add.* Juozapavičiaus 9, Vilnius 232686; tel. 355 868.
- **VEIVERYTĖ, Sofija**, painter; b. 1926; grad. Kaunas Applied and Decorative Art Inst.; lecturer , Vilnius Art Acad., 1951 — 85; Prof.; author of figure compositions, portraits, mural paintings. *Add.* (h) Kuosų 4 — 1, Vilnius 232055; tel. 741 669.
- **VELIKONIS, Virmantas**, Chair., Lith. Agric. Union, 1990 — ; b. 1939; grad. Lith. Agric. Acad., agron.; Chair., *Ramygala* collective farm, 1977 — . *Add.* (h) Garuckų km., Ramygala 235333; tel. 921 58.
- **VĖLIUS, Norbertas**, folklorist (mythology); b. 1938; grad. Vilnius Univ.; DSc. (Philol.); Inst. of Lith. Lit. and Folklore, 1962 — ; Chair., Soc. for Lith. Ethnic Culture, 1990 — ; works: *Mitinės lietuvių sakmių būtybės* (Mythical Beings of the Lith. Legends, 1977), *Senovės baltų pasaulėžiūra* (The World Outlook of the Ancient Balts, 1983; 1989 in Engl.), *Chtoniškasis lietuvių mitologijos pasaulis* (The Chtonic Lith. Mythological World, 1987). Ed. more than 10 publ. of Lith. folklore. *Add.* (h) Konarskio 21 — 23, Vilnius 232009; tel. 652 962.
- **VERBA, Robertas**, film dir, cameraman; b. 1932; grad. Moscow Inst. of Cinematography; Lith. Film Studio, 1960 — ; author of film essays, documentaries and educ. films, on agric. and culture hist. *Add.* (h) Žirmūnų 129 — 42, Vilnius 232012; tel. 773 228.
- **VIELIUS, Vytautas Adolfas**, architect; b. 1933; grad. Vilnius Art Acad.; Chief Arch. of designs, Design Inst. of Ind. Constr., 1980 — ; co-designer of original commercial, cultural, educ. buildings in Vilnius and a memorial in Kaunas. *Add.* (h) Vytenio 13 — 60, Vilnius 232006; tel. 639 054.
- **VILČIAUSKAS, Sigitas**, Dir-Gen., leather and footwear co *Elnias*, 1988 — ; b. 1943; grad. Kaunas Technol. Univ., eng. (mech.); Šiauliai Machine-Tool Plant, 1960 — 88; was deported with parents to Siberia, 1949. *Add.* (h) Varpo 29 — 34, Šiauliai 235400; tel. 387 20.
- **VILDŽIŪNAS, Vladas**, sculptor; b. 1932; grad. Vilnius Art Acad.; teaches at it, 1988 — ; author of portraits, monuments, decorative park sculpture (incl. Los Angeles). *Add.* (h) Lobio 13 — 1, Vilnius 232021; tel. 777 451.
- **VILEMAS, Jurgis**, Dir, Inst. of Phys. and Eng. Problems of Energy Research, 1981 — ; b. 1938; grad. Moscow Power Inst., nuclear eng.; DSc. (Eng.), Prof., Acad., Lith. Acad. of Sci.; research in nuclear thermal dynamics. *Add.* (h) Kranto 52 — 2, Kaunas 233002; tel. 741 975.
- **VILKAS, Eduardas**, Dir, Inst. of Econ., 1985 — ; b. 1935; grad. Vilnius Univ., math. and econ.; DSc. (Phys. & Math.), Prof., Acad., Lith.

Acad. of Sci.; Inst. of Math. and Cybernetics, 1958 − 84; research in theory of probabilities, game theory and math. econ.; Lith. SC Deputy. *Add.* (h) Kareivių 18 − 44, Vilnius 232012; tel. 776 759.

▪ **VILUTIS, Mikalojus Povilas**, graphic artist; b. 1944; grad. Vilnius Art Acad.; teaches at it, 1988 − ; his works (mostly serigraphs) are grotesque, of expressive composition, contrasting colours; many prints acquired by foreign collectors. *Add.* (h) Justiniškių 49 − 13, Vilnius 232056; tel. 229 007.

▪ **VINTYS, Bronius**, Dir-Gen., ent. *Dovana*, 1971 − ; b. 1934; grad. Kaunas Technol. Univ., eng. (mech.); at the ent. since 1967. *Add.* (h) Didlaukio 19 − 27, Vilnius 232057; tel. 778 418.

▪ **VIRBICKAS, Juozas**, Dir, Inst. of Ecology, 1990 − ; b. 1939; grad. Vilnius Univ., hydroecologist, ichthyologist; DSc. (Biol.); at the Inst. since 1964; works on hydroecology, thermoecology, ichthyology; 7 books; Mem., Int. Cttee of Baltic Biol.; Chair., Soc. of Lith. Ecologists. *Add.* (h) Kalvarijų 134 − 14, Vilnius 232042; tel. 765 389.

▪ **VIRBICKAS, Raimundas**, Dir, television plant *Tauras*, 1988 − ; b. 1950; grad. Kaunas Technol. Univ., eng. (radio mech.); at the plant since 1968. *Add.* (h) Aušros al. 13 − 5, Šiauliai 235400; tel. 385 16.

▪ **VISAKAVIČIUS, Marijonas**, Chair., Lith. Confederation of Free TU, 1990 − ; b. 1944; operator, ind. amalgamation *Azotas*, 1979 − 90. *Add.* Gynėjų 3, Vilnius 232710; tel. 615 260.

▪ **VYŠNIAUSKAITĖ, Angelė**, ethnographer; b. 1919; grad. Vilnius Univ. and Vilnius Pedag. Inst.; CSc. (Hist.); Inst. of Lith. Hist., 1948 − ; works on the traditions of Lith. family, cultivation and processing of flax and customs connected with it, on the hist. of Lith. ethnography; 8 books (*Lietuvių etnografijos bruožai*, Outline of Lith. Ethnography, 1964). *Add.* (h) Antakalnio 83 − 22, Vilnius 232040; tel. 744 817.

▪ **VYŠNIAUSKAS, Petras**, clarinettist, saxophonist; b. 1957; grad. Lith. Conservatoire, teaches at it, 1988 − ; leader of Vyšniauskas Jazz Quartet, 1980 − 88; plays jazz band trio (P.Vyšniauskas; Ch.Ramond, double bass, K.Kugel, percussion instruments), 1989 − . *Add.* (h) Justiniškių 80 − 37, Vilnius 232017; tel. 410 120.

▪ **VIŠOMIRSKIS, Romanas**, Dir, Inst. of Chem. and Chem. Technol., 1976 − ; b. 1928; grad. Vilnius Univ., phys.-chem.; DSc. (Chem.), Prof., Acad., Lith. Acad. of Sci.; at the Inst. since 1954; research in the kinetics of electro-chem. deposition of metals. *Add.* (h) Žirgo 5 − 4, Vilnius 232040; tel. 747 475.

▪ **VITKUS, Kęstutis**, microsurgeon; b. 1952; grad. Vilnius Univ.; its lecturer, 1985 − ; Head of Reconstructive and Plastic Microsurgery Clinic; DSc. (Med.), Prof.; together with his father M.Vitkus began microsurgery operations in Lithuania *Add.* (h) Sruogos 20, Vilnius 232040; tel. 769 541.

▪ **YEGOROV, Ivan**, Chair., Lith. Supreme Old Faith Council, 1974 − ; b. 1905; grad. Ecclesiastic Courses of Vilnius Teachers' Sem.; Mem.,

Christian Peace Conference. *Add.* (h) Naujininkų 24, Vilnius 232030; tel. 690 700.

▪ **YEMELYANOV, Vasilii**, Ed., newspaper *Echo Litvy*, 1970 − ; b. 1937; grad. Kaunas Technol. Univ.; taught at it, 1960 − 70. *Add.* (h) Donelaičio 20 − 3, Vilnius 232009; tel. 637 542.

▪ **ZALATORIUS, Albertas**, lit. critic; b. 1932; grad. Vilnius Univ.; DSc. (Philol.); Inst. of Lith. Lit. and Folklore, 1961 − ; studies: *Lietuvių apsakymo raida ir poetika* (The Development and Poetics of Lith. Short Story, 1971), *XX a. lietuvių novelė* (Lith. Short Story of the 20th Cent., 1980), coll. of articles *Prozos gyvybė ir negalia* (The Vitality and Feebleness of Prose, 1988); Dep. Chair., *Sąjūdis* Seim Council, 1990 − . *Add.* (h) Savičiaus 14 − 1, Vilnius 232024; tel. 222 628.

▪ **ZAVADSKAS, Edmundas Kazimieras**, Rector, Vilnius Technol. Univ., 1990 − ; b. 1944; grad. Kaunas Technol. Univ., eng. (constr.); DSc. (Eng.), Prof.; research in constr. eng. and automated technol. design; was exiled with father to Vorkuta, 1955 − 59. *Add.* (h) Viesulo 13 − 201, Vilnius 232050; tel. 452 438.

▪ **ZELKEVIČIUS, Benjaminas**, football coach; b. 1944; grad. Lith. Inst. of Physical Training; player of Vilnius *Žalgiris* team, 1963 − 73, Chief Coach, 1977 − ; his team was the champ. of University Games (Zagreb, 1987). *Add.* (h) Grybo 3a − 17, Vilnius 232040; tel. 741 900.

▪ **ZINGERIS, Emanuelis**, Chair., Foreign Affairs Cttee of SC, 1990 − ; b. 1957; grad. Vilnius Univ., spec. in Lith. philol.; worked at Vilnius Univ. (Kaunas branch), 1985 − 88; Dir, Jewish Museum, 1989 − ; Chair., Soc. of Jewish Culture in Lithuania; Lith. SC Deputy. *Add.* Gedimino pr. 53, Vilnius 232026; tel. 628 729.

▪ **ZINKEVIČIUS, Zigmas**, linguist (Lith. philol.); b. 1927; grad. Vilnius Univ.; lectures at it, 1950 − ; DSc. (Philol.), Prof., Acad., Lith. Acad. of Sci.; Mem., Swedish Royal Acad. of Letters, Hist. and Antiquities; has co-authored, with A.Girdenis, a new classification of dialects of the Lith. lg. (publ. in 1966); books: *Lietuvių dialektologija* (Lith. Dialectology, 1966), *Iš lietuvių istorinės akcentologijos* (From the Lith. Hist. Accentology, 1975), *Lietuvių antroponimika. Vilniaus lietuvių asmenvardžiai XVII a. pradžioje* (Lith. Antroponimics. The Lith. Personal Names in Vilnius at the Beginning of the XVII Cent., 1977), *Lietuvių kalbos istorija* (Hist. of the Lith. Lg., 1984 − 88, vols 1 − 3); compiled textbooks for higher sch. *Add.* (h) Justiniškių 41 − 24, Vilnius 232056; tel. 410 877.

▪ **ZUBOVAS, Vytautas**, Dir-Gen., Dept of Conservation of Hist. Properties, 1990 − ; b. 1948; grad. Kaunas Technol. Univ., arch.; Dir, Klaipėda Inst. of Design and Restoration, 1981 − 90. *Add.* Upės 3, Vilnius 232005; tel. 354 058.

▪ **ZURBA, Algimantas**, E-in-C, magazine *Moksleivis*, 1989 − ; writer; b. 1942; grad. Vilnius Univ.; his novels *Šimtadienis* (Hundred Day Party, 1975), *Integralas* (Integral, 1981), short stories, publicistic books deal with the problems of spiritual maturity of the youth, relations between generations. **Add.** (h) Mildos 31 – 3, Vilnius 232055; tel. 358 915.

▪ **ŽALAKEVIČIUS, Vytautas**, film dir, dramatist; b. 1930; grad. Moscow Inst. of Cinematography; works at Lith. Film Studio and *Mosfilm*; producer, *Studija 2000*, 1990 – ; films on social and pol. issues: 'No One Wanted to Die' (prize at Karlovy Vary Festival, 1966), 'Liberty is a Sweet Word' (prize at Moscow Festival, 1975). **Add.** (h) Šilo 62 – 4, Vilnius 232055; tel. 749 653.

▪ **ŽEBRIŪNAS, Vytautas Arūnas**, film dir; b. 1930; grad. Vilnius Art Acad.; Lith. Film Studio, 1959 – ; leader of *ARS* film assoc., 1990 – ; films marked by lyricism, poeticism, elegy, a mix of tragic and humorous situations. Prizes: film 'Living Heroes' (Karlovy Vary, 1960), 'The Last Day of the Holidays' (Locarno, 1965; Cannes, 1966). **Add.** (h) Vaižganto 4/1 – 3, Vilnius 232001; tel. 625 793.

▪ **ŽEIMANTAS, Liubomiras Viktoras**, E-in-C, magazine *Lietuvos ūkis*, 1988 – ; b. 1931; CSc. (Hist.), Doc.; lecturer at Vilnius Univ., 1967 – 88. **Add.** (h) Architektų 60 – 13, Vilnius 232043; tel. 447 042.

▪ **ŽELVYS, Rimantas**, psychologist; b. 1959; grad. Vilnius Univ., CSc. (Psychology); Dir, Inst. of Perfection of Public Educ. Workers, 1990 – ; research in problems of med., teen-agers and youth psychology. **Add.** Radvilaitės 5 – 32, Vilnius 232001; tel. 763 831.

▪ **ŽEMAITAITIS, Gediminas**, Dir, stockings factory *Koton*, 1965 – ; b. 1931; grad. Kaunas Technol. Univ., eng. (electromech.). **Add.** (h) Vasario 16-osios 7 – 3, Kaunas 233000; tel. 225 600.

▪ **ŽEMAITIS, Juozas**, Roman Catholic bishop; b. 1926; grad. Kaunas Priest Sem.; ordained in 1949; Apostolic Administrator of the Diocese of Vilkaviškis, 1989 – . **Add.** Armino 6, Marijampolė 234520; tel. 566 75.

▪ **ŽEMAITYTĖ, Aldona**, Ed., weekly *Dienovidis*, 1990 – ; b. 1945; grad. Vilnius Univ., journalist; worked on the staff of the weekly *Literatūra ir menas*, 1972 – 88; with her parents was deported to Siberia. **Add.** Pilies 23a, Vilnius 232001; tel. 223 101.

▪ **ŽEPKAITĖ, Regina**, historian; b. 1925; grad. Vilnius Univ.; DSc. (Hist.); Inst. of Lith. Hist., 1961 – ; works on the int. situation and foreign policy of Lithuania in the 20th cent.; 7 books (*Lietuva ir didžiosios valstybės 1918 – 1939 m.*, Lithuania and the Great Powers in 1918 – 1939; 1986), textbooks. **Add.** (h) Antakalnio 83 – 34, Vilnius 232040; tel. 741 640.

▪ **ŽIDONIS, Vilius**, Min. of Material Resources, 1991 – ; b. 1933; grad. Kaunas Technol. Univ.; lectured at it, 1962 – 91; eng. (mech.); DSc. (Eng.), Prof.; research on technol. of food and chem. ind., packing machines; 120 inv. **Add.** Tumo-Vaižganto 8a/2, Vilnius 232640; tel. 628 830.

▪ **ŽILINSKAITĖ, Vytautė**, writer; b. 1930; grad. Vilnius Univ.; in the coll. of the satirical and humorous short stories *Angelas virš miesto* (The Angel Above the City, 1967), *Karuselėje* (Merry-Go-Round, 1970), *Kvaitulys* (Giddiness, 1984) the criticism of philistinism and moral vices goes together with the gen. problems of contemporary contradictions of the soc.; irony, paradox, conditionality mark the short stories; books for children; books transl. into Ger., Russ., Hung., Est., Latv. and other lgs. **Add.** (h) Mildos 31 – 12, Vilnius 232055; tel. 357 535.

▪ **ŽINTELIS, Gintautas**, engineer (electrical); b. 1943; grad. Kaunas Technol. Univ.; its lecturer, 1970 – ; DSc. (Eng.), Corr. Mem., Lith. Acad. of Sci.; research in automated design of computing machinery. **Add.** (h) Vitkausko 26 – 21, Kaunas 233031; tel. 759 782.

▪ **ŽOROMSKIS, Kazimieras**, painter; b. 1913; grad. Vilnius and Vienna Art Acad.; Prof.; resident of USA, 1946 – 86; instructor of higher art sch.; his works blend elements of various modernistic trends (expressionism, abstractionism, opart, photorealism); exh. in USA, Spain; some works acquired by Butler Inst. of American Art (Youngstown), Georgia Museum of Art (Athens), Pembrook Library (Pembrook), Moscow museums. **Add.** (h) Pylimo 8/2 – 37, Vilnius 232001; tel. 628 939.

▪ **ŽUKAUSKAS, Algirdas**, Vice-Pres., Lith. Acad. of Sci., 1966 – ; b. 1923; grad. Kaunas Univ., eng. (mech.); DSc. (Eng.), Prof., Acad., Lith. Acad. of Sci.; worked out the simulation methods of thermal exchange in liquids; author of 8 scientific studies, 5 of them in Engl. **Add.** (h) Valančiaus 4/9 – 3, Vilnius 232000; tel. 630 498.

▪ **ŽVYBAS, Eimutis**, Dir, plant *Ekranas*, 1990 – ; b. 1957; grad. Kaunas Technol. Univ., eng. **Add.** (h) Kniaudiškių 14 – 20, Panevėžys 235309; tel. 201 55.

▪ **ŽVIRGŽDAS, Stasys**, photographer; b. 1941; grad. Moscow N.Krupskaya Folk Art Univ.; author of photomontages and landscape photography; personal exh. abroad, winner of many prizes; AFIAP, 1988. **Add.** (h) Gerovės 9 – 2, Vilnius 232041; tel. 674 054.

HELPFUL WORDS AND PHRASES

ENGLISH	ESTONIAN	LATVIAN	LITHUANIAN
■ GENERAL	■ ÜLDIST	■ VISPĀRĪGĀ NODAĻA	■ BENDRASIS SKYRIUS
Yes	jah	jā	taip
No	ei	nē	ne
Yes, I am	jah, ma olen	jā, es esmu	taip, aš esu
No, I am not	ei, ma ei ole	nē, es neesmu	ne, aš nesu
Yes, I have	jah, mul on	jā, man ir	taip, aš turiu
No, I haven't	ei, mul ei ole	nē, man nav	ne, aš neturiu
I can	ma saan (võin)	es varu	aš galiu
I cannot	ma ei saa (ei või)	es nevaru	aš negaliu
How much?	Kui palju?	Cik?	Kiek?
How many?			
How far?	Kui kaugel?	Cik tālu?	Ar toli?
How long?	Kui kaua?	Cik ilgi?	Ar ilgai?
I want ..	ma tahan ..	es gribu ..	Aš noriu ..
I do not want ..	ma ei taha ..	es negribu ..	aš nenoriu ..
Please ..	palun ..	lūdzu ..	prašom
Thank you	tänan	paldies	ačiū
Sunday	pühapäev	svētdiena	sekmadienis
Monday	esmaspäev	pirmdiena	pirmadienis
Tuesday	teisipäev	otrdiena	antradienis
Wednesday	kolmapäev	treśdiena	trečiadienis
Thursday	neljapäev	ceturtdiena	ketvirtadienis
Friday	reede	piektdiena	penktadienis
Saturday	laupäev	sestdiena	šeštadienis
What time is it now?	Mis kell praegu on?	Cik ir pulkstenis?	Kiek valandų?
■ FORMS OF ADDRESS	■ KÕNETUSSÕNAD	■ UZRUNAS	■ KREIPINIAI
Sir!	Härra!	Kungs!	Pone!
Madam!	Proua!	Kundze!	Ponia!
Ladies and Gentlemen!	Daamid ja härrad!	Dāmas un kungi!	Ponios ir ponai!
Mr. Brown!	Härra Brown!	Brauna kungs!	Pone Braunai!
Mrs. Brown!	Proua Brown!	Brauna kundze!	Ponia Braun!
Ms. Brown!	Proua Brown!	Brauna kundze!	Ponia Braun!
Miss Brown!	Preili Brown!	Brauna jaunkundze!	Panele Braun!
Doctor!	Doktor!	Doktor!	Daktare!
Professor!	Professor!	Profesor!	Profesoriau!
■ FORMULAS OF POLITENESS	■ VIISAKUSVÄL- JENDID	■ PIEKLĀJĪBAS IZTEICIENI	■ MANDAGUMO FORMULĖS
Apologies	**Vabandamine**	**Atvainošanās**	**Atsiprašymas**
I beg your pardon	Palun vabandust	Piedodiet, lūdzu	Prašom atleisti
Pardon	Vabandust		Atleiskite
Excuse me	Vabandage	Atvainojiet	Atsiprašau
I am sorry	Vabandust		
That's all right	Sellest pole midagi	Nekas	Nieko tokio
Never mind	Pole viga		

Requests	Palumine	Lūgumi	Klausimas
May I ask you a question?	Kas ma tohin teilt midagi küsida?	Vai drīkstu jautāt?	Ar galima paklausti?
May I come in?	Kas ma tohin sisse tulla?	Vai drīkstu ienākt?	Ar galima jeiti?
Come in, please	Tulge sisse, palun	Lūdzu ienāciet	Prašom jeiti
What can I do for you?	Mida ma võin teie heaks teha?	Ar ko varu pakalpot?	Kuo galiu padėti?
Could you do me a favour?	Kas te võite mulle teene osutada?	Vai jūs varētu man izdarīt pakalpojumu?	Gal malonėtumėte padėti?
Would you kindly tell me.. show me..	Kas te ei ütleks mulle..? näitaks mulle..?	Vai jūs, lūdzu, man nepateiktu..? neparādītu..?	Gal galėtumėte man pasakyti..? parodyti..?

Thanks	Tänamine	Pateicība	Padėka
Thank you	Tänan	Paldies	Ačiū
Thanks	Aitäh		
Thank you very much	Tänan teid väga	Ļoti pateicos	Labai ačiū
Thank you for your kindness	Tänan teid lahkuse eest	Pateicos par jūsu laipnību	Ačiū, jūs labai malonus
Don't mention it Never mind	Pole tänu väärt	Nav par ko	Nėra už ką

■ MEETING PEOPLE	■ TERVITUSED	■ SATIKŠANĀS	■ SUSITIKIMAI
How do you do? Hallo!	Tere!	Sveicināti!	Sveiki!
Good morning!	Tere hommikust!	Labrīt!	Labas rytas!
Good afternoon!	Tere päevast!	Labdien!	Laba diena!
Good evening!	Tere õhtust!	Labvakar!	Labas vakaras!
Good night!	Head ööd!	Ar labu nakti!	Labanakt!
Good bye!	Head aega!	Uz redzēšanos!	Viso gero!
So long!	Nägemiseni!	Visu labu!	Iki pasimatymo!
Pleased to meet you	Meeldiv teiega tutvuda	Patīkami ar jums iepazīties	Malonu susipažinti
Let me introduce myself	Lubage mul end tutvustada	Atļaujiet stādīties priekšā	Leiskite prisistatyti
Please introduce me to..	Palun tutvustage mind..	Lūdzu, iepazīstiniet mani ar..	Prašom pristatyti mane..
May I introduce you to my wife?	Lubage mul teid tutvustada oma naisega	Atļaujiet jūs iepazīstināt ar manu sievu	Leiskite pristatyti jus mano žmonai
I am from ..	Ma olen ..	Es esmu no ..	Aš esu iš ..
Come and see me	Tulge mind vaatama	Atnāciet pie manis	Aplankykite mane
Will you help me please?	Kas te aitaksite mind, palun?	Lūdzu, vai jūs man nepalīdzētu?	Gal galėtumėte man padėti?
Will you take me to ..?	Kas te viiksite mind..?	Vai jūs mani neaizvestu uz ..?	Gal nuvežtumėte mane į ..?
Wait a little Just a minute	Oodake natuke	Mazliet pagaidiet	Truputėli palaukite
Willingly	Meeleldi	Labprāt	Mielai
With pleasure	Hea meelega		Su malonumu
Certainly	Muidugi	Protams	Žinoma

■ LANGUAGE	■ KEEL	■ VALODA	■ KALBA
Can you speak English? German?	Kas te räägite inglise keelt? saksa keelt?	Vai jūs runājat angliski? vāciski?	Ar kalbate angliškai? vokiškai?
What languages do you know?	Mis keeli te oskate?	Kādas valodas jūs protat?	Kokias kalbas jūs mokate?
Does anybody speak English here?	Kas keegi oskab siin inglise keelt?	Vai kāds šeit runā angliski?	Ar čia kas nors kalba angliškai?

I do not speak Russian	Ma ei oska vene keelt	Es neprotu runāt krieviski	Aš nemoku kalbėti rusiškai
Speak slowly, please	Rääkige aeglaselt, palun	Runājiet lēnāk, lūdzu	Prašom kalbėti lėčiau
Will you repeat it, please?	Palun, korrake seda veel	Lūdzu, atkārtojiet to vēlreiz	Prašom pakartoti dar kartą
Do you get me?	Kas te saate aru?	Vai jūs mani saprotat?	Ar mane suprantate?
Sorry, I didn't understand you	Vabandust, ma ei saanud aru	Piedodiet, es jūs nesapratu	Atsiprašau, aš nelabai supratau
What is it called in English?	Kuidas see inglise keeles on?	Kā to sauc angliski?	Kaip tai vadinama angliškai?
We need an interpreter	Me vajame tõlki	Mums ir vajadzīgs tulks	Mums reikia vertėjo

■ IN TOWN	■ LINNAS	■ PILSĒTĀ	■ MIESTE
guidebook	turistijuht	ceļvedis	turisto vadovas
district	linnaosa	rajons	rajonas
suburb	eeslinn	priekšpilsēta	priemiestis
street	tänav (tn.)	iela	gatvė (g.)
road	tee	ceļš	kelias
avenue	puiestee (pst.)	prospekts (prosp.)	prospektas (prosp.), alėja (al.)
boulevard	puiestee (pst.)	bulvāris (bulv.)	bulvaras (bulv.)
highway	maantee (mnt.)	lielceļš, šoseja (šos.)	autostrada, plentas (pl.)
square	väljak	laukums (lauk.)	aikštė (a.)
river	jõgi	upe	upė
bridge	sild	tilts	tiltas
What transport is there to ..?	Mis liiklusvahend viib ..?	Ar ko var aizbraukt uz ..?	Kuo nuvažiuoti į..?
bus (tram, trolleybus) stop	bussi- (trammi-, trolli-) peatus	autobusa (tramvaja, trolejbusa) pietura	autobuso (tramvajaus, troleibuso) stotelė
Tell me when to get off, please	Öelge, palun, millal maha minna	Lūdzu, pasakiet, kad man jāizkāpj	Prašom pasakyti, kada man išlipti
I have lost my way	Ma olen eksinud	Es esmu apmaldījies	Aš paklydau
taxi rank	taksopeatus	taksometru stāvvieta	taksi stotelė
route	marsruut	maršruts	maršrutas
near	lähedal	tuvu	arti
far	kaugel	tālu	toli
forward	edasi	uz priekšu	pirmyn
straight	otse	taisni	tiesiai
to the right (left)	paremale (vasakule)	pa labi (kreisi)	į dešinę (į kairę)
Please, get me a taxi	Palun, hankige mulle takso	Lūdzu, izsauciet man taksometru	Prašom iškviesti man taksi
Can you take me to the airport, please?	Kas te viiksite mind lennujaama, palun?	Vai jūs neaizvestu mani uz lidostu, lūdzu?	Atsiprašau, ar negalite mane nuvežtij aerouostą?
Where is the closest petrol station?	Kus on lähim bensiinijaam?	Kur ir tuvākā degvielas uzpildes stacija?	Kur yra artimiausia degalinė?
car park	autoparkla	autostāvvieta	automobilių stovėjimo aikštelė
Will you translate that notice, please?	Tõlkige see silt, palun	Lūdzu, pārtulkojiet šo uzrakstu	Prašom išversti šį užrašą
Could you tell me, please, how to get to	Kas te ütleksite, palun, kuidas minna ..	Vai jūs, lūdzu, man nepateiktu, kā nokļūt uz ..	Gal galėtumėte man pasakyti, kaip nuvykti į..
the hotel?	hotelli?	viesnīcu?	viešbutį?
the centre?	keskusesse?	centru?	centrą?
the airport?	lennujaama?	lidostu?	aerouostą?
the post office?	postkontorisse?	pastu?	paštą?
the church?	kirikusse?	baznīcu?	bažnyčią?
the art gallery?	kunstimuuseumi?	mākslas muzeju?	dailės muziejų?
N. street?	N. tänavale?	N. ielu?	N. gatvę?
the National theatre?	Rahvusteatrisse?	Nacionālo teātri?	Nacionalinį teatrą?
the railway terminal?	raudteejaama?	dzelzceļa staciju?	geležinkelio stotį?
Information office	Teadete büroo	Uzziņu birojs	Informacijos biuras

Where can I inquire about something left in a taxi?	Kust saab küsida taksosse unustatu kohta?	Kur es varētu painteresēties par taksometrā atstātajām mantām?	Kur aš galėčiau pasiterauti dėl taksi paliktų daiktų?
lavatory	WC	tualete	tualetas
toilet	tualett		
booking office	piletikassad	kases	kasos

■ SHOPPING. SERVICE	■ OSTMINE. TEENINDUS	■ IEPIRKŠANĀS. SADZĪVES PAKAL-POJUMI	■ PREKYBA. APTARNAVIM
Where can I buy some souvenirs?	Kust saab osta meeneid?	Kur var nopirkt suvenīrus?	Kur aš galėčiau nusipirk suvenyrų?
At what time do they open (close) the shops?	Mis kell kauplused avatakse (suletakse)?	Kad atver (slēdz) veikalus?	Kada atidaromos (uždaromos) parduotuvės?
food store	toidupood	pārtikas veikals	maisto prekės
department store	kaubamaja	universālveikals	universalinė parduotuvė
bookshop	raamatupood	grāmatu veikals	knygynas
second-hand bookshop	raamatuantikvariaat	grāmatu antikvariāts	antikvariatas
books on art	kunstiraamatud	mākslas grāmatas	dailės albumai
How much is it? What is the price of..	Kui palju see maksab? Mis hind on?	Cik tas maksā?	Kiek kainuoja?
baker's (bread shop)	leivapood	maizes veikals	duonos parduotuvė
drugstore, chemist's	apteek	aptieka	vaistinė
optician's (optometrist's)	prillipood	briļļu veikals	optika
hairdresser's barber's	juuksur	frizētava	kirpykla
shoe repair	kingaparandaja	apavu labošana	avalynės taisykla
post office	postkontor	pasts	paštas
telephone	telefon	telefons	telefonas
telegraph	telegraaf	telegrāfs	telegrafas
market	turg	tirgus	turgus
I would like to..	Ma tahaksin..	Es vēlētos..	Aš norėčiau..
cheap	odav	lēts	pigus
expensive	kallis	dārgs	brangus

■ MEALS	■ EINESTAMINE	■ MALTĪTES	■ VALGYMAS
restaurant	restoran	restorāns	restoranas
café	kohvik	kafejnīca	kavinė
eating house	söökla	ēdnīca	valgykla
snack bar	einelaud	bufete	bufetas
national dishes	rahvusroad	nacionālie ēdieni	nacionaliniai patiekalai
meat dishes, main courses	liharoad	gaļas ēdieni	mėsos patiekalai
soup	supp	zupa	sriuba
fish	kala	zivis	žuvis
vegetables	köögiviljad	saknes	daržovės
fruits	puuviljad	augļi	vaisiai
desserts	magusroad	saldie ēdieni	saldumynai
drinks	joogid	dzērieni	gėrimai
juice	mahl	sulas	sultys
wine	vein	vīns	vynas
ice cream	jäätis	saldējums	ledai
menu	menüü	ēdienkarte	valgiaraštis
water	vesi	ūdens	vanduo
sugar	suhkur	cukurs	cukrus
salt	sool	sāls	druska
I'd like the menu, please	Palun menüüd	Lūdzu, ēdienkarti	Prašom valgiaraštį
Could you bring the bill, please?	Palun arvet	Lūdzu, rēķinu	Gal galėtumėte pateikti sąskaitą?

■ MEDICAL AID	■ ARSTIABI	■ MEDICĪNISKĀ PALĪDZĪBA	■ MEDICINOS PAGALBA
ambulance	esmaabi	ātrā palīdzība	greitoji pagalba
first aid post	esmaabipunkt	medicīnas punkts	medicinos punktas
dentist	hambaarst	zobārsts	dantų gydytojas
hospital	haigla	slimnīca	ligoninė
Please, call a doctor (ambulance)	Palun, kutsuge arst (kiirabi)	Lūdzu, izsauciet ārstu (ātro palīdzību)	Prašom pakviesti gydytoją (greitąja pagalbą)
Is there a doctor near here?	Kas arst on siin lähedal?	Vai šeit nav ārsts?	Ar čia yra kur nors gydytojas?

■ CUSTOMS. CUR- RENCY EXCHANGE	■ TOLL. VALUUTAVAHETUS	■ MUITA. VALŪTAS APMAIŅA	■ MUITINĖ. VALIU- TOS KEITIMAS
What items are liable for duty?	Mille eest peab tolli maksma?	Kādi priekšmeti tiek muitoti?	Už kokius daiktus reikia mokėti muitą?
What duty must I pay?	Kui palju ma pean tolli maksma?	Cik liela muita man ir jāmaksā?	Kiek reikia mokėti muito?
Where is the nearest currency exchange office?	Kus on lähim valuuta- vahetuskontor?	Kur ir tuvākais valū- tas apmaiņas punkts?	Kur yra artimiausias valiutos keitimo punktas?
What is the exchange rate of an English pound sterling?	Mis on Inglise nael- sterlingi vahetuskurss?	Kāds ir apmaiņas kurss anglų sterliņu mārciņai?	Koks yra Anglijos svaro sterlingų keitimo kursas?
US dollar?	USA dollari vahetus- kurss?	ASV dolāram?	JAV dolerio?

NB On page 87, the authors of the Estonian, Lithuanian and Latvian anthems have been erroneously printed under the Latvian anthem. We apologize.